Scout the World in Santa Monica!

AFCI
ASSOCIATION OF FILM COMMISSIONERS INTERNATIONAL

LOCATIONS TRADE SHOW 2004
Santa Monica Civic Auditorium

APRIL 16 - 17 - 18, 2004
Santa Monica, California USA

For visitor and exhibitor information check our website at
www.afci.org

Tel: (323) 852-4747   Fax: (323) 852-4904
E-mail: maggie@afci.org

International
Film Guide 2004

THE ULTIMATE ANNUAL REVIEW OF WORLD CINEMA

edited by DANIEL ROSENTHAL

founding editor PETER COWIE

VIRGIN BOOKS
LONDON

SILMAN-JAMES PRESS
LOS ANGELES

57th Locarno International Film Festival.

August 4-14 2004.

Locarno: 360° of captivating cinema

President: Marco Solari | Director: Irene Bignardi | Vice Director: Teresa Cavina | Head of Communication: Doris Longoni

Address: via Luini 3a CH-6601 Locarno Tel. +41 91 756 21 21 Fax +41 91 756 21 49 http://www.pardo.ch e-mail: info@pardo.ch

Contents International Film Guide 2004

Editor

Daniel Rosenthal

Founding Editor

Peter Cowie

Consulting Editor

Derek Elley

Editorial Assistant

Sara Tyler

Sales Director

Jerry Odlin

Sales Manager

Lisa Ray

Publishing Director

Richard Woolley

Cover Design

Button One to One

Photo Consultants

The Kobal Collection

tel +44 (0) 20 7624 3300

Editorial and Business Offices
Button Publishing
246 Westminster Bridge Road
London SE1 7PD
tel +44 (0) 20 7401 0410
fax +44 (0) 20 7401 0249
e info@buttonpublishing.com

ISBN 1-902-04996-9 (United Kingdom)
ISBN 1-879505-75-4 (United States)
British Library Cataloging in
Publication Data
Variety International Film Guide 2004
1. Rosenthal, Daniel 1971-

Distributed in the UK by
Virgin Books

Published in the US by
Silman-James Press
tel +1 323 661 9922 fax 661 9933

Copyright © 2003 by
Button Publishing Ltd

'Variety International Film Guide' is a
trademark of Reed Elsevier Properties
Inc. and is used under license.

Printed and bound in Dubai by
Emirates Printing Press

You Can't Beat the Sound

All around the world, audiences are being thrilled by Dolby® sound. We remain committed to making films sound better than ever before.

Image taken from *Perspectives* – the new Dolby cinema trailer.

Contents International Film Guide 2004

International Liaison

Africa (Algeria, Morocco, Tunisia): Roy Armes
Argentina: Alfredo Friedlander
Armenia: Susanna Harutiunian
Australia: Peter Thompson
Austria: Roman Scheiber
Azerbaijan, Belarus, Georgia, Ukraine: Goga Lomidze
Belgium: Erik Martens
Bosnia & Herzegovina: Rada Sesic
Brazil: Nelson Hoineff
Bulgaria: Pavlina Jeleva
Canada: Brendan Kelly
Chile: Andrea Osorio Kleiner
China: Shelly Kraicer
Colombia: Pedro Adrián Zuluaga
Croatia: Tomislav Kurelec
Cuba: Luciano Castillo, Alberto Ramos
Czech Republic: Eva Zaoralová
Denmark: Ann Lind Andersen
Egypt: Fawzi Soliman
Estonia: Jaan Ruus
Finland: Antti Selkokari

France: Michel Ciment
Germany: Jack Kindred
Greece: Yannis Bacoyannopoulos
Hong Kong: Tim Youngs
Hungary: John Nadler
Iceland: Olafur H. Torfason
India: Uma da Cunha
Iran: Jamal Omid
Ireland: Michael Dwyer
Israel: Dan Fainaru
Italy: Lorenzo Codelli
Japan, South Korea: Frank Segers
Kazakhstan, Uzbekistan: Eugene Zykov
Latvia: Andris Rozenbergs
Lebanon, Syria: Mohammed Rouda
Lithuania: Grazina Arlickaite
Luxembourg: Marlene Edmunds
Malaysia: Baharudin A. Latif
Mexico: Carlos Bonfil
Nepal: Uzzwal Bhandary
Netherlands: Pieter van Lierop
New Zealand: Peter Calder
Norway: Trond Olav Svendsen
Pakistan: Aijaz Gul

Peru: Isaac León Frías
Philippines: Tessa Jazmines
Poland: William Roderick Richardson
Portugal: Martin Dale
Puerto Rico: José Artemio Torres
Romania: Cristina Corciovescu
Russia: Kirill Razlogov
Serbia & Montenegro: Goran Gocic
Singapore: Yvonne Ng
Slovakia: Hana Cielová
Slovenia: Ziva Emersic
South Africa: Martin Botha
Spain: Jonathan Holland
Sri Lanka: Amarnath Jayatilaka
Sweden: Bengt Forslund
Switzerland: Michael Sennhauser
Thailand: Anchalee Chaiworaporn
Turkey: Atilla Dorsay
United Kingdom: Philip Kemp
United States: Eddie Cockrell
Uruguay: Jorge Jellinek
Venezuela: Andreína Lairet, Suzanne García

Front Cover Photographs (clockwise, from top left)
Nicole Kidman in **The Hours** *(Paramount/Miramax/Kobal/Clive Coote); Zhang Ziyi in* **Hero** *(Beijing New Picture Film Co./Miramax/Kobal);*
Douglas Silva in **City of God** *(Globo Filmes/Kobal); Oksana Akinshina, left, and Elina Benenson in* **Lilya 4-ever** *(Memfis Film/Per-Anders*
Jörgensen); Chiwetel Ejiofor in **Dirty Pretty Things** *(BBC/Celador Productions/Kobal); Daniel Brühl in* **Good Bye, Lenin!** *(X Filme Creative Pool).*
All images on p.321 appear courtesy of the Kobal Collection.

Notes from the Editor

Waiting to go into a screening at the Cinemaxx theatre during the Berlin Film Festival in February 2003, my eye was drawn to the monitors behind the box-office counter, which were relaying fuzzy, black-and-white pictures of the movies playing in the auditoria. I could make out what looked like a Latin American street scene, a pair of European lovers and an Asian family, and was struck by how different those screens must look for the 50 weeks of the year when the festival is not in town: filled with Hollywood imports and one or two mainstream local titles, just like thousands of other multiplexes the world over.

That contrast seemed as good a visual metaphor as any for *IFG*'s approach to film. For the first 40 years of its life, under founding editor Peter Cowie, this book has been committed to recording, criticising and celebrating the Babel-like diversity of film-making, not just the movies that emerge from LA, and that focus is unchanged in this 41st edition, my first as editor.

As ever, our World Survey reflects the ebb and flow in the fortunes of more than 70 national film industries. In China, independent producers are emerging as a major force. In Azerbaijan and Belarus, the governments have responded to intense lobbying from film-makers for state support. Norway's feature output is on course to double, while Slovenia's directors hope that the country's entry into the EU in 2004 will bring instant access to much-needed subsidies.

Elsewhere, the outlook is bleaker. Directors in Bosnia and Herzegovina are still obliged to import 35mm camera equipment at absurd cost. Producers in Pakistan will take time to recover from the closure of the 30-year-old National Film Development Corporation. Full-length scripts in Puerto Rico are confined exclusively to television.

Daniel Rosenthal

This year's reports also remind us that censorship still poses a clear and present danger to creative freedoms. It is most evident in our dossier on Iran, some of whose directors risk imprisonment or exile to show their work uncut, and has reared its head in Mexico, where Catholic leaders tried and failed to ban the sight of a priest in love in *The Crime of Father Amaro*, and in Chile, where audiences were finally permitted to watch Scorsese's *The Last Temptation of Christ*.

Our correspondents also highlight cinema's undimmed power to stir debate on key figures and incidents in a nation's history. Gregor Jordan's *Ned Kelly* had Australians arguing over the iconic status of their most famous outlaw. Atom Egoyan's account of the Armenian genocide, *Ararat*, became a huge talking point – and commercial hit – in Armenia. Most remarkably of all, Estonia's *Names in Marble*, the story of young volunteers' courage in the 1918 war of independence, surpassed *Titanic* as the country's all-time box-office champion.

Public attitudes to recent or contemporary events were also challenged by two of our

Total HelpArt

Jan Hrebejk's **Pupendo**: *acclaim and a mass audience*

Directors of the Year: Jan Hrebejk's *Pupendo* encouraged a generation of Czechs to re-examine their behaviour under communism in the 1980s and Lukas Moodysson's *Lilya 4-ever* spurred Swedes to address the suffering of child prostitutes. Both also pulled off a hat-trick achieved by a very select band: winning acclaim from national and international critics *and* attracting a mass audience at home.

The exceptional nature of such successes is confirmed by our annual World Box-Office Survey, as Hollywood's dominance continues unopposed in too many territories. Some do manage to buck the trend, notably South Korea, where increasingly slick commercial film-making is supported by a screen quota system, and Serbia and Montenegro, whose cinemagoers devour homegrown stories that yoke domestic concerns to Hollywood genre conventions. In Bulgaria, Croatia, Portugal and Taiwan, however, local features account for no more than 2% of ticket sales, and in English-speaking markets like Australia, Canada and New Zealand, the battle against the American studios is only marginally less one-sided.

Most British films also struggle to find an audience at home, and the celebration of revenue over content grows daily, with Hollywood titles marketed to UK audiences largely on the strength of their chart triumph in the US. "Jim Carrey's highest-ever opening weekend comedy gross!" hollered print ads for *Bruce Almighty* in June 2003 – not in the trade press, but in tabloids like the *Sun* and *Evening Standard*.

As another blockbuster season ended with *Pirates of the Caribbean* heading for a global gross of $600m-plus, it would be heartening to think that producer Jerry Bruckheimer's essentially old-fashioned romp – no masterpiece, but at least enjoyable and inoffensive – had vastly exceeded studio expectations because it drew such positive word-of-mouth from the legions who felt short-changed by *The Hulk* and the *Charlie's Angels* and *Tomb Raider* sequels, or the tedious, hollow *Matrix Reloaded*. Might *Pirates* signal the start of an anti-CGI backlash?

UK distributors concerned by the dearth of popular local features are at least seeing signs of a renewed interest in foreign-language fare. If films as diverse as *Good Bye, Lenin!*, *Belleville Rendez-vous* and *Etre et avoir* can break into the British box-office Top 15 in one three-month period, as they did in summer 2003, and if French-owned UGC Cinemas, the one multiplex chain in Britain that consistently programmes specialised titles, can see its Glasgow site generate a remarkable 33% of its business from arthouse films, then for those dedicated to cinematic plurality the news cannot all be bad.

The vagaries of corporate takeovers and fickle culture ministries – not to mention audiences – may mean that the coming year reverses some or all of these trends. Whatever happens, *IFG* and its correspondents will continue to track every new development with inquisitive enthusiasm. – *Daniel Rosenthal*

Elliot Marks/Disney/Jerry Bruckheimer Inc.

Pirates of the Caribbean: *start of a blockbuster backlash?*

Columbia/Marvel/Zade Rosenthal/Kobal

Comic-book adaptation **Spider-Man** *was the biggest hit of 2002, grossing $821m, but even that vast sum was dwarfed by the combined takes for the first two* Harry Potter *and* Lord of the Rings *films. World Box-Office Survey begins on p.321.*

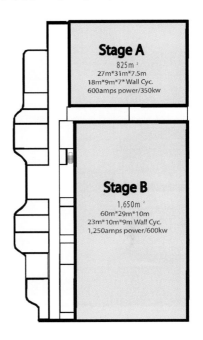

Directors of the Year

Christopher Guest by Eddie Cockrell

Columbia/Deana Newcomb/Kobal

Plug the name "Christopher Guest" into the search engine of the Internet Movie Database, and you'll find on his extensive filmography page a photo of Nigel Tufnel, the sincere yet clueless lead guitarist he played in director Rob Reiner's landmark and largely improvised 1984 independent film *This Is Spinal Tap*. While certainly Guest's most popular and enduring characterisation – and supremely emblematic of his brand of underdog comedy, which treats passionate eccentrics with mischievous dignity – Nigel is only the tip of the iceberg in a prolific career that has spanned some 35 years and every contemporary artistic medium.

Writer, actor, composer, arranger, comedian, director: from live theatre through the glory days of the *National Lampoon* humour machine, from early bit parts in movies through tentative steps behind the camera and the triumphant improvisational troika of *Waiting for Guffman*, *Best in Show* and *A Mighty Wind* – three films in six years which herald something genuinely new and exciting in American film comedy – Guest's oeuvre has a conceptual continuity worthy of Coleridge or Zappa, and reveals a determined, perceptive and canny Renaissance man who respects and honours the foibles of

entertainment history, even as he re-imagines the very nature of the creative process.

CHRISTOPHER HADEN-GUEST was born into aristocracy on February 5, 1948, in New York City. His father was Lord Peter Haden-Guest, a card-carrying member of the British House of Lords who'd been a ballet dancer and a publications editor at the United Nations; and his mother, Lady Jean Haden-Guest, was Jean Hindes, who subsequently served as vice-president of CBS from 1976 to 1986. Guest studied music, art and drama from an early age, and a trip to England as a teenager brought him work at the BBC and exposure to the comedy of, among others, Peter Sellers.

Back Stateside, he did time at Bard College and the New York University School of the Arts before embarking on a career that could easily fill an essay twice this length. Highlights include a handful of Broadway shows; spot-on musical spoofs and groundbreaking comedy material for nearly 60 episodes of *The National Lampoon Radio Hour*; a Best Musical Score Obie nomination for his work on *National Lampoon's Lemmings* (an irreverent and hugely influential musical revue that re-imagined Woodstock as a mass suicide set to music); five *NatLamp*-branded record albums of topical sketches and musical spoofs; an Emmy for co-writing Lily Tomlin's 1975 ABC TV special; and a player on ABC's short-lived variety series *Saturday Night with Howard Cosell* (NBC's rival Saturday variety show became *Saturday Night Live* and featured Guest in 1984-85).

It was during this time that he met and befriended future collaborators Michael McKean (with whom he'd write spoofs of folk and rock songs) and Fred Willard. In 1977, Guest was hired to play the college roommate of Michael

"Meathead" Stivic (Rob Reiner), son-in-law of outspoken bigot Archie Bunker (Carroll O'Connor) on the TV sitcom *All in the Family*, which led to a friendship that endures today (Guest's three most recent improvisational films were bankrolled by Castle Rock Entertainment, of which Reiner is a founding partner). Throughout his career, Guest has consistently returned to collaborations with friends. "We're not faking a friendship," he told the *New Zealand Herald* in July 2003 of his 35 years with McKean and 28 with Spinal Tap bassist Harry Shearer.

A decade of small- to medium-sized roles in Hollywood films ran parallel to these other projects: uncredited as a resident in Arthur Hiller's *The Hospital* (1971); a young policeman in both Peter Yates' *The Hot Rock* (1972) and Michael Winner's *Death Wish* (1974); the "Boy Lover" in Mike Nichols' *The Fortune* (1975); in support of future collaborator Bob Balaban in Claudia Weill's charming *Girlfriends* (1978); Jeb Stuart Magruder in the mini-series *Blind Ambition* (1979), about Nixon's downfall; treacherous real-life outlaw Charlie Ford, to his brother Nicholas' Bob Ford in Walter Hill's bloody Western siblingfest *The Long Riders* (1980); supporting Andy Kaufman in Allan Arkush's mawkish misfire *Heartbeeps* (1981). Of this dramatic urge, Guest told Nitrate Online in October 2000: "I like acting... I wouldn't even mind being on a TV show. Not as the main lead, but as the guy who comes in from next door every once in a while, does his little thing, and then leaves."

A style is born

After working again with Reiner on the largely forgettable 1982 TV movie *Million Dollar Infield*, Spinal Tap was born. The saga of two long-time British chums (Guest and McKean) whose heavy metal band is falling apart during a disastrous American tour, the film has become a touchstone of self-reflexive, contemporary pop culture comedy on the basis of its two chief strengths: the authentic musicianship of the fictitious band (Guest, McKean, Shearer and a revolving series of doomed drummers) and the obvious improvisational nature of every scene (Guest calls it "riffing", after the spontaneous creative process of the classic screen comedians).

Post-*Tap,* Guest worked on SNL, other TV collaborations with gifted comedians Martin Short and Billy Crystal (who'd been in *Tap*); modest but distinctive parts in Frank Marshall's jaunty *Little Shop of Horrors* (1986), Robert Altman's weird *Beyond Therapy* (1987) and a pair of Reiner movies (Guest played the fiendish Count Rugen in 1987's cherished, though overpraised fairy tale parody *The Princess Bride* and the intense Dr Stone in a single, vivid scene in 1992's *A Few Good Men*). There's more – lots more – suggesting Guest was soaking up the moviemaking atmosphere, looking for a way to blend his still-nascent collaborative creative process with the strict demands of Hollywood.

After honing his technical skills as a director on some fondly remembered but relatively obscure TV shows (*Morton & Hayes*, and the fairytales of Shelley Duvall's *Tall Tales and Legends*), Guest made his feature directing debut with the genial Hollywood satire *The Big Picture* (1989), starring Kevin Bacon as an award-winning film student determined to make a studio picture by playing the Hollywood game. Both it and the subsequent 1993 HBO production *Attack of the 50 Ft. Woman* (an off-kilter though respectful

Michael McKean, *left, and Kevin Bacon in* **The Big Picture**

remake of Nathan Juran's cheesy 1958 sci-fi chestnut that sees Daryl Hannah grow to take revenge on cloddish husband Daniel Baldwin) display a disarming sincerity in place of the expected irony, as well as a heartfelt appreciation for those toiling on the margins of showbusiness.

Chris Farley and Matthew Perry in **Almost Heroes**

Guest's only later directorial effort outside the improvised trilogy is *Almost Heroes* (1998), a funny enough spoof of the Lewis and Clark expedition that suffers from being the film that SNL star-turned-Hollywood-comedian Chris Farley had just completed when he died of a drug overdose at 33 (emulating the premature end of Guest's former *NatLamp* collaborator John Belushi). That tragedy aside, there's a vaudevillian exuberance to the proceedings, even as Guest seems to chafe under the restrictions of scripted comedy – no matter how broadly and skilfully it's acted. "I liked the script," Guest told Nitrate Online. "The movie just didn't work. You never know what's going to work."

Am dram thank you ma'am

By the mid-1990s, Guest was kicking around ideas with Canadian-born actor-writer Eugene Levy, veteran of the legendary SCTV comedy troupe (which also included John Candy and Catherine O'Hara) and a high-profile character actor in such contemporary fare as the

American Pie films (he plays Jim's Dad). They settled on a *Tap*-like, improvisatory approach that balances the risks of the unknown with the rewards of fresh, uncharted comedic results.

Their first collaboration, *Waiting for Guffman* (1997), established the template for their experiment (don't call it a "mockumentary", Guest is said to hate the word). In the small town of Blaine, Missouri, Broadway refugee Corky St Claire (Guest, riffing on gay characters he'd played on radio and SNL) rallies a fairly untalented but enthusiastic gaggle of townspeople to perform a sesquicentennial tribute to their burg, known heretofore as the stool capital of the world (footrests, not the other kind). As the company gets wind that Guffman will be scouting the play for possible Broadway relocation, the pressures mount. The remarkable thing about the film is how rich and self-assured it is: 60 hours of Super-16 footage edited down over a year and a half, with songs by the same Guest-McKean-Shearer team that wrote the Spinal Tap music (mind-bendingly, the climactic "Red, White and Blaine" revue was the only part of the film actually rehearsed in advance).

A pet project

After *Almost Heroes,* Guest reassembled the *Guffman* cast, with a few new additions, for *Best in Show* (2000). The episodic story of owners preparing their pets for a breed showcase took

Guest as Corky St Claire in **Waiting for Guffman**

eight months to edit from the 60 hours of footage captured during a five-week shoot. By now, the improvisation was "almost a live television technique", Guest told the BBC. "I had a microphone to talk with the cameraman. It was all hand-held and I actually told him who to focus on... I could hear a joke developing. It was exciting because it happened right then."

How, precisely, does the preparation for this kind of comedy work? Here's Guest himself, talking with Levy on the Region 1 *Best in Show* DVD: "Eugene and I sit for many months to work out the story, which has a beginning, a middle and an end... All the scenes are delineated, are on cards, everything tracks, everyone has to know who they are in relation to the other people. The difference is there's no dialogue written... Things can change in the beginning of the movie, [but] once you get into the story it becomes so intricately constructed that you can't just move anything around because it will impact something else... once people are on the road to go to the show, you're following the map that you've laid out. Which is the most important thing in a film where there's no dialogue written, because the actors need... to have a basis of reality that you can improvise from."

Eugene Levy and Catherine O'Hara in **Best in Show**

Guest has gathered a group of actors willing and able to work in this way. In addition to Guest and Levy and old friends McKean and Willard, the core company includes Balaban, Michael Hitchcock, Catherine O'Hara and Parker Posey. Since *Guffman*, new recruits have included Ed Begley Jr, Jennifer Coolidge,

John Michael Higgins, Jane Lynch and Jim Piddock. Able support is provided by instantly recognisable character actors such as Shearer, Lewis Arquette, Paul Benedict, Paul Dooley, Brian Doyle-Murray and Deborah Theaker. And there's one actor, Scott Williamson, who seems to have a bit part in just about everything Guest's directed. This is certainly the freshest group of comedy performers since Preston Sturges' 1940s heyday (tellingly, Guest and McKean were featured on the 2001 Criterion DVD commentary track of Sturges' immortal *Sullivan's Travels*).

Songs with the *Wind*

A Mighty Wind (2003) takes the concept to new levels. Following the death of legendary concert promoter Irving Steinbloom, beloved 1960s acoustic trio The Folksmen (Guest, McKean and Shearer, reviving an act they'd first tried out on TV in the mid-1980s) agree to join acoustic conglomerate The New Main Street Singers and estranged romantic duo Mitch & Mickey (Levy and O'Hara) in a memorial concert at New York City's Town Hall. The road to revival is, of course, a bumpy one.

The film is an extraordinary piece of work, with a level of cultural ephemera (fictitious album covers, that sort of thing) and dramatic substance (Levy and O'Hara shine) new to the form. All three of these modest yet groundbreaking films are available on DVD, with enough bonus material to give fans a vivid glimpse into Guest's painstaking methodology and the conceptual continuity that finds characters, situations, clues and trivia scattered from one work to the next.

If there's a flaw to this technique, it's in the rhythm, and this is particularly noticeable during *Best in Show*. Many sequences begin with fairly normal interview situations, then spiral into bizarre verbal riffing that stops the flow dead rather than advances the narrative. That this flaw is largely absent in *A Mighty Wind* is further testament to the strength of the story and everyone's comfort level with the non-stop improvisation.

Castle Rock/Doane Gregory/Kobal

"Many of Chris' movies are about people who are... I wouldn't say obsessive, but they're passionate about something that may not be very popular," says John Michael Higgins in the *Mighty Wind* press-kit, neatly summing up Guest's overarching theme. "I believe that there is great value in finding something not so fashionable to get passionate about in your life."

Guest guards his personal life with some ferocity. At Rob Reiner's house in 1984, he married actress Jamie Lee Curtis, star of *A Fish Called Wanda* and *True Lies*. Some profiles claim the actress saw Guest's picture in *Rolling Stone* and was immediately smitten. In any event, it's a touchy subject: "I don't talk about the family," he told *The Onion* in the 1990s. The couple has two adopted children, Annie and Thomas. In addition to actor Nicholas, the director has a half-brother, Anthony Haden-Guest, a reporter, writer and cartoonist.

Upon his father's death in 1996, Guest assumed the short-lived title of Fifth Baron Haden-Guest

of Saling in the County of Essex in the peerage of the United Kingdom; nearly all hereditary seats were eliminated in 1999. "Well, 650 of us were given the pink slip, actually," Guest told writer Gavin Edwards in April 2003, with the dry, absurdist wit typical of his press interviews. "I got to go to Parliament before the axe came down. The peers all dress up in their scarlet robes. It's like a 1950s Technicolor movie, but you're in the movie, wearing a scarlet robe... The robe was handed down through the family. Now it's in our closet, safely tucked away." Guest being Guest, the urge for one final riff is irresistible: "I still have a letter somewhere, asking me to send the hall pass back to them."

EDDIE COCKRELL is a Maryland-based film critic and programming consultant who reviews for *Variety* from the Berlin, Karlovy Vary, Montreal and Toronto film festivals. His writing also appears on the Nitrate Online and indieWIRE websites and in several American film festival catalogues.

Castle Rock/Suzanne Tenner

Left to right: John Michael Higgins, Jane Lynch, Parker Posey and Chris Moynihan in **A Mighty Wind**

Christopher Guest Filmography

1989
THE BIG PICTURE
Script: Michael Varhol, CG, Michael McKean, from a story by Varhol, CG. Direction: CG. Photography: Jeff Jur. Editing: Marty Nicholson. Production Design: Joseph T. Garrity. Players: Kevin Bacon (Nick Chapman), Emily Longstreth (Susan Rawlings), J.T. Walsh (Allen Habel), Jennifer Jason Leigh (Lydia Johnson), Michael McKean (Emmet Sumner), Martin Short (Neil Sussman; uncredited), Kim Miyori (Jenny Sumner), Teri Hatcher (Gretchen), Dan Schneider (Jonathan Tristan-Bennet), Jason Gould (Carl Manknik), Tracy Brooks Swope (Lori Pressman), Don Franklin (Todd Marvin), Gary Kroeger (Mark), Alice Hirson (Mrs Chapman), Grant Owens (Mr Chapman), Fran Drescher (Polo Habel), Eddie Albert, Sr (MC.), Stephen Collins, Elliott Gould (Attorneys). Produced by Michael Varhol for the Aspen Film Society. 100 mins.

1993
ATTACK OF THE 50 FT. WOMAN
Script: Mark Hanna, Joseph Dougherty. Direction: CG. Photography: Russell Carpenter. Editing: Harry Keramidas. Production Design: Joseph T. Garrity. Players: Daryl Hannah (Nancy Archer), Daniel Baldwin (Harry Archer), William Windom (Hamilton Cobb), Christi Conaway (Louise "Honey" Parker), Paul Benedict (Dr Victor Loeb), O'Neal Compton (Sheriff Denby), Frances Fisher (Dr Theodora Cushing), Lewis Arquette (Mr Ingersol). Produced by Debra Hill for Bartleby Ltd, Home Box Office and Warner Bros. Television. 89 mins.

1997
WAITING FOR GUFFMAN
Script: CG, Eugene Levy.

Direction: CG. Photography: Roberto Schaefer. Editing: Andy Blumenthal. Production Design: Joseph T. Garrity. Music and lyrics: Michael McKean, Harry Shearer, CG. Players: Lewis Arquette (Clifford Wooley), Bob Balaban (Lloyd Miller), CG (Corky St Claire), Matt Keeslar (Johnny Savage), Eugene Levy (Dr Allan Pearl), Catherine O'Hara (Sheila Albertson), Parker Posey (Libby Mae Brown), Fred Willard (Ron Albertson), Paul Benedict (Not Guffman), David Cross (UFO expert), Paul Dooley (UFO abductee), Miriam Flynn (Costume designer), Michael Hitchcock (Steve Stark). Linda Kash (Mrs Allan Pearl), Don Lake (Phil Burgess, Blaine historian), Larry Miller (Glenn Welsch, Mayor), Brian Doyle-Murray (Red Savage), Deborah Theaker (Gwen Fabin-Blunt), Scott Williamson (Tucker Livingston). Produced by Karen Murphy for Pale Morning Dun Productions. 84 mins.

1998
ALMOST HEROES
Script: Mark Nutter, Tom Wolfe, Boyd Hale. Direction: CG. Photography: Adam Kimmel, Kenneth MacMillan. Editing: Ronald Roose. Production Design: Joseph T. Garrity. Players: Chris Farley (Bartholomew Hunt), Matthew Perry (Leslie Edwards), Eugene Levy (Guy Fontenot), Bokeem Woodbine (Jonah), Lisa Barbuscia (Shaquinna), David Packer (Bidwell), Harry Shearer (Narrator). Produced by Denise Di Novi for Di Novi Pictures. 90 mins.

2000
BEST IN SHOW
Script: CG, Eugene Levy. Direction: CG. Photography: Roberto Schaefer. Editing: Robert Leighton. Production Design: Joseph T. Garrity. Players: Bob Balaban (Dr Theodore W. Millbank III), Jennifer Coolidge (Sheri Ann Cabot), CG (Harlan Pepper), John Michael Higgins

(Scott Donlan), Michael Hitchcock (Hamilton Swan), Eugene Levy (Gerry Fleck), Jane Lynch (Christy Cummings), Michael McKean (Stefan Vanderhoof), Catherine O'Hara (Cookie Fleck), Parker Posey (Meg Swan), Fred Willard (Buck Laughlin), Ed Begley Jr (Hotel Manager), Patrick Cranshaw (Leslie Ward Cabot), Linda Kash (Fay Berman), Don Lake (Graham Chissolm), Larry Miller (Max Berman), Jim Piddock (Trevor Beckwith), Jay Brazeau (Dr Chuck Nelken), Cody Gregg (Zach Berman). Produced by Karen Murphy for Castle Rock Entertainment. 90 mins.

2003
A MIGHTY WIND
Script: CG, Eugene Levy. Direction: CG. Photography: Arlene Donnelly Nelson. Editing: Robert Leighton. Production Design: Joseph T. Garrity. Music: CG, Harry Shearer, Michael McKean, Eugene Levy, Annette O'Toole, Catherine O'Hara, John Michael Higgins, Jeffrey CJ Vanston. Music Supervision: Jeffrey CJ Vanston. Players: Bob Balaban (Jonathan Steinbloom), Ed Begley, Jr (Lars Olfen), Jennifer Coolidge (Amber Cole), Paul Dooley (George Menschell), CG (Alan Barrows), John Michael Higgins (Terry Bohner), Michael Hitchcock (Lawrence E. Turpin), Don Lake (Elliott Steinbloom), Eugene Levy (Mitch Cohen), Jane Lynch (Laurie Bohner), Michael McKean (Jerry Palter), Larry Miller (Wally Fenton), Christopher Moynihan (Sean Halloran), Catherine O'Hara (Mickey Crabbe), Jim Piddock (Leonard Crabbe), Parker Posey (Sissy Knox), Harry Shearer (Mark Shubb), Deborah Theaker (Naomi Steinbloom), Fred Willard (Mike LaFontaine), Mary Gross (Ma Klapper), Paul Benedict (Martin Berg), Scott Williamson (PBN TV Director). Produced by Karen Murphy for Castle Rock Entertainment. 90 mins.

Jan Hrebejk by Eddie Cockrell

Total HelpArt

I f Czech director Jan Hrebejk's filmography to date had a motto, it might be something like "All the Nostalgia, None of the Sentimentality". With four episodic, period-set features in a decade – movies awash with cultural iconography and music, that nevertheless revolve around life-and-death issues of personal relationships and political pressures, inspired in large part by real-life anecdotes – Hrebejk has established himself as among the most socially conscious movie-makers in an impressively revitalised Czech cinema.

Indeed, Hrebejk is the first Czech since Ewald Schorm in 1971 to be selected as an IFG Director of the Year, suggesting that the aggregate international attention garnered by *Big Beat* (1993), *Cosy Dens* (1999), the Oscar-nominated *Divided We Fall* (2000) and *Pupendo* (2003) – not to mention the awards and success enjoyed by a handful of other Czech films – is helping to put this exciting national cinema back on the map.

That his films also rank among the most financially successful recent domestic releases confirms his prominence in contemporary Czech culture at large. Hrebejk and his team are smart enough to create popular entertainments, yet shrewd enough to know that these films serve as guideposts for a newly Westernised society as it analyses and grapples with a complex, often harrowing past.

Beneath the cultural ephemera that coat his movies like a thick, tasty frosting lie very real issues of love, loyalty, deceit and tolerance in the face of political and social turmoil. Yet non-Czechs don't need specialist historical knowledge to understand and enjoy Hrebejk's films – although it helps to have a basic grasp of the key political phases of European history from the 1930s onwards, identified by Czech émigré writer Josef Skvorecky (who left for Canada in 1969) as "liberal democracy until 1938, Nazism 1939-45, the uneasy democratic socialism of 1945-48, Stalinism between 1948 and 1960, the liberalisation of communism 1960-67, the crazy attempt to square the circle in 1968, the Attila-the-Hun solution of the Panzers in August 1968, the colonisation of Regnum Bohemiae which had begun before we left..." Add to that the peculiar, Orwellian complacency of early 1980s Czech society embodied in *Pupendo*, and Hrebejk's career arc comes into sharp focus.

Friends first, then colleagues

JAN HREBEJK was born on June 27, 1967 in Prague. While studying at the Stepánská academic school, he met and befriended a boy one year older than himself, aspiring writer Petr Jarchovsky. Later, as both attended the famed Film Academy of Performing Arts (FAMU), Hrebejk made three short films from scripts by Petr Zelenka (later a prominent film-maker): *Everything You Always Wanted to Know About Sex and Are Afraid to Experience* (1988), *Year 1948* (1989) and *Don't Do Anything Unless You Have a Good Reason* (1991).

In 2002, Zelenka, whose *Buttoners* played to great acclaim on the international festival circuit, remembered their student years during a Radio Prague interview: "FAMU gives you time to think about whatever you want to think about. It doesn't teach you anything, which was quite cruel... But it was probably true that we learned more from criticising each other – there were five of us [in the scriptwriting class] – than from actual professors. So it gave us time and it gave us sort of a small family."

Meanwhile, Jarchovsky wrote a script for fellow student Igor Chaun, part of an ongoing series called "Non-Mysterious Stories". Hrebejk and Jarchovsky were then reunited on a script set in a communist youth organisation. Called *Let Us Sing a Song* (the Czech title, *Pejme písen dohola,* is a complex pun), this 1990 feature marked the directorial debut of their colleague Ondrej Trojan.

The *Beat* generation

Appropriately, Hrebejk's debut feature, *Big Beat* (*Sakalí léta*), is about revolution. In a working-class Prague neighbourhood circa 1959, flamboyant rock'n'roller Bejby (literally, "Baby", played by Martin Dejdar, now the Czech voice of Bart Simpson) shakes up a group of youngsters aching for an original form of expression – a "Big Beat" – amidst the politically induced repression of the day. With this film, Hrebejk and Jarchovsky announce their film-making strategy: an episodic narrative, acted with relish and framed with period trappings, escalates into an exaggerated, yet oddly logical tale of individual yearning versus societal strictures (significantly, the closing credits divide story credit among the director, scripter, source writer Petr Sabach and composer-lyricist Ivan Hlas).

Though *Big Beat* had limited festival exposure abroad, at home it won four Czech Lions (Best

Rock'n'roll shakes up Prague in **Big Beat**

Ivan Maly/Space Films

Original Film Score, Best Actor for Josef Abrhám's long-suffering cop father, Best Director and Best Film) and spent more than six months in the country's box-office top 10.

Moving forward from the Stalinist era to the eve of the 1968 Soviet invasion, *Cosy Dens* (*Pelísky*) is dedicated "to everyone whose friends, lovers, parents and children disappeared overnight as you remained here alone". The caricatured and necessarily heavy-handed metaphors of *Big Beat* give way to a more bittersweet and quintessentially Czech mix of grim reality and absurdist comedy, embodied once again in the title, the approximate English translation of a phrase meaning "a small or secure space".

In a spacious Prague neighbourhood, two very different families live in the same building. Sebek (actor-singer Miroslav Donutil) is a simple but disciplined military officer who constantly clashes with his neighbour, Kraus (Jirí Kodet), a former resistance fighter who's lost none of his outspokenness. Their teenaged children teeter on the edge of two generations, grappling simultaneously with acute embarrassment at their parents' strident ideologies and the increasingly pervasive influence of Western – and home-grown – rock'n'roll.

Predictably, the film dominated the box-office and won a clutch of awards at home. But as the

Miroslav Donutil and Simona Stasova in **Cosy Dens**

first Hrebejk film to travel extensively, it focused attention on both its technical prowess and tonal echoes of classic 1960s Czech cinema. *Cosy Dens* is also notable as Hrebejk's first professional collaboration with former school chum-turned-producer Ondrej Trojan, as well as an early release from Space Films, the first private production and distribution company in the post-communist country.

A miracle in Bohemia?

A masterfully balanced comedic drama about the hard choices faced by Czech citizens during the waning days of the Second World War, *Divided We Fall* (*Musíme si pomáhat*) confronts an incendiary topic with grace, style, compassion and the exquisitely practical wit for which Czech films are rightly renowned.

In a Nazi-occupied Bohemian village, childless couple Marie and Josef Cízek (Anna Sisková, Boleslav Polívka), try to lead a normal life in the face of his diagnosed sterility and the chaos swirling just outside their windows. When David Wiener (Csongor Kassai), the only surviving member of a neighbouring Jewish family long since deported, escapes from Theresienstadt and shows up on their doorstep seeking shelter, they overcome their trepidation and hide the emaciated young man in a small store room.

Increasing the tension are unannounced visits by Cízek's pre-war pal Horst Procházka (Jaroslav Dusek), a boorish collaborator and hirsute Hitler lookalike (the actor sports the first of his three bizarre hairstyles in a Hrebejk film) who cracks his knuckles constantly, demonstrates Nazi war strategy with pieces of food and lusts after Marie with increasingly undisguised vigour. He also begins to suspect the Cízeks' secret.

Devising a plan for continued access to Marie that is half revenge and half subterfuge, Horst attempts to move emotionally shattered Nazi clerk Albrecht Kepke (Martin Huba) from his lodgings at the Wiener house to the Cízeks' spare bedroom. Marie blocks the strategy, announcing to Josef's astonishment her imminent need for the room as a nursery. With no choice left, they persuade David, who has developed a rapport with Marie, to impregnate her as quickly as possible to stave off the Nazis.

David delivers, but the childbirth is disrupted and forever influenced by the German withdrawal and subsequent witch-hunt for collaborators, which the Cízeks cannot escape. In a shattering, complex coda, Josef pushes his new baby in a stroller through the rubble that was his street, pausing to display him for a family that looks very much like the Wieners.

Boleslav Polívka in the final scene of **Divided We Fall**

Hrebejk and Jachovsky again bring to life a key period in Czech history with palpable authenticity and a rich, unerringly truthful complexity of character. The night-time village streets are as murky as the morals of those who survive there, vividly evoking one fearful citizen's rueful observation of "what abnormal times can do to normal people." Thus, the deadly serious business of weeding Jews out of the population is leavened with often audacious humour: a forbidden pig carcass must be eaten quickly to avoid detection; Marie hides the fugitive next to her in bed when her husband arrives home drunk with Horst and Kepke in tow.

Czech media mainstay and Hrebejk regular Polívka reaches a new high as Cízek, a bundle of nervous tics and ironic asides, aware that his furtive looks and smart mouth could get him and his wife into deadly trouble (the performance was reportedly based on the actor's father). Polívka dances through the conflicting emotions of a man who knows what he needs to do but is unclear if he possesses the necessary dignity.

Another flurry of awards followed, but, more importantly, the film picked up an American distributor and was one of the final five foreign film Oscar nominees. Tellingly, *Divided We Fall* is the most formally titled of Hrebejk's films, the literal Czech phrase "we must help each other" morphing into the hugely ironic conclusion of Procházka's mantra-like "united we stand". Hrebejk told kamera.co.uk: "'Divided we fall' is in the American constitution, so perhaps the pathos and irony is actually even bigger... Therefore I like this English title very much."

Coming to terms with compromise

Perhaps Hrebejk's most mature work to date, and a huge popular success since its domestic theatrical bow in late March 2003, *Pupendo* explores the complex, grey issues of guilt and complicity, loyalty and honesty that Czechs have grappled with since the 1968 Soviet invasion and the subsequent repressive socialist government that collapsed with 1989's Velvet Revolution.

By the early 1980s, at the height of Reagan-era Cold War tensions, Czechs who came of age around the Prague Spring of 1968 were settling into lives of compromise and dashed dreams. For sculptor Bedrich Mára (Boleslav Polívka), this means that instead of pursuing his obvious talent (he was once known as "the best head man in the country"), an unspecified political gaffe has resulted in his marginalisation within Prague's art world. All that remains of whatever defiance he once may have had are the Frank Zappa and John Lennon posters on his walls.

Stripped of his prestigious academy post and not even listed on the official Artists Association roster, Mára shares a cramped riverside flat with cynical but loving wife Alena (Eva Holubová) and two children, one of whom is deaf. Each day he rows across the Vltava River to his studio on Liben Island, where he cranks out dozens of ceramic piggy banks, or just fishes. Mara's classmate, Magda (Vilma Cibulková), has it much better, having married blustery but ambitious Míla Brecka (Jaroslav Dusek), now a respected school principal. A card-carrying communist only to secure advancement and comfort for his wife and two kids, Comrade Míla doesn't really subscribe to the party line, but justifies it to himself (as many did at the time) by vowing to work for change from within.

By chance, Bedrich meets down-on-his-luck art historian Alois Fábera (Jirí Pecha), and their subsequent friendship prompts the academic to begin an article on the sculptor, and for Mára himself to consider accepting a surprise commission to sculpt a party functionary. Though conditions appear to be softening somewhat, the deadly seriousness of socialist life is brought home when a chunk of Alois' smuggled essay on Bedrich's work is read out on Voice of America and the family must suffer a new round of ostracism.

Yet again, Hrebejk and Jarchovsky (who share a "film by" credit) mix dark humour and grim drama in equal measure. The title comes from the childish prank of slapping a heavy coin on the bare stomach of a victim who has been promised something pleasurable, a startling, if tenuous metaphor for socialism's illusion of stability and prosperity, which became the sting of repression. So, too, the rigidity of 1980s Czech lives is spoofed at every turn, though much of the humour is so insular as to be puzzling to an outsider.

Various sub-plots involve the adventures of the couples' offspring, who recognise the futility of their parents' lives and live their own accordingly; and the dream of travel, which provides a distinctive coda set at Hungary's desolate Balaton Lake (similar to the ambiguous dénouement of *Divided We Fall*).

As he did in *Divided We Fall*, Dusek holds the screen with a turn that cannily subverts self-importance with flashes of pathos; his pivotal scene with Polívka, as they drunkenly compose a written "message to the future" denouncing socialism, to be embedded in the hideous mural Mára is slapping on to a school wall, is among the film's emotional high points. At press time,

Pupendo was smashing all existing domestic box-office records on its way to a tour of international film festivals (it's already copped the Golden Kingfisher best film award at the Plzen national film days).

Beyond the big screen

Parallel with his film-making activities, Hrebejk has been active in television and on the stage. With his long-time cameraman Jan Malír he created the children's television series *Where Stars Are Falling* in 1996. During the same period, Hrebejk and Jarchovsky also collaborated on three award-winning original stories for the *Bachelors* TV show. In 1997, he made his stage debut directing Christopher Hampton's *Les Liaisons Dangereuses*, starring Vilma Cibulková, following up with a theatre version of Woody Allen's *Bullets over Broadway* and a revival of *Amadeus*. He contributed video skits to the portmanteau feature *Czech Soda* '98, culled from the satirical current affairs TV

Total Help Art

Left to right: Jirí Pecha, Vilma Cibulková and Boleslav Polívka in **Pupendo**

programme, and has also directed numerous music videos, commercials and documentaries.

The Hrebejk-Jarchovsky-Trojan collaboration continues apace on two fronts: the producer's second directorial effort, *Zelary* (with a script by Jarchovsky), was scheduled for an autumn 2003 release. Hrebejk himself was at press time in production on *Loop the Loop*, his first feature set in the present, which he describes as "three interweaving tragi-comic stories about the loss and recovery of love, friendship and family". Waiting in the wings is the long-gestating *I Served the English King*, from the 1990 novel by Bohumil Hrabal (whose novel *Closely Watched Trains* became the Oscar-winning 1966 film).

In interviews, Hrebejk often comes across as earnest and intense, a film-maker singularly concerned with the successful delivery of a message in which he and his team have invested much thought. "My search for substance," he writes in a director's statement attached to preliminary *Loop the Loop* information, "is a journey towards an unclear-cut, tragi-comic reflection of our lives, towards strong but unforced emotion." In other words, all of the nostalgia, none of the sentimentality.

Jan Hrebejk Filmography

1993
SAKALÍ LÉTA
(**Big Beat,** aka **Years of the Jackal,** aka **Jackal Years**)
Script: Petr Jarchovsky, from short stories by Petr Sabach. Direction: JH. Photography: Jan Malír. Editing: Jan Mattlach. Music, Lyrics: Ivan Hlas. Players: Jakub Spalek Kaspar (Eda), Martin Dejdar (Bejby), Josef Abrhám (Prokop), Sylva Tománková (Bejbina), Jan Semotán (Ksanda), Jitka Asterová (Milada), Jirí Ornest (Milada's husband), Jan Kacani (Reddy), Pavel Janousek (Neumann), Sasa Rasilov (Peterka), Zdenek Vencl Kaspar (Babka), Václav Jakoubek (Petykoluna), Radek Holub Kaspar (Gang leader), Radek Smejkal (Restaurant owner's assistant), Anna Kreuzmannová (Auntie Juricková), Raoul Schránil (Chief Kaláb), Petr Bratka (Marína), Dominik Prouza (Carda), Jan Halas (Peterka Senior), Zuzana Michnová (Peterková). Produced by Jirí Jezek for Nova, Polytechna and Space Films. 109 mins.

1999
PELÍSKY
(**Cosy Dens,** aka **Cozy Dens**)
Script: Petr Jarchovsky, from his story using motifs from the book Hovno horí (literally, Shit Burns)
by Petr Sabach. Direction: JH. Photography: Jan Malír. Editing: Vladimír Barák. Music: various. Players: Miroslav Donutil (Sebek), Jiri Kodet (Kraus), Simona Stasová (Sebková), Emília Vásáryová (Krausová), Boleslav Polívka (Uncle), Jaroslav Dusek (Sasa Maslan), Eva Holubová (The teacher), Stella Zázvorková (Grandmother), Marek Morvai Javorsky (Péta), Michael Beran (Michal), Jirí Krejcík (Professor), Kristyna Nováková (Jindriska), Sylvie Koblízková (Uzlinka), Ondrej Brousek (Elien), Boris Hybner (Magician), Miroslav Kaman (Cop), Richard Tesarík (Boris). Produced by Pavel Borovan, Ondrej Trojan (also Executive Producer) for Czech Television and Total HelpArt. 116 mins.

2000
MUSÍME SI POMÁHAT
(**Divided We Fall**)
Script: Petr Jarchovsky, from his story. Direction: JH. Photography: Jan Malír. Editing: Vladimír Barák. Music: Ales Brezina. Players: Boleslav Polívka (Josef Cízek), Anna Sisková (Marie Cízková), Csongor Kassai (David Wiener), Jaroslav Dusek (Horst Procházka), Martin Huba (Dr Albrecht Kepke), Jirí Pecha (Frantisek Simácek), Simona Stasová (Libuse Simácková), Richard Tesarík (Captain),

Vladimír Marek (SS Officer), Jiri Kodet (Doctor Fischer-Rybár). Produced by Ondrej Trojan (also Executive Producer) and Pavel Borovan for Total HelpArt and Czech Television. 123 mins.

2003
PUPENDO
Script: Petr Jarchovsky, loosely based on the work of Petr Sabach. Direction: JH. Photography: Jan Malír. Editing: Vladimír Barák. Music: various, including Oskar Petr, Wolfgang Amadeus Mozart. Players: Boleslav Polívka (Bedrich Mára), Eva Holubová (Alena Márová), Jaroslav Dusek (Míla Brecka), Vilma Cibulková (Magda Brecková), Jirí Pecha (Alois Fábera), Lukás Baborsky (Matej Mára), Vojtech Svoboda (Bobes Mára), Nikola Pesková (Pavla Brecková), Matej Nechvátal (Honza Brecka), Jan Drozda (Jirka Ptácník), Pavel Liska (Vláda Ptácník), Zuzana Krónerová (Zdena Gabalová), Zuzana Michnová (Vlasticka), Sona Cervená (Frau König), Matej Ruppert (Delivery man), Hana Seidlová (Teacher), Bohumil Klepl (Motycka), Boris Hybner (Krauze). Produced by Pavel Borovan and Jaroslav Kucera for Czech Television, Ondrej Trojan for Total HelpArt. 126 mins.

Kim Jee-woon by Adrien Gombeaud

Cineclick Asia

G hosts, murderers, vampires... a list of the characters in Kim Jee-woon's work makes it hard to believe that until the release of his latest movie, Koreans considered him a mainstream comedy specialist (his first films were all major domestic hits). This commercial comedy etiquette probably explains why, unlike his countrymen Im Kwon-taek or Kim Ki-duk, little is known about Kim Jee-woon in the West, where distributors tend to think that Asian arthouse cinema has more potential than popular titles, and where his strange world therefore remains largely undiscovered.

KIM JEE-WOON was born on July 6, 1964 in Seoul. He began his career on stage as an actor and then as director of two plays in 1994-95: *Hot Sea* and *Movie Movie*. He also started to write screenplays and submit them to competitions. The turning point in his career came in 1997, when *Wonderful Season* won the Premiere "Best Screenplay" prize and *The Quiet Family* won Best Screenplay in the first scenario contest run by popular Korean film magazine *Cine21*. *Wonderful Season* has yet to be filmed, but Kim would make his directorial debut with *The Quiet Family*.

His competition success coincided with the opening of the first multiplex in Seoul and a period in which the Korean film industry began to surge forwards, mostly because the *chaebols* (conglomerates such as Samsung and Daewoo) had opened new film-making divisions. This burgeoning industry needed new blood, and many of today's established names made their directorial debuts between 1996 and 1998: Hong Sang-soo with *The Day the Pig Fell into the Well* (1996), Kim Ki-duk with *Crocodile* (1996), Lee Chang-dong with *Green Fish* (1997). Like many of these young directors, Kim had almost no film background, and *The Quiet Family* resembles other Korean debuts made in 1996-98 – a low-budget movie based on a very solid script with a tone that is unusual for Korean cinema.

It's too *Quiet*...

The viewer enters *The Quiet Family* like a mad insect attacked by the light. In a very long shot, we fly across the rooms of an elegant chalet. Suddenly, we stop. Beneath us, lying on a couch, a young girl silently stares upwards. Her dark eyes seem to ask: "What are you doing here?" Then, bored: "All right, you can stay if you really want." She seems to be sucking the power out of the camera, and will be our silent guide throughout the story. Not only has Kim pushed us into his house, he has given us the keys to his cinematic kingdom. Most of what we see in his next films is already evident: an isolated location, a young girl, an ability to address and manipulate the spectator.

We are in a rural boarding house recently opened by the Kang family after the father's dismissal from his office job. It's nice... but empty. Two weeks after the opening, the first guest shows up. The next morning he is dead.

Golden Network

Left to right: Choe Min-Shik, Na Mun-hee, Song Kang-ho and Park Im-hwan in **The Quiet Family**

To protect the business' reputation, the Kangs decide not to tell the police, and bury the corpse in the forest. The next day a young couple wants to spend the night, but only because this is a romantic enough place in which to commit suicide. Somehow all the guests die, and digging becomes a habit.

Released on April 25, 1998, *The Quiet Family* became a surprise hit, with 343,948 admissions in Seoul. It had not been an easy film to promote. Two of the leading actors, Song Kang-ho and Choi Min-shik, now major stars, were

then almost unknown. Besides, even if comedy was a popular local genre, there had never been a Korean comedy with such a morbid plot. But this special movie caught the mood of the times as few films do.

In 1998, loaded with a $200 billion deficit and caught up in the Asian economic meltdown, Korea entered what people called the "IMF times". Slowly these three letters became a curse, appearing on walls, in the news and in restaurants ("IMF menu"). In *The Quiet Family*, the Kangs fight hard to survive (as many Korean families were doing in real life) in the midst of piled-up corpses, getting used to – and maybe even enjoying – an extreme situation. In his next film, Kim would dig deeper in his exploration of Korea's social crisis, and unearth the most fascinating character in contemporary Korean cinema: the foul king.

King of the ring

The Foul King takes place in the wrestling community, but Kim's past as a stage actor and director was probably a source of inspiration –

Cinedick Asia

Song Kang-ho, centre, as the masked hero of **The Foul King**

not only because wrestling has more to do with acting than with sport, but also because *The Foul King* deals with an identity crisis, just like many films about actors, from *Opening Night* to *Mulholland Drive.*

Im Tae-ho (Song Kang-ho) is a shy, weak bank employee, constantly humiliated by his boss, laughed at by his colleagues and dumped by girls. His life takes a radical turn when he decides to join a wrestling team. Behind a tiger mask, he becomes "Ultra X", aka "The Foul King", a character who cheats constantly, inventing mean and funny tricks in doomed attempts to defeat the heroes of the ring. Ostensibly a comedy, this is really a voyage into the twisted arcades of a schizophrenic mind. The bank and wrestling ring reveal two aspects of the same character, but ultimately both locations are the same; Ultra X and Im Tae-ho are both programmed to lose. "The first time you rise up, the second time you stay down. This is how the game ends," says his coach. In a dream, Im sees himself as Elvis "The King" Presley. He starts to sing with a deep, masculine voice but the microphone breaks and his voice rises up in comically embarrassing fashion.

Suddenly, Ultra X refuses to be King of the Losers any longer. In one last bout against a major star of the ring, Yu Pi-ho, he decides to win. The match becomes a wild catfight, Ultra X's mask is torn apart, revealing Im's angry, bleeding face – but the result is a tie. Im has not won, but by avoiding defeat has changed the prewritten script. Later, when he tries to take revenge against his boss he slips and ends up on his knees. Without the mask, there is no way Im can win. He has literally lost face.

In a very simple way Kim had again addressed questions that torment so many Koreans. How much of my life do I control? Is my face a mask and my suit a costume? But the film's impact also owes a lot to Song Kang-ho. Im's character allows him to give an outstanding, clownish performance, his expressions switching from fear to joy, deception to hate, surprise to enthusiasm in a comically frenetic rhythm. He is not really acting, he is making faces... or should I say masks.

In classical Korean theatre, actors were masked. The mask is a very familiar theme in Korean fiction. In Yi Chong-jun's novel *The Prophet* (1975), a bartender forces her clients to wear masks, and one gives "prophecies that are so exact that people obey by themselves, so that the prophecy becomes true". *The Foul King* suggests that you become what you are told to become. You are what you wear. When the film came out on DVD, the special edition box-set included a bonus gift: a mask.

Between a laugh and the fear

The Foul King was number one at the box-office for six months and seen by more than two million people. Kim now had major commercial clout, but it took him three years to complete another feature. During that time he participated in two interesting omnibus projects. With the internet growing incredibly fast in Korea in 2001, three renowned directors – Kim, Ryu Seung-won (*Die Bad*) and Jang Jin (*The Happenings* and *The Spy*) – each agreed to direct an online short for a website, cine4m.com. The project gave Kim the freedom to make *Coming Out,* an underground, insolent, funny and sexy little film. Downloaded by more than a million viewers, it is possibly his richest and most complicated piece to date.

It tells the story of a young girl who makes a videotape to tell her parents that she is a vampire. The narrative sprays out in multiple directions – the girl's confession, an interview with her brother and another video shot by a vampire – and ends in a white room with a lesbian sex scene that makes the title explicit.

Coming Out is very much an "internet film". In front of his computer the viewer is usually alone in the privacy of his home. The confession plot allows Kim to develop the intimate film/viewer relationship established in *The Quiet Family.* The videotape images and the text that sometimes appears on screen produce a disturbing yet delicious web-cam effect. But the internet allows one person to speak to the whole world, so the girl's confession is also public. *Coming Out* contains a great deal of blood, but is mainly a comedy with some hilarious moments, like the last shot of the girl in a cafeteria, naturally pouring fresh blood on a hot dog. The vampirism reminds us of a constant in Kim's characters: they are all incurably contaminated. Instead of struggling in vain against what they are, they accept and experience their disease to the full.

In 2002, Applause Pictures (Hong Kong), Bom film productions (Korea) and Cinemasia (Thailand) teamed up for a pan-Asian project, *Three*, asking three Asian directors (Kim, Thailand's Nonzee Nimibutr and Hong Kong's Peter Ho San-chan) to film a short ghost story. Kim's short, *Memories,* was his first work completely removed from the comedy genre. It tells the story of a man who's lost his memory and a woman looking for her way home following a car accident, and Kim deploys as many kinds of horrific images and sounds as possible. But besides a few purely terrifying images (a woman plunging her finger into her own head), *Memories* is haunted by the deep and pathetic beauty of a desperate woman running in search of her own death.

Cineclick Asia

Kim Hye-su in **Memories**

Bridging genres

In early summer 2003, Kim's belated third feature was finally released. Grossing $6.4m in just one week, *A Tale of Two Sisters* (*Changwha, hongryeong*) had the biggest opening ever in Korean film history and two months later

DreamWorks bought the remake rights for $1m. It is a horror movie that describes the passionate relationship between two pre-teen sisters, who, after their mother's suicide, have spent a long time in a mental institution. While they were away, their father has remarried and when they come back home they must face their very strict new stepmother (Yeom Jung-ha), who seems to scare the younger sister Su-yeon (Mun Geun-young), leading Su-mi (Im Soo-jeong), the elder, to try to protect her. The house is old, large and elegant and after the mother's ghost appears in the closet where she hanged herself, it starts to reveal the tragic origins of the conflict between the sisters and the stepmother.

Cineclick Asia

Yeom Jung-ha as the stepmother in **A Tale of Two Sisters**

The story and aesthetic are in the tradition of *Little Red Riding Hood* and there is an almost unreal, European atmosphere, with numerous nods to Hitchcock (*Rebecca* or *Psycho* for the house, but also "Freudian films" like *Marnie* or *Spellbound*). The first minutes are full of a powerful, almost romantic sensuality; one can almost smell the wax on the shiny wooden floor, feel the fresh air and hear the bees flying over the lake. Later we realise that we have not visited a house but a girl's vision. From this beautiful opening to the frightening nightmare scenes, Kim has never done anything so technically accomplished. However, *A Tale of Two Sisters* is more a synthesis of his previous works than a fundamental change of direction. The sisters and the association of female blood with guilt recall *Coming Out*; the house comes from *The Quiet Family*; the denial of reality from *Memories*.

After three features and two shorts, Kim has clearly emerged as a film-maker who keeps to one path and for whom genres are not a list of conventions but structures large enough to give his ideas and obsessions free rein and universal application. By straddling horror and comedy he has created a world in which laughter meets violence and jokes leave a bitter taste of blood. It is a complex, dark and funny universe, but a very coherent one, with its fractured families, twisted, ridiculous bodies and disturbed, suffering characters. Kim keeps methodically challenging his audience, sketching the large painting of a fascinating, multi-faceted monster, a creation of his mind that may also be a self-portrait.

ADRIEN GOMBEAUD is based in Paris, where he writes for *Positif* and the daily financial paper *Les Echos*. He has written a thesis on contemporary Korean cinema, and is director of *Tan'gun*, a bi-annual publication on Korean culture and society.

Kim Jee-woon Filmography

1998
CHOYONG HAN KAJOK (The Quiet Family)
Script and Direction: K J-w. Photography: Jeong Gwang Sok. Editing: Ko Im-pyo. Production Design: Oh Sang-man. Music: Jo Yeong-wuk. Players: Park Im-hwan (Kang Tae-gu. Father), Na Mun-hee (Mrs Kang), Song Kang-ho (Kang Yeong-min. The son), Choe Min-shik (Uncle), Go Ho-gyong (Kang Mi-na), Lee Yun-seong (Kang Mi-su). Produced by Lee Un for Myeong Film. 99 mins.

2000
BANCHIK WANG (The Foul King)
Script and Direction: K J-w. Photography: Hong Kyeong-pyo. Editing: Go Im-pyo. Production Design: Oh Sang-man. Music: Uh Uh Boo project. Players: Song Kang-ho (Im Taeho/Ultra X), Chang Jin-young (Chang Min-young), Park Sang-myeon (Tae Baek-san). Produced by Oh Jung-wan for Bom Film Productions. 112 mins.

2001
COMING OUT
Script and Direction: K J-w. Photography: Choi Young-hwan. Editing: Ahn Byun-geun. Production Design: Na Sun-kyung. Players: Ku Hye-ju (Vampire elder sister), Shin Ha-kyun (Younger brother), Jang I-ji (Younger brother's girlfriend), Lee Seu-li (Middle school girl who gets her blood sucked). Produced by Kim Seong-je for Suda Dilm Productions. 40 mins.

2002
MEMORIES
[Part of the portmanteau film Three] Script and Direction: K J-w. Photography: Alex Hong (Hong Kyung-pyo). Editing: Chung Yun-chul. Production Design: Yi Chung-mun. Music: Cho Sung-woo. Players: Kim Hye-su, Jeong Bo-sok. Produced by Oh Jung-wan for Bom Film Productions. 40 mins.

2003
CHANGWHA, HONGRYEONG (A Tale of Two Sisters)
Script and Direction: K J-w. Photography: Lee Mogae. Editing: Go Im-pyo. Production Design: Cho Gum-hyeon. Music: Yoon Byoung-ho. Players: Im Soo-jong (Soo-mi), Mun Geun-young (Su-yeon), Yeom Jung-ha (Eun-joo), Kim Kap-su (Mu Hyeon). Produced by Oh Ki-min and Oh Jung-wan for Bom Film Productions. 115 mins.

Cineclick Asia

Im Soo-jeong as the elder sibling in **A Tale of Two Sisters**

Lukas Moodysson by Bengt Forslund

Memfis Film/Per-Anders Jörgensen

After making just three feature films, Lukas Moodysson has secured an impressive international reputation. His films have all been sold to between 30 and 40 countries and have sometimes been released with surprising success outside Sweden. In Sweden, having secured the blessing of Ingmar Bergman and the critics, he is generally regarded as the leader of a "new wave" of promising directors, all of whom made their debuts around the millennium.

Being a leader is nothing new for Moodysson, who has never suffered from lack of ego. When he had a collection of his poems, *It Doesn't Matter Where the Lightning Strikes,* published at the age of 17, he left school to be a writer – stamped by some critics as a genius. Two more poetry volumes followed and at 20 a novel, *White Blood,* followed shortly by two new collections of poetry. Such productivity did not pass unnoticed – especially as the author was young and mighty. *White Blood* was a surrealistic orgy of sex, drugs and Russian ice-hockey and Moodysson became something of the leader of a literary protest movement, "The Malmö Gang", named after the capital of the southern part of Sweden.

But that was long ago and Moodysson, now 34, looks back at this *Sturm und Drang* period with a certain scepticism. "Today I find *White Blood* quite bad," he has said. "I don't want anyone to read it." He is now back in Malmö, where his career began, but his life is very different. Today he is a family man, close to his wife Coco – his "consigliere" according to the credits in his movies – and his two kids. Anxious for his privacy, he is reluctant to give interviews, but his self-confidence is intact. He knows his value, trusts his intelligence and intuition. He says nothing about each new project before or during production. The press are forbidden from visiting the set and the actors are not allowed to give interviews. He talks through his films.

The road to the movies

LUKAS MOODYSSON was born on January 17, 1969, in Åkarp, a village just outside Malmö. His grandfather was a farmer, but his father left the countryside for the city, where he married a librarian and worked as an engineer, specialising on submarine motors.

The Moodyssons divorced a few years after having Lukas, who then lived with his mother. A left-wing feminist, she brought up her son in a home full of books. Movies came later and his most direct inspiration for becoming a director was David Lynch's *Twin Peaks* serial, shown in Sweden in the early 1990s. In 1992, he applied to the director's course at the Dramatic Institute in Stockholm and his talent was obvious from the outset; he was one of only four applicants out of several hundred to win a place at the first attempt. Very much a lone wolf, he was not happy to be back in an institutional environment, but he persevered and learned the technical side of his craft; storytelling gifts are something else – they come from the inside.

His examination film, *Showdown in the Underworld,* is unexceptional cinematically but has a good and original story and is well cast. Thus the hallmarks of his feature films are already discernible, making him, in many respects, the opposite of Lars von Trier. For Moodysson it's more important to reach the public with what he has to say than by how he says it. In *Showdown in the Underworld,* a divorced father has invited his young son, whom he hasn't seen for four years, to dine at a Chinese restaurant. The son is a vegetarian – like Moodysson – and that is their first problem. Gradually the son realises that the restaurant is just a cover for his dad's brothel operations, and by introducing his son to "love" through one of the hookers, the father tries to attract the son to his business.

One of those who saw the originality in *Showdown...* was Lars Jönsson at Memfis Film (today the leading production company in Sweden, it has also co-produced with Zentropa and Lars von Trier), who asked Moodysson to make another short, a test for a possible feature. *Talk* is the English title of the film, but that's a bit too straight compared with the original, *Bara prata lite* (literally, *Just Chat a Bit*).

Memfis Film/Ola Kjelbye

Sten Ljungren as the lonely protagonist of **Talk**

The film deals with a lonely middle-aged man who has just lost his job. He tries to talk to strangers on the bus about his former employment but they are just disturbed. One day the doorbell rings. A young girl from a religious sect wants to tell him about her beliefs. The man is not interested in religion, but suddenly has someone to talk to and invites her in. He is so happy to have someone around that when she wants to leave he gets angry and accidentally kills her. In the last scene we see them together: a television, a corpse and a lonely man. Lonely people on the edge of life are also one of Moodysson's preoccupations.

The love that dares speak

With *Fucking Åmål,* Moodysson made the hit of the year in Sweden in 1998, with almost 900,000 admissions. The title? Well, Åmål is one of the smallest cities in Sweden, far out in the west, and its name is sometimes used as a synonym for "the end of the world", as Wim Wenders used the American city Paris in *Paris, Texas.* "Fucking" doesn't need an explanation, but did mean that in the "sensitive" UK and US markets, the film was released as *Show Me Love.* Maybe it was a change for the better. One Japanese distributor contacted the Swedish Film Institute asking if they could buy the rights to Moodysson's *Fucking a Male.*

This tale of two terminally bored teenage girls (Rebecka Liljeberg and Alexandra Dahlström) coming out as lesbians at an Åmål school was successful for several reasons. Movies about schooldays are often popular because we all remember our own education, especially if the films are realistic, with attractive young actors. *Show Me Love* was certainly such a film, sensitively exploring adolescence and the courage that it takes to be different, but I doubt it would have been such a big hit without its lesbian theme – and the happy ending.

It was daring of Moodysson to introduce questions of homosexuality into a story of 15-year-olds, and he was fortunate that the film came at a moment when both children and parents were ready to see and discuss the issue openly. *Show Me Love* can certainly only have helped broaden the understanding of homosexual love and the problems it may bring, at home, in school, in society.

Memfis Film/Åke Ottosson

Rebecka Liljeberg, left, and Alexandra Dahlström in
Show Me Love

Everyone in Sweden had heard about *Fucking Åmål* by the end of 1998, but it wasn't until the Swedish Golden Bug awards gala in January 1999 that Moodysson became as famous as his film. Not because the movie deservedly took four of the most important prizes (Best Film, Director, Script and Actress, shared between the two leads), but because Moodysson accepted his honours wearing Mickey Mouse ears and shocked the audience and millions of television viewers with a 'thank you' speech in which he attacked the gala for being pretentious and people in general for eating meat, not paying their taxes and driving their cars too fast.

Together, something can be done

Curiosity is always an incentive for Moodysson, curiosity about other people and their feelings. He may use small parts of his own life in his films (who doesn't?), but the most remarkable aspect of his career is how different his films are and how he deals so sympathetically with worlds that he cannot know first-hand: the young lesbian girls of *Show Me Love* and, in *Together*, the politically aware, progressive, post-'68 generation, trying to live as a commune in Stockholm in 1975.

Moodysson had certainly heard about this movement, but to the poet of the late 1980s it seemed naïve and stupid – until he happened to see an exhibition about the communes in Gothenburg. He was impressed by all the different things that young people fought for in the 1970s and he eventually decided to make a positive film about it – a comedy with a heart that ends by stressing the necessity of togetherness in society, friendship and family. *Together* gave him his international breakthrough, doing well at the box-office in many countries, including the UK and the US

Memfis Film/Per-Anders Jörgensen

Michael Nyqvist and Lisa Lindgren in **Together**

(Hollywood bought the rights for a yet-to-be-produced remake).

Togetherness is also the theme of the three-hour, four-part television serial *The New Country* (*Det nya landet,* 2000), which Moodysson co-wrote with another promising scriptwriter, Peter Birro, for director Geir Hansteen Jörgensen. An entertaining road movie with a great deal to say about present-day Sweden, it followed Ali, a 15-year-old Somali, and Massoud, 40, an Iranian, on the run through Sweden in a rusty Mazda, both about to be expelled as illegal immigrants.

An angel in hell

It's typical of Moodysson that the longest and most revealing interview he has given to date appeared in *Situation,* a magazine sold by the homeless. In it, he said: "To poke about relations and emotional life is important, but you also have to grasp the big connections, understand why things are like they are. If you have talent, you cannot use it only for your own sake, you have a responsibility. Many people live in misery. I don't want to depress them even

more. A certain form of entertainment is also necessary and it is necessary to give hope. It's a difficult world to live in, but not a world without hope." The interview came out after the premiere of *Together* in August 2000 and if there is precious little hope to be found in the bleak plot of Moodysson's latest film, *Lilya 4-ever,* there is much to be drawn from a film-maker using his talent to take a stand against criminality and injustice.

Lilya is based on the real-life case of a teenage Russian girl who committed suicide after being brought to Sweden and used as a prostitute. A fatherless Russian teenager, Lilya (the astonishing Oksana Akinshina), lives with her mother in a poor and dreary suburb. When the mother leaves for America with her boyfriend, Lilya has to move to a rundown flat with no electricity or heating. Her only friend is a younger boy, Volodya (Artiom Bogucharskij), who's been thrown out by his widowed father. Together they find a bit of warmth and hope and one day she falls in love with an apparently sympathetic man, Andrei, who says he can promise her a new life and a good job in Sweden.

Oksana Akinshina and Artiom Bogucharskij in **Lilya 4-ever**

When she arrives, however, she is met by a Russian pimp who takes her passport and locks her up in a small flat, taking her out only to sell her body to man after man. When she finally "escapes" she has no money, no passport, no language. Her only solution is to jump from a motorway bridge and in that moment she and Volodya are reunited as angels. Moodysson has the talent to bring off this audacious, potentially mawkish finale, so that you leave the cinema with tears in your eyes, convinced that even in death there is hope, that something can be learned, something can be done. In Sweden, the film won Golden Bugs and has been widely discussed in schools and specially screened for members of parliament, so that even if this kind of human trafficking is not easy to stop, the powers-that-be are at least more aware of it.

In spring 2003, *Lilya 4-ever* opened in the US to excellent reviews, leading to renewed invitations for Moodysson to make films there. But he has no intention of leaving Sweden and June 2003 saw the release of the feature documentary he made with his friend, well-known documentarist Stefan Jarl. *Terrorists* consists of prison interviews with young students gaoled for their part in demonstrations at the EU meeting attended by George Bush in Gothenburg in 2002. Moodysson was scheduled to begin shooting his next fiction feature in autumn 2003. Once again, the title and subject matter were a secret. He continues to do things his own way.

BENGT FORSLUND was a well-known film producer for 30 years at Svensk Filmindustri, the Swedish Film Institute and Nordic Film & TV Fund. He is also a film historian and the author of several books, including *Swedish Television Drama 1954-2004* and volumes on Victor Sjöström and Sven Nykvist.

Lukas Moodysson Filmography

1995
EN UPPGÖRELSE I DEN UNDRE VÄRLDEN
(Showdown in the Underworld)
Script and Direction: LM.
Photography: Carl Sundberg.
Players: Stefan Sauk (Father),
Hampus Pettersson (Son),
Camilla Lundén (Hooker).
23 mins.

1997
BARA PRATA LITE (Talk)
Script and Direction: LM.
Photography: Ulf Brantås.
Players: Sten Ljunggren
(The man), Cecilia Frode
(The girl). 14 mins.

1998
FUCKING ÅMÅL
(Show Me Love)
Script and Direction: LM.
Photography: Ulf Brantås.
Editing: Michal Leszczylowski.
Players: Alexandra Dahlström
(Elin), Rebecka Liljeberg (Agnes),
Ralph Carlsson (Agnes' father),
Maria Hedborg (Agnes' mother),

Axel Zuber and Sam Kessel in **Together**

Memfis Film/Per-Anders Jörgensen

Jill Ung (Elin's mother), Erica Carlson (Jessica, Elin's sister), Mathias Rust (Johan), Stefan Hörberg (Markus). Produced by Lars Jönsson for Memfis Film. 89 mins.

2000
TILLSAMMANS (Together)
Script and Direction: LM.
Photography: Ulf Brantås.
Editing: Michal Leszczylowski.
Players: Lisa Lindgren (Elisabeth), Michael Nyqvist (Rolf), Emma Samuelsson (Eva, Elisabeth's daughter), Sam Kessel (Stefan, Elisabeth's son), Gustav Hammarsten (Göran), Anja Lundqvist (Lena), Jessica Liedberg (Anna), Shanti Roney (Klas), Olle Saari (Erik), Ola

Norell (Lasse), Axel Zuber (Tet), Cecilia Frode (Signe), Lars Frode (Sigvard). Produced by Lars Jönsson for Memfis Film. 106 mins.

2002
LILJA 4-EVER (Lilya 4-ever)
Script and Direction: LM.
Photography: Ulf Brantås.
Editing: Michal Leszczylowski.
Players: Oksana Akinshina (Lilya), Artiom Bogucharskij (Volodya), Ljubov Agapova (Lilya's mother), Llia Sinkarjova (Lilya's aunt), Elina Benenson (Natasha), Pavel Ponomarjov (Andrei), Tomas Neumann (Witek). Produced by Lars Jönsson for Memfis Film. 109 mins.

Christopher Nolan by Philip Kemp

Summit Entertainment/Kobal

When he was 27, Christopher Nolan started directing his first feature film – a black-and-white shoestring affair starring a cast of unknowns and shot on 16mm over the space of a year with the help of his friends. Five years later he was in Hollywood, directing Oscar-winners Al Pacino, Robin Williams and Hilary Swank. This would be a remarkable career trajectory by any standards – but is all the more striking given that Nolan has never had any formal film-making training.

CHRISTOPHER NOLAN was born in London on July 30, 1970, to an English father and an American mother. The movie-making bug emerged early. Aged seven, he and his younger brother Jonathan were borrowing their father's Super 8 camera to make films starring Action Man figures. Science-fiction was a favourite genre, much influenced by *Star Wars.* In 1989, his surrealist short *Tarantella* was screened on PBS in America. While reading English Literature at University College, London, Nolan continued making films with a group of friends who had formed a film society. Another of his shorts, *Larceny,* was shown at the 1996 Cambridge Film Festival.

The group raised funds by showing second-run films, then used the surplus revenue to buy film stock and maintain their equipment. "It was a great place to experiment and to learn, because there was no structure," Nolan later recalled. Members would be given ten minutes' worth of film to make a three- to four-minute movie. "It was a very, very good exercise for focusing on exactly what you need."

In 1997, Nolan embarked on his first feature, *Following,* using the same micro-budget guerrilla tactics. Shooting at weekends on found locations around London, he completed the 70-minute film for a sum variously reported as anything from $5,000 to $10,000. Not that the finished article betrays those slender resources; a lean, mean psychological thriller, it more than made up in tightly knit intricacy for what it lacked in plush production values. Directing from his own script – and acting as his own DP – Nolan plays sophisticated games with perception and exposition. With a cunning that David Mamet might admire, the film constantly keeps us guessing as to who's doing what to whom until, as the trap springs shut in the last reel, we suddenly realise the full diabolical ingenuity of the scam.

A thirtyish, unemployed drifter, Bill, fancying himself as a novelist, takes to following people at random in the streets. He tells himself he's "gathering material", but it's evident that he's just trying to stave off boredom and a sense of futility. Then one of his "followees" confronts him – a sharp-suited individual who calls himself Cobb and announces that he's a professional burglar. Invited along to watch Cobb at work, Bill becomes increasingly complicit, especially when an attractive young blonde gets involved in the increasingly labyrinthine plot. Only when it's far too late does Bill finally perceive the affair's hidden complexities.

Christopher Nolan

Jeremy Theobald in **Following**

So far, so noirish. But what makes *Following* more than a moody, low-rent retread of so many classic noirs is the way Nolan tells his story. He ingeniously fragments his narrative, flipping back and forth in time as the various pieces of the jigsaw drop into place. At first it's confusing, but very soon we realise that the appearance of his hero – whether or not Bill is clean-shaven or his face is bruised – indicates where we are in the sequence of events. At the same time it shows how Nolan (as his next film would confirm) loves to keep his audience guessing, leaving them as bemused as his protagonist.

"My concept," Nolan explains, "was to write a thriller that has absolutely no padding whatsoever, and no gratuitous characterisation. To me it's the classic film noir model: you define the characters by what they do to each other – by their actions, not their psychology. And of course it's not a new idea at all, but it's an idea that's often forgotten in modern cinema, strangely."

As for *Following*'s tiny budget, according to Nolan: "Whatever low figure you've heard, it probably cost less... Like most people on the film, including the actors, I was working full-time – making corporate videos, which gave us the money to buy the 16mm stock – so we were only able to shoot on Saturdays. Sundays we rested!

"Right from the start, it was always going to be fragmented. I'm just very interested in narrative, which I see as a controlled release of information. You don't *have* to release it chronologically, you can do it in far more interesting ways, as we do in real life when we're speaking... And films have done that for years – look at *Citizen Kane* – but over the last few decades TV, which tends to be very linear, has held that back. Fortunately, I think that's changing now."

In the UK, despite critical praise, *Following* received cursory treatment from its distributor, Alliance, being presented on a single screen in London before a perfunctory national release. Luckily the film was seen by Peter Broderick of Next Wave Films, an American outfit set up to support tyro film-makers, who put up money to create a 35mm show print, polish the sound mix and generally raise the film's profile on the festival circuit; it won awards at Rotterdam, Dinard, Newport and Slamdance.

Something to remind me...

Given the contrasting responses to *Following* in Britain and the US, it's hardly surprising that Nolan promptly relocated to the States, a move made easier by his dual nationality. "No one in the US ever asked me *why* I made my film," he noted on a return visit to London. "That's the first thing everyone in England does. It makes it so difficult here when you're starting out. But I've always made films: I did as a kid, and I'll always carry on. It's incredible to believe, but someone's going to pay me to make the next one."

The next one, based on a short story Nolan's brother Jonathan had started writing, was *Memento,* about a man suffering from short-term memory loss. Not amnesia, as Nolan is at pains to point out; an amnesiac can be anybody or anything, whereas his protagonist, Leonard Shelby, knows perfectly well who he is and what happened to him prior to the traumatic event – the rape and murder of his wife – that triggered his memory loss. Now, determined to avenge his wife, he sets out to solve the killing – but since he can't remember anything he's found out, he constantly sends messages to himself, using polaroids, scraps of paper and even tattoos (some in mirror writing) to recall his findings.

Nolan's masterstroke was, as with *Following,* to adopt a challengingly audacious narrative tactic. He reduces the audience to the same bewildered state as his hero by telling the story backwards: we open with Leonard killing the man he believes to be his wife's murderer, then jump backwards in five-minute sections to retrace his steps towards this conclusion.

Even by the end of the film, however, the solution is ambiguous depending on what we choose to believe. As Nolan notes: "The thing that divides people is visual memory versus verbal memory. If you believe what you've seen in the film, you come to one conclusion. If you believe what you've heard, you come to another... What I'm finding is that most people are very reluctant to abandon the idea of their visual memory. People believe their eyes more than their ears." By detaching us from the conventional narrative flow, Nolan turns his thriller material into a meditation on memory, identity and the nature of truth.

Predictably, producers to whom Nolan sent his script reacted nervously, suggesting he rewrite the plot as a conventionally ordered story. But a positive response came from Aaron Ryder at Newmarket, and Nolan was able to proceed with a budget of $4.5m and a potent cast: Guy Pearce, fresh from his success in *L.A. Confidential,* as Leonard, a just-post-*Matrix* Carrie-Anne Moss as his possibly fatale helper, and Joe Pantoliano as his ambiguous friend. Actors, says Nolan, "seem much more able to tap into the subjective nature of [*Memento*] than producers and executives, because they read it from the point of view of a character they would play."

Memento had a small budget by Hollywood standards, and was filmed fast – in fact, to almost exactly the same schedule as *Following*, 25 days

Carrie-Anne Moss and Guy Pearce in **Memento**

(albeit consecutive ones). Nolan was able to bring in his composer from *Following*, David Julyan, even though he had no Hollywood track record (and, like Nolan, no formal training). Nolan's judgment was vindicated: Julyan's score powerfully enhances the film's sense of anxiety and dislocation.

Once the film was finished, distributors, like producers, reacted with incomprehension. "I'd kind of expected that," remarked Nolan. "I'd always joked to the producers that, if we did it right, a lot of people weren't going to like it." Enthused critical reaction to festival screenings, a standing ovation at Venice and some vigorous backstage lobbying by Steven Soderbergh gained the film a release, and it proved an unexpected box-office hit, grossing $26m in the US alone.

Nolan had again proved he could revitalise well-worn noir conventions through the audacity of his treatment, to create startlingly vivid images, to credit his audiences with the intelligence and persistence to follow challenging ideas – and to elicit outstanding performances, especially a gaunt and tormented Pearce. Nolan himself seems to have been taken aback by the film's

appeal: "It seems to have a passionate following. We always imagined it would be a bit of a cult movie. But there's such a wide audience beyond that who have seen it and appreciated it."

The innocent sleep

On the strength of *Memento*'s success, Nolan was offered the chance at a big-budget mainstream movie with A-list Hollywood stars. At first sight the assignment hardly looked promising: Nolan, a brilliant interpreter of his own material, would be working to someone else's script, and a second-hand one at that. The brooding Norwegian thriller, *Insomnia* (1997), directed by Erik Skjoldbjærg and starring Stellan Skarsgård, had scored a low-level international success, but Hollywood's track record on remakes of European foreign-language movies was dire. Moreover, Hillary Seitz's script – which relocates the action to Alaska – was almost entirely linear, with none of the ingenious chronological games of Nolan's first two films.

Nolan, though, took eagerly to the project, sensing a chance to "do something a bit different with that concept" and admiring Seitz's achievement in

Al Pacino and Hilary Swank in **Insomnia**

Alcon Ent/Section Eight/Rob McEwan/Kobal

"Americanising it without selling out the darkness of the original material". Indeed, the remake sticks quite closely to the original's plot. A veteran LA cop, Dormer (Pacino), and his partner, Eckhart (Martin Donovan), are sent to Alaska to investigate the killing of a schoolgirl. There's tension between them – Eckhart intends to give evidence to Internal Affairs that may jeopardise Dormer's career. A stakeout goes wrong; chasing the killer through the fog, Dormer accidentally shoots Eckhart dead. He blames the shooting on the killer (Robin Williams), but the latter has seen what really happened and starts to apply blackmail.

For once, a Hollywood remake proved as good, if not better than its European source. In narrative terms, *Insomnia* is Nolan's most conventional movie to date, but it connects with his previous treatments of a central character's state of mind. Dormer has to face up to his own identity: the star LAPD detective his reputation suggests or a corrupt opportunist? And just how accidental was his shooting of his partner? Nolan makes atmospheric use of his majestic Alaska locations to suggest the oppression that steadily encroaches on Dormer's mind, unable to sleep thanks to his own demons and the 24-hour daylight.

As Dormer, dead behind the eyes even before the fatal shooting, Pacino gives one of his finest, least mannered performances in years, and Williams, at long last shedding his relentlessly twinkly screen persona, makes a chillingly calculating villain. David Julyan again contributed the score, weaving together orchestral and electronic sonorities to suggest the encroaching insomniac unreality.

Tense and accomplished though it is, *Insomnia* is undoubtedly the least distinctive and original of Nolan's films. The evidence suggests that he's a director better suited to working on his own material. Yet *Insomnia*, as he no doubt intended, proved that he could handle a large budget and A-list cast, and should have earned him the freedom to explore even more challenging and personal projects. The news, at press time, that he is to direct the fifth entry in the *Batman* series hardly arouses delight, but it may just be that Nolan can surprise us all by revitalising this weary franchise.

PHILIP KEMP is a freelance writer and historian, and a regular contributor to *Sight & Sound*.

Christopher Nolan Filmography

1998
FOLLOWING
Script, Direction and Photography: CN. Editing: Gareth Heal, CN. Music: David Julyan. Production Design: Tristan Martin. Players: Jeremy Theobald (The young man, Bill), *Alex Haw* (Cobb), *Lucy Russell* (The blonde), *John Nolan* (The policeman). *Produced by CN, Jeremy Theobald, Emma Thomas. 70 mins.*

2000
MEMENTO
Script and Direction: CN. Photography: Wally Pfister. Editing: Dody Dorn. Music: David Julyan. Production Design: Patti Podesta. Players: Guy Pearce (Leonard Shelby), *Carrie-Anne Moss* (Natalie), *Joe Pantoliano* (Teddy), *Mark Boone Jr* (Burt). *Produced by Suzanne Todd, Jennifer Todd. 109 mins.*

2002
INSOMNIA
Script: Hillary Seitz. Direction: CN. Photography: Wally Pfister. Editing: Dody Dorn. Music: David Julyan. Production Design: Nathan Crowley. Players: Al Pacino (Will Dormer), *Robin Williams* (Walter Finch), *Hilary Swank* (Ellie Burr), *Martin Donovan* (Hap Eckhart). *Produced by Paul Junger Witt, Edward L McDonnell, Broderick Johnson, Andrew A Kosove. 118 mins.*

Iranian Cinema Now

The decade since *IFG*'s 1993 dossier on Iranian cinema has been marked by international triumphs for the country's films, the ever-changing face of censorship and the hopes and disappointments of Mohammad Khatami's presidency, as **JUDY STONE** reports.

"Iranian cinema is probably the most extraordinary phenomenon of the last 10 to 15 years," Alberto Barbera, consultant to Italy's National Museum of Cinema, recently wrote in *Film International*, the invaluable English-language quarterly published in Tehran. Leading the way internationally is Abbas Kiarostami, who became the first Iranian to win the Palme d'Or for *Taste of Cherry* in 1997, but whose two recent films have not been screened in Iran. Mohsen Makhmalbaf's magical *Gabbeh* (1996) entranced viewers in many countries and his *Kandahar* (2001) introduced audiences to a hitherto unknown world.

After 9/11, Iran was named by President Bush as part of the "axis of evil", and the acceleration of international tensions inevitably took a renewed toll on the cultural scene. Since 2000, more than 90 Iranian newspapers and magazines have been banned, including *Film Report* and *World Cinema*, and scores of journalists arrested, as powerful conservative clerics have stepped up their fight against reformist elements and student demonstrators.

Afghan tales through Iranian eyes

In the last decade, previously unmentionable approaches have been taken in films dealing with women. There have been ground-breaking portrayals of Kurdish lives and, perhaps most striking of all, many films dealing with

Aziz Saati

Mohsen Makhmalbaf's **The Cyclist**

Afghanistan. The last category of films was foreshadowed by Makhmalbaf's *Cyclist* (1989), about a homeless Afghan refugee's race to collect money to pay for medical treatment for his ailing wife. His prescient *Kandahar*, which followed a Canadian-Afghan woman's search for her sister, was released just before the start of the coalition air attacks on Afghanistan. It also made headlines for the questionable casting of Hassan Tantai, an Afro-American Muslim, born David Belfield, who had confessed on American television to the 1980 murder

Wild Bunch

Mohsen Makhmalbaf's **Kandahar**

in Washington, D.C. of Ali Akbar Tabatabai, a former Iranian diplomat opposed to the Islamic regime. The film won the Cannes festival's Ecumenical prize and UNESCO's Fellini Award.

Makhmalbaf's elder daughter, Samira, who at 17 drew international attention in 1997 at Cannes with her debut *The Apple* and shared the 2001 Cannes Jury Prize for *Blackboards*, went on to win the same prize outright for *At Five in the Afternoon*, about a young woman in devastated Kabul who attends a secular school and dreams of becoming president, a goal symbolised by her repeated changes into high-heeled white shoes. The 2003 Venice festival showed *The Joy of Madness*, a documentary by Samira's 14-year-old sister, Hana, which revealed Samira's sometimes high-handed methods in dealing with the reluctant non-professional Afghans in her cast. It also portrays a people living in fear, through interviews with a mullah, a family and two women.

Abolfazi Jalili's *Delbaran*, top prize winner at the 2001 Festival of Three Continents, portrays the courage of a 14-year-old Afghan refugee who helps out at a café and service station while the police chief searches for illegal border-crossers. More daring is 2002's *Abjad* (*The First Letter*), Jalili's autobiographical memoir of an adolescent Muslim, frustrated in his artistic desires, who falls in love with a Jew, daughter of a cinema owner, before the Islamic revolution sends her family into exile.

Majid Majidi's **Baran**

Majid Majidi's *Baran* (2000) is set in an Iranian factory that employs Afghan illegals, including a girl disguised as a boy. When a young Iranian helper discovers her secret he is transformed by the knowledge. Majidi's vividly revealing documentary, *Barefoot to Herat* (2002), takes place in two ill-equipped refugee camps in western Afghanistan, where people face cold, hunger and death.

Hassan Yekapanah's appealing *Djomeh* (1999), co-winner of the Cannes Camera d'Or for best first feature, follows an illegal Afghan dairy farm worker who falls hopelessly in love with an Iranian shopkeeper's daughter. After the film's Afghan star, Jalil Nazari, accepted an invitation to a Hamburg festival he could not return to Iran, an ordeal sensitively documented in Mahoud Behraznia's *Heaven's Path* (2000).

Novem Productions

Emkan (Mehdi Morady) faces the Mullah of Saveh in Abolfazi Jalili's **Abjad**

In *Paradise Is Somewhere Else* (2003), Abdolrasol Golbin sympathetically presents an Afghan teenager and his new Iranian buddy, who desperately wants to escape a sheep herder's existence, and shows how fate conspires against them.

These Afghani ordeals are matched in Bahman Ghobadi's devastating portrayal of young Kurds trying to save a crippled youngster in *A Time for Drunken Horses* (1999), co-winner, with *Djomeh*, of the Camera d'Or in 2000. Ghobadi's *Marooned in Iraq* (2002) has breathtaking shots of the rugged mountainous landscape and surprising moments of humour, as Kurdish musicians wander across the Iran-Iraq border in search of their long-lost vocalist, who has defied the ban on woman singers.

Fariborz Kamkari's debut feature, *Black Tape*, subtitled *The Videotape Fariborz Kamkari Found in the Garbage*, won praise at Edinburgh and criticism in the *New York Times* for its unusual presentation of an uneasy relationship between a young Kurdish woman trying to reclaim her Kurdish identity and her older husband, who turns out to be her former torturer.

A time for female voices

Feminine issues have been addressed in new ways by both male and female directors, including Rakhshan Bani-Etemad, Tamineh Milani and Manijeh Hekmat (all profiled later in this dossier). Kiarostami's controversial *Ten* (2002), shot on video, was his first exploration of women's lives. Dariush Mehrjui takes on patriarchal oppression and the desperation of three young women in *Bemani* (2002).

In Rasul Sadr Ameli's *The Girl in the Sneakers* (1998), his teenage heroine runs away from home after she and her boyfriend are stopped in a park by police who arrest him; her outraged parents prohibit any more unseemly behaviour. Sadr Ameli's *I'm Taraneh 15* (2002) is a heartening look at the courageous decision of a divorced young woman to keep her baby.

Film critic Nasser Saffarian presented an

Rasul Sadr Ameli's **I'm Taraneh 15**

impressive three-part documentary on the late Farough Farroukhzad, who broke taboos with her erotic poetry and made an influential documentary about lepers, *The House Is Black* (1962). Veteran director Naser Taghvai (*Captain Korshid*, 1987) returned after a 15-year break with *Blank Page* (2002), the portrait of a restless woman who longs to become a screenwriter in spite of her husband's opposition.

Bahram Beizai (*Bashu – The Little Stranger*, 1985) won the Iranian critics' 2001 Best Film prize for *Killing Rabids*, his first production in 10 years, but foreign critics reacted negatively to its murky approach to contemporary problems. Criticising restrictions that make it virtually impossible to show the reality of relationships between men and women, Beizai has declared that "the greatest loss of our cinema is the loss of love... That is why our films are lifeless."

Mohsen Makhmalbaf's wife, Marziyeh Meshkini, won several awards from Italian critics for her debut feature *The Day I Became a Woman* (2000), a three-part exploration into a woman's three stages of life. Kim Longinotto and Ziba Mir-Hosseini's *Divorce Iranian Style* (1998), inspired by *Marriage on Trial*, a book by the London-based Iranian anthropologist Ziba Mir-Hosseini, goes into an Iranian divorce court to hear several women trying to change their lives. And a father's answer to the 1991 American film *Not Without My Daughter*, starring Sally Field, is recorded in Bozorg Mahmoody's documentary,

Without My Daughter (2002), a "letter" to the child he has not seen for 16 years.

Mariam Shahriar's brave *Daughters of the Sun* (1999) is the story of a girl who shaves her head, disguises herself as a boy and goes to work in a rural factory, only to find herself the object of a female co-worker's affections. It was kept from being shown at the Fajr film festival, but beat 65 other debuts to win Best First Feature at Montreal in 2000. The film was sent to 40 other festivals but has not been screened in Iran.

The shadow of censorship

Shahriar's experience resembles the fate of other prize-winning productions, among them Jafar Panahi's banned *The Circle*, which have not been shown in Iran, either because of censorship or the severe shortage of cinemas for arthouse films. Although Iran is among the world's top 15 countries in terms of feature production, it has only approximately 315 screens for a population of 67 million. About 70 to 80 films are made annually, but on average only six to 10 are arthouse productions sent to festivals. About half of these are sent by the Farabi Cinema Foundation, the rest by independent Iranian companies or non-Iranian distributors.

In the US, the best introduction to Iranian cinema was provided by Jamsheed Akrami's *Friendly Persuasion* (2000), a documentary featuring interviews with 14 leading film-makers who try to answer the question: "How could humane images emerge in such a tense and problem-filled society?" The directors point out that repression, the Islamic revolution, the eight-year Iran-Iraq war and economic problems have made people more sensitive to – and artists more likely to focus on – personal relationships. *Friendly Persuasion* is ultimately an indictment of film censorship.

Akrami, who left Iran prior to the Shah's downfall in 1979 and now teaches at William Paterson University in New Jersey, has also helped bring Iranian films to New York's Film Society of Lincoln Center. Not only did he introduce the

work of Amir Naderi, the first Iranian to attract international attention, with *The Runner* (1985), but he also showed two of the three innovative films Naderi made in Manhattan after settling there in the late 1980s.

In "New Directors, New Directions", Akrami introduced Fereydoun Geyrabni's *Red* (2000), about an oppressed woman fighting against her abusive husband, and Behrooz Afkhami's *Hemlock*, the controversial tale of an unstable nurse's relationship with a married man, which became the highest-grossing film of 2000 in Iran (it was also the first film to have been made by an Iranian member of parliament).

Akrami also screened Maziar Miri's *The Unfinished Song* (2002), which had difficulties with the censors for its focus on an officially banned female singer. Other films seen at Lincoln Center included: Iraj Karimi's *Going By* (2001), a road movie with a nod to Kiarostami, *One More Day* (2000), Babak Payami's first feature, about a quiet relationship between a man and woman who see each other every morning at a bus stop, Mohammad Ali Talebi's *You Are Free* (2001), an examination of juvenile delinquency, Bahman Kiarostami's *Tabaki* (2001), a revealing portrait of professional mourners and Niki Karimi's *To Have or Not To Have* (2001), about childless couples.

The way the absence of female companionship adversely affects the lonely lives of soldiers and miners is intuitively addressed by Ali-Reza Amini in two films, *Letters in the Wind* (2002) and *Tiny Snowflakes* (Locarno Jury Prize, 2003). Parviz Shahbazi's *Deep Breath* (2003) sheds a rare light on the hopelessness of the young generation, exploring the self-destructive lethargy of a college student and his trouble-making friend.

Banned for four years, *Snowman*, an undistinguished black comedy directed by Davud Mirbagheri, grossed a record $500,000 in 1997, even though Islamic militants were infuriated by its depiction of an Iranian man who has disguised himself as a woman in Turkey in the hope of marrying an American and emigrating. It was attacked in several cities as immoral, despite a politically correct ending in which the man falls in love with an Iranian woman and returns with her to Iran.

Parviz Shahbazi's **Deep Breath**

Truths stranger than fiction

In 2003, the Edinburgh and Tribeca (New York) festivals screened Maziar Bahari's *Along Came a Spider*, a shocking documentary about a psychopath who killed 16 prostitutes in Mashad and won ideological sympathy among Islamic militants. HBO bought the US rights and the film may well be screened in Iran, according to Akrami, who notes that Bahari was allowed to interview the killer on condition he would not discuss the sexual aspects of the case: "There is no mention that the killer was also a rapist. That changes his image from a psychopath to a Muslim zealot with a mission."

Although not part of official programmes, a few provocative independent films do manage to reach audiences off the beaten track. *The Tree that Remembers* (Canada/Iran/US), a searing 2001 documentary on Iranians who have survived emigration after years in prison, is part of a touring UN Film Festival. Its director, Masoud Raouf, was himself a political prisoner in Iran and embarked on the work after reading about a young Iranian student who hanged himself from a tree on the outskirts of a small Canadian town.

Elli Safari's documentary, *Medium of Love* (2002) is a portrait of the unorthodox cleric Ali Afsahi, who taught a course in modern film, showing classic clips of sex and violence, as well as controversial ones from Oliver Stone's *Natural Born Killers*. His work was based on the belief that students should understand the roots of violence and learn about love and life in other societies. In 2000, he was arrested, defrocked and imprisoned for four months. The documentary was broadcast in Holland, where Safari now lives, and presented at the 2002 London festival. In January 2003, Afsahi was arrested again, held in prison overnight and ordered to apologise for what he had said in the documentary or face a ten-year sentence that was still hanging over him at press time. He lost his job and was ordered not to work in film again.

Taking it to the streets

The widespread appreciation of Iranian films abroad brought out three Iranian pickets during a programme at the Pacific Film Archive in Berkeley, California, in 2003. The protesters argued that the international exposure of such memorable productions masks the hard facts of right-wing censorship and imprisonments by the repressive Iranian government. Their disapproval reflected objections voiced in 1993 and 1994 by Parviz Sayyad, Los Angeles-based director of *The Mission* (1982), that Iranian film seasons and festival appearances "buy face and honour for a regime without either".

One of the protesters, Moslem Mansouri, had brought along a DVD of his secretly shot documentary, *Trial* (2002), a captivating film about the brick-making villagers of Khosro. For 10 years, the workers had a joyous hobby – participating in unauthorised 8mm movies about their humdrum lives – until the government put a stop to it. Their local film-maker, Ali Matini, had written 110 unauthorised books about his community and directed 18 movies with his amateur actors. Then, in 1992, he was arrested and released months later, on condition that he never make another movie; the villagers were ordered not to co-operate with him.

But Matini and his players got together once more to show their activities in *Trial*. Mansouri had also been arrested in 1981 for his political views and imprisoned for two years. Between 1994 and 1998 he produced eight documentaries, including *Close-Up, Long Shot*, a portrait of Hoossein Sabzian, who played the movie-obsessed Mohsen Makhmalbaf impersonator in Kiarostami's *Close-Up*. *Trial* was enthusiastically added to the Pacific Film Archive season and won the Tribeca Festival's prize of $25,000 worth of post-production services.

Regime changes

In Tehran, film-makers had chafed under confusing regulations and stifling restrictions, as management of cinema affairs changed hands three times between 1994 and 1997. They had hoped for improvement after Khatami's election in 1997. Ataollah Mohajerani, a moderate, was appointed head of the Ministry of Culture and Islamic Guidance and named Seifollah Daad as deputy minister for cinema. Daad, with 15 years' experience as a director, came into office vowing to ease restrictions, get rid of bureaucracy and support the Iranian presence at festivals – a matter of some controversy among hard-liners.

Daad's administration loosened restrictions, giving a green light to many of the films mentioned above, and released some previously banned films. However, in early 2001 Mohajerani was replaced, and in June Daad resigned under pressure from conservatives. Mohammad-Hassan Pezeshk, one of the most experienced managers at the Farabi Cinema Foundation, took over.

There were some rumblings about several movies selected for the 2002 Fajr festival that were later censored by the Culture Ministry, and reports that conservatives were put on the next Fajr selection committee to prevent a repeat of the situation. Not shown, but the subject of much anticipation was Mani Haghighi's *Abadan* (2001), an engaging, independently financed low-budget movie about an 80-year-old man's desire to escape Tehran, and his daughter, and visit Abadan. The director, who was educated in Canada, is the son of cinematographer Nemat Haghighi and grandson of director Ebrahim Golestan.

Three days before the 2003 Fajr festival, film-makers were shocked to learn that Mohammad Mehdi Heydarian, considered a "severe believer" in Islamic and revolutionary values, had been appointed to succeed Pezeshk, who was suffering from throat cancer. Heydarian had been director of the General Office for Observation and Evaluation when Khatami was minister of culture (1983-92) and went on to found Sima Film, the production body for Iranian TV, which is known for its hostile attitude toward Iranian films and film-makers.

In his new post, Heydarian soon became embroiled in a newspaper quarrel with Jafar Panahi, who refused to cut 17 minutes from *Crimson Gold*, the fact-based story of a pizza delivery man (played by Hossein Emadeddiin), and refused to obey an order not to take the film to Cannes, where it won the Un Certain Regard Jury prize.

Hossein Emadeddin in **Crimson Gold**

Jafar Panahi Productions

A few months later, Babak Payami reported that he had been arrested by "polite" armed men who confiscated the 35mm negative of his new work, *The Silence Between Two Thoughts* (2003), which is set during Afghanistan's Taliban regime and deals with Islamic rules governing the execution of a virgin. Payami smuggled out a video and it premiered at Venice (where his *Secret Ballot* had won the Silver Lion for best director in 2001, but was never screened in Iran). Payami said that when he complained about his treatment to Culture Ministry officials they claimed they had no knowledge of the events in question. He is not returning to Iran.

Recently, there have been reports that films may not now show so much as one lock of a woman's hair slipping out from under the obligatory *hejab* (scarf). It's cover-up all the way, as Iranian film-makers confront increasing restrictions at home, even as they continue to win acclaim abroad.

"The future of Iranian cinema will be decided by the ongoing battle between the film-makers and the Islamic fundamentalists controlling the media," suggests Jamsheed Akrami. "Along with the press, cinema has proven itself to be a potent medium for initiating social change. While the fundamentalists have succeeded in muzzling the press and exercising full control over radio and television, they have had a much tougher time with the socially committed film-makers who, despite domestic bans imposed on their films, have had little difficulty in finding international arenas for raising their voices."

JUDY STONE, a former (long-time) film critic for the *San Francisco Chronicle*, is the author of *Eye on the World* (Silman-James Press, 1997), interviews with 200 film-makers from 40 countries, and *The Mystery of B. Traven* (iUniverse.com, Inc.). Her extensive interviews with Iranian film-makers will appear in her next book, alongside conversations with authors from many countries.

The Film-Makers

RAKHSHAN BANI-ETEMAD, director.

Born in Tehran, 1954. Widely regarded as Iran's foremost woman film-maker, she rejects being slotted into a feminist sidebar even though four of her features and a recent documentary have all dealt with women's issues. In her daring *Nargess* (1992), a romantic triangle involves a young thief, his older lover and partner in crime and a strong-willed young woman. *The Blue-Veiled* (1994) depicts community opposition to the love between a poor farm worker and her wealthy, older boss. In *May Lady* (1998), a domineering son is suspicious about the man who keeps telephoning his divorced mother, a film-maker who documents women's problems. After Bani-Etemad graduated in directing from Tehran's College of Dramatic Arts, she made TV documentaries from 1984 to 1987, on consumer culture, the urban employment of rural migrants, drug addiction and economic measures during wartime. She still considers social documentary her favourite genre. Her most recent fiction feature, *Under the Skin of the City* (2000), dramatises the struggle of a working-class mother trying to keep her family together.

During the 2001 campaign to re-elect President Mohammad Khatami she made *Our Times*, a two-part documentary on the teenage campaign to re-elect him and the attempt by a destitute single mother to run for president. "What sets Ms Bani-Etemad apart from other Iranian film-makers," a review in *The Iranian* noted, "is that while she portrays the depth of despair she never condescends and never victimises her characters."

BAHMAN FARMANARA, director, producer and actor.

Born in Tehran, 1942. Bahman Farmanara came back to cinematic life playing himself as a dying

Mitra Mahasseni

Rakhshan Bani-Etemad

man in *Smell of Camphor, Fragrance of Jasmine* (2000), his first feature in 22 years. At 16, his wealthy father had sent him to study in England and then to film school at the University of Southern California. He won acclaim for his first feature, *Prince Ehtejab* (1977), about a decadent aristocratic family under the dying Qajar dynasty. The Shah's censors banned his *Tall Shadows of the Wind* (1978), in which a scarecrow multiplies and terrorises a village. It was banned again after the Islamic revolution in 1979.

Bahman Farmanara in **Smell of Camphor, Fragrance of Jasmine**

Farmanara spent the next ten years as a producer and distributor in Canada and the US and since 1990 has run his family's textile business in Tehran. Every time he submitted a film script it was rejected. One week after his last submission was refused, the depressed Farmanara wrote an outline about a director who was not allowed to work for 20 years, has a heart condition and proposes a film about his own funeral. A week later the idea for *Smell of Camphor*... was approved.

His *House Built on Water* (2001), which touches on a troubled father-son relationship, Aids, drug addiction, and the 'serial murders' of intellectuals, won top honours at the Fajr festival in 2002, despite its odd mixture of a poetic element, thriller excitement and Koran mysticism. It became a hit after 17 elements were heavily censored, including references to the lack of a future for the young. Somehow the film still illustrated the saying "Life without hope is like a house built on water." Which may well describe the atmosphere for many in Iran.

MANIJEH HEKMAT, director and producer.

Born in Arak, 1962. Although she was an assistant director on 11 features and producer of five, she didn't come to international attention until threatened with imprisonment if she held a private screening of *Women's Prison* (2001), her directorial debut, during the 2002 Fajr festival. Several months later, a print found its way to Singapore and went on to acclaim at the Venice festival and 50 other international showcases, winning Rotterdam's first Amnesty International Prize.

After a two-year struggle with censors, a cut version of the film, which alludes to crime, corruption, prostitution, drug addiction and homosexuality, became a hit in Iran, playing to more than 1.3 million viewers. After hardline religious groups protested, a theatre was burned down and the film was pulled off screens in 10 cities, including finally Tehran.

Although the film dramatises the 17-year relationship between a tough jailor, initially assigned to suppress a prison riot and a feisty, long-term inmate, Hekmat thought of prison as a microcosm of society. The nine minutes cut for domestic consumption included the shot of a prisoner being led off to execution and another scene in which women are smoking. It inexplicably preserved a moment that implied a Lesbian sexual attack.

On June 23, 2003, there was a disheartening postscript to the global praise for *Women's Prison* when Zahra Kazemi, a Canadian-Iranian mother and photo-journalist who was taking pictures outside Tehran's notorious Evin prison, which confines men and women, was arrested and severely beaten. She died in custody on July 11.

ABBAS KIAROSTAMI, director.

Born Tehran, 1940. Graduated in painting from Tehran University's Faculty of Fine Arts and worked initially in painting, graphics and book illustration. He founded the film department of the Institute for the Intellectual Development of Children and Young Adults, directing his first production, *Bread and the Alley*, in 1970. From the time of *Where Is the Friend's House?* (1986), *Life and Nothing More* (1992), *Through the Olive Trees* (1994) and *Close-Up* (1990), until his ground-breaking twelfth feature, *Ten*, he has been hailed internationally as one of this era's great film-makers. Nevertheless, he has been criticised at home for his deliberate ambiguity, designed to stimulate the viewer's response to a film.

He became the first Iranian to win the Palme d'Or in 1997 for *Taste of Cherry*, a re-affirmation of life that resists the temptation of death. *A.B.C. Africa* (2001), his video documentary on children orphaned by the Aids crisis in Uganda received good reviews abroad, some negative criticism in Iran and won Martin Scorsese's year-end accolade as the "movie that stayed most strongly in my mind... a cinematic poem on the human capacity to move beyond tragedy."

Kiarostami became headline news in 2002 when the US refused to give him a visa to attend *Ten*'s premiere at the New York Film Festival. The *New York Times* editorially condemned that action. The film, which deals provocatively with women's lives, has not been screened in Iran, following Kiarostami's refusal to cut 40%, including scenes involving a prostitute and a cantankerous boy arguing with his divorced mother.

Abbas Kiarostami

When Kiarostami arranged a private screening at a 215-seat hall, 3,500 people turned up, some pushing their way in, breaking the doorkeeper's arm. His *The Wind Will Carry Us* (1999) has still not received a theatrical release because of the censors' objection to a scene in which a woman is dimly pictured milking a goat, while the protagonist recites a few lines of erotic poetry.

The director has also supplied ideas and/or scripts for several films, including Alireza Raisian's *Abandoned Station* and *The Journey*, Mohammad Ali Talebi's *The Wind and the Willow* and Jafar Panahi's *The White Balloon* and *Crimson Gold*.

Three documentaries by other film-makers have enhanced his "unpredictable" reputation: Yuji Mohara's *A Week with Kiarostami*, a rare look at the director on location for *The Wind Will Carry Us*, along with a substantial interview; Jamsheed Akrami's *A Walk with Kiarostami*, tracking the director as still photographer, engrossed in the natural beauty of Ireland's Galway Bay, and Mahmoud Benraznia's *Close-Up Kiarostami*, with tributes from stars, directors and festival chiefs, as well as remarks from hostile local critics.

In a considerable artistic departure, Kiarostami combined film and theatre for a unique staging in Rome in 2003 of the *Ta'zeyeh*, a traditional passion play about the murder of Hussein, grandson of the prophet Mohammed. In addition to his many festival awards, he has been made a Commander of Art and Literature in France, and Italy's National Museum of Cinema in Turin honoured him with a two-week retrospective of all his films, as well as video installations, photography and poetry. It also premiered two of five shorts, combining film and still photographs, on the theme of water, a flow designed, he says, to awaken "the ability to look and see, to listen and to hear; in short, a forgotten art: how to use our senses."

MAJID MAJIDI, director and actor.

Born in Tehran, 1959. Began acting as a youngster, but to please his father enrolled in

Tehran University's engineering school – only to switch to the drama department, later dropping out when the universities were shut down. When film production resumed in the 1980s, he appeared in three Makhmalbaf productions, memorably starring in *Boycott* (1985) as an imprisoned revolutionary forced to reconsider his early beliefs.

He won international acclaim with his heart-tugging but unsentimental features *Children of Heaven* (1997), an Oscar nominee, and *The Color of Paradise* (1998), but changed direction with *Baran* (2000), a stark depiction of exploited Afghans in an Iranian factory. All three won the Montreal World Film Festival's Grand Prize of the Americas.

His interest in Afghanistan dates back to *Baduk*, his 1991 debut feature about child slavery, when he saw dead Afghan refugees on the road near the Iran-Pakistan border. That interest is movingly manifested in his new documentary feature, *Barefoot to Herat*, filmed during visits to two Afghan refugee camps in 2001 and 2002. Witnessing the Afghanis' struggle to survive,

Majid Majidi

Majidi asked: "How will the collective human conscience justify their fate?"

MAKHMALBAF FILM HOUSE

In 1996, writer, director and producer Mohsen Makhmalbaf (born in 1957 in Tehran) took a break from making such well-known films as *Gabbeh* (1995) and started a school for selected students, including his daughters, Samira and

Maysam Makhmalbaf

Samira Makhmalbaf (behind camera) shooting **At Five in the Afternoon**

Hana, and his photographer son Maysam (the middle child), as well as his second wife, Marziyeh Meshkini.

The school's 30 classes range from philosophy, poetry, swimming and cooking to practical film-making. Makhmalbaf demands absolute concentration. Whatever a student's designated activity at a given point, that is all they do for eight hours a day for at least a month. The results are visible in the prizes won by Samira's *Apple* (1998), *Blackboards* (2000) and *At Five in the Afternoon* (2003), 14-year-old Hana's *Joy of Madness* (2002) and Meshkini's *The Day I Became a Woman* (2000).

Although Makhmalbaf's touch is evident in their work, they have already progressed more rapidly than he did. He did not make his first film (*Nasouh Repentance*) until 1982. Imprisoned under the Shah's regime from 1974-79 for attacking a policeman, he began writing for radio and stage, works later collected in his three-volume *A Dumb Man's Dream*. He has become one of the most prolific and controversial directors, usually depicting political and social themes, while evolving from his commitment to fundamentalism to a realisation that "truth is not found in a single place!"

DARIUS MEHRJUI, director.

Born in Tehran, 1940. Graduated in philosophy, UCLA. His *The Cow* (1969) was the first Iranian film to win an international prize at the Venice festival. It won approval from the Ayatollah Khomeini and helped to open an exploratory new path towards realism in Iranian film-making, although that has not protected him from censorship in the course of a long career that has been marked by four films unusually sympathetic to women: *Banoo* (1992), *Sara* (1993), *Pari* (1995) and *Leila* (1997).

He once accused censors of seeing sexual symbols in everything – noting their objection to the red-lettering of *Sara* on a poster because "it's like a woman's period." Mehrjui's latest, *Behmani*, with its focus on three young women destroyed after rebelling against masculine

restrictions, was ignored by the national jury at the Fajr festival in 2002, but impressed foreign guests. The story was inspired by reports of the high rate of suicide by fire among young women in a tribal community on the Iraq border. Mehrjui said he gave it a more or less happy ending "because I didn't want to show these people without any hope."

Darius Mehrjui

TAMINEH MILANI, director.

Born in Tabriz, 1960. She has a degree in architecture from the University of Tehran. She may always remain best known internationally for having endured seven days in prison on shadowy charges after her controversial sixth film, *The Hidden Half* (2000), had already opened in Tehran.

She started working as a set designer, script girl and assistant director. Her debut feature, *Children of Divorce*, was co-winner of Best First Film at Fajr and she came to international attention with *The Legend of a Sigh* (1990). *Two Women* (1999) won a Fajr prize for Best Script after being turned down for seven years. The first and best of her feminist trilogy, it drew unprecedented cheers from Tehran audiences for its focus on a woman's struggle for an education and an identity beyond marriage and motherhood.

The Hidden Half enraged hardliners by opening up the taboo subject of the Islamic revolution's

Tamineh Milani's **Two Women**

imprisonment and execution of dissidents in the 1980s. But some critics were turned off by the tangled plot, involving a former radical student, now married to a judge, and her youthful attraction to a married intellectual.

Criticism increased at the melodramatic, anti-male tone of *The Fifth Reaction* (2002), about a desperate young widow on a cross-country car chase to outwit her dictatorial father-in-law's attempts to gain custody of her two sons. "I try," the outspoken Milani has said, "to make films that will create a movement so there will be discussions and debates."

JAFAR PANAHI, director.

Born in Mianeh (Azerbaijan province), 1960. Took a BA in directing from the faculty at IRIB (Islamic Republic of Iran Broadcasting). One sentence may have been prophetic in Panahi's charming first feature, *The White Balloon* (1995). When a little girl is told "It's not good for girls to watch snake charmers", she replies: "I wanted to see what's not good for me to watch." The Iranian watch-keepers relegated the film to theatres that showed only children's films, even though it won Cannes' Camera d'Or for best first film and the International Critics Prize.

It was submitted as Iran's official entry for the Foreign-Language Oscar, but, angered by an anti-Iranian bill in the US Congress, the Iranian government unsuccessfully pressured the Academy to withdraw it. Panahi was forbidden to attend the Sundance Festival or to do telephone interviews with American reporters.

Later, at Rotterdam, he was discreetly circumspect, but ensuing events brought out a less diplomatic side.

Jafar Panahi

The production of his third feature, *The Circle* (2000), a sharply critical look at the problems experienced by two women on the day they get out of prison, was subjected to "devastating quarrels and fights" and rejected by the Fajr festival. It later won the Golden Lion at Venice, was released in more than 30 countries – and banned in Iran.

Panahi has since refused to make changes demanded in his fourth feature, *Crimson Gold* (2002), from a Kiarostami idea, and suggested by the true story of a pizza delivery man who fatally shot himself during a bungled armed robbery. As seen through the delivery man's eyes, the film presents a bleak look at class divisions, homelessness, illegal drinking and the overly zealous morals police. Against orders, Panahi smuggled a copy to Cannes where it won the jury prize in Un Certain Regard.

Profiles by **JUDY STONE.**

Unless otherwise credited, all pictures appear courtesy of the Farabi Cinema Foundation.

The Most Successful Iranian Films
at International Festivals, 1993-2002

Film	Awards
The Color of Paradise (Majid Majidi, 1999)	17
The Father (Majid Majidi, 1996)	15
The Jar (Ebrahim Forouzesh, 1994)	14

Majid Majidi's **Children of Heaven**

Ebrahim Forouzesh's **The Jar**

The Circle (Jafar Panahi, 2000)	11
The Key (Ebrahim Forouzesh, 1986)	9
The White Balloon (Jafar Panahi, 1995)	9
The Paper Airplane (Farhad Mehranfar, 1995)	
Sara (Dariush Mehrjui, 1991)	8

Children of Heaven (Majid Majidi, 1996)	8
Kandahar (Mohsen Makhmalbaf, 2001)	8
Baran (Majid Majidi, 2001)	8
The Willow and the Wind (Mohammad Ali Talebi, 1999)	8
The Mirror (Jafar Panahi, 1997)	8
The Day I Became a Woman (Marziyeh Meshkini, 2000)	8

Jafar Panahi's **The White Balloon:** *winner of 11 international awards*

The Most Successful Iranian Film-makers at International Festivals, 1993-2002

Director	Appearances	Awards
Abbas Kiarostami	895	19
Mohsen Makhmalbaf	495	29
Dariush Mehrjui	316	10
Rakhshan Bani-Etemad	228	9
Majid Majidi	191	50
Bahram Beizaie	156	3
Abolfazl Jalili	150	14
Ebrahim Forouzesh	137	33
Mohammad Ali Talebi	118	22
Jafar Panahi	116	28

Reza Mir-Karimi, Farhad Mehranfar and Rassul Sadr-Ameli each won 13 international festival awards in this period.

Ebrahim Forouzesh: 137 festival appearances

Iranian Box-Office Top Ten 2002

		$
1.	Redcap and Sarvenaz	677,600
2.	The Pastry Girl	478,365
3.	Bread, Love and Motorcycle 1,000	458,750
4.	I'm Taraneh 15	405, 375
5.	The Last Supper	316, 625
6.	Women's Prison	312, 750
7.	The Intruder	298, 375
8.	Low Heights	262, 875
9.	Blue	226, 200
10.	Sam and Nargess	226, 200

All titles are Iranian.

Population:	67 million
Admissions:	7.07 million
Total box-office:	$5.3m
Local films' market share:	50%
Screens:	315
Avge. ticket price:	$0.70

All figures except population are for Tehran only.

*The puppet hero of box-office smash **Redcap and Sarvenaz***

Iranian Feature Production 1984-2003 (films per year)

1984 – 30	1994 – 45
1985 – 41	1995 – 62
1986 – 43	1996 – 63
1987 – 52	1997 – 54
1988 – 42	1998 – 54
1989 – 48	1999 – 54
1990 – 56	2000 – 60
1991 – 45	2001 – 87
1992 – 52	2002 – 76
1993 – 56	2003 – 82

Industry Directory

All Tel/Fax numbers require (+98 21)
prefix. All companies are in Tehran

Producer-Distributors

Hedayt Film Institute, Mr Morteza
Shayesteh, 15 Khaled, Eslamboli St.
Tel: 872 7188.

Jozan Film Co. Mr Masoud Jafari
Jozani, 20 Razmandegan Alley,
Fajr St, Motahari St.

Rasaneh Filmsazan Mr Seyyed
Gholamreza Moosavi, 36 Khosro
Alley, Ostad Nejat Ollahi St.
Tel: 880 5576.

Novin Far Film Institute Mr
Hoosang Noorollahi, th 15, 4fl,
Jomhoori Ave. Tel: 641 2644.

Pooya Film Institute Mr Abdollah
Alikhanird, 10, 3 fl Jomhoori.
Tel: 670 3574.

Guya Film Institute Mr Seyyed
Mohammad Qazi, 1st fl, 105
Ramsarst, Somayyeh Ave.
Tel: 884 7555.

Shokufa Film Institute Mr Jafar
Agha, Babaeyan, 18 Abureihan St,
Enqelab St. Tel: 641 6939.

Avishan Film Institute Mr Abbas
Panahandeh, 17 Fateh Alley,
Babataher St, Fatemi St.
Tel: 896 0927.

Rasaneh Omid Film Institute
Mr Sirous Taslimi, 23 Tajbakhsh
Alley, Mirdamad Ave. Tel: 227 6746.
Fax: 227 67616.

Laleh Barg Cinema Institute
Mr Gholam, Hossein Bolouriyan, 3rd
fl, 79 Iran, Shahr St, Enqelab St.

Sepahan Film Cinema Institute
Mr Ebrahim Bank, 3rd fl, 26 Razi St,
Jomhoori Ave. Tel: 670 6268.

**Eyma Film Art & Cultural
Development Co.** Mr Hossein,
Zandbaf, 1st fl, 6 Varavinist,
Motahari St. Tel: 830 0724.

Rasaneh Nikan Institute Mr Bijan
Emkaniyan, 1 Marivan St, South
Sohrevardi Ave. Tel: 881 2121 4.

Baharan Film Institute Mr Akbar
Sadeghi, 18/1 Bahar, Mastiyan St,
Hafte, Tir Sq. Tel: 882 4432.

Rahe – Erfan Cinema Institute Mr
Mohsen Mosaferchi, 1st fl, 26 Ansari
Alley, Jomhoori Ave. Tel: 646 3622.

**Negin Shahr Film Production
Institute** Mr Jalaleddin Ghezel
Ayagh, 1/36 Kabkaniyan St,
Keshavarz Blvd. Tel: 896 8181.

Sabz Film Art & Cultural Institute
Mr Rassul Sadr Ameli, 1st fl,
17 Mazandarani St, Hafte Tir Sq.
Tel: 882 5838.

**Faradis – Barin Distribution
& Production Institute**
Mr Manoochehr Mohammadi, 1st fl,
113 Malayeripour St, North Mofateh
St. Tel: 830 7732.

Farabi Cinema Foundation Mr
Reza Dad, 75 Sie, Tir Ave, Tehran
11358. Tel: 670 1010. Fax: 670
8155. e: fcf1@dpi.net.ir.

**Sureh Cinema Development
Organization** 13 Somayyeh Ave,
1599819613, Tehran. Tel: 880
52957. Fax: 880 529
e: scdo@hotmail.com.

**Institute for the Intellectual
Development of Children and
Young Adults** Mr Mohsen
Chiniforoushan, Hejab St, Fatemi
Ave, Tehran, 14156. Tel: 896 7392.
Fax: 882 1121.
e: intl_affairs@jamejam.net.

Gol Film Co. Mr Hamid Reza
Ashtiyanipour, 2nd fl, 2 Maragheh
St, Ostad Nejatollahi St, Enghelab
St. Tel: 880 1976.

Sheherazad Media International
Ms. Katayoon Shahabi, 2, 3rd
Sarvestan, Pasdaran Ave, Shariati
St, Tehran, 16619, Iran. Tel: 285
8962. Fax: 285 8962.

Behnegar Institute Mr Ahmad
Mosazadeh, 78 East Motahari Ave,
Tehran, 15667. Tel: 843 0860.
Fax: 206 1137.
e: info@behnegar.com.

Producers

Sina Cultural Film Institute
Mr Manouchehr Asgari Nassab, 2nd
fl, 113 Malayeri Pour Ave, Hafte Tir
Sq, Tehran, Iran. Tel: 883 2392.
Fax: 884 8805.

Nemayish Film Company
Mr Habiblohe Sahranavard, 1st fl,
4 Motahari Ave, Shariati St, Tehran,
Iran. Tel: 868 73.

Khat-o-Modj Company Mr Alireza
Davoud Nezhad, 74 Habibi Alley,
Soroush St, Ebn Yamin St, North
Sohrevardi Ave, Tehran, Iran.
Tel: 876 2055. Fax: 876 8082.
e: info@lineandwave.com.

Andishe Film Institute Mr Mohsen
Vaziri, 723/2, 5 Andishe Ave,
Shariati St. Tel: 840 5398.
Fax: 843 5462.

Seventh Art & Cultural Institute
Mr Karim Atashi, 334 khajeh
Nasyredine Toosi Ave, Taleghani St,
Shariati St. Tel: 750 3797.

Tamasha Institute Mr Taghi Aligholi
Zadeh, 8, 9 Alley, Arabali Ave,

Khoramshahr St. Tel/Fax: 873 3844.
e: info@tamasha.net.

**Art And Literature House For
Children** Ms. Freshteh Taerpour,
1st fl, 24 Sadar Alley, Tonkabon St,
Enghlab St. Tel/Fax: 753 2181.

Fanose Kheyal Cinema Institute
Mr Gholamreza Azadi, 16 Sanaey
Alley, North Ghandi St.
Tel: 879 2309.

Neshane Film Production Co.
Mr Iraj Taghipoor, 57 Sodmand St,
Shariati St. Tel: 750 1640. Fax: 750
8932. e: info@neshane.com.

Afagh Film Institute Mr Amir
Hossein Sharifi, 23 Amini St, Valie
Asr Ave. Tel: 879 8588.

Aryan film Production Institute
Mr Yadollah Shahidi, 3rd flr, 8/1
Shahin St, Mirzay-eshirazi.
Tel: 881 1920. Fax: 832 0755.

Tuba Visual & Cultural Institute
Mr Roholah Baradari, 6 Niyayesh St,
Tuhid St, Tuhid Sq. Tel: 693 9476.
Fax: 692 1303.

Sobhan Film Mr Saeed Hajimiri,
I,45 Noori Alley, Jami St, Vali e
Asr ave. Tel/Fax: 649 0534.
e: info@sobhanfilm.com.

Sahara Cultural Film Institute
Mr Majid Modarresi, 39 Niloufar St,
Apadana Ave. Tel: 876 6110. Fax:
876 0488. e: modaresi@dpir.com.

Bamdadofilmco Ms. Manijeh
Hekmat, 1st fl, 17 Mazandarani Ave,
Hafte Tir Sq. Tel: 830 9538.

Amrooz Film Mr Davoud Rashidi,
3rd fl, 27 Palizi St, Sohrevardi St.
Tel: 866 639.

Mehrab Film Corporation
Mr Jamal Shorjeh, 86-25 Ave/
Jehan, Ara Ave, Doctor Fatemi.
Tel: 800 0076.

Makhmalbaf Film House Mr
Mohsen Makhmalbaf, 6th fl, 32-16
North Felestin. Tel: 895 8384.

Boshra Film Art & Institute
Mr Seyyed Jamal Sadatyyan, 13
Lyda Ave, Vanak Sq, ValieAsr Ave.
Tel: 887 0290. Fax: 888 6822.

Yekta Film Production Institute
Mr Hossein Tavakoli, niya 1st fl,
441 next Bahar Shiraz Shariati.

Aftab – Negaran Film Production
Mr Ahmad Reza Takhtkeshian,
2nd fl, 505 next 51 Alley, seyyed
Jamaleddin Asadabadi.
Tel: 806 7515.

Panjereh Abi Filmmaking
Mr Mohammad Ali Talebi, 3rd fl,
444 Boluri Alley, Manzarieh
Niyavaran. Tel: 229 9597.

DVD Round-Up

TWO-DISC SPECIAL EDIT

STRAW DOGS
A FILM BY SAM PECKINPAH

by Daniel Rosenthal

While the phenomenal world-wide growth in DVD retail continues to be driven by seven-figure sales for the likes of *Harry Potter* and *The Lord of the Rings*, and even a middling action-adventure like *Daredevil* is given the two-disc treatment, the format's most important contribution to film culture, rather than Hollywood coffers, continues to be its three Rs: restorations, reissues and revelations.

For all viewers, particularly the younger generation, the opportunity to discover or return to the classics in pristine transfers then explore immediately their production or critical reception through commentaries, interviews and documentaries has the potential to transform living rooms into a combination of arthouse rep cinema, festival Q&A session and film school. The first newspaper profiles in which a gifted tyro director explains how DVD inspired his passion for movie-making may not be far away.

Silent Cinema

D. W. Griffith begins this year's round-up, thanks to a magnificent, seven-disc box-set, **Griffith Masterworks** (Kino on Video, Region 1), that could fill a weekend of fairly concentrated viewing. *The Birth of a Nation* and *Intolerance* are included, the former's Klan scenes as shocking as ever, and the set also offers Lillian Gish as the abused Limehouse waif in *Broken Blossoms* and more than 20 of Griffith's short films.

The vast reissue of Charlie Chaplin's feature films came just too late for inclusion here, but Chaplin completists will covet **The Essany**

Films – Volumes 1 and 2 (British Film Institute, Region 2), a pair of two-disc sets compiled after a nine-year hunt for the best available materials, containing six hours' worth of the shorts that Chaplin made between 1915 and 1918, including his first appearance as the Tramp.

Fritz Lang's endlessly influential **Metropolis** (Kino on Video, Region 1; Eureka Video, Region 2) appears in a two-disc set after a marathon restoration process in Germany. It's a joy to see Lang's astounding vision of a mechanised, divided society in such clean form. This version is a third longer than previous reissues and is accompanied by Gottfried Huppertz's original 1927 score. Extras include documentaries on the making of the film and the restoration.

European Classics

Roman Polanski had only just graduated from film school when he shot **Knife in the Water** (1962, Criterion, Region 1) in the Polish lake district. Faithfully observing the Greek unities,

UFA/Kobal

Metropolis: *beautifully restored for DVD*

this riveting study of machismo is a classic three-handed play, set over 24 hours, as middle-aged husband, young wife and even younger hitch-hiker play power games on the couple's yacht. Polanski and co-writer Jerzy Skolimowski's memories of the production, in video interviews, are fascinating, and the second disc in this set contains a selection of Polanski's short films from 1957-62.

The compassion and economy of Ermanno Olmi's storytelling in **Il Posto** (1961) and **I Fidanzati** (1962, both Criterion, Region 2) are wondrous to behold. In the former, the teenaged Domenico (wide-eyed Sandro Panseri), secures the job of the title with a faceless Milan corporation (actually the Edison company, for whom Olmi worked at the time) and in the latter the ruggedly handsome Carlo Cabrini is the oil plant worker sent to Sicily while his fiancée pines for him in Milan. Olmi's video recollections supply invaluable background.

Olmi's generosity of spirit was matched by Federico Fellini in his 1951 debut, **The White Sheikh** (Criterion, Region 1), the delightful tale of naïve, provincial newlyweds (Leopoldo Trieste and Brunella Bovo) and their Roman misadventures, she with the eponymous star (Alberto Sordi) of her favourite *fumetti* photo strip, he with his big-city relatives.

Alberto Sordi, as **The White Sheikh,** *woos Brunella Bovo*

In a new interview on this disc, given shortly before he died, Trieste recalls Fellini taking a phone call from Ingmar Bergman and remarking: "I hear Bergman's voice and I see a skull." Such a dark thought could easily come to mind after immersing oneself in the madness, suicidal despair and psycho-sexual games endured by

the characters in **A Film Trilogy by Ingmar Bergman** (Criterion, Region 1) This superb four-disc box set, an outstanding work of restoration and publishing even by Criterion's exalted standards, contains *Through a Glass Darkly* (1961), *Winter Light* (1962) and *The Silence* (1963), each with a video introduction from *IFG*'s founding editor, Peter Cowie, and *Ingmar Bergman Makes a Movie*, the five-part Swedish Television documentary made during the production of *Winter Light*.

There is insufficient space here to do justice to the achievements of director, cast and crew in even one of the films, but I will single out the genius of Sven Nykvist, particularly in his lighting of the claustrophobic hotel in the breathtakingly erotic *The Silence*, and the raw acting of Gunnar Björnstrand and Harriet Andersson, as the solipsistic novelist and his schizophrenic daughter in *Through a Glass Darkly*.

Gunnar Björnstrand and Harriet Andersson play father and daughter in **Through a Glass Darkly**

After witnessing a country priest's crisis of faith in *Winter Light*, it's a relief to turn to a less bleak, child's-eye view of rural Sweden, in Lasse Hallström's **My Life as a Dog** (1985, Criterion, Region 1), as 12-year-old Ingemar (the charming Anton Glanzelius) is sent to stay with his uncle after his mother falls ill. A repeat viewing emphasises Hallström's delicate, humane touch, ironically compromised in recent years by the Hollywood career this film earned him.

Jules Dassin's thrilling and, unusually for a crime film, moving **Rififi** (1955, Arrow Films, Region 1) created the blueprint from which many a heist movie has been built (Michael Mann's *Heat* tops the list of its more recent descendants), and this sparkling reissue includes Dassin on sprightly form in a new video interview.

Akira Kurosawa

Several of Akira Kurosawa's major works have recently emerged on DVD, including his celebrated transpositions of Shakespeare. The haunted greys and driving rain of his samurai *Macbeth*, **Throne of Blood** (1957, Criterion, Region 1), regain much of their original clarity, but his apocalyptic *King Lear*, **Ran** (1985, Wellspring, Region 1), appears in a disappointing transfer that leaves Emi Wada's Oscar-winning costumes and the most precisely colour co-ordinated battle scenes in movie history looking uncomfortably flushed.

Nippon Herald/Greenwich/Kobal

Peter, left, and Tatsuya Nakadai as 'Fool' and 'Lear' in Kurosawa's Shakespeare-inspired **Ran**

The British Film Institute's latest Kurosawa reissues for Region 2, each one introduced with personable expertise by Alex Cox, take in perhaps his funniest film, **Sanjuro** (1962), **Red Beard** (1965), his final collaboration with Toshiro Mifune (as a country doctor in the late 19th century) and **Ikiru** (1952), featuring his other most loyal and resourceful player, the careworn Takashi Shimura, as the cancer-stricken hero.

American Tales

Merchant Ivory's Henry James adaptations do not stand up well against their later treatments of E. M. Forster. The sterile and stilted **The Europeans** (1979), with Lee Remick over-acting as the gold-digger who shakes up a reserved New England family, and **The Bostonians** (1984; both Criterion, Region 1), with Vanessa Redgrave and Christopher Reeve fighting for the heart and mind of young liberationist Madeleine

Potter in post-Civil War Boston, lack either the vigour of *A Room with a View* or the emotional force of *Howards End*, although both are near-flawless in their craftsmanship. Video interviews with Merchant, Ivory and screenwriter Ruth Prawer Jhabvala accompany both discs.

Merchant Ivory/Kobal

Christopher Reeve in **The Bostonians**

The two-disc, tenth anniversary reissue of Clint Eastwood's **Unforgiven** (Warners, Regions 1 & 2) contains *All on Accounta Pullin' a Trigger*, a new documentary with contributions from Eastwood, Morgan Freeman, Gene Hackman and writer David Webb Peoples, who acknowledges the influence on his script of another film in which an iconic Western star challenged the heroic status of his previous roles: Don Siegel's *The Shootist*, with John Wayne's dying gunslinger a close relative of Eastwood's William Munny in *Unforgiven*.

Warner Bros/Kobal

Morgan Freeman and Clint Eastwood in **Unforgiven**

In 1980, Richard Rush drew praise from François Truffaut and almost every critic in America for **The Stunt Man** (Anchor Bay, Regions 1 & 2), which stands alongside Truffaut's own *Day for Night* as one of the most vibrant and perceptive films about film-making. Steve Railsback, with a thick Texan accent and a thousand-yard stare, is the Vietnam vet

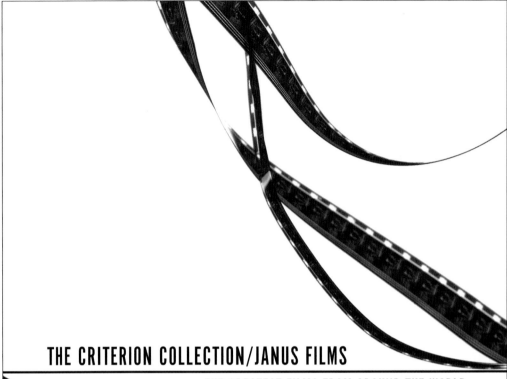

THE CRITERION COLLECTION/JANUS FILMS

THE GREATEST FILMS FROM AROUND THE WORLD

 JANUS FILMS

THE CRITERION COLLECTION
www.criterionco.com

undertaking absurdly dangerous stunts for a First World War action-romance directed by megalomaniac Eli Cross (Peter O'Toole on irrepressible form) and Barbara Hershey is at her most beguiling as the film's leading lady. Rush's script constantly wrong-foots the viewer, as does the second disc's two-hour documentary, *The Sinister Saga of the Stunt Man*.

Fox/Kobal

Steve Railsback, Richard Rush and Barbara Hershey on location for Rush's **The Stunt Man**

Visions of Britain

Two influential films written by Alan Sillitoe are now enjoying a new lease of (gritty) life on DVD. The devil-may-care exploits of factory worker Arthur Seaton (Albert Finney) in Karel Reisz's **Saturday Night and Sunday Morning** (1960, British Film Institute, Region 2) troubled the censors, particularly the scenes of adultery and tips on DIY abortion, and a superb commentary by historian Robert Murphy covers this and many other topics. Another Murphy commentary helps the viewer keep pace with Tony Richardson's **The Loneliness of the Long Distance Runner** (1962, British Film Institute, Region 2), as another great anti-hero, Tom Courtenay's borstal boy, loses the climactic cross-country race.

When Derek Jarman's artistry was anchored by another writer's gifts for story and character, as in his film of Marlowe's *Edward II*, the effect was mesmerising, but in **Jubilee** (1977, Criterion, Region 1) the combination of fifth-form agit prop, sexual violence and cod-Shakespearean dialogue is almost unwatchable – all self-indulgent sound and fury, signifying nothing beyond the enjoyment of cast and crew. This 25th anniversary reissue, including a new documentary by Jarman actor Spencer Leigh,

should nonetheless be an important resource for historians of punk.

Jubilee's lawless London is less terrifying than picturesque Cornwall in Sam Peckinpah's **Straw Dogs**, banned for 18 years in the UK and now reissued in two special editions (Criterion, Region 1; Fremantle Media, Region 2). What starts out as a thoughtful anatomy of the marriage between Dustin Hoffman's American mathematician and Susan George's seductive Cornish girl is transformed into something far darker – and much less convincing – by the notorious rape scene and the Hoffman character's self-defensive discovery of his inner violence.

Among the wealth of extras on the two editions, the highlight (on the two-disc Region 1 set) is Paul Joyce's *Sam Peckinpah: Man of Iron*, a BBC documentary so clear and comprehensive that it survives the removal, for copyright reasons, of all the Peckinpah film clips included when it was originally broadcast.

ABC Pictures/Cinerama Releasing/Kobal

Dustin Hoffman and Susan George in **Straw Dogs**

Documentaries

Almost half a century after its release, the shock of Alain Resnais' half-hour Holocaust documentary, **Night and Fog** (1955, Criterion, Region 1), is undimmed. The cuts between black-and-white stills and newsreels from the 1940s and Sacha Vierny and Ghislain Cloquet's colour footage of the abandoned, overgrown buildings at Auschwitz and Majdanek are like jolts from a nightmare to a waking dream. Novelist and camp survivor Jean Cayrol's commentary, given pitch-perfect delivery by Michel Bouquet, apologises for explaining the fingernail scratches on the ceiling of a gas chamber, "but you have to know", and everyone has to see *Night and Fog* at least once.

One wonders what someone of Resnais' integrity would have made of Robert Flaherty's methods in making **Man of Aran** (1934, Home Vision Entertainment, Region 1). *How The Myth was Made*, the 1970s documentary on this disc, dwells on Flaherty the master manipulator, who talked of 'casting' the right Aran islanders as though he were Selznick in search of Scarlett,

Robert Flaherty's **Man of Aran**

and engineered the tension of the unforgettable shark-fishing episode like Michael Bay cutting together a gun battle. If you can forgive the artifice it remains a great work; it has certainly aged far better than Flaherty's **Louisiana Story** (1948, Home Vision Entertainment, Region 1), which now plays like a twee cross between *National Geographic* and *Huckleberry Finn*.

Finally, **Lost in La Mancha** (2002, Optimum Releasing, Region 2), which saw co-directors Keith Fulton and Louis Pepe graduating with first-class honours from their more pedestrian assignments on 'Making of' featurettes for the likes of *Three Kings*. Their gain was Terry Gilliam's loss as his Spanish shoot for *The Man Who Killed Don Quixote* was derailed and shut down by leading man Jean Rochefort's illness, a flash flood and other mishaps. This joins the *Apocalypse Now* saga, *Hearts of Darkness*, and the *Fitzcarraldo* story, *Burden of Dreams*, as one of the finest of film-making true stories. Sadly, this time we can't judge the trials and tribulations against their masterful end product.

Other Recent Releases

Key to Abbreviations: [R1: Region Code; ACI: Archive Cast/Crew Interview; AD: Archive Documentary; ADI: Archive Director Interview; CC: Cast/Crew Commentary; DC: Director's Commentary; NCI: New Cast/Crew Interview; ND: New Documentary; NDI: New Director Interview; NDT: New Digital Transfer; NST: New Subtitle Translation; RC: Restoration Comparison; SC: Scholar's/Critic's Commentary; SG: Stills Gallery; TT: Theatrical Trailer.]

Ali: Fear Eats the Soul (*Rainer Werner Fassbinder, 1974*) [Criterion, R1. AD; NDT; NIx2; NST; TT; 2 Discs.]
Fassbinder's updated reworking of Douglas Sirk's *All That Heaven Allows*.

An Actor's Revenge (*Kon Ichikawa, 1962*) [BFI, R1.]
Bare bones reissue for over-the-top tale of a vengeful kabuki female impersonator (Kazuo Hasegawa, in his 300th screen appearance).

Andrei Rublyov (*Andrei Tarkovsky, 1966*) [Ruscico, R9. ADx3; ND; SG.]
The life of the 15th-century icon painter, accompanied by documentaries on the film and its historical background.

An Angel at My Table (*Jane Campion, 1990*) [Artificial Eye, R2. DS; ND; SG; TT.]
Devastating account of the troubled life of New Zealand author Janet Frame (Kerry Fox).

The Animatrix (*Various directors, 2003*) [Warners, R1&2.]
Nine animated shorts, based on and inspired by *The Matrix* and Japanese *anime*, that will chiefly appeal to Wachowski obsessives. Mahiro Maeda's gruesome *The Second Renaissance – Parts I and II* is the only tale to emulate the menace of the original *Matrix*.

The Bitter Tears of Petra von Kant (*Rainer Werner Fassbinder, 1972*) [Wellspring, R1. AD; SC.]
Verdi and the Walker Brothers supply the

Gainsborough/Kobal

Tango/Kobal

Hanna Schygulla, left, and Margit Carstensen in
The Bitter Tears of Petra von Kant

soundtrack to Fassbinder's stylised exploration of
sexual obsession and manipulation.

Black and White in Color (*Jean-Jacques
Annaud, 1976*) [Home Vision Entertainment, R1.
NCI; NDI.]
Annaud won an Oscar for this blackly comic First
World War satire, set on the Ivory Coast. The main
bonus feature is just that: producer Arthur Cohn's
Oscar-winning documentary about a trekking
expedition, *The Sky Above, the Mud Below*
(1961).

The Color Purple (*Steven Spielberg, 1985*)
[Warners, R1&2. NDx4; SG; TTx3.]
Spielberg's first bid to be taken seriously as more
than the king of popcorn entertainment, with
Danny Glover a world away from *Lethal Weapon*
heroics as a brutal husband.

Come and See (*Elem Klimov, 1985*) [Ruscico, R9.
AD; NDI, NCIx2; SG.]
The horrific Second World War conflict between
Partisans and Germans in Byelorussia, seen
through the eyes of 16-year-old Flyora (Aleksei
Kravchenko). Justly billed as "a crowning
achievement of 1980s Soviet cinema".

Coup de grâce (*Volker Schlöndorff, 1976*)
[Criterion, R1. NCI; NDI; NDT; NST.]
Repression and depression loom large in the
relationship between a young aristocrat
(Margarethe von Trotta) and a Prussian soldier in
Latvia, 1919.

Les Dames du Bois du Boulogne (*Robert
Bresson, 1945*) [Criterion, R1. NDT; NST; SG.]
Strong echoes of *Les liaisons dangereuses* in
Bresson's melodrama about the aristocrat, her
ex-lover and the prostitute. An arrestingly
beautiful transfer.

Fargo (*Joel Coen, 1996*) [MGM, R1&2. CC; ND;
ADI; SG; TT.]
The Coens' Oscar-winning "true story" of kidnap
and murder, with an appropriately quirky
documentary and a sharp commentary from
cinematographer Roger Deakins.

Hiroshima mon amour (*Alain Resnais, 1959*)
[Criterion, R1. AI; NDT; NI; NST; SC.]
Resnais' masterpiece of love, time and memory;
astonishing to think it was his fiction feature debut.
Extras include a detailed commentary from *IFG*'s
Peter Cowie and vintage interviews with Resnais
and star Emmanuelle Riva.

Mosfilm/Kobal

Aleksei Kravchenko in **Come and See**

The Honeymoon Killers (*Leonard Kastle, 1969*) [Criterion, R1. NDI; NDT; TT.] Dark story with a fearless performance by Shirley Stoler as the obese spinster who falls for Tony Lo Bianco.

The Hustler (*Robert Rossen, 1961*) [Fox, R1&2; NCC; ND; SG; TT.] Perhaps Paul Newman's greatest performance, as flawed pool genius Fast Eddie Felson. Bonus features include trick-shot analysis.

Indiscretion of an American Wife/Terminal Station (*Vittorio De Sica, 1954*) [Criterion, R1. NDT; SC; TT.] Double-bill offering both versions of Jennifer Jones and Montgomery Clift's Roman liaison: De Sica's 89-minute *Terminal Station* and *Indiscretion…*, the 72-minute cut re-edited by David O. Selznick without De Sica's permission.

The Merchant of Four Seasons (*Rainer Werner Fassbinder, 1972*) [Wellspring, R1. ADx2.] The histrionic, almost am-dram performances (Hannah Schygulla excepted) undermine the essential power of this *Woyzeck*-like story of a fruit seller's descent into a personal hell. Includes documentary *The Many Women of Fassbinder.*

The Mission (*Roland Joffé, 1986*) [Warners, R1&2. AD; DC. 2 discs.] Joffé delivers a fine full-length commentary on a film whose power owes much to Chris Menges Oscar-winning camerawork and Ennio Moriccone's unforgettable score. Includes the BBC *Omnibus* programme about the location shoot.

One Flew Over the Cuckoo's Nest (*Milos Forman, 1975*) [Warners, R1&2. DC; DS; ND; NDT; TT. 2 Discs.] Forman's commentary and a lengthy documentary explain the intensive methods that helped to make this adaptation of Ken Kesey's novel one of the great American films of the 1970s.

Ossessione (*Luchino Visconti, 1947*) [BFI, R2. SC.] The late Massimo Girotti smoulders as the drifter in Visconti's magnificent version of Cain's *The Postman Always Rings Twice*.

Quai des Orfèvres (*Henri-Georges Clouzot, 1947*) [Criterion, R1. ACI; ADI; NDT; TT.]

A jealous husband, murder and *un flic* – the recipe for a Parisian *noir* classic.

La Règle du jeu (*Jean Renoir, 1939*) [BFI, R2. AD.] Includes a 1987 French documentary on the making of Renoir's matchless blend of country-house comedy and state-of-the-nation satire.

The Sacrifice (*Andrei Tarkovsky, 1986*) [Artifical Eye, R2. AD; SG. 2 Discs.] Tarkovsky's final film, with Erland Josephson as the retired actor making a pact with God to avert nuclear apocalypse. Includes *Sacrifice* co-editor Michal Leszczylowski's remarkable documentary *Directed by Andrei Tarkovsky*.

Singin' in the Rain (*Gene Kelly, Stanley Donen, 1951*) [Warners, R1&2. CC; AD; ND; SG. 2 Discs.] Sensationally good treatment of a Hollywood classic. Includes commentary from Donen, Debbie Reynolds and others; extensive documentaries.

Solaris (*Andrei Tarkovsky, 1972*) [Ruscico, R9. NCI; ND; SG.] Timely opportunity to compare Tarkovsky's original adaptation of Stanislav Lem's philosophical sci-fi novel with Steven Soderbergh's leaner Hollywood remake.

La terra trema (*Luchino Visconti, 1948*) [BFI, R2.] The almost unbearably harsh lives of Sicilian fishermen and their families inspire an impassioned neo-realist masterpiece.

Z (*Constantin Costa-Gavras, 1968*) [Wellspring, R1. DC; NDT; NI; RC; SG; TT.] Still the political thriller against which all entries in the genre should be judged. ∎

Visconti's **La terra trema**

Books Round-Up

by Daniel Rosenthal

That John Boorman's autobiography, **Adventures of a Suburban Boy** (Faber, London and New York), is beautifully written will come as no surprise to anyone with *Money into Light* (1985), his production diary for *The Emerald Forest*, on their shelves. What distinguishes *Adventures...* as a great memoir full stop, not simply a great film book, is Boorman's ability to tell his story from two seamlessly edited perspectives.

As he takes us through his childhood in Blitz-stricken London, comically dull National Service, apprenticeship directing BBC documentaries and on to Hollywood, *Point Blank* and beyond, with stopovers in the South Pacific, Ireland (where he eventually made his home) and the Amazon, we experience the highs and lows of his younger selves as though standing beside them. Yet the immediacy of the recollections is always tempered by the rueful wisdom of Boorman today, at 70: acutely self-aware, incapable of self-pity.

He confirms that the young boy's wartime rites of passage in *Hope and Glory* were the purest autobiography, and reveals how the love triangle in that film – involving his father, mother and his father's best friend, whom his mother wished she had married – has been a constant preoccupation, surfacing in his earliest love affairs and his treatment of the Arthur, Guinevere and Lancelot story in *Excalibur* (still the finest cinematic account of the Grail legend). He acknowledges the recurrent intervention of blind fate in his career (had an MGM executive not been distracted by an urgent phone call from David Lean, *Point Blank* might never have been made), portrays his friend Lee Marvin with love and humour and is generally unsparing in his

Columbia/Kobal

In **Adventures of a Suburban Boy**, *John Boorman recalls making* Hope and Glory, *with Sebastian Rice-Edwards as his younger self*

praise or criticism of collaborators on both sides of the camera.

By choosing to shuttle between Hollywood and home turf, he joined the ranks of British directors denied "stability or continuity. Our lives frittered away on movies we fail to make." A typical example of the book's honesty and generosity comes when, having described the time and effort he invested in one of those unrealised projects, a putative 1970s adaptation of *The Lord of the Rings*, he hails Peter Jackson's *The Fellowship of the Ring* as "of such scope and magnitude that it can only be compared to the building of the great Gothic cathedrals. My concept shrivels by comparison."

Art Linson has followed up his first Tinseltown memoir, *A Pound of Flesh – Perilous Tales of How to Produce Movies in Hollywood* (1994), with the even more enjoyable **What Just Happened?**

(Bloomsbury, London and New York). It is subtitled *Bitter Hollywood Tales from the Front Line* and covers 1996-2000, when Linson's flops outnumbered his hits. He begins with misbegotten wilderness thriller *The Edge*, whose scriptwriter David Mamet's bemused question after a pitch meeting at Fox gives the book its title and whose production was briefly jeopardised by the 'war of Alec Baldwin's beard', a classic tale of star vanity and insecurity. Then comes Alfonso Cuarón's modernised, muddled *Great Expectations* (18 major script revisions in four months), before Linson redeems himself briefly with *Fight Club* and slips back down the ladder with *Pushing Tin* and the disastrous *Sunset Strip*.

Merrick Morton/Fox/Kobal

Art Linson tells the story of Fight Club *in* **What Just Happened?**

Like Boorman, Linson has a fine line in self-deprecation ("If you didn't have De Niro's home phone number you might not have a producing career," suggests one associate), and his tales are framed by a mischievous, novelistic device that's very much in the *Fight Club* spirit (the first rule of reviewing *What Just Happened?* is that you do not talk about the trick in *What Just Happened?*).

A touch of Linson's narrative coherence would have improved Peter Bart and Peter Guber's **Shoot Out – Surviving Fame & [Mis]Fortune in Hollywood** (Putnam's, New York; Faber, London), in which pearls of wisdom and personal observations from the *Variety* editor-in-chief and the producer of *Batman* and *Rain Man* are rather

haphazardly strung together. There are, nonetheless, some great inside stories about star salaries, script development and duplicitous agents.

Several of the stories in *Shoot Out* date from the days when Bart worked at Paramount as number two to Robert Evans, whose star-studded memoir **The Kid Stays in the Picture** (Faber, London) has been reissued to mark the release of the film documentary of the same name. Evans' seen-it-all authority could hardly be in starker contrast to the shocked tone adopted by Eric Hamburg in **JFK, Nixon, Oliver Stone and Me** (Public Affairs, New York). An idealistic Congressional aide and speechwriter in the late 1980s, Hamburg's obsession with the Kennedy assassination helped convince the director of *JFK* to give him a job in 1993 and he swiftly learned that nothing on Capitol Hill had prepared him for Stone's unpredictable mood swings. The Washington outsider's perspective on film-making is a refreshing one, and Hamburg's book is a useful companion to the more academic analyses of Stone's films in **Oliver Stone's USA – Film, History and Controversy** (University Press of Kansas), edited by Robert Brent Toplin.

Biography and Interviews

Sam Spiegel's life of reinvention, deportation orders, unpaid bills, serial marriage and prodigious womanising would have been a gift to a biographer even if he had not sustained a producing career that earned him an unprecedented three Best Picture Oscars, for *On the Waterfront*, *The Bridge on the River Kwai* and *Lawrence of Arabia*. So it's disappointing to report that in **Sam Spiegel – Biography of a Hollywood Legend** (Little, Brown, London and New York), Natasha Fraser-Cavassoni fails to bring either the man or the producer into sharp focus.

Fraser-Cavassoni, who met the producer while working as a company assistant on his last film, *Betrayal* (1983), adapted from the adultery play by her step-father, Harold Pinter, dutifully chronicles Spiegel's acts of "appalling selfishness" and innumerable affairs (his appetite for nubile

Columbia/Kobal

Sam Spiegel: subject of Natasha Fraser-Cavassoni's
Biography of a Hollywood Legend

starlets grew as he aged). Her grasp of
Hollywood history and the film-making process,
however, is comparatively sketchy, and her prose
is littered with stylistic howlers.

In a different class, and appearing in Britain two
years after its publication in the US, is Joseph
McBride's **Searching for John Ford – A Life**
(Faber, London), an appropriately epic (700
pages) study of a man whose movies helped
define the world's vision of the American West
and who, in McBride's words, "used film-making
as his refuge from reality, a way to create a safe,
privileged, mythical world that functioned
according to his own private rules."

Ford's admirers include Martin Scorsese, who, as
an instructor at New York University's Film School
in 1969, upped the Hollywood content of a
student viewing schedule dominated by Fellini
and Bergman, telling his class "Now look at these
American films by Ford and Hawks, they're
wonderful!" This story appears in the third revised
edition of **Scorsese on Scorsese** (Faber, London
and New York), edited by Ian Christie and David
Thompson, whose new chapters on *Kundun*,
Bringing Out the Dead and *Gangs of New York*
improve what was already one of the best in
Faber's invaluable directors series.

The series' other new entry this year is **Herzog
on Herzog** (Faber, London and New York). In the
briefest of forewords, Werner Herzog explains

that, faced with "the stark alternative to see a
book on me compiled from dusty interviews with
all the wild distortions and lies, or collaborating – I
choose the much worse option, to collaborate."
Editor Paul Cronin's reward for some deeply
researched questions is disarming candour from
his subject, on his debt to Lotte Eisner, his love-
hate relationship with Klaus Kinski and the insane
endeavours of *Fitzcarraldo*: "Probably no one will
ever need to do again what we did," Herzog
concedes. "I am a Conquistador of the Useless."

Scorsese features again in Laurent Tirard's
Moviemakers' Master Class (Faber, London and
New York), a collection of interviews with 20 of
the world's most accomplished film-makers.
Originally published in French film magazine
Studio, these fascinating pieces will tell you the
differences between John Boorman, Sydney
Pollack and the Coens' treatment of actors, or
John Woo and Wong Kar-wai's approaches to
camerawork.

The excellent **Story and Character – Interviews
with British Screenwriters** (Bloomsbury, London)
edited by Alistair Owen, suggests that the road to
hell may not, after all, be paved with unfilmed
screenplays. Shawn Slovo, garlanded for *A World
Apart*, and excoriated for *Captain Corelli's
Mandolin*, has no fewer than 13 scripts on her CV
that have not reached the screen, yet tells Owen
proudly: "I haven't been out of work since
[1986]… I've been writing productively, earning a
good living and having a good time." Owen's
other subjects include the Midas-like Richard
Curtis and Simon Beaufoy, who recalls how, after
his gentle comedy *The Full Monty* had stormed
the US box-office, he was telephoned by Dino De
Laurentiis – and asked to write a *Conan the
Barbarian* sequel.

History and Criticism

With **French Cinema – From Its Beginnings to
the Present** (Continuum, New York and London),
Rémi Fournier Lanzoni sets out to address what
he saw as "an increasing need for an English-
language book" on more than 100 years of Gallic
film-making, and fills the gap with a thoroughly
readable and comprehensive study that tracks

every major commercial and artistic development from the Lumières to the emergence of young guns like Mathieu Kassovitz and Eric Zonca.

Ryan Gilbey, one of the best of the younger generation of British film critics, adores 1970s American cinema, and in **It Don't Worry Me – Nashville**, *Jaws*, *Star Wars* and beyond (Faber, London) writes with his customary finesse and attention to detail on ten of that decade's most influential directors (Coppola, Lucas, Spielberg, Malick, De Palma, Altman, Kubrick, Allen, Demme and Scorsese).

For **Writers at the Movies** (Marion Boyars, London and New York), editor Jim Shepard invited 25 fellow novelists (including Lorrie Moore and J. M. Coetzee) and poets (including Michael Ryan and Lawrence Raab) to submit an essay on a memorable film. Moore attempts to defend the indefensible in her love letter to *Titanic*, while Ryan conducts a moving post mortem examination on *Dead Man Walking*. It's consistently rewarding to read such gifted writers taking a break from their day jobs.

Dead Man Walking features in **Writers at the Movies**

Film Studies

The Wallflower Press' *Directors' Cuts* series (London and New York) has already covered David Lynch and Nanni Moretti, and now includes Aleksandar Dundjerovic's **The Cinema of Robert Lepage – The Poetics of Memory**, a clear-sighted study of Quebec's polymath genius, and **The Cinema of Kathryn Bigelow – Hollywood Transgressor**, edited by Deborah Jermyn and Sean Redmond. The Bigelow book embodies the

best and worst of academic approaches to film, offering a fine case study of the writing, production, marketing and distribution problems behind the millennial mess that was *Strange Days*, alongside essays bogged down in pretentious critical theory. The director's low-budget vampire Western *Near Dark*, for example, is earnestly discussed as "a reflexive text… that is often self-consciously interrogating conservative and patriarchal ideologies."

Emma Wilson occasionally adopts an equally off-putting prose style in **Cinema's Missing Children** (Wallflower Press, London and New York), a set of thought-provoking essays about recent films – including *All About My Mother* and *The Son's Room* – whose protagonists must confront the death of young sons or daughters. Wilson's analysis of the "mortuary aesthetic" in Michael Winterbottom's *Jude* is particularly illuminating.

Wallflower's impressively wide-ranging list also includes Sylvie Blum-Reid's **East-West Encounters – Franco-Asian Cinema and Literature** (in-depth studies of films such as *Emmanuelle*, *Indochine* and *The Scent of Green Papaya*), Leon Hunt's **Kung Fu Cult Masters**, which explores chop-socky flicks from Bruce Lee to Ang Lee, Valerie Orpen's clear, concise introduction to **Film Editing – The Art of the Expressive**, which contains extreme close-ups on *Rear Window* and *Raging Bull*, and Joel W. Finler's third, newly revised edition of **The Hollywood Story**, one of the best histories of the dream factory.

Kathryn Bigelow's Near Dark *and* Stange Days *are assessed in* **Hollywood Transgressor**

Dennie Todd/Working Title/Kobal

Firooz Zahedi/Fox/Kobal

Reference

DV-wielding teenagers with *El Mariachi* and *The Blair Witch Project* posters on their bedroom walls are presumably the prime target audience for **The Guerrilla Film Makers Movie Blueprint** (Continuum, London and New York), in which indie director Chris Jones (co-author of the *Guerilla Film Makers Handbook*) provides a 27-step guide (including budget, scheduling, catering and festival submissions), clearly illustrated with charts and diagrams.

Emanuel Levy's **All About Oscar** (Continuum, London and New York) has enough facts, anecdotes, themed analysis ("The Luck of the British", "Is the Oscar a White Man's Award?") and appendices ("Best Picture Winners by Genre" etc.) to satisfy the most obsessive Academy fan.

Edited by Brian McFarlane, the Australian scholar who has been a distinguished contributor to Pommie film history for more than 30 years, **The Encyclopedia of British Film** (Methuen/British Film Institute, London) instantly establishes itself as a standard reference work: 5,800 entries by 120 contributors covering stars, directors, studios and much more besides, with an Introduction by McFarlane to set this mammoth work and its selection criteria in context.

McFarlane's associate editor on the *Encyclopedia*, Anthony Slide, has continued his 35-year, "personal odyssey" through the pre-sound era with **Silent Players – A Biographical and Autobiographical Study of 100 Silent Film Actors and Actresses** (The University Press of Kentucky). This century of brief, sympathetic profiles begins with "sad little creature" Mignon Anderson and ends with King Kong's main squeeze, the "competent, compliant and, above all, intelligent" Fay Wray. Each essay is accompanied by a beautifully reproduced half- or full-page portrait or scene still.

Screenplays

Frida – Bringing Frida Kahlo's Life and Art to Film (Newmarket Press, New York; Pocket Books, London) is a handsome companion to the Julie Taymor film that deservedly took Oscars for its Make-Up and Elliot Goldenthal's vibrant Latino score. It includes the script and more than 170 illustrations (stills and paintings by Kahlo and Diego Rivera). Less glossy but equally absorbing is **The Donnie Darko Book** (Faber, London and New York), which supplements Richard Kelly's screenplay for his unsettling tale of teen angst with stills, artwork by Kelly and a lengthy director interview.

David Hare offers a fascinating account of the adaptation process in the introduction to his dazzling screenplay for **The Hours** (Talk Miramax Books, New York; Faber, London), which for my money was robbed of the Best Adapted Screenplay Oscar by Ronald Harwood's **The Pianist** (Faber, London and New York), now published in the same volume as *Taking Sides*, adapted by Harwood from his play about Wilhelm Furtwängler and Nazi complicity.

Finally, four titles that will be on many Christmas lists. **Movies of the '70s**, edited by Jürgen Müller, is another of Taschen's photo-led celebrations, focusing on 120 films (mostly from the US, with some European and Asian titles). Design lecturer Emily King's wonderful **Movie Poster** (Mitchell Beazley, London) is a four-part, chronological compilation that traces the evolution of an art form whose primary task, as King writes, is "to connect with the people on the street, not with the images on the screen."

Jeffrey Vance's **Chaplin – Genius of the Cinema** (Harry N. Abrams, New York and London) is a magnificently produced tribute with extensive biographical and critical text, 500 pictures (some previously unpublished) and a comprehensive filmography.

At £39:95/$69.95, Edward Buscombe's **Cinema Today** (Phaidon, London and New York) is even dearer than Vance's book, but offers equally good value for money. With the help of more than 700 immaculately reproduced photographs, one of the most authoritative and knowledgeable of film historians tackles the last 30 years in 20 chapters. This is a glorious doorstop of a book, to be dipped into and savoured.

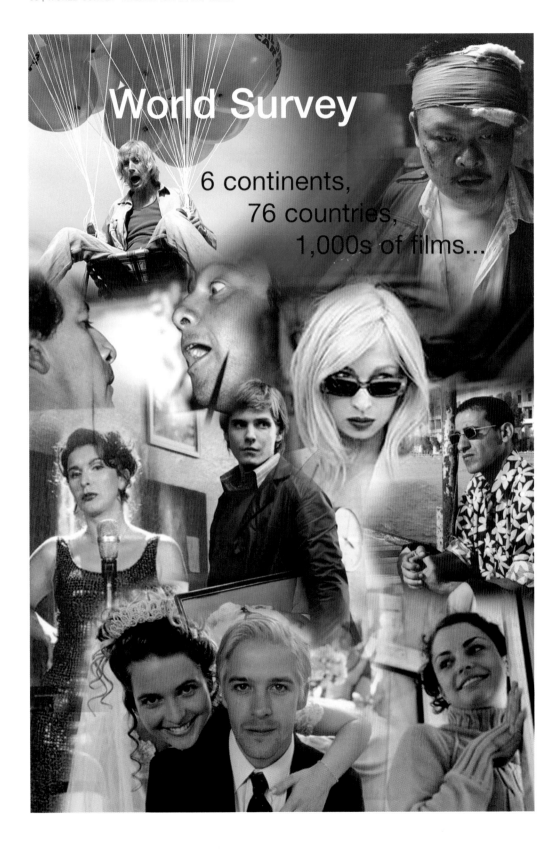

World Survey

6 continents,
76 countries,
1,000s of films...

Algeria Roy Armes

Recent Films

RACHIDA
[Drama, 2002] Script and Dir:
Yamina Bachir-Chouikh. Phot:
Mustapha Belmihoub. Players:
Ibtissem Djouadi, Bahia Rachedi,
Hamid Ramas, Abdelkader
Belmokadem. Prod: Arte France
Cinéma/Ciné-Sud Promotion
(Thierry Lenouvel; France)/Ciel
Production (Algeria).

Rachida

LA VOISINE (The Neighbour)
[Drama, 2002] Script: Hadjira
Mouhoub and Ghaouti
Bendeddouche. Dir:
Bendeddouche. Phot: Allal
Yaiaoui. Players: Linda Yasmine,
Aïda Guechoud, Rania, Fatiha
Soltane, Nadia Kherbache, Amal
Bouguera, Prod: Agence
Artistique et Audio-Visuel
(3A,V).

L'ATTENTE DES FEMMES
(Women's Expectations)
[Drama, 2001] Script and Dir:
Naguel Belouad. Phot: Bachir
Selami. Players: Sonia, Doudja
Achachi, Salima Seddiki, Tounes
Ait Ali, Abdallah Bouzida,
Kamel Rouini. Prod: 3B
Productions (Paris).

LA FILLE DE KELTOUM
(Keltoum's Daughter)
[Drama, 2002] Script and Dir:
Mehdi Charef. Phot: Alain
Levent. Players: Cylia Malki,
Baya Belal, Jean-Roger Milo,

A lgerian cinema continues to operate at subsistence level, with no sign of its production and distribution infrastructures being restored. But at least Ghaouti Bendeddouche's **The Neighbour** *(La voisine),* one of the films left incomplete when the production organisations were shut down in 1998, was finally screened at the major Arab film festival, the Journées Cinématographiques de Carthage in Tunis. The film, which shows the dramatic impact of the arrival of a beautiful newcomer on the cloistered, regulated life of a group of women in the Casbah, is described by its director as "a human comedy and voyage into the emotional and social malaise of Algeria".

Very impressive, too, was **Rachida**, the first feature of former film editor Yamina Bachir-Chouikh (b. 1964), who had worked on numerous Algerian documentaries and features, including two of the best-known films made by her brother, Mohamed Chouikh, *The Citadel* and *The Desert Ark*. Incredibly, she is the first Algerian woman to shoot a 35mm feature in Algeria (the work of Assia Djebbar and Hafsa Zina-Koudil was in 16mm). *Rachida* is the story of a young female teacher whose attempts to create a positive life for herself are constantly thwarted by the threat and reality of violence. Another newcomer, based this time in Europe, Naguel Belouad, shot for eight weeks in Algeria (he is one of a tiny handful of film-makers active there), but, curiously, in **Women's Expectations** *(L'attente des femmes)*, he chose not to explore the burning contradictions of contemporary Algerian society. Instead, he offers a study of the sufferings of women within polygamy in 1920s Algeria.

The novelist and film-maker Mehdi Charef, whose previous five films had all shown aspects of immigrant life in Europe, followed his

Marc Detiff

Mehdi Charef's **Keltoum's Daughter**

Fatma Ben Saidene, Deborah Lamy. Prod: Cinétévé/Studiocanal France/Arte France (France).

FRONTIÈRES (Frontiers)
[Drama, 2001] Script: Mostéfa Djadjam and Agnès de Sacy. Dir: Djadjam. Phot: Pascal Lagriffoul. Players: Lou Dante, Clarisse Luambo, Ona Luyenke, Dioucounda Koma. Prod: Vertigo Productions (France).

LETTRES D'ALGÉRIE (Letters from Algeria) *[Drama, 2002] Script and Dir: Aziz Kabouche. Phot: Philippe Bouyer. Players: Lilah Dadi, Abbès Zahmani, Cécilia Hornus. Prod: Plaisanterie Privée/3B Production.*

AU-DELÀ DE GIBRALTAR (Beyond Gibraltar) *[Drama, 2001] Script: Taylan Barman, Mourad Boucif and Gérard Preszow. Dir: Barman and Boucif. Phot: Michel Baudour. Players: Mourad Maimmuni, Bach Lan Le Ba-Thi, Abdeslam Arbaoui, Rachida Chbani, Samir Rian, Nabil Ben Yadir. Prod: Saga Film/Arte Belgique/RTBF (Belgium)/Studio L'Equipe/Météore Films (Belgium).*

WESH WESH – QU'EST-CE QUI SE PASSE? (Wesh Wesh – What's Happening) *[Drama, 2002] Script: Rabah Ameur-Zaïmèche and Madjid Benaroudj. Dir: Ameur-Zaïmèche. Phot: Olivier Smittarello, Karim Albaoui. Players: Rahah Ameur-Zaïmèche, Ahmed Hammouda, Braim Ameur-Zaïmèche, Farida Mouffok, Ali Mouffok. Prod: Sarrazink Production (France).*

LA MAÎTRESSE EN MAILLOT DE BAIN (The Mistress in a Swimming Costume) *[Drama, 2002] Script and Dir: Lyèce Boukhitine. Phot: Denis Rouden. Players: Eric Savin, Franck Gourlat, Lyèce Boukhitine, Paco Cabezas, Frédéric Graziani. Prod: Fidélité Productions (France).*

excellent *Marie-Line* with a much more uneven work, **Keltoum's Daughter** (*La fille de Keltoum*), yet another tale of a young woman who quits the security of Europe, in this case to seek out in Algeria the mother who she thinks has selfishly abandoned her.

Journeys' ends

Several features have been made by new film-makers of Algerian origin now resident in Europe. Mostéfa Djadjam (b. 1952), a former actor who played the lead in Merzak Allouache's second film, *The Adventures of a Hero* (*Les aventures d'un héros*) in the 1970s, directed **Frontiers** (*Frontières*), a powerful study of a group of six would-be emigrants from various parts of Africa and the difficulties they experience even before reaching Europe.

Aziz Kabouche's **Letters from Algeria** (*Lettres d'Algérie*) deals with the emotional troubles of a theatre group, comprising a young director and three actors, who set out to base a play on the "Letters from Algeria" section of the newspaper *Le Monde*. Two self-taught young film-makers also offered their views on immigrant life in the communities within which they grew up. Mourad Boucif (b. 1967), working with a childhood friend, the Turkish immigrant Taylan Barman, offered a look at young love in the immigrant community in Belgium, **Beyond Gibraltar** (*Au-delà de Gibraltar*), while Rabah Ameur-Zaïmèche (b. 1968) mined his own family's life in poor Paris suburbs in **Wesh Wesh – What's Happening?** (*Wesh wesh – Qu'est-ce qui se passe?*).

A rather different tone was adopted in another debut film, **The Mistress in a Swimming Costume** (*La maîtresse en maillot de bain*), written and directed by the actor Lyèce Boukhitine. Boukhitine turned away from the specific problems of immigrant life to look instead at the more general problems of French thirtysomethings in a small provincial town.

With 16 new features and a mass of shorts released by film-makers of North African origin since the beginning of 2000, this is a flourishing area. Eleven of the 16 directors involved are newcomers making their first feature. All but one (Mostéfa Djadjam) were born in the 1960s, none is film school-trained and over half have a background in acting. These newcomers are making full use of the opportunities offered by the structure of the French film industry, but it is arguable that their real links to North Africa are becoming more and more tenuous.

ROY ARMES is Emeritus Professor of Film at Middlesex University, London. He has written widely on cinema for 38 years. His current project is *Post-Colonial Images: Studies in North African Film*, scheduled for publication in English and French in 2004.

Argentina Alfredo Friedlander

The Year's Best Films

Alfredo Friedlander's selection:
Minimal Stories
(Dir: Carlos Sorín)
Seaside Resorts
(Documentary. Dir: Mariano Llinás)
Heritage
(Dir: Paula Hernández)
Kamchatka
(Dir: Marcelo Piñeyro)
Common Places
(Dir: Adolfo Aristarain)

Recent and Forthcoming Films

HISTORIAS MÍNIMAS
(Minimal Stories)
[Comedy-drama, 2002] Script: Pablo Solarz. Dir: Carlos Sorín. Phot: Hugo Colace. Players: Javier Lombardo, Antonio Benedictis, Javiera Bravo, Aníbal Maldonado, César García, Enrique Otranto, Julia Solomonoff. Prod: Guacamole Films/Wanda Vision (Spain).
Thousand of miles south of Buenos Aires, three lonely characters travel on their own: an old man looking for his missing dog, a salesman with a big birthday cake and a very poor woman who has won a TV contest. Their stories and dreams intertwine on the deserted routes of Patagonia.

APASIONADOS (Passionate)
[Comedy, 2002] Script: Alex Ferrara, Juan José Jusid, Marcela Guerty, Raúl Becerra. Dir: Jusid. Phot: Porfidio "Popy" Enriquez. Players: Pablo Echarri, Nancy Duplaá, Natalia Verbeke, Héctor Alterio, Pablo Rago, Camila

Argentina is slowly recovering from an unprecedented economic and political crisis, that touched its lowest point during 2002, which saw also an 8% reduction in the number of releases (217) compared to 2001. Almost half were distributed by the five majors, including all of the year's ten biggest hits, and this was one of the worst years ever for independent distributors.

The amount of local films released (48) was slightly higher than 2001, and they made up 20% of total releases. Unfortunately, even though total cinema attendance went up by 2%, this increase was not reflected in the box-office share for Argentine movies (just under 10% of the total revenue). **Passionate** (*Apasionados*) was the only local movie appearing among the ten with the highest admissions.

During 2002 Argentinean movies were shown in many festivals, winning more than 50 international awards. At Berlin in 2003 two films, **Kamchatka** (Argentina's offical entry for the 2002 Foreign-Lanugage Film Oscar) and **Mercano, the Martian**, were shown in non-competitive sections. At the 50th San Sebastian International Film Festival, the excellent **Minimal Stories** (*Historias mínimas*) received, among other accolades, the Special Jury Award, and the Silver Shell for best actress went to Mercedes Sampietro for **Common Places** (*Lugares comunes*), directed by the veteran Adolfo Aristarain, who also shared the Silver Shell for best script.

Federico Luppi and Mercedes Sampietro in **Common Places**

Passionate

Fiardi Mazza. Prod: Telefé/Buena Vista International/Patagonik Film Group/Alquimia Producciones (Spain).
A young air hostess asks her best friend a very special favour: could she lend her new boyfriend for just one night?

KAMCHATKA
[Drama, 2002] Script: Marcelo Figueras. Dir: Marcelo Piñeyro. Phot: Alfredo Mayo. Players: Ricardo Darín, Cecilia Roth, Fernanda Mistral, Héctor Alterio, Tomás Fonzi, Matías del Pozo, Milton de la Canal. Prod: Buena Vista International/Patagonik Film Group.
Argentina, 1976. Harry, 10, and his younger brother move with their parents to a house on the outskirts of Buenos Aires. They live happily until the day their father and mother have to leave them with their grandparents.

BALNEARIOS (Seaside Resorts)
[Documentary, 2002] Script, Dir and Prod: Mariano Llinás. Phot: Lucio Bonelli.
In his first movie, Llinás shows, with plenty of humour, various seaside resorts. Lifeguards, sand castles and old-fashioned hotels are some of the curious ingredients in these authentically nostalgic vignettes.

HERENCIA (Heritage)
[Comedy-drama, 2001] Script and Dir: Paula Hernández. Phot: Víctor Kino González. Players: Rita Cortese, Adrián Witzke, Julieta Díaz, Héctor Anglada, Martín Adjemián, Cutuli. Prod: Rojo Films/Rolo Azpeitía.
Olinda (Cortese) is an Italian immigrant who came to Buenos Aires in the 1950s and owns a small restaurant. She meets

Not so festive

In March 2003, the 18th International Film Festival of Mar del Plata lacked the glamour of previous years, with poor foreign guest participation. Only Kate Winslet and several film directors were invited and the jury headed by Spanish director Ventura Pons chose Spain's *Volverás* as Best Film. The FIPRESCI jury preferred the impressive *Facing the Truth*, the first of Danish director Nils Malmros' nine movies to be shown in Argentina.

Only one month later, the fifth Buenos Aires International Film Festival (BAFICI), devoted to independent films, took place. The winner of the Official Section was the fresh and original *Waiting for Happiness*, directed by Abderrahmane Sissako from Mauritania (already a 2002 prize-winner at Cannes). The festival was superbly attended, with virtually every screening a sell-out. The Audience Award went to **The Blonde People** (*Los Rubios*), which treats a subject still fresh in the memories of many: the disappearance of thousands of people during the military government of the late 1970s. There were several documentaries among the many first or second features presented at BAFICI in 2002, including **Seaside Resorts** (*Balnearios*), which was well-regarded by critics and audiences for its originality and humour.

Clearly, the Argentinian film industry is still alive, but the outlook is mixed. On the one hand, we have a crowd of well-established directors (Aristarain, Piñeyro, Agresti, Puenzo, Lecchi) who are preparing or have recently released new projects. On the other hand we see a huge number of newcomers who are ready for their debuts but are not sure if their movies will ever be seen by the public.

ALFREDO FRIEDLANDER is a freelance film critic who writes regularly for the monthly *Cinetop* magazine. He also broadcasts on movie history and is, above all, a film buff.

Antonio Benedictis, left, in **Minimal Stories**

Paula Hernández's **Heritage**

Peter (Witzke), a young German who revives her hopes and lost memories.

LUGARES COMUNES
(Common Places)
[Drama, 2002] Script: Adolfo Aristarain, Kathy Saavedra. Dir: Aristarain. Phot: Porfirio Enríquez. Players: Federico Luppi, Mercedes Sampietro, Valentina Bassi, María Fiorentino, Osvaldo Santoro, Pepe Soriano, Claudio Rissi, José Luis Alfonso. Prod: Adolfo Aristarain, Gerardo Herrero (Tornasol Films/Spain)/Shazam S.A.
A professor of literature, compelled to retire for political reasons in Buenos Aires, travels to Spain with his wife. There he meets his son, who left Argentina looking for a better life. Their meeting will show how little they have in common.

EL CUMPLE (Birthday Party)
[Drama, 2002] Script and Dir: Gustavo Postiglione. Phot: Fernando Zago. Players: Raúl Calandra, Bárbara Peters, Miguel Franchi, Natalia Depetris, Tito Gómez, Gerardo Dayub, Adriana Frodella, Gustavo Girado. Prod: GAP.
Pablo (Calandra) turns 38. His best friend prepares a party in which different characters and their stories will merge. Paula, a young student with a video camera, collects images that result in a film-within-the-film.

Gustavo Postiglione's **Birthday Party**

MERCANO, EL MARCIANO
(Mercano, the Martian)
[Animated feature, 2002] Script: Juan Antín, Lautaro Núñez de Arco. Dir: Antín. Prod: Universidad del Cine.
Mercano, the Martian started as a series of TV shorts, created by Juan Antín and Ayar Blasco. The film is about an alien who arrives accidentally in Buenos Aires, where he becomes one of many marginal beings and witnesses Argentina's ongoing crisis.

SAMY Y YO (Samy and Me)
[Comedy, 2002] Script and Dir: Eduardo Milewicz. Phot: Marcelo Camorino. Players: Ricardo Darín, Angie Cepeda, Alejandra Flechner, Henny Trayles, Cristina Benegas, Alejandra Darín. Prod: Bulevares.
Samuel Goldstein (Ricardo Darín) is almost 40 and his life is a mess. He can hardly stand his mother and wife and his job as a TV screenwriter is a total failure. But his whole life changes when he meets the exuberant Mary (Cepeda).

LUCA VIVE (Luca Lives)
[Drama, 2002] Script: Carlos Polimeni, Daniel Ritto, Jorge Coscia. Dir and Phot: Coscia. Players: Daniel Ritto, Tom Lupo, Valeria de Luque, Lorena Damonte, Emir Omar Chabán, Adriana Pérez, Ada Quiñónes. Prod: Palcos Producciones.
Luca Prodan was a very popular rock singer in Argentina who died tragically. The movie recreates his last days of "sex, drugs and rock'n'roll" and earlier moments/from his life.

EL FONDO DEL MAR
(The Bottom of the Sea)
[Comedy, 2002] Script and Dir: Damián Szifrón. Phot: Lucio Bonelli. Players: Daniel Hendler, Gustavo Garzón, Dolores Fonzi, Daniel Valenzuela, José Palomino, Diego Peretti, Alejandra Fiore. Prod: Aeroplano S.A.
Road movie about an obsessive young man who pursues his girlfriend to find the secret lover he believes she is seeing.

ANY Y LOS OTROS
(Ana and the Others)
[Drama, 2003] Script and Dir: Celina Murga. Phot: Marcelo Lavintman, José María Gómez. Players: Camila Toker, Ignacio Uslengui, Juan Cruz Díaz La Barba, Natacha Massera. Prod: Celina Murga, Carolina Konstantinovsky.
After an absence of several years, Ana travels to the town where she was born, buys a local newspaper containing a photo taken by a former lover and starts looking for him.

POTESTAD (Legal Authority)
[Political drama, 2003] Script: Ariel Sienra, Luis César D'Angiolillo. Dir and Prod: D'Angiolillo. Phot: María Inés Teyssie. Players: Eduardo Pavlovsky, Lorenzo Quinteros, Luis Machín, Noemí Frenkel, Alejo García Pintos, Susy Evans.
During Argentina's military dictatorship, a doctor, Eduardo (Pavlovsky), finds his daily reality is a distorted mosaic of disturbing events. An original look at repression.

LOS RUBIOS
(The Blonde People)
*[Political semi-documentary,
2003] Script and Dir: Albertina
Carri. Phot: Catalina Fernández.
Player: Analía Couceyro. Prod:
Cine Ojo.*
The blonde people are Albertina
Carri's parents, who disappeared
in 1977, when she was four. This
film deals with the emptiness left
by their disappearance.

VALENTIN
*[Drama, 2002] Script and Dir:
Alejandro Agresti. Phot: José
Luis Cajaraville. Players: Carmen
Maura, Rodrigo Noya, Julieta
Cardinali, Jean Pierre Noher,
Max Urtizberea, Fabián Vena,
Carlos Roffe, Lorenzo Quinteros,
Alejandro Agresti. Prod: First
Floor Features (Amsterdam)/De
Productie (Rotterdam)/Rossini
Wisznia Agresti (Buenos
Aires)/DMVB Films
(Paris)/Duque y Castelao
Productions (Rome-Madrid)/Surf
Film (Rome).*
Valentín, eight, dreams of
becoming an astronaut and

finding new parents after his
mum and dad divorce and leave
him with his granny in a huge
old house.

ILUSIÓN DE MOVIMENTO
(Movement Illusion)
*[Drama, 2001] Script and Dir:
Héctor Molina. Phot: Fernando
Zago. Players: Carlos Resta,
Matías Grapa, Darío
Grandinetti, Mónica Alfonso,
Tito Gómez, Raúl Calandra,
Melina Mailhou. Prod: Gustavo
Postiglione, Miren Martinetti.*
After several years away, a man
returns to the city of Rosario
to meet the seven-year-old child
whom he has never seen and
whose mother disappeared
during the dictatorship.

CAJA NEGRA (Black Box)
*[Drama 2002] Script, Dir and
Phot: Luis Ortega. Players:
Dolores Fonzi, Edgardo Couget,
Eugenia Bassi, Silvio Bassi,
Mariano Maradei, Oscar
Bangertef. Prod: Villa Vicio SRL.*
This is a story of ordinary people.
A girl approaches her father, who

has been treated badly in life and
is given food and lodging by the
Salvation Army. She also takes
care of a very old woman who
offers her advice. Special Jury
Prize in Mar del Plata (2002).

Quotes of the Year

"To arrive at Buenos Aires
and see what is happening
to Argentinian cinema is
a fantastic experience. The
enthusiasm shown by local
directors and audiences
gives me the impression that
good things will continue
to happen here."
SIMON FIELD, *director of the
Rotterdam Film Festival, during
the Buenos Aires Independent
Film Festival in 2003.*

"The movie business is to
art what golf is to sports,
because you require plenty
of money for both."
ADRIAN CAETANO, *director
of* Bolivia *and* The Red Bear.

The 51st Silver Condor Awards
Presented in Buenos Aires on
July 22, 2003

Film: *Minimal
Stories/Historias Mínimas*
(Carlos Sorín).
First Film: *Herencia/Heritage*
(Paula Hernández).
Director: Carlos Sorín
(*Minimal Stories*).
Original Screenplay: Pablo
Solarz (*Minimal Stories*).
Adapted Screenplay: Adrián
Caetano (*Bolivia*).
Actor: Julio Chávez (*A Red
Bear*).
Actress: Rita Cortese
(*Heritage*).
Supporting Actor: Enrique
Liporace (*Bolivia*).

Supporting Actress: Julieta
Díaz (*Heritage*).
Male Newcomer: Antonio
Benedictis (*Minimal Stories*).
Female Newcomer: Mimí
Ardú (*El bonaerense*).

Pablo Trapero's thriller **El bonaerense**
won two Silver Condors

Cinematography: Hugo
Colace (*Minimal Stories*).
Music: Nicolás Sorín (*Minimal
Stories*).
Sound: Carlos Abbate and
José Luis Díaz (*Minimal
Stories* and *Kamchatka*).
Editing: Nicolás Goldbart
(*El bonaerense*).
Art Direction: Margarita Jusid
(*Minimal Stories*).
Animated Feature: *Mercano
the Martian* (Juan Antín).
Video Film: *Seaside Resorts*
(Mariano Llinás).
Foreign Film: *Talk to Her*
(Pedro Almodóvar).
Special Awards: Susana
Freire, Elsa Daniel, María
Vaner, Vicente Vigo, Duilio
Marzio and Cineclub Santa Fe
(on its 50th anniversary).

Armenia Susanna Harutyunyan

Recent and Forthcoming Films

JIVANU VERADARDZE
(Return of Jivani)

[Docu-drama, 2003] Script: Harutyun Khachatryan, Mikayel Stamboltsyan, Valery Gasparyan. Dir: Khachatryan. Phot: Vrezh Petrosyan. Players: Mikayel Dovlatyan, Artashes Hovsepyan. Prod: Hayfilm Studio.
Made in the style of a documentary investigation rather than a conventional biopic, the film looks at modern Armenia through the eyes of poet and philosopher Jivani (1846-1909). We follow the construction of a monument to Jivani and its transportation from Yerevan to Javakhk, his birthplace.

Harutyun Khachatryan's
Documentarist

TAK ERKIR – TSURT DZMER
(Hot Country, Cold Winter)

[Drama, 2004] Script: David Safaryan, Yana Drouz. Dir: Safaryan. Phot: Jarek Raczek, Armen Khachatryan, Ashot Mkrtchyan. Players: Ashot Adamyan, Yana Drouz, Karen Janibekyan. Prod: Studio DS and Armenfilm Studios (Armenia)/NFM Production-Distribution (Netherlands)/Studio 217 (Russia)/HFF Potsdam-Babelsberg Production (Germany).

In 2004, Armenia will celebrate the 80th anniversary of the production of the first Armenian film. Since 1924, film production has continued on a fairly consistent basis, and the state has always been the principal source of production finance, even after the transition to a new market economy encouraged producers to seek alternative funding. In 2003, the Ministry of Culture gave support, on a non-competitive basis, of around $700,000 (383m Drams) to the movie industry. The money is shared between the two state-owned studios, Hayfilm and Hayk, with around two thirds of the subsidy allocated to fiction features, about 25% to animation and the remainder shared between documentary production and the promotion of Armenian cinema at festivals and markets.

This limited funding explains why Armenian films generally take three to four years to make. This applies to the docu-drama **Documentarist**, directed by Harutyun Khachatryan. Its hero is a documentary director who with a small crew compiles a mosaic of diverse images representing 1990s Armenia: child beggars, disabled children abandoned by their parents, refugees, homeless dogs put down without a trace of pity. This fine film shows the tragedies of a society in transition, but not without hope amid the despair. Released in Armenia at the end of 2002, it was nominated for the NIKA award of the Russian Film Academy (for best film from the CIS and Baltic states). Meanwhile Harutyun Khachatryan's docu-drama about Armenia's celebrated poet and philosopher Jivani, **Return of Jivani** (*Jivanu veradardze; see IFG 2003*), should finally be released in cinemas in the middle of 2004.

The two new features completed in 2002-03 had begun production in 2000-01, only to hit financial problems that stalled both for almost two years. David Safaryan's international co-production **Hot Country, Cold Winter** is a psychological drama that takes audiences back to Yerevan in the 1990s, when the capital had no electricity because of civil war and an energy blockade. The main protagonists in these extreme circumstances are a middle-aged couple whose desperate and often very funny attempts to keep warm alternate with flashbacks to their childhood in the 1960s.

Virgin births

Director Edgar Baghdasaryan spent two years looking for the right

Tigran and Katya endure a hard winter during a prolonged power cut. They laugh, cry, reminisce, get angry and make up – anything to forget the cold and the dark – and help their family and neighbours to do the same.

MARIAM

[Drama, 2004] Script and Dir: Edgar Baghdasaryan. Phot: Vahagn Ter-Hakobyan. Players: Janet Harutyunyan. Prod: Hayfilm Studio.

Mariam (the Armenian name for the Virgin Mary) is a young woman who dwells on her virginity and behaves so strangely that those around her, even her psychotherapist, cannot understand her. The psychotherapist thinks the only way to cure her disorders is to awaken her sensuality, but Mariam resists the idea. The child she gives birth to at the end of the film does not appear to have been conceived from the sperm of an earthly donor; it's unclear whether the birth means the end or the beginning of the world.

LOVEMBER

[Lyrical drama, 2004] Script and Dir: Tigran Xmalyan. Phot: Arten Melkuyan. Players: Sergey Danielyan, Anush Stepanyan, Khoren Abrahamyan. Prod: Yerevan Film Studio.

Love story about a street musician and a nurse who try to give birth to God. According to their plan she has to get pregnant by every man they meet during one month in 2000AD, in Yerevan.

Quote of the Year

"Documentarist is my return after 10 years [in which] I was occupied with anything but cinema. [This award] is proof that I have been forgiven for my 'unwitting treachery'."
HARUTYUN KHACHATRYAN, *after receiving a Special Mention from the Documentary Jury at Karlovy Vary, July 2003.*

Actress Yana Drouz, director David Safaryan and cinematographer Ashot Mkrtchyan shooting Hot Country, Cold Winter

leading actress to play a virginal teacher at a school for the deaf in **Mariam**, hoping to find someone who could not only learn sign language but also make genuine contact with deaf and dumb children. Having auditioned players from Armenia, Georgia and several other countries, he finally chose an unknown, Janet Harutyunyan, who was born and brought up in Iran, studied in Armenia and now lives there. *Mariam* is a modern take on the story of the Virgin Mary (called Mariam in Armenia) and through the story of this pure creature it openly confronts the cult of sex and sensuality that presently overwhelms our lives. Among the new projects launched in 2003 is **Lovember**, written and directed by Tigran Xmalyan, which also explores the story of the Virgin Mary in modern terms and reflects a trend for Armenian artists to seek for new meaning in biblical stories.

In September 2002, the whole country was preoccupied with Atom Egoyan's eagerly awaited account of the Armenian genocide, **Ararat**, whose premiere was held in Yerevan, with the director and his wife and lead actress, Arsine Khanjian, welcomed by the President. The film became a box-office phenomenon, attracting 50,000 admissions at Yerevan's Moscow cinema alone, comfortably outperforming *Men in Black II* and *Spider-Man* and going on to become the country's all-time box-office record holder. It also aroused heated discussions in Armenian society, both because of its subject matter and because of our preoccupation with the Armenian diaspora (Egoyan is one of its most prominent representatives) and our desire to regain a clear cultural identity, symbolised by the very popular slogan "One Nation – One Culture".

SUSANNA HARUTYUNYAN graduated in film criticism from Moscow State Cinema Institute in 1987. She has been film expert of the daily *Respublika Armenia* since 1991 and is president of Armenia's Association of Film Critics and Cinema Journalists.

Australia Peter Thompson

The Year's Best Films

Peter Thompson's selection:

Japanese Story
(Dir: Sue Brooks)

Garage Days
(Dir: Alex Proyas)

Ned Kelly
(Dir: Gregor Jordan)

The Rage in Placid Lake
(Dir: Tony McNamara)

Till Human Voices Wake Us
(Dir: Michael Petroni)

Recent and Forthcoming Films

GARAGE DAYS
[Drama, 2002] Script: Alex Proyas, Dave Warner, Michael Udetsky. Dir: Proyas. Phot: Simon Duggan. Players: Kick Gurry, Maya Stange, Pia Miranda, Russell Dykstra, Brett Stiller, Chris Sadrinna. Prod: Proyas, Topher Dow/Mystery Clock. Follows the (almost) universal dream of every youth to become a rock star.

CRACKERJACK
[Comedy, 2002] Script: Mick Molloy and Richard Molloy. Dir: Paul Maloney. Phot: Brent Crockett. Players: Mick Molloy, Judith Lucy, Bill Hunter, Samuel Johnston, John Clarke. Prod: Mick Molloy, Stephen Luby/Million Monkeys/AFFC/Film Victoria/Macquarie/Molloy Boy/Network Ten/Showtime.

BAD EGGS
[Comedy, 2003] Script and Dir: Tony Martin. Phot: Graeme Wood. Players: Mick Molloy, Bob Franklin, Judith Lucy, Alan Brough, Bill Hunter, Marshall

Nicole Kidman's Oscar for *The Hours* helped to keep Australia in the spotlight over the last 12 months – or at least out of the shadows – as the country's cinematic identity continues to rest largely with its high-flying actors (although the brilliant cinematographer Dion Beebe was Oscar-nominated for *Chicago*).

By mid-2003, Kidman had *seven* films lined up after *The Hours,* including Lars von Trier's underwhelming *Dogville* and Anthony Mingella's *Cold Mountain.* Russell Crowe had at least two films set after Peter Weir's *Master and Commander* and Cate Blanchett three set for release in 2004 after *Veronica Guerin* and the final part of *The Lord of the Rings* trilogy. Eric Bana became Ang Lee's *Hulk.* Hugh Jackman plays the monster-hunter in *Van Helsing* and Heath Ledger has rejoined *A Knight's Tale* director Brian Helgeland for *The Order.* Gaining ground on this leading pack is Naomi Watts, with James Ivory's *Le Divorce* and Alexander González Iñárritu's *21 Grams* among the four new films confirming her versatility.

The constant hope is that the stars' box-office appeal in American or British films will raise awareness of Australian projects. Australians who have frequently led the battle for the 'cultural exception' from the rising tide of so-called free trade (beginning with the 'Make It Australian' campaign 30 years ago), invariably declare their commitment to local films, even after becoming working exiles, and Ledger, Watts, Geoffrey Rush, Rachel Griffiths, Anthony LaPaglia, Toni Collette, Radha Mitchell and Guy Pearce have returned home recently to act in Australian films.

Ledger as legend

Ledger, Watts, Rush and Griffiths lent their weight to Gregor Jordan's eagerly anticipated **Ned Kelly**, which opened in March 2003. Combined British and Australian investment gave financial muscle that translated into an unusually full canvas, peopled by a large international cast, with Englishmen Orlando Bloom and Phillip Barantini and Ireland's Laurence Kinlan (*Intermission*) and Kerry Condon (*Angela's Ashes*) making up Kelly's extended family.

Born in 1854 and hanged in 1880, bushranger Kelly is the closest Australia has to an iconic national myth. He personified the struggle

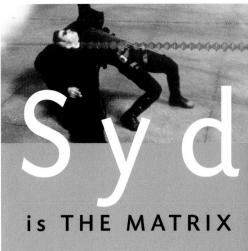

Orlando Bloom, centre, and Heath Ledger, right, in **Ned Kelly**

between the British colonial (Protestant) establishment and the working-class poor, many of them Irish Catholics arriving, like Ned's father, as convicts. By 14, Ned was in trouble with the police and by 19 a fully-fledged outlaw, robbing banks with his brother Dan and their friends Joe Byrne and Steve Hart. So fearful were the authorities of the bushranger's enduring popularity that *The Story of the Kelly Gang* (1906), the world's first full-length feature film, was banned. But Ned continued to stir the public imagination and inspire writers, artists (notably Sidney Nolan) and film-makers; Tony Richardson's *Ned Kelly* (1970) starred Mick Jagger, and Yahoo Serious modernised the myth in *Reckless Kelly* (1993).

Unfazed by these antecedents, Jordan, who found success four years ago with Ledger in the crime drama *Two Hands,* opted for a down-to-earth approach, working from a screenplay based on Robert Drewe's novel *Our Sunshine*. At odds with the latter's title, *Ned Kelly* is frequently dark, with Oliver Stapleton's brooding images drained of colour. What Jordan's film lacks in profundity, it makes up for in energy, and the most stirring moments depict the gang, hardly more than boys, riding the wild country they know better than their pursuers. Ledger is a marvellous, even definitive Ned, full of rough but eloquent passion.

Massively promoted in Australia, the film performed disappointingly, earning less than $9m, respectable for an Australian film, but not one budgeted at $19m (it didn't help that it opened as the Iraq War played out live on television). *Ned Kelly* also stirred up heated, partisan debate about Kelly's status, which was inevitable and desirable but overshadowed the film's substantial virtues. In its wake, the low-budget spoof **Ned** proved that nothing is sacred. Writer-director-actor Abe Forsythe laboured the obvious in his good-natured, Python-esque farce. But the film flopped.

Personal growth department

Like *Ned Kelly,* Russell Mulcahy's **Swimming Upstream** sticks

Napier. Prod: Stephen Luby, Tony Martin, Greg Sitch/Million Monkeys/Double Yolker/Macquarie/Movie Network.

BLURRED
[Teen comedy, 2002] Script: Stephen Davis, Keir Shorey. Dir: Evan Clarry. Phot: Phil Cross. Players: Matthew Newton, Jess Gower, Kristian Schmid, Craig Horner, Veronica Sywak. Prod: Chris Brown, Chris Fitchett/Pictures in Paradise. After the stress of their final school exams, teenagers unwind – and in some cases unravel – on Queensland's Gold Coast.

TAKE AWAY
[Comedy, 2003] Script: Dave O'Neil, Mark O'Toole. Dir: Marc Gracie. Phot: Peter Zakharov. Players: Vince Colosimo, Stephen Curry, Rose Byrne, Nathan Phillips. Prod: David Redman/Mondayitis. Tony and Trev, owners of rival fish shops, fight habitually but unite when a multinational food business threatens them both.

TILL HUMAN VOICES WAKE US
[Drama, 2001] Script and Dir: Michael Petroni. Phot: Roger Lanser. Players: Guy Pearce, Helena Bonham Carter, Frank Gallacher, Lindley Joyner. Prod: Thomas Augsberger, Matthias Emcke, Shana Levine, Dean Murphy, Nigel Odell, David Redman/AFFC/East Finance Group/Film Victoria/Instinct Ent./Key Ent./Globe/Melbourne Film Office.

NED KELLY
[Drama, 2003] Script: John Michael McDonagh based on the novel Our Sunshine by Robert Drewe. Dir: Gregor Jordan. Phot: Oliver Stapleton. Players: Heath Ledger, Orlando Bloom, Naomi Watts, Joel Edgerton, Laurence Kinlan, Phillip Barantini, Kerry Condon, Kris McQuade, Rachel Griffiths, Geoffrey Rush. Prod: Nelson Woss, Lynda

House/Universal/Studio
Canal/Working Title.

Geoffrey Rush in **Swimming Upstream**

SWIMMING UPSTREAM

*[Drama, 2003] Script: Anthony
Fingleton and Diane Fingleton.
Dir: Russell Mulcahy. Phot:
Martin McGrath. Players:
Geoffrey Rush, Judy Davis, Jesse
Spencer, Tim Draxl, David
Hofner, Craig Horner, Brittany
Byrnes. Prod: Howard Baldwin,
Karen Baldwin, Paul
Pompian/Crusader Ent.*

GETTIN' SQUARE

*[Comedy, 2003] Script: Chris
Nyst. Dir: Jonathan Teplitsky.
Phot: Garry Phillips. Players:
Sam Worthington, David
Wenham, Freya Stafford, Gary
Sweet, Timothy Spall. Prod:
Martin Fabinyi, Tim White, Trish
Lake/United Int./Studio
Canal/Universal.*
A young crim and two of his
prison mates try to go straight
after their release, but are caught
between corrupt cops and former
gangster associates.

JAPANESE STORY

*[Drama, 2003] Script: Alison
Tilson. Dir: Sue Brooks. Phot:
Ian Baker. Players: Toni Collette,
Gotaro Tsunashima, Matthew
Dyktysnski, Lynette Curran.
Prod: Sue Maslin/Palace/Logo/
AFFC/PMP/Screenwest/
Film Victoria.*

ALEXANDRA'S PROJECT

*[Thriller, 2003] Script and Dir:
Rolf de Heer. Phot: Ian Jones.
Players: Gary Sweet, Helen
Buday, Bogdan Koca. Prod: de
Heer, Julie Ryan, Domenico
Procacci/Vertigo/Fandango/
Palace/SAFC.*
A suburban housewife takes
revenge on her husband.

to the facts. It's based on the true story of Anthony Fingleton, who
used his prowess as a champion swimmer to pave his way to
Harvard and a showbusiness career in New York. The film
concentrates on his youth in 1950s Brisbane and his struggle
to win approval and ultimate emancipation from his belligerent,
alcoholic father, Harold, played with steely intelligence by Geoffrey
Rush. Jesse Spencer is the young Tony, Judy Davis his long-
suffering but resilient mother and Tim Draxl his favoured
brother, John. Mulcahy opts for flashy visual treatment of the boy's
frequent bouts in the pool but it's not really a sporting film.
The real battle is within the family, poisoned by Harold's addiction.
Swimming Upstream is handicapped by its 'Movie of the Week'
affinities, but the leads all deliver high-powered performances.

In a quieter, more thoughtful vein, Michael Petroni's **Till Human
Voices Wake Us** also enlists international star power, teaming
Guy Pearce with Helena Bonham Carter (at her most beguiling)
in a story about repressed memory and desire. He is buttoned-
up psychiatrist Sam Franks and she is Ruby, a mysterious,
otherworldly figure who reminds him irresistibly of his lost
childhood sweetheart. Petroni delivers a wonderful evocation
of place, with subtle, compelling lead performances, but if there's
an audience for such gentle, contemplative material, it wasn't
found in Australia. The film was re-edited for its US release,
abandoning Petroni's chronological progression and inter-cutting
the experiences of Pearce's character as a child, but that still
wasn't enough to please many reviewers.

Although not released in Australia at the time of writing,
Japanese Story promises to be a prestige hit with critics and
a sleeper with audiences. Screened in Un Certain Regard at
Cannes in 2003, it's a genuine surprise. Director Sue Brooks,
writer Alison Tilson and producer Sue Maslin previously
collaborated on the sparse, folksy, shaggy dog's tale *Road to
Nhill*, but *Japanese Story* is far more ambitious, taking as its
starting point the complicated relationship between Australia
and Japan, mortal enemies 60 years ago, but now close
trading partners.

Toni Collette and Gotaro Tsunashima fall in love in **Japanese Story**

Sandy (Toni Collette), a geologist, becomes an unwilling guide for businessman Tachibana (Gotaro Tsunashima) as he tours remote mines in the Outback. She finds him inscrutable but slowly falls in love. It's an intensely physical infatuation, beautifully conveyed by stunning imagery, but the film takes a totally unexpected turn and digs deep into the nature of love and mortality. Collette's performance is unforgettable.

Parochial fun and games

Serious films with artistic pretensions have a solid tradition in Australia, going back to the industry's 1970s revival and beyond. But parochial comedies that debunk such aspirations have a better commercial track record. The classic example is *Crocodile Dundee,* and Paul Hogan has tried, with mixed results, to escape his own creation, re-locating to Los Angeles and appearing in films like *Flipper*. At press time he was about to star alongside Michael Caton (*The Castle*) and Pete Postlethwaite in Dean Murphy's 'ocker' comedy *Strange Bedfellows*. Caton and Hogan are two straight guys who pose as a gay couple to dodge tax and Postlethwaite is the inspector who tries to bust their scam.

Ten years ago, David Caesar (*Dirty Deeds*) made a gentle comedy about lawn bowls called *Greenkeeping* and one of the biggest homegrown successes of 2002 was the broad, knockabout comedy **Crackerjack**, which concerns a bunch of salt-of-the-earth characters trying to save their bowls club from developers. It cashed in on the popularity of local comedian Mick Molloy, who will next be seen in *Bad Eggs,* as an undercover cop who decides to take on police corruption (a ubiquitous subject in Australia). Another highly successful comedian, Nick Giannopoulos, is hoping to repeat the considerable success of his first film *The Wogboy* (2000) with **The Wannabes**, and early indications are that it could be a popular local hit. Giannopoulos directs and stars as a loser who dreams of fame. Faintly resembling *The Ladykillers* (1955), it's generally played for the broadest of laughs.

Comedy boomlet

Almost half the films made in Australia in the 12 months to May 2003 were comedies, most of them with fairly modest budgets, but some upping the ante with superior production values. *Gettin' Square* is directed by Jonathan Teplitsky who established himself with the romantic comedy *Better Than Sex* (2000) and it again features David Wenham. *The Night We Called It a Day,* directed by Paul Goldman (*Australian Rules,* 2002), stars Dennis Hopper as Frank Sinatra and is loosely based on Ol' Blue Eyes' visit to Australia in 1974, when unions retaliated against his perceived arrogance by closing down his concerts. Both films were unseen at press time.

THE RAGE IN PLACID LAKE
[Comedy, 2003] Script and Dir: Tony McNamara. Phot: Ellery Ryan. Players: Ben Lee, Miranda Richardson, Rose Byrne, Garry McDonald. Prod: Marian Mcgowan/Rapacious.
Placid Lake's parents have bequeathed him a life of obligatory nonconformity. But his unlikely best friend Gemma could help him escape.

HORSEPLAY
[Comedy, 2003] Script: Stavros Kazantzidis, Allanah Zitzerman. Dir: Kazantzidis. Phot: David Eggby. Players: Marcus Graham, Tushka Bergen, Jason Donovan, Bill Hunter, Natalie Mendoza, Abbie Cornish. Prod: Zitzerman/ AFFC/Macquarie/PMP.
His wife hates him, his mistress despises him and he's lost his job, but small-time horse trainer Max still attempts one more big scam.

THUNDERSTRUCK
[Comedy, 2003] Script: Darren Ashton, Shaun Angus Hall. Dir: Ashton. Phot: Geoff Hall. Players: Damon Gameau, Stephen Curry, Callan Mulvey, Ryan Jonson, Sam Worthington. Prod: Jodi Materson/Eddie Wong/Wildheart.
After a near-death experience, five boys, all devoted AC/DC fans, make a pact to bury whoever dies first next to their idol, the band's original singer Bon Scott. Eleven years later, they have to fulfil their promise.

UNDER THE RADAR
[Comedy-thriller, 2003] Script: Steve Pratt. Dir: Evan Clarry. Phot: Philip Cross. Players: Steady Eddy, Chloe Maxwell, Nathan Phillips, Clayton Watson, Rory Williamson. Prod: Chris Brown, Chris Fitchett/Pictures in Paradise.
Three boys and a girl, all in their early twenties, leave their homes on a pilgrimage to coastal beaches, craving excitement.

THE NIGHT WE CALLED IT A DAY

[Comedy, 2003] Script: Peter Clifton, Michael Thomas. Dir: Paul Goldman. Phot: Danny Ruhlmann. Players: Dennis Hopper, Melanie Griffiths, Joel Edgerton, Rose Byrne, Portia de Rossi, David Hemmings, David Field. Prod: Peter Clifton, Nik Powell, Emile Sherman/Icon/Ocean.

THE WANNABES

[Comedy, 2003] Script: Chris Anastassiades, Ray Bosley, Nick Giannopoulos. Dir: Giannopoulos. Phot: Dan Burstall. Players: Giannopoulos, Russell Dykstra, Isla Fisher, Felix Williamson. Prod: Tom Burstall, Giannopoulos/G.O./Macquarie.

Radha Mitchell in **Visitors**

VISITORS

[Drama, 2003] Script: Everett de Roche. Dir: Richard Franklin. Phot: Ellery Ryan. Players: Radha Mitchell, Ray Barrett, Phil Ceberano, Tottie Goldsmith, Dominic Purcell, Susannah York. Prod: Franklin/Bayside.
After six months at sea on an unassisted solo circumnavigation, Georgia Perry's 44-foot sloop is becalmed for several days. Cabin fever sets in, blurring the border between fact and fantasy.

TRAVELLING LIGHT

[Drama, 2003] Script and Dir: Kathryn Millard. Players: Pia Miranda, Sacha Horler, Tim Draxl, Kestie Morassi, Heather Mitchell, Marshall Napier, Simon Burke, Joanne Priest, Anna Torv, Tamblyn Lord. Prod: Helen Bowden/TOI-TOI.
Two sisters dream of a life beyond their small-town,

Of the films I've seen, **Danny Deckchair** is probably the most likely of this year's crop to be a hit. Danny (Rhys Ifans from *Notting Hill*) is a no-hoper stuck in a dead-end relationship who becomes a media sensation by disappearing into a stormy sky on a deckchair suspended by helium balloons. While a nationwide search unfolds, Danny discovers a new life, and a new persona, in an idyllic country town, where he falls in love with a lonely parking cop (Miranda Otto). Writer-director Jeff Balsmeyer brings great energy and imagination to his feature directing debut. It's folksy, almost cartoonish at times, but Ifans and Otto, who changes from plain Jane to dazzler, both endow their characters with genuine depth.

Rhys Ifans takes off as **Danny Deckchair**

Double-edged swords

If you had walked around Australia's capital cities in 2002-03, you could not have failed to notice the impact of the *Star Wars* and *Matrix* cycles, the most commercially successful of the many runaway Hollywood productions that have swelled the coffers of high-end Australian companies in recent years. Obviously, there are positive spin-offs. Local commercials-makers, for example, are now exploiting Australian resources to draw work from Asia and even North America.

But it's all very fragile. The Australian dollar was climbing again in mid-2003, making our facilities less of a bargain. Like the success of our actors overseas, foreign productions tend to distract people from the underlying realities. Australian film-making depends on government subsidy and protective regulation, but these have been gradually undermined, especially at the hands of John Howard's mean-minded, right-wing government.

A footnote: the next big Australian star may well be Rose Byrne. With five films due for release in 2003 and a starring role opposite Brad Pitt in *Troy* in 2004, it will be hard to miss her.

PETER THOMPSON is a writer, film-maker and critic who appears regularly on Australian television.

suburban existence. Change beckons when they meet Lou, an American beat poet.

THE HONOURABLE WALLY NORMAN

[Comedy, 2003] Script: Andrew Jones, Rick Kalowski. Dir: Ted Emery. Phot: David Foreman. Players: Kevin Harrington, Shaun Micallef, Greig Pickhaver. Prod: Jonathan Shteinman, Emile Sherman/Wally.

Timid, small-town meat worker Wally finds himself nominated for parliament and finds hidden strengths.

YOU CAN'T STOP THE MURDERS

[Comedy, 2003] Script: Gary Eck, Anthony Mir. Dir: Mir. Phot: Justin Brickle. Players: Eck, Mir, Akmal Saleh, Richard Carter, Kirsty Hutton, Robert Carlton. Prod: Anastasia Sideris/Big Mo/Miramax/SBSI/Showtime. Police in a tiny Australian town are baffled by a series of murders. Someone is killing inhabitants who share the same occupations as disco legends the Village People, and there is one job left – the cop.

WATERMARK

[Drama, 2003] Script: Kerry Rock, Georgina Willis. Dir: Willis. Phot: Paul Kolsky, David

Perry. Players: Jai Koutrae, Sandra Stockley, Ruth McDonald, Ellouise Rothwell. Prod: Kerry Rock/Potoroo.

A COLD SUMMER

[Drama, 2003] Script: Teo Gebert, Paul Middledich, Olivia Pigeot, Susan Prior. Dir: Middledich. Phot: Steve Arnold. Players: Gebert, Pigeot, Prior. Prod: Grace Yee, Middledich/Eltham Strathmore.

DANNY DECKCHAIR

[Romantic comedy, 2003] Script and Dir: Jeff Balsmeyer. Phot: Martin McGrath. Players: Rhys Ifans, Miranda Otto, Justine Clarke, Rhys Muldoon. Prod: Andrew Mason/City/Macquarie.

DEEPER THAN BLUE

[Drama, 2003] Script and Dir: Sandra Sciberras. Phot: Greg Parish. Players: Colin Friels, Genevieve Picot, Bruce Myles, Robert Taylor, Kate Whitbread. Prod: Whitbread/Max's Dreaming. Lives are changed when a young boy is rushed to hospital unconscious.

UNDEAD

[Horror-comedy, 2003] Script, Dir and Prod: Peter and Michael Spierig. Phot: Andrew Strahorn. Players: Felicity Mason, Mungo McKay, Rob Jenkins, Lisa

Cunningham, Dirk Hunter, Emma Randall.
Alien pestilence from meteors wakes the living dead.

THE CROP

[Comedy, 2003] Script: George Elliot. Dir: Scott Patterson. Players: Elliot, Holly Brisley, Rhys Muldoon, Tahnee Stroet, Bruce Venables, Tony Barry. Prod: David Wood/Miracle. Nightclub owner Ronnie finds he's going broke because the police have introduced random breath testing. His customers have taken to smoking dope instead of boozing. So Ronnie decides to go into horticulture.

LOVE'S BROTHER

[Comedy, 2003] Script and Dir: Jan Sardi. Players: Giovanni Ribisi, Adam Garcia, Amelia Warner, Silvia de Santis, Eleanor Bron, Paola Dionisotti, John Bluthal, Barry Otto. Prod: Jane Scott, Sarah Radclyffe/ Love's Brother

Quotes of the Year

"Before Australian film-makers are allowed to hire equipment or people they should be made to get their scripts right."
ALEX MESKOVICH, exhibitor.

Australian Film Institute Awards 2002

Film: Rabbit-Proof Fence (Producers: Phillip Noyce, Christine Olsen, John Winter).
Direction: Ivan Sen (Beneath Clouds).
Original Screenplay: Roger Monk (Walking on Water).
Adapted Screenplay: Phillip Gwynne, Paul Goldman (Australian Rules).
Actress: Maria Theodorakis (Walking on Water).
Actor: David Gulpilil (The Tracker).

Supporting Actress: Judi Farr (Walking on Water).
Supporting Actor: Nathaniel Dean (Walking on Water).
Cinematography: Allan Collins (Beneath Clouds).
Editing: Reva Childs (Walking on Water).
Original Music Score: Peter Gabriel (Rabbit-Proof Fence).
Production Design: Chris Kennedy (Dirty Deeds).
Sound: Bronwyn Murphy, Craig Carter, Ian McLoughlin, John Penders (Rabbit-Proof Fence).

Costume Design: Tess Schofield (Dirty Deeds).
Foreign Film: The Lord of The Rings: The Fellowship of the Ring.
Byron Kennedy Award for Excellence: Rachel Perkins.
Raymond Longford Life Achievement: Dr Patricia Edgar.
Young Actor: Emily Browning (Halifax f.p (Playing God)).
Global Achievement: Mel Gibson.

Austria Roman Scheiber

The Year's Best Films

Roman Scheiber's selection:

Jesus, You Know
(Docu. Dir: Ulrich Seidl)

**Blind Spot. Hitler's
Secretary** (Docu. Dirs: André
Heller, Othmar Schmiderer)

Time of the Wolf
(Dir: Michael Haneke)

Blue Moon
(Dir: Andrea Dusl)

Wicked Cells
(Dir: Barbara Albert)

Recent and Forthcoming Films

BÖSE ZELLEN (Wicked Cells)
*[Drama, 2003] Script and Dir:
Barbara Albert. Phot: Martin
Gschlacht. Players: Kathrin
Resetarits, Ursula Strauss, Georg
Friedrich, Gabriela Schmoll.
Prod: coop 99 Filmproduktion.*

DER GLÄSERNE BLICK
(Dead Man's Memories)
*[Thriller, 2002] Script and Dir:
Markus Heltschl. Phot: Christian
Berger. Players: Sylvie Testud,
Miguel Guilherme, Sonja Romei.
Prod: TTV Film/Agora Film (D).*

**IM TOTEN WINKEL. HITLERS
SEKRETÄRIN**
(Blind Spot. Hitler's Secretary)
*[Documentary, 2002] Script and
Dir: André Heller, Othmar
Schmiderer. Phot: Schmiderer.
Featuring: Traudl Junge.
Prod: Dor Film.*

KALTFRONT (Cold Front)
*[Thriller, 2003] Script and Dir:
Valentin Hitz. Phot: Martin
Gschlacht. Players: Georg
Friedrich, Viviane Bartsch, Edita
Malovcic. Prod: coop 99
Filmproduktion.*

Steven Gaydos of *Variety,* a long-time observer of European film-making, recently noted that "the Austrians are enjoying perhaps the greatest flowering of cinematic talent in 70 years." Danish producer Vibeke Windeloev, one of the driving forces behind *Breaking the Waves* and *Dancer in the Dark,* believes that "Austria is probably the most interesting European film country at the moment." Film-makers like Michael Haneke, Ulrich Seidl, Barbara Albert, Virgil Widrich and many others have captured international attention over the past couple of years and continue to keep the local industry energised.

Haneke kept rolling with another disturbing picture, once again premiered at Cannes, about the coldness of the world; on this occasion, however, the devastation is not primarily internal-psychological, but external. The time of the apocalypse, when all values disintegrate and the highest become the lowest, is known in Germanic mythology as the **Time of the Wolf** (*Wolfzeit*). Fleeing a disaster, a middle-class family (father, mother, played by Isabelle Huppert, and two children) travel from the city to their private country refuge, believing themselves to be escaping the general chaos. Quickly and painfully they learn how mistaken they have been. An odyssey through a devastated country begins, and their stops resemble the stations of the cross.

Barbara Albert, acclaimed for her debut *Northern Skirts* (*Nordrand,* 1999), links the stories of very different characters and families in **Wicked Cells** (*Böse Zellen*). In a vaguely defined, small Austrian town, the characters search for structure in their lives, briefly evading loneliness in talk shows, department stores and competitions. The dead still influence the living. A catastrophe forces a new beginning

*Isabelle Huppert, right, in Michael Haneke's **Time of the Wolf***

and guilt cries out for redemption. Virgil Widrich followed his Oscar-nominated short, *Copy Shop,* with a *tour de force* through trash film history. **Fast Film** is a stop-go animated recycling project: hundreds of action, Western and other Hollywood B-movie scenes mixed up and reinvented as an outstanding new film fantasy.

Christ and the Führer

Ulrich Seidl, director of the internationally acclaimed *Dog Days* (*Hundstage*), presented another of his provocative TV documentaries. **Jesus, You Know** (*Jesus, du weisst*) is a portrait of six people who feel a close relationship to Christ, intimately observing them talking to their most important contact. Seidl said: "I wanted to deal with my own very Catholic youth and education. I didn't want to show extreme or sectarian people, but average religious human beings." He creates an ironic perspective as the six believers talk: camera and viewers take the position of Jesus. **Blind Spot. Hitler's Secretary** (*Im toten Winkel*) by André Heller and Othmar Schmiderer was nominated for Best Documentary at the European Film Awards. For the first time, Hitler's private secretary, Traudl Junge, appeared on camera to talk of her life and work for the Führer. It was also the last time: she died a few days after the premiere in Berlin, aged 81.

The biggest home-made box-office hit of 2002 was Harald Sicheritz's **Poppitz,** a satirical tragi-comedy about a car salesman (Roland Düringer) picking the worst possible time for a vacation (shaky situation at work, marriage on the rocks). But these everyday troubles are nothing compared to the stress awaiting him at the "all-inclusive vacation paradise" called Cosamera. Some 440,000 Austrians wanted to see this nightmare of a movie, filled with bad performances and Austria's typical, boring 'cabaret' humour – sadly familiar from Sicheritz's earlier films.

Led by the first two *Lord of the Rings* films, total admissions rose from 18.98 million in 2001 (the best result since the late 1970s) to 19.32 million. The two most successful Austrian arthouse pictures were *Dog Days* (104,000 admissions) and *The Piano Teacher* (95,000). The quality of recent Austrian films is reflected in growing interest from European distributors. Austrian movies have an increasing presence in Eastern Europe, and Italian cinemagoers have been offered *Be My Star* (*Mein Stern*), *Blind Spot, The Piano Teacher, Dog Days* and Andrea Dusl's **Blue Moon,** an atmospheric odyssey through Eastern Europe (brilliant sound design by electronics guru Christian Fennesz), which follows a money courier (Josef Hader), who falls in love with and pursues a mysterious young woman (Viktoria Malektorovych) to the Ukraine.

ROMAN SCHEIBER is an editor of Austria's monthly movie magazine *RAY.*

NOGO
[Drama, 2002] Script and Dir: Sabine Hiebler, Gerhard Ertl. Phot: Helmut Wimmer. Players: Meret Becker, Oliver Korittke, Jasmin Tabatabai, Jürgen Vogel, Mavie Hörbiger. Prod: Dor Film.

Dor Film/Petro Domenigg

Marie Bäumer and Roland Düringer in **Poppitz**

POPPITZ
[Comedy, 2002] Script: Roland Düringer, Harald Sicheritz. Dir: Sicheritz. Phot: Helmut Pirnat. Players: Roland Düringer, Marie Bäumer, Kai Wiesinger, Nora Heschl. Prod: Dor Film.

WOLFZEIT (Time of the Wolf)
[Drama, 2002] Script and Dir: Michael Haneke. Phot: Jürgen Jürges. Players: Isabelle Huppert, Béatrice Dalle, Patrice Chéreau, Olivier Gourmet. Prod: Wega Film.

Viktoria Malektorovych in **Blue Moon**

BLUE MOON
[Drama, 2001] Script and Dir: Andrea Dusl. Phot: Wolfgang Thaler. Players: Josef Hader, Viktoria Malektorovych. Prod: Lotus Film.

Quote of the Year

"International success is the cream on the milk pot of national film production. To keep it simple: the milk is necessary to get the cream. If the cow gives no milk, there is no cream either."
MICHAEL HANEKE, *director.*

Azerbaijan Goga Lomidze

Recent and Forthcoming Films

RASSTREL OTMENIAETSA
(*literally*, **Execution Cancelled**)
[Thriller, 2002] Script: Isi Meliqzade and Alecper Muradov. Dir: Muradov. Players: Nasiba Zeinalova, Fuad Poladov, Yashar Kuliev, Mirvari Novruzova, Taliat Rakhmanov, Meliq Dadashev. Prod: Azerbaijanfilm/ Studio Aidyn.

OVSUNCHU (Wizard)
[Adventure, 2003] Script: Natig Rasulzade and Oktai Mirkasimov. Dir: Mirkasimov. Phot: Kianan Mamedov. Players: Bakhtiar Khanizade, Fuad Poladov, Ayan Mirkasimova. Prod: Azerbaijanfilm/Yeni Film.

Bakhtiar Khanizade in **Wizard**

YUKHU (The Dream)
[Comedy, 2002] Script: Ficret Aliev and Kasim Safarogly. Dir: Aliev. Phot: Valry Kerimov. Players: Nasiba Zeinalova, Siyavush Aslant, Yashar Nuri, Ayan Mirkasimova. Prod: Azerbaijanfilm/Vakhid Film.

As in every other former Soviet republic, the market share for local films in Azerbaijan is tiny, with cinemas running the latest hits from the US, Russia, France, India and Hong Kong. A few foreign films are dubbed into Azerbaijani but most come from Russian distributors with Russian subtitles. The 75 or so cinemas that remain open (compared with almost 800 in 1960) urgently need modern equipment, and the whole country has just one Dolby cinema, in Baku (home to a total of 16 movie theatres).

As Jamil Farajev, head of the Cinema Department at the Ministry of Culture, has noted, after a decade of reorganisation the local production and distribution sectors are still trying to refine their infrastructures. This important, oil-producing country undoubtedly has obstacles to surmount in its film industry, but progress has been made and the government now spends about $600,000 (3 billion Manat) per year on film – enough to finance about three fiction features, two documentaries and two animated features.

In 2002, four feature-length films were completed, including former cinematographer Alecper Muradov's directorial debut **Rasstrel Otmeniaetsa** (literally, *Execution Cancelled*), which tells the factually based story of Khan (Fuad Poladov), an Azeri Robin Hood who was active in the countryside after the Second World War.
This folk hero robbed the rich to support the poor and gained great authority and influence. The movie stars popular Azeri actors Nasiba Zeinalova, Mirvari Novruzova, Taliat Rakhmanov and Meliq Dadashev. *Rasstrel* took ten years to complete, and because some of the early footage disintegrated or became damaged in that time many scenes had to be reshot. Muratov studied as a cameraman at Moscow's VGIK and has worked on ten feature and 50 documentary films.

Doctor and Goliath

The script for **Wizard** (*Ovsunchu*) by Oktay Mirkasimov (a graduate of Moscow's VGIK who has made around 20 films in the last 35 years) was written in 1989, shooting started in 2000, but the completed film opened theatres only on January 31, 2003. It is set during the Sovietisation of Azerbaijan in 1920-21 and the hero, a philosopher and doctor, comes into conflict with the new reality of a communist country. He helps people and leads a spiritual life, a proud man whose deep-rooted moral values cannot be shaken by the commonplace outrages of those times. The film has a David versus Goliath motif, but shows that a single person cannot defeat a harsh regime such as Bolshevism. In this Russian/Israeli/Kazakh co-production there are notable performances by Bakhtiar Khanizade, as the doctor, and Ayan Mirkasimova, as a deaf girl.

The other two films of last year were comedies. Ficret Aliev's **The Dream** (*Yuchu*) is a lyrical tale of a man dreamily in love with a woman for whom he will do anything. Jangir Mechtiev's **Chaji Gara,** based on a nineteenth-century Azeri literary classic by Mirza Fatali Akhundov (the founder of Azeri theatre), which began shooting a decade ago, takes an ironic look at local society in the mid-nineteenth century.

Young love in Ficret Aliev's **The Dream**

In the autumn of 2002, a number of international film festivals and retrospectives were held in Baku, most notably October's 2nd International Film Festival of Audiovisual Production, jointly organised by the Film Directors' Guild and the Youth Ministry, with a major focus on young and debutant film-makers.

Finally, an epic $12m Azerbaijani-US-Dutch adaptation of *Ali and Nino,* from the bestselling 1930s novel by Kurban Said, is scheduled to open in cinemas in autumn 2004. Dutch director Pieter Verhoeff has said he has been dreaming for 20 years of filming this romantic story of Georgian beauty Nino and Azeri intellectual Ali, who fall in love in the 1910s, and believes that the story of antagonism between Christian and Muslim will be particularly powerful today.

GOGA LOMIDZE lives in the Netherlands, where he teaches Russian and works as a freelance translator.

Belarus Goga Lomidze

Recent and Forthcoming Films

PRIKOVANNY (Chained)
[Drama, 2002] Script and Dir: Valery Rybarev. Players: Vladimir Gostiukhin, Alla Kliuka, Tatiana Titova.

Chained

VREMIA GONA (Hunting Season)
[Short, 2001] Script and Dir: Andrei Golubev. Players: Ivan Matskevich, Kirill Zakharov, Dmitri Pustilnik, Olga Shantsyna.

Quote of the Year

"The actors, some of whom had turned down bigger projects, got symbolic salaries."
DMITRI ZAITSEV, *director, on the making of his low-budget* Between Life and Death.

Between Life and Death

In 2004, Belarus celebrates a major anniversary: the 80th birthday of its film industry. That industry is now dominated by the state studio, Belarusfilm, which was a successful producer of youth and war films in the Soviet period. In those days annual output was around 15 features, as well as a great deal of animated and documentary work, but in the mid-1990s a major financial crisis brought production to a standstill.

Since 2000, following the widely approved appointment as studio chief of experienced film engineer Viacheslav Shenko, the situation has improved markedly. With the aid of about $1m a year in state subsidy, Belarusfilm now produces an average of three fiction features, ten documentaries and four animations per year. It also has a degree of financial security from hosting numerous Russian TV series, including two commissions in 2002 from the Russian TV giant RTR (22 episodes of *Law* and 12 episodes of *Kamenski*).

However, the studio's pride and joy in 2002, hailed by one local journalist as "the first domestic blockbuster", was Dmitri Zaitsev's **Between Life and Death** *(Mezhdu zhizniu i smertiu),* a cute, low-budget crime thriller set in the mid-1940s. Its hero, Yanek (popular Russian actor Evgeni Sidihin), is arrested by mistake and imprisoned. He escapes and sets out to track down the bad guy.

The Belarus-Russian co-production **Chained** *(Prikovanny),* directed by Valeri Rybarev, won acclaim at Russia's Kinoshok Film Festival in 2002. The drama touches on incest as Pavel, an isolated war veteran, thinks he has found a new love only to discover that the girl is his daughter, who's determined to reunite Pavel with her mother, Pavel's first love, and may bring him salvation after the traumas of his war experiences.

Hollywood films dominate local cinemas, *The Two Towers, Men in Black II* and *Attack of the Clones* accounting for a large chunk of the 11 million admissions at Belarus' 152 cinemas in 2002. In November 2002, the annual Minsk International Film Festival took place, with 17 films from 10 countries in competition, including work by Andrey Konchalovski and Pavel Todorovski. ∎

Belgium Erik Martens

The Year's Best Films

Erik Martens' selection:
After Life
(Dir: Lucas Belvaux)
On the Run
(Dir: Lucas Belvaux)
Step by Step
(Dir: Philippe Blasband)
Any Way the Wind Blows
(Dir: Tom Barman)
Girl (Dir: Dorothée van
den Berghe)

Recent and Forthcoming Films

ALIAS
[Thriller, 2002] Script: Paul Koeck and Christoph Dirickx. Dir: Jan Verbeyen. Phot: Philip Van Volsem. Players: Hilde De Baerdemaeker, Geert Hunaerts, Veerle Dobbelaere, Hilde Van Mieghem, Werner De Smedt. Prod: Another Dimension of an Idea.

ANY WAY THE WIND BLOWS
[Comedy-drama, 2003] Script and Dir: Tom Barman. Phot: Renaat Lambeets. Players: Natali Broods, Matthias Schoenaerts, Eric Kloeck, Diane De Belder, Frank Vercruyssen, Jonas Boel, Dirk Roofthooft, Sam Louwyck. Prod: Corridor.

DES PLUMES DANS LA TETE
(Feathers in My Head)
[Drama, 2002] Script and Dir: Nicolas de Thier. Phot: Virginie Saint-Martin. Players: Sophie Museur, Francis Renaud, Ulysse de Swaef, Alexis Den Doncke. Prod: JBA Productions/ Magellan Production.

With no success comparable to 2002's Belgian triumph at Cannes (Olivier Gourmet's Best Actor award for Jean-Pierre and Luc Dardenne's *Le fils*), the past year felt slightly anticlimactic (not least because local audiences showed hardly any interest in *Le fils*). In 2003, Cannes screened only a handful of Belgian films, mostly minority participants such as Sylvain Chomet's Official Selection title, the animated feature *Les Triplettes de Belleville,* the story of an orphaned boy and his passion for bicycles. The only film that actually tasted Belgian was the warmly received Directors' Fortnight entry **Feathers in My Head** (*Des plumes dans la tête*), by newcomer Nicolas de Thier, about a family struck by the disappearance of their six-year-old child.

Earlier in the year, a Belgian short, Dirk Beliën's *Gridlock (Fait d'hiver)*, was nominated at the Academy Awards. It mixes humour, drama and suspense in the tale of a young manager who gets stuck in a traffic jam on his way home. He uses his mobile phone to call his wife, unaware that he is about to cause irreparable damage. On the whole, however, Belgian films did not perform well abroad; nor did they flourish at home.

Then, on October 2, 2002, came the death of André Delvaux, one of Belgium's most important film-makers during the past four decades. Like few others, he managed to give his films a more international drive, yet they also successfully brought together the French- and Dutch-speaking communities of Belgium. Today, this kind of co-operation is the exception rather than the rule.

For the Flemish (i.e. Dutch-speaking) community, 2002-03 has been a period of transition. New film institutions have been put in place, and everyone is curious to see how they will perform. The introduction of a tax shelter, allowing film investment to be partially tax-deductible, comes long after similar schemes in other European countries (some of which are now being scaled back), but has nevertheless prompted optimistic expectations that private money will be injected into the underfinanced Belgian production sector.

Triple vision

The year's most interesting achievement, and my personal favourite, was a dazzling trilogy from Belgian actor-director Bruno

HOP

*[Social drama, 2002] Script and
Dir: Dominique Standaert. Phot:
Remon Fromont. Players:
Kalomba Mboyi, Ansou
Diedhiou, Sjarel Branckaerts,
Antje de Boeck, Jan Decleir,
Emile Mpenza. Prod: Executive
Productions/Signature
Films/Sokan.*

Kassablanka

KASSABLANKA

*[Drama, 2002] Script: Guy Lee
Thys. Dir: Guy Lee Thys and
Ivan Boeckmans. Phot:
Guillaume Vandenberghe.
Players: Roy Aernouts, Mo
Barich, Amid Chakir, Patricia
Chenut, Tanja Cnaepkens. Prod:
Fact & Fiction.*

MEISJE (Girl)

*[Drama, 2002] Script: Dorothée
Van den Berghe and Peter van
Kraaij. Dir: Van den Berghe.
Phot: Jan Vancaillie. Players:
Charlotte Vanden Eynde, Els
Dottermans, Frieda Pittoors,
Matthias Schoenaerts, Nico
Sturm, Wim Opbrouck. Prod:
Lumière Productie/K-2/
Motel Films.*

SCIENCE FICTION

*[Drama, 2003] Script: Chris
Craps and Jean-Claude van
Rijckeghem. Dir: Dany Deprez.
Players: Koen De Bouw, Wendy
van Dijk, David Geclovicz, Fran
Michiels, Ilse Van Hoecke, Staf
Coppens. Prod: A Private View.*

UN COUPLE EPATANT

(Amazing Couple) *[Comedy,
2002]* / **CAVALE (On the Run)**
[Drama, 2002] / **APRES LA VIE
(After Life)** *[Drama, 2002]
Script and Dir: Lucas Belvaux.
Phot: Pierre Milon. Players:
Ornella Muti, François Morel,*

Belvaux, who lives in Paris and also found the bulk of his budget in France. He uses an audacious concept, with three films sharing the same central event: the escape from prison of an extreme left-wing terrorist, Bruno Le Roux (Belvaux), who runs off to Grenoble to attend to urgent business.

In **On the Run** (*Cavale*) he is the main character, whereas in **After Life** (*Après la vie*) the lead is a police officer running the investigation. The tone of the third part is completely different: **Amazing Couple** (*Un couple épatant*) is more a comedy of manners, a story of supposed marital betrayal and all other kinds of misinterpretations. Fascinatingly, each film influences our perception of the others. When you see them in a different order, you experience them differently, so that, for example, the good guy in film one can become a bad guy in film two.

Philippe Blasband's directorial debut, **Step by Step** (*Un honnête commerçant*), is another production of considerable originality. Blasband already had a reputation as a writer of adventurous scripts like *Une liaison pornographique* and *Thomas est amoureux,* which demonstrated his gift for ingenious dialogue and striking concepts. The film is a thriller of sorts, in which two police inspectors interrogate a businessman who pretends to be 'honest', though the truth appears somewhat different. The conflict in this film is all in the words. The camerawork is unfashionably rigid, and the film could sometimes use some air, but as a debut feature it is undeniably a fine achievement.

Philippe Noiret, left, in **Step by Step**

Shoot the messages

In Dominique Standaert's **Hop,** Justin is a 13-year-old illegal refugee from Burundi, on the run from the authorities. Shot on Sony HD, the film makes a plea for inter-racial understanding and takes a firm stand against racism and the "fortress Europe" ideology, but unfortunately becomes overburdened by its message. The remaining titles concentrate on youngsters in their teens or twenties. They are all Dutch-language projects, continuing the recent trend in which many films in Flanders and the Netherlands have explicity targeted the youth market.

Dominique Standaert's Hop

Ideologically speaking, **Kassablanka,** by Guy Lee Thys and Ivan Boeckmans, comes very close to Standaert's *Hop.* In a housing block called Kassablanka the different communities find it hard to live together. There's a lot of racism in the air and the gaps between the various ethnic groups are very wide. When Wout falls in love with Leilan, the girl-next-door of North African origin, his view on life alters completely. The film has some nice scenes but is far too simple, and, like *Hop,* puts too much weight on its message.

To some extent this also applies to **Science Fiction**, Dany Deprez's follow-up to his first feature, *De Bal. Science Fiction* is a nicely crafted film dominated by one central metaphor: children are often aliens to their parents and vice versa. Andreas truly believes that his parents come from another planet. On the one hand, screenwriters Chris Craps and Jean-Claude van Rijckeghem take the metaphor very literally, on the other, they sustain the ambiguity until the end. The idea is nice, but there could have been more life to it.

In the two last films, we move from kids in their early teens to kids in their late twenties. Dorothée Van den Berghe's first feature, **Girl** (*Meisje*), evokes a young girl's mental universe. The titular heroine is the introverted Muriel (Charlotte Vanden Eynde), who is confronted with two other women from different generations: Laura, who could

Dominique Blanc, Gilbert Melki, Catherine Frot, Lucas Belvaux. Prod: Agat Films & Cie/Canal+/CNC/Cofimage 12/Entre Chien et Loup/Natexis Banques Populaires Images 2/RTBF/Rhône-Alpes Cinéma.

Lucas Belvaux's Cavale

UN HONNETE COMMERCANT (Step by Step)
[Crime thriller, 2002] Script and Dir: Philippe Blasband. Phot: Virginie Saint-Martin. Players: Benoît Verhaert, Philippe Noiret, Yolande Moreau, Frédéric Bodson, Serge Larivière, Patrick Hastert. Prod: Artémus Productions/Media Services/RTBF/Samsa Film.

VERDER DAN DE MAAN (Sea of Silence)
[Drama, forthcoming] Script: Jacqueline Epskamp. Dir: Stijn Coninx. Phot: Walther van den Ende. Players: Bert André, Anneke Blok, Jappe Claes, Neeltje de Vree, Annet Malherbe, Wim Opbrouck, Huub Stapel, Johanna ter Steege. Prod: Broadcasting Agency/Isabella Films/KRO/Lichtblick Film- und Fernsehproduktion/Sophimages/ Zentropa Productions.
In a Dutch village in the 1960s, a Catholic farmer's family tries to cope with setbacks in daily life.

THE EMPEROR'S WIFE
[Drama, forthcoming] Script: Paul Ruven. Dir: Julien Vrebos. Phot: Toni Malamatenios. Players: Jonathan Rhys-Meyers, Max Beesley, Rosana Pastor, Leticia Dolera, Claire Johnston, Alexander Macqueen, Johnny de Mol, James Auden. Prod: A-Films/Delux Productions/ Fu Works/Spice Factory Ltd/Staccato Films/Terras/

The Emperor's Wife BV.
The emperor of the land of 1,001 nights is looking for a new wife.

DE ZAAK ALZHEIMER
(The Alzheimer Case)
[Thriller, 2003] Script: Erik Van Looy, Carl Joos, based on a novel by Jef Geeraerts. Dir: Van Looy. Phot: Players: Carl Joos, De Bouw, Werner De Smedt, Jan Decleir, Jo Demeyere. Prod: MMG.
Police inspectors tackle a murder case involving a contract killer who appears to be suffering from Alzheimer's.

CRUSADE IN JEANS
[Drama, forthcoming] Script: Wright Bernstein. Dir: Ben Van Bogaert. Players: Jamie Bell, Jan Decleir, Stany Crets. Prod: Kinepolis Film Productions.
Boy travels back in time and finds himself in the midst of the Children's Crusade.

HOT DOGS
[Drama, forthcoming] Script and Dir: Frédéric Brival. Phot: Michaël Inzillo. Players: Brival, Fabrice Rodriguez, Nicolas Gob, Isabelle Colassin. Prod: Cinargo/CCCP.
A young film-maker becomes involved in the life of a gigolo whose portrait she is shooting.

LE TANGO RASHEVSKI
[Drama, forthcoming] Script: Philippe Blasband, Sam Garbarski. Dir: Garbarski. Phot: Jean-Paul Kieffer. Players: Natan Cogan, Tania Garbarski, Hippolyte Girardot, Michel Jonasz, Daniel Mesguich, Ludmila Mikaël, Rudi Rosenberg, Jonathan Zaccaï, Prod: Archipel/Entre Chien et Loup/Samsa Film.
When grandmother Rashevski dies, the family is completely bereft.

LA FEMME DE GILLES
[Drama, forthcoming] Script: Philippe Blasband based on the works of Madeleine Bourdhouxe. Dir: Frédéric Fonteyne. Players: Stefano Accorsi. Prod: Artémis/RTBF/Cinéart/Nord-

be Muriel's mother, and Laura's mother, who could indeed be Muriel's grandmother. The way bodies are dealt with in this film is quite impressive: Van den Berghe puts her "girls" in all their nakedness before the camera and makes them look naked beyond skin depth. It is this Patrice Chéreau touch that lingers in the memory for weeks. The female characters, especially Muriel, are nicely drawn; the male characters, especially Muriel's two young lovers, lack substance.

Finally there is **Any Way the Wind Blows,** a highly anticipated film from Tom Barman, a major name on the Belgian rock scene. Like Van den Berghe in *Girl*, Barman is basically interested in the evocation of a state of mind. As we follow eight characters, who all seem to be pretty lost, throughout a hot day in June, Barman captures something that is more than simply private experience, slightly less than the zeitgeist. He makes some interesting choices in his use of music and puts some drive in the film. From time to time, the metaphysics are over the top, but we go with the flow.

ERIK MARTENS is a freelance film critic. His work appears in Flemish quality newspaper *De Standaard*, in leading entertainment weekly *Focus Knack* and on Flemish public radio Klara. He is editor-in-chief of the Belgian Film Archive's Flemish film history DVD project.

Ouest Productions/Canal + France/Samsa Film/Lucky Red.
Belgium, 1930s. A young woman discovers that her husband is having an affair with her sister.

STEVE & SKY
[Drama, forthcoming] Script and Dir: Felix Van Groeningen. Phot: Ruben Impens. Players: Titus De Voogdt, Delfine Bafort, Johan Heldenbergh, Romy Bollion. Prod: Favourite Films.
Steve, 22, is in jail because of an Ecstasy deal. Sky, 22, likes to talk to her fish. Jean Claude is in a wheelchair. Three people stuck in a moment.

THE WEDDING PARTY
[Drama, forthcoming] Script: Jean Van Hamme, Dominique Deruddere, Charlie Higson based on the strip cartoon Lune de Guerre *by Jean Van Hamme. Dir: Deruddere. Prod: MMG.*
Belgium's Joseph Plateau Awards 2002 are listed on p.151.

Quotes of the Year

"It's amazing how little you know about people. I have a friend who's a film-maker. I've known him for years. Yesterday I found out that he has a job at the Ministry of Finance."
LUCAS BELVAUX, *director, explaining why all the characters in his films lead double lives.*

"Our films are made throughout Europe, in cellars and attics. We got rid of the idea of the big studio. Everybody can work at home. We have people in Poland, Spain, Ireland, England, Sweden, Canada, Hungary. What binds us is the way we work."
PIET DE RYCKER, *Belgian animator, on making animated films in Europe.*

Bosnia and Herzegovina Rada Sesic

The Year's Best Films

Rada Sesic's selection:

Fuse (Dir: Pjer Zalica)

Remake (Dir: Dino Mustafic)

To and Fro
(Short. Dir: Jasmila Zbanic)

Sarajevo's Dog
(Docu. Dir: Haris Prolic)

The North Went Mad
(Short. Dir: Aida Begic)

Recent and Forthcoming Films

REMAKE

[Drama, 2003] Script: Zlatko Topcic. Dir: Dino Mustafic. Phot: Mustafa Mustafic. Players: Ermin Bravo, Alexandar Seksan, Miralem Zubcevic, Zijah Sokolovic, Jasna Diklic. Prod: Enes Cviko/Forum Sarajevo.
Structured as a film-within-a-film, this exciting war drama tells two parallel stories of a father and son who in the span of 50 years are both imprisoned by their neighbours, tortured, humiliated and saved by luck.

GORI VATRA (Fuse)

[Drama, 2003] Script and Dir: Pjer Zalica. Phot: Mirsad Herovic. Players: Adis Beslagic, Bogdan Diklic, Izudin Bajrovic, Senad Basic, Jasna Zalica. Prod: Zijo Mehic/ReFresh.
Unemployment and economic crises are reaching their peak in post-war Tesanj, home to Muslims, Serbs and Croats. On the way to visit American soldiers, Bill Clinton is going to become the town's godfather in seven days, but democracy has to be established first. At the same time, the mystery of a missing son haunts a retired fireman and leads

osnia and Herzegovina has had independent cinema production for the last 50 years, but its directors have always had to rent 35mm cameras from Serbia or Croatia. Today, camera rental can amount to 30% of a film's entire budget – a crazy situation given the republic's amazing recent successes, most notably the Oscar for Danis Tanovic's *No Man's Land* and the European Academy Award for Ahmed Imamovic's short, *10 Minutes,* about the devastating difference between the same 10 minutes of life in Rome and in Sarajevo. Directors and producers hope such accolades will help them to find greater financial support at home and from international partners.

Much still needs to change, because in the eight years since the end of the war, Bosnia averaged only one feature film every three years. That 2002-03 harvested three new features owed more to coincidence than any premeditated changes in the film industry. Two of the three films had their scripts approved for financial support several years ago, only to languish on the shelf while producers managed to find Turkish, German or French co-producers but could not get their hands on the money promised by the local authorities.

History repeats itself

Encouragingly for the future of Bosnian cinema, all three new features are the debuts of directors who had established themselves through very profound and accomplished shorts and documentaries. The first to reach cinemas was Dino Mustafic's **Remake**, which had generated

Dino Mustafic's war drama **Remake**

to the story's dramatic climax.

LJETO U ZLATNOJ DOLINI
(*literally,* **Summer in the Golden Valley**)
[Drama, 2003] Script and Dir: Srdjan Vuletic. Prod: Refresh/Arkadena.

NAZAD-NAPRIJED (To and Fro)
[Short fiction, 2002] Script and Dir: Jasmila Zbanic. Phot: Christine A. Maler. Players: Sara Djuric, Fatima Fazlagic, Sasa Djuric. Prod: Damir Ibrahimovic, Jasmila Zbanic/Deblokada.
A Bosnian family expelled from their home returns to the ruined house, allowing Zbanic to ponder in very intriguing manner our notions of "home".

SJEVER JE POLUDIO
(The North Went Mad)
[Short drama, 2003] Script: Aida Begic, Elma Tataragic. Dir: Aida Begic. Phot: Erol Zubcevic. Players: Izeta Gradjevic, Miralem Zubcevic, Admir Glamocak. Prod: Amra Baksic, Elma Tataragic/Centre for Contemporary Arts.
A young girl dies in an accident and her friends start panicking. All night, several different people get involved in this horrific, absurd situation.

SARAJEVSKI PAS
(Sarajevo's Dog)
[Documentary, 2002] Script: Eldar Emric, Haris Prolic. Dir: Prolic. Phot: Eldar Emric. Prod: Semsudin Cengic/Flash.
Ronny the dog is old and ill but his owners are reluctant to put him down because he is the only living memory of their son, who fell in the battle for Sarajevo in 1993.

BEZ KALORIJA (Sugar Free)
[Short fiction, 2002] Script and Dir: Ines Tanovic. Phot: Almir Djikoli. Players: Ajla Frljuckic, Lana Baric, Tanja Smoje. Prod: Mina Salkic/RTV Federacija BiH/ASU Sarajevo/Refresh/ Document Sarajevo.

considerable buzz after its premiere at Rotterdam (it finished sixth out of 150 entries in the festival's audience poll) and went on to box-office success throughout Bosnia.

This moving film is based on the autobiographical script by Sarajevo-based Zlatko Topcic. He describes his own destiny as well as his father's during two wars, the Second World War and the 1990s conflict that broke up the former Yugoslavia. The story unfolds against a background of concentration camps, ethnic cleansing and torture, and deals with friendship, betrayal, disappointment and the disorientation of a generation. There is a brilliant lead performance from newcomer Ermin Bravo as an aspiring young scriptwriter whose life is turned upside down by war and imprisonment.

Another Bosnian debut, Pjer Zalica's **Fuse** (*Gori vatra*), is a post-war drama that brims with charm and humour but leaves a bitter aftertaste. The story is situated in Tesanj, a small town facing a severe economic crisis. The unemployment rate is at its peak. At the same time the people who left Bosnia during the war are returning to face the mistrust of their former neighbours and colleagues. The mystery surrounding the fate of certain missing people threatens the peace, and the only chance for prosperity is the possible visit of Bill Clinton, who is supposed to become the town's godfather.

Pjer Zalica's tragi-comedy **Fuse**

Zalica has made an exciting tragi-comedy, with several characters whose initially separate stories develop into one common fate at the end. The funny, bold and succinct dialogue offers a potent critique of society, and Zalica builds the suspense very slowly towards a final catharsis which affects the audience almost as profoundly as the protagonists. Cameraman Mirsad Herovic skilfully creates melancholic visuals that perfectly complement the director's approach.

The third debut (unreleased at press time) is **Ljeto u zlatnoj dolini** (literally, *Summer in the Golden Valley*), from Srdjan Vuletic, who won an award for a short at Berlin in 2000. His story deals with contemporary Sarajevo, as a young man who has to settle his late father's debts gets more and more involved in the underworld, of which he knows nothing.

Refugees' return

The production of shorts has been flourishing. Jasmila Zbanic directed and co-produced a very poetic film, *To and Fro (Nazad-naprijed)*, which, with hardly any dialogue, tackles the very sensitive issue of returning refugees. Powerful visuals are the only means the director uses to ponder the question of whether those who left can ever truly return "home". Her film was made with the help of the Cine Bosnia fund, part of the Göteborg Festival, as was the new project of Aida Begic, whose previous short was selected for Cannes. Begic's *The North Went Mad*, which premiered at Göteborg, is a slightly absurd drama about a young girl who dies accidentally. Everybody who comes into contact with the corpse thinks they were responsible for her death and tries to get rid of it as soon as possible. In 2003, Cine Bosnia has backed Alma Becirovic's script for *Saturday Night*.

In the documentary field, Haris Prolic's **Sarajevo's Dog** *(Sarajevski pas)*, produced by the independent company Flash, distinguishes itself from the other non-fiction subjects, most of which were made for Bosnian Television. The film is about the destiny of an old dog that has to be put to sleep by his owners, an old couple. The dog, however, is the only possession left to them by their son, a Bosnian soldier who fell in the last war. The film was selected for the competition at IDFA in Amsterdam.

Production is obviously moving slowly forward, but it is still determined by accidental meetings or friendships between potential partners. To make the situation easier and more professional for all concerned, the Sarajevo Film Festival started in 2002 an extraordinary initiative, Cine Link. Inspired and supported by Rotterdam's CineMart project, Cine Link is a platform for all good scripts from Bosnia and Herzegovina, Croatia, Serbia and Montenegro. They were selected by an international committee and were pitched to potential producers during the 9th Sarajevo Film Festival last August and the industry waits eagerly to see what emerges.

RADA SESIC writes for *Skrien* and *Dox* magazines, lectures at the University of Amsterdam, helps to programme the Rotterdam Festival and is a co-organiser of IDFA in Amsterdam. She also makes short films and documentaries.

Tale of a young woman so influenced by media-promoted fashion trends that she becomes obsessed with her looks, watching her diet and exercising exhaustingly. Until one day…

ZIVOT OD MILUTINA
(The Life of Milutin)
[*Short drama, forthcoming*]
Script and Dir: Dejan Strika.
Phot: Milan Knezevic. Players: Dragoslav Medojevic, Aleksandar Blanic, Radmila Smiljanic. Prod: AU Banja Luka/Nezavisna TV Banja Luka. Satirical vision of an ordinary man's life, from his birth to his education, communist upbringing and then the turbulent years of war.

Quotes of the Year

"I am sorry to say it, but most film industry people, especially from the Anglo-Saxon world, didn't even know where Bosnia was before Danis Tanovic got an Oscar [for *No Man's Land*]."
PIERRE SPENGLER, *producer, explaining why it's so hard to promote Bosnian movies.*

"We have a tremendous problem with bureaucracy. One has to waste a lot of time to get certain permissions and you're never sure whether you have the right document. That's a very hard and exhausting job and I salute every producer who challenges this situation."
PJER ZALICA, *director, explaining why the shooting of his* Fuse *was postponed three times.*

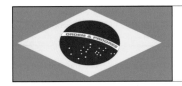

Brazil Nelson Hoineff

Recent and Forthcoming Films

CARANDIRU

[Drama, 2003] Script: Hector Babenco, Victor Navas, Fernando Bonassi, based on the book by Dráuzio Varella. Dir: Babenco. Phot: Walter Carvalho. Players: Luiz Carlos Vasconcellos, Rodrigo Santoro, Wagner Moura, Caio Blat. Prod: Hector Babenco/Daniel Filho/Columbia TriStar Films of Brazil/Globo Filmes.
Based on the book *Estação Carandiru*, written by a doctor who worked as a volunteer in the São Paulo House of Detention. The doctor's encounters with his patients become a window on the everyday life of the criminal underworld.

Zeca Guimarães in **God is Brazilian**

DEUS É BRASILEIRO
(God is Brazilian)

[Comedy, 2003] Script: Carlos Diegues, João Ubaldo Ribeiro, based on the short story by Ribeiro. Dir: Diegues. Phot: Affonso Beato. Players: Antônio Fagundes, Wagner Moura, Paloma Duarte, Bruce Gomlevsky. Prod: Renata de Almeida Magalhães/Rio Vemelho Productions/Columbia TriStar Films of Brazil/Globo Filmes.

The new government that took office in January 2003 had an immediate impact on the film industry. President Lula and the Workers Party were elected with strong support from artists and intellectuals, and Lula appointed as Minister of Culture one of Brazil's most famous and irreverent composers and performers, Gilberto Gil. Six months later, actor Jose Wilker was appointed president of Riofilme, the municipal agency for film production and distribution.

Because virtually all local production continues to rely on federal and state tax laws, and public companies are, through these laws, the biggest investors in film, the comments of director Caca Diegues in the *O Globo* newspaper five months after Lula's election sparked nationwide discussion over the criteria for official sponsorships of films. Diegues accused the new minister for social communication (the department responsible for government advertising and "propaganda"), Luiz Gushiken, of establishing rules for investment by public companies that would favour government propaganda rather than the artistic qualities of the projects. His comments led the president to call a meeting between ministers Gushiken, Gil and film industry figures, and to ensure that cultural activities would be conducted by the Ministry of Culture, not Social Communications.

The decision divided the industry, important film-makers like Nelson Pereira dos Santos claiming that those who spoke for the industry at the crisis meeting were merely promoting their own interests and that the new government was in danger of repeating the sins of its predecessor, by always favouring the same small group of producers. This distracting dispute, combined with the new government's hesitation in defining new rules for state sponsorship, slowed production in the first half of 2003, suggesting that feature film output would slip below the 30-plus level achieved in the previous two years.

Millions can't be wrong

In terms of attendance for local films, the 12 months from mid-2002 were outstanding for Brazilian cinema, with four local films selling more than two million tickets each: Fernando Meirelles' *City of God* (*Cidade de Deus*), Caca Diegues' *God is Brazilian* (*Deus é*

Brasileiro), Hector Babenco's *Carandiru* and Paulo Sergio Almeida's *Xuxa and the Gnomes* (*Xuxa e os duendes*). All four were co-produced by Globo Filmes, confirming the group's dominance of the audio-visual industry (Globo president Roberto Marinho died in August 2003, aged 98, and was immediately succeeded by his son, Roberto Irineu Marinho).

Rodrigo Santoro, left, and Gero Camilo as prisoners in **Carandiru**

Inspired by a best-selling novel by MD Dráuzio Varella, who worked closely with the prisoners at Carandiru, the biggest detention facility in Brazil, **Carandiru** portrays the lives of its thousands of inmates and the rebellion that led to an assault by military police, killing more than 110 people. **God is Brazilian** is a farce about the day when God (vividly played by Antônio Fagundes) visits Brazil as a common man to get in touch with the population.

A huge success internationally, **City of God** explores three decades in the daily life of Cidade de Deus, the Rio de Janeiro slum inhabited by many young drug dealers. Meirelles, with a long track record in commercials, shows children getting involved in crime to escape poverty, and in some cases ultimately killing for the pleasure of it. The density of the novel by Paulo Lins on which the film is based is often replaced by a stylised aesthetic, which was criticised in several quarters in Brazil for being too beautiful and poetic compared to the cruel reality of the drug lords in today's Rio.

These four hits were distributed by the local arms of US majors, including Warners, Fox and Columbia, and their increasing influence can be seen in the fate of some of the best recent Brazilian films, which were released by smaller companies and fared less well at the box-office (such as Beto Brant's thriller *The Trespasser*), or failed to secure national distribution at all, as in the case of newcomer Renato Falcão's **Margarette's Feast** (*A festa de*

After deciding to take a holiday, God comes to the north-east of Brazil, where he intends to choose someone to take his place. In His search for one of the few saintly people left in the world, He will be helped by an unscrupulous man and a passionate woman.

O HOMEM QUE COPIAVA
(The Man Who Copied)
[Comedy, 2003] Script and Dir: Jorge Furtado. Phot: Alex Sernambi. Players: Lázaro Ramos, Leandra Leal, Pedro Cardoso, Luana Piovani. Prod: Nora Goulart/Luciana Tomasi/Casa de Cinema de Porto Alegre/Columbia TriStar Films of Brazil/Globo Filmes.
A photocopier operator has to raise some money to win the girl he loves. He works on several different plans, and to his surprise all of them work out.

Cláudia Abreu and Murilo Benício in **The Man of the Year**

O HOMEM DO ANO
(The Man of the Year)
[Comedy-drama, 2003] Script: Rubem Fonseca, based on the novel by Patricia Mello. Dir: José Henrique Fonseca. Phot: Breno Silveira. Players: Murilo Benício, Cláudia Abreu, Jorge Dória, Natália Lage. Prod: Conspiração Filmes/Leonardo Monteiro de Barros/Warner Bros.
After killing a local drug dealer an unemployed man (Benício) accidentally becomes a folk hero hitman and crime lord – but at great personal cost.

LISBELA E O PRISIONEIRO
(*literally*, **Lisbela and
the Prisoner**)
*[Comedy, 2003] Script: Guel
Arraes, Jorge Furtado, João
Falcão, based on the play by
Osman Lins. Dir: Arraes. Phot:
Uli Burtin. Players: Selton Mello,
Débora Falabella, Marco Nanini,
Bruno Falcão. Prod: Paula
Lavigne/Natasha Filmes/Fox
Filmes do Brasil/Globo Filmes.*
In a very small town in the
north-east of Brazil, a very young
woman is about to marry a rich
man. But, one day, an artist and
singer arrives in town and falls
desperately in love with the
bride-to-be.

O CAMINHO DAS NUVENS
(*literally*, **The Way of the Clouds**)
*[Comedy, 2003] Script: David
França Mendes. Dir: Vicente
Amorim. Phot: Gustavo Hadba.
Players: Cláudia Abreu, Wagner
Moura, Ravi Ramos Lacerda,
Sidney Magal. Prod: Luiz Carlos
Barreto/Buena Vista Films of
Brazil/Globo Filmes.*
The adventures of a man, his
wife and their five children, who
travel from the north-east to São
Paulo riding bicycles. The man
wants to find a job that will pay
him enough money to raise his
family with dignity. Based on
a true story.

1972
*[Comedy-musical, 2003] Script:
Ana Maria Bahiana, José Emílio
Rondeau. Dir: Rondeau. Phot:
Marcelo Durst. Players: Raphael
Rocha, Dandara Ohana Guerra,
Bem Gil, Louise Cardoso. Prod:
Grupo Novo de Cinema/Tarcísio
Vidigal/Ana Maria
Bahiana/Buena Vista Films
of Brazil.*
A surprising love story set
against Rio de Janeiro's nascent
early 1970s rock scene, at
the height of the military
dictatorship.

Margarette), a small jewel crafted in 1920s style. Falcão, who lives
in New York, tells the story of a man who wants to buy a gift for his
wife, despite the fact that he has just lost his job. With an inspiring
lead performance from Hique Gomez, who also wrote the
wonderful *chorinhos* music (a Brazilian genre born in the nineteenth
century), the film creates a Chaplinesque atmosphere, bringing
emotion and joy to the common audience.

The year's biggest controversy involved Ancine (the National
Agency for Film), created in September 2002 and directed by film-
maker Gustavo Dahl. Two ministries, Industry and Development
& Culture, were battling for control of Ancine and President Lula
repeatedly postponed a final decision on the issue (at press time
it was still unresolved). The agency has been playing an important
role in the establishment of the national policy for cinema and had
entered into fruitful negotiations with pay-TV broadcasters through
Article 39, a law that encourages TV companies to invest 3% of
their revenues in the co-production of local programmes,
including films.

NELSON HOINEFF is president of the Association of Film Critics
of Rio de Janeiro and film critic for the daily *Jornal do Brasil* and
www.criticos.com.br

Douglas Silva as the murderous "L'il Dice" in City of God

OS NARRADORES DE JAVÉ
(**The Story Tellers**)
*[Comedy, 2003] Script: Luiz
Alberto de Abreu, Eliane Caffé.
Dir: Caffé. Phot: Hugo Kovensky.
Players: José Dumont, Gero
Camilo, Ruy Rezende, Nelson
Xavier. Prod: Vânia
Cattani/Bananeira Filmes/Gullane
Filmes.*

A man tries to save his small
home town, threatened with
destruction by the construction
of a dam, by collecting old stories
from its inhabitants.

Bulgaria Pavlina Jeleva

The Year's Best Films

Pavlina Jeleva's selection:
Under the Same Sky
(Dir: Krassimir Krumov)
Warming Up
Yesterday's Lunch
(Dir: Konstantin Bonev)
Emigrants (Dir: Ivailo Hristov)
One Calorie of Tenderness
(Dir: Ivanka Gravcheva)
Whose Is This Song?
(Documentary. Dir:
Adela Peeva)

Recent and Forthcoming Films

PODGRIAVANE VA
VCHERASHNIA OBIAD
(Warming up Yesterday's Lunch)
*[Drama, 2002] Script: Mile
Nedelkovski. Dir: Konstantin
Bonev. Phot: Konstantin Zankov.
Players: Svetlana Yancheva,
Biliana Kazakova, Snejina
Petrova, Roussi Chanev.
Prod: Gala Film (Bulgaria)/
Digitprop (Macedonia).*

EDNA KALORIA NEJNOST
(One Calorie of Tenderness)
*[Drama, 2003] Script: Georgi
Danailov. Dir: Ivanka Gravcheva.
Phot: Alexander Lazarov. Players:
Maria Kavardjikova, Tzvetana
Maneva, Valentin Ganev, Plamena
Getova, Marin Yanev.
Prod: Niki Film, with the support
of Bulgarian National Television/
Boyana Film Company.*

PATUVANE KAM YERUSALIM
(Journey to Jerusalem)
*[Drama, 2003] Script: Yurii
Dachev. Dir: Ivan Nitchev. Phot:
Georgi Nikolov. Players: Elena
Petrova, Alexander Morfov, Vassil
Vassilev-Zueka, Bernd Michael*

At the 25th national film festival, Golden Rose, in Varna in October 2002, critics and audiences were cheered by a revival in local production. Unfortunately, the revival of creativity was in contrast to the rather low level of state funding and poor distributor and audience support for domestic films, which claimed barely 1% of the total box-office gross.

The top prize at Varna, the Golden Rose, went to **Emigrants**, directed by popular actor Ivailo Hristov from a script by director Ljudmil Todorov (*Running Dogs*, 1989; *Emilia's Friends*, 1996). Its three talented young leads, Deyan Donkov, Valery Iordanov and Ivan Radoev, shared the Best Actor prize for their portrayals of three unemployed friends, who take odd jobs and dream of emigrating with the help of a mythical uncle in Argentina. Full of fresh humour and showing intelligent irony towards everyday life in Bulgaria, *Emigrants* was instantly held up as a symbol of hope for the new Bulgarian cinema.

The second most acclaimed film was Konstantin Bonev's debut, **Warming up Yesterday's Lunch** (*Podgriavane va vcherashnia obiad*), written by gifted, Skopje-based novelist Mile Nedelkovski. Beautifully shot by Konstantin Zankov, the film tells the story of a woman who decides to speak in front of a young film crew and reveals personal secrets from different political regimes, from before and immediately after the communist era.

Following the success of his co-production with Germany and Greece, *After the End of the World*, Ivan Nichev presented **Journey to Jerusalem** (*Patuvane kam Yerusalim*) and once again deals with the Holocaust, through the story of two young Jews, David and Elsa, who make a dangerous journey towards the Black Sea and a ship bound for Palestine. For **Drugiat nash vazmozhen zhivot** (literally, *This Other Possible Life of Ours*), director Rumiana Petkova was able to bring Vania Tzvetkova, one of the most popular Bulgarian actresses, back home from her base in the US to play a woman falling in love with the same man after 20 years apart.

Written by Georgy Danailov and directed by the eminent Ivanka Grabcheva, **One Calorie of Tenderness** (*Edna kaloria nejnost*) boasted a sensitive leading performance by Maria Kavardjikova as Nadejda (which means 'hope'), a middle-aged divorcee, who, after

Lade. Prod: *Cinemascope – 1, Nichev (Bulgaria)/Saxonia-Media (Germany).*

DRUGIAT NASH VAZMOZHEN ZHIVOT (*literally,* **This Other Possible Life of Ours**) [Drama, 2003] *Script: Nevelina Popova. Dir: Rumiana Petkova. Phot: Svetla Ganeva. Players: Vania Tzvetkova, Ivan Ivanov, Irini Jambonas, Ljuben Chatalov, Valentin Tanev. Prod: Doli Media Studio, with the support of Bulgarian National Television.*

POD EDNO NEBE (**Under the Same Sky**) [Drama, 2003] *Script and Dir: Krassimir Kroumov. Phot: Emil Hristov. Players: Marta Kondova, Krassimir Dokov, Roumen Traikov, Nikolay Ouroumov, Leontina Arditi. Prod: Bulgarian National Television.*

CHIA E TAZI PESSEN (**Whose Is This Song?**) [Documentary, 2003] *Script and Dir: Adela Peeva. Prod: Adela Media (Bulgaria)/Periscope Production NV (Belgium).*

RAZSLEDVANE (Investigation) [Drama, 2003] *Script and Dir: Iglika Triffonova. Phot: Rali Ralchev. Players: Svetlana Yancheva, Krassimir Dokov. Prod: KLAS Film (Bulgaria)/ Move-a-Mountain (Germany).* A murderer and a woman detective face off in a merciless moral battle that ends with his confessing his crime.

Quote of the Year

"The difference between me and a waiter is that I can always say: 'I won't serve this table.'"

EMIL HRISTOV, *cinematographer for hire.*

Maria Kavardjikova as a divorcee in **One Calorie of Tenderness**

building a successful scientific career, sets out to find a second husband, much to the consternation of her grown-up son and daughter and best friend.

Even before it was broadcast by its producer, Bulgarian National Television, Krassimir Krumov's drama **Under the Same Sky** (*Pod edno nebe*) was called in by various international festivals. Tender and poetical, the film deals with the real-life economic plight of Bulgarian Turks, by following Rufie, a poor 15-year-old village girl who disguises herself as a boy and tries to enter Turkey illegally to rejoin her father, who has returned there in search of work. Adela Peeva's documentary **Whose Is This Song?** (*Chia e tazi pessen*) follows the director's curious geographical and spiritual journey through a couple of Balkan countries in which everyone pretends to be the owner of the same popular song.

The seventh edition of the Sofia Film Festival, in March 2003, introduced an international competition for first and second films and welcomed many international guests, including Otar Iosseliani and Petr Zelenka. The country's most important festival (176 films, 11 awards), Sofia was among the first beneficiaries of the EU's Media Plus programme, following Bulgaria's admission in June 2002.

PAVLINA JELEVA has been a professional film critic and journalist since 1978, contributing to many Bulgarian newspapers and magazines. Having been national representative at the Eurimages Board and FIPRESCI, she now runs her own film company.

Canada Brendan Kelly

The Year's Best Films

Brendan Kelly's selection:

The Barbarian Invasions
(Dir: Denys Arcand)

Québec-Montréal
(Dir: Ricardo Trogi)

Looking for Leonard
(Dirs: Matt Bissonnette,
Steven Clark)

**How My Mother Gave Birth
to Me During Menopause**
(Dir: Sébastien Rose)

20h17 rue Darling
(Dir: Bernard Emond)

Recent and
Forthcoming Films

THE BLUE BUTTERFLY
*[Drama, 2002] Script: Pete
McCormack. Dir: Léa Pool.
Phot: Pierre Mignot. Players:
William Hurt, Pascale Bussières,
Marc Donato. Prod: Francine
Allaire, Arnie Gelbart, Claude
Bonin, Michael Haggiag.*
A terminally ill 10-year-old boy
persuades a renowned
entomologist to take him on a
trip to the rainforests of Central
and South America in search of
the mythic and elusive Blue
Morpho butterfly.

COMMENT MA MERE
ACCOUCHA DE MOI
DURANT SA MENOPAUSE
(How My Mother Gave Birth
to Me During Menopause)
*[Comedy, 2002] Script and Dir:
Sébastien Rose. Phot: Nicolas
Bolduc. Players: Micheline
Lanctôt, Paul Ahmarani. Prod:
Roger Frappier, Luc Vandal.*
At 30, Jean Charles still lives on
rather intimate terms with his
mother and sister, but his new

French-language Canadian cinema is on a major-league roll. Too bad the same can't be said for Canadian film-makers toiling away in English. The box-office success of the Robert Lantos-produced curling comedy *Men with Brooms* in 2002 continues to look like the exception that proves the rule that Canadians outside largely French-speaking Quebec have little enthusiasm for homegrown cinema. Atom Egoyan's ambitious Armenian genocide drama, *Ararat*, and David Cronenberg's *Spider* both elicited tons of media coverage in Canada, then failed to generate much action at cash registers. The lesson? Audiences still have little appetite for the dark, twisted *auteur* cinema that's been English Canada's calling card for the past 20 years.

English-Canadian films fail utterly to dent the total supremacy of Hollywood fare at cinemas outside Quebec, accounting for a woeful 1% of ticket sales for English-language films. However, French-language Canadian films in 2002 grabbed a 12% share of the Canadian market for all French-language films.

But there are some glimmers of hope for English-Canadian film. Deepa Mehta's light and entertaining tribute to Bollywood musicals, *Bollywood/Hollywood*, garnered good results in autumn 2002. *Mambo Italiano*, director Emile Gaudreault's adaptation of the hit coming-out-of-the-closet play, also did well on home turf and has been sold to more than 20 countries, including the US. Lantos, one of Canada's leading producers, is also pushing Canadian cinema to new levels of visibility with his expensive (by local standards) projects, notably the thriller *The Statement*, directed by Norman Jewison and starring Michael Caine.

Stone turns to gold

The unequivocal success story of recent years remains *le cinéma Québecois*. In 2002, total box-office for Quebec film surged to $10m (C$15m), up 50% on 2001, and local pics' share of the province's total gross rose to 8% (from 6% in 2002). The year's flagship Québecois hit was **Séraphin: Heart of Stone** (*Séraphin, un homme et son péché)*, a period drama that set an all-time record for Quebec cinema of more than $5.4m.

Set in late nineteenth-century rural Quebec, *Séraphin* is a solid,

girlfriend should change all that. Or maybe not.

FOOLPROOF

[Thriller, 2002] Script and Dir: William Phillips. Phot: Derek Rogers. Players: Ryan Reynolds, Kristin Booth, Joris Jarsky, James Allodi, David Suchet. Prod: Seaton McLean, Bill House.
An ingenious trio who plot foolproof robberies as high-tech games must battle for their lives when a notorious gangster blackmails them into executing a $20m heist.

LA GRANDE SEDUCTION
(Seducing Doctor Lewis)

[Comedy-drama, 2002] Script: Ken Scott. Dir: Jean-François Pouliot. Phot: Allen Smith. Players: Raymond Bouchard, David Boutin, Benoît Brière, Pierre Collin, Lucie Laurier, Bruno Blanchet, Rita Lafontaine, Clemence Desrochers, Donald Pilon. Prod: Roger Frappier, Luc Vandal.
A resident of a tiny port village in Quebec tries to convince a multinational corporation to set up a factory on the outskirts of town.

THE GREAT GOOSE CAPER

[Family comedy, 2002] Script: Charles Dennis. Dir: Nicolas Kendal. Phot: Andy Collins. Players: Chevy Chase, Joan Plowright, James Purefoy. Prod: Alex Brown, Wendy Hill-Tout.
A story about a young boy recovering from the loss of his mother who must save the life of a goose to redeem himself.

moving melodrama about a young woman, Donalda (Karine Vanasse), who nobly agrees to marry a miserable, old and psychopathic miser, Séraphin (Pierre Lebeau), in order to save her father and the family business from ruin, despite her continuing, clandestine love for another man, Alexis (Roy Dupuis). Director Charles Binamé – previously known for hip, urban pics like *Eldorado* – takes a more traditional approach with this adaptation of a classic Quebec novel from the 1930s and pays careful attention to historical detail. Lebeau oozes unpleasantness and aggression in a memorable turn in the lead role.

One of the most satisfying aspects of the film's record-breaking run was that it showed that audiences in Quebec will shell out for serious drama. For the past 15 years, virtually all the local hits have been salty, low-brow comedies like *La Florida* and the *Les boys* ice-hockey franchise. Quebec moviegoers' renewed enthusiasm for upscale fare was confirmed by the runaway success of Denys Arcand's **The Barbarian Invasions** (*Les invasions barbares*), one of the most accomplished Canadian films in years. After misfiring with his showbiz satire *Stardom*, Arcand returns to fine form with this sequel to his 1987 global arthouse hit *The Decline of the American Empire* (*Le déclin de l'empire Américain*). It reunites many of the same Montreal intellectuals from the earlier film, but this time the focus is on Rémy (Rémy Girard), who is dying from an unnamed disease.

Arcand's smart, witty film deals with heavy issues but manages to remain remarkably accessible. This is populist arthouse craft at its best. Arcand touches on strained father-son relations, the generation gap between baby-boomers and their offspring and Canada's decrepit health-care system and yet still includes some of the funnier lines heard in Canadian film in a long while. The film is also blessed with fine performances, including Girard as the ailing womaniser, comic-turned-actor Stéphane Rousseau as his successful and resourceful son and Marie-Josée Croze as a heroin addict with a heart of gold (she took Best Actress at Cannes in 2003, while Arcand took Best Screenplay).

Chevy Chase in **The Great Goose Caper**

Stéphane Rousseau, left, and Rémy Girard in **The Barbarian Invasions**

Odeon Films

Sex as comedy

First-time feature director Ricardo Trogi's **Québec-Montréal** is a refreshing comedy. This high-IQ road movie follows nine twentysomething men and women (three friends, two colleagues, two lovers and a young couple disillusioned with their relationship) as they head down the highway from Quebec City to Montreal in four cars. They talk up a storm about love and, especially, sex, and with its R-rated bedroom chatter, the picture has drawn comparisons to that other Quebec classic full of racy sex talk, *The Decline of the American Empire.* Trogi's film is unpretentious, often hilarious and finally moving.

Julie Le Breton and Tony Conte in **Québec-Montréal**

Mambo Italiano is an even lighter comedy, but manages to be a fun, if slight riff on many of the same ethnic themes covered in *My Big Fat Greek Wedding,* with a gay twist. Director and co-writer Emile Gaudreault and co-writer Steve Galluccio have adapted Galluccio's hit play into a fast-moving, engaging flick that's not high art but has more audience appeal than all too many English-Canadian titles.

One of the bigger recent disappointments was **The Favourite Game**, writer-director Bernar Hébert's loose adaption of the 1963 Leonard Cohen novel. The film is Hébert's first mainstream narrative pic after years of crafting award-winning experimental art films and he fumbles the transition. A key problem is lead actor J.R. Bourne, who plays the Cohen-esque main character, Leo. He should be a romantic dreamer, but in Hébert and Bourne's hands, just comes off as an egotistical jerk.

Cohen's spirit and name also hover over another recent Canadian film, debutant writer-directors Matt Bissonnette and Steven Clark's **Looking for Leonard**. This no-budget story about small-time hoodlums, a strange computer programmer (Joel Bissonnette) and a woman obsessed with Leonard Cohen (Kim Huffman) is memorably far-fetched and captures the off-kilter charm of early Jim Jarmusch, with the help of some droll dialogue and strong acting, particularly from Huffman and Bissonnette.

LES INVASIONS BARBARES (**The Barbarian Invasions**) *[Comedy-drama, 2002] Script and Dir: Denys Arcand. Phot: Guy Dufaux. Players: Marie-Josée Croze, Rémy Girard, Louise Portal, Stéphane Rousseau, Dorothée Berryman. Prod: Denise Robert, Daniel Louis.*

JE N'AIME QUE TOI (*literally,* **I Love Only You**) *[Drama, 2003] Script and Dir: Claude Fournier. Phot: René Verzier. Players: Noémie Godin-Vigneau, Michel Forget, Dorothée Berryman, Jean-Nicolas Verreault, France Castel, Normand Chouinard. Prod: Marie-José Raymond.*
A novelist with writer's block meets a mysterious young woman who becomes his muse.

LITTORAL (*literally,* **Coastal**) *[Drama, 2003] Script: Wajdi Mouawad, Pascal Sanchez. Dir: Mouawad. Phot: Romain Winding. Players: Steve Laplante, Miro, Isabelle Leblanc, Pascal Contamine, Manon Brunelle, David Boutin, Gilles Renaud. Prod: Brigitte Germain.*
A young Montrealer of Lebanese origin decides to take his dad's body back to Lebanon to bury him in his home village.

LUCK *[Comedy-drama, 2002] Script and Dir: Peter Wellington. Phot: Luc Montpellier. Players: Sarah Polley, Luke Kirby. Prod: Simone Urdl, Jennifer Weiss.*
A young man convinced of his bad luck tests his hypothesis by gambling with love and money.

MY LIFE WITHOUT ME *[Drama, 2002] Script and Dir: Isabel Coixet. Phot: Jean-Claude Larrieu. Players: Sarah Polley, Mark Ruffalo, Scott Speedman, Deborah Harry, Maria de Medeiros, Amanda Plummer. Prod: Gordon McLennan, Esther Garcia.*
Ann's modest life with two kids and a husband takes a dramatic turn when her doctor tells her that she has cancer and only two months to live.

NEZ ROUGE
(*literally,* **Red Nose**)
[*Comedy, 2003*] *Script: Sylvie Pilon, Sylvie Desrosiers. Dir: Erik Canuel. Phot: Bernard Couture. Players: Patrick Huard, Michele Barbara Pelletier, Pierre Lebeau, Jean L'Italien. Prod: Jacques Bonin, Claude Veillet.*
Romance is in the air when a critic and a first-time novelist meet.

NOTHING
[*Black comedy, 2002*] *Script: Andrew Miller, Andrew Lowery. Dir: Vincenzo Natali. Phot: Derek Rogers. Players: David Hewlitt, Andrew Miller, Gordon Pinsent. Prod: Noah Segal, Steve Hoban.*

OWNING MAHOWNY
[*Drama, 2002*] *Script: Maurice Chauvet, based on the book* Stung *by Gary Ross. Dir: Richard Kwietniowski. Phot: Oliver Curtis. Players: Philip Seymour Hoffman, Minnie Driver, Maury Chaykin, John Hurt. Prod: Andras Hamori, Seaton McLean, Alessandro Camon.*
Polite, mild-mannered Dan Mahowny is an assistant bank manager with a head for numbers and a devastating appetite for gambling.

PIGGY BANK BLUES
[*Comedy-drama*] *Script: Tim Burns. Dir: John N. Smith. Phot: Pierre Letarte. Players: Jane Curtin, Peter MacNeill, Sheila McCarthy, Patrick McKenna, Pascale Montpetit, Mary Walsh. Prod: Lorraine Richard, Greg Dummett, Sam Grana.*

QUEBEC-MONTREAL
[*Comedy, 2002*] *Script: Jean-Philippe Pearson, Patrice Robitaille, Ricardo Trogi. Dir: Trogi. Phot: Steve Asselin. Players: Isabelle Blais, Patrice Robitaille, Jean-Philippe Pearson, Stéphane Breton. Prod: Nicole Robert.*

Writer-director Bernard Emond's **20h17 rue Darling** is a dark, desperate and also curiously compelling drama. Great Quebec actor Luc Picard plays a burned-out former journalist and recovering alcoholic whose life is thrown for a loop when his apartment building mysteriously blows up. Picard does a great job of making you care about this screwed-up guy, no small feat considering the character is a whiner who would simply be irritating in a lesser actor's hands.

Cronenberg's **Spider** is an impressive piece of work that showcases one of the finest performances in Ralph Fiennes' career to date. In the title role, Fiennes has the unenviable task of portraying a schizoid Londoner who is inarticulate (with gusts down close to catatonic), and he somehow makes Spider real and engrossing. But the film itself isn't particularly involving and, in the end, the script, penned by Patrick McGrath from his own novel, has little to say beyond the obvious point that Spider is one seriously unhappy schizophrenic.

BRENDAN KELLY reports on the Canadian film scene for *Variety*. He also writes about entertainment for *The Montreal Gazette* and is a columnist on CBC Radio.

SERAPHIN, UN HOMME ET SON PECHE
(**Seraphin: Heart of Stone**)
[*Drama, 2002*] *Script: Charles Binamé, Pierre Billon. Dir: Binamé. Phot: Jean Lepine. Players: Pierre Lebeau, Karine Vanasse, Roy Dupuis. Prod: Lorraine Richard.*

Séraphin: Heart of Stone

THE STATEMENT
[*Drama, 2003*] *Script: Ronald Harwood, based on the novel by Brian Moore. Dir: Norman Jewison. Phot: Kevin Jewison. Players: Michael Caine, Jeremy Northam, Tilda Swinton, Alan Bates, John Neville, Charlotte Rampling. Prod: Robert Lantos, Norman Jewison.*
The story of Pierre Brossard (Caine), a former war criminal in Vichy France, now on the run from hitmen and the police.

Quotes of the Year

"I'd like to work with Atom Egoyan. I can't talk about one frame of *The Sweet Hereafter* without crying. [It's] untouched by sticky studio fingers. And he likes swarthy chicks – so tell him to call me."

NIA VARDALOS, *Winnipeg-born writer-star of* My Big Fat Greek Wedding.

"It was shocking to me. I've been going to the States for years, and normally when you say you're from Canada, you just get a blank stare. Now it is, amongst many, fairly negative, hostile."

MICHAEL DONOVAN, *one of the producers of* Bowling for Columbine, *on anti-Canadian sentiment following the film's Oscar win and the country's refusal to join the Iraq war coalition.*

Chile Andrea Osorio Klenner

The Year's Best Films

Andrea Osorio Klenner's
selection:

Sex with Love
(Dir: Boris Quercia)
Paradise b
(Dir: Nicolás Acuña)
**Ogú and Mampato in Rapa
Nui** (Dir: Alejandro Rojas)
Saturday (Dir: Matías Bize)
And Cows Fly
(Dir: Fernando Lavanderos)

Recent and Forthcoming Films

TAXI PARA TRES
(A Cab for Three)
*[Drama, 2001] Script and Dir:
Orlando Lübbert. Players:
Alejandro Trejo, Daniel Muñoz,
Fernando Gómez-Rovira. Prod:
Orlando Lübbert Producciones
Audiovisuales.*

A Cab For Three

SEXO CON AMOR
(Sex with Love)
*[Comedy, 2003] Script and Dir:
Boris Quercia. Phot: Antonio
Quercia. Players: Alvaro
Rudolphy, Sigrid Alegría,
Patricio Contreras, Boris
Quercia, María Izquierdo. Prod:
Diego Izquierdo/Chile
Chitá/Lado Izquierdo/Cine Cien.*

PARAÍSO B (Paradise b)
[Suspense, 2002] Script: Luis

It seems odd to talk of a Chilean cinema industry when barely one in 20 of the movies released in 2002 was a domestic production, and 96.6% of total box-office receipts were for overseas films. And yet the outlook for local film-makers looks promising. After several years under discussion in Congress, a new Audiovisual Promotion Bill was expected to become law by the end of 2003. It would give Chile an autonomous organisation responsible for all audiovisual projects, gathering all subsidies (worth just under $2m in 2002) into one fund, determined annually according to the national budget.

Also, a new cinema classification law was passed in 2002, establishing a classification system by age group (No Under-7s; 14+;18+, etc.) to replace the previous, stricter censorship legisation under which some 1,090 films had been banned – among them Scorsese's *The Last Temptation of Christ*, which was finally released in Chile in 2003.

Since the phenomenal box-office success of Cristián Galaz's *The Sentimental Teaser (El chacotero sentimental)* in1999 (the last year in which Chliean cinema was covered by *IFG*), the country has been waiting for another local hit, and it came with Boris Quercia's **Sex with Love** (*Sexo con amor*). Within eight weeks of its release in March 2003 it had surpassed 794,000 admissions, beating *The Sentimental Teaser*'s previous record of 792,000 (a total built up over 30 weeks).

Boris Quercia's **Sex with Love** *set a box-office record*

Emilio Guzmán, Daniel Pizarro, Nicolás Acuña. Dir: Acuña. Phot: David Bravo. Players: Nelson Villagra, Leonor Varela, Juan Pablo Ogalde, Fernando Gómez-Rovira. Prod: Fernando Acuña/Promocine/NuevaImagen/Chilefilms.
Leo and Pedro, childhood mates, work under the orders of "The Chief", a gangster in the horse gambling business. Everything changes for Leo when Gloria (Pedro's sister and Leo's great love) returns to town.

Eternal Blood

SANGRE ETERNA
(Eternal Blood)
[Horror-thriller, 2002] Script: Jorge Olguín and Carolina García. Dir: Olguín. Phot: José Luis Arredondo. Players: Juan Pablo Ogalde, Blanca Lewin, Patricia López, Carlos Bórquez. Prod: Verónica Cid/Angelfilms S.A.
Camilla, a journalism student, joins a group of youngsters in a role-playing game called "Eternal Blood". They fall under the influence of Dahmer, who performs vampire rituals.

Quote of the Year

"The scene was inspired by an Italian sex survey. The results revealed that apart from the bed, the washing machine is the favourite place where people like to make love."

BORIS QUERCIA, writer-director and star of Sex with Love, explains one of its more controversial scenes.

In his second feature, Quercia directs and performs and his excellent script relies on simple, funny dialogue to project an X-ray image of Chilean society's attitudes towards sex and sexuality. It is impossible not to identify with at least one of the characters as a group of parents face up to introducing the topic of sex to their elementary school-age children – even though sex is far from a fully resolved issue in their own lives. Quercia's fresh comedy achieves a feat rare amongst Chilean productions: making audiences laugh out loud.

Hail to the thief

The Chilean film community could take great pride in 2001, when **A Cab for Three** (Taxi para tres) by Orlando Lübbert won the Golden Shell at the San Sebastian Film Festival. It is a story of marginality, represented by two bandits who assault a taxi driver, asking the Chilean delinquents' notorious question, "Steering wheel or trunk?" (forcing their victim to choose between becoming a driver or a hostage). Tempted by easy money, the man becomes the gang's getaway driver. Lübbert masterfully portrays an underworld reality that many have never seen, filled with characters constantly searching, like all of us, for a better life.

Nicolás Acuña also introduces the audience to marginalised characters in **Paradise b** (Paraíso b), a love story which shows an exquisite sobriety in the development of its story and characters. Among the many fine actors in both films, the young and gifted Fernando Gómez-Rovira stands out as Pedro, a low-ranking criminal in Paradise b, and as Coto, one of the bandits in A Cab for Three.

In a completely different vein is Jorge Olguín's **Eternal Blood** (Sangre eterna). In his second horror outing, Olguín brought off a remarkable achievement: raising the finance for the first Chilean vampire movie and then developing the necessary creativity and technology to generate the impressive special effects required by the script. Eternal Blood was good enough to win the Best Special Effects prize at the 2003 Malaga Fantastic Film Festival and became the second Chilean movie released on DVD in the US.

Among other recent productions was Chile's first animated feature, **Ogú and Mampato in Rapa Nui** (Ogú y Mampato en Rapa Nui), launched in 2002. Alejandro Rojas brings to the screen Mampato, the 12-year-old boy whose time-travelling adventures have been familiar to Chileans in cartoon strip form since 1968. Early 2003 saw the release of Matías Bize's **Saturday** (Sábado), Chile's first real-time production and one without budgetary problems: it was made for $40.

ANDREA OSORIO KLENNER is a journalist, producer and Programme Co-ordinator of the Valdivia International Film Festival.

China Shelly Kraicer

The Year's Best Films

Shelly Kraicer's selection:
Tiexi District (Dir: Wang Bing)
Hero (Dir: Zhang Yimou)
Gone Is the One Who Held Me Dearest in the World
(Dir: Ma Xiaoying)
Blind Shaft (Dir: Li Yang)
Cala My Dog
(Dir: Lu Xuechang)

Li Yang's **Blind Shaft**

Recent and Forthcoming Films

**TIANDI YINGXIONG
(Warriors of Heaven and Earth)**
[Swordplay, 2003] Script: He Ping. Dir: He. Phot: Zhao Fei. Players: Jiang Wen, Vicki Zhao Wei, Wang Xueqi. Prod: Columbia Pictures Film Production Asia/Huayi Brothers & Taihe Film Investment/Xi'an Film Studio Group.

ZI HUDIE (Purple Butterfly)
[Drama, 2003] Script and Dir: Lou Ye. Phot: Wang Yu. Players: Zhang Ziyi, Liu Ye, Toru Nakamura, Li Bingbing. Prod: Dream Factory/Shanghai Film Studio.

L ed by the astonishing box-office breakthrough of Zhang Yimou's *Hero,* and sustained by an impressive new breadth of production, the state of mainland Chinese cinema continued to flourish in the past year. Despite the SARS-enforced closure of cinemas in Beijing and partial closure in Shanghai, in the spring of 2003, prospects seem equally strong for 2004.

While international festivals tend to showcase and support the production of underground independent Chinese cinema, the nation's mainstream studios continue to churn out a mixture of dutifully propagandistic, morale-boosting works alongside some genuinely interesting fare. Staking out the middle ground are intrepid private companies supporting commercial, populist, vitally creative films that can be released locally and that should be better known internationally.

Headlining China's new films were productions from three acknowledged "Fifth Generation" masters. Zhang Yimou's **Hero** (*Yingxiong*) is a spectacular historical martial arts fantasy about a group of mythical assassins: two lone swordsmen, Sky (Jet Li) and Nameless (Donnie Yen), a pair of lovers, Flying Snow (Maggie Cheung) and Broken Sword (Tony Leung Chiu-wai), and Sword's student, Moon (Zhang Ziyi). They oppose the future first Emperor of China (Chen Daoming) and his brutal accumulation of power and territory. This Who's Who of East Asia's premiere marquee names and thousands of extras are supported by state-of-the-art (Australian and US) special effects. Zhang's masterful co-ordination of dazzling cinematography and spectacular action herald a welcome return to form.

Zhang Ziyi and Tony Leung Chiu-wai in **Hero**

KONGQUE (Peacock)
*[Drama, 2003] Script: Li Qiang.
Dir: Gu Changwei. Phot: Yang
Shi. Players: Zhang Jingchu,
Feng Shuo, Lu Yulai. Prod: Asian
Union Film.*

SHOUJI (Cell Phone)
*[Comedy, 2003] Script: Liu
Zhenyun, Feng Xiaogang. Dir:
Feng. Players: Ge You, Xu Fan.
Prod: Columbia Pictures Film
Production Asia/China Film Co-
Production/Huayi Brothers &
Taibe Film Investment.*

LÜ CHA (Green Tea)
*[Romance, 2003] Script: Wang
Shuo, Wang Qinan, based on the
novel by Jin Renshun. Dir: Zhang
Yuan. Phot: Christopher Doyle.
Players: Jiang Wen, Vicki Zhao
Wei. Prod: Asian Union Film.*

XIANG ER KUI (Sunflower)
*[Drama, 2003] Dir: Zhang Yang.
Prod: Ming Productions/Asian
Union Film/Raintree Pictures.*

WO XIN FEIXIANG (Rainbow)
*[Drama, 2003] Script and Dir:
Gao Xiaosong. Players: Li
Xiaolu, Chen Daoming,
Zheng Yu.*

**MOLI HUAKAI
(Jasmines Bloom)**
*[Drama, 2003] Script: Zhang
Xian, Hou Yong, based on the
novel by Su Tong. Dir: Hou.
Phot: Yao Xiaofeng. Players:
Zhang Ziyi, Joan Chen, Jiang
Wen, Liu Ye. Prod: Century
Hero Film Investment/Beida
Huayi/Wanji Communications/
Jin Yingma.*

**ZUN ZHI NANFANG
(South of the Clouds)**
*[Drama, 2003] Script and Dir:
Zhu Wen. Players: Li Xuejian,
Jin Zi. Prod: Century Hero
Film Investment.*

ERDI (Drifters)
*[Drama, 2003] Script and Dir:
Wang Xiaoshuai. Phot: Wu Di.
Players: Duan Long, Shu Yan,
Zhao Yiwei, Tang Yang.
Prod: People Workshop/Arc
Light Films.*

The highest-grossing Chinese film ever released on the mainland, *Hero*'s popularity demonstrates the growing effectiveness of mass media campaigns: unprecedented advertising (plus strict control over piracy) provoked long queues at theatres. While audiences embraced the film, most Chinese critics found fault with its reliance on spectacle over storytelling, and many found its message disturbingly government-friendly.

Chen Kaige opts for full-bore populism with **Together** (*He ni zai yiqi*), the story of a rural teenage violin prodigy struggling to "make it" in Beijing. Formally mainstream genre material, it is saved from excessive sentimentality by Chen's typically polished technique and by some finely nuanced performances.

Springtime in a Small Town (*Xiao cheng zhi chun*), Tian Zhuangzhuang's return after eight years to directing, is a stately remake of Fei Mu's 1948 masterpiece of the same title. The new film is a sedate, subtle, elegant and gorgeously crafted drama of barely restrained passion. It celebrates a self-consciously classical style with a purpose. Retrospectively radical, it tries to heal the wounds separating China's traditional past from its post-revolutionary present.

A rich underground seam

While the Masters' new works all received the Film Bureau's approval for screening in China, a number of provocative underground films, many with Western co-financing, could play in festivals outside China only. With a *nine*-hour running time and a tough subject – the collapsed lives of workers laid off from bankrupt state-owned factories in north-eastern China's grim rust belt – Wang Bing's DV documentary **Tiexi District** (*Tiexi qu*) may have few commercial prospects. But it's a masterpiece: the first great Chinese film of the twenty-first century. Wielding his camera with a lyricism, intimacy and humanely poetic sensibility, Wang crafts heartfelt, intensely observed stories of workers, their families

Wang Bing's DV documentary **Tiexi District**

and their neighbours, struggling to survive in a post-industrial nightmare-scape.

Industrial exposé also features in Li Yang's **Blind Shaft** (*Mang jing*), a darkly powerful drama of murder, revenge and coming-of-age, set in China's illegal private mines. Two partners plan to murder a young co-worker, but become ineluctably drawn into a complex miasma of corrupted innocence, free-floating male sexuality and unexpected sympathy. *Blind Shaft*'s tight, edgy filming style, insurgent location shooting and richly sympathetic performances herald a stunning debut.

Less carefully realised, perhaps, but at least as unique, are gay activist and film academic Cui Zi'en's wittily provocative digital video features. He finished at least four in 2002-03. These melodrama/comedies of uninhibited gay love and liberation (with Chinese characteristics) may be rough documents of cinema as politics. But his latest, **Feeding Boys, Ayaya** (*Aiyaya, qu bu ru*), shows a new maturity, broadening his vision and giving space for his characters to mature.

Indies, women to the fore

Independent producers of commercial movies form the most vital sector of Chinese cinema today. Privately funded, Lu Xuechang's **Cala My Dog** (*Kala shi tiao gou*) is ostensibly an authentic Beijing neighbourhood comedy about a worker trying to retrieve his unlicensed dog, picked up in a police sweep. The film challenges the censors with (and gets away with) a surprisingly bold, dark critique of urban China's empty everyday lives.

Women first-time directors share the vanguard of commercial cinema. **Gone Is the One Who Held Me Dearest in the World** (*Shijieshang zuiteng wode nage ren qu le*), Ma Xiaoying's

Ma Xiaoying's **Gone Is the One Who Held Me Dearest in the World**

XIN XIN (Two Hearts)
[Drama, 2003] Script and Dir: Sheng Zhimin. Phot: Zhang Xi. Players: Jin Xin, Qin Qin, Li Bin, Li Wei. Prod: Sheng Zhimin Film Workshop.

MUDIDI SHANGHAI (Welcome to Destination Shanghai)
[Drama, 2003] Script, Dir and Phot: Andrew Cheng. Players: Yang Zhiying, Cui Zi'en, Zhou Yi.

CHONGCHU YAMAXUN (Charging Out Amazon)
[Drama, 2002] Script: Zhao Junfang, Wang Gehong. Dir: Song Yeming. Phot: Dong Yachun. Players: Hou Yong, Mu Lixin. Prod: August First Film Studio.

TIANSHANG CAOYUAN (Heavenly Grassland)
[Drama, 2002] Script: Chen Ping. Dir: Sai Fu, Mai Lisi. Phot: Ge Ritu. Players: Na Renhua, Ning Cai, Guersireng, Tumen. Prod: China Film Group/Inner Mongolia Film Studio/CCTV Movie Channel.

XI SHI YAN (Eyes of a Beauty)
[Drama, 2002] Script: Guan Hu, Zhou Guangrong. Dir: Guan. Phot: Wu Di. Players: Ma Yili, Huang Yiqun, Yang Qianqian, Liu Juyong. Prod: Beijing Jiatong Century Movie and TV Cultural Communication Co.

RUOMA DE SHIQISUI ` (When Ruoma Was Seventeen)
[Drama, 2002] Script: Meng Jiazong. Dir: Zhang Jiarui. Phot: Ma Dongge. Players: Li Min, Yang Zhigang, Zhu Linyuan, Li Cui. Prod: Beijing Youth Film Studio/Liang Li Film & Television Co.

JIAZHUANG MEI GANJUE (Shanghai Women)
[Drama, 2002] Script: Peng Xiaolian, Xu Minxia. Dir: Peng. Phot: Lin Liangzhong, Zhu Dongrong. Players: Lu Liping, Zhou Wenqian, Sun Haiying. Prod: Shanghai Film Studio.

JIDI YINGJIU (Red Snow)
[Adventure, 2002] Script: Jiang Hao. Dir: Zhang Jianya. Players: Karen Mok, Shao Bing, Dunzu Duoqi, Zhu Lei, Lin Lin. Prod: Shanghai Film Studio.

WODE MEILI XIANGCHOU (Far From Home)
[Drama, 2002] Script: Ya Zi, Liu Yi, based on a story by Manfred Wong. Dir: Yu Zhong. Phot: Xu Bin. Players: Xu Jinglei, Liu Xuan, Daniel Chan. Prod: Beijing Forbidden City Film.

The 22nd Golden Rooster Awards

Film:
Charging Out Amazon
(Song Yeming);
Pretty Big Feet
(Yang Yazhou).
Director:
Chen Kaige (*Together*);
Yang Yazhou (*Pretty Big Feet*).
Actor:
Ning Cai (*Heavenly Grassland*).
Actress:
Tao Hong (*Life Show*); Ni Ping (*Pretty Big Feet*).
Supporting Actor:
Wang Zhiwen (*Together*).
Supporting Actress:
Yuan Quan (*Pretty Big Feet*).
Screenplay: Si Wu (*Life Show*).
Cinematography:
Dong Yachun
(*Charging Out Amazon*).
Sound Recording:
Lü Jiajin
(*Springtime in a Small Town*).
Art Direction:
Quan Rongzhe
(*Charging Out Amazon*).
Music:
San Bao (*Heavenly Grassland*).
Editing: Zhou Ying (*Together*).
Foreign Film Dubbing:
Pearl Harbor.
Directing Debut:
Huang Hong (*A Father with His Twenty-Five Children*).
Film for Children:
June Boy (Liuyue nanhai).
Science Education Film:
Abyss: Truth About Evil Cuts
(*Shen yuan: xie jiao de ben zhi*).

remarkably assured debut, is a luminously photographed story of a middle-aged woman coming to terms with her mother's senile dementia. Its sophisticated plotting and fabulous cast pack an authentic emotional wallop, not least thanks to Siqin Gaowa's performance as the daughter. Her extraordinary expressive range and theatrical intensity mark this as the great performance of the year, in any language.

Screen star and youth idol Xu Jinglei shows her serious side as director of **Me and Dad** (*Wo he baba*), a tale of a daughter getting to know her seedy but roguishly affectionate father. This intimate, quirky drama is by turns quietly sad and vibrantly alive, offering both popular and critical appeal.

At the self-consciously "arty" end of the commercial spectrum are Sun Zhou's **Zhou Yu's Train** (*Zhou Yu de huoche*) and Meng Jinghui's *Chicken Poets* (*Xiang jimao yiyang fei*). With a baroquely non-linear narrative steeped in swooning, rich romanticism, *Train* provides Gong Li with a fine showcase for her revitalised acting career, as a porcelain painter torn between two men, a would-be poet and a veterinarian whom she meets on the train. She excels against a lushly photographed backdrop that offers considerable pleasure whenever the story threatens to become incomprehensible.

Chicken Poets' virtues are less balanced. This story of an avant-garde poet with writer's block who, inspired by a singing muse and a Mephistophelian vendor of a "How to Write Poetry" CD-ROM, becomes a media star, is all stylistic flourishes, and its brilliant set-pieces seem empty. Other notable independent commercial films include former underground trailblazer Zhang Yuan's dark psychological drama, **I Love You** (*Wo ai ni*), which showcases a shattering performance by Xu Jinglei as a borderline-crazy newlywed; Chen Daming's droll black comedy **Man Hole** (*Jing gai'er*), and Jiang Qinmin's magical realist **Sky Lovers** (*Tianshang de lianren*), a charming tale of love and devotion set in an enchanted mountainside, which avoids preciousness with a beguiling sense of fancy.

Friends of the state

China's state-run studios continued to produce a range of films, from dour propaganda fests to engaging entertainments. The best was Huo Jianqi's **Life Show** (*Shenghuo xiu*), winner of Golden Roosters for Best Actress (Tao Hong) and Screenplay. Huo displays his typically fine eye for driving a story pictorially. His atmospheric evocation of a Chongqing night market vividly tells a complicated story of a roast-duck vendor whose domestic and romantic lives intersect in unpredictable ways.

Studios seem to feel that there can never be enough tales involving dedicated teachers at hardscrabble rural schools. Two current instalments don't rise much above the genre's stolid limitations (city folk learn valuable lessons from putative bumpkins, and vice versa). Yang Yazhou's **Pretty Big Feet** (*Meili de da jiao*), winner of four Golden Roosters, at least avoids the hamfisted histrionics and twitchy camera affectations of Huang Hong's **A Father with His Twenty-Five Children** (*Ershiwuge haizi yige die*), an unworthy winner of the Rooster for Best Directing Debut.

Enterprise culture

On the industry side, in the face of impending WTO-mandated relaxation of China's tightly controlled film import restrictions, the local commercial sector is consolidating its strengths. Trailblazers included Feng Xiaogang's box-office-friendly New Year's comedies and indie production companies such as IMAR and Electric Orange, with their skilful marketing of commercially funded, audience-friendly pictures set in contemporary urban China.

Today's independents are approaching critical mass, a development spurred by a major 2002 policy change that freed them from the formal requirement of partnering with a state-owned studio. The *People's Daily* reported in May 2003 that private investment now accounts for one third of China's feature film production (and four fifths of its TV dramas). Private companies such as Asian Union Films, Beijing Forbidden City Film and Huaiyi Brothers & Taihe Film Investment can now finance a range of appealing films that are finding an urban audience, films which could build a sustainable domestic market for popular and substantial local cinema.

In distribution news, China Film Group's monopoly on the import and distribution of foreign films was finally broken in 2003, and the newly established Hua Xia Film Distribution Company will now share China Film's import capability. Exhibition infrastructure is also receiving a boost. The government reported that 30 digital cinemas are expected to be completed by the end of 2003, with plans for a further 70. And in a move that might hint at a less censorious atmosphere for movies with "mature" themes, a new, state-backed classification system based on content was being mooted at press time. If introduced, it would obviate the need to censor every film released in China to suit general audiences.

SHELLY KRAICER writes about Chinese-language cinema from Toronto. He is the editor of the *Chinese Cinema Digest* and the website www.chinesecinemas.org.

The One Hundred Flowers Awards

(voted by readers of *Popular Cinema* magazine)

Film:
Judge Mama (Dir: Mu Deyuan);
A Father with His Twenty-Five Children (Dir: Huang Hong);
Big Shot's Funeral (Dir: Feng Xiaogang).
Actor:
Ge You (*Big Shot's Funeral*).
Actress:
Zhou Xun (*A Pinwheel without Wind*).
Supporting Actor:
Ying Da (*Big Shot's Funeral*).
Supporting Actress:
Yuan Li (*Pure Sentiment*).

Quote of the Year

"Seven or eight years ago, art-comes-first was the byword among film-makers. Mainland cinema was dominated by talk about art and politics, and business was never mentioned. Recently, everyone's begun to talk about business. But it's still an ongoing process."
ZHANG YIMOU, *director.*

Colombia Pedro Adrián Zuluaga

The Year's Best Films

Pedro Adrián Zuluaga's selection:

The First Night
(Dir: Luis Alberto Restrepo)

Bad Love
(Dir: Jorge Echeverri)

Zona 2 MI-17 (Documentary. Dirs: Nelson Restrepo et al)

Despair – Polyphony of a Family (Documentary. Dir: Gustavo Fernández)

Like Cat and Mouse
(Dir: Rodrigo Triana)

Recent and Forthcoming Films

COMO EL GATO Y EL RATÓN (Like Cat and Mouse)
[Comedy, 2002] Script: Jörg Hiller. Dir: Rodrigo Triana. Phot: Sergio García. Players: Jairo Camargo, Patricia Maldonado, Manuel José Chávez, Gilberto Ramírez. Prod: Clara María Ochoa Producciones S.A.

HUMO EN TUS OJOS (Smoke in Your Eyes)
[Drama, 2002] Script, Dir and Prod: Mauricio Cataño Panesso. Phot: Mauricio Cataño Panesso and Enrique Forero. Players: Ana María Kámper, Helios Fernández. Elvira, a mature woman, flees from society and from herself, taking refuge in solitude and fantasy to live life to the full.

LA PRIMERA NOCHE (The First Night)
[Drama, 2001] Script: Luis Alberto Restrepo and Alberto Quiroga. Dir: Restrepo. Phot: Sergio García. Players: Carolina Lizarazo, John Alex Toro, Hernán Méndez, Enrique

In the 1980s, the relative commercial success of Colombian cinema was mainly supported by a trend that originated in television and used popular humour as a means of attracting larger audiences. Very popular TV actors such as Carlos Benjumea teamed up with directors such as Gustavo Nieto Roa to make a number of simple and effective comedies. With this improved commercial success, the illusion of a national movie industry was created. This phenomenon, recalled by some as *benjumeism*, after the actor who symbolised its virtues and vices, did not create solid foundations for a diverse industry, and finally died when state subsidies dried up because of the neoliberal economic policies of the early 1990s.

More recently, a phenomenon similar to *benjumeism* has developed, as television has again lent themes, actors and even audiences to the big screen. Dago García, a producer and scriptwriter, started supporting experimental films such as *The Woman on the Upper Floor* (*La mujer del piso alto*, 1995) and Biased Position (*Posición viciada*, 1998), but soon focused his interests towards a strictly commercial cinema, in the soccer movie *Maximum Penalty* (*La pena máxima*, 2001) and *It's Better Being Rich Than Poor* (*Es mejor ser rico que ser pobre*, 2000), which dealt with the neverending "talent" of the common people for celebrating.

In 2002, García and Ricardo Coral-Dorado, his favourite director, presented **I Look for You** *(Te busco)*, which reaffirmed their commitment to the mass market, tracing the adventures and

Nuns become involved in murder in the controversial **Dirty Habits**

misfortunes of a tropical music band in the early 1980s. Gustavo, an unemployed man, wants to be part of this orchestra and is desperately in love with its singer, Jazmín. He decides to create an orchestra of his own to win Jazmín, with the aid of his five-year-old nephew (from whose point of view the story is told). The newly created orchestra is made up of Gustavo's drunkard and loser friends. Though presented in a stiff and schematic way, this is a lively portrait, reflecting García's view that "popular culture is a source of humour, and [demonstrates] the solidarity that exists among the popular classes".

Shakespeare in Bogotá?

Rodrigo Triana's **Like Cat and Mouse** (*Como el gato y el ratón*) was described by some as a tropical *Romeo and Juliet*, set in the poor neighbourhoods of Bogotá. But the tragic component here is replaced by an air of comedy, in a grotesque portrait of two families, the Brocheros and the Cristanchos, longstanding friends who become irreconcilable enemies when electricity arrives in the neighbourhood and disputes arise from its use and indiscriminate abuse. In the background, a love story between the sons of the two families develops. This also ends up in abuse and sentimental humiliation, and stokes the neverending family feud. Unfortunately, what could have been a powerful and symbolic social portrait delivers only cheap, sterile laughs.

The lowest point of domestic cinema, however, came with **After Party – The Movie**, a digital feature co-directed by Guillermo Rincón and TV actor and director Julio César Luna. Here, an upper-class family has to deal with innumerable misfortunes. Narration, acting and technical aspects all fall to very low standards and the film is worth mentioning only because it found minimal distribution in 2003, whereas the fine drama **Dirty Habits** (*Hábitos sucios*) struggled to reach cinemas at all, largely because of its controversial subject: a real-life convent murder case.

Fortunately, Luis Alberto Restrepo's **The First Night** (*La primera noche*) has great narrative maturity, free from lowest common denominator tricks and melodramatic excess. This is the story of a young peasant couple, Toño and Paulina, driven from their land by the ongoing war in Colombia between government troops, paramilitaries and left-wing guerrillas. They head for the city, taking with them not only the wounds of military and social conflict but also their own contradictions as a couple. Recurring flashbacks contrast two equally unbearable realities: the one they have left behind and the one they must now endure.

Also aimed at discerning adults is Jorge Echeverri's **Bad Love** (*Malamor*). As in his previous, very personal films, Echeverri's theme

Carriazo. Prod: Luis Alberto Restrepo/Congo Films.

TE BUSCO (I Look for You)
[*Comedy, 2002*] *Script: Dago García. Dir: Ricardo Coral-Dorado. Phot: Juan Carlos Vásquez. Players: Robinson Díaz, Andrea Guzmán, Álvaro Bayona. Prod: Dago Producciones.*

HÁBITOS SUCIOS
(Dirty Habits)
[*Drama, 2002*] *Script and Dir: Carlos Palau. Phot: Alejandro Vallejo. Players: Carmiña Martínez, Andrea Quejuan, Alexandra Escobar, Adelaida Otálora. Prod: Carlos Palau and Angela Marken.*
The story of a Colombian catholic nun accused of killing another nun in a convent in November 1999. Fiction and reality become interwoven in a film that looks inside and outside the convent for the motives for a crime that the justice system could never clear up.

AFTER PARTY – THE MOVIE
[*Drama, 2002*] *Script: Ricardo Pachon and Juan Carlos Morales. Dir: Guillermo Rincón and Julio César Luna. Phot: Ricardo Pachón. Players: Julio Medina, Danilo Santos, Camilo Sáenz. Prod: PR Producciones.*

After Party – The Movie

SUMAS Y RESTAS
(Additions and Subtractions)
[*Drama, 2002*] *Script: Hugo Restrepo and Víctor Gaviria. Dir: Gaviria. Phot: Rodrigo Lalinde. Players: Juan Uribe, Fabio Restrepo. Prod: La Ducha Fría (Colombia)/A.T.P.I.P. (Spain).*
Santiago, a well-off engineer,

is seduced into a get-rich-quick world of random violence by his childhood friend, El Duende (The Goblin), now a drug dealer.

MALAMOR (Bad Love)
[Drama, 2003] Script, Dir and Prod: Jorge Echeverri. Phot: Oscar Bernal and Echeverri. Players: Cristina Umaña, Fabio Rubiano.

APOCALIPSUR
[Drama, 2003] Script and Dir: Javier Mejía. Phot: Juan Carlos Orrego. Players: Andrés Echavarría, Marisela Gómez, Pedro Pablo Ochoa. Prod: Perro a Cuadros Producciones.
In 1992, Medellín is a dangerous place. The Flaco has to flee to London because his mother is threatened. After a few months he returns but things have not changed. Friends go to the airport to pick him up in a van that becomes a refuge for everyone.

Quote of the Year

"Films are made to be screened. So I imagine that I will screen *Dirty Habits* on walls and on sheets put up in parks, because three years' work cannot be left up in the air."
CARLOS PALAU, *director of* Dirty Habits, *reacting to the refusal of Cine Colombia, the country's largest exhibitor, to screen his film.*

A displaced family is at the heart of **The First Night**

is once again the impossibility of a successful relationship. An adolescent actress puts everything at stake to make her mother, Hache, return her love, but keeps failing. Natural scenery of exquisite beauty, especially the Sierra Nevada de Santa Marta, helps to create the pessimistic atmosphere in a film that, like Echeverri's *Terminal* (2001), is the closest thing Colombia has to authentic *auteur* cinema.

Colombian film-makers must currently overcome enormous challenges to shoot and edit their films and find distribution, but new legislation which will benefit their industry at production, distribution and exhibition levels was on its way to becoming law in mid-2003. Following the model successfully used in other Latin American countries, the law recommends tax measures which will allocate funds for the promotion of domestic productions. It is hoped that these measures will brighten the future, and yet the debate surrounding them polarised various factions and revealed an industry whose simplest collective dreams are likely to become shipwrecked by insane personal interests.

PEDRO ADRIÁN ZULUAGA is editor of *Kinetoscopio* magazine, published by the Centro Colombo Americano in Medellín. He also directs the centre's film programme.

Croatia Tomislav Kurelec

The Year's Best Films

Tomislav Kurelec's selection:
Fine Dead Girls
(Dir: Dalibor Matanic)
**God Forbid a Worse Thing
Should Happen**
(Dir: Snjezana Tribuson)
24 Hours (Dirs: Kristijan Milic,
Goran Kulenovic)
Winter in Rio
(Dir: Davor Zmegac)
The General's Imperial Smile
(TVM. Dir: Stjepan Hoti)

Recent and
Forthcoming Films

24 SATA (24 Hours)
*[Two thrillers, 2002] Script: Ivan
Pavlicic, Goran Kulenovic. Dir:
Kristijan Milic, Goran Kulenovic.
Phot: Mario Sablic. Players:
Marinko Prga, Hrvoje Keckes,
Kristijan Topolovec, Janko
Rakos, Robert Roklicer, Lucija
Serbedzija, Igor Stikovic, Sven
Sestak, Thomas Krstulovic, Bojan
Navojec. Prod: Interfilm/Croatian
Television (HRT).*

FINE MRTVE DJEVOJKE
(Fine Dead Girls)
*[Drama, 2002] Script: Mate
Matisic, Dalibor Matanic. Dir:
Matanic. Phot: Branko Linta.
Players: Nina Violic, Olga
Pakalovic, Ivica Vidovic, Milan
Strljic, Inge Appelt, Kresimir
Mikic. Prod: Croatian Television.*
Lesbian drama (with elements of
black comedy) about two young
students who rent an apartment
hoping to find peace, but find it
becomes hell.

NE DAO BOG VECEG ZLA
(God Forbid a Worse Thing
Should Happen)

In this country of 4.3 million, there are only around 50 cinemas screening films on a daily basis. Fifteen years ago there were 188, and in Zagreb alone four cinemas closed in the first half of 2003, to be adapted for theatre performances. No wonder total cinema attendance fell by 10% in 2002-03. In their struggle to survive, cinemas are oriented solely towards commercial Hollywood films, although not even this guarantees success.

Is television to blame? Viewers can choose from at least four films a day on terrestrial television, before we even consider cable and satellite options. Is the price of a cinema ticket too high? At around $3, the average cost of a trip to the movies is far too steep for the average Croatian. Whatever the reasons, it's not just theatrical exhibition that is suffering. DVD and VHS distributors have seen a drop in sales as pirated copies make an unwelcome comeback (it was thought the pirates had been defeated several years ago).

While Croatian films aired on national television a year after their theatrical premiere generally achieve a 30% audience share and number among the most popular broadcasts, in cinemas the same films will sell fewer than 10,000 tickets; some do not even shift 1,000. This trend has continued despite the rise in the number and quality of Croatian films produced in 2001-02 and shown at the Pula Film Festival in July 2002 – a season that marked one of the best since Croatian independence in 1992.

Dalibor Matanic's **Fine Dead Girls** (*Fine mrtve djevojke*) was the year's best film and the first Croatian feature to depict a lesbian couple. In a Zagreb suburb, the women's neighbours turn against

Surburban scandal has a tragic outcome in **Fine Dead Girls**

[Drama, 2002] Script: Goran Tribuson, based on his autobiographical novel. Dir: Snjezana Tribuson. Phot: ? Players: Ivo Gregurevic, Filip Curic, Luka Dragic, Mirjana Rogina, Ivo Gregurevic, Semka Sokolovic-Bertok, Goran Navojec. Prod: Croatian Television.
Nostalgic story of a boy's coming-of-age, 1960-68.

POTONULO GROBLJE
(The Sunken Cemetery)
[Horror, 2002] Script: Mladen Juran, Goran Tribuson, Ivan Salaj, based on Tribuson's novel. Dir: Juran. Phot: Slobodan Trninic. Players: Sven Medvesek, Barbara Nola, Jiri Menzel, Asim Bukva. Prod: Interfilm.
A fortysomething man's search for his identity leads to murders and supernatural events.

Winter in Rio

PREZIMITI U RIU
(Winter in Rio)
[Drama, 2002] Script and Dir: Davor Zmegac. Phot: Goran Trbuljak. Players: Mustafa Nadarevic, Leona Paraminski, Sven Medvesek, Ranko Zidaric, Zarko Savic. Prod: Maxima Film/Croatian Television.
In today's Zagreb, a veteran of the war for Croatian independence tries to restore relations with his daughter.

SERAFIN, SVJETIONICAREV SIN (Seraphim, the Lighthouse Keeper's Son)
[Period drama, 2002] Script and Dir: Vicko Ruic. Phot: Silvio Jesenkovic. Players: Vjekoslav Jankovic, Barbara Prpic, Ivo Gregurevic, Vanja Drach, Nada Gacesic Livakovic, Mia Begovic. Prod: Maydi film i video/Croatian Television/Synchro.

SJECANJE NA GEORGIJU

them when they realise the nature of their relationship. Instead of continuing with boring lives filled with gossip and bickering – all the while adhering to the norms of civilised behaviour – the neighbours reveal the dark side of human nature that leads to rape and murder.

Matanic focuses on the intolerance and hatred that are a recognisable facet of contemporary Croatian society. He and his cameraman, Branko Linta, adopt an almost documentary approach to the unfolding drama, supplementing it with thriller elements and occasional comic or grotesque situations. The director paces the film with an extraordinary sense of rhythm, creates very true-to-life characters and has a fine eye for detail. Despite its provocative theme and undeniable quality, *Fine Dead Girls* could not even sell 13,000 tickets at cinemas, far below the 50,000 admissions achieved by its director's debut, *The Cashier Wants a Holiday* (2000).

Snjezana Tribuson's **God Forbid a Worse Thing Should Happen**

The second best film in the past season had an even worse commercial fate. Snjezana Tribuson's **God Forbid a Worse Thing Should Happen** (*Ne dao bog veceg zla*) is a nostalgic evocation of adolescence in a small provincial town in the 1960s. Based on the screenplay of her sibling and renowned Croatian author, Goran Tribuson, it vividly recreates the atmosphere of their youth with a palette of interesting characters.

With the aid of discreet comic detail, everyday events seen through the eyes of the protagonists from ages 11 to 18 receive unexpected significance. The more obviously dramatic events (their uncle's arrest, their father losing his job) and the major socio-political changes in communist Yugoslavia are de-emphasised, becoming merely the framework for the youths' day-to-day reality (girls gradually take centre stage) in this fascinating portrayal of ordinary lives.

Premium exports

Two visually arresting but dramatically unexceptional films which received negative reviews in Croatia and aroused minimal public interest were more successful abroad. Directed as an art film and shown at the Montreal Film Festival, Vicko Ruic's **Seraphim, the Lighthouse Keeper's Son** (*Serafin, svjetionicarev sin*) is a historical drama set at the start of the twentieth century, about a young man who grows up with his family on a small island where his father kept the lighthouse. The son becomes an officer in the Austro-Hungarian army, of which Croatia was then a part, and his fear of his authoritarian dad contributes to a tragic love story.

Mladen Juran's horror film **The Sunken Cemetery** (*Potonulo groblje*) won a prize at the Sci-Fi Film Festival in Brussels. It portrays a middle-aged man who returns to his hometown after years of roaming Europe in search of inner peace and a sense of identity, and with a wish to make amends for mysterious events in his childhood. This quest results in numerous murders.

Davor Zmegac's thriller **Winter in Rio** (*Prezimiti u Riu*) follows the attempt of a homeless and desperate veteran of the Homeland War (1991-95) to present himself as a respectable citizen in the eyes of his daughter, who has come home for a visit. To succeed, he has to confront fellow veterans who have acquired their wealth through crime. Despite its interesting theme and direction, the film lacks a credible screenplay.

The debut film of Kristijan Milic and Goran Kulenovic, **24 Hours** (*24 sata*), attracted attention at Pula. Comprised of two medium-length films, it offers an aggressive and authentic portrayal of the way in which Croatian youth vents its dissatisfaction with the status quo. Milic's *Safe House* is a Tarantino-like story of violence in which three policemen spend the night guarding a witness in a deserted warehouse, aware that, because of collusion between the authorities and organised criminals, they will come under attack from another group of police officers.

Kulenovic's *Straight to the Bottom* shows a day in the life of four young friends who meet at a bar not long after graduating from

(**Remembrance of Georgia**) *[Drama, 2002] Script: Nino Skrabe. Dir: Jakov Sedlar. Players: Boris Miholjevic, Almira Osmanovic. Prod: Orlando Film/Studio Guberovic/ Capistrano film.*

DOKTOR LUDOSTI (*literally,* **Doctor of Craziness**) *[Comedy-drama] Script and Dir: Fadil Hadzic. Phot: Slobodan Trninic, Players: Pero Kvrgic, Igor Mesin, Elizabeta Kukic, Predrag Vusovic, Olga Pakalovic. Prod: Alka Film.* Two hours in the office of a psychiatrist whose patients' diverse conditions are representative of the madness of our times.

DUGA MRACNA NOC (*literally,* **The Long Dark Night**) *[Drama, 2003] Script and Dir: Antun Vrdoljak. Phot: Vjekoslav Vrdoljak. Players: Goran Visnjic, Boris Dvornik, Goran Navojec, Bernarda Oman, Goran Grgic, Ivo Gregurevic, Mustafa Nadarevic. Prod: Druzba/Croatian Television.* Set between 1940-54, an epic chronicle of four families divided by war, ideology, nationality and race (Croatian, Jewish, German).

ISPOD CRTE (*literally,* **Below the Line**) *[Drama, 2003] Script and Dir: Petar Krelja. Phot: Karmelo Kursar. Players: Rakana Rushaidat, Leona Paraminski, Filip Sovagovic, Jasna Bilusic, Relja Basic. Prod: Vedis/ Croatian Television.* Drama about a bourgeois Zagreb family torn apart by the dramatic changes in Croatia during the 1990s.

KONJANIK (*literally,* **The Horseman**) *[Period drama, 2003] Script: Branko Ivanda, Ivan Aralica. Dir: Ivanda. Phot: Slobodan Trninic. Players: Zrinka Cvitesic, Niksa Kuselj, Goran Grgic, Dragan Despot, Dejan Acimovic, Gordana Gadzic. Prod: Telefilm/Croatian Television.*

Love story between a Muslim girl and a Croat boy against a turbulent eighteenth-century background.

KRALJEVA OSTAVSTINA
(*literally,* **The King's Legacy**)
[*Horror, 2003*] *Script: Krsto Papic, Mate Matisic, based on the stories of Aleksander Grin. Dir: Papic. Phot: Goran Trbuljak. Players: Leon Lucev, Lucija Serbedzija, Filip Sovagovic, Ivo Gregurevic. Prod: Ozana Film/Croatian Television.*
A kind of sequel to Papic's succesful horror *Izbavitelj* (*The Rescuer*, 1976). Rats become men and try to rule the world, in a metaphor for the rise of totalitarianism.

NOCAS JE NOC
(*literally,* **Tonight's the Night**)
[*Arthouse road movie, 2003*] *Script and Dir: Zvonimir Juric. Phot: Vjeran Hrpka. Players Bojan Navojec, Daria Lorenci, Natasa Dangubic, Rakan Rushaidat. Prod: Propeler Film/Croatian Television.*
One night, two former lovers meet in the park and start to talk about male-female relationships, but then a miracle-maker appears and joins their conversation.

OVCE OD GIPSA
(*literally,* **The Gypsum Sheep**)
[*Thriller, 2003*] *Script: Jurica Pavicic, Vinko Bresan, Zivko Zalar, Ivo Bresan, based on Pavicic's novel. Dir: Vinko Bresan. Phot: Zalar. Players: Leon Lucev, Alma Prica, Drazen Kühn, Marinko Prga, Mirjana Karanovic, Kresimir Mikic. Prod: Interfilm/Croatian Televison.*
Former soldiers of the war for Croatian independence kill a Serb and kidnap his young daughter.

TU (*literally,* **Here**)
[*Drama, 2003*] *Script: Zrinko Ogresta, Josip Mlakic. Dir: Ogresta. Phot: Davorin Gecl. Players: Jasmin Telalovic, Ivan Herceg, Marija Tadic, Filip Jurcic, Zlatko Crnkovic. Prod: Interfilm/Croatian Television.*

A local loser tries to rob a bar in **24 Hours**

school. One is unemployed, one is a barman, one is a local loser who is trying to rob the bar and the fourth, once a local thug, has become a policeman. The plot becomes more complex when a former female classmate and beauty queen enters the inn. This is less a thriller, more a study of everyday life, revealing the very thin line between good and bad.

The two directors' striking presentations of Croatian youths' authentic feelings of disappointment have marked them as the new hopes of national cinema. However, of the many singled out in this way in recent years, few have managed to live up to the hype. With only six films being produced each year, space for manoeuvre is limited, especially in view of the fact that those who do get to make films often make bad ones, such as Jakov Sedlar's **Remembrance of Georgia**, boringly adapted from a stage play about a famous, elderly actor who receives an unexpected visit form a nun in his apartment on New Year's Eve.

TOMISLAV KURELEC has been a film critic since 1965, mostly on radio and television. He has directed five short films and many television items.

Six different stories, each characteristic of Croatia today.

GENERALOV CARSKI OSMIJEH (The General's Imperial Smile)
[*TV Drama, 2002*] *Script: Zlatko Krilic. Dir: Stjepan Hoti. Phot: Dragan Markovic. Players: Niksa Kuselj, Zeljko Vukmirica, Eliza Gerner, Slavko Juraga, Dijana Bolanca. Prod: Croatian Television.*

Quote of the Year

"I am surprised that the Croatian film industry has not taken advantage of the gold mine of human fates, which can be used to make films: Vukovar, Dubrovnik and all the horrors that happened here."

FADIL HADZIC, *director (b. 1922), who returned to film-making after a 19-year break with* Doktor Ludosti.

Cuba Luciano Castillo & Alberto Ramos

The Year's Best Films

Alberto Ramos' selection:

Havana Suite
(Dir: Fernando Pérez)

Family Video
(Dir: Humberto Padrón)

Nothing More
(Dir: Juan Carlos Cremata)

Honey for Oshún
(Dir: Humberto Solás)

Between Hurricanes
(Dir: Enrique Colina)

Thais Valdés in **Nothing More**

Recent and Forthcoming Films

MIEL PARA OSHÚN
(Honey for Oshún)
[Drama, 2001] Script: Elia Solás. Dir: Humberto Solás. Players: Jorge Perugorría, Isabel Santos, Mario Limonta. Prod: Audiovisuales ICAIC Producción-Distribución (ICAIC)/El Paso Producciones (Spain)/Televisión Española /Canal+.
Roberto returns to Cuba after 32 years, longing to meet the mother who supposedly abandoned him.

VIDEO DE FAMILIA
(Family Video)
[Drama, 2001] Script and Dir: Humberto Padrón. Players: Enrique Molina, Verónica Lynn, Elsa Camp. Prod: ICAIC/BAY VISTA/Producciones AcHePé.
Raulito lives abroad. On his birthday, his relatives in Cuba

Under the harsh economic conditions of the 1990s, co-production with European partners became fundamental to the survival of Cuban cinema. At the same time, the services offered by the skilled professionals of the Cuban Institute of Cinematographic Art and Industry (ICAIC), at very competitive costs, turned Cuban studios into a perennial temptation for foreign producers, channelling fresh capital into the state-run film industry.

Through these two methods, local film-making endured, and Cuban directors can now forge ahead without giving up their dedication to talent and intellectual rigour and Costa-Gavras' dictum that the artist "cannot live in society without trying to understand it and talk about its problems". Cuban master Tomás Gutiérrez Alea (1928-1996) was one director who insisted on the importance of social criticism, often through the caustic humour that is a common response to the contradictions of Cuban life. His *Strawberry and Chocolate* (*Fresa y chocolate*, 1993) treated the previously taboo subject of homosexuality and introduced a flavour of tolerance to Cuban cinema.

Juan Carlos Tabío co-directed *Strawberry and Chocolate* and, after the fraudulent optimism of *Waiting List* (*Lista de espera*, 2000), based on a short story by Arturo Arango, he and Arango collaborated again on this year's anodyne **Aunque estés lejos** (approximately translated as *Though You're Far Away*), in which Tabío looks once again at film-making, as in *The Elephant and the Bicycle* (*El elefante y la bicicleta*, 1994).

In the past, critics regretted that comedy was the rare bird of Cuban cinema, while "historicist" dramas were the norm. However, since the 1990s crisis that balance has been reversed, and many critics now object that comic perspectives predominate. Some 20 social comedies have been made since the absurd decision by the government to demonise Daniel Díaz's playful, nonsense treatment of social ills in *Alice in Wonder Town* (*Alicia en el pueblo de Maravillas*, 1990).

After *A Paradise under the Stars* (*Un paraíso bajo las estrellas*, 1999), Gerardo Chijona has shot *Love by Mistake* (*Perfecto amor equivocado*), a sequel to *Adorable Lies* (*Adorables mentiras*, 1991), his bright feature debut, which humorously explored two-faced

shoot a collective video-letter for him and his sister reveals that her brother is gay.

Liberto Rabal and Zulema Clares in Nights of Constantinople

LAS NOCHES DE CONSTANTINOPLA
(Nights of Constantinople)
[Comedy, 2001] Script: Manuel Rodríguez, Orlando Rojas. Dir: Rojas. Players: Liberto Rabal, Verónica Lynn, Vladimir Villar. Prod: ICAIC/ El Paso Producciones (Spain).
A young writer's prudish grandmother accidentally learns that he has won an erotic literature competition.

Jacqeline Arenal in Regards

MIRADAS (Regards)
[Drama, 2001] Script: Sigfredo Ariel, Enrique Álvarez. Dir: Álvarez. Players: Mijail Mulkay, Jacqueline Arenal. Prod: Audiovisuales ICAIC Producción-Distribución/El Paso Producciones (Spain).
Iván, a photographer, has just burned all of his photographs when his girlfriend calls from Miami and says she needs to sell more stills to buy her plane ticket out of Cuba.

NADA + (Nothing More)
[Comedy, 2001] Script: Manuel Rodríguez, Juan Carlos Cremata. Dir: Cremata. Players: Thais Valdés, Nacho Lugo. Prod: ICAIC/DMVB Films (France)/PHF Films (Spain).
Carla works at the post office. Her parents have entered her in a USA-sponsored visa lottery.

behaviour in Cuban society. Enrique Colina follows in Chijona's footsteps in his debut feature **Between Hurricanes** (*Entre ciclones*), shown at Critics' Week in Cannes 2003. Another feature debut, Juan Carlos Cremata's **Nothing More** (*Nada+*), was invited to the Directors' Fortnight in Cannes in 2002 and has won several festival awards.

Reeling in the years

Among the Cuban film-makers to have used history to comment on the present was Humberto Solás with *Explosion in a Cathedral* (*El siglo de las Luces*, 1990) and the same spirit inspires the remarkable documentarist Rigoberto López in his fiction feature debut, **Scent of an Oak** (*Roble de olor*), a nineteenth-century love story that sets off contemporary echoes.

Fernando Pérez, nominated by critics as the best Cuban film-maker of the 1990s, has gradually moved forward through time, setting

Lia Chapman and Jorge Perugorría in Scent of an Oak

Clandestines (*Clandestinos*, 1987) and *Hello, Hemingway* (1990) in the recent past, then moving to the present in his medium-length feature *Madagascar* (1994) and the full-length *Life is a Whistle* (*La vida es silbar*, 1998). He brings his peculiar sensibility to bear on complex contemporary reality in **Havana Suite** (*Suite Habana*), a barely classifiable movie, shot on digital video, which blurs the boundaries between fiction and documentary. Audiences embraced it and local critics said it was worthy of comparison with domestic masterpieces such as Alea's *Memories of the Underdevelopment* (*Memorias del subdesarrollo*, 1968).

The trend in *Havana Suite* and other fiction films to address contemporary issues, regardless of likely official disapproval or injunction, may be a response to the dearth of socially concerned documentaries (the fall of the Berlin Wall sounded the death knell for Cuban documentary production, because the DDR had supplied cheap film stock).

Juan Padrón's **More Vampires in Havana** (*Más vampiros en La Habana*) is a feature animation sequel to his international hit *Vampires in Havana* (*Vampiros en La Habana*, 1985). After exploring the richness of Cuban musical culture in an earlier film about the famous quartet Los Zafiros, Manuel Herrera is back on familiar ground with **Bailando el cha cha cha** (literally, *Dancing the Cha-cha-cha*), a tale of love and hate in a notorious dance hall, set in pre-revolution Havana, 1952.

In an effort to stimulate the flourishing of new talents, ICAIC co-funded **Family Video** (*Video de Familia*, 2001), the graduation project of Humberto Padrón at the Faculty of Audiovisual Communication. ICAIC also supported young newcomers Pavel Giroud, Lester Hamlet and Esteban García Insausti (who have some experience in documentary, short fiction and music videos) on the DV-shot **Loves on the Run** (*Amores en fuga*), whose three stories encompass suspense, drama and the musical.

The new *Filmography* produced by ICAIC represents a precious source of information about an essential part of Cuban cultural patrimony. It records that between 1959 and 2002, Cuba produced 220 features, 1,180 documentaries, 337 animated productions and 41 public information films (shot in the early 1960s for a mass, semi-literate audience). In 2002, there were 4.89 million admissions at the country's 376 cinemas (equivalent to less than one annual visit for every two Cubans) and total box-office was $2.8m.

LUCIANO CASTILLO is a film critic and scholar, director of the mediatheque at the EICTV film school, Havana, and editor-in-chief of *Cine Cubano* magazine. **ALBERTO RAMOS** is a film critic and editor of *ECOS* magazine.

AUNQUE ESTÉS LEJOS

[*Comedy, 2003*] *Script: Arturo Arango, Juan Carlos Tabío. Dir: Tabío. Players: Antonio Valero, Mirtha Ibarra, Bárbaro Marín. Prod: ICAIC/Tornasol Films (Spain)/DMVB (France).*
Alberto, a Spanish actor, Mercedes, a film producer, and her lover Pedro, a screenwriter, are looking for a plot on which to base a movie. When Pedro proposes a story about his colleagues' personal experiences, they agree.

ROBLE DE OLOR
(Scent of an Oak)
[*Drama, 2003*] *Script: Rigoberto López, Eugenio Hernández Espinosa. Dir: López. Players: Jorge Perugorría, Lia Chapman, Raquel Rubí. Prod: ICAIC/Igeldo Komunikazioa (Spain)/Les Filmes du Village (France).*
Cuba, early nineteenth century. A beautiful black woman born in Santo Domingo and a romantic German tradesman are involved in an intense love story.

Hopeless, she reads the letters of desperate people and tries to comfort them.

SUITE HABANA **(Havana Suite)**
[*Drama, 2003*] *Script and Dir: Fernando Pérez. Prod: Wanda Films (Spain)/ICAIC.*
The lives of several people who meet in present-day Havana reveal that there are many invisible and different Havanas.

ENTRE CICLONES
(Between Hurricanes)
[*Comedy, 2003*] *Script: Enrique Colina, Eliseo Altunaga, Antonio José Ponte. Dir: Colina. Players: Mijail Mulkay, Mario Balmaseda, Indira Valdés. Prod: ICAIC/Igeldo Komunikazioa (Spain)/Les Filmes du Village (France).*
After a hurricane destroys his Havana flat, Tomás, an optimistic, wicked young mulatto, gets involved in conflict.

MÁS VÁMPIROS EN LA HABANA **(More Vampires in Havana)**
[*Animation, 2003*] *Script and Dir: Juan Padrón. Prod: ICAIC/Estudios ISKRA S.L.*
In 1923, the scientist Von Dracula invented "Vampisol", a formula allowing vampires to be safely exposed to sunshine. Pepe, his Cuban nephew, after discovering "Vampisol", must face a mob of Nazi vampires in Havana.

Czech Republic Eva Zaoralová

The Year's Best Films

Eva Zaoralová's selection:
Year of the Devil
(Dir: Petr Zelenka)
Faithless Games
(Dir: Michaela Pavlátová)
Pupendo (Dir: Jan Hrebejk)
Forest Walkers
(Dir: Ivan Vojnár)
Village B (Documentary
short. Dir: Filip Remunda)

Recent and Forthcoming Films

CERT VÍ PROC
(Devil Knows Why)
*[Fairy tale, 2003] Script: Ondrej
Sulaj, Roman Vávra. Dir: Vávra.
Phot: Ramúnas Greicius. Players:
Tána Pauhofová, Iva Janzurová,
Stepán Kubista, Josef Somr,
Csongor Kassai, Jirí Lábus. Prod:
Verbascum/Mediarex
Movie/Czech TV/Bamac/Slovak
TV/Barrandov Studio.*

DEVCÁTKO (Girlie)
*[Tragi-comedy, 2002] Script and
Dir: Benjamin Tucek. Phot:
Antonín Chundela. Players:
Dorota Nvotová-Láberová, Jana
Hubinská, Ondrej Vetchy, Mário
Kabos, Pavel Kikincuk. Prod:
Daniel Tucek/Golden
Down/Czech TV.*

FIMFÁRUM JANA WERICHA
(The Fimfarum of Jan Werich)
*[Family animation, 2002] Script:
Aurel Klimt, Jirí Kubícek. Dir:
Klimt, Vlasta Pospísilová. Phot:
Vladimír Malík, Zdenek Pospísil.
Art Dir: Martin Velísek, Petr
Pos. Prod: Aurel Klimt, Martin
Vadas/Krátky Film Praha/Studio
Jirího Trnky.*

The Czech film industry does not receive direct state support. The country's population of 10 million provides a somewhat restricted local theatrical market and Czech films have difficulty penetrating the international market. Nevertheless, the country still managed to produce more than 20 features in 2002, with another eight reaching cinemas in the first few months of 2003 and at least ten more scheduled for release by 2004.

Czech Television is prominently involved in this minor production miracle, co-financing most Czech films. However, in some cases, a desire to invest is also generated amongst commercial producers by local films' popularity with audiences. For example, Petr Zelenka's category-defying "false documentary" *Year of the Devil* (*Rok Dabla*) was among the ten most popular films of 2002, and the Czech Film Academy presented it with five Czech Lions. It also won Best Film at Karlovy Vary in 2002 and in Trieste and Siberia in 2003.

The sci-fi fairy tale **Max, Sally and the Magic Phone** (*Mach, Sebestová a kouzelné sluchátko*), directed by the experienced Václav Vorlícek and based on an extremely successful Czech animated TV series, also broke into the top ten. It was particularly thanks to attractive casting that audiences, rather than critics, welcomed young Andrea Sedlácková's **Seducer** (*Musím te svést*), about a bankrupt entrepreneur who, on the brink of divorcing his wife, a government minister, asks a womanising friend to seduce her. Ivan Trojan's performance as the husband earned him the Czech Lion for Best Actor.

Alice Nellis' bittersweet comedy *Some Secrets* (*Vylet*) was also highly popular among audiences and won two Czech Lions and the New Directors' Prize at San Sebastian. The tragi-comedy **Girlie** (*Devcátko*), the debut of Benjamin Tucek, enjoyed popular and critical acclaim at the Rotterdam IFF in 2003, as did Ivan Vojnár's **Forest Walkers** (*Lesní Chodci*), a film romance set on the fringes of society and aimed at the intellectual audience. Vojnár employs a largely amateur cast, a documentary style and philosophical reflection.

The nostalgic comedy by Vladimír Michálek, *Autumn Spring* (*Babí léto*), met with enthusiastic applause at a number of American festivals in 2002 and was purchased for US distribution. Several festival prizes in Europe and the US went to Jana Sevcíková's documentary **Old Believers** (*Staroverci*, 2001), which examines the spiritual traditions of descendants of Russian emigrants in a remote Romanian village.

An abnormal tale of 'normalisation'

Jan Hrebejk followed up his triumphant *Cosy Dens* (*Pelísky*, 1999) with **Pupendo**, another tragi-comic film based on the work of writer Petr Sabach. With an untranslatable (and barely intelligible even in Czech) title denoting the adolescent initiation "ritual" experienced by Hrebejk and co-scriptwriter Petr Jarchovsky, the story, centred around a sculptor, is set in the early 1980s, when Czechs were still experiencing "normalisation" – a process which censored artistic endeavours and put a clamp on civil freedoms. Straight after its premiere, Hrebejk's film won the national festival FINALE in Plzen and became a huge hit.

One of the **Old Believers**

Demons abound in Roman Vávra's popular fairy tale **Devil Knows Why**

Devil Knows Why (*Cert ví proc*), conceived by the young Roman Vávra as a "film for all the family", delighted audiences and critics with the tale of Philip, the hero who must defeat Lucifer and his devilish minions to save the kingdom of King Dobromil the Good and earn the hand of his daughter, Princess Annie. **The Pied Piper** (*Krysar*), by cinematographer-director Frantisek A. Brabec, was received somewhat more inconsistently. Brabec conceived his feature-length version of the legend as a challenge: he began filming on the morning of December 31, 2002, and completed it on the morning of January 1, 2003. He may have earned a place in the *Guinness Book of Records*, but only a few appreciated this experiment, which resembled a lengthy video clip.

Audiences were also unsure what to make of the directorial debut of actor Jan Kraus, **Small Town** (*Mestecko*), a satirical comedy in

KDO BUDE HLÍDAT HLÍDACE? DALIBOR ANEB KLÍC K CHALOUPCE STRYCKA TOMA (Who Will Guard the Guard? Dalibor, or the Key to Uncle Tom's Cottage) [Social documentary, 2002] Script and Dir: Karel Vachek. Phot: Karel Slach. Prod: Negativ/Czech TV.

KRYSAR (The Pied Piper) [Thriller, 2003] Script: F. A. Brabec, Ivana Nováková. Dir and Phot: Brabec. Players: Petr Jákl, Ester Geislerová, Richard Krajco, Karel Dobry, Stanislav Tyser. Prod: J.B.J. Film/Dioptra a.s.

LESNÍ CHODCI (Forest Walkers) [Romance, 2003] Script: Ivan Vojnár, based on the novel by Martin Rysavy. Dir: Vojnár. Phot: Ramúnas Greicius. Players: Jirí Schmitzer, Jitka Prosperi, Zdenek Novák, Petra Poláková, Miroslav Bambusek. Prod: GAGA Production/Czech Television/Synergia Film/Studio Virtual/Margo Film Paris/ ALEF Film +Media Group/ Filmservice Slovakia.

MESTECKO (Small Town) [Comedy, 2003] Script and Dir: Jan Kraus. Phot: Divis Marek. Players: Otmar Brancuzky, Vlastiml Brabec, Ivo Hybl, Rostislav Novák, Norbert Lichy. Prod: Czech TV/S Pro Alfa Film.

MUSÍM TE SVÉST (Seducer) [Comedy, 2002] Script and Dir: Andrea Sedlácková. Phot: Vladimír Holomek. Players: Ivana Chylková, Jan Kraus, Ivan Trojan. Prod: Czech TV/Daniel Závorka/Vision Production.

Jan Kraus' **Small Town**

NEVERNÉ HRY
(Faithless Games)
*[Romance, 2003] Script: Dina
Diosi. Dir: Michaela Pavlátová.
Phot: Martin Strba. Players:
Zuzana Stivínová, Peter Bebjak,
Ady Hajdu, Jana Hubinská,
Kristinka Svarinská. Prod:
Negativ/Czech TV/Ars Media
(Slovakia)/Slovak TV.*

ZELARY
*[Drama, 2003] Script: Petr
Jarchovsky, based on the novel
by Kveta Legátová. Dir: Ondrej
Trojan. Phot: Asen Sopov,
Players: Ana Geislerová, Gyorgy
Cserhalmi, Jaroslava Adamová,
Iva Bittová. Prod: Total HelpArt
T.H.A./Barrandov Biografia/
Czech TV/Dorfilm/ALEF Film.*

Andrea Sedláčková's **Seducer**

Frantisek A. Brabec's **The Pied Piper:** *shot in just 24 hours*

which a successful television personality comments on the transition of society from stagnant communism to "untamed" capitalism in a style more akin to a popular television entertainment show. The fascinating experiment by debuting Tomás Hejtmánek, **Feelings** (*Sentiment*), hovers on the border between documentary and fiction. It is based on Hejtmánek's interviews with a legendary figure in Czech film history, Frantisek Vlácil (1924-2001), who made the famous epic *Marketa Lazarová* (1967). In another unusual but highly popular and critically acclaimed film, **The Fimfarum of Jan Werich** (*Fimfárum Jana Wericha*), five animated stories based on tales by celebrated actor and author Jan Werich are directed by different film-makers.

Among films awaiting release when this report went to press, **Faithless Games** (*Neverné hry*), the feature debut of Michaela Pavlátová, a well-known, award-winning creator of animated films, describes with great sensitivity the "fatigue" of an intimate relationship. It is probably heading for a festival career rather than mainstream success.

Youth has its day

Young people aged 16 to 25 should certainly appreciate **One Hand Can't Applaud** (*Jedna ruka netleska*), in which writer-director David Ondrícek re-introduces the themes and cast from his 2000 hit *Loners* (*Samotári*). Both of Ondrícek's films, like Bohdan Sláma's forthcoming *Happiness* (*Stestí*), capture the emotions of various strata of contemporary Czech youth. Sláma, whose debut *Wild*

Bees (*Divoké vcely*, 2001) enjoyed success at home and abroad, portrays characters lingering on the fringes, struggling for their existence so painfully that they do not even dare to dream. Ondrej Trojan is expected to create a real stir with *Zelary*, a 1940s love story based on the book by Kveta Legátová who, at the age of 80, was hailed as the Czech literary discovery of the new millennium.

The Czech Film Center was launched in Prague early in 2003, to help Czech producers to promote their films at foreign festivals, and to provide interested parties with information about Czech film production. It will also organise promotional events. The Center was established and is run by the Association of Audiovisual Producers, with support from the Czech Ministry of Culture. MEDIA Desk, whose Prague office opened on January 2, 2003, acts as an important mediator to help give Czech producers and distributors access to EU funding. Meanwhile Czech studios and locations – in particular the hugely popular, unspoilt streets and squares of Prague – continue to attract revenue from visiting international productions.

EVA ZAORALOVÁ is editor of the magazine *Film a doba* and the author of many essays and books on Italian, French and Czech cinema. She is also artistic director of the Karlovy Vary International Film Festival.

Quote of the Year

"The Czech film industry – in spite of its small market and the fact that we dismantled its studios and structure after the Velvet Revolution – is still alive."

ZDENEK SVERAK, *scriptwriter and actor.*

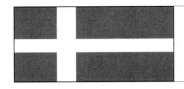

Denmark Ann Lind Andersen

The Year's Best Films

Ann Lind Andersen's selection:

Dogville (Dir: Lars von Trier)
Inheritance (Dir: Per Fly)
Open Hearts
(Dir: Susanne Bier)
Okay (Dir: Jesper W. Nielsen)
Facing the Truth
(Dir: Nils Malmros)

Recent and Forthcoming Films

RECONSTRUCTION
[Romantic drama, 2003] Script: Christoffer Boe, Mogens Rukov. Dir: Boe. Phot: Manuel Claro. Players: Nikolaj Lie Kaas, Maria Bonnevie. Prod: Nordisk Film in co-operation with TV2/Danmark.

REMBRANDT
(Stealing Rembrandt)
[Comedy-drama, 2003] Script: Jannik Johansen, Anders Thomas Jensen. Dir: Johansen. Phot: Erik Kress. Players: Lars Brygmann, Jacob Cedergren. Prod: Fine & Mellow Productions.

FORBRYDELSER (Crimes)
[working title]
[Drama, 2003] Script: Annette K. Olesen, Kim Fupz Aakason. Dir: Olesen. Phot: Bøje Lomholdt. Players: Ann Elenora Jørgensen, Trine Dyrholm, Sonja Richter. Prod: Zentropa Productions.

DOGVILLE
[Drama, 2003] Script and Dir: Lars von Trier. Phot: Anthony Dod Mantle. Players: Nicole Kidman, Lauren Bacall, Paul Bettany, James Caan. Prod: Zentropa Productions.

When Danish director Martin Strange Hansen received his Academy Award for Best Short Fiction Film for *This Charming Man*, a humorous, politically astute comment on racism and fear of strangers, he made no reference to the war in Iraq. Instead, he attacked the proposed closure of Denmark's Short Film Fund, without which, he said, "my film would never have been made", and which had already bred previous Oscar-winners *Ernst and the Light* (1996), *Wolfgang* (1997) and *Election Night* (1998) and given numerous directors the chance to develop.

The prospect of the fund's closure, together with a first draft of the new Financial Law for Film and Media that cut back state support, seemed like a heavy double blow. The draft, however, met with such strong criticism from industry figures that culture minister Brian Mikkelsen ultimately chose to re-order his priorities and channel more money to Danish film.

Under the new legislation, the two national public service TV stations, DR and TV2, are committed to investing $30.7m (DKR200m) in the production of Danish films over the next four years. Added to the Danish Film Institute's budget, this extra funding means that Danish feature films will receive $143m for a four-year period in which between 80 and 100 feature films are planned – continuing the upward trend which should see 24 Danish films released theatrically in 2003, compared to 19 in 2002. Hansen's fears for short films were allayed by the news that some $30m had been earmarked for Shorts and Documentaries (almost 10% more than originally announced), although there is still concern that fewer new projects will be produced in these fields than in the last four-year period.

One of the reasons for the great dissatisfaction with the government's first draft – and the minister's subsequent change of direction – is that Danish cinema is thriving. In addition to Hansen's Oscar, the country claimed the Camera d'Or at Cannes in 2003, thanks to debutant Christoffer Boe's **Reconstruction**, an ambitious and stylish psychological drama about a man who loses his past and must put his faith in love in order to gain a future. Our local hero and genius, Lars von Trier, received a lot of attention for his latest, *Dogville*, and the continued success of the Dogme movement has helped Danish films to gain wider exposure on the domestic market, with two representatives in the box-office Top Ten for 2002 and a further six in the Top 20, to give homegrown films a 24% market share. Hollywood blockbusters took 67% and helped total box-office increase by one million to 12.9 million admissions in 2002.

Rolf Konow/Nordisk Film

Nicole Kidman and James Caan in **Dogville**

Chastity still sells

Some of the best Danish films of 2002 were made according to the Dogme rules – or almost, one might say, given the widespread debate on whether a film is still authentic Dogme if the rules aren't followed precisely. But as Susanne Bier, director of *Open Hearts*, asked: "Isn't this matter of cheating irrelevant if the result is good?" And her results were indeed excellent (and very popular: 700,000 admissions) in her compelling and deeply moving **Open Hearts** (*Elsker dig for evigt*). It had outstanding performances from Mads Mikkelsen, as a married doctor who has an affair with the fiancée of a paralysed accident victim, and Paprika Steen as his wife. Steen also took the lead in **Okay**, Jesper W. Nielsen's heartwarming Dogme entry, as the outwardly hardheaded but emotionally fragile social worker Nete, whose father falls terminally ill. In the process of dealing with his disease she has to reconsider her concept of family and, in the end, herself.

Another of the country's most prominent actresses, Sidse Babett Knudsen, was the centre of young director Natasha Arthy's **Old, New, Borrowed and Blue** (*Se til venstre, der er en svensker*). Arthy had earlier enjoyed great success with a feature film and TV series for kids, but fared less well with this Dogme comedy about a girl who meets an ex-lover the day before her wedding. *Old, New, Borrowed and Blue*'s silly tone is meant to amuse but doesn't, and it was aptly described by one local film critic as "Dogme Light".

Despite audiences' continuing appetite for Dogme fare, Zentropa

FEAR X
[Thriller, 2003] Script: Nicolas Winding Refn, Hubert Selby Jr. Dir: Refn. Phot: Larry Smith. Players: John Turturro, Deborah Unger, James Remar. Prod: NWR.

AT KENDE SANDHEDEN (Facing the Truth)
[Drama, 2002] Script: Nils Malmros, John Mogensen. Dir: Malmros. Phot: Jan Weincke. Players: Jens Albinus, Peter Schrøder. Prod: Nordisk Film.

SKAGERRAK
[Romantic drama, 2003] Script: Søren Kragh-Jacobsen, Anders Thomas Jensen. Dir: Kragh-Jacobsen. Phot: Erik Kress. Players: Iben Hjejle, Bronagh Gallagher, Martin Henderson. Prod: Nimbus Film.

Ole Kragh-Jacobsen

Iben Hjejle in **Skagerrak**

DE GRØNNE SLAGTERE (The Green Butchers)
[Comedy-drama, 2003] Script and Dir: Anders Thomas Jensen. Phot: Sebastian Blenkov. Players: Mads Mikkelsen, Nikolaj Lie Kaas. Prod: M & M Productions.

ARVEN (Inheritance)
[Drama, 2003] Script: Per Fly, Kim Leona, Dorte Høgh, Mogens Rukov. Dir: Fly. Phot: Harald Gunnar Paalgard. Players: Ulrich Thomsen, Lisa Werlinder, Gita Nørby. Prod: Zentropa Productions.

Per Arnesen

Ulrich Thomsen in **Inheritance**

ELSKER DIG FOR EVIGT
(Open Hearts)
[Drama, 2002] Script: Susanne Bier, Anders Thomas Jensen. Dir: Bier. Phot: Morten Søborg. Players: Mads Mikkelsen, Sonja Richter, Paprika Steen. Prod: Zentropa Productions.

OKAY
[Drama, 2002] Script: Kim Fupz Aakeson. Dir: Jesper W. Nielsen. Phot: Erik Zappon. Players: Paprika Steen, Ole Ernst, Troels Lyby. Prod: Bech Film/Angel/Scanbox.

IT'S ALL ABOUT LOVE
[Drama, 2003] Script: Thomas Vinterberg, Mogens Rukov. Dir: Vinterberg. Phot: Anthony Dod Mantle. Players: Joaquin Phoenix, Claire Danes, Sean Penn. Prod: Nimbus Film International, co-produced with FilmFour/Zentropa Entertainments9/Senator Films/Key Films/Shochiku/Pathé Distribution/Memfis Film/Isabella Films/Film i Väst/Egmont Entertainment/DR TV-Drama Danish Broadcasting Corporation/VPRO TV.

SE TIL VENSTRE, DER ER EN SVENSKER
(Old, New, Borrowed and Blue)
[Comedy, 2003] Script: Kim Fupz Aakeson. Dir: Natasha Arthy. Phot: Rasmus Videbæk. Players: Sidse Babett Knudsen, Björn Kjellmann, Søren Byder. Prod: Nimbus Film.

LYKKEVEJ (Move Me)
[Drama, 2003] Script and Dir: Morten Arnfred. Phot: Dirk Brüel. Players: Birthe Neumann, Jesper Lohmann. Prod: Nordisk Film/TV2/Denmark.

Productions have decided that the 10th Danish feature in this form should be the last. It is from Annette K. Olesen, director of the fine *Minor Mishaps*, has the working title *Crimes (Forbrydelser)* and is a story about women in prison.

The leading men

Meanwhile, Dogme's two most celebrated progenitors, Lars von Trier and Thomas Vinterberg, have abandoned the vows and moved on to highly experimental films, with very different results. With **It's All About Love**, Vinterberg told a dystopic love story about an ice-skating champion, Elena (Claire Danes), and her soon-to-be-ex-husband, John (Joaquin Phoenix), who get involved in a clone production scheme. There is no denying Vinterberg's will and courage in going in a completely different direction from *Festen*, but he failed to draw the daring story, great visual scenes and technical experimentation into a coherent, satisfying whole.

Per Arnesen/Nordisk Film

Joaquin Phoenix and Claire Danes in **It's All About Love**

For von Trier everything fell into place with **Dogville**. This story of a mountain village disrupted by a stranger, Grace (the excellent Nicole Kidman, grasping both the stubborn wilfullness and fragility of her character), is more than just another portrait of a masochistic and victimised woman like the ones in *Breaking the Waves* and *Dancer in the Dark*. It is an exploration of the goodness and evil in us all when we are given the power to rule over the lives of others. *Dogville* is undoubtedly one of the most important films in Danish film history, on a par with Dreyer, because its stylistic experimentation (chalk lines on the floor instead of scenery) and profound storytelling take cinema into new and uncharted grounds.

While some change tack, others, such as Per Fly, continue doing what they have always liked best. With **Inheritance** (*Arven*), Fly delivered the second film in his social-realistic class trilogy. Following *The Bench* (about the working class), *Inheritance* made the problems of the upper class vivid and understandable, thanks in great part to the leading performance of Ulrich Thomsen (the eldest son in *Festen*) who plays a son who reluctantly inherits the family steel factory and is forced to choose betwen familial obligations and following his heart.

Anders Thomas Jensen's fine ear for dialogue means that in spite of his youth he has already become a respected script doctor employed on many Danish films, and from time to time he also directs his own scripts, most recently **The Green Butchers** (*De grønne slagtere*), a very stylish black comedy with cannibalistic undertones.

While von Trier, Vinterberg, Fly and Jensen's most recent features indicate that a wave of more stylised work is sweeping in to replace the realistic puritanism of Dogme, several films with stories taken from everyday reality were scheduled for release in the second half of 2003. Let us hope the two trends can continue in parallel.

ANN LIND ANDERSEN is a film journalist and critic for *Berlingske Tidende*. She holds a Master's degree in Arts and Aesthetics.

Quote of the Year

"As I see it, being an artist is like being a terrorist. As a terrorist… I can either take up arms and blow up a petrol station. Or I can make something that inspires and affects people. I don't believe in throwing bricks, but in making films!"

NICOLAS WINDING REFN, *director.*

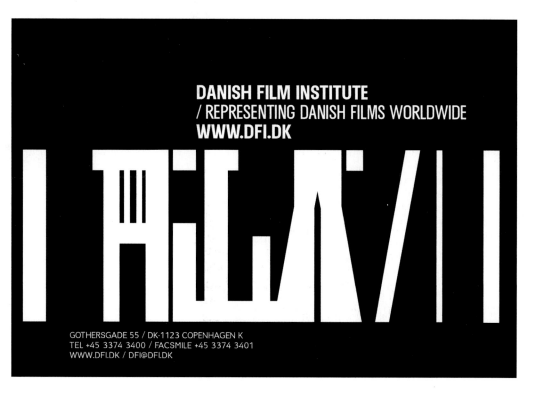

Egypt Fawzi Soliman

The Year's Best Films

Fawzi Soliman's selection:
His Excellency the Minister
(Dir: Samir Seif)
Mafia (Dir: Sherif Arafa)
The Desire
(Dir: Ali Badrakhan)
Women Who Loved Cinema
(Documentary. Dir:
Marianne Khoury)

Recent Films

MAALI AL WAZIR
(His Excellency the Minister)
*[Drama, 2002] Script: Wahid
Hamed. Dir: Samir Seif. Phot:
Ramsis Marzouk. Players:
Ahmad Zaki, Hesham Abdel
Hamid Lebleba. Prod: Egyptian
Media Production Co.*

AL LIMBI
*[Comedy, 2002] Script: Ahmad
Abdallah. Dir: Wael Ihsan.
Phot: Mohsen Nasr. Players:
Mohamed Saad, Hasan Hosni,
Able Kamel. Prod: Al Sobki for
Film Production.*

MOHAMI KHULÀA
(Khul Lawyer)
*[Comedy, 2002] Script:
Wahid Hamed. Dir: Mohamed
Yassin. Phot: Ayman Abu El
Makarem. Players: Hani Ramzi,
Ola Ghanem, Dalia El Beheri.
Prod: Al Arabia.*

KHARIF ADAM
(Adam's Autumn)
*[Drama, 2002] Script: Alaa
Azzam. Dir: Mohamed Kamel el
Qaliubi. Phot: Ramsis Marzouk.
Players: Hesham Abdel Hamid,
Hasan Hosni, Sawsan Badr,
Jihan Fadel. Prod: Egyptian
Media Production Co.*

Egyptian cinema is in crisis. The number of films produced in 2002 fell to just 22. Some productions have stalled through lack of funding and others sit on the shelf for years as distributors increasingly devote their resources to releasing American films in new cinemas (97 foreign titles screened in 2002). Although sound and picture quality has improved, most local films lack intellectual ambition and favour easy comedy – a trend which peaked with the year's top box-office hit **Al Limbi**, starring Mohamed Saad as an illiterate, inefficient drunk whose antics persuaded one local MP to ask for an export ban on the film. Other critics suggested that the film succeeded because young people saw in Saad's character a bitter, believable caricature of their own shabby circumstances.

Sandra Nashaat's comedy sequel **Thieves in Thailand**

Another successful comedy was **Meedo Troubles** (*Meedo mashakel*), with Ahmad Helmi – a kind of Egyptian Peter Sellers – as a luckless hero who ends up in many comic scrapes (he's even accused of being a terrorist). **Thieves in Thailand** (*Haramiya fi Tailand*), the third film by young Sandra Nashaat, re-teams most of the characters from her previous work, *Thieves in Kindergarten*. A famous painting is smuggled to Thailand; chases and contrived comic situations ensue. The prominent comedy star Adel Imam is directed by his son, Rami, in **Prince of Darkness** (*Amir al zalam*), playing a blind man who helps blind orphans. In **Fish Tail** (*Dheil al samaka*), scriptwriter Wahid Hamed comically exposes sections of Egyptian society by following a young electricity meter-reader as he meets various characters.

In **Khul Lawyer** (*Mohami khulàa*), Hani Ramzi plays a young divorce lawyer (*khulàa* refers to a Muslim woman's right to divorce) who finds himself in amusing situations, highlighting contradictions between rural and urban societies. After his fine debut *Omar 2000* undeservedly flopped, young Ahmad Atef bounced back with **How to Make Girls Love You** (*Ezzay tekhalli al banat tehebak*), delivering love stories, Red Sea and Swiss scenery and MTV-style songs and dances.

No laughing matters

The more earnest and creative side of the industry was represented mainly by two films produced by Media City and screened at the 2002 Cairo International Film Festival. Samir Seif's **His Excellency the Minister** (*Maali al wazir*) has a courageous, satirical script by Wahid Hamed, which cleverly blends dream and reality to attack political corruption, in the story of a minister elected by chance because of a mix-up over names. The other Media City film, **Adam's Autumn** (*Kharif Adam*), directed by M. Kamel el Qaliubi, swept the board at the national film awards in April 2003. It revolves around *Thaar* (blood feuds) that rage between 1948 and 1967 in a remote village whose inhabitants are so obsessed with settling past scores that they cannot enjoy the present. This is a poetic epic and a condemnation of a powerless society in which nothing seems to improve.

The shortage of finance spurred several directors to use digital video. Mohamed Khan in **Young Thief** (*Clifty*) delivers a social comedy about an habitual city swindler. Yusri Nasrallah in **The Sun's Gate** (*Bab al shams*) adapts Lebanese writer Elias Khoury's novel about twentieth-century massacres and expulsions, through the eyes of two generations of fathers and sons. Asmaa Al Bakri's **Violence and Derision** is a drama about a fictional coastal city ruled by a tyrant.

State-backed documentary production has also dwindled, but private producer Ashikat Al-Cinema backed Marianne Khoury's **Women Who Loved Cinema**, about six strong-willed women whose adventurous streak changed the face of the film industry in early twentieth-century Egypt. *Tuesday 29 February*, the story of one day in the life of a young wife who revolts against tradition, earned Gihan El Aasar the Best Short Film prize at the national film festival. Egypt's most important director, Youssef Chahine, began work on *The Anger*, about his relationship with the US, where he studied film.

FAWZI SOLIMAN is a film journalist and critic who has contributed to magazines and newspapers in Egypt and the Arab world. He has served on the FIPRESCI jury of many film festivals.

DHEIL AL SAMAKA (Fish Tail)
[Social drama, 2003] Script: Wahid Hamed. Dir: Samir Seif. Phot: Ayman Abo El Makarem. Players: Hanan Turk, Amr Waked, Sari Al Naggar. Prod: Media City/Wahid Hamed Films.

HARAMIYA FI TAILAND (Thieves in Thailand)
[Comedy, 2003] Script: Nabil Amin. Dir: Sandra Nashaat. Phot: Ihab Moh Ali. Players: Karim Abdel Aziz, Magid Kedwani, Hanan Turk. Prod: Oscar.

MEEDO MASHAKEL (Meedo Troubles)
[Comedy, 2003] Script: Ahmad Abd Allah. Dir: Mohamed Al Naggar. Phot: Ayma Abo El Makarem, Mohamad Lotfi. Players: Hasan Hosni, Ahmad Helmi, Sherin. Prod: Areean Screen.

Ahmad Helmi in **Meedo Troubles**

IZZAY TEKHALLI AL BANAT TEHEBAK (How to Make Girls Love You)
[Romantic comedy, 2003] Script: Ahmed El Beih. Dir: Ahmad Atef. Phot: Hani Salama, Ahmad Eid, Nour, Sommaya El Khashab, Hind Sabri. Prod: Kamel Abou Ali.

Quote of the Year

"A trend of comic films has risen to amuse people – and ignore any problems relevant to life and society."
DAOOD ABD EL SAYED, *director.*

Spotlight on Baltics

Baltic Films is the umbrella organisation of three film bodies of Estonia, Latvia and Lithuania. We intermediate Baltic films to festivals, provide information about local film production and studio facilities, represent the films at the leading markets.

Our main activities include:
- **Baltic Event** – screenings of yearly feature production
- **Baltic Sea Documentary Forum** – co-production forum of documentaries (www.bmc.lv)
- **Transit Zero** – international filmmakers meetings in Baltic region (www.transitzero.org)

Other international activities taking place in Baltic countries:
- **Black Nights Film Festival** (annual in December, www.poff.ee) Tallinn
- **Arsenals International Film Festival** (biannual in September, www.arsenals.lv) Riga
- **European Documentary Film Symposium** (biannual in September, www.latfilma.lv) Riga

- **Bimini International Animated Film Festival** (annual in April, www.bimini.lv) Riga
- **Vilnaus Pavasaris International Film Festival** (annual in March, www.kino.lt) Vilnius
- **Tinklai Intrenational Short Film Festival** (annual in September/October, www.tinklai.net) Vilnius, Klaipeda

ESTONIA · LATVIA · LITHUANIA

Baltic Films

BALTIC FILMS – YOUR BRIDGE TO BALTIC FILMMAKERS

Estonia Jaan Ruus

A KGB-trained spy faces
unemployment in **Agent Wild Duck**

The Year's Best Films

Jaan Ruus' Estonian
selection:

Agent Wild Duck
(Dir: Marko Raat)

Names in Marble
(Dir: Elmo Nüganen)

The Last Soldiers of the
Continuation War
(Documentary. Dir: Enn Säde)

Arvo Pärt. 24 Preludes for
a Fugue (Documentary.
Dir: Dorian Supin)

Button's Odyssey (Animated
short. Dir: Mati Kütt)

Recent and
Forthcoming Films

SOMNAMBUUL (Broken Sleep)
[Psychological drama, 2003]
Script: Madis Kõiv, Sulev Keedus.
Dir: Keedus. Phot: Rein Kotov.
Players: Katariina Lauk-Tamm,
Evald Aavik, Ivo Uukkivi, Jan
Uuspõld. Prod: F-Seitse
(Estonia)/Kinotar (Finland).
A woman finds refuge in dreams
during the Second World War.

BROIDIT (Brothers)
[Psychological drama, 2003]
Script and Dir: Esa Illi. Phot:
Marita Hällfors. Players: Max
Bremer, Aaro Vuotila, Marianne
Kütt, Milka Alroth.

In 2002, **Names in Marble** (*Nimed marmortahvlii*) sold 136,000
tickets, beating *Titanic's* previous all-time record of 133,000. This
romantic Estonian film about the schoolboy volunteers who helped
win the 1918 War of Independence against the Bolsheviks is
a traditional tale played on simple chords (innocent, idealistic
children go to war). It hails noble heroism and appeals to pure
audience feelings. But it is also a valuable social document, giving
back to Estonians a sense of their national history and educating
people in other parts of Eastern Europe about a war they never
would never have studied in Soviet classes.

Well-known Russian cameraman Sergey Astakhov has captured
Estonia in a very refreshing way, while director Elmo Nüganen, one
of the country's best theatre directors, has masterfully let the
energy of young theatre school graduates flow on to the screen.
Another popular production, released in 2003, is the cross-dressed
comedy **Made in Estonia** (*Vanad ja kobedad*), the feature debut of
commercials director Rando Pettai. Beloved TV actors Henrik
Normann and Madis Milling play six male and female roles in
operetta-like sketches that ran in Estonian cinemas for 21 weeks.

The director's fear of the actor

While *Names in Marble* owes much to its acting, younger Estonian
directors seem rather afraid of actors, and so concentrate on highly
stylised work. Marko Raat's largely fictional **Agent Wild Duck**
(*Agent Sinikael*) is an off-beat drama about an economic espionage
bureau which makes money manipulating the public. A punctual,
old-fashioned KGB-trained spy loses his job as new trends are
introduced, and the film becomes a sarcastic portrait of yuppie
society. But the action is so unreal that it never moves beyond an
intellectual exercise and the actors resemble the director's puppets.

As part of the campaign to cure society's amnesia about local film
history (suppressed in Soviet times), there was public celebration
of the 90th anniversary of Estonian cameraman Johannes
Pääsuke's earliest footage, shot in 1912. The first domestic
animation production, *Adventures of the Doggie-Juku* (*Kutsu-Juku*
seiklusi), made in 1931 in Disney style, was restored and rereleased
with the cult historical adventure about a peasants' uprising,
The Last Relic (*Viimne reliikvia*, 1969), which was popular in Soviet

Prod: Kinotar (Finland)/F-Seitse (Estonia).

Karl and Marilyn

KARL JA MARILYN
(Karl and Marilyn)
[Animation, 2003] Script and Dir: Priit Pärn. Prod: Eesti Joonisfilm.
Marx meets Marilyn Monroe...

TÄNA ÖÖSEL ME EI MAGA
(We Will Not Sleep Tonight)
[Psychological thriller, 2004] Script: Kristian Taska, Mihkel Ulman, Jaan Tätte. Dir: Ilmar Taska. Phot: Istvan Borbas. Players: Peter Franzén, Maria Avdjusko, Priit Võigemast, Carmen Kass. Prod: Kristian Taska Production.

SIGADE REVOLUTSIOON
(The Revolution of Pigs)
[Coming-of-age comedy, 2004] Script: Jaak Kilmi, René Reinumägi. Dir: Kilmi. Phot: Arko Okk. Players: Jass Seljamaa, Lilian Alto, Evelin Kuusik, Uku Uusberg, Vadim Albrant. Prod: Rudolf Konimois Film.
Student Brigade reunion in 1986.

ETTEVAATUST, SIGA
(Beware of the Pig)
[Comedy, forthcoming] Script: Peep Pedmanson. Dir: Aku Louhimies. Prod: Ruut Pictures.
Middle-aged Estonian farmer organises a pig hunt for the Finns as a front for drug smuggling.

Quote of the Year

"Without parrots and hit-men, the world would have missed out on a lot."
TARMO TEDER, *film critic and scriptwriter, celebrating two of the most popular character types in Estonian animation.*

times because of its allegorical references.

Concerted promotion of Estonian cinema (including the introduction of a Cinema Bus, which toured all 15 districts in summer 2002) and the success of *Names in Marble* helped domestic productions claim a record 11% market share. Total admissions rose by 20.1%, despite the decision by MPDE, the monopolistic distribution company owned by Finnkino (it claims 87% of Estonian admissions), to raise by 10% ticket prices that were already among the highest in Eastern Europe. Of the 97 new films screened, 78 were American productions or co-productions.

Television channels have begun to show more and more domestic documentaries, and are serving as co-producers. Viewers were particularly engaged by Andres Maimik's **Welcome to Estonia** (provocative conversations with public figures in the style of Britain's Ali G), and Urmas E. Liiv's **The Other Arnold** (*Teine Arnold*), about media manipulation. With **Juri Vella World** (*Juri Vella maailm*), about a spiritual leader of the Nenet nation in Siberia, ethnographer Liivo Niglas follows the tradition of several Estonians who have made films about our kinsmen, the Hantis and the Nenets.

Estonian animation takes pride in a new generation of film-makers (Ülo Pikkov, Priit Tender, Kaspar Jancis, Mait Laas), whose work shines at international festivals alongside that of masters now in their forties and fifties (Priit Pärn, Mati Kütt, Riho Unt, Rao Heidmets). The animation studios, Eesti Joonisfilm and Nukufilm, have secured their financial positions by producing series for international TV stations.

Production continues to depend almost completely on state subsidies. In 2002, the state allocated $2.86m (EEK 47.5m), of which the Estonian Film Foundation (EFF) contributed $2.1m (no change from 2001). Additional funding has come from Estonia's entry into the EU's MEDIA Plus programme. The popularity of *Made in Estonia,* which received half its budget from private sources, revived the debate about private finance, several years after the banks decided that it was hopeless to grant loans to production companies. Martin Aadamsoo, the new managing director of the EFF, is preparing to establish a film foundation based on private capital. Some industry figures are unhappy that subsidy has gone to mainstream films, but these are the projects that have brought Estonian viewers back to the cinemas and ensured that domestic film production is no longer marginalised in the national culture.

JAAN RUUS is a film critic for the biggest Estonian weekly, the Tallinn-based *Eesti Ekspress*, and is president of Estonian FIPRESCI.

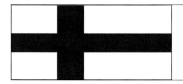

Finland Antti Selkokari

The Year's Best Films

Antti Selkokari's selection:
The Man without a Past
(Dir: Aki Kaurismäki)
Blue Corner (Dir: Matti Ijäs)
Lovers and Leavers
(Dir: Aku Louhimies)
Upswing
(Dir: Johanna Vuoksenmaa)
Screaming Men
(Documentary. Dir:
Mika Ronkainen)

Recent and Forthcoming Films

RAID
*[Thriller, 2003] Script: Tapio
Piirainen, Harri Nykänen. Dir:
Piirainen. Phot: Timo Heinänen.
Players: Kai Lehtinen, Oiva
Lohtander, Mari Rantasila,
Juha Muje. Prod: Claes Olsson,
Kinoproduction.*
An underworld character avenges
the death of his girlfriend.

**MOSKU LAJINSA VIIMEINEN
(Mosku – The Last of His Kind)**
*[Lapland-set Western, 2003]
Script: Olli Soinio. Dir: Tapio
Suominen. Phot: Robert
Nordström. Players: Kai
Lehtinen, Maria Järvenhelmi,
Uula Laakso, Petter Sairanen.
Prod: Fantasiafilmi Oy.*

**PAHAT POJAT
(Bad Boys – A True Story)**
*[True crime comedy-drama, 2003]
Script: Pekka Lehtosaari, based
on an original idea by Anssi
Miettinen and Pekka Lehtosaari.
Dir: Aleksi Mäkelä. Phot: Pini
Hellstedt. Players: Peter Franzén,
Niko Saarela, Lauri Nurkse,
Jasper Pääkkönen, Vesa-Matti
Loiri. Prod: Solar Films.*

The bottom line shows that in 2002 the stated goal of the Finnish Film Foundation to diversify the thematic range of national film-making is paying off at cinemas. Total admissions rose from 6.6 million to 7.7 million and the market share for local films rose from 10% to a stunning 17%, although Finnish exhibitors and distributors have a long way to go before repeating the achievement of 1999, when local films grabbed a quarter of all admisssions.

Three local films broke into the year's top ten: *Rolli and the Spirit of the Woods*, a children's fantasy epic, (see *IFG 2003*), the romantic drama *Me and Morrison* (see *IFG 2003*) and *Lovers and Leavers*, a smoothly made thirtysomething romantic comedy that smartly exploited its Helsinki locations and was aimed at the 15 to 35, predominantly female age group, telling an urban story of pop culture and romantic obessions.

Johanna Vuoksenmaa, after demonstrating a sure hand on several short fiction films and TV series, made an impressing feature debut with **Upswing** (*Nousukausi*), a featherlight entertainment about a yuppie couple tricked into taking an extreme holiday in a slum, which naturally turns into nightmare. Peter Flinckenberg photographed the film with such a deft hand it was hard to believe that he was fresh out of film school. *Upswing* did healthy business after its February 2003 premiere, with more than 150,000 admissions.

Petteri Summanen and Tiina Lymi as a yuppie couple in Upswing

Child's play pays

For years Finnish cinema has differed from those of other Nordic countries like Sweden and Denmark by not putting much emphasis

HAAVEIDEN KEHÄ
(Blue Corner)
[Drama, 2002] Script: Matti Ijäs, Heikki Reivilä. Dir: Ijäs. Phot: Kari Sohlberg. Players: Sulevi Peltola, Rea Mauranen, Petteri Summanen, Mikko Alanko, Antti Litja. Prod: Dada-Filmi.

EILA
[Drama, 2003] Script: Tove Idström. Dir: Jarmo Lampela. Phot: Harri Räty. Players: Sari Mällinen, Ilkka Koivula, Hannes Suominen, Kristiina Halkola, Kari Hietalahti. Prod: Tero Kaukomaa, Blind Spot Pictures. A cleaning woman sues the state after she is unlawfully dismissed.

NÄKYMÄTÖN ELINA – SOM OM JAG INTE FANNS
(Elina – As If I Didn't Exist)
[Drama, 2003] Script: Kjell Sundstedt, based on a novel by Kerstin Johansson i Backe. Dir: Klaus Härö. Phot: Jarkko T. Laine. Players: Natalie Minnevik, Bibi Andersson, Marjaana Maijala, Henrik Rafaelsen. Prod: Filmlance International (Sweden)/Claes Olsson, Kinoproduction Oy (Finland). Finnish-speaking schoolgirl confronts the Swedish teacher who's banned Finnish.

KAHLEKUNINGAS
(The Handcuff King)
[Drama, 2002] Script and Dir: Arto Koskinen. Phot: Hans Welin. Players: Miikka Enbuske, Emil Lundberg, Lina Hofverberg, Heikki Hela, Maija Junno, Arttu Kapulainen. Prod: Claes Olsson, Kinoproduction. Period coming of-age story.

HEINÄHATTU JA VILTTITOSSU
(Hayflower and Quiltshoe)
[Children's drama, 2002] Script: Kaisa Rastimo, Marko Rauhala, based on children's books by Sinikka and Tiina Nopola. Dir: Rastimo. Phot: Tuomo Virtanen. Players: Katriina Tavi, Tilda Kiianlehto, Minna Suuronen, Antti Virmavirta. Prod: Marko Rauhala, Kinotaurus Oy.

on children's films, but that seems to be changing. Helped by its high production values and the simultaneous success of fantasy epics like the Lord of the Rings and Harry Potter movies, Rolli was the big kids' hit of 2002, with almost 260,000 admissions.

Less ambitious in scale than Rolli, Kaisa Rastimo's **Hayflower and Quiltshoe** (Heinähattu ja Vilttitossu) did fair business (205,000 admissions). It's based loosely on popular children's books by sisters Sinikka and Tiina Nopola and its eponymous heroines are sisters trying to catch the attention of their absent-minded parents. Their efforts hit the spot with audiences hungry for sympathetic, yet not too saccharine family entertainment. Rastimo took an impressively realistic approach, which did not shy away from the family's internal conflicts. The film's charm is very much based on credible lead performances by Katriina Tavi and Tilda Kiianlehto and a lavishly colourful set design by Kati Ilmaranta.

Katriina Tavi, right, and Tilda Kiianlehto as **Hayflower and Quiltshoe**

The producers smartly harnessed young patrons to the marketing wagon by issuing press releases filled with complimentary comments left on the film's website by satisfied kids. The same technique was adopted by the producers of **One-Way Ticket to Mombasa** (Menolippu Mombasaan), which attracted many teen fan letters with its story of two cancer-stricken teenage boys breaking free from hospital and living life to the full while hitting the road. This was by-the-numbers storytelling, but the flair shown by lead actors Joonas Saartamo and Antti Tarvainen made them overnight heartthrobs and lured an impressive 146,000 cinemagoers. In the wake of these three hits, no fewer than seven children's films were in pre-production in summer 2003.

The sound of Arctic madness

A documentary making its way on to the festival circuit was Mika Ronkainen's **Screaming Men** (Huutajat), about a male choir founded in the late 1980s as an in-joke between punk rock musicians in Oulu, the largest town in northern Finland. Instead of singing, they scream the verses of whichever national anthems take their fancy. The film shows how the choir's conductor and composer, Petri Sirviö, and the 'singers' are opposed to extreme forms of nationalism, which has landed them in hot water when they have performed their own arrangements of certain anthems. Ronkainen, a former member of the choir, skilfully balances the tone between absurd and serious.

Matti Ijäs showed a deft touch with **Blue Corner** (*Haaveiden kehä*). The actors' performances carry the story of a middle-aged, disillusioned, left-wing idealist (Sulevi Peltola) coaching his sons to be boxers. Peltola's performance won the Jussi prize for Best Actor and he does a wonderful job of conveying both the father's disillusionment and his determination to pass something noble to his sons, who have developed different survival tactics to cope with his relentless perfectionism: Jamppa (Petteri Summanen), the first-born, drifts through urban landscapes to get as far away from his dad as possible; Kusti (Mikko Alanko) worships his older brother. Ever the humanist, Ijäs tells the story with a tenderness reminiscent of Aki Kaurismäki, emphasising the shameful and painful twists and turns in human lives.

Sulevi Peltola as a disciplinarian father in **Blue Corner**

Finally, Jörn Donner, having said in 2001 that he was retiring from directing and producing after a 50-film career, may be making a comeback. At the Festival of Finnish films in Turku in April 2003 he announced his ambition to produce an epic about Petrograd, the name for St Petersburg during the 1914-24 interregnum before the Soviets turned the city into Leningrad.

ANTTI SELKOKARI is a Helsinki-based freelance film critic and journalist. He contributes to *Aamulehti*, Finland's second best-selling daily newspaper.

MENOLIPPU MOMBASAAN
(One-Way Ticket to Mombasa)
[Teen drama, 2002] Script: Hannu Tuomainen, Atro Lahtela. Dir: Tuomainen. Phot: Pekka Uotila. Players: Antti Tarvainen, Joonas Saartamo. Prod: Hannu Tuomainen, Cinemaker.

One Way Ticket to Mombassa

NOUSUKAUSI (Upswing)
[Comedy-drama, 2003] Script: Mika Ripatti. Dir: Johanna Vuoksenmaa. Phot: Peter Flinckenberg. Players: Tiina Lymi, Petteri Summanen, Antti Virmavirta, Juha Veijonen. Prod: Lasse Saarinen, Kinotar.

HELMIÄ JA SIKOJA
(Pearls and Pigs)
[Family drama, 2003] Script and Dir: Perttu Leppä. Phot: Jyrki Arnikari. Players: Mikko Leppilampi, Laura Birn, Unto Helo, Jimi Pääkallo. Prod: Jarkko Hentula, Talent House.

SIBELIUS
[Biopic, 2003] Script and Dir: Timo Koivusalo. Phot: Pertti Mutanen. Players: Martti Suosalo, Miina Turunen, Seela Sella, Vesa Vierikko. Prod: Timo Koivusalo, Artista Filmi.

LAPSIA JA AIKUISIA
(Producing Adults)
[Drama, 2003] Script: Pekko Pesonen. Dir: Aleksi Salmenperä. Phot: Tuomo Hutri. Players: Minna Haapkylä, Minttu Mustakallio, Kari-Pekka Toivonen. Prod: Tero Kaukomaa, Blind Spot Pictures.

Quote of the Year

"I won't be seen there."

AKI KAURISMÄKI, *nominated for* The Man without a Past, *announcing that he would not be attending the Oscars ceremony, in protest at American foreign policy.*

France Michel Ciment

The Year's Best Films

Michel Ciment's selection:
Bon Voyage
(Dir: Jean-Paul Rappeneau)
La Petite Lili
(Dir: Claude Miller)
Raja (Dir: Jacques Doillon)
Feelings
(Dir: Noémie Lvovsky)
Twenty-Nine Palms
(Dir: Bruno Dumont)

Frédérique Barraja

*Julie Depardieu and Jean-Pierre
Marielle in* La petite Lili

Recent and Forthcoming Films

LE COÛT DE LA VIE
(The Cost of Living)
*[Comedy, 2002] Script and Dir:
Philippe Le Guay. Phot: Laurent
Machuel. Players: Vincent
Lindon, Fabrice Luchini, Lorant
Deutsch, Géraldine Pailhas,
Isild Le Besco. Prod: Les Films
des Tournelles.*

DANCING
*[Fantasy, 2002] Script and Dir:
Patrick Mario Bernard, Xavier
Brillat, Pierre Trividic. Phot:
Brillat, Emmanuel Caula.
Players: Bernard, Trividic, Peter
Bonke. Prod: Ex Nihilo.*

The outlook for French cinema was more cloudy than usual in the wake of the crisis that shook Canal+ and its reduced investment in feature production in 2002-03. Several technical firms (labs in particular) also faced financial strife as they were not paid by bankrupt clients, and in summer 2003 a general strike by the *intermittents* (part-time arts workers) halted many festivals and even some film shoots.

In addition, Cannes, the great showcase for French cinema, proved counter-productive this year. The selection of six domestic films in competition (almost a third of the entire selection, plus the disastrous *Fanfan la Tulipe* as opening film) seemed arrogant, with only four features representing the rest of Europe. When the jury, led by Patrice Chéreau and containing French actors Karin Viard and Jean Rochefort, declined to give a single prize to a French film, it confirmed the old, well-known remark of Festival president Gilles Jacob: while an Italian juror will never leave the table before he is sure an Italian film has a prize, a French juror will not stop until it is confirmed that none of his countrymen will be rewarded.

A small (-1.4%) decline in cinema admissions to 184.5 million and a more striking drop in the market share for French films (35%, against 41.4% in 2001, an exceptional year) hinted at possible problems in the future, but the health of national cinema on all fronts seems sound compared with France's European neighbours. French film-makers still secured by far the largest market share in Europe, and audiences showed the strongest resistance to Hollywood films (which took 45% of the market).

Fifteen French films sold more than one million tickets (20 in 2001), while 23 American films (as in 2001) achieved the same goal, with five at more than five million. Some 488 features were released, but the dominance of the top titles has increased: 100 films took 83% of the box-office and 30 accounted for 55%. Average per capita attendance is still roungly three times a year, with a 2.8% drop in Paris and a 5.3% increase outside the capital (a result of the development of suburban multiplexes). The multiplexes now claim 43% of the box-office and, as expected, have led to the closure of small cinemas (at least 65 in 2002).

The more encouraging figures, however, concern export sales, revealing an increasing interest in French films (with the exception of the UK, which ranks 16th on the list). Some 55 million tickets were sold for French films abroad (a 350% increase compared with 1995), 60% of them in Europe, 22% in the US, 10% in Latin America and 8% in Asia. An interesting feature is the burgeoning market in eastern Europe, following the initial rush towards Hollywood fare following the collapse of communism.

Feature production held fairly steady at 163 films (167 in 2001), with total investment of €862m (€965m in 2001). Fifty-four of the films involved an international co-production deal. As usual, creative renewal was assured, with 67 first features (27 supported by the 'Advance on Receipts' subsidy scheme), although the prevalence of first and second features (60% of total production) is problematic because most newcomers are shooting on a shoestring and may struggle to sustain their careers.

Leading ladies

As usual there were promising debuts. Marina de Van's **In My Skin** (*Dans ma peau*) explores a territory familiar to Georges Franju. A woman with a stable professional and sentimental life starts to show signs of mental disorder by mutilating herself after she accidentally cuts her leg. Rarely has a character's relationship to her body been so sensitivity portrayed, and de Van, who wrote, directed and played the lead, shows a rare talent for suggesting the unspeakable.

No less daring is the first feature from Emmanuelle Bercot (who acted in Claude Miller's *The Class Trip* and Tavernier's *It All Starts Today*). Like de Van, she wrote, directed and took the lead role in **Clément,** a female take on the Lolita syndrome that details the passion of a 30-year-old woman for a 13-year-old boy, who candidly seduces the adult in a game both perverse and innocent, finally leaving her stranded with her doomed infatuation.

A pair of gay artists are at the centre of **Dancing**

Christophe Henry/Lazennec

Marina de Van in **In My Skin**

DANS MA PEAU (In My Skin)
[*Drama, 2002*] *Script and Dir: Marina de Van. Phot: Pierre Barougier. Players: de Van, Laurent Lucas, Léa Drucker. Prod: Lazennec Productions.*

ETRE ET AVOIR
(To Be and to Have)
[*Documentary, 2001*] *Dir: Nicolas Philibert. Phot: Laurent Didier. Prod: Maïa Films.*

LA FLEUR DU MAL
(The Flower of Evil)
[*Drama, 2001*] *Script: Caroline Eliacheff, Louise L. Lambrichs. Dir: Claude Chabrol. Phot: Eduardo Serra. Players: Nathalie Baye, Benoît Magimel, Suzanne Flon, Bernard Le Coq. Prod: MK2.*

L'IDOLE (The Idol)
[*Psychological drama, 2001*] *Script: Samantha Lang, Gérard Brach. Dir: Lang. Phot: Benoît Delhomme. Players: Leelee Sobieski, James Hong, Jean-Paul Roussillon, Jalil Lespert. Prod: Fidélité Productions.*

IL EST PLUS FACILE POUR UN CHAMEAU...
(It's Easier for a Camel...)
[*Comedy-drama, 2002*] *Script: Valeria Bruni-Tedeschi, Noémie Lvovsky, Agnès de Sacy. Dir: Bruni-Tedeschi. Phot: Jeanne Lapoirie. Players: Bruni-Tedeschi, Chiara Mastroianni, Jean-Hugues Anglades. Prod: Gemini Films.*

RETOUR A KOTELNITCH
(Return to Kotelnitch)
[Documentary, 2003] Script and
Dir: Emmanuel Carrère. Phot:
Philippe Lagnier. Prod: Les Films
des Tournelles.

**NI POUR NI CONTRE (BIEN
AU CONTRAIRE)**
[Thriller, 2001] Script: Cédric
Klapisch, Alexis Galmot. Dir:
Klapisch. Phot: Bruno
Delbonnel. Players: Marie
Gillain, Vincent Elbaz, Zinedine
Soualem. Prod: Vertigo
Productions.

PETITES COUPURES
(Small Cuts)
[Drama, 2001] Script and Dir:
Pascal Bonitzer. Phot: William
Lubtchansky. Players: Daniel
Auteuil, Kristin Scott-Thomas,
Pascale Bussières. Prod: Rezo
Productions.

LA PETITE LILI
[Drama, 2003] Script: Claude
Miller, Julien Boivent. Dir: Miller.
Phot: Gérard de Battista.
Players: Bernard Giraudeau,
Nicole Garcia, Ludivine Sagnier,
Jean-Pierre Marielle. Prod: Les
Films de la Boissière.

LES SENTIMENTS (Feelings)
[Drama, 2002] Script and Dir:
Noémie Lvovsky. Phot: Jean-
Marc Fabre. Players: Nathalie
Baye, Jean-Pierre Bacri, Isabelle
Carré. Prod: Auteurs Réalisateurs
Producteurs (ARP).

SON FRÈRE (His Brother)
[Drama, 2003] Script: Patrice
Chéreau, Anne-Louise Trividic,
after Philippe Besson. Dir:
Chéreau. Players: Bruno
Todeschini, Eric Caravaca. Prod:
Azor Films.

SWIMMING POOL
[Comedy-thriller, 2003] Script
and Dir: François Ozon. Phot:
Yorik Le Saux. Players: Charlotte
Rampling, Ludivine Sagnier,
Charles Dance. Prod: Fidélité
Productions.

TIRESIA
[Drama, 2003] Script and Dir:
Bertrand Bonello. Phot: Josée

Dancing, a joint effort by Pierre Trividic, Patrick-Mario Bernard and Xavier Brillat, also revealed a formidable trio of new talents, who had already directed an exceptional literary portrait of H. P. Lovecraft. Their first feature is inspired by the work of this great American writer, with its sense of the uncanny and its suggestive rendition of a fantastic atmosphere. A pair of homosexual artists who live in an isolated former dance-hall on the coast begin to have visions and progressively lose their sense of reality. The film has a rare sophistication worthy of Alain Resnais.

Another great master, Maurice Pialat (who died at the beginning of 2003), is a source of inspiration for newcomer Xavier Giannoli, whose **Les corps impatients** focuses on the body of a young woman suffering from a fatal illness and the body of her lover, who has an affair with another girl. Giannoli's film is not without its weaknesses – especially in the script – but it reveals a keen observation of joys and torment.

Left-wingers and bicycle thieves

In a lighter mode, the actress Valeria Bruni-Tedeschi directed a brilliant first feature, **It's Easier for a Camel...** (Il est plus facile pour un chameau...), with obvious semi-autobiographical elements (the author comes from a wealthy Italian family and lives mostly in France, having fled the Red Brigades with her parents when they were threatened). She plays the lead, a whimsical woman living with an extreme left-wing husband of modest origins and facing her family, who enjoy a leisurely and mostly idle existence. The film has charm, fantasy and a rich sense of humour, which evokes Hollywood's elegant screwball comedies.

The Tour de France is the backdrop for **Belleville Rendez-vous**

Comedy is also the key element of **Belleville Rendez-vous** (Les Triplettes de Belleville), the animated feature that thrilled Cannes. Sylvain Chomet, already celebrated for his short The Old Lady and the Pigeons (La vieille dame et les pigeons), has achieved with his first feature a blend of nostalgia for the popular arts of the 1950s, satirical scenes and a poetic realism reminiscent, like *Amélie*, of the French school of film-making. Set against the background of the Tour de France and an American metropolis, it is a ravishing tale of a young boy kidnapped by a gang of hoodlums as he rides his bicycle, and saved by three former music-hall performers.

Another remarkable foray was **Return to Kotelnitch** (*Retour à Kotelnitch*) by Emmanuel Carrère, a well-known novelist who has already inspired Claude Miller (*The Class Trip*) and Nicole Garcia (*The Adversary*). The film started as a documentary about a Hungarian prisoner-of-war who remained for 50 years in a Russian town, Kotelnitch, some 500 miles from Moscow. After one of the protagonists, a young woman, was murdered with her child, Carrère returned to interview her friends and family. His investigation reveals a great deal about himself, his ancestors and his Russian roots. Part non-fiction novel, part self-portrait, it is an unusual experience in storytelling.

Some of French cinema's elder statesmen, in their seventies or eighties, are as active as their younger colleagues. Alain Resnais has been finishing a film based on a 1930s operetta (*Pas sur la bouche*), Eric Rohmer a spy thriller set in the same period and Jacques Rivette a metaphysical mystery story. Agnès Varda has shot a sequel to *The Gleaners and I* (*Les glaneurs et la glaneuse*), interviewing the protagonists of her film two years later.

Jean-Paul Rappeneau, with **Bon Voyage,** offered one of the best films of the year, a supreme example of classical cinema, a story both epic and intimate about a politician, a movie star, a German spy, an ex-convict, a writer and a professor, all caught in Bordeaux during the French debacle of 1940. With formidable energy and

Jérôme Prébois

Grégori Derangère and Isabelle Adjani in **Bon Voyage**

Deshaies. *Players: Lucas Belvaux, Clara Chovaux. Prod: Haut et Court.*

LES TRIPLETTES DE BELLEVILLE
(Belleville Rendez-vous)
[Animation, 2002] Script and Dir: Sylvain Chomet. Prod: Les Armateurs.

TRISTAN
[Thriller, 2003] Script: Olivier Dazat. Dir: Philippe Harel. Phot: Mathieu Poirot-Delpech. Players: Mathilde Seigner, Nicole Garcia, Jean-Jacques Vanier. Prod: Les Films de la Suane.

TWENTY-NINE PALMS
[Drama, 2003] Script and Dir: Bruno Dumont. Phot: George Lechaptois. Players: David Wissak, Katerina Golubeva. Prod: 3B Productions.

UNE FEMME DE MENAGE
(A Cleaning Woman)
[Romantic comedy, 2003] Script and Dir: Claude Berri. Phot: Eric Gautier. Players: Jean-Pierre Bacri, Emilie Dequenne, Brigitte Catillon. Prod: Hirsch.

RENE
[Drama, 2001] Script, Dir and Phot: Alain Cavalier. Players: Joël Lefrançois, Nathalie Malbranche, Nathalie Grandcamp. Prod: Camera One.

BON VOYAGE
[Historical drama, 2003] Script: Jean-Paul Rappeneau, Patrick Modiano. Dir: Rappeneau. Phot: Thierry Arbogast. Players: Isabelle Adjani, Gérard Depardieu, Grégori Derangère, Virginie Ledoyen, Yvan Attal. Prod: ARP.

CARNAGE
[Drama, 2002] Script and Dir: Delphine Gleize. Phot: Crystel Fournier. Players: Chiara Mastroianni, Clovis Cornillas, Lio, Jacques Gamblin. Prod: Balthazar Productions.

CE JOUR-LÀ (That Day)
[Comedy-drama, 2003] Script and Dir: Raoul Ruiz. Phot: Acacio de Almeida. Players:

Bernard Giraudeau, Elsa
Zylberstein, Jean-François
Balmer. Prod: Gemini Films.

LES CHOSES SECRETES
(Secret Things)
[Drama, 2002] Dir and Script:
Jean-Claude Brisseau. Phot:
Wilfrid Sempé. Players: Sabrina
Seyvecou, Roger Mirmont,
Coralie Revel. Prod: Les
Aventuriers de l'Image.

CHOUCHOU
[Comedy, 2003] Script: Merzak
Allouache, Gad Elmaleh. Dir:
Allouache. Phot: Laurent
Machuel. Players: Gad Elmaleh,
Catherine Frot, Roschdy Zem,
Claude Brasseur. Prod: Les Films
Christian Fechner.

CLEMENT
[Drama, 2003] Script and Dir:
Emmanuelle Bercot. Phot:
Crystel Fournier. Players: Bercot,
Kevin Goffette, Lou Castel.
Prod: Arte France Cinéma/Moby
Dick Films/Telecip.

EAGER BODIES
[Drama, 2003] Script and Dir:
Xavier Giannoli. Phot: Yorick
Le Saux. Players: Laura Smet,
Nicolas Duvauchelle,
Marie Denarnaud. Prod:
Elizabeth Films.

a dazzling sense of rhythm, Rappeneau blends comedy and drama with a perfection reminiscent of Hollywood in its heyday.

At the other extreme, his friend Alain Cavalier, who started as his assistant and screenwriter, has all but abandoned fiction films for minimalist portraits shot on DV, such as his latest effort, **René,** about an obese comedian who tries to lose weight. The director is interested in the relationship of his character with his massive body (echoing the focus in his other films on the hands or faces of his protagonists).

Claude Chabrol, on top form for several years now, achieved a new level of commercial and artistic success with **The Flower of Evil** (La fleur du mal), a new variation on his favourite theme, the evil at the heart of provincial bourgeois life, spiced here with a satire on local politics, which allows a wonderful performance by Nathalie Baye as a candidate for office. Claude Berri was equally inspired in **A Cleaning Woman** (Une femme de ménage), about the relationship between a grumbling middle-aged divorcee (Jean-Pierre Bacri) and his young charwoman (Emilie Dequenne), to whom he is reluctantly attracted. This showed Berri's cold, bittersweet, economical observation at its best.

Emilie Dequenne and Jean-Pierre Bacri in **A Cleaning Woman**

Lili, fraternity and inequality

The generation of directors who emerged in the 1970s also made their presence strongly felt. Claude Miller's **La Petite Lili,** a modern adaptation of Chekhov's The Seagull set in the world of cinema, shows the director at his best: energetic, sensitive and playful as he portrays his group of characters, from the outsider, Lili (Ludivine Sagnier), to the eccentric uncle (Jean-Pierre Marielle) and the mother (Nicole Garcia), torn by emotional and family conflicts at a peaceful seaside resort.

Patrice Chéreau's **His Brother** (*Son Frère*) won Best Direction at Berlin for its portrayal of two brothers who have little in common but are drawn together by a fatal illness. Following *Intimacy*, Chéreau again forsakes his baroque style in favour of a dense, concentrated study of behaviour, with a powerful physicality in the hospital scenes and the brotherly relationship.

Jacques Doillon in **Raja** dealt again with the infatuation of an older man (Pascal Greggory) for a younger woman, but this time the girl is Moroccan and works in Marrakech for a rich Frenchman. A modern version of *The Devil Is a Woman*, this is also a non-politically correct view of the relationship between South and North, rich and poor, with Doillon's habitual gift for bringing out the best from professional or amateur actors.

Alain Corneau's **Fear and Trembling** (*Stupeur et tremblements*), adapted from Amélie Nothomb's autobiographical novel, tells the hilarious and frightening story of Amélie (brilliantly played by Sylvie Testud), a young interpreter working for a big company in Tokyo. Unable to grasp the complex codes of Japanese society, she goes from one humiliating experience to the next. Corneau's impeccably rigorous style records this downfall to the strains of Bach's *Goldberg Variations*.

Sylvie Testud, right, plays a hapless interpreter in **Fear and Trembling**

In **Secret Things** (*Choses secrètes*), Jean-Claude Brisseau weaves an erotic tale about two girls who use their sexual expertise to climb up the social ladder. As usual, the director's obsessive, outspoken and direct approach disconcerted some, but proved subversive and quite original. In contrast, André Téchiné's **Strayed** (*Les égarés*) plays on all the nuances of grey to evoke the story of a Mother Courage of the Second World War: a widow (convincingly portrayed by Emmanuelle Béart) who wanders the French countryside with her two children as the German army approaches, and meets and gradually falls in love with a stranger.

French César Academy Awards 2003

Film: *The Pianist*.
Director: Roman Polanski (*The Pianist*).
Actor: Adrien Brody (*The Pianist*).
Actress: Isabelle Carré (*Se souvenir des belles choses*).
Supporting Actor: Bernard Le coq (*Se souvenir des belles choses*).
Supporting Actress: Karin Viard (*Embrassez qui vous voudrez/Summer Things*).
Young Actor: Jean-Paul Rouve (*Monsieur Batignole*).
Young Actress: Cécile de France (*L'auberge espagnole/Pot Luck*).
European Film: *Talk to Her*.
First Fiction Film: *Se souvenir des belles choses* (Zabou Breitman).
Foreign Film: *Bowling for Columbine*.
Short Film: *Peau de vache* (Gérald Hustache-Mathieu).
Screenplay: Constantin Costa-Gavras (*Amen*).
Music: Wojciech Kilar (*The Pianist*).
Cinematography: Pawel Edelman (*The Pianist*).
Editing: Nicolas Philibert (*Etre et avoir/To Be and to Have*).
Sound: Jean-Marie Blondel, Gerard Hardy, Dean Humphreys (*The Pianist*).
Art Direction: Allan Starski (*The Pianist*).
Costumes: Philippe Guillotel, Tanino Liberatore, Florence Sadaune (*Astérix et Obélix: Mission Cléopâtre*).
Honorary Awards: Bernadette Lafont, Spike Lee, Meryl Streep.

Michel Ciment adds: *The artistic quality of the year would have made every member of the French film industry happy if the sudden death at the Berlin Film Festival in February 2003 of Daniel Toscan du Plantier (pictured above), the producer and foremost promoter of French cinema abroad, had not cast a shadow over the whole profession.*

Raoul Ruiz was at Cannes and Venice with, respectively, **That Day** (*Ce jour-là*) and **A Place among the Living** (*Une place parmi les vivants*). The former is a surreal fantasy set in Switzerland about a serial killer (Bernard Giraudeau) who has escaped from an asylum, is hired to murder a rich heiress but ends up protecting her and getting rid of several other characters. The latter, shot in Bucharest, is another murder story, which evokes the picturesque Paris of the 1950s and a mysterious death in the Red Light district.

From desert *Palms* to the *Pool*

Some of the best surprises of the year came from directors with three or four films to their credit, among them Lucas Belvaux's bold trilogy of comedy, thriller and melodrama (*Un couple épatant-Cavale-Après la vie*; see also Belgium section), with the same characters reappearing as major or minor figures. Analogous in structure to Durrell's *Alexandria Quartet,* it is a fascinating experience. Bruno Dumont's **Twenty-Nine Palms**, shot in the American desert, is a worthy successor to *La vie de Jésus* (*The Life of Jesus*) and *L'humanité*, confirming his unique visual style and puritan obsession with sex, as he portrays the journey of a disintegrating couple towards its tragic conclusion.

As prolific as Raoul Ruiz, François Ozon turns again to a murder story that skilfully blends fantasy and reality in **Swimming Pool,** with Charlotte Rampling as a crime novelist (she could have imagined the plot of Ozon's *8 Women*) whose quiet sojourn at her publisher's villa in the south of France is fatally disrupted by his beautiful, promiscuous young daughter (Ludivine Sagnier). Bertrand Bonello's **Tirésia** is a modern reworking of the Greek legend about a man transformed into a blind woman by the wrath of a goddess, before being endowed with the gift of prophecy. Bonello has made a strange, haunting film, under the influence of Bresson.

This survey ends on two noteworthy comedies. Philippe Le Guay's **The Cost of Living** (*Le coût de la vie*), in the style of Altman or Paul Thomas Anderson's choral films, explores money through several characters, from the miser to the profligate. Noémie Lvovsky's *Feelings* (*Les Sentiments*) is a screwball comedy involving an older couple (Jean-Pierre Bacri, Nathalie Baye) and a younger one (Isabelle Carré, Melvil Poupaud) that turns into a Pialat-like tragedy. Many shades of emotion are vividly rendered in this brilliant film, as Lvovsky switches easily from smiles to tears, helped by four excellent performers.

MICHEL CIMENT is president of FIPRESCI, a member of the editorial board of *Positif*, a radio producer and author of a dozen books on cinema.

Georgia Goga Lomidze

Recent and Forthcoming Films

COMME UN NUAGE
(Like a Cloud)
*[Drama, 2003] Script and Dir:
Mikheil Kobakhidze. Players:
Tina Kobakhidze, Cyr Chevalier,
Pierre Belot, Patricia Colin,
Frédéric Lagnau. Prod: Hugues
Desmichelles/Parabole S.A.*

SARKMELI (The Window)
*[Drama, 2003].
Script: J. Aqimidze, Tina
Menabde and Kakha Melitauri.
Dir: Menabde, Melitauri.
Phot: K. Chelidze.
Prod: M. Alavidze/National
Centre of Cinematography
(NCC).*

GANKHETQILEBIS VASHLI
(The Apple of Discord)
*[Animation, 2002] Script and
Dir: Bondo Shoshitaishvili.
Phot: Sh. Kiladze. Prod:
Shoshitaishvili/NCC.*

PORTRETI (The Portrait)
*[Drama, 2003] Script and
Dir: G. Ckonia. Phot:
T. Erqomaishvili. Prod:
T. Glonti/NCC.*

MGLIS AGSAREBA
(Confession of the Wolf)
*[Drama, 2003] Script and Dir:
R. Nanaeishvili. Phot: M. Sturua.
Prod: Tamaz Laitidze/NCC.*

EQVSI DA SHVIDI
(The Eyes – Restless Century)
*[Drama, 2002] Script and
Dir: Geno Caava. Phot:
M. Mednikovi. Prod: Zura
Shubladze/NCC.*

**KIDEV ERTI
QARTULI ISTORIA**
(One More Georgian History)
*[Drama, 2002] Script:
L. Imedashvili, Erekle*

After a decade of recession and decline, Georgia's cinema network has begun to show signs of recovery. All the cinemas remain in the hands of independent owners and in 2002 most did well, with Tblisi's newly-restored cinemas (including four with Dolby) enjoying great success thanks to the *Harry Potter*, *Lord of the Rings* and James Bond franchises. The majority of the American films are imported from Russia, dubbed or subtitled in Russian. But a new local law insists that no film can be released unless some prints are dubbed into Georgian (a lucrative new sideline for local actors!). Holllywood titles claim almost 90% of the market, and although French, Russian and Spanish films are popular they are hard to find in cinemas.

The National Centre of Cinematography (NCC), the most important local producer since its creation in April 2001, used its 2002 budget of $250,000 (500,000 Lari) to support 11 feature films, as well as several animations and shorts. For 2003, film-makers should have access to NCC funds of $400,000. Veteran studio Georgian Film remains the largest production centre. In 2002 it rented some of its studios to Imedi A Holding, the new Georgian media corporation that owns satellite TV and radio stations and newspapers. Its Art Imedi wing has promised to create 500 new jobs in film-making.

One of Georgia's veterans, Guguli Mgeladze, directed the quasi-autobiographical **Enki – Benki**, a tragi-comedy about a film director (played by Otari Megvinetukhucesi, one of Georgia's finest actors) who cannot raise the money to complete his latest film and so makes a deal with some very dodgy customers. This is Mgeladze's 15th feature. He made his acting debut at 14 in Mikheil Chiaureli's legendary *Giorgi Saakadze* (1942) and in the 1950s acted in Russian films made by such acclaimed directors as Pudovkin and Gerasimov.

April 2003 saw the long-delayed premiere of Erekle Badurashvili's **One More Georgian History** (*Kidev erti qartuli istoria*), which had begun shooting in 1998 but which then had its financing cut by Georgian Film. Badurashvili's drama examines three different periods in Georgian history: the 1920s, 1990s and the present day.

Badurashvili. Dir: Badurashvili. Phot: N. Nozadze. Prod: Zaza Gomarteli/NCC.

TBILISI – ISTANBUL
[Drama, 2003] Script and Dir: L. Zaqareishvili. Phot: G. Magalshvili. Prod: Temo Giorgobiani/NCC.

Enki – Benki

ENKI – BENKI
[Drama, 2002] Script and Dir: Guguli Mgeladze. Phot: M. Magalshvili. Prod: Rezo Nikolaishvili/NCC.

QALAQIS DACEMA
(Fall of the City)
[Drama, 2002] Script: Gio Mgeladze, Rezo Tabukashvili. Dir and Phot: Mgeladze. Prod: G. Saladze/NCC.

EINE EROTISCHE GESCHICHTE (An Erotic Tale)
[Short, 2002] Script and Dir: Dito Tsintsadze. Phot: Lorenz Haarmann. Players: Lasha Baqradze, Silvina Buchbauer, Tobias Oertel. Prod: Ziegler Film/WDR.

Quote of the Year

"Young people with heart and intellect, who do not want to put up with corruption, no longer work in film production."

OTAR IOSSELIANI *on the new generation of film-makers.*

European unions

Georgian directors continue to thrive by making co-productions with France, Germany and Russia. After Otar Iosseliani's festival successes with *Monday morning* (*Lundi matin*), Mikheil Kobakhidze, one of the finest directors from the former Soviet Union, now resident in Paris, has been in France to complete his new project, *Comme un nuage* (*Like a Cloud*). The director was absent from film-making between 1969 and 2000, when he made a short, *En chemin*, and the new feature is described by producers Parabole as "a movie which transports the viewer from an idyllic childhood in harmony with nature to the hell of an extravagant city".

Two Georgian film-makers have been busy in Germany. Nana Jorjadze, a 1996 Academy Award nominee, has worked with her regular producer Oliver Damian on *Tears of Don Juan*, and Dito Tsintsadze's new film *Schussangst* was scheduled for release in autumn 2003. In 2002, Tsintsadze made a short, *An Erotic Tale*, for a highly acclaimed German erotic TV series. It's a funny story of a frustrated writer, Nico, in search of erotic adventure for his new novel who ends up in a *ménage à trois* with the beautiful Sonja and her ex-husband.

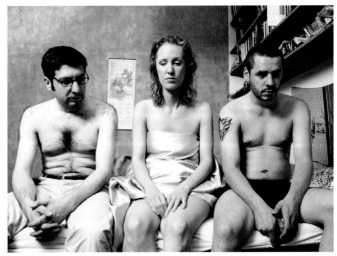

Three's company in Dito Tsintsadze's **An Erotic Tale**

The ongoing programme of DVD reissues by RUSCICO has included Georgian classics *Father of a Soldier* (1964) by Rezo Chkheidze, a Second World War drama about a Georgian peasant, which drew more than 20 millions admissions on its original release in the USSR. Also available are Sergo Parajanovi's *Legend of Surami Fortress* (1984), a colourful patriotic drama, and *Ashugi Qaribi* (1988), Parajanovi's love song to Azeri, Armenian and Georgian cultures. ∎

Germany Jack Kindred

The Year's Best Films

Jack Kindred's selection:
Good Bye, Lenin!
(Dir: Wolfgang Becker)
Naked (Dir: Doris Dörrie)
Angst (Dir: Oskar Röhler)
Soloalbum
(Dir: Gregor Schnitzler)
Anatomy 2
(Dir: Stefan Ruzowitzky)

Recent and Forthcoming Films

DER ALTE AFFE ANGST
(Angst)
[Drama, 2002] Script and Dir:
Oskar Röhler. Phot: Hagen
Bogdanski. Players: André
Hennicke, Marie Baeumer,
Ben Becker, Mariek Zielcke,
Vadim Glowna. Prod: Bioskop
Film, Munich.

Ben Becker in **Angst**

ANATOMIE 2 (Anatomy 2)
[Thriller, 2002] Script: Andreas
Berger. Dir: Stefan Ruzowitzky.
Phot: Barnaby Metschurat.
Players: Joachim Bissmeier,
Herbert Knaup, Roman Knizka,
Wotan Wilke Möhring, Rosel
Zech, Franka Potente. Prod:

By and large, 2002 was not a bad year for Germany's film exhibitors, but it was a dismal year for local films, with no domestic blockbusters and a string of stock-in-trade, low-budget titles failing to pull in the crowds. Box-office revenues, compiled by the Federal Film Board, totalled a respectable $902m (€960m), down $25m on 2001, and admissions fell by 14 million to 163.9 million, largely because of the surging home video market and widespread unemployment. Nevertheless, it was still the industry's second-best result since reunification.

American distributors captured 80% of the market, but with no stand-out spectator magnet like the Western spoof *Manitou's Shoe* (10.5 million admissions in 2001), the market share of home-grown productions dropped to a meagre 11.9%, from 18.4% in 2001. Last year's best local performer was the children's movie *Bibi Blocksberg* (two million admissions), while the teen comedy sequel *More Ants in their Pants* and Caroline Link's Oscar-winner *Nowhere in Africa* both went past the one-million benchmark for a hit in Germany. Link's surprise win and the three Oscars for Roman Polanski's *The Pianist* boosted domestic box-office returns and export sales for both titles.

There was a major setback when Sony Pictures Entertainment threw in the towel on its Berlin-based production arm, Deutsche Columbia Pictures Filmproduktion, following a disastrous series of feature film flops, including the entertaining sequel *Anatomy 2*, whose tally of 725,000 admissions was a major disappointment compared to the original *Anatomy*'s haul of nearly two million in 2000. Defying gloomy warnings of over-screening in the multiplex sector, the leading Kinopolis chain opened a $165m, 14-screen theatre in downtown Munich.

Becker rebuilds the Wall

The first three months of 2003 brought new hope with the phenomenal success of **Good Bye, Lenin!**, whose 5.7 million admissions in its first seven weeks of release surpassed all Hollywood titles and pushed first-quarter attendance to a five-year high. Shot in Friedrichshain, near Alexanderplatz in the heart of what was East Berlin, Wolfgang Becker's film is a tragi-comedy about German reunification as seen from an East German

Deutsche Columbia TriStar Film Production.

DAS FLIGENDE KLASSENZIMMER
(The Flying Classroom)
[Children's adventure, 2002] Script: Henriette Piper, Franziska Buch, Uschi Reich. Dir: Tomy Wigand. Phot: Peter von Haller. Players: Ulrich Noethen, Sebastian Koch, Piet Klocke, Anja Kling. Prod: Bavarian Filmverleih & Produktions, Munich.

EPSTEINS NACHT
(Epstein's Night)
[Drama, 2002] Script: Jens Urban. Dir: Urs Egger. Phot: Lukas Strebel. Players: Mario Adorf, Guenter Lamprecht, Bruno Ganz, Otto Tausig, Annie Girardot, Nina Hoss. Prod: MTM Medien & Television, Munich/Constantin, Munich.
Jochen Epstein is released after 15 years in jail for murder, but his troubles really begin as he encounters his former co-inmates from a concentration camp.

FARLAND *[working title]*
[Drama, 2003] Script and Dir: Michael Klier. Phot: Hans Fromm. Players: Laura Tonke, Richy Mueller, Daniel Brühl, Karina Fallenstein. Prod: Zero Film.
Low-budget story explores the social and mental problems of people in and around Berlin.

GOOD BYE, LENIN!
[Comedy-drama, 2002] Script: Bernd Lichtenberg, Wolfgang Becker. Dir: Becker. Phot: Martin Kukula. Players: Daniel Brühl, Katrin Sass, Maria Simon, Chulpan Khamatova, Florian Lukas. Prod: X Filme Creative Pool, Berlin.

HERR LEHMANN (Berlin Blues)
[Comedy, 2002] Script: Sven Regener. Dir: Leander Haussmann. Phot: Frank Griebe. Players: Christian Ulmen, Detlev W. Buck, Katja Danowski, Tim Fischer, Uwe-Dab Berlin. Prod: Boje Buck Produktion, Berlin.
Haussmann's second feature about love, friendship and loss,

Daniel Brühl in **Good Bye, Lenin!**

perspective. The plot involves a young man (Daniel Brühl) and his ailing mother, who has been in a coma for nine months. After she awakes, she is unaware that reunification has taken place. To avoid shocking her, the son recreates the DDR in the family apartment.

The movie had a surprise resonance among some ex-East Germans, evoking nostalgia that the dreary communist state was not all bad. It won the Blue Angel at Berlin for Best European Film and the talent of relative newcomers Becker and leading man Brühl, branded as a "shooting star" by the press, has generated new hope for made-in-Germany productions.

A potential blockbuster, produced, directed and co-written by Michael "Bully" Herbig, is in the pipeline, reuniting the team behind *Manitou's Shoe*. A parody of the *Star Trek: Enterprise* series, the title, *(T)raumschiff Surprise – Period 1*, is a play on the German words for dream and spaceship, and the storyline has Earth facing invasion in the year 2304. Mankind's last hope rests with the feeble crew of the spaceship *Surprise*, who roam the universe in total boredom.

Von Trotta recreates *Rosenstrasse*

Director Margarethe von Trotta, of New German Cinema fame, has come up with a major project, *Rosenstrasse*, based on the true story of German women whose public protest saved their Jewish husbands from deportation to Nazi death camps. Rosenstrasse 2-4 was a Jewish community centre in Berlin where intermarried Jews were imprisoned in 1943 and the site of the protest by 6,000 wives who faced down Nazi security forces and demanded the safe return of their husbands. With Hitler's agreement, propaganda minister Joseph Goebbels ordered the men's release, to avoid public outcry at shooting women in the streets. The cast is led by Katja Riemann as a young pianist and member of Goebbels' social elite, who witnessed the Rosenstrasse protest, and by Maria Schrader as a present-day New York journalist researching the fate of her own family in Nazi Germany.

Producer Bernd Eichinger unveiled plans to film *The Downfall – Hitler and the End of the Third Reich* (*Der Untergang – Hitler und das Ende des Dritten Reiches*), Professor JoachimFest's book about Hitler's last days in the Berlin bunker. Eichinger's adaptation is directed by Oliver Hirschbiegel (*The Experiment*) and stars Swiss actor Bruno Ganz as Hitler, Juliane Köhler as Eva Braun and Alexandra Maria Ladra as Traudl Junge, Hitler's secretary, whose memoirs were another source for Eichinger's script.

The documentary **Hitler's Jewish Soldiers** (*Hitlers Jüdische Soldaten*, working title) is another movie delving into Germany's Nazi past, based on research by Texan historian Bryan Mark Rigg, who had discovered that while some of his German relatives were murdered in Auschwitz, others had fought for Hitler. It is directed, with some re-enacted scenes, by Heike Mundzeck.

Fear and disrobing

Director Oskar Roehler's **Angst** (*Der alte Affe Angst*), has impotence as the underlying theme in a battle of the sexes. Hyped as "a modern love story", the plot involves a stage director, Robert (André Hennicke), and his girlfriend, Marie (Marie Baeumer), a nurse in a children's clinic, who fight constantly over their differing attitudes towards life. Marie fails in her erotic attempts to revitalise their love life and finally leaves Robert after she learns of his one-night stands with prostitutes. After their emotions have been exhausted, they get together again, united in a hope for a new beginning.

Doris Dörrie's **Naked** (*Nacht*) is a sex comedy involving 2 unhappy couples, Amelia and Felix (Heike Makatsch, Benno Fürmann), and Annette and Boris (Alexandra Maria Lara and Jürgen Vogel), who have been close friends for years. The former pair are in the throes of a divorce and the latter's marriage is in crisis despite the husband's success on the stock exchange. The movie reaches its comic climax when the couples make a high-stakes bet as to whether two of them, blind-folded, can pick out their naked partners using only their hands. *Naked* drew nearly one million cinemagoers.

At the urging of parent company Sony in Culver City, director Stefan Ruzowitzky took the helm of **Anatomy 2** (*Anatomie 2*), in a bid to repeat the success of his first *Anatomy*. Barnaby Metschurat starred as Jo, who begins his internship at a large Berlin clinic. Urged on by a nurse (Heike Makatsch), Jo reluctantly performs an illegal operation on a child and is invited by the clinic's sinister director (Herbert Knaup) to join his weekly "salon", a grisly research project which threatens Jo's life.

after his successful debut *Sonnenallee* (*Sun Alley*, 2000).

HITLERS JUEDISCHE SOLDATEN
(**Hitler's Jewish Soldiers**)
[*Docu-drama, 2003*] *Script and Dir: Heike Mundzeck. Phot: Rupert Lehmann. Prod: Trigon Film, Hamburg.*

NACKT (**Naked**)
[*Drama, 2001*] *Script and Dir: Doris Dörie. Phot: Frank Griebe. Players: Heike Makatsch, Benno Fürmann, Alexandra Maria Lara, Jürgen Vogel, Nina Hoss. Prod: Constantin Film Produktion, Munich.*
A party game between 2 couples takes on a new dimension as facades are torn down.

PLAYA DEL FUTURO
(*literally* **Beach of the Future**)
[*Action road movie, 2003*] *Script: Peter Lichtefeld, Dagmar Benke. Dir: Lichtefeld. Phot: Frank Griebe. Players: Hilmi Soezer, Oliver Mario, Kari Vanaanen, Nina Petri, Peter Lohmeyer. Prod: Bosko Biati Film Berlin.*
Penniless in Spain, Jan Holz pursues the boss who's run off without paying him.

SIE HABEN KNUT
(**They've Got Knut**)
[*Drama, 2003*] *Script: Daniel Nocke. Dir: Stefan Krohmer. Phot: Benedict Neuenfels. Players: Valerie Koch, Hans-jochen Wagner, Ingo Haeb, Alexandra Neldel. Prod: Home Run Pictures, Stuttgart.*
A tale of forgotten ideals in Germany's turbulent 1980s, when love and politics were inseparable.

SCHATTEN DER ZEIT
(**Shadows in Time**)
[*Romantic drama, 2003*] *Script and Dir: Florian Gallenberg. Phot: Juergen Juerges. Players: Prashant Narayanna, Tannishtha Chatterjee, Tilotama Shome, Vijay Raz. Prod: Diana Film, Munich.*

SOLOALBUM
[*Romantic Comedy, 2002*] *Script: Jens-Frederik Otto. Dir: Gregor*

Schnitzler. Phot: Gero Steffen.
Players: Matthias Schweighoefer,
Nora Tschirner, Christian
Naethe, Oliver Wnuk. Prod:
Goldkind Film, Munich.

Concorde

Matthias Schweighofer and Sandy
Mölling in **Soloalbum**

VERRUECKT NACH PARIS
(Crazy About Paris)
[Comedy-drama, 2002] Script
and Dir: Eike Besuden, Pago
Balke. Phot: Piotr Lenar. Players:
Paula Kleine, Wolfgang
Goettsch, Frank Grabski,
Dominique Horwitz, Corinna
Harfouch. Prod: Geisberg
Studios, Bremen.

WIR (We)
[Drama, 2003] Script and Dir:
Martin Gypkens. Phot: Eva
Fleig. Players: Oliver Bockern,
Rike Schmidt, Jannek Petri, Knut
Berger, Karina Plachetka. Prod:
Credofilm, Berlin.
Old school friends come to terms
with adult responsibilities, failed
loves and unpaid phone bills.

(T)RAUMSCHIFF SURPRISE –
PERIOD 1 (literally, **Spaceship**
Surprise – Period 1)
[Star Trek parody, 2003] Script:
Michael "Bully" Herbig, Alfons
Biedermann, Rick Kavanian. Dir:
Herbig. Phot: Stephan Schuh.
Players: Rick Kavanian,
Christian Tramitz, Til Schweiger,
Anja Kling, Michael Herbig.
Prod: Bavaria Film, Munich.

DER UNTERGANG –
HITLER UND DAS ENDE DES
DRITTEN REICHES
(The Downfall – Hitler and the
End of the Third Reich)
[Historical drama, 2003] Script:
Bernd Eichinger. Dir: Oliver
Hirschbiegel. Phot: Rainer
Klausmann. Players: Bruno Ganz,
Alexandra Maria Ladra, Juliane

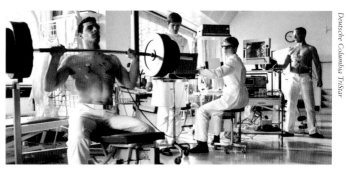

Deutsche Columbia TriStar

Strange experiments in horror sequel **Anatomy 2**

Berlin-born director Gregor Schnitzler delivered **Soloalbum,**
a romantic comedy of young love and disillusion. Ben (Matthias
Schweighoefer), a sophisticated 24-year-old editor of a thriving pop
magazine, appears to have it all. But suddenly, his girlfriend of three
years, Katharina (Nora Tschirner), severs the relationship and plunges
the egotistical Ben into an identity crisis. Comic situations arise as he
tries simultaneously to forget Katharina and win her back.

Hopes were high at press time for East German-born Leander
Haussmann's second feature *Berlin Blues (Herr Lehmann)*,
a rollicking comedy set in West Berlin just before the collapse of the
Wall in 1989. It stars Christian Ulmen, Katja Danowski, Detlev Buck
and Janek Rieke as a group of beer-loving social misfits in the
wide-open Berlin district of Kreuzberg who must confront the end
of an era as Berliners pour through the breach in the Wall.

JACK KINDRED, former *Variety* bureau chief in Germany and
senior editor for the German Press Agency, covers film, TV and
video from his Munich outpost.

Köhler, Ulrich Noethen, Corinna
Harfouch, Daniel Brühl. Prod:
Constantin Productions, Munich.

ROSENSTRASSE
(literally, **Rose Street**)
[Historical Drama 2002] Script
and Dir: Margarethe von Trotta.
Phot: Franz Rath. Players: Maria

Martin Feifel and Katja Riemann
in **Rosenstrasse**

Schrader, Katja Riemann,
Jürgen Vogel. Prod: Meyer Film,
Hamburg, Get Reel, Holland/
Studio Hamburg.

Quote of the Year

"My seven-month-old
daughter was seriously ill
in hospital and she was
more important to me than
the Oscar."
CAROLINE LINK, director,
explaining why she did not
attend the ceremony where
Nowhere in Africa was named
Best Foreign-Language Film.

German Film Awards 2003

Film: *Good Bye, Lenin!*
Director: Wolfgang Becker (*Good Bye, Lenin!*).
Actor: Daniel Brühl (*Good Bye, Lenin!* and
Elephant Heart/Elefantenherz).
Actress: Hannelore Elsner
(*My Last Film/Mein letzter Film*).
Supporting Actor: Florian Lukas
(*Good Bye, Lenin!*).
Supporting Actress: Corinna Harfouch
(*Bibi Blocksberg*).
Documentary: *Rivers and Tides*
(Thomas Riedelsheimer).
Children's Film: *The Flying Classroom/
Das fliegende Klassenzimmer*.
Foreign Film: *The Hours* (US).
Cinematography: Thomas Riedelsheimer
(*Rivers and Tides*).
Editing: Peter Adam (*Good Bye, Lenin!*).
Music: Yann Tiersen (*Good Bye, Lenin!*).
Production Design: Lothar Holler
(*Good Bye, Lenin!*).
Best Screenplay (Filmed): *Do Fish Do It?/
Fickende Fische* (Almut Getto).

Corinna Harfouch as Rabia the witch in **Bibi Blocksberg**,
*for which she won Best Supporting Actress at the German
Film Awards.*

Best Screenplay (Unfilmed): *Napola*
(Maggie Peren, Dennis Gansel).
Prize of Honour: Ulrich Gregor, film historian.
Audience Award (German Film):
Good Bye, Lenin!.
Audience Award (Actor of the Year):
Daniel Brühl.

Bavaria Film Verleih/Constantin Film

European Film Awards 2002

Film: *Hable con ella* (*Talk to Her*).
Director: Pedro Almodóvar (*Talk to Her*).
Actor: Sergio Castellitto, *Bella Martha* (*Mostly
Martha*; Germany) and *L'Ora di Religione...*
(*My Mother's Smile*; Italy).
Actress: The cast of *8 Femmes*.
Screenwriter: Pedro Almodóvar (*Talk to Her*).
Cinematographer: Pawel Edelman (*The Pianist*).
Achievement in World Cinema: Victoria Abril,
actress (Spain).
Lifetime Achievement Award: Tonino Guerra,
screenwriter (Italy).
Discovery – Fassbinder Award: *Hukkle*
(György Palfi, Hungary).
Documentary Award – Prix Arte: *Etre et Avoir*
(*To Be and to Have*, Nicolas Philibert, France).
***Screen International* Award (Non-European
Film):** *Divine Intervention*
(Elia Suleiman, Palestine).
European Short Film: *10 Minutes*
(Ahmed Imamovic, Bosnia & Herzegovina).

People's Choice Awards
Director: Pedro Almodóvar (*Talk to Her*).
Actor: Javier Camara (*Talk to Her*).
Actress: Kate Winslet (*Iris*).

Belgium – Joseph Plateau Awards 2002

Film: *Le Fils* (*The Son*, Luc and
Jean-Pierre Dardenne).
Director: Luc and Jean-Pierre Dardenne
(*The Son*).
Actor: Olivier Gourmet
(*The Son* and *Une part de ciel*).
Actress: Antje De Boeck (*Hop*);
Els Dottermans (*Meisje*).
Composer: Daan (*Meisje*);
Vincent D'Hondt (*Hop*).
Screenwriter: Danis Tanovic (*No Man's Land*).
Short Film: *Snapshot* (Jakob Verbruggen).
Documentary: *Iran. Sous le voile des
apparences* (Thierry Michel).
Joseph Plateau Box-Office Prize: *Alias*
(Jan Verheyen).

ESPRESSO SOCIETY STUDIO

Greek Film Centre
Focus on
Greek Cinema

10, Panepistimiou Ave. 106 71 Athens, Greece
Tel. 00210 3648.007, 3631.733 Fax 00210 3614.336
e-mail: info@gfc.gr http: www.gfc.gr

Greece Yannis Bacoyannopoulos

The Year's Best Films

Yannis Bacoyannopoulos'
selection:

Hard Goodbyes: My Father
(Dir: Penny Panayotopoulou)

Lilly's Story
(Dir: Robert Manthoulis)

Loser Takes All
(Dir: Nikos Nikolaidis)

Think it Over
(Dir: Katerina Evangelakou)

The World Again
(Dir: Nikos Cornilios)

Loser Takes All

Recent and Forthcoming Films

TO LIVADI POU DAKRIZI
(The Weeping Meadow)
[Drama, 2003] Script and Dir: Theo Angelopoulos. Phot: Andreas Sinanos. Players: Alexandra Aidini, Nikos Poursanidis, Giorgos Armenis, Vassilis Kolovos. Prod: Angelopoulos/Intermedias/Bac Films/Storie.
The first part of Angelopoulos' epic, lyric Trilogy is set in

Films in Greece are increasingly becoming just another consumer product. As the exhibition boom continues (but only in the form of multiplexes in the major provincial towns) cinemas are becoming part of Fun Parks in which a movie is just one of the choices available to the young people who make up an ever greater proportion of the audience. They watch films en masse while consuming popcorn and carrying on running commentaries, and it seems the only films that can survive in such relaxed viewing conditions are dazzling productions with special effects, thrills and spills. All of them of course American. For the first year ever, in 2002-03 the 20 top-grossing films in Greece were all American.

In this climate the traditional single-screen theatres face extinction and the only "resistance" comes from arthouse cinemas specialising in European and other international films. These include the Greek Film Centre's network, Film Centre, and the Ministry of Culture's Municipal Movie network. In this way a small but loyal audience is being reached by challenging films such as *Irréversible, Bowling for Columbine* and *The Man without a Past.*

However, Greek productions (24 new films were screened in 2002) are lost in the void between these two fields, and audiences no longer even bother to find out whether they might in fact enjoy a Greek film. Even the popular local comedies that in recent years had revived a successful genre of old Greek cinema and garnered a substantial share of the box-office have suffered a devastating drop, as evidenced by the failure of Nikos Perakis' **Liza and All the Others**.

Yet on the artistic front the outlook was far from negative. Established directors presented interesting works and emerging film-makers also produced solid achievements, with women to the fore (it was telling that for the first time both the first and second prizes of the State Cinema Awards for Best Film went to female directors, with an almost equal share of the votes).

Our father, who art...

Penny Panayotopoulou's **Hard Goodbyes: My Father** racked up the most admissions for a Greek film, many individual state prizes and much critical acclaim following its international screenings.

Panayotopoulou adopts a structure that appears loose, with frequent rifts and new starting points. Yet everything gradually fuses into a dual portrait: a mother, still young, and her little boy (Yorgos Karayannis, who won the Leopard for Best Actor at Locarno), who face, both together and separately, the painful aftermath of the sudden death of the husband and father in 1960s Athens. The universe of lies and false illusions in which the 10-year-old boy seeks shelter echoes with romantic authenticity.

A son and mother face their grief in **Hard Goodbyes: My Father**

A dense and well-written script clearly etches the portraits of the many characters in Katerina Evangelakou's romantic family comedy **Think it Over**. It's a film of humour and acute psychology, built around a woman who, at 40, experiences her first major existential crisis and re-examines the choices she made in her adolescence and the subsequent direction her life has taken (a choice between pastry-making and love?). Her mother and sisters, who must all manage men, are major presences in an environment that is intrinsically feminine.

Yannis Economidis' first feature, **Matchbox**, drew critics' attention. The director confined the drama of a working-class family tearing into each other and collapsing in a stiflingly closed space; a naturalistic, modern *kammerspiel*. The words rattle at an ever faster pace. Everything takes place at full volume, in a constant state of crisis, of hysteria.

Made with a large group of young amateur actors, Nikos Cornilios' **The World Again** is an uneven film that nonetheless has substantial and unexpected virtues. Cornilios observes the world of adolescence and the road to maturity with bold originality. He does not immerse us in the sort of retro-reminiscence to which we have become accustomed. The kids in the story set off on a journey that is a learning experience in the world of unspoiled nature, as well as

Greece, 1919-49. With reference to the Theban Cycle it follows the fate of Hellenism through the story of two people who first meet as children in 1919, during the flight of the Greeks from Odessa, and are repeatedly separated and reunited by great historical events.

KOKKINI PEMPTI
(Red Thursday)
[Drama, 2003] Script and Dir: Christos Siopachas. Phot: Rostislav Pyroumov. Players: Paschalis Tsarouchas, Clare Day, Sergei Vinogradov, Demetris Tzoumakis, Alkis Kritikos, Patrick Myles. Prod: Cyprus Film Advisory Board/Greek Film Centre/Studio Classica/Hellenic Broadcasting Corp./Arctinos Ltd/Christos Siopachas.
Smuggler Angelos had a dream: to save enough money to buy a shiny new coach. He meets and marries Mary, an Englishwoman, but before the honeymoon is over Angelos finds himself sharing a gaol cell with Alexei, a Russian adventurer.

MATIA APO NICHTA
(Eyes of Night)
[Drama, 2003] Script and Dir: Pericles Hoursoglou. Phot: Stamatis Giannoulis. Players: Yannis Karatzoyannis, Vangelio Andreadaki, Hekavi Douma, Nikos Karimalis, Spyros Stavrinidis, Dimitris Mavropoulos. Prod: Greek Film Centre/Pericles Hoursoglou/CL Productions.
Chronis, a truck-driver, always wants to travel. Eleftheria, 35, is desperate to have a baby. Into their lives comes a third lonely person, Vallia, a country girl who hitches a ride to Athens in Chronis' truck.

GAMILIA NARKI
(Wedding Torpor)
[Drama, 2003] Script and Dir: Dimitris Indares. Phot: Dimitris Katsaitis. Players: Fanny Mouratidi, Natalia Stylianou, Alexandros Logothetis, Ana Dimitrievich. Prod: Greek Film

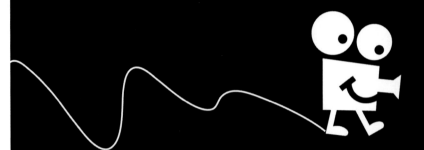

a process of mourning, as they search for the grave of the mother of one of the group in remote, picturesque cemeteries. The experiences prove painful. They are observed with an oblique gaze, and come across as poetic enigmas.

Teenagers on the road to adulthood in **The World Again**

Bridging the gulf

The generation of mature film-makers was represented with remarkable quality. Robert Manthoulis, a French resident for the past 30 years, with a massive filmography mostly in the documentary field, returned with a fiction feature that is a bridge between Greek "exiles" and their distant homeland. In **Lilly's Story**, a director tries to make a film about a humble heroine of the resistance against the Greek junta. In so doing he unravels the life experiences of persecuted Greeks of all eras, in both western and eastern countries. Manthoulis favours the fine thread of memory, both dramatic and humorous, over the socio-political charge that one might customarily expect from such a subject. This is a relaxed, calmly articulated film, both realistic and mythic, with faith in the spiritual resources of its heroes.

At the other end of the spectrum lies Nikos Nikolaidis' **Loser Takes All**, which brings to life for the umpteenth time the rebellious youth of the 1960s and their individualistic anarchism. Nikolaidis boldly transfers them to the present day. The tired hero meets a youthful counterpart and together they move on the fringes of the law, with admiring women, and confront weird killer crooks. Nikolaidis presents a variation of the doomed American film noir, but with personality, a genuine romanticism and admirable technical economy.

YANNIS BACOYANNOPOULOS began writing on film in 1960 and for 28 years has been the film critic of the Athens daily *Kathimerini* and the Hellenic Broadcasting Corporation.

Centre/Dimitris Indares/CL Productions.
Thomas and Lily, in their mid-thirties with a child, are in their seventh "difficult" year of marriage. The sudden departure of their home help and the arrival of Irina, a captivating foreigner, as her replacement, create a chain of explosive situations.

POLITIKI KOUZINA
(A Touch of Spice)
[Drama, 2003] Script and Dir: Tassos Boulmetis. Players: George Corraface, Ieroklis Michallidis, Renia Loizidou, Stelios Mainas, Tassos Bantis, Theodora Tzimou. Prod: Greek Film Centre.
The hero is Fanis Iakovidis, a charming professor of astrophysics, in his forties with a great talent for cooking.

ENA TRAGOUDI DE FTANI
(A Song Is Not Enough)
[Drama, 2003] Script and Dir: Elissavet Chronopoulou. Phot: Christos Alexandris. Players: Gogo Brebou, Yannis Kokiasmenos, Alexandra Karoni, Fenia Papadodima, Anna Koutsaftiki, Stratoula Theodoratou, Costas Kappas, Babis Yotopoulos. Prod: Greek Film Centre/Elissavet Chronopoulou/CL Productions.
In 1972, Irene is arrested by the military regime for resistance activities and sent to Korydallos prison. When she is released in August 1973 she finds that nothing in her life is the same.

I THEATRINES (The Thespians)
[Drama, 2003] Script: Viki Demou, Panayotis Portokalakis. Dir: Portokalakis. Phot: Yannis Drakoularakos. Players: Lena Kitsopoulou, Giorgos Karamichos, Laertis Vasileiou, Maria Protopappa, Christos Stergioglou, Dimitris Petropoulos. Prod: Hellenic Broadcasting Corp./CL Productions/Panayotis Portokalakis/Greek Film Centre.
In medieval Greece, Antonina,

a beautiful Byzantine actress, lives a lighthearted life, playing in a constant game of seduction with those around her, until she meets and marries General Andronicus. Then she falls in love with Theodosius, a guest and friend of Andronicus' son Photios, and a devastating scandal ensues.

OLO TO VAROS
TOU KOSMOU
(All the Weight of the World)
[Drama, 2003] Script and Dir: Thanos Anastopoulos. Phot: Ilias Konstantakopoulos. Players: Layia Giourgou, Ioanna Sobzyk, Maria Zorba, Ioanna Tsirigouli, Minas Hadzisavvas, Renos Mandis, Fotis Spyros, Nikos Georgakis. Prod: Fantasia Audiovisual Ltd/Greek Film Centre.
A story about 10 urban people, each carrying a different emotional burden.

HANI (Inn)
[Drama, 2003] Script and Dir: Giorgos Bakolas. Phot: Odysseas Pavlopoulos. Players: Dimitris Alexandris, Dimitris Xanthopoulos, Giorgos Moroyannis, Michalis Yannatos, Constantina Takalou, Aspasia Alevra, Meleti Georgiadi, Antonis Vlissidis, Alexandros Moukanos. Prod: Greek Film Centre/Hellenic Broadcasting Corp./Giorgos Bakolas, Nikos Sekeris.
In a city in the Ottoman Orient in the early 1900s, a load of gold sovereigns leads two Greeks, Zissos and Apostolos, on an adventurous journey. The inn is their stopover in the middle of the adventure.

I YENEI TIS SAMOTHRAKIS
(The Valiants of Samothrace)
[Comedy, 2003] Script and Dir: Stamatis Tsarouchas. Phot: Spyros Papatriantafyllou. Players: Renos Haralambidis, Dimitris Piatas, Costas Santas, Tassos Palantzidis, Rigas Axelos. Prod: Midnight Films Ltd/Greek Film Centre/Hellenic Broadcasting Corp.
The tragi-comic misadventures of a company of conscripts serving

in a battalion of "undesirables" who are suddenly caught up in the 1974 mobilisation and transferred to Cyprus to face the Turkish invasion. But they end up in Samothrace.

MIA YPEROCHI MERA
(It's a Wonderful Day)
[Drama, 2003] Script: George Karadinakis, Dimitris Vakis. Dir: Dinos Mavroidis. Phot: Antonis Linardatos. Players: Efi Mouriki, Irene Balta, Spiros Konstantopoulos, Vladimiros Kyriakidis, Pemy Zouni, Konstantinos Markoulakis, Giorgos Karamichos. Prod: New Greek Television/Alpha TV/Mythos Productions Ltd (Athens)/Greek Film Centre.
Six characters, all torn between reality and dreams, attempt to communicate, in six parallel stories that unfold over 24 hours in present-day Athens.

NYFES (Brides)
[Drama, 2003] Script: Ioanna Karistiani Voulgari. Dir: Pantelis Voulgaris. Phot: Giorgos Arganitis. Players: Damian Lewis, Victoria Haralambidou, Andrea Ferreol, Evi Soulidou, Dimitris Katalifos, Steven Berkoff. Prod: Cappa Productions/Alco Films.
Summer, 1922. Photographer Norman Harris is sailing first-class to America on SS King Alexander. In third class are 700 brides-to-be, each carrying a photograph of the bridegrooms they have never met. Norman and one of the brides, Niki, gradually fall in love.

Quotes of the Year
"You can even get Donna Karan on sale. So why not *Think it Over?*"
KATERIN EVANGELAKOU, *director, proposing a reduction in cinema ticket prices for Greek films, to help them compete with American movies.*

"There is a negative prejudice from audiences [towards Greek films]. If *Matchbox* had been in English it might have had more widespread appeal."
YORGOS TZIOTZIOS, *distributor and critic, analysing the poor commercial performance of one of the year's better films.*

Hong Kong Tim Youngs

The Year's Best Films

Tim Youngs' selection:
Just One Look (Dir: Riley Ip)
Golden Chicken
(Dir: Samson Chiu)
Infernal Affairs (Dirs:
Andrew Lau and Alan Mak)
New Blood (Dir: Soi Cheang)
Shark Busters
(Dir: Herman Yau)

Recent and Forthcoming Films

RUNNING ON KARMA
[Romantic comedy, 2003] Dir: Johnnie To, Wai Ka-fai. Players: Andy Lau, Cecilia Cheung. Prod: China Star, Milkyway Image.

THE FLOATING LANDSCAPE
[Drama, 2003] Dir: Carol Lai. Players: Ekin Cheng, Karena Lam, Liu Ye, Su Jin, Huang Jue, Ben Luk. Prod: Filmko.

LOST HORIZONS
[Romance, 2003] Dir: Derek Chiu. Players: Francis Ng, Anita Yuen, Ruby Lin, Oh Ji-ho. Prod: Mandarin.

HEROIC DUO
[Action, 2003] Dir: Benny Chan. Players: Leon Lai, Ekin Cheng, Francis Ng, Karena Lam, Xu Jing Lei. Prod: Universe.

MY DREAM GIRL
[Romantic drama, 2003] Dir: Raymond Yip. Players: Vicky Zhao, Ekin Cheng, Vincent Kok, Mark Lui, Niki Chow. Prod: Universe/Shanxi Film Studio.

SCREAMING
[Horror, 2003] Dir: Soi Cheang. Players: Charlene Choi, Gillian Chung, Wong You-nam. Prod: Universe.

The runaway success of police thriller *Infernal Affairs* at Christmas 2002 brought much-needed cheer to the Hong Kong film industry after a difficult year. As Andrew Lau and Alan Mak's movie raked in more than $7m (HK$55m) over the holiday season, the film-making community was reminded that Hongkongers will still crowd into cinemas for excellent local films.

The months before Christmas were less positive, with production and audience numbers down. Some 92 local films reached the city's cinemas in 2002, down from 126 in 2001, and more than a third of these were shot on DV. The traditionally strong summer yielded lacklustre returns against the soccer World Cup, home video and a poor economic climate, and mainstream cinemagoers found little to attract them in the off-peak months that followed, a period in which release schedules kept changing and low-budget films, including DV titles, opened with minimal or no fanfare ahead of prompt video release.

In September, exhibitors cut ticket prices on Tuesdays and Wednesdays to woo back audiences, while industry figures held crisis meetings at the Revitalising Hong Kong Film Industry Forum. A government response, the Film Guarantee Fund, which guarantees half of film-makers' bank loans (up to $333,000), was announced in January 2003 and launched in April.

Just as the strong box-office returns from Christmas 2002 and Chinese New Year 2003 were boosting the industry and production was stepping up a gear, the Easter outbreak of Severe Acute Respiratory Syndrome (SARS) dealt a major blow. Box-office takings crashed and releases were shuffled or delayed. The government's "Cinema Capital in April" promotional initiative also suffered when the Hong Kong-Asia Film Financing Forum was cancelled because of SARS-related travel fears. Normality had returned by June, however, when the first local summer movies brought queues back to cinemas.

'Tis the season to see movies

Infernal Affairs, which shared Christmas slots with Zhang Yimou's *Hero* (see China section), was bolstered by exceptionally positive word of mouth. After the initial attraction of an all-star cast,

PAPA LOVES YOU
[Drama, 2003] Dir: Herman
Yau. Players: Tony Leung Ka-fai,
Charlene Choi, Eric Tsang. Prod:
China Star.

THE TWINS EFFECT
[Action-horror, 2003] Dir: Dante
Lam. Players: Charlene Choi,
Gillian Chung, Ekin Cheng,
Anthony Wong, Josie Ho,
Jackie Chan. Prod: EMG.

INFERNAL AFFAIRS II
[Thriller, 2003] Dir: Andrew
Lau, Alan Mak. Players: Edison
Chen, Shawn Yue, Francis Ng,
Eric Tsang, Anthony Wong.
Prod: Media Asia.

ANNA & SHAOLIN
[Action comedy, 2003] Dir:
Raymond Yip. Players:
Ekin Cheng, Miriam Yeung.
Prod: Universe.

TURN LEFT, TURN RIGHT
[Drama, 2003] Dir: Johnnie To,
Wai Ka-fai. Players: Gigi Leung,
Takeshi Kaneshiro. Prod: Warner
Bros/Raintree Pictures/
Milkyway Image.

STAR RUNNER
[Romantic action-musical, 2003]
Dir: Daniel Lee. Players:
Vannessa Wu, Kim Hyun Ju.
Prod: Filkmo/Sil-Metropole.

2046
[Drama, 2003] Dir: Wong Kar-
wai. Players: Maggie Cheung,
Zhang Ziyi, Tony Leung Chiu-
wai. Prod: Jet Tone.

THE SWORD SEARCHERS
[Period action, 2003] Dir: Ching
Siu-tung. Players: Nicholas Tse,
Jackie Chan. Prod: Mandarin.

SILVER HAWK
[Action, 2003] Dir: Jingle Ma.
Players: Michele Yeoh, Richie
Ren, Brandon Chang. Prod:
Han Entertainment.

HIT TEAM 2
[Action, 2003] Dir: Dante Lam.
Players: Aaron Kwok, Eason
Chan, Xu Jing Lei.
Prod: Universe.

JIANG SHI
[Horror, 2003] Dir: Law Chi-

including Andy Lau and Tony Leung Chiu-wai, the well-refined
script by Felix Chong and Alan Mak about gangsters infiltrating
the police force sparked glowing recommendations. Superb
performances, slick production values and minimalist set-pieces
added to the appeal of the movie, which was selected as Hong
Kong's entry for the Best Foreign-Language Film Oscar.

Andy Lau (left) and Tony Leung Chiu-wai in hit thriller **Infernal Affairs**

Johnnie To and Wai Ka-fai continued their tradition of presenting
holiday hits. After recording a summer 2002 box-office winner
with **My Left Eye Sees Ghosts**, a supernatural romantic comedy
starring Sammi Cheng and Lau Ching-wan, the co-directors did
even better at Chinese New Year 2003 with **Love for All Seasons**,
again starring Cheng, this time as a mainland Chinese nun who has
her heart broken by a Hong Kong playboy (Louis Koo). Also playing
at New Year were Vincent Kuk's clever feng shui comedy **My
Lucky Star**, starring Miriam Yeung and Tony Leung Chiu-wai, and
Gordon Chan's period comedy **Cat and Mouse**, starring
Andy Lau alongside Cecilia Cheung.

Economic uncertainty, rising unemployment and falling property
prices gained headlines in Hong Kong in 2002-03, and several film-
makers explored social issues for more drama-oriented work.
Samson Chiu's **Golden Chicken** (another Christmas 2002 release)
achieved this most successfully by charting Hong Kong's
fluctuating fortunes, as narrated by a prostitute, delightfully played
by Sandra Ng. As she rose through the red-light ranks to a glitzy
nightclub in boom years, before taking up self-sufficient one-
woman brothel work today, her highs and lows echoed those
of the city.

In the lower-budget arena, Herman Yau's **Shark Busters** took
a more direct approach. Starting out as a routine police thriller, Yau
then shifts focus on to individual cops' struggles with their personal
finances. With real-life scenarios adapted for the screen, audiences
witnessed policemen dealing with devalued property and spiralling
debts, and fighting back against ruthless loan sharks.

Sandra Ng as the prostitute heroine of **Golden Chicken**

A languid *Look* back

Nostalgia became a cultural trend in Hong Kong as citizens and film-makers remembered better times while also looking forward. Among several nostalgic productions, Riley Ip's **Just One Look** was the most accomplished. Shot in a peaceful island setting, the film placed rising young stars in a 1970s village in the story of a boy growing up. It not only provided a charming look back at an old community but also paid tribute to past moviegoing experiences: a small cinema has a key position in the film's landscape.

leung. *Players: Anthony Wong, Brandon Chang, Kei Yeung. Prod: Han Entertainment.*

LOVE UNDERCOVER 2
[Comedy, 2003] Dir: Joe Ma. Players: Miriam Yeung, Daniel Wu, Woo Fung, Raymond Wong, Hui Shiu-hung, Lam Suet. Prod: Mei Ah/Media Asia.

MISS TO
[Drama, 2003] Dir: Raymond To. Players: Daniel Wu, Michelle Reis, Lydia Shum. Prod: Universe.

Quote of the Year
"Word of mouth – about the quality of a movie – is what really matters in the end."
WOODY TSUNG WAN-CHI, *chief executive of the Motion Picture Industry Association, on the success of* Infernal Affairs.

The 22nd Hong Kong Film Awards

Best Film: *Infernal Affairs.*
Best Director: Andrew Lau Wai-keung, Alan Mak Siu-fai (*Infernal Affairs*).
Best Screenplay: Alan Mak Siu-fai, Felix Chong Man-keung (*Infernal Affairs*).
Best Actor: Tony Leung Chiu-wai (*Infernal Affairs*).
Best Actress: Angelica Lee Sum-kit (*The Eye*).
Best Supporting Actor: Anthony Wong Chau-sang (*Infernal Affairs*).
Best Supporting Actress: Rene Liu (*Double Vision*).
Best New Actor: Eugenia Yuan Lai-kei (*Three: Going Home*).
Best Cinematography: Christopher Doyle (*Hero*).
Best Art Direction: Huo Ting-xiao, Yi Zhen-zhou (*Hero*).
Best Editing: Danny Pang, Pang Ching-hei (*Infernal Affairs*).
Best Sound: Tao Jing (*Hero*).
Best Costume and Make-Up: Emi Wada (*Hero*).
Best Action Choreography: Ching Siu-tung (*Hero*).
Best Special Effects: *Hero.*
Best Original Score: Tan Dun (*Hero*).
Best Original Song: "*Infernal Affairs*" from *Infernal Affairs*.
Best Asian Film: *My Sassy Girl* (South Korea).
Outstanding Young Director Award: Law Chi-leung (*Inner Senses*).
Lifetime Achievement Award: actors Walter Cho Tat-wah, Shek Kin.

Among action movies and thrillers, a notable return was the girls-with-guns genre, popular in the 1980s and 1990s. Corey Yuen's **So Close** brought together an attractive cast, led by Shu Qi, Vicky Zhao and Karen Mok, in a fun modern action scenario (two women avenging the death of their father), all presented with nods to old-style local action film-making. Ching Siu-tung's **Naked Weapon** had pistol-packing, scantily-clad girls but lacked local flavour (nearly all the dialogue was in English).

On a much smaller scale, Easter 2003 saw the release of Johnnie To's **PTU**, a highly stylised police thriller two years in the making and focused on a single night's action, as tactical unit policemen secretly help a comrade who loses his gun in a street fight. It manages to entertain with off-beat humour as tense set pieces unfolded.

On the up and up

The low number of 35mm movie productions in 2002-03 meant less scope for auspicious debuts on either side of the camera. Nonetheless, several films showcased the city's rising talent. In the horror genre, young director Soi Cheang (*Horror Hotline, Diamond Hill*) released his bleakest work yet, **New Blood**. Favouring serious chills instead of commonplace horror-comedy, Cheang presented a dark, atmospheric piece charting three people's misfortunes arising from their good deeds. With an outstanding performance by up-and-coming starlet Niki Chow, Cheang offered viewers some of Hong Kong's most nightmarish celluloid imagery of recent years.

Producer-director Joe Ma, having already turned singer-actor Miriam Yeung into an audience favourite in comedies like *Love Undercover,* worked with Twins (popular singing duo Charlene Choi and Gillian Chung) in **Summer Breeze of Love**, a teen romance comedy as lightweight as its title. Ma's 2003 slate kicked off with Choi on her own as a superstar singer in **Diva Ah Hey**, an enjoyable drama about the making of pop idols.

The 2003 summer season was ushered in with **Truth or Dare: 6th Floor Rear Flat**, a debut mainstream feature by Barbara Wong. Previously known for her documentary *Women's Private Parts,* Wong helmed a confident and lively film about youth that hit all the right notes with its target audience. The cast occupying the flat of the title included new singers and popular radio DJs and showcased some of Hong Kong's best young acting talent.

TIM YOUNGS is a Hong Kong-based editor and writer who serves as Hong Kong consultant to the Far East Film Festival, Udine.

Hungary John Nadler

The Year's Best Films

John Nadler's selection:
Cloud over the Ganges (Dir: Gabor von Dettre)
Forest
(Dir: Benedek Fliegauf)
A Long Weekend in Pest and Buda (Dir: Karoly Makk)

Recent and Forthcoming Films

MAGYAR VANDOR
(Hungarian Vagabond)
[Historical comedy, 2004] Script: Gabor Harmat. Dir: Gabor Herendi. Players: Károly Gesztesi, János Gyuriska, János Greifenstein, Zoltán Seress, Gyözö Szabó, Tibor Szervét, István Hajdu. Prod: Herendi, Skyfilm Hungary.
Based on the legends of the seven Asian tribes that founded Hungary more than 1,000 years ago, Herendi's film has the seven great chiefs sleeping late on the day of departure from Asia to Europe, waking to find that their people have left without them. In a frantic bid to catch up, the chiefs cross Europe and time, encountering Hungarians at every crucial stage of their history.

ROMA COP
[Crime drama, 2004] Script: Gabor Dettre, Akos Kertesz. Dir: Dettre. Phot: Ferenc Pap. Players: Zoltan Mucsi, Ildiko Toth, Lajos Kovacs, Antal Cserna, Anna Györgyi. Prod: Uj Budapest Filmstúdió.
Roma, an ethnic Gypsy, is raised in an upper middle-class Hungarian family, studies law and joins the police in a bid to help his fellow Roma. When

H ungarian directors, producers and distributors all viewed 2002-03 as a pivotal year for the nation's post-communist film industry, which currently has money and talent in abundance. Professionals only disagreed over the amount of progress Hungarian cinema had made in its path towards commercial viability.

According to Agnes Havas, managing director of Budapest-based Skyfilm Studio, the record-breaking success of Gabor Herendi's glossy comedy **A Kind of America** (*Valami Amerika*; see *IFG 2003*), which pulled 526,114 admissions in 2002, has established a new standard for Magyar producers. "It was more successful by far than any other Hungarian movie in the post-communist period," explained Havas, whose company backed *A Kind of America* (the story of a Hungarian-American who comes home and pretends to be a Hollywood mogul). "And it was successful because this movie actually introduced a new era of targeting young Hungarian audiences with subject matter they like."

Hungarian film has had to recover from numerous setbacks since the collapse of communism in 1989. Hungary's newfound market freedom allowed almost unfettered access for the major Hollywood distributors and their films, causing box-office receipts for domestic features to fall dramatically in the 1990s. Now the industry is finding its legs again. Not every professional credits *A Kind of America* alone for the evolution of Hungarian film, but even the most respected auteurs admit that change is in the air.

Skyfilm Studio

Gabor Herendi's box-office smash **A Kind of America**

investigating a crime, the 'Roma Cop' finds himself at the heart of a 'whodunnit' and a crisis of identities. Does his allegiance lie with Gypsies or Hungarians?

SORSTALANSÁG (Fateless)
[Historical drama, 2004] Script: Gyorgy Spiro, Imre Kertesz, based on Kertesz's novel. Dir: Lajos Koltai. Prod: Peter Barbalics, Magic Media.
Based on Nobel Prize-winning novel, the movie chronicles the coming of age of a teenage Jewish-Hungarian boy in a Nazi concentration camp. The title comes from the protagonist's realisation that by stealing their freedom and self-determination, the Nazis had deprived their Jewish prisoners of their individual fates.

BEING JULIA
[Drama, 2003] Script: Ronald Harwood. Dir: István Szabó. Phot: Lajos Koltai. Players: Annette Bening, Jeremy Irons, Maury Chaykin. Prod: Robert Lantos, Serendipity Point Films.
Julia Lambert is a successful British actress married to her agent, Michael. Facing middle age and fading appeal to her husband, son and audience, she begins a scandalous love affair with a much younger man. When she realises she has been manipulated by her young lover, she plans her revenge. Based on a Somerset Maugham story.

MAGYAR SZÉPSÉG
(Hungarian Beauty)
[Drama, 2002] Script: Péter Gothár, Pal Zavada. Dir: Gothár. Phot: Francisco Gazon. Players: Gabor Mate, Dorottya Udvaros, Eniko Borcsok. Prod: Jozsef Berger, Istvan Kardos, Mythberg Films/Duna Film Production.
A tale of two neighbouring families in contemporary Budapest, the movie explores changing values in post-communist Hungary. A bored, middle-aged Hungarian couple have affairs with much younger lovers. As in the film's model,

"There is more and more movement towards commercially viable products," notes director Gabor Dettre, who was scheduled to begin principal photography on his *Roma Cop* in autumn 2003. Dettre cautions that Hungary is not in a position to "go Hollywood" overnight, but says that greater commercial success and stability are inevitable. "It's automatic growth – really the same direction other film industries such as Denmark and France are moving in."

Socialist security

Ironically, Hungarian film-makers are finding independence and profits through the helping hand of the socialist-led coalition government of Prime Minister Peter Medgyessy. The Medgyessy administration channelled emergency funding into the coffers of a host of Hungarian features that were scheduled to premiere in 2003 but lacked the money for completion. What is more, during the Hungarian Film Week (the nation's annual domestic cinema festival) in February 2003, Medgyessy announced that his government would pump in $20m (Ft. 5bn) to shore up the industry by the end of the year, and introduce a new film law. He also vowed to allocate additional state support of between $7m and $9m per year until 2006.

The new film law is expected to rejuvenate the industry, and on the eve of its passage in autumn 2003 had the blessing of local professionals and Hollywood. The Americans are supporting it because legislators dropped a plan to impose a tax on ticket sales that would have been used to fund Hungarian productions. Heeding Hollywood's warning that this levy would cause box-office inflation and a drop in attendance, the bill's authors have devised new ways of bringing funds to Hungary's cash-strapped auteurs.

"There are a lot of new ideas in this bill on finding money for film production – like special state councils that will distribute money," said Peter Balint, managing director of distributors UIP Dunafilm. "But the important thing to the Hollywood industry is that there will be no taxation." Tinseltown executives will also be pleased to see sections of the bill that will reportedly make it easier and cheaper for foreign productions to shoot in Hungary.

Local flavours stay fresh

These concessions to commercial viability have not caused Magyar cinema to lose its personality or flavour. The 35 features screened at the 2003 Film Week highlighted the unique vision of Hungarian auteurs. The only fest entry that paid lip service to Hollywood was Péter Gothár's **Hungarian Beauty** (*Magyar Szépség*). It explored the lives, stresses and loves of two modern Magyar families and was Gothar's bid to translate the cinematic language of Sam

Mendes' *American Beauty* into Hungarian. It earned him the top award at the festival.

Gothár was the only veteran to be honoured at the fest. The jury and audiences ignored the works of mature masters like Miklós Jancsó and Károly Makk and threw enthusiastic support behind new and unknown film-makers like Benedek Fliegauf, whose experimental low-budget **Forest** (*Rengeteg*) won the Gene Moskowitz Prize awarded by foreign critics. Fliegauf has since won audiences at home and festival awards abroad for this innovative depiction of the lives of young Hungarians.

Even Herendi, after *A Kind of America* made him the Magyar equivalent of Steven Spielberg, is determined to tell uniquely Hungarian stories. In his forthcoming *Hungarian Vagabond* (*Magyar Vandor*), which completed principal photography in late August 2003, Herendi is creating Hungary's answer to *Monty Python and the Holy Grail,* with a time-travelling historical comedy. The historical references make the film tailor-made for a home audience, but producers Skyfilm Studio will hope that the zany slapstick will also play well with foreign audiences, following the precedent set by *A Kind of America,* which was released in the US.

Location shooting for Gabor Herendi's **Hungarian Vagabond**

JOHN NADLER has been writing for *Variety* from eastern Europe since the mid-1990s. He is also Balkan correspondent for Canada's CanWest Newspapers and the author of *Searching for Sofia: A Tale of Obsession, Murder, and War* (Doubleday Canada, 2003).

Quote of the Year

"I'm always encouraging my staff to take chances. I'd rather they try new things and fail than get complacent."

V. J. MURRAY, *co-owner of the Budapest-based UCICE cinema chain, which operates 103 screens in Hungary, the Czech Republic and Slovakia.*

American Beauty, the plot revolves around the murder of the protagonist.

RENGETEG (Forest)
[Drama, 2002] Script: Benedek Fliegauf, Judit Sos. Dir: Fliegauf. Phot: Zoltan Lovasi. Players: Rita Braun, Barbara Csonka, Edit Lipcsei, Katalin Meszaros, Ilka Sos, Barbara Thurzo. Prod: Andras Muhi, Inforg Studio.
This atmospheric depiction of a group of young Hungarians quickly became a favourite on the festival circuit and was selected as Hungary's nominee for the Academy Award for Best Foreign Film. An experimental movie shot in close-ups and made up of seven vignettes beginning and ending with a seemingly commonplace but terrifying event. The cast are amateurs.

34th Hungarian Film Week Awards (2003)

Main Prize: *Hungarian Beauty* (Péter Gothár).
Best First Film: *Happy Birthday* (Csaba Fazekas).
Simo Sandor Best First Film Prize: *Forest* (Benedek Fliegauf).
Best Visual Expression: *Dancing Figure* (Ferenc Grunwalsky).
Best Director of Photography: Tamas Sas (*Happy Birthday*).
Best Screenplay: *Rose's Song* (Andor Szilagyi).
Best Young Screenplay: *Bro* (Zsombor Dyga and Balazs Lovas).
Best Producer: Andras Muhi (*Forest* and *Libiomfi*); Gyorgy Budai (*A Bus Came* and *Libiomfi*).
Best Actor: Zoltan Mucsi (*Libiomfi*).
Best Actress: Eszter Onodi (*Happy Birthday*).
Best Supporting Actor: Lajos Kovacs (*Fool's Song* and *Rinaldo*).
Main Prize for Short and Experimental Films: *The Rubberman (*Karoly Ujj Meszaros*).*
Best Documentary: *The End of the Road (*Tamas Almasi*).*

Iceland Olafur H. Torfason

The Year's Best Films

Olafur H. Torfason's
selection:

Noi the Albino
(Dir: Dagur Kári Pétursson)
The Sea
(Dir: Baltasar Kormákur)
A Man Like Me
(Dir: Róbert I. Douglas)
Pohossibilities (Docu. Dir:
Ari Alexander Ergis
Magnússon)
Pam, Noi and their Men
(Docu. Dir: Ásthildur
Kjartansdóttir)

Recent and Forthcoming Films

OPINBERUN HANNESAR
(The Revelation of Hannes)
*[Drama, 2003] Script and Dir:
Hrafn Gunnlaugsson. Players:
Vidar Víkingsson, Helga Braga
Jónsdóttir, Jóhanna Vigdís
Arnardóttir. Prod: F.I.L.M.*

Hrafn Gunnlaugsson, director of
The Revelation of Hannes

VEDMALID (The Wager)
*[Comedy, 2003] Script and Dir:
Sigurbjörn Adalsteinsson (aka
Sigur-Björn). Phot: Arnar Thor
Thorisson. Players: Kristine
Alexandria, Chris Devlin, Burt
Young, Priscilla Lee Taylor,
Dennis Maynard, Dian Bachar,
Ryan McTavish. Prod: Prophecy
Pictures LLC/Icelandic Film
Corporation.*

O n January 1, 2003 the tasks previously managed by the Icelandic Film Fund were taken over by the Icelandic Film Centre (IFC) and the National Film Archive, and IFC director Laufey Gudjónsdóttir took over from Thorfinnur Ómarsson, the Fund's director since 1996; Thorarinn Gudnason was appointed director of the archive. The structural reforms were intended to make IFC operate as efficiently as possible in handling applications and allocation of funds for the development, production, promotion and/or distribution of Icelandic films.

The average annual film production in Iceland remains at five fiction features and the trend of tackling rural rather than urban stories continues, with three films set in fishing communities. Baltasar Kormákur's **The Sea** (*Hafid*), a family drama set in a fishing village, enjoyed spectacular success despite its dark tones in juxtaposing the different views and values of the generations. The ageing entrepreneur, working for the common people's sake, seems tyrannical to his family when it comes to administering his fishing quota. *The Sea* stayed on top of the box-office chart for weeks and received wider international distribution than any other Icelandic film in history. It received eight EDDA awards (the Icelandic Oscars), was Iceland's entry for the Academy Awards and won the FIPRESCI prize at Istanbul.

Hélène de Fougerolles and Hilmir Snaer Gudnason in **The Sea**

Noi the Albino (*Nói albínói*), feature film debut of Dagur Kári Pétursson, instantly became a festival hit (numerous prizes and more than 30 invitations), earning rave reviews and several international distribution deals. Nói, the 17-year-old hero, dreams of escaping an isolated fishing village with a girl, but most of his enterprises fail. This warm winter picture appealed to audiences, juries and critics alike, winning more than 10 awards, including three at Gothenburg and five at the Angers European First Film. American director Bradley Rust Gray's **Salt** took the Caligari Prize at Berlin for its tale of two sisters who have spent their lives in a remote fishing town but want to move to Reykjavik.

To China with love

Fridrik Thór Fridriksson had limited success at home with *Falcons* (*Fálkar*; see *IFG 2003*), but it was well received abroad. In Róbert I. Douglas' **A Man Like Me** (*Madur eins og ég*), a shy Reykjavík postal worker falls in love with a Chinese waitress at a local restaurant and secretly follows her all the way to China. Encouraged by his colourful friends and relatives, he seems at last to break out of his reclusive existence.

French-Icelandic director Sólveig Anspach's **Stormy Weather**, premiered in Un Certain Regard at Cannes 2003, explores the deep relationship between two women, a non-speaking mental patient (Didda Jónsdóttir) and her doctor (Elodie Bouchez), in France. When the patient's identity is revealed she is sent to her home country, Iceland, but the doctor follows her to finish the treatment. A considerable part of *Stormy Weather* was filmed in Anspach's birthplace, the Vestmannaeyjar islands.

Baltasar Kormákur, Didda Jónsdóttir and Elodie Bouchez in **Stormy Weather**

Gudny Halldorsdóttir's **Stella Runs for Parliament** (*Stella í frambodi*) is a deeply satirical comedy, the sequel to the 1986 hit *The Icelandic Shock Station* (*Stella í orlofi*), which Halldorsdóttir wrote. Stella accidentally floats from her image-building consulting company into politics, and meets a bunch of weird males who need assistance. **No Such Thing** (aka *Monster*) by Hal Hartley, produced and shot in Iceland and New York City, showed an American journalist tracing her fiancé in Iceland and encountering a strange creature. It had little success at the box-office and no mercy from reviewers.

KALDALJÓS (Cold Light)
[Drama, 2003] Script: Freyr Thormodsson, Hilmar Oddsson. Dir: Oddsson. Phot: Sigurdur Sverrir Pálsson. Players: Ingvar Sigurdsson, Kristbjörg Kjeld. Prod: Icelandic Film Corporation.

1.0 (One Point O)
[Thriller, 2003] Script and Dir: Jeff Renfroe, Marteinn Thorisson. Phot: Christopher Soos. Players: Jeremy Sisto, Deborah Unger, Lance Henriksen, Udo Kier. Prod: Armada Pictures/VIP Medienfonds 2 Filmgeschäftsführung GmbH.

Fridrik Thor Fridriksson, director of **Niceland**

NÆSLAND (Niceland)
[Drama, 2004] Script: Huldar Breidfjord. Dir: Fridrik Thor Fridriksson. Phot: Morten Søborg. Players: Gary Lewis, Martin Compston, Peter Capaldi, Carrie Fox. Prod: Zik Zak Filmworks/ Nimbus Film (Denmark)/Tradewind Pictures (Germany)/Film & Music Entertainment (UK).

Í TAKT VID TÍMANN
(Keeping up with the Times)
[Comedy, 2004] Script: Águst Gudmundsson and players. Dir: Gudmundsson. Players: Eggert Thorleifsson, Egill Ólafsson, Jakob F. Magnússon, Ragnhildur Gísladóttir, Tómas R. Tómasson. Prod: Ísfilm.

STRAKARNIR OKKAR
(Eleven Men)
[Comedy, 2004] Script: Jón Atli Jónasson, Róbert I. Douglas. Dir: Douglas. Prod: Icelandic Film Company/Solarfilms Inc. (Finland)/Borealis Production AS (Norway)/Film & Music Entertainment (UK).

ÓVINAFAGNADUR
[a.k.a. **THORDUR KAKALI**]
(A Gathering of Foes)
[Drama, forthcoming] Script:
Einar Kárason. Dir: Fridrik Thór
Fridriksson. Prod: Icelandic Film
Corporation.

Oskar Jónasson, director of
The Silent Magician

SKARI SKRÍPÓ
(The Silent Magician)
[Comedy, 2004] Dir: Oskar
Jónasson. Prod: Icelandic Film
Corporation.

DÍS (Goddess)
[Comedy, 2004] Script and Dir:
Silja Hauksdóttir. Prod: Sögn ehf.

NÓI ALBÍNÓI (Noi the Albino)
[Drama, 2002] Script and Dir:
Dagur Kári Pétursson. Phot:
Rasmus Videbaek. Players:
Tómas Lemarquis, Thröstur Leó
Gunnarsson, Elín Hansdóttir.
Prod: Zik Zak Filmworks, in co-
operation with M&M
Productions (Denmark), The
Coproduction Office (Germany)
and The Bureau (UK).

MADUR EINS OG ÉG
(A Man Like Me)
[Comedy, 2002] Script and Dir:
Róbert I. Douglas. Phot: Pawel
Gula. Players: Jón Gnarr,
Stephanie Che (Yuen Yuen).
Prod: Icelandic Film Company.

HAFID (The Sea)
[Drama, 2002] Script: Baltasar
Kormákur and Olafur Haukur
Símonarson. Dir: Kormákur.
Phot: Jean-Louis Vialard.
Players: Gunnar Eyjólfsson,
Kristbjörg Kjeld, Hilmir Snaer
Gudnason. Prod: Blue Eyes
Productions, in co-operation
with Emotion Pictures (France)
and Filmhuset (Norway).

Among the small-budget digital features were Eiríkur Hauksson's **1st of April** (*Fyrsti apríll*), in which a prank has grave consequences, **U.S.S.S.** by Eiríkur Leifsson, a blood-stained, puerile copy-cat action film introducing a number of young actors and musicians, and **Didda and the Dead Cat** (*Didda og daudi kötturinn*), a family movie by Helgi Sverrisson and Kristlaug Sigurdardóttir, about a 9-year-old who acquires super-sight after a bath in cod-liver oil.

In the eye of the beholder

More and more documentaries are being screened in cinemas. At the EDDA ceremony, Best Documentary went to the controversial **In the Shoes of the Dragon** (*Í skóm drekans*) by Olafur Sveinsson and Hrönn Sveinsdóttir, about the latter's participation in a Miss Iceland contest. Its public screenings were only permitted after the faces of judge Claudia Schiffer and several contestants were blurred. Ólafur Sveinsson took the esteemed Culture prize of the Reykjavík daily newspaper DV for his documentary **Hlemmur,** about the daily life of a group of misfits.

Hrafnhildur Gunnarsdóttir and Thorvaldur Kristinsson's **Straight Out – Stories from Iceland** (*Hrein og bein*) used interviews with young gay people describing their experiences of coming out. It shared the Stu and Dave's Excellent Documentary Award at the San Francisco International Lesbian and Gay Film Festival. Other festival successes included Ágúst Gudmundsson's *Seagulls' Laughter* (*Mávahlátur*), which took Ecumenical Prize at the Nordic Film Days in Lübeck, Germany. Its teenage star, Ugla Egilsdóttir, was named Best Actress at Karlovy Vary. Róbert I. Douglas' *The Icelandic Dream* (*Íslenski draumurinn*) was Best Film at Black Point, Wisconsin. Best Short Film at the EDDAs was *The Little, Ugly Caterpillar* (*Litla lirfan ljóta*), Iceland's first computer-generated animation.

Among forthcoming attractions, *The Revelation of Hannes* (*Opinberun Hannesar*) is written and directed by veteran film-maker Hrafn Gunnlaugsson from a short story by Iceland's Prime Minister, Davíd Oddsson. When his office computer, containing supposedly top-secret material, is stolen, Hannes, a lifetime clerk at the State Investigations department, tries to solve the case himself but becomes the main suspect.

British actors Gary Lewis and Martin Compston star in Fridrik Thór Fridriksson's English-language *Niceland* (*Næsland*), set in Iceland and Germany. A happy couple in their early twenties find their lives turned upside down when their cat goes missing. Ágúst Gudmundsson's comedy *Í takt vid tímann* (with the working English title of *Keeping up with the Times*) is a sequel to his *On Top* (*Med allt á hreinu*), the 1982 comedy usually regarded as Iceland's most popular film ever. In the new film, pop group Studmenn hit the road again.

Cold Light (*Kaldaljós*), written and directed by Hilmar Oddsson, is based on a bestselling novel by Vigdis Grimsdóttir, one of Iceland's most popular writers. Filmed in Seydisfjördur, deep in the eastern fjords, it describes the difficult experiences of a guilt-ridden character as a boy and as a man. Billed as "Iceland's first Hollywood movie", *The Wager* (*Vedmálid*) is a romantic comedy shot in Hollywood about a young producer who bets a colleague that he can make a movie in three days, release it in a month and make a fortune. Cue lots of frenetic action.

Goddess (*Dís*) is the debut feature of Silja Hauksdóttir, based on the best-selling book that she co-wrote with Birna Anna Björnsdóttir and Oddny Sturludóttir. It's set in 2000 and describes the millennial atmosphere through the experiences of Dís, who, in her early twenties, suffers, like so many of her generation, from having too many options. Finally, Róbert I. Douglas' *Eleven Men* (*Stákarnir okkar*) follows an all-gay soccer team from an amateur league as they take on big professional sides.

OLAFUR H. TORFASON (b. 1947) studied film in Copenhagen. Since 1987 he has been film critic for the Icelandic National Broadcasting Service and is on the editorial board of the film magazine *Land & synir*.

STELLA Í FRAMBODI
(Stella Runs for Parliament)
[Comedy, 2002] Script and Dir: Gudny Halldorsdóttir. Phot: Hálfdán Theodórsson. Players: Edda Björgvinsdóttir, Thorhallur Sigurdsson, Gisli Runar Jonsson. Prod: Umbi.

STORMY WEATHER
[Drama, 2003] Script: Roger Bohbot and Solveig Anspach. Dir: Anspach. Phot: Benoît Dervaux. Players: Elodie Bouchez, Sigurlaug Jónsdóttir, Baltasar Kormákur, Ingvar E. Sigurdsson, Christophe Sermet, Natan Cogan. Prod: Ex Nihilo/Les Films du Fleuve/

Sögn/Blueeyes Productions.

SALT (Salt)
[Drama, 2003] Script and Dir: Bradley Rust Gray. Phot: Anne Misawa. Players: Brynja Gudnadóttir, Davíd Örn Halldórsson, Melkorka Huldudóttir. Prod: Soandbrad/Cut&Paste.

U.S.S.S.
[Action, 2003] Script and Dir: Eiríkur Leifsson. Players: Davíd Gudbrandsson, Jón Marinó, Sirry Jónsdóttir, Felix Eyjólfsson, Thorsteinn Vidarsson, Baldur Bragason. Prod: Hugvargur/Púra.

FYRSTI APRÍLL (1st of April)
[Drama, 2003] Script and Dir: Eiríkur Hauksson. Prod: Hauksson/Icelandic Film Corporation.

Quotes of the Year

"Soccer is the ultimate art form and nothing else comes close to it. Soccer is so beautiful, so cruel, so poetic."
JÓN ATLI JÓNASSON, *writer of football comedy* Eleven Men.

"This begging for money abroad also implies that you have to chisel out your films in the form of an obnoxious European mediocrity."
MARGRÉT RÚN GUDMUNDSDÓTTIR, *director, on a problem facing the Icelandic industry.*

India Uma da Cunha

The Year's Best Films

Uma da Cunha's selection:

A Passion Play
(Dir: Rituparno Ghosh)

A Nation Without Women
(Dir: Manish Jha)

Raghu Romeo
(Dir: Rajat Kapoor)

Tale of a Naughty Girl
(Dir: Buddhadeb Das Gupta)

Mr and Mrs Iyer
(Dir: Aparna Sen)

Recent and Forthcoming Films

CHOKHER BALI
(A Passion Play)
[Bengali. Period drama, 2003]
Script: Rituparno Ghosh, based
on a novel by Rabindranath
Tagore. Dir: Ghosh. Phot: Abhik
Mukhopadhyay. Players:
Aishwarya Rai, Prosenjit
Chattopadhyay, Tota
Roychowdhury, Raima Sen.
Prod: Shree Venkatesh Films.
Set between 1902 and 1905,
when the partition of Bengal was
a serious threat. A beautiful
small-town woman, rejected as a
bride by two urbane bachelor
friends, reappears in their lives a
year later as an embittered
widow and creates a vortex of
conflicting passions.

Amol Palekar's **Eternity**

ANAAHAT (Eternity)
[Marathi. Period drama, 2002]
Script: Dr Sameer Kulkarni,

The gulf between the markets for Indian films at home and abroad continues to widen. Domestic revenues seem to shrink by the week. But the UK and US yield profits from the cross-continental applause for what is termed "Bollywood"; the Indian diaspora makes the cash registers ring.

Last year was a time of serious reckoning. The number of new feature films actually fell. Producers lost at least $60m on their big-budget star vehicles in 2002, and distributors, exhibitors and the music industry lost perhaps twice as much. A staggering 95% of the new releases bombed and only two created a ripple, the low-budget *Raaz* and the big-budget *Devdas*. The reasons? Outdated film formulas, limp scripts, the sagging popularity of once mega-stars, and above all, a cinema-savvy public exposed to home and world cinema through television and video.

Television has been taking its toll, piracy is still rampant, foreign imports (no longer to be aped) set new and more expensive production standards. Old-time movie despots suddenly found they were no longer arbiters of taste and had only a superficial understanding of their markets. Stories needed to quicken the rhythms of the heart, they discovered, not just set feet a-tapping. It was a bad season.

All is not, of course, lost. The export market is a sun rising in the west. The Indian market is still largely impervious to Hollywood's global dominance. The Indian government is taking the industry seriously. English-language films, made in India or abroad by Indian expatriates, enjoyed a boom, propelled by audience acceptance of the so-called cross-over film. Big-banner and small independent producers came out with a spate of "Indian-English" pictures reflecting the life and preoccupations of Indian society, including Subhash Ghai's *Jogger's Park,* Mahesh Manjrekar's *It Rained One Night,* Mahesh Dattani's *Morning Raga,* Pamela Rooks' *Dance Like a Man* and Kaizad Gustad's *Boom!.* Younger film-makers, headier and hardier than their elders, are joining the fray, V. K. Prasad's *Freaky Chakra* and debuts such as Prakash Belawadi's sombre *Stumble* and Sujoy Ghosh's peppy *Jhankar Beats* securing modest releases.

Indians living abroad, with film-school training and film scripts in hand,

Arif, left, and Shohana, centre, play dancers in **Dance Like a Man**

look homewards as co-production alliances increase. Chicago's Satish Menon shot his Malayalam film *Bhawam* (based on *A Streetcar Named Desire*) in India and won Kerala's top awards. Manish Jha's debut, **Mathrabhoomi** (*A Nation Without Women*), a French co-production, appeared in Venice's Critics' Week. The $40m **The Invaders**, to be directed by Roland Joffe, is on the cards. So are *Marigold,* to be produced by US-based Siddharth Jain of Hyperion Films, and *Opium Royale,* from Emmanuel Pappas' Kundalini Pictures, which aims to be an erotically charged comedy of manners, directed by Digvijay Singh and Naman Ramachandran. *One-Dollar Curry* is being co-produced by India's ZEE TV network, with France TV and Silhouette Films.

The world is watching

Many countries showed their appreciation of Indian cinema. *Time* magazine rated Bhansali's *Devdas* fourth among its ten "Best of the World" films and placed Mira Nair's *Monsoon Wedding* fifth of 10 "Best of Cinema from the West". France made Kerala's Adoor Gopalakrishnan a Commander of the Order of Arts and Letters, the second Indian after Satyajit Ray to be so honoured. His latest film, the Indo-French *Shadow Kill* (*Nizalkuthu*), had a mid-2003 release in Paris. Naseeruddin Shah played a lead role alongside Sean Connery in *The League of Extraordinary Gentleman*. The Indian hit, *Chalte, Chalte,* reached number seven in the UK's box-office chart.

Mira Nair and Deepa Mehta turned to literature, shooting *Vanity Fair* and *The Republic of Love,* respectively, in London. Also there, Gurinder Chadha started shooting her Indianised *Pride and Prejudice,* casting India's top star Aishwaria Rai as its heroine. Some Indians moved themes and shoots abroad. Mahesh Manjrekar set his **It Rained That Night** (a re-make of a Hindi film which underlined double standards on infidelity) in New York state. Rajiv Rai shot his big-budget **Asambhav** almost entirely in Switzerland's Ticino area.

Sandhya Gokhle. Dir: Amol Palekar. Phot: Debu Deodhar. Players: Anant Nag, Deepti Naval, Sonali Bendre, Pradeep Welankar, Shrirang Godbole, Dr Vilas Ujavne. Prod: Rohit Sharma, Amol Palakar, Sarth (India)/Mimesis (US).
Drama, set in the 1500s, about a woman's sexual desire, controlled on male terms, especially so in a royal family which demands a heir.

RAGHU ROMEO
[Hindi. Comedy, 2003] Script and Dir: Rajat Kapoor. Phot: Rafey Mahmood. Players: Vijay Raaz, Saurabh Shukhla, Maria Goretti, Sasa Siddiqui. Prod: Cyberspace/NFDC.
Raghu, a waiter at a cheap dance joint, escapes his unbearably exploited daily life in television, and begins to believe in the real-life existence of TV soap-opera queen Neeta. In the process, he almost loses his real-life love, dancer Sweety, who in turn is lusted after by an inept gunman.

ABAR ARANYE
(A Journey to the Forest Again)
[Bengali. Social drama, 2003] Script, Dir and Phot: Goutam Ghosh. Players: Soumitra Chatterjee, Sharmila Tagore, Subhendu Chatterjee, Samit Bhana, Gulshan Ara Champa, Rupa Ganguly, Tabu. Prod: Rainbow T Sarkar Combine.
Ghosh made a documentary on Satyajit Ray when he was filming *Aranyer Din Ratri/Days and Nights in the Forest* (1969) and now takes the characters from that film and sees how life has treated them almost 30 years on.

FAIR IS FOUL
[Hindi. Social drama, 2003] Script: Abbas Tyrewala, Vishal Bharadwaj. Dir: Bharadwaj. Phot: Hemant Chaturvedi. Players: Irfan Khan, Tabu, Naseeruddin Shah, Om Puri, Pankaj Kapoor. Prod: Kaleidoscope Entertainment Pvt Ltd.
Shakespeare's *Macbeth*

transported to the underworld of today's Mumbai, where a gang is led by Abbaji, an ageing don revered by his followers. His young mistress Nimmi desires his second-in-command, Maqbool, and uses him to get rid of Abbaji.

MATRABHOOMI
(A Nation Without Women)
[Hindi. Social drama, 2003]
Script and Dir: Manish Jha.
Phot: Venu Gopal. Players:
Sushant Singh, Tulip Joshi,
Sudheer Pandey, Mukesh Bhatt,
Aditya Srivastava, Piyush
Mishra. Prod: Star Management
Group (India)/Ex-Nihilo
(France).
In a village now devoid of women because of infanticide against girls, a frustrated father and his five sons exult when a young bride appears, exploiting her with a chilling violence.

MORNING RAGA
(Music of the Seasons)
[Indian English. Social drama,
2003] Script and Dir: Mahesh
Dattani. Phot: Rajiv Menon.
Players: Shabana Azmi, Lillette
Dubey, Perizad Zerobian, Prakash
Rao. Prod: K. Raghavendra Rao
for RK Teleshow.
After the accidental death of two village women, the tragedy inextricably links three people who bond and cope through the uniting force of music.

DEVI AHILYA BAI
[Hindi. Period biography, 2002]
Script: Shama Zaidi, Nachiket.
Dir: Nachiket and Jayoo. Phot:
Navroze Contractor. Players:
Mallika Prasad, Sadaashiv
Amrapurkar, Bharti Jaffrey,
Shabana Azmi, Ganesh Yadav.
Prod: NFDC.
The sixteenth century. The story of Ahilya, whose father-in-law (the head of state) refuses to submit her to the prevailing practice that requires a widow to commit suicide by throwing herself on her husband's funeral pyre. Instead he grooms her to become the unique ruler enshrined today in temples.

Seasons of Indian films are becoming common annual events in cities outside India. Christina Marouda in early 2003 launched the Los Angeles Indian Film Festival. Two years earlier, Luca Marziali had started his successful "River to River" event in Florence, held in December. Buddhadeb Das Gupta, in Karlovy Vary, and Girish Karnad, in Locarno, were on prestigious international juries.

Regional loyalties

The regional Indian film, reflecting variegation within a certain Indian-ness, has been pushed firmly to the sidelines by the starry glow of the international bandwagon. But diehard believers hold the flag aloft. From Bengal, Rituparno Ghosh's eagerly awaited *Chokher Bali* competed at Locarno 2003. Shyam Benegal has been making *Netaji – The Last Hero,* a big-budget epic on Bengal's charismatic freedom fighter Subhash Chandra Bose. Goutam Ghosh's intriguing *A Journey to the Forest Again* (*Abar aranye*), taking a Satyajit Ray film forward in time, is ready. Govind Nihalani is busy with the shoot of his first star-studded film, *Dev,* and Amol Palekar has completed his period film *Anahat,* shot in the temple city of Hampi.

Shyam Benegal's historical epic **Netaji – The Last Hero**

To return to the state of the film industry, which accounts for 24% of India's entertainment business. It grew by a meagre 6.4% in 2002. Film production fell by a whopping 70 films (943, down from 1013). That number contracts further when it contains 140 films dubbed from one language to another, of which 40 were US/UK imports. *Spider-Man* in Hindi did better than most local films, as did *xXx, Men in Black II, Stuart Little II* and *Bend it Like Beckham.* Hindi films (representing 60% of total box-office) led with 218, followed by the four South Indian languages: Tamil (178), Kannada (113), Telugu (107) and Malayalam (101). Bengal followed next with 47, Marathi (20), Assamese (17), Gujarati (15), Chatisgarhi (14), English (12). There were 290 imported films, almost 50 more than in 2001.

"Let's be professional"

India's never-say-die film community faced its sinking fortunes with customary resilience. To cater to the affluent diaspora market of twenty million homesick fans, producers are learning that they must show greater accountability and upgrade their image and operations. Lack of transparency and piracy have been major problems for film financing backed by reliable sources. In 2001, the Indian government had conferred industry status upon Bollywood, making it eligible for bank financing, and the state-run Industrial Development Bank of India allocated a sizeable amount to film production in 2001-02, spread over seven projects floated by the likes of Crest Communication, Padmini Telemedia, VR Projects and D Rama Naidu.

Seeing the benefits of corporatisation, Mukta Arts Limited, the film production company promoted by producer-director Subhash Ghai, raised public money through an IPO in 2000-01. Pritish Nandy Communications Limited and Padmalaya Telefilms Limited also raised capital from the public to venture into film production. Zee Telefilms, which had previously produced small TV movies, made its foray into cinematic feature film production with *Gadar Ek Prem Katha,* one of the biggest blockbusters of 2001.

US majors expanded their activity and range, starting to distribute Indian films as well as their own imports. Columbia Tristar took the lead by releasing seven films in 2002, including Bollywood's *Pyaar Mein Kabhie Kabhie, 16 December* and *Agnivarsha,* and Fox and Warners have followed suit. The impact of Bollywood has been strong enough for the government to declare the entertainment industry a high-priority growth area. In 2002, the top brass from the Information and Broadcasting Ministry joined film industry leaders in delegations to Cannes, London, Los Angeles, Tokyo and Berne to woo co-production investors.

Ironically, after withstanding the horrors of 2002, it was a horror film that revived the shaken industry. In early 2003, Ram Gopal Verma's **Ghost** (*Bhoot*), which sought to frighten the wits out of its audience using special effects (minus song and dance), was a major hit. In typical, naïve imitation, a dozen horror films were immediately greenlit. Alongside Verma, young actress-turned-producer Pooja Bhatt is another beacon. As producer, her big success, **Jism,** oozed sex and sizzle, and she is following up with her directing debut, *Paap – Through Sin She Found Love.*

UMA DA CUNHA heads Medius (India) Services, which provides casting, promotional and executive services for films shot in India. She edits *Film India Worldwide* magazine and is a film researcher on Indian cinema and a consultant and programmer for festivals.

NETAJI – THE LAST HERO
[Hindi/English. Biographical drama, 2003). Script and Dir: Shyam Benegal. Phot: Rajan Kotari. Players: Sachin Khadekar, Partap Sharma, Yashwant Sinha, Jishu Sengupta, Divya Dutta. Prod: Sahara India Ltd.
The life of Bengali freedom fighter Netaji Subhash Chandra Bose, an ardent nationalist who opposed non-violent resistance, raised an Indian National Army and set a government in exile against the British.

DEV (*literally,* God)
[Hindi. Comedy-drama, 2002] Script: Meenakshi Sharma. Dir and Phot: Govind Nihalani. Players: Amitabh Bachchan, Om Puri, Kareena Kapoor, Fardeen Khan, Amrish Puri, Rati Agnihotri. Prod: Entertainment One/Applause Entertainment, in association with Udbhav Dreamzone.
Hard choices confront the officers in the higher echelons of the Indian police force.

ARIMPARA
(A Story That Begins at the End)
[Malayalam. Social drama, 2002] Script: Murali Nair and Madhu Aspara, based on O. V. Vijayan's story "The Wart". Dir: Nair. Phot: M J Radhakrishnan. Players: Nedumudi Venu, Sona Nair, Bhagyanath, Rajan Sithara, Bharatan Narakkal. Prod: NFDC (India)/ NHK (Japan)/ Murali Nair Productions.
In remote Kerala, a happy family of three headed by a farmer sees their lives ruined because of a monstrous wart that grows on the patriarch's chin.

MEENAXI – A TALE OF THREE CITIES
[Hindi. Social musical, 2002] Script: Faiza Husain, Owais Husain. Dir: Owais Husain, M. F. Husain. Phot: Santosh Sivan. Players: Tabu, Raghuvir Yadav, Nadira Babbar, Kunnal Kapoor. Prod: Culture of the Street Films.
The film delves into the limitless world of creative endeavour and

its vicissitudes.

1:1.6, AN ODE TO LOST LOVE
[Hindi. Social drama, 2002]
Script, Dir and Phot: Madhu
Ambat. Players: Atul Kulkarni,
Gulshan Grover, Mausumi,
Sonali Kularni, Rati Agnihotri.
Prod: NFDC.
A cinematographer meets actress
Sushmita (who reminds him of
his lost love) and her mother.
He embarks on his directorial
debut with a film that analyses
the creative process and is
tragically reinforced by real
events during filming

AALO (Light of Hope)
[Bengali. Drama, 2002] Script
and Dir: Tarun Mazumdar. Phot:
Shakti Bandhopadhya. Players:
Rituparna Sengupta, Abhishek
Chatterjee, Kunal Mitra, Soumili
Biswas, Bhaswar Chatterjee.
Prod: PRISM Entertainment.
Rural Bengal, 1950s. A beautiful,
urban young woman tries to
improve the lives of poor,
illiterate women.

HAVA ANYE DE
(Let the Wind Blow)
[Hindi. Social drama, 2003]
Script and Dir: Partho Sengupta.
Phot: Jean-Marc Ferrière.
Players: Anikhet Vishwasrao,
Nishikant Kamat, Tanishtha
Chatterjee. Prod: Mystique
Media Ltd (India)/Santocha
Productions (France), with Fonds
Sud of the French Foreign
Ministry.
A cynical Indian youth's reaction
to the growing tensions with
Pakistan lead to nuclear war
between the two countries.

BHAVAM (Emotions of Being)
[Malayalam. Social drama, 2002]
Script and Dir: Satish Menon.
Phot: Sunny Joseph. Players:
Mita Vashisht, Murali Menon,
Jyotismayee Siddique. Prod:
Satish Menon/Visual
Possibility/Kerala State Film
Development Corp.
A disillusioned journalist and his
wife, a college lecturer numbed
by her listless students, feel
stifled by economic and political

Nana Patekar, left, and Ajay Devgan in horror hit **Ghost**

opportunism. Their circumstances
worsen when her mysterious
sister pays a surprise visit.

Tigmanshu Dhulia's **To Achieve**

HAASIL (To Achieve)
[Hindi. Political thriller, 2003]
Script and Dir: Tigmanshu
Dhulia. Phot: Rafey Mehmood.
Players: Jimmy Shergill, Hrishitaa
Bhatt, Irfan Khan, Ashutosh
Rana. Prod: Karma Network.
In a politically driven, crime-
ridden, traditional university
town, two students fall in
love and are torn apart by
a benefactor who turns out
to be a traitor.

DUBAI RETURN
[Hindi. Black comedy, 2003]
Script: Vinay Chaudhry, Rajesh
Devraj, Ravi Deshpande, Aditya
Bhattacharya. Dir: Bhattacharya.
Phot: Sanjay Kapoor. Players:
Irfan Khan, Vijay Maurya, Razak
Khan, Divya Dutta, Ritu
Shivpuri. Prod: Destiny
Pictures/Aditya Bhattacharya.

The story of Aftab Angrez,
the most celebrated killer in
Mumbai, who actually hadn't
bumped off anyone.

MADNESS IN THE DESERT
[Documentary, 2003] Script and
Dir: Satyajit Bhatkal. Phot: Bimal
Biswas, Prakash Bhat, Madhu N.,
Satyajit Bhatkal. Featuring: the
cast and crew of Lagaan. Prod:
Aamir Khan Prods.
The making of box-office hit
Lagaan: four turbulent years in
the life of its director, Ashutosh
Gowariker, star-producer Aamir
Khan and their team.

Quotes of the Year
"Film-makers here don't
know how to use me.
I don't fall into any premeditated categories.
I find myself chronically
incapable of playing larger-
than-life characters."
NASEERUDDIN SHAH, *actor.*

"The light is very beautiful
here. There are some
amazing locations. Yet there
is nothing to give away that I
am shooting [outside India]."
SAMEER KARNIK, *director,
while filming his debut,*
Why Did We Fall in Love?,
in Scotland.

Iran Jamal Omid

Recent and Forthcoming Films

A LIGHT BURNS HERE
[Religious drama, 2003] Script, Dir and Prod: Reza Mirkarimi. Phot: Hamid Khozouie Abyane. Players: Habib Rezayi, Saeed Poursamimi, Allah-Qoli Nazari.
The custodian of a village shrine seeks a substitute when he has to go to a nearby town for medical treatment. But the villagers, who have lost faith, offer no help and finally he enlists his mentally retarded nephew.

ONE FLEW OVER THE CUCKOO'S NEST
[Social drama, 2003] Script and Dir: Ahmad Reza Motamedi. Phot: Mohammad Aladpoush. Players: Ezzatollah Entezami, Ali Nasirian, Parviz Parastouyi, Niki Karimi. Prod: Mohammad Reza Takhtkeshiyan.
Mostofi forces his step-niece to divorce her husband, then tries to bring one of his friends into the story.

Mioyagi Ya in **Carpet of the Wind**

CARPET OF THE WIND
[Drama, 2003] Script: Mohammad Soleymani. Dir: Kamal Tabrizi. Phot: Hassan Pouya. Players: Reza Kianian, Takaeki Inuki, Mioyagi Yu, Fariba Kamran. Prod: Ali Reza Shojanoori.

The economic crisis that has been plaguing film-making in Iran for the past few years still persists, and cinema attendance in 2002 fell to 20 million (the annual figure was once 80 million). At a time when relatively easy access to more than 400 television stations has helped reduce per capita involvement in movie going and other communal cultural events to 20 minutes per year, government officials have acknowledged that drastic action is required to promote the moviegoing habit, upgrade the hopelessly outdated and uncomfortable cinemas (more than 200 of Iran's 270 theatres urgently need attention) and produce more entertaining films.

One of the first measures, the introduction of half-price tickets for some weekday screenings, failed to boost attendance. Another measure, the increase in film imports, to offer audiences a greater variety of films, might arrest the spate of cinema closures, because provincial theatres' attempts to programme popular movies are hindered by producers, who sell Iranian films to television immediately after their first-run public screenings in Tehran. Also, video clubs offer tapes of the films several months before they go on release in the provinces.

Despite these problems, production continues at a surprisingly high level. According to figures from the Farabi Cinema Foundation, in May 2003 83 film projects were in various stages of production. Judging by the experiences of previous years, it is safe to estimate that around 60 films will be completed by 2004, of which a third will probably struggle to find theatrical distribution.

Box-office receipts for Iranian films were low, with the exception of Iraj Tahmasb's record-breaking combination of live-action and animation, **Redcap and Sarvenaz**, which grossed $677,600. Two thirds of the 40 local titles released in 2002 failed to recoup their costs, despite an increase in ticket prices. Even with 25% of production costs covered by government loans, it is hard in this difficult economic climate to explain the increase in feature production.

Makhmalbaf's Afghan trilogy

Whatever the problems at home, Iranian cinema continues to be

highly successful on the international scene. Four Iranian films were screened at Cannes in 2003, led by Samira Makhmalbaf's **At Five in the Afternoon**, which earned her the Jury Prize for the second time (following *Blackboards*) and represented her third encounter with Afghanistan. In 1988 she performed in her father Mohsen's *The Cyclist,* which depicted the plight of Afghani immigrants, and the result of her own trip to the country was *God, Construction, Demolition,* one of the episodes in the portmanteau film *11'09"01.*

At Five in the Afternoon focuses on Nogreh, an Afghan woman caught between tradition and the modern world. Wrapped in a blue burqa, she slips off to school in secret, wearing high-heeled shoes, and dreams of one day becoming president. Her father finds the irreligious "blasphemy" of post-Taliban Kabul unbearable and, when his son is reported dead in a landmine blast, he flees into the desert with Nogreh, his step-daughter and her sick baby. Makhmalbaf says that she wanted to show the reality and not the media-presented clichés of Afghanistan, and not to pass judgment on father or daughter, and in this sense *At Five...* recalls the impartiality of her first film, *The Apple.*

Mamad Haghighat's *Two Angels* was in the Critics' Week and Jafar Panahi's **Crimson Gold** took top prize in Un Certain Regard. It is based on a real-life incident and is partly an extension of his previous film, *The Circle,* which depicted the sad lot of various women. Here, Panahi focuses on men from various social groups who, like the women in *The Circle,* seem to be stuck in an unbreakable vicious circle. Hossein, a pizza delivery man, enters a high-class jewellery shop to buy a gift for his fiancée. He leaves when he meets a cold reception from the owner, who is one of the people to whom he delivers pizza. Later he returns armed with a gun and tragedy follows. In spite of certain effective and thought-provoking moments, the film lacks the overall impact of *The Circle.*

Parviz Shahbazi, already known to local viewers for the moving *Traveller from the South* and *The Whisper,* made his first international impact with **Deep Breath** in the Cannes Directors' Fortnight. It deals with the crisis facing the young generation (a favourite recent theme for Iranian film-makers), but Shahbazi approaches the subject from a different angle and creates a remarkable picture of young people in a society in transition through the story of Kamran, a melancholy student, and Mansur, his simple-hearted friend and companion. During their aimless wanderings, they meet Aida, a cheerful and lively student who can lift Mansur's spirits. The spiritual confusion of a group of well-to-do young people is conveyed through realistic and unobtrusive dialogues, a meticulous sound mix, precise editing and fine performances.

TAKE A LOOK AT THE SKY SOMETIMES
[Fantasy, 2003] Script: Farhad Towhidi. Dir: Kamal Tabrizi. Phot: Farhad Saba. Players: Reza Kianian, Atila Pesyani, Haniye Tavassoli. Prod: Mohammad Reza Takhtkeshiyan.

CRIMSON GOLD
[Social drama, 2003] Script: Abbas Kiarostami. Dir and Prod: Jafar Panahi. Phot: Hossein Jafarian. Players (non-professionals): Hossein Emadeddin, Kamyar Vaziri.

WHITE NIGHTS
[Drama, 2003] Script: Saeed Aqiqi. Dir: Farzad Motamen. Phot: Jamshid Alvandi. Players: Mahdi Ahmadi, Haniye Tavassoli, M. Shah-Ebrahimi. Prod: Hossein Zandbaf.

Mansour Shahbazi, left, and Saeed Amini in **Deep Breath**

DEEP BREATH
[Drama, 2003] Script and Dir: Parviz Shahbazi. Phot: Ali Loqmani. Players: Mansour Shahbazi, Maryam Palizban, Saeed Amini. Prod: Amir Samavati.

AT FIVE IN THE AFTERNOON
[Drama, 2003] Script and Dir: Samira Makhmalbaf, based on a story by Mohsen Makhmalbaf. Phot: Ebrahim Ghaffuri. Players: Aqeleh Rezayi, Abdol-Ati Yusofzai, Marziye Amiri. Prod: Makhmalbaf Film Productions.

LEGEND OF THE WAR-STRICKEN TOWN
[War drama, 2003] Episode One: A Small Dream. Script: Habib Ahmadzadeh. Dir: Parviz Sheikh-Tadi. Phot: Naser Mahmoud Kolaye. Players: Reza Shafiyijam,

Mehdi Faghih, Mina Jafarzadeh.
Prod [all episodes]: Saeed Saedi
(Fadak Film).
A toy shop salesman looks back
in judgement on his 80 years
of life.
Episode Two: God's Jokes.
Script: H. Ahmadzadeh,
Abdolhassan Barzideh. Dir: A.
Barzideh. Phot: M. Kolaye.
Players: Mohammad Reza
Davudnezhad, Ali Sadeghi,
Hamid Azarang.
During the siege of Abadan in the
Iran-Iraq war, a young scout
decides to send his possessions to
his family, but discovers that a
burglar has broken into his house.
Episode Three: The Third
Narration. *Script and Dir:*
Rakhshan Bani-Etemad. Phot:
Morteza Poursamadi. Players:
Gohar Kheirandish.
Leyla, whose husband left for
the war 16 years ago, meets the
mothers and husbands of
disabled war veterans.

MEETING THE PARROT
[Drama, 2003] Script and Dir:
Alireza Davudnezhad, based on a
sketch by Qodratollah Mirzayi.
Phot: Alireza Zarrindast.
Players: Mohammad Reza
Hajjar, Mahaya Petrossian,
Afarin. Prod: A. Davudnezhad,
Hassan Tavakkolnia.
A woman struggles to save her
husband's life.

BUDDHA'S MURMURS
[Drama, 2003] Script and Dir:
Hossein Qasemi Jami. Phot: Saed
Nikzat. Players: Naser Ruintan,
Ayesheh Jalili, Yunos Heydari.
Prod: Ali Agha Owjani,
Mohammad Akramiye.
A young Iranian humanitarian
aid worker witnesses the plight
of homeless children in
Afghanistan.

TEARS IN THE COLD
[War drama, 2003] Script and
Dir: Azizollah Hamidnezhad.
Phot: Mohammad Davudi.
Players: Parsa Pirouzfar,
Golshifteh Farahani. Prod: Amir
Hossein Sharifi (Afaq Film).
During the Iran-Iraq war, a

Tabrizi's Carpet rite

Kamal Tabrizi, who is gradually making his presence felt after
a quarter-century of film-making, completed a serious TV series
of social relevance, *Time of Rebellion,* and two feature films.
Focusing on the most original and ancient Persian art, carpet
weaving, **Carpet of the Wind** follows a Japanese carpet merchant
who travels to Iran to arrange for the weaving of a special kind
of carpet. He encounters setbacks, which are finally overcome with
the aid of his Iranian friend and a group of carpet weavers. With
uniformly fine performances and beautiful backdrops of ancient
architecture, this is a deceptively simple film that explores the issue
of dialogue between nations.

In Tabrizi's **Take a Look at the Sky Sometimes** (also presented
to an enthusiastic reception at the Fajr Festival), several ghosts,
including the spectre of a man from ancient times, help people to
lead a good life and to die with decorum. The ghosts also help one
another to purge any dark spots they may have carried from life.
In Tabrizi's view, death can be as sweet as a loving kiss; or even
the most hilarious moment of life. This is a rather talkative and
somewhat protracted comedy, with moments of biting satire that
expose the shortcomings of the contemporary world.

Reza Kianian, left, and Asghar Taqizadeh in **Take a Look at the Sky Sometimes**

Farzad Motamen's **White Nights** is a free adaptation of Feodor
Dostoyevsky's romantic novel, set in contemporary Iranian society
and including quotations from classic and modern Iranian poets.
It is a simple film about a man, a woman, a city and love, with
a sedate pace and a meticulous expressive style that has not yet
attracted the attention and acclaim it deserves.

After the exhilarating satire of his debut feature *The Child and the*
Soldier and the fresh subject matter of *Under the Moonlight,* Reza
Mirkarimi addresses religious faith in *A Light Burns Here,* which
lacks the frankness of approach and warmth of *Under the*

Moonlight but is still attractive and thoughtful. It is a great pity that the high quality of these films and their international acclaim provide scant motivation for local cinema attendance.

JAMAL OMID has been active for more than four decades as a film critic, author (15 books, including the *History of Iranian Cinema: 1900-1979*) and film-maker (screenwriter and executive producer). He is programme director of the Fajr International Film Festival.

soldier faces a mountain ordeal.

THE CRIME
[Drama, 2003] Script and Dir: Mohammad Ali Sajjadi. Phot: Hossein Maleki. Players: Jamshid Hashempour, Mitra Hajjar, Azita Lachini. Prod: Hassan Tavakkolnia (Yekta Film).
Siavash, a disturbed and rebellious student, murders a man he hates.

THE FASCINATION OF FLIGHT
[Drama, 2003] Script: Pouran Darakhshandeh, Mohammad Hadi Karimi. Dir and Prod: Darakhshandeh. Phot: Farhad Saba. Players: Jamshid Mashayekhi, Bahram Radan, Shahab Hosseini, Hessam Navab Safavi.
A young writer explores drug and Aids problems among young people.

TINY SNOWFLAKES
[Drama, 2003] Script and Dir: Alireza Amini. Phot: Turaj Aslani. Players: Mohsen Tanabandeh, Majid Bahrami, Behruz Khalili. Prod: A. Amini (Centre for Promotion of Documentary & Experimental Filmmaking).
Two mine guards are drawn to a woman teacher.

THE DUEL
[War drama, 2003] Script and Dir: Ahmad Reza Darvish. Phot: Bahram Badakhshani. Players: Saeed Rad, Pezhman Bazeghi, Parivash Nazariye, Anushirvan Arjomand. Prod: Farhang Tamasha Institute.
Zeynal, a war veteran released after 20 years' captivity in Iraq, is accused of committing crimes at the start of the war.

A PLACE TO LIVE
[War drama, 2003] Script and Dir: Mohammad Bozorgnia (based on a story by Jamal Omid). Phot: Hossein Jafarian. Players: Ezzatollah Entezami. Prod: Sima Film.
After Iraq's invasion of Iran, an elderly farmer overcomes his initial reluctance to fight when his young son is captured.

GAVKHOUNI
[Drama, 2003] Script and Dir: Behruz Afkhami, based on a story by Jafar Modarres Sadeqi. Phot: Mohammad Aladpoush. Players: Bahram Radan, Bahareh Rahnama, Ezzatollah Entezami. Prod: Ali Moallem.
A young man is haunted by nightmarish memories of his dead father and his hometown, Isfahan.

A FEW WISPS OF HAIR
[Drama, 2003] Script and Dir: Iraj Karimi. Phot: Mohammad Reza Sokut. Players: Fariba Kamran, Behnaz Jafari, Afsaneh Chehreh-Azad. Prod: Mohammad Sadeq Azin, Behruz Salimi.
Her student son's problems force a recently divorced mother to contact friends and relatives whom she previously shunned.

THE FAR AWAY WOMAN
[Drama, 2003] Script and Dir: Ali Mosaffa. Phot: Homayoun Pilevar. Players: Leila Hatami, Homayoun Ershadi, Turan Mehrzad. Prod: Ruhollah Baradari, Iraj Jamshidi.
A man looks back on his married life on the night before he is due to meet his ex-wife and child.

SHE WON'T TALK
[Crime drama, 2003] Script: Shadmehr Rastin, Ahmad Amini. Dir: Amini. Phot: Hassan Pouya. Players: Katayun Riahi, Laleh Eskandari, Shahab Hosseini, Shohreh Soltani. Prod: Gholamreza Gomroki (Deja Film).
A woman on trial for murder remains silent in court as her lawyer tries to prove her innocence.

THE FAMILY FARM
[War drama, 2003] Script and Dir: Rasul Mollaqolipour. Phot: Rasul Ahadi. Players: Mehdi Ahmadi, Ateneh Faqih Nasiri. Prod: Habibollah Kasesaz.

THE WINNING CARD
[Drama, 2003] Script: Khashayar Alvand. Dir: Sirus Alvand. Phot: Asghar Rafiyijam. Players: Fariborz Arabnia, Baran Kowsari, Atila Pasiyani. Prod: Alvand, Rasul Sadre Ameli.

SQUEAKING SHOES
[Melodrama, 2003] Script and Dir: Shapour Qarib. Phot: Seyed Mohammad Rowzati. Players: Akbar Abdi, Kobra Farrokhi, Dariush Asadzadeh. Prod: Bahram Mohammadi Pour.

Reza Mirkarimi's **A Light Burns Here**

Ireland Michael Dwyer

The Year's Best Films

Michael Dwyer's selection:

Intermission
(Dir: John Crowley)
In America (Dir: Jim Sheridan)
Song for a Raggy Boy
(Dir: Aisling Walsh)
Chavez – Inside the Coup
(TV Doc. Dirs: Kim Bartley,
Donnacha O' Briain)
Veronica Guerin
(Dir: Joel Schumacher)

Dylan Moran in **The Actors**

Recent and Forthcoming Films

THE ACTORS
*[Comedy, 2003] Script and
Dir: Conor McPherson. Phot:
Seamus McGarvey. Players:
Michael Caine, Dylan Moran,
Michael Gambon, Miranda
Richardson, Lena Headey,
Michael McElhatton. Prod:
Company of Wolves.*

bl,.m
*[Drama, 2003] Script: Sean
Walsh, based on* Ulysses *by
James Joyce. Dir: Walsh. Phot:
Ciaran Tanham. Players: Stephen
Rea, Angeline Ball, Hugh
O'Conor, Patrick Bergin. Prod:
Odyssey Pictures.*

A chill wind of uncertainty blew through the Irish production sector for the first four months of 2003. Production was down, and the majority of films going ahead were produced under the Irish Film Board's schemes for low- and micro-budget features. Even more unsettling was the confirmation that the tax incentive scheme, under Section 481 of the Finance Act, was to be discontinued from the end of 2004, on the orders of the Department of Finance.

Producers' fears were finally allayed in May, when the new arts minister John O'Donoghue opened the Irish Pavillion at Cannes and announced: "Film production is and will remain important to Ireland." He promised "a complete review of the existing incentive structures, of where they position us strategically and competitively, and where we need to position ourselves after 2004 to ensure that we remain attractive as a filming location." He did not refer directly to an alternative to Section 481, but his positive approach and awareness of the urgency of the situation were greeted with applause and evident relief.

A month later, there was more good news with the arrival of two major Hollywood productions in Ireland: Jerry Bruckheimer's epic *King Arthur*, directed by Antoine Fuqua, and Peter Howitt's romantic comedy *The Laws of Attraction*, starring Pierce Brosnan and Julianne Moore.

The exhibition boom has continued, with cinema admissions for 2002 reaching 17.3 million, the highest ever recorded (up 8.6% on 2001), and a record 28 films passing the €1m mark at the box-office. Admissions are projected to exceed 18 million in 2003, and by June four films had comfortably grossed more than €2m (including *Gangs of New York* and *The Matrix Reloaded*), with six others passing €1.5m.

Prisoners of God

Irish productions found it extremely difficult to compete against so many high-profile Hollywood movies in this crowded market. The only one to make over €1m in 2002 was **The Magdalene Sisters**, a UK/Irish production set entirely in Ireland and featuring an Irish cast, but shot in Scotland by a Scottish director, Peter Mullan.

Tough and deeply unsettling, Mullan's film is unflinching in depicting the degradation and brutality experienced by inmates at one of the Magdalene laundries run by callous nuns in 1960s Dublin County. Its focus is on four young women, all vulnerable victims of a rigidly patriarchal and deeply conservative society, and the largely unfamiliar cast is uniformly convincing.

Aidan Quinn, centre, in Aisling Walsh's **Song for a Raggy Boy**

The male experience of comparable hardship was confronted in Irish director Aisling Walsh's powerful **Song For a Raggy Boy**, an unflinching dramatisation of fierce cruelty to boys at a forbidding Christian Brothers institution in late 1930s Cork. In sharp contrast to Mullan's depiction of all nuns as ogres, Walsh's more balanced film features a single sadist, a glacial teacher (Iain Glen), and surrounds him with men too old or too scared to interfere, until an idealistic new teacher (Aidan Quinn) rocks the boat.

A more romanticised view of mid-twentieth-century Ireland is presented in Bruce Beresford's **Evelyn**. This old-fashioned, factually based drama features Pierce Brosnan as a working-class Dubliner who won a landmark court case in 1953 to retain the custody of his three children after his wife left him for another man. The screenplay simplifies the more complex aspects of the case, and there are more than a few anachronisms.

Evelyn was a box-office disappointment, as was Conor McPherson's contemporary Dublin comedy **The Actors**. Expanded by McPherson from a storyline by Neil Jordan, this tall tale features Michael Caine and Dylan Moran as down-at-heel Dublin actors using their gifts for disguise and accents to pull off a scam. Moran, a stand-up comic and TV actor in his first cinema role, is amusing, but Caine is miscast and the absurdist humour mostly falls flat.

The latest works from some of Ireland's most high-profile directors were set and shot in other countries: Neil Jordan's *The Good Thief*

COWBOYS AND ANGELS
[Comedy-drama, 2003] Script and Dir: David Gleeson. Phot: Volker Tittel. Players: Michael Legge, Allen Leech, Amy Shiels, Frank Kelly. Prod: Wide Eye Films.
A bored young civil servant moves in with a gay fashion student and becomes a star on the catwalk.

DEAD BODIES
[Thriller, 2003] Script: Derek Landy. Dir: Robert Quinn. Phot: Donal Gilligan. Players: Andrew Scott, Kelly Reilly, Sean McGinley, Gerard McSorley. Prod: Distinguished Features.

GOLDFISH MEMORY
[Comedy-drama, 2003] Script and Dir: Liz Gill. Phot: Ken Byrne. Players: Flora Montgomery, Keith McErlean, Sean Campion, David Gaynor, Stuart Graham, Fiona O'Shaughnessy. Prod: Goldfish Films.

THE HALO EFFECT
[Drama, 2003] Script and Dir: Lance Daly. Phot: Ivan McCullough. Players: Stephen Rea, Grattan Smith, Kerry Condon, Simon Delaney. Prod: Fastnet Films.
The proprietor of a downmarket café tries to cope with incompetent staff, his gambling addiction and some loan sharks.

HEADRUSH
[Comedy-thriller, 2003] Script and Dir: Shimmy Marcus. Phot: Owen McPolin. Players: Wuzza Conlon, Gavin Keilty, Laura Pyper, Tom Hickey. Prod: Zanzibar Films.
Two disillusioned young Dubliners hope to solve all their problems by smuggling drugs for a local gangster.

IN AMERICA
[Drama, 2002] Script and Dir: Jim Sheridan. Phot: Declan Quinn. Players: Paddy Considine, Samantha Morton, Sarah Bolger, Emma Bolger, Djimon Hounsou. Prod: Hell's Kitchen.

INTERMISSION
[Drama, 2003] Script: Mark O'Rowe. Dir: John Crowley. Phot: Ryszard Lenczewski. Players: Colin Farrell, Cillian Murphy, Colm Meaney, Kelly MacDonald, Shirley Henderson, Brian F. O'Byrne, Ger Ryan. Prod: Parallel Films/Company of Wolves.

LAWS OF ATTRACTION
[Romantic comedy, 2004] Script: Robert Harling, Aline Brosh McKenna, Karey Kirkpatrick. Dir: Peter Howitt. Phot: Adrian Biddle. Players: Pierce Brosnan, Julianne Moore, Michael Sheen, Parker Posey, Frances Fisher. Prod: Deep River Productions/Irish Dreamtime/Intermedia Film.
Two New York divorce lawyers become romantically involved.

MYSTICS
[Comedy, 2003] Script: Wesley Burrowes. Dir: David Blair. Phot: Donal Gilligan. Players: David Kelly, Milo O'Shea, Maria Doyle Kennedy, Liam Cunningham. Prod: MR Films/Murphia Pictures.
Two veteran fraudsters claim to be able to communicate with the dead.

SONG FOR A RAGGY BOY
[Drama, 2003] Script: Aisling Walsh and Kevin Byron Murphy, based on the book by Patrick Galvin. Dir: Walsh. Players: Aidan Quinn, Iain Glen, John Travers, Marc Warren, Alan Devlin, Dudley Sutton. Prod: Subotica Entertainment.

TIMBUKTU
[Road movie, 2003] Script: Paul Freaney. Dir: Alan Gilsenan. Phot: P. J. Dillon. Players: Eva Birtwhistle, Karl Geary, Liam O'Maonlai. Prod: Yellow Asylum Films/MR Films.
A young woman and her transvestite friend search for her brother in the Sahara.

VERONICA GUERIN
[Drama, 2002] Script: Mary Agnes Donoghue. Dir: Joel

in the south of France, Damien O'Donnell's *Heartlands* in the north of England, and Thaddeus O'Sullivan's *The Heart of Me* in London. None made a significant commercial impact.

Tales of two cities

Jim Sheridan's fifth feature **In America** is set in New York but was filmed mostly on Irish locations doubling for Manhattan. Sheridan's charming, semi-autobiographical comedy-drama follows the experiences of an Irish immigrant couple (Paddy Considine and Samantha Morton) and their young daughters (sisters Sarah and Emma Bolger) during their first year in New York. Devoid of whingeing self-pity, it charts their progress through a series of hard knocks to deliver a celebration of love, friendship, innocence and resilience that is deeply moving and very funny.

*Samantha Morton, right, in Jim Sheridan's **In America***

The first two films produced under the Irish Film Board's low-budget initiative, *Dead Bodies* and *Goldfish Memory*, capture a distinctively modern Irish urban milieu far removed from the misty-eyed, stage-Irish tradition. Director Robert Quinn's debut feature **Dead Bodies** is a dark, stylish and satisfyingly unpredictable thriller of deceit, desperation and corruption set in present-day Dublin. It features the versatile Andrew Scott in an intriguing portrayal of a self-absorbed young man renewing his relationship with a demanding ex-girlfriend who proves even more self-obsessed and pushes his patience to the limit.

Writer-director Liz Gill's **Goldfish Memory**, the follow-up to her debut *Gold in the Streets*, chronicles the complicated sexual and romantic liaisons of young Irish people as they switch partners – and in several cases, sexual preferences – in their quest for love. This light and breezy romantic comedy features a spirited young cast led by Flora Montgomery and Keith McErlean.

The darker side of Dublin life is charted in Joel Schumacher's gritty, factually based **Veronica Guerin**, featuring Cate Blanchett as the eponymous Irish investigative reporter who, at the age of 36, was murdered by a drug-dealing gang in 1996. This is the second movie to deal with Guerin's life and death, following John Mackenzie's *When the Sky Falls* (2000), starring Joan Allen, which failed to secure a US release. The superior new film is anchored by Blanchett's complex portrayal of Guerin as a brave, dogged and unconventional reporter who was also rather naïve and ultimately reckless.

The most impressive of all recent Irish productions is **Intermission**, which marks an immensely assured joint feature film debut for two bright Irish theatre talents, writer Mark O'Rowe and director John Crowley. With cinematic flair and vigorous pacing, their smartly plotted, dark comedy-drama skilfully juggles and interweaves more than a dozen characters into one edgy Dublin mosaic. In a flawless ensemble cast, an understated Cillian Murphy oozes screen presence as a lovelorn supermarket assistant, Colm Meaney brilliantly captures the tragi-comic character of the absurdly vain detective who is the enthusiastic subject of a TV documentary, and Ireland's hottest acting property, Colin Farrell, is scarily volatile as an unscrupulous young criminal.

Colm Meaney, left, and Colin Farrell in **Intermission**

MICHAEL DWYER has been Film Correspondent with *The Irish Times* in Dublin since 1988. He is the co-founder and artistic director of the Dublin International Film festival, which had its inaugural outing in March 2003.

Schumacher. Phot: Brendan Galvin. Players: Cate Blanchett, Gerard McSorley, Ciaran Hinds, Brenda Fricker, Colin Farrell. Prod: Jerry Bruckheimer Films.

Cate Blanchett as **Veronica Guerin**

Quotes of the Year

"I'm convinced it could have had mass appeal, especially when you look at the rubbish that gets made today. It astonishes me that a script of that calibre is just lying there and not getting made."
DAMIEN O'DONNELL, *director, on the collapse of his nineteenth-century drama* Edgardo Mortara, *just weeks before filming was to begin.*

"I am enchanted, but as I am still in the game and might win the lovely bugger outright, would the Academy please defer the honour until I am 80?"
PETER O'TOOLE's *initial response on hearing he was to receive an honorary Oscar.*

"Making the character a publicist was a very good idea because in a very short space you get to show his potential for being an asshole every day."
COLIN FARRELL *on his role in* Phone Booth.

Israel Dan Fainaru

The Year's Best Films

Dan Fainaru's selection:
James' Journey to Jerusalem (Dir: Ra'anan Alexandrowicz)
Broken Wings (Dir: Nir Bergman)
Yossi and Jaegger (Dir: Eitan Fox)
Nina's Tragedies (Dir: Savi Gabizon)
Ben's Biography (Dir: Dan Wolman)

Ben's Biography

Recent and Forthcoming Films

NINA'S TRAGEDIES – A SAD COMEDY
[Comedy-drama, 2003] Script and Dir: Savi Gabizon. Phot: David Grufinkel. Players: Ayelet Zorer, Yoram Hatav, Anath Waxman, Alon Aboutboul, Shmil Ben Ari, Evgenya Dodina, Dov Navon. Prod: Anath Assouline, Savi Gabizon.
Coming-of-age tale in a family where the father has gone back to religion, the mother consoles herself in the arms of a new lover every day and the beloved aunt, Nina, nurses a secret passion for the man who came to tell her that her husband had been killed in action.

Whoever said muses are silent when cannons roar didn't know the first thing about Israeli cinema. In the last couple of years, while the country has undergone possibly its worst ever security and economic crisis, the film-making muses have never been more prolific. At home, the tendency of Israeli audiences to look at their own films is ever more pronounced – and not just at one single hit, as in previous years.

Though *Broken Wings* was 2002's box-office locomotive (250,000 admissions), there were quite a few wagons attached to it. Menahem Golan's adaptation of an A. B. Yehoshua novel, **Open Heart**, was clobbered by the critics but did quite nicely (60,000 admissions), as did a local comedy, **The Wisdom of the Pretzel** (40,000), and **Bonjour Monsieur Shlomi** (40,000 and counting), a gentle, intelligent coming-of-age picture by Shemi Zarchin. In all, Israeli films accounted for just under 5% of the total attendance (9.58 million).

Internationally, Israeli films are no longer considered nuisances, but are courted – and not only the works of Amos Gitai, whose international reputation has mostly relied on solid European support. Beyond the various awards raked by Dover Kosashvili's debut, *Late Marriage*, its successful theatrical distribution in America proved there are audiences for Israeli films outside the close circuit of the Jewish communities. Nir Bergman's *Broken Wings,* following a similar pattern, indicates that *Late Marriage* was more than just an accident, and films such as **Yossi and Jaegger**, Eytan Fox's moving homosexual love story in a military bunker on the Lebanon border, and *James' Journey to Jerusalem* (see *IFG 2003*) have subsequently crossed borders with some success. Documentaries, too, seem to be doing marvellously well abroad, among them July Gerstel's **My Terrorist** (sold to 20 countries), while the 'mockumentaries' of Avi Mograbi are being released theatrically in France.

One reason for this abrupt turning of the tide is the belated implementation of the Cinema Law. Painfully born in 2000, it is supposed to allocate to the film industry 50% of the annual franchise fees paid (as a percentage of their income) by commercial television companies. Despite the sharp fall in TV revenues that reflects the crisis throughout the Israeli economy, the funds passed on to the Cinema Authority are still, at around $14m (NS 61m) a year, far larger than ever before.

Another positive factor is the competition between several film funds, offering alternatives for new projects. Each may have a specific purpose (feature films, documentaries, marginal projects or TV dramas), but collaboration between them is increasingly prevalent, often with good reason, since it wastes time and money if they all dabble in promotion, distribution and international sales. The third reason is that many of the younger film-makers have given up preaching, whether on political or social topics, in favour of more personal stories (what preaching remains comes from a more intimate standpoint).

James and Nina, Jerusalem-bound

Of the outstanding features at the 2003 Jerusalem Film Festival, **James' Journey to Jerusalem**, released almost a year after it was completed, was inexplicably slaughtered by the Israeli critics after its successful screening in the Directors' Fortnight at Cannes, but, regardless of local scribes' opinions, it is heading for an international career.

Savi Gabizon, whose two previous films have been major hits at home, once again won the festival's Wolgin Award, this time with his bittersweet **Nina's Tragedies – a Sad Comedy**, yet another coming-of-age story (a tremendously popular field here), which combines laughter and tears with many other topical issues (Russian immigration, the return to religious roots and war casualties). Gabizon manipulates the story a bit too much for its own good and engineers some excessive coincidences, but this is nevertheless a smooth, professional satire, with a polyphonic plot and some remarkable performances, most particularly from Ayelet Zorer as Nina, who has everything it takes to become the country's next leading star actress.

Ayelet Zorer and Alon Aboutboul in **Nina's Tragedies**

BEN'S BIOGRAPHY
[Comedy, 2003] Script, Dir and Prod: Dan Wolman. Phot: Itamar Hadar. Players: Gal Zayid, Avigail Michaeli, Rivka Gur, Sharon Alexander.

A GIFT FROM HEAVEN
[Drama, 2003] Script and Dir: Dover Kosashvili. Phot: Loren Dayan. Players: Yuval Segal, Lior Ashkenazi, Dover Kosashvili, Moni Moshonov, Menashe Noy. Prod: Marek Rozenbaum, Transfax Prod.
The complicated relations between several Georgian immigrant families in Israel who stay faithful to their old ways.

JAMES' JOURNEY TO JERUSALEM
[Social satire, 2003] Script: Ra'anan Alexandrowicz, Sami Douanis. Dir: Alexandrowicz. Phot: Sharon de Mayo. Players: Siyabonga Melongisi Shibe, Arie Elias, Salim Daw. Prod: Amir Harel, Lama Prod.
A young black African comes to visit the Holy Sites in Jerusalem, is mistaken for an illegal worker and put to work and finally blends into the system.

BONJOUR MONSIEUR SHLOMI
[Coming-of-age comedy, 2003] Script and Dir: Shemi Zarchin. Players: Oshri Cohen, Esti Zackheim, Arie Elias, Albert Iluz, Aya Cohen. Prod: Eitan Even, Evanstone Prod.
A teenager who's thought to be slightly retarded toils hard to bring peace to his embattled, impoverished family, when suddenly he is told he is a mathematical genius.

Oshri Cohen and Aya Cohen in
Bonjour Monsieur Shlomi

THE GLOW
[Socio-political satire, 2003]
Script and Dir: Igal Bursztyn.
Phot: Giora Nikh. Players: Assi
Dayan, Tinker Bell, Rivka
Michaeli, Yair Rubin. Prod: Eyal
Shirai/Cinema Postprod.

TURN LEFT AT THE END OF THE WORLD
[Social drama, 2003] Script: Avi
Nesher, Sara Ezer, Runy Porath-
Shuval. Dir: Nesher. Phot: David
Gurfinkel. Players: Aure Atika,
Jean Ben-Gigi, Permit Setai,
Krutika Desai, Neta Gerti, Liraz
Charchi, Israel Katurza, Robi
Porath-Shuval, Rotem Abohav,
Nadav Abeksis, Mariano
Adelman, Nati Ravitz. Prod: Avi
Nesher/Samuel Hadida/Artomas
Communications/United
King/Davis Films.
In 1969, two immigrant
communities, one Moroccan, one
Indian, learn to live together in
a small Israeli town.

WALKING ON WATER
[Drama, 2003] Script: Gal
Ochovski. Dir: Eytan Fox. Phot:
Toby Hochstein. Players: Lior
Ashkenazi, Kenneth Baker,
Carolina Peters. Prod: Amir
Harel/Lama Prod.
The friendship between a
Mossad agent and a young
German tourist visiting Israel,
who is the nephew of a Nazi war
criminal wanted by the Israeli
authorities.

THE GOSPEL ACCORDING TO GOD
[Political satire, 2003] Script and
Dir: Assi Dayan. Phot: Ofer
Inov. Players: Dayan, Gil
Kopatsch, Tinker Bell, Tzofit
Grant. Prod: Yoram Kislev/Haim
Mekleberg/Hallas Prod.
Redemption Day is here, God is
supposed to send his Son back
to earth, but Jesus is less than
enthusiastic about his task. He'd
rather follow European soccer
than save souls.

MISS ENTEBBE
[Drama, 2003] Script: Dana
Shatz, Omri Levy. Dir: Levy.
Phot: Gabriel Vagon. Players:

Another Jerusalem premiere, Dan Wolman's intensely personal **Ben's Biography**, may look a bit too much like a transition from stage to screen (the script has been produced as a play), but somehow, once you accept its strange, almost surrealist narrative (long flashbacks designed to explain the extreme hang-ups of an adult accountant whose twisted upbringing has left him unable to stand touching or being touched), it offers moving and bitterly sarcastic moments.

State of the nation

Soon after the festival, Amos Gitai unveiled **Alila**, a collage of prototypes representing parts of Israeli society. Typically intellectual and sometimes declamatory, yet more affecting than is usual with Gitai, it has some nice performances that transcend the script, and displays his customary concern with structure (every scene made up of one shot, opening and closing with a dissolve). All in all a balanced, though not very flattering portrait of the insecurities, doubts and passions of today's Israelis.

Igal Bursztyn's **The Glow** (originally made for television) is a surrealist satire on Israel's obsession with security and the ideological decadence of a generation born and bred under the military myth. A retired, legendary commander, now a ministerial adviser, takes his mistress for a weekend in the country with friends from his glorious army past and finds himself surrounded by strange, threatening phenomena. This is a modest production whose reflections on contemporary Israel sometimes go over the top (what satire doesn't?), and at press time awaited a theatrical release to follow its TV premiere.

Assi Dayan and Tinker Bell in **The Glow**

There are several intriguing titles among the 20 new Israeli features that were in various stages of production at press time. Some are by veterans, including Eytan Green's *Henry's Dream,* about the belated film-making debut of a frustrated movie fan, *Turn Left at the End of the World,* which marks the return home of Avi Nesher after 20 years' writing and directing in the US, and Assi Dayan's *Gospel According to God,* which promises to be as wild and challenging as any of his earlier political allegories. Itzhak "Zeppel" Yeshurun's *Noa Is No Longer 17* is a sequel to his earlier hit, *Noa at 17,* about the collapse of the kibbutz mentality.

Among the younger generation, Dover Kosashvili's second picture, **A Gift from Heaven**, was a highly controversial item at the Jerusalem Festival, Eytan Fox has been finishing *Walking on Water* (partly shot in Germany), and Joseph Cider, whose debut, *Time of Favor*, did remarkably well, deals once again with nationalist-orthodox motives in *Around the Bonfire.* Producer Marek Rozenbaum is back as a director for the second time with *To Dance,* and Shachar Segal, once the bright new hope of the local cinema, who for a long time preferred to make commercials instead of features, is almost ready to unveil his first full-length effort, *A Small Step.*

The industry's next major goal is to improve local exhibition of Israeli films. Dealing with Globus Group and Israeli Theatres, the giants who control the vast majority of screens, has proved terribly frustrating. Both chains either represent or have long-term arrangements with the American majors, so their enthusiasm for local fare is limited and, even for the most attractive pictures, their terms are so tough that producers who distribute their own films (for lack of better solutions), refuse to invest in advertising after the initial release, for what they see as an unfair share of the profits. Possible solutions include the launch of theatres dedicated to domestic productions, or a law introducing a quota of Israeli films for all local screens. Needless to say, the exhibitors don't like the sound of either idea.

DAN FAINARU is co-editor of Israel's only film magazine, *Cinematheque,* and a former director of the Israeli Film Institute. He was editor-in-chief of the late *European Film Reviews* and reviews regularly for *Screen International.*

Merva Avrahami, Merav Gruber, Igal Naor, Alon Olearchik, Yael Abekessis. Prod: Renen Schorr. When Arab terrorists hijack an El Al flight to Entebbe, the son of a woman passenger and his two good friends, all aged 12, kidnap an Arab boy and hold him hostage in a bid to secure the mother's release.

NOA IS NO LONGER 17
[Social drama, 2003] Script and Dir: Itzhak "Zeppel" Yeshurun. Phot: Amnon Salomon. Players: Shmulik Shilo, Irith Tzur, Dina Doron, Dalia Shimko, Maya Maron, Ronnie Buchsbaum. Prod: Yeshurun/Avi Kleinberger. When a bankrupt kibbutz is put up for sale, all those who had once fiercely defended or attacked it close ranks and help the veterans save what little they can from the debacle.

HENRI'S DREAM
[Drama, 2003] Script and Dir: Eitan Green. Phot: Yaron Shachaf. Players: Menashe Noy, Jonathan Hashiloni, Igal Elkabetz. Prod: Uri Sabbag/Einath Bikel/Perlite Prod. Henri, 50, head of maintenance at a film school, is about to direct a first film, and he will need a miracle to prevent it turning out to be a disaster.

ALILA
[Drama, 2003] Script: Amos Gitai, Marie-Josée Sanselme. Dir: Gitai. Phot: Renato Berta. Players: Yael Abekessis, Amos Lavie, Uri Klauzner, Hanna Laszlo, Yossi Karmon, Ronit Elkabetz. Prod: Laurent Truchot/Michel Popper/Michael Tapuach. A collage of stories set in an old building in a Tel Aviv slum, each story representing a segment of contemporary Israeli society.

Italy Lorenzo Codelli

The Year's Best Films

Lorenzo Codelli's selection:
The Best of Youth
(Dir: Marco Tullio Giordana)
Farewell of the Past
(Documentary. Dir:
Marco Bellocchio)
A Heart Elsewhere
(Dir: Pupi Avati)
**Horse Fever – Mandrake
Style** (Dir: Carlo Vanzina)
The Last Customer
(Documentary. Dir:
Nanni Moretti)

Recent Films

A CAVALLO DELLA TIGRE
(Jail Break)
*[Comedy, 2002] Script: Carlo
Mazzacurati, Franco Bernini,
from Luigi Comencini's 1961
movie. Dir: Mazzacurati.
Players: Fabrizio Bentivoglio,
Paola Cortellesi. Prod:
Rodeo Drive/Rai Cinema.*

L'ANIMA GEMELLA
(Match Made in Heaven)
*[Comedy, 2003] Script:
Domenico Starnone, Sergio
Rubini. Dir: Rubini. Phot: Paolo
Carnera. Players: Valentina
Cervi, Violante Placido, Sergio
Rubini. Prod: Medusa Film/
Cecchi Gori Group.*

CALLAS FOREVER
*[Drama, 2002] Script: Martin
Sherman, Franco Zeffirelli. Dir:
Zeffirelli. Phot: Ennio Guarnieri.
Players: Fanny Ardant, Jeremy
Irons, Joan Plowright. Prod:
Cattleya/Medusa Film/Alquimia
Cinema (Spain)/Media Pro
Pictures (Romania).*

This was a season to celebrate. Compared to 2001-02, attendance for Italian movies almost doubled in 2002-03, reaching around 30% of the gross for the first time since 1987-88. Moreover the top three hits were all home-made comedies. The lowbrow farce **Christmas on the Nile** (*Natale sul Nilo*) was the customary holidays package from Aurelio De Laurentiis' Filmauro, exploiting ageing clowns Christian De Sica and Massimo Boldi's bawdy repertoire.

Then came Roberto Benigni's **Pinocchio**, a big-budget revisitation of Carlo Collodi's classic. It had great visual flair – camerawork by Dante Spinotti, sets and costumes by the late Danilo Donati – but its heartless vacuity disappointed most fans of both the wooden puppet and the Tuscan comic genius. Still, Silvio Berlusconi's Medusa Film orchestrated a record-breaking 800-theatres release which guaranteed the film's commercial impact. A third blockbuster, **The Legend of Al, John & Jack** (*La leggenda di Al, John & Jack*), was smartly overbooked by the same company for Christmas. This surreal gangster spoof starred the beloved Milanese trio of Aldo, Giovanni & Giacomo in their most Marx Bros-like vehicle to date.

Subtlety lives

Happily, audiences' rediscovery of Italian cinema extended to a few subtler films, too, such as Ferzan Ozpetek's **Facing Window** (*La finestra di fronte*) and Gabriele Muccino's *Remember Me* (*Ricordati di me*). Wartime experiences and a hidden gay passion connect with

Nicoletta Romanoff in Gabriele Muccino's **Remember Me**

a contemporary straight romance in Ozpetek's easy-to-digest melodrama; not the most original film from the Istanbul-born director, although the late, great Massimo Girotti shines as a philosopher-cook. Muccino, rightly acclaimed for his former megahit *The Last Kiss* (2001), chose a serious mood for **Remember Me**, a harsh, rather skin-deep attack on a TV-dominated society. The film's neuropathic, disintegrating family miraculously finds a safety valve at the end and Nicoletta Romanoff's cynical, go-getting teenager is the pearl among a bubbly cast.

Popular Roman comedian-director Carlo Verdone was back in vogue thanks to **It's Not Our Fault** (*Ma che colpa abbiamo noi*), which delivers subdued mockery of therapy group members trying to cure their various depressions. Back to his favourite dreams of a mythical past, Pupi Avati painted **A Heart Elsewhere** (*Il cuore altrove*), one of his most personal watercolours. This Hawksian, bittersweet fairy tale, set in 1920s Bologna, deals with the impossible attraction between a naïve teacher and a gorgeous blind girl. An ironic hymn to diversity, it was well received at Cannes. Carlo Vanzina and his brother, screenwriter Enrico, revamped their father Steno's 1976 humorous classic *Febbre da cavallo* with **Horse Fever – Mandrake Style** (*Febbre da cavallo – la Mandrakata*), a very worthy follow-up reuniting a crowd of Roman character actors. The Vanzinas Bros' **Sunday Lunch** (*Il pranzo della domenica*) was an uneven family sitcom.

Vanessa Incontrada and Neri Marcoreè in **A Heart Elsewhere**

Three cons and a diva

Some established film-makers stumbled. Formerly brilliant Carlo Mazzacurati remade Luigi Comencini's 1961 black comedy *A cavallo della tigre*; unfortunately he showed neither teeth nor topicality in **Jail Break** (*A cavallo della tigre*), a dull yarn about a petty bank robber and two lifers dogged by misfortune after they escape from prison. **Callas Forever** was another average tableau by Franco Zeffirelli, remembering slices of his past career.

IL CUORE ALTROVE
(**A Heart Elsewhere**)
[Romance, 2003] Script and Dir: Pupi Avati. Phot: Pasquale Rachini. Players: Neri Marcorè, Vanessa Incontrada, Giancarlo Giannini. Prod: Duea Film/ Rai Cinema.

DILLO CON PAROLE MIE
(**Ginger and Cinnamon**)
[Comedy, 2003] Script: Ivan Cotroneo, Stefania Montorsi, Daniele Luchetti. Dir: Luchetti. Phot: Paolo Carnera. Players: Stefania Montorsi, Martina Merlino, Giampaolo Morelli. Prod: Studio Canal Urania/ Medusa Film/Tele+.

EL ALAMEIN
[War drama, 2002] Script and Dir: Enzo Monteleone. Phot: Daniele Nannuzzi. Players: Pier Francesco Farina, Emilio Solfrizzi, Paolo Briguglia. Prod: Cattleya.

**FEBBRE DA CAVALLO –
LA MANDRAKATA**
(**Horse Fever – Mandrake Style**)
[Farce, 2002] Script: Carlo Vanzina, Enrico Vanzina. Dir: Carlo Vanzina. Phot: Claudio Zamarion. Players: Luigi Proietti, Rodolfo Laganà, Carlo Buccirosso, Enrico Montesano. Prod: Solaris Cinematografica/ Warner Bros Italia/International Video 80.

LA FELICITÀ NON COSTA NIENTE (**Happiness for Free**)
[Drama, 2003] Script: Francesco Bruni, Mimmo Calopresti, Heidrun Schleef. Dir: Calopresti. Phot: Arnaldo Catinari. Players: Mimmo Calopresti, Francesca Neri, Vincent Perez. Prod: Bianca Film/Rai Cinema/Europa Corp. (France)/Canal+/Ventura Film (Switzerland)/TSI- Televisione Svizzera.

LA FINESTRA DI FRONTE
(**Facing Window**)
[Drama, 2003] Script: Gianni Romoli, Ferzan Ozpetek. Dir: Ozpetek. Phot: Gianfilippo Corticelli. Players: Massimo Girotti, Giovanna Mezzogiorno, Raoul Bova, Filippo Nigro. Prod:

Niccolò Ammaniti's best-selling thriller, more than Gabriele Salvatores' conventional staging, made a moderate success of **I'm Not Scared** (*Io non ho paura*), in which a child discovers in a hollow a boy who's been kidnapped by his own parents. Roberto Faenza concocted for middlebrow European tastes **The Soul Keeper** (*Prendimi l'anima*), about psychoanalyst Carl Gustav Jung's affair with his patient Sabina Spielrein. Daniele Luchetti assembled an enjoyable beach party, **Ginger and Cinnamon** (*Dillo con parole mie*), starring his witty wife Stefania Montorsi.

My Name Is Tanino, Paolo Virzì's lite odyssey of a Sicilian teenager pursuing the American Dream in the mid-West, and Sergio Rubini's **Match Made in Heaven** (*L'anima gemella*), a bizarre satirical fantasy about two Southern belles magically switching bodies with one another, were kept on the shelf for more than a year because of producer Vittorio Cecchi Gori's ongoing problems with justice. As a player, Rubini could not save Piergiorgio Gay's flat literary adaptation **The Power of the Past** (*La forza del passato*).

Gloomy Mimmo Calopresti starred as an architect looking for redemption in his soporific, Antonionesque pensum **Happiness for Free** (*La felicità non costa niente*). With one eye perhaps on Ken Russell, Michele Placido gave full freedom of excess to Stefano Accorsi and Laura Morante as romantic poets in **A Journey Called Love** (*Un viaggio chiamato amore*). As working-class movies are a dying species, one must acknowledge that Riccardo Milani's **The Place of the Soul** (*Il posto dell'anima*) gently hit some of its targets, notably the crimes of multinational conglomerates, in the story of dismissed labourers driving out their multinational company's top bosses.

Zero for politics

Silvio Berlusconi's regime, with its vice-like grip on television and newspapers, has a sedative effect on would-be political movies, or at least on the handful that can even secure finance and distribution nowadays, such as Ferdinando Vicentini Orgnani's **Ilaria Alpi – The Cruellest of Days** (*Ilaria Alpi – Il più crudele del giorni*) and Renzo Martinelli's **Piazza of the Five Moons** (*Piazza delle cinque lune*). The former 'exposes' how and why two TV reporters were killed in Somalia, the latter how and why Aldo Moro was kidnapped and murdered by the Red Brigades. Both directors deliver poor imitations of Francesco Rosi's and Oliver Stone's approaches, merely losing themselves in a foggy maze of conspiracy theories about the CIA and other 'evil forces'. Enzo Monteleone's **El Alamein** starts off criticising the Fascist colonial war and ends up heralding army heroism.

On the rise are explicitly right-wing pamphlets devoted to "honest

R & C Produzioni/Redwave Films (UK)/Afs Films (Turkey)/Clap Filmes (Portugal).

LA FORZA DEL PASSATO
(The Power of the Past)
[Drama, 2002] Script: Lara Fremder, Piergiorgio Gay, based on the novel by Sandro Veronesi. Dir: Gay. Phot: Luca Bigazzi. Players: Sergio Rubini, Bruno Ganz, Sandra Ceccarelli. Prod: Albachiara/Istituto Luce.

IL GIOCO DI RIPLEY
(Ripley's Game)
[Thriller, 2003] Script: Charles McKeown, Liliana Cavani, based on the novel by Patricia Highsmith. Dir: Cavani. Phot: Alfio Contini. Players: John Malkovich, Dougray Scott, Ray Winstone, Chiara Caselli. Prod: Cattleya/Baby Films (UK).

ILARIA ALPI – IL PIÙ CRUDELE DEI GIORNI (Ilaria Alpi – The Cruellest of Days)
[Political drama, 2003] Script: Marcello Fois, Ferdinando Vicentini Orgnani, based on a book by Giorgio Alpi, Luciana Alpi, Mariangela Gritta Grainer, Maurizio Torrealta. Dir: Orgnani. Phot: Giovanni Cavallini. Players: Giovanna Mezzogiorno, Rade Sherbedgia, Erica Blanc, Angelo Infanti. Prod: Lares Video/ Gam Film/Emme Produzioni/ Rai Cinema.

IO NON HO PAURA
(I'm Not Scared)
[Drama, 2003] Script: Francesca Marciano, Niccolò Ammaniti, from the novel by Ammaniti. Dir: Gabriele Salvatores. Phot: Italo Petriccione. Players: Giuseppe Cristiano, Mattia Di Pierro, Diego Abatantuono. Prod: Colorado Film/Cattleya/ Alquimia Cinema (Spain)/ The Producers Films (UK).

LA LEGGENDA DI AL, JOHN & JACK
(The Legend of Al, John & Jack)
[Comedy, 2002] Script: Aldo, Giovanni, Giacomo, Massimo Venier, Walter Fontana, Paolo Cananzi. Dir: Aldo, Giovanni

Giacomo, Massimo Venier. Phot:
Arnaldo Catinari. Players: Aldo,
Giovanni, Giacomo. Prod:
A.Gi.Di/Medusa Film.

**MA CHE COLPA ABBIAMO
NOI (It's Not Our Fault)**
[Comedy, 2003] Script: Piero
De Bernardi, Pasquale Plastino,
Fiamma Satta, Carlo Verdone.
Dir: Verdone. Phot: Danilo
Desideri. Players: Verdone,
Margherita Buy, Anita Caprioli.
Prod: Virginia/Warner Bros. Italia.

Carlo Verdone in It's Not Our Fault

**LA MEGLIO GIOVENTÙ
(The Best of Youth)**
[Family saga, 2003] Script: Sandro
Petraglia, Stefano Rulli. Dir:
Marco Tullio Giordana. Phot:
Roberto Forza. Players: Luigi Lo
Cascio, Alessio Boni, Maya Sansa,
Jasmine Trinca, Adriana Asti,
Sonia Bergamasco, Fabrizio
Gifuni. Prod: Rai Fiction.

MY NAME IS TANINO
[Comedy, 2003] Script: Paolo
Virzì, Francesco Bruni, Francesco
Piccolo. Dir: Virzì. Phot: Arnaldo
Catinari. Players: Corrado
Fortuna, Mimmo Mignemi.
Prod: Cecchi Gori Group/
Whizbang Films Inc. (US).

**NATALE SUL NILO
(Christmas on the Nile)**
[Farce, 2002] Script: Neri
Parenti, Fausto Brizzi, Lorenzo
De Luca, Marco Martani,
Andrea Margiotta. Dir: Parenti.
Phot: Gian Lorenzo Battaglia.
Players: Christian De Sica,
Massimo Boldi. Prod:
Filmauro/Lola Films (Spain).

PERDUTO AMOR (Lost Love)
[Drama, 2003] Script: Manlio
Sgalambro, Franco Battiato.
Dir: Battiato. Phot: Marco

individuals struggling against corruption", such as Pasquale
Squitieri's **A Second Chance** (L'avvocato De Gregorio) and Luca
Barbareschi's **The Chameleon** (Il trasformista). The Culture
Ministry's grants system is being reformed to allocate more funds
to financially successful companies and less (or none at all) to new
producers. Not that anybody seems to give a damn for such
matters when more than half of the annual output is still drowned
by a distribution system mishandled by a bunch of power-brokers
who ensure that some 60 Italian features a year will never be seen
beyond festivals or one-off, accidental screenings.

Youth has its day

In such a climate it might seem paradoxical that a brave enterprise
like Marco Tullio Giordana's **The Best of Youth** (La meglio
gioventù), produced for Rai TV by Angelo Barbagallo (Nanni
Moretti's usual partner at Sacher Film), could even see the light of
the day. Rai 1 refused to broadcast this six-hour mini-series, but
Cannes selected it, it won Un Certain Regard's main award and it
then secured a theatrical release in many countries, including Italy.
An outstanding, multilayered family saga written as a kind of
autobiography by Sandro Petraglia and Stefano Rulli (inspired by
Visconti's Rocco and His Brothers), it covers the last 40 years of
national troubles, and three generations' highs and lows. An epic
look at the Eternal Youth in all of us is powerfully orchestrated by
Giordana and, all by itself, The Best of Youth brings back a Golden
Age when the public broadcasting network regularly supported
ambitious, experimental works by Rossellini, Fellini, Taviani, Olmi,
Bertolucci and Co.

Marco Tullio Giordana, left, directs Sonia Berganasco in The Best of Youth

Marco Bellocchio and Nanni Moretti directed two small-scale,
digital documentaries, undoubtedly among their most
accomplished creations. **Addio del passato** (literally, Farewell of
the Past) is an expressionist portrait à la Grosz of Piacenza,
Bellocchio's beloved/hated birthplace, and its flaming fervour for

Giuseppe Verdi's operas. **The Last Customer**, which records an old Manhattan pharmacy's final hours, shows Moretti exorcising his fear of losing his dear Nuovo Sacher – a renowned art theatre in Rome threatened with a state eviction order. During the last two years Moretti has become a leader of *girotondi* (ring-arounds), a mass movement protesting against scandalous new laws.

There are some promising debutants to keep an eye on, including Emanuele Crialese after **Grazia's Island** (*Respiro*), successfully released abroad, and Costanza Quatriglio after **The Island** (*L'isola*), both quite similar, folksy stories of children and mothers on the timeless, sundrenched Sicilian archipelago. Daniele Vicari announced himself with **V Max**, a proletarian drama set in Pier Paolo Pasolini's landscapes. Francesco Patierno made **Pater Familias**, a stark neo-realist sketch. Famous singer-composer Franco Battiato turned to directing with **Lost Love** (*Perduto amor*), an intimate self-portrait enriched by evocative pop songs.

The 10th anniversary of Federico Fellini's passing saw his legend re-evaluated by several remarkable books: Tullio Kezich's *Federico Fellini, la vita e i film* (Feltrinelli), Enzo de Castro's *Fellini in cento pagine* (Edizioni dell'Oleandro), Mario Longardi's *Più stelle che in cielo* (Gremese), Bernardino Zapponi's *Il mio Fellini* (Marsilio), Veniero Rizzardi's *L'undicesima musa. Nino Rota e i suoi media* (Rai-Eri) and *Drawing Dreams: Dante Ferretti Production Designer* (Cinecittà Holding). Nanni Moretti's *Caro diario* (Edizioni del Centro Studi, Lipari) is an in-depth coffee-table album devoted to *Dear Diary* (1993).

LORENZO CODELLI is on the board of Cineteca del Friuli and is a regular contributor to *Positif* and other periodicals.

Valeria Golino, Vincenzo Amato, Francesco Casisa. Prod: Fandango/Les Films de Tournelles (France).

RICORDATI DI ME
(Remember Me)
[Drama, 2003] Script: Gabriele Muccino, Heidrun Schleef. Dir: Muccino. Phot: Marcello Montarsi. Players: Fabrizio Bentivoglio, Laura Morante, Nicoletta Romanoff, Monica Bellucci, Gabriele Lavia. Prod: Fandango Film/Medusa Film/Buena Vista (France)/Vice Versa Film (UK).

IL POSTO DELL'ANIMA
(The Place of the Soul)
[Comedy, 2003] Script: Domenico Starnone, Riccardo Milani. Dir: Milani. Phot: Arnaldo Catinari. Players: Silvio Orlando, Michele Placido, Paola Cortellesi. Prod: Albachiara/Rai Cinema/Bianca Film.

UN VIAGGIO CHIAMATO AMORE (A Journey Called Love)
[Romance, 2002] Script: Heidrun Schleef, Diego Ribon, Michele Placido. Dir: Placido. Phot: Luca Bigazzi. Players: Laura Morante, Stefano Accorsi, Alessandro Haber, Galatea Ranzi. Prod: Cattleya/Rai Cinema/Stream.

Pontecorvo. Players: Corrado Fortuna, Donatella Finocchiaro. Prod: L'Ottava.

PIAZZA DELLE CINQUE LUNE
(Piazza of the Five Moons)
[Political thriller, 2003] Script: Renzo Martinelli, Fabio Campus. Dir: Martinelli. Phot: Blasco Giurato. Players: Donald Sutherland, Giancarlo Giannini, Stefania Rocca. Prod: Martinelli Film Company/Istituto Luce/Spice Blue Star/Box Films.

PINOCCHIO
[Comedy, 2002] Script: Vincenzo Cerami, Roberto Benigni, from the novel by Carlo Collodi. Dir: Benigni. Players: Benigni,

Nicoletta Braschi, Carlo Giuffrè, Peppe Barra. Prod: Melampo Cinematografica/Cecchi Gori Group/Miramax Italia.

IL PRANZO DELLA DOMENICA (Sunday Lunch)
[Comedy, 2003] Script: Enrico Vanzina, Carlo Vanzina. Dir: Carlo Vanzina. Phot: Claudio Zamarion. Players: Massimo Ghini, Barbara De Rossi, Rocco Papaleo, Elena Sofia Ricci. Prod: Rai Cinema/International Video 80.

RESPIRO (Grazia's Island)
[Drama, 2002] Script and Dir: Emanuele Crialese. Phot: Claudio Zamarion. Players:

Quotes of the Year

"*A Heart Elsewhere* is a kind of summary of my whole youth and perhaps quite a bit of my adult life."
PUPI AVATI, *director*.

"I didn't know what was happening to me, but now I understand. So I'm at work on a movie about my own trials which will name all the names. I'm not afraid of anybody."
VITTORIO CECCHI GORI, *'re-born' producer*.

Italy – Donatello Awards 2003

Film: *Facing Window* (*La finestra di fronte*).
Director: Pupi Avati (*A Heart Elsewhere/Il cuore altrove*).
Debuting Director: Daniele Vicari
(*V Max/Velocita massima*).
Producer: Domenico Procacci (*Respiro*).
Actress: Giovanna Mezzogiorno
(*Facing Window*).
Actor: Massimo Girotti (*Facing Window*).
Supporting Actor: Ernesto Mahieux
(*The Embalmer/L'imbalsamatore*).
Supporting Actress: Piera Degli Esposti
(*The Hour of Religion – My Mother's Smile/L'ora di religione – Il sorriso di mia madre*).
Script: Ugo Chiti, Matteo Garrone, Massimo Gaudioso (*The Embalmer*).
Cinematography: Daniele Nannuzzi
(*El Alamein*).
Music: Andrea Guerra (*Facing Window*).
Art Direction: Danilo Donati (*Pinocchio*).

Tartan Films Distribution

Emanuele Grialese's **Respiro**, *for which Domenico Procacci was named Best Producer at the Donatellos 2003*

Costume Design: Danilo Donati (*Pinocchio*).
Editing: Cecilia Zanuso (*El Alamein*).
Sound: Andrea Giorgio Moser (*El Alamein*).
Short Film: *Racconto di guerra* (Mario Amaura); *Rosso Fango* (Paolo Ameli).
Foreign Film: *The Pianist*.
David School Prize: *Facing Window*.

Kobal

MASSIMO GIROTTI, *pictured above in Visconti's* Ossessione *(1943), died on January 5, 2003, aged 84. He was posthumously named Best Actor at the Donatello Awards 2003 for his performance as an amnesiac in Ferzan Ozpetek's* Facing Window.

Japan Frank Segers

The Year's Best Films

Frank Segers' selection:
The Twilight Samurai
(Dir: Yoji Yamada)
A Snake of June
(Dir: Shinya Tsukamoto)
Alive (Dir: Ryuhei Kitamura)
Bright Future
(Dir: Kiyoshi Kurosawa)
***When The Last Sword
Is Drawn*** (Dir: Yojiro Takita)

Bright Future

Recent and Forthcoming Films

BATTLE ROYALE 2
*[Drama, 2003] Script: Kenta
Fukasaku, Norio Kida. Dir: Kinji
Fukasaku, Kenta Fukasaku.
Phot: Junichi Fujisawa. Players:
Tatsuya Fujiwara, Riki Takeuchi,
Beat Takeshi, Ai Maeda. Prod:
Kimio Kataoka, Mitsuru Kawase.*
Three years after *Battle Royale*'s
survivors, Nanahara Shuya and
Nakagawa Noriko, escaped from
the island, the world has
descended into an Age of
Terrorism. A year after the
destruction of the Capitol, a
motley bunch of 42 juvenile
delinquents and truants is
abducted by the military, trapped
inside a vast tent and forced to
put on military uniforms and
lethal electronic necklaces.

The notion that the Japanese film industry has been running on auto-pilot these last few years, powered exclusively by Hollywood films and domestic animation, should be rejected. Yes, Japan's film establishment has been resistant to the idea that original, live-action production is important, if not vital, and to do it right you have to spend major money and take risks. But that resistance is starting to crumble.

For one thing, there have been top-level changes at the three major studios – Toho, Toei and Shochiku – with each new regime proclaiming the importance of production. Tsuyoshi Okada, president of Toei (and the son of former Toei chairman and industry guru Shigeru Okada), has said that one way to improve the less than perfect health of the company's film division is to spend more on its upcoming productions. At Toho, new president Hideyuki Takai has put great faith in several young directors unashamedly tackling subjects of popular appeal to mainstream audiences. At Shochiku, president Nobuyoshi Otani has promised to push output to about 10 titles annually, with more resources devoted to each film.

Are these execs deluded – given that only one Japanese title, the animated **The Cat Returns** (*Neko no ongaeshi*), made 2002's list of the top 10 box-office hits? And what about other key statistics: the market share for local titles, including animation, was a disappointing 27.1% (down from 39% in 2001) and the 293 Japanese live-action films released in 2002 took just 8% of the market. Of these about 100 were soft-core films playing specialised venues, and only about 50 were big-studio films, the remaining arthouse titles tending to turn up on the festival circuit and then virtually disappear on limited release at home.

The studio execs carefully hedge their bets by noting that the emphasis is largely on fewer, better-financed films, and pointing out that because Japan, unlike Korea, does not boast a feisty independent sector the majors are in a strong position to lure big-money corporate backers to support these more expensive new productions.

The emphasis on enlarging attendance through "event" films from the Japanese majors comes at a time when Japan has more screens than at any time since 1972 (2,635, up 50 from 2001). But

ODORU DAISOSASEN II
(Bayside Shakedown 2)
[Drama, 2003] Script: Ryoichi Kimizuka. Dir: Katsuyuki Motohiro. Players: Yuji Oda, Toshiro Yanagiba. Prod: Fuji TV. Motohiro's sequel to the highly successful 1998 feature version of a popular TV series about a tough detective working the Bayside Precinct. Pretty boy Yuji Oda returns in the lead.

UNTITLED HOU HSIAO HSIEN PROJECT
[Drama, 2003]. Dir: Hou Hsiao Hsien. Prod: Shochiku Co.

CLUB SHINCHUGUN
(Out of this World)
[Drama, 2003] Dir: Junji Sakamoto. Phot: Norimichi Kasamatsu. Players: Peter Mullan, Masato Hagiwara, Joe Odagiri. Prod: Shochiku Co./Eisei Gekijo, Kadokawa Daiei Pictures/Asahi Broadcasting/FCB Worldwide/Sedic International/Kino. In 1947, musically talented youngsters in Japan befriend Allied forces, including American GIs, in the hope of being hired for various functions as jazz musicians (jazz performances were banned during the war).

CASSHERN
[Sci-fi action, 2003] Dir: Kazuaki Kiriya. Prod: Shochiku Co. Music video director Kiriya's feature debut, adapted from a highly popular 1970s animation about an eponymous human-turned-robot who battles valiantly to save war-torn Earth.

GET UP!
[Drama, 2003] Dir: Kazuyuki Izutsu. Phot: Hideo Yamamoto. Players: Toshiyuki Nishinda, Takako Tokiwa. Prod: Cine Qua Non.

CHILSIK NO NATSU
[Drama, 2003] Dir: Kiyoshi Sasabe. Players: Kiri Mizutani, Yasuyo Mimura. Prod: Premier International.

GEGE
[Drama, 2003] Dir: Itsumichi Isomura. Players: Takao Osawa,

total attendance remained almost flat at 161 million admissions, and there is concern that the building boom may have gone too far.

With digital broadcasting scheduled to begin in Japan at the end of 2003, broadband services picking up steam and home video growing by 10% in 2002, thanks to DVD, execs are preoccupied with supplying films as software for these expanding platforms – and to maximise revenues they must make original titles, not simply import foreign product on limited rights deals.

Min Tanaka, left, and Hiroyuki Sanada in **The Twilight Samurai**

Yamada's *Samurai* sunset

The local "event" film of 2002 came from one of Japan's most seasoned directors, the commercial mainstay of Shochiku, 70-year-old Yoji Yamada. His **The Twilight Samurai** (*Tasogare seibi*) commanded strong numbers at the box office and had the critics in ecstasy; it took 12 of the 13 Japan Academy Awards and was voted best Japanese film of 2002 in the prestigious *Kinema Junpo* magazine critics' poll.

The European, socially conscious, humanist style of the 1950s and 1960s, an approach out of fashion in Japan nowadays, infuses Yamada's comedies (the 48-title *Tora-san* series), as well as **Twilight Samurai**, his first foray into traditional costume drama. There's the standard quotient of swordplay, but the main character – a principled, low-level samurai trying to support two young children and a senile mother on his minuscule earnings – incorporates qualities found in the stalwart, good-hearted protagonists of so many of Yamada's previous 77 titles. It is Yamada's most inventive and satisfying work in years. Why he has not yet had a major retrospective at an A-list festival is a mystery. Yojiro Takita's **When the Last Sword Is Drawn** (*Mibu gishi den*), lacks the soul of Yamada's picture, but still delivers stylish, large-scale samurai action, complete with Edo-period settings, ace swordsmen and Byzantine clan politics.

Kiichi Nakai, centre, in **When the Last Sword Is Drawn**

Toei's biggest summer film of 2003 was the late Kinji Fukasaku's *Battle Royale II – Requiem*. He died while shooting this sequel to his hugely successful, controversial and violent 2000 title about high-school students taken to a remote island, given weapons and told to kill each other. His son, Kenta Fukasaku, took over and on its wide release in July it comfortably outperformed the original film.

Battle Royale II's sadistic high-school principal, Takeshi Kitano, is following up two directorial flops – *Brother* and *Dolls* – with *Zatoichi*, a feature film version of a popular TV hero, a blind masseur and master swordsman, which suggests that Kitano is aiming for a commercial hit at all costs. The original television series aired from 1962, and ran for 26 episodes until 1989.

A *Snake*, a jellyfish and a dinosaur

Despite the relatively narrow commercial confines of live-action Japanese cinema, a surprisingly diverse menu of challenging new entries surfaced over the last year. Most intriguing was Shinya Tsukamoto's erotically charged **A Snake of June** (*Rokugatsu no hebi*), about the conjugal recharging of a balding, bespectacled, workaholic husband (Yuji Kotari) and his lissome, very proper social-worker wife (sensationally portrayed by Asuka Kurosawa). Tsukamoto, opting for black-and-white cinematography shot largely in pouring rain, lends a distinctly noirish feel to this tale of the wife's sexual blackmail by a deranged stalker, much to the husband's forbidden pleasure. A compelling psychological mystery, skilfully told.

Ryuhei Kitamura's **Alive** is a polished screen version of Tsutomu Takahashi's *manga* about a condemned murderer who survives by becoming a subject in a gruelling scientific experiment. Special effects and existentialism in one tidy package. Kiyoshi Kurosawa directed **Bright Future** (*Akarui mirai*), one of the two Japanese films

Yuriko Ishida. Prod: Fuji Television/Toho/Gentosha/Dentsu/Altamira Pictures.

DRAGON HEAD
[Drama, 2003] Dir: George Iida. Phot: Junichiro Hayashi. Players: Satoshi Tsumabuki, Sayaka.

ROBOCON
[Drama, 2003] Script and Dir: Tomoyuki Furuyama. Prod: Robocon Production Committee.

ASHURA NO GOTOKU
[Drama, 2003] Script: Tomomi Tsutsui. Dir: Yoshimitsu Morita. Phot: Nobuyasu Kita. Players: Shinobu Otake, Hitomi Kuroki. Prod: Ashira No Gotoku Production Committee.

HACHIGATSU NO KARIYUSHI
[Drama, 2003] Script: Yume Takagari. Dir: Iwao Takahashi. Phot: Masakazu Oka. Players: Ryuhei Matsuda, Haruka Suenaga. Prod: Gaga Communications, VAP.

9 SOULS
[Drama, 2003] Script and Dir: Toshiaki Toyoda. Players: Ryuhei Matsuda, Yoshio Harada. Prod: Tohokushinsha Film/Eisei Gekijo/Film Makers/Little More.

THE HUNTER AND THE HUNTED
[Drama, 2003] Script: Yoshiko Kobayashi, Katsuhiko Manabe. Dir: Izuru Narushima. Phot: Takahide Shibanushi. Players: Koji Yakusho, Akira Emoto. Prod: Groove Corp./Culture Publishers/Eisei Gekijo/Japan Home Video.

ANTENNA
[Drama, 2003] Script: Takashi Ujita, Kazuyoshi Kumakiri. Dir: Kumakiri. Phot: Takahide Shibanushi. Players: Ryo Kase, Akemi Kobayashi. Prod: Groove Corp./Office Shirous.

SAYONARA KURO
[Drama, 2003] Script: George Matsuoka, Emiko Hiramatsu, Katsumi Ishikawa. Dir: Matsuoka. Phot: Norimichi Kasamatsu. Players: Satoshi Tsumabuki, Ayumi Ito. Prod:

Cine Qua Non/Dentsu/
Eisei Gekijo/Hapinet Pictures/
Artist Film.

**JOSE TO TORA TO
SAKANA TACHI**
*[Drama, 2003] Script: Aya
Watanabe. Dir: Isshin Inudo.
Players: Satoshi Tsumabuki,
Chizuru Ikewaki. Prod:
IMJ Entertainment.*

ZATOICHI
*[Drama, 2003] Script and Dir:
Takeshi Kitano. Players: Beat
Takeshi [Kitano], Tadanobu
Asano. Prod: Bandai
Visual/Tokyo FM/
Dentsu/TVAsahi/Saito
Entertainment/Office Kitano.*

Takeshi Kitano as **Zatoichi**

Quote of the Year

"Though this battle may cost
me my life, I will give it
without a shred of regret."
KINJI FUKASAKU, *as he began
directing* Battle Royale II *in
December 2002. He died at 72
on January 12, 2003, and the
film was completed by his only
son, Kenta.*

in the main competition at Cannes in 2003, alongside **Shara**
(*Sharasojyu*) from the promising 34-year-old, Naomi Kawase.

Kurosawa is always a provocative storyteller and *Bright Future*'s
tale of an emotionally unstable young factory worker's attachment
to a convicted murderer's pet jellyfish and the killer's father (yes, in
that order) provides low-key fascination and a tough, convincing
performance from Asano Tadanobu. And where would another year
in Japanese cinema be without the latest instalment of Toho's most
famous franchise, **Godzilla: Godzilla Against Mechagodzilla**,
directed by Masaaki Tezuka, has the renowned dinosaur battling
a robotic, supercharged version of himself.

Shochiku scored a special coup by organising a retrospective of 33
newly printed Yasujiro Ozu films at specialised venues in Tokyo and
at the Berlin and New York film festivals. The event, marking the
centenary of Ozu's birth in Tokyo on December 12, 1903, also
prompted Taiwanese director Hou Hsiao Hsien to undertake with
Shochiku's backing an as-yet untitled drama to start shooting in
summer 2003, dedicated to the film master.

Hideyuki Hirayama's **Out**, about an abused wife who kills and
dismembers her husband, surprised many by being selected as
Japan's foreign-language Oscar entry, ahead of Hayao Miyazaki's box-
office sensation *Spirited Away* (which went on to win Best Animated
Feature). Miyazaki is completing *Howl's Moving Castle*, scheduled for
release in summer 2004 and based on a 1986 novel about a girl who
is transformed into an old woman by a wizard's spell.

FRANK SEGERS is a freelance writer who for many years
specialised in Far Eastern entertainment issues for *Variety*. He is
now a regular contributor to *Moving Pictures* and *The Hollywood
Reporter*, covering Japan and South Korea.

School kids prepare to fight in **Battle Royale II**

Kazakhstan Eugene Zykov

The Year's Best Films

Eugene Zykov's selection:

My Brother Silk Road
(Dir: Marat Sarulu)

Leila's Prayer
(Dir: Satybaldy Narymbetov)

Three Brothers
(Dir: Serik Aprymov)

Do Not Cry
(Dir: Amir Karakulov)

***Umai – Mother-Goddess
of Fertility***
(Short. Dir: Narym Igilik)

Leila's Prayer

Recent and Forthcoming Films

OSTROV VOZROZHDENIJA
(**Renaissance Island**)
*[Drama, 2003] Script: Rustem
Abdrashev, based on the poem
by Joras Abdrashev.
Dir: Abdrashev. Phot: Khasan
Kydyraliev. Players: Temirzhan
Danyarov, Zhanel Makazhanova,
Mereke Uly Sayat. Prod: Kazakh
Film Studios.*
A teenager enjoys his first
romance in contrast to the
cynical love affairs around him.

K azakh cinema is gaining prominence, with a number of local films securing festival honours in 2002-03. Serik Aprymov's *Three Brothers* took Best Film in Delhi and Amir Karakulov's *Do Not Cry* won Best Director and Critics' Choice awards at Kinoshock in Russia. Saken Narymbetrov's **Leila's Prayer** (*Lelanyn koze*) was deservedly nominated for a Nika (Russian Oscar) for Best Film from the CIS and Baltics. This is a wonderful film about a teenage girl with a magically powerful imagination, who gradually learns to use her gift to defend herself or to have fun. Marat Sarulu's Kyrgyz-Kazakh co-production *My Brother Silk Road* won awards at the Festival des Trois Continents, Nantes and the Asian Film Festival in Vesul.

Kazakh festival activity is also on the increase. In addition to the annual, purely domestic The Stars of Shaken event each October, the second Eurasia International Festival is planned for Almaty in 2004. In 2002-03 a number of European Film Weeks were held in major Kazakh cities to help local filmgoers recall Soviet-era traditions of popular West European cinema. Meanwhile the European presence in Kazakh movie theatres has grown from 5% of titles to almost 20%. Russian and Asian repertoire accounts for 11% of titles, and seven out of ten are American. By early 2004 multiplexes and upgraded movie-houses are expected to showcase more Kazakh films, but, inevitably, American titles dominate these venues and, led by blockbusters such as *The Matrix Reloaded*, admissions for the first half of 2003 were up by almost 15% on the second half of 2002, according to leading distributor Otau Cinema.

Young, gifted and Kazakh

In April 2003 the strategic position of chairman of the 300-strong Kazakh Film-Makers' Union was taken by Amir Karakulov, 35, winner of the Young Director's Main Award at the Tokyo Film Festival for *The Last Holidays* as well as the Kinoshock prize for *Do Not Cry*. Also an experienced producer of TV commercials for leading European agencies, Karakulov leads a 'new wave' of pragmatic young talents in the local film industry, mostly graduates of the Moscow or Almaty film academies. At Kazakh Film, Karakulov took charge of the new Debut Film Studios, which released the contemporary drama **Renaissance Island**, directed by film academy graduate Rustem Abdrashev.

SARDAR (*literally*, **Leader of 1,000 Warriors**)
[Historical epic, 2003] Dir: Bulat Kalymbetov. Phot: Khasan Kadyraliev, Renat Kosai. Prod: Studios Suar (Urumchi)/Kazakh Film Studios.
In a vicious war between two tribes only love is a peace-maker.

You Need a Puppy

TEBE NUZHEN SCHENOK (You Need A Puppy)
[Family, 2003] Script and Dir: Kanymbek Kasymbekuly, Alibek Amseuly, Esken Elubaev. Phot: Marat Tokhtabakiev. Players: Azamat Omarov, Atageldi Ismailov, Tamara Kosubaeva. Prod: Kazakh Film Studios.
A heartwarming story of a village boy who saves puppies, meets friends and wins his parents' respect.

MALEN'KIE LYUDI (Little People)
[Drama, 2003] Script and Dir: Nariman Turebayev. Phot: Boris Troshev. Players: Erzhan Bekmuratov, Oleg Kerimov. Prod: Kazakh Film Studios/Kadam Studios (Kazakhstan)/Minima Cinema (France).
Life is harsh for two young men in today's Kazakhstan.

In search of the young audience, Kazakh Film released **You Need a Puppy** (*Tebe nuzhen schenok*), which did well at the box-office, and its production slate also included two big-budget epics in the Kurosawa tradition, with exotic locations and armies of extras on horesback. Released in 2003, **Sardar** (in ancient Kazakh the word means 'leader of 1,000 warriors') evokes the war between the Kazakhs and the Jungars. In summer 2003 shooting began on the Kazakh/US/Russian co-production *The Nomad (Kochevnik)*.

A few more international projects are in development. Shooting and post-production will be based in France for *Tracker*, the screen-version of Alexander Pushkin's classics about a tracker whose daughter runs away with a French traveller.

Murat Nugmanov's independent Scythe National Producers' Centre released four shorts by first-time directors, with support from Kazakh Film and a local affiliate of the Soros Foundation. Sunflowers is about the miraculous love between a young girl and her grandmother and the equally traditional *Apple* is an amusing look at two pedestrians who show their ambitions in the street. More innovative are *Sparrow from Mtsentovo*, a bittersweet tale of survival by a modern young Kazakh woman, and *Umai – Mother Goddess of Fertility*, which showcases an old woman who relives her life in flashbacks as she looks through cherished belongings shortly before her death.

EUGENE ZYKOV is a Moscow-based freelance writer. He heads a Moscow-based information agency, which provides PR, analysis, location and production services for the film and TV industries.

KOCHEVNIK (The Nomad)
[Historical epic, forthcoming]
Script: Roustam Ibragimbekov.
Dir: Ivan Passer. Prod: Kazakh
Film Studios/Ibrus (Russia)/
Ask Film (US).

OKHOTNIK (Hunter)
[Drama, 2003] Script and Dir: Serik Aprymov. Phot: Khasan Kydyraliev. Prod: East Cinema in association with Kazakh Film Studios/NHK/Fond Sud/ Fondazione Montecinema Verita.
Man vs nature in a remote village.

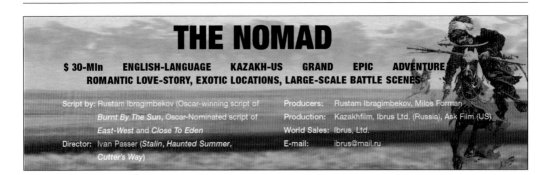

Latvia Andris Rozenbergs

Recent and Forthcoming Films

SAUJA LOZU
(A Handful of Bullets)
[Drama, 2001] Script: Lauris Gundars. Dir: Una Celms. Phot: Janis Eglitis. Players: Janis Murnieks, Kristine Nevarauska, Harijs Spanovskis. Prod: Kaupo Filma/Latsfilm AB (Sweden).
Love triangle amidst post-Soviet chaos.

Laila Pakalnina's **The Python**

PITONS (The Python)
[Drama, 2003] Script and Dir: Laila Pakalnina. Phot: Gints Berzins. Players: Mara Kimele, Ilze Pukinska, Januss Johansons, Juris Zagars. Prod: Hargla (Latvia)/Acuba Film (Estonia).
In an average school in the post-Soviet era, somebody has defecated in the attic. The tyrannical headmistress investigates.

ATVED MANI MAJAS
(Take Me Home)
[Drama, 2003] Script: Margarita Pervenecka. Dir: Arvids Krievs. Phot: Davis Simanis. Players: Kristine Nevarauska, Girts Krumins, Martins Freimanis. Prod: Kaupo Filma.
Seduced by sex, drugs and gambling, several characters enter into conflict with society.

HONEY BABY
[Drama, 2003] Script: Mika Kaurismäki, Ulrich Mayszies,

After Latvia joined Eurimages and the MEDIA programme in 2002, the National Film Centre, in co-operation with the various non-governmental film-makers' organisations, was asked to submit a proposal for boosting state support for international co-productions. So in November the future of the film sector seemed bright, until the newly elected government suddenly decided to suspend the funding of the film branch altogether. Only after a major outcry did the cabinet agree to set funding at slightly less than its previous, insufficient level, with the result that total state support of around $960,000 a year is less than the average budget for a European fiction feature.

While film executives reached for their heart pills, business somehow continued as usual. Laila Pakalnina, an award-winner at Cannes in 1996 and 1998, finished her second feature **The Python** (*Pitons*), a drama representing school as a model of a totalitarian society. It was scheduled for release in autumn 2003, as were Mika Kaurismäki's *Honey Baby* (Latvia's first Eurimages co-production), a modern reworking of the Orpheus and Eurydice myth, and Arvids Krievs' *Take Me Home* (*Atved mani majas*), from a debut screenplay by recent Academy of Culture graduate Margarita Pervenecka. Her script attacks the infantilism of her generation and its inability adequately to respond to the challenges of life. But Krievs, one of Latvia's best directors, has never strictly followed his scripts and this is unlikely to be an exception.

Kristine Nevarauska in **Take Me Home**

Eike Gorezecka. Dir:
Kaurismäki. Phot: Timo
Salminen. Players: Henry
Thomas, Irina Björklund. Prod:
Stamina Media GmbH
(Germany)/Twenty Vision
Filmproduktion GmbH
(Germany)/Marianna Films OY
(Finland)/Eho Filma (Latvia).
Road-movie love story inspired
by Orpheus and Eurydice.

RIGAS SARGI
(The Guards of Riga)
[Historical action drama, 2004]
Script: Andris Kolbergs.
Dir: Aigars Grauba.
Prod: Platforma Filma.

FLASHBACK
[Documentary, 2002] Script and
Dir: Herz Frank. Phot: Herz
Frank and Victor Griberman.
Prod: EFEF/Kaupo Filma.
Faced with a life-threatening
heart condition, documentary
film-maker Herz Frank made
this magnificent confession.

FOTO: INTA RUKA
(Photo: Inta Ruka)
[Documentary, 2003] Script and
Dir: Arvids Krievs. Phot: Davis
Simanis. Prod: Kaupo Filma.
Inta Ruka is a cleaner in the
Swedish Embassy in Riga, but
for 20 years has taken
internationally acclaimed
photographs.

SEKOTAJI (Followers)
[Documentary, 2003] Script:
Elvita Ruka, Andis Miziss. Dir:
Miziss. Phot: Agris Birzulis, Andris
Prieditis, Maris Maskalans. Prod:
Vides filmu studija (Environment
Film Studio).
In the depths of the Siberian taiga,
a former soviet militiaman has
proclaimed himself a new Christ.

Quote of the Year

"I can't stand young guys
saying about Latvia 'I hate
this country'. We want to
show that our statehood
was gained at great cost."

AIVARS EKIS, *producer,*
launching historical drama
The Guards of Riga.

Pitch perfect?

Pitching sessions were held by the Film Centre and the expert
commissions had a tough job picking winners from 32 fiction, 60
documentary and 24 animation projects. The most interesting
competition was in the fiction sector and two audience-friendly
projects were approved. The first, *The Guards of Riga* (*Rigars sargi*),
is an action film that was brilliantly pitched by the producer and
manager of a private TV channel, Aivars Ekis. It dramatises November
11, 1919, a crucial date in the battle for Latvian independence,
when Latvian riflemen, most of them inexperienced volunteers,
somehow managed to defeat a larger, better-armed force of German
and Russian mercenaries. Ekis and director Aigars Grauba will be
following the same formula they used successfully in *Dangerous
Summer*: simple human drama against the background of a major
historical event.

The other project is *Waterball for the Fat Tomcat* (*Udensbumba
resnajam runcim*), a warm-hearted and humorous family film that is
the latest collaboration between scriptwriter Alvis Lapins and director
Varis Brasla, who have a rare gift for understanding children. It's the
tale of little Marta, who uses a plastic flask full of water to scare away
the fat cat that chases little birds. Marta's mother has to become
a hairdresser in Riga after losing her job as a cultural organiser, leaving
Marta at the mercy of her disciplinarian sister Biruta – and giving her
a multitude of targets for the waterbomb.

Regrettably, a MEDIA-developed project, *Celebration of Life*, from
producer Antra Cilinska and director Peteris Krilovs, had to be
postponed for another year because the earlier support for *Guards
of Riga* and *Waterball* meant that the production funding assigned
to fiction films had almost run out. The script by Lauris Gundars
was the best I've read in the 12 years since independence.
A young, successful businesswoman is invited to the funeral of the
mother who entrusted her upbringing to others in the hope that she
might have a better life. The young lady meets several people who
have played central roles in the life of her mother, which comes to
represent the whole history of Latvia since 1939.

Sadly, some 10 days after the pitching competition in March 2003,
the well-known documentary director Ansis Epners died, aged 65.
Despite everything, it is encouraging to note that producers, directors
and film executives now meet regularly to discuss promoting Latvian
films at Cannes, Annecy or Karlovy Vary, in a matter-of-fact way that
was absolutely unimaginable only a few years ago.

ANDRIS ROZENBERGS has directed seven fiction films and
a dozen documentaries. He is Head of the Film Registry at Latvia's
National Film Centre.

Lebanon Mohammed Rouda

The Year's Best Films

Mohammed Rouda's
selection:

Dreams of the Exile
(Dir: Mai Masri)

In the Shadows of the City
(Dir: Jean Khalil Chamoun)

When Maryam Spoke
(Dir: Assad Fouladkar)

Recent Films

AHLAM AL MANFA
(Frontiers of Dreams and Fears)
*[Documentary, 2001] Script and
Dir: Mai Masrei. Prod: Nour
Prods, with ITVS Prods.*
The lives of Palestinians living
in a camp in Beirut, through the
eyes and experiences of 14 year-
old Mona.

ARDH MAJHOULA
(Terra Incognita)
*[Drama, 2002] Script and Dir:
Ghassan Salhab. Phot: Jacques
Boulquin. Players: Carole
Abboud, Abla Khoury, Walid
Sadek. Prod: Agat Films/
CIE Films.*
A group of young women and
men, who all witnessed the war,
reflect on the past.

MIN HON MARRA AL HOB
*[Drama, 2003] Script and Dir:
Borhan Alawiya. Phot: Raymond
Fromon. Players: Fadi Abi
Khalil, Rymond Hosni, George
Ka'di. Prod: Jal Film/
Alexie Films/B. A. Films.*
Coming out of the war, two men
find themselves unable to cope
with peacetime. After their wives
leave them, they decide to treat
society as it treats them, with
revenge and contempt.

TAIF AL-MADINA
(In the Shadows of the City)

Four Lebanese features went into production in 2002 and are ready now for local and international exposure as the latest offerings from an industry that, despite its market limitations, never stopped functioning, even during the bleakest days of the civil war (1976-91). Some Lebanese directors gained international recognition in this period, through their determination to make films about the war, including the late Maroun Bagdadi (*Little Wars*, *The Veiled Man*) and Ziad Al Doweiri (*West Beirut*). Others made their first films during the war and continued in peacetime, among them Randa Shahal Sabbag, Samir Habshi and Jean Khalil Chamoun. Others joined the parade after the war stopped, including Ghassan Salhab, responsible for **Beirut Phantoms** (*Ashbah Beirut*), a drama about a man believed to have died during the war who's found still trying to reassemble his shattered life, and **Terra Incognita** (*Ardh majhoula*).

The four new films are Borhan Alawiya's **Love Passed from Here** (*Min hona marra alhob*), Randa Shahal Sabbag's **The Kite** (*Ta'ira min warak*), Mahmoud Hojeij's **The Silent Majority** (*Al akthariya al samita*) and Bahij Hojeij's **Girdle of Fire** (*Zinnar el-nar*). Alawiya, the eldest of this group, began his career in the early 1970s and, like many others, moved to Europe during the war, where he found backing to make documentaries in Egypt and Lebanon. *Love Passed from Here* is his first fiction feature in more than 20 years and its late 2003 release was eagerly anticipated in Lebanon, where he now lives.

Plus ça change...

The inherent problems for Lebanese production are unchanged. While Egyptian cinema towered over all other neighbouring cinemas in the last two decades, Lebanese producers stood little chance of recouping their investments in 100% local production from the tiny domestic theatrical market, and were obliged to forge partnerships with Egypt, Syria and, in a few cases, Turkey. This is still the case, even after the end of Egyptian dominance, and now all directors need co-production money, most of it from France. Despite this shortage of finance, the last three years have been very productive even before taking into account the dozens of amateur and student films, some of them very impressive, that are made every year.

*[War drama, 2002] Script and
Dir: Jean Khalik Chamoun.
Phot: Youcef Sahraoui. Players:
Majdi Machmouchi, Christine
Choueiri, Ammar Chalk, Ahmad
Itani. Prod: Nour Prods/Cine-
Sud, Jean Khalik Chamoun.*
In 1975, a 12-year-old boy
emigrates from southern
Lebanon to Beirut, seeking refuge
from Israeli shellings, just as war
reaches the capital.

LAMMA HIKYIT MARYAM
(When Maryam Spoke)
*[Drama, 2002] Script, Dir and
Prod: Assad Fouladkar. Phot:
Joseph Shemali. Players:
Bernadette Habeib, Talal Al Jordi,
Renee Deek, Umaya Laboud.*
A husband and wife are forced to
divorce, despite their mutual love,
because his family blames her for
their failure to have children.

ZINNAR EL-NAR
(Girdle of Fire)
*[Drama, 2003] Script and Dir:
Bahij Hojeij, based on the novel*
Despotism *by Rachid El-Da'eef.
Phot: Maxime Oroux. Players:
Nidaa' Wakim, Hasan Farhat,
Bernadette Hadeeb, Abdallah
Al Homsy.*
During the civil war a university
professor tries to isolate himself
from the war, but finds he
must act.

Quote of the Year

"Because of the limited
budget, I asked all my actors
to lower their already small
salaries. In return I promised
to finish the film fast and it
took me just two weeks."
*ASSAD FOULAKAR, director
of* When Maryam Spoke.

There have even been some local hits, including **Most Unbearable** (*Asaal shee*). Directed by Shadi Hanna and based on a popular TV comedy series and packed with ironic, sometimes political jokes, it sold 120,000 tickets in 2001. In 2002, Samir Habshi followed his highly artistic debut *The Hurricane* (*Al asifa*) with a teenage romantic comedy, **A Trip** (*Mishwar*), which sold almost 75,000 tickets.

Jean Khalil Chamoun, who like his wife, Mai Masri, is an acclaimed documentary director, made his first fiction film, **In the Shadows of the City** (*Tayf al-madina*), but this impressive war drama sold fewer than 9,000 tickets. Randa Shahal Sabbag made **Civilisées** (*Al motahadiroon*), which started production in 1999 and was seen on the festival circuit in 2000 before premiering in Lebanon in 2001 after the censors cut more than a third of its 100 minutes, mainly for its foul language and a story (the difficult love between a Christian girl and a Muslim fighter during the war) that the censors considered offensive towards ex-warring parties. In 2002-03, **When Maryam Spoke** (*Lamma hikyit Maryam*) brought international festival acclaim for the talented Assad Fouladkar.

When Maryam Spoke

Many Lebanese films, especially the better ones, are still reflecting on the civil war and its aftermath. The industry hopes that the government, through the National Centre of Cinema (established in the early 1970s), may increase its film subsidies, but that is unlikely, given the harsh economic conditions in a country that was once the jewel of the Middle East.

MOHAMMED ROUDA is a Lebanese-born film critic and the author of *Book of Cinema* (four volumes, 1984-94) and *Hollywood and the Arabs* (2001). He first wrote for *IFG* in the 1970s.

Lithuania Grazina Arlickaite

The Year's Best Films

Grazina Arlickaite's selection:
Utterly Alone
(Dir: Jonas Vaitkus)
Sunday. The Gospel According to Lift-Man Albert
(Short. Dir: Arunas Matelis)
The Life of Venecijus and Ceasar's Death
(Dir: Janina Lapinskaite)
Last Car
(Short. Dir: Audrius Stonys)
Trolleybus Town (Docu. Dir: Giedre Beinoriute).

Recent and Forthcoming Films

PASKUTINIS VAGONAS (Last Car)
[Short drama, 2002] Script and Dir: Audrius Stonys. Phot: Rimvydas Leipus. Players: Juozas Budraitis, Arnas Vysockis. Prod: Litnek Studio.
A father and his son, wandering musicians, busk their way through every carriage of a train until, in the last compartment, they are confronted by an aggressive gang – an encounter that changes their lives forever.

SEKMADIENIS. EVANGELIJA PAGAL LIFTININKA ALBERTA (Sunday. The Gospel According to Lift-Man Albert)
[Documentary, 2003] Script and Dir: Arunas Matelis. Phot: Rimvydas Leipus, Andrejus Trukanas, Vytautas Survila. Prod: Nominum, in association with LKS (Lithuania)/HBF (The Netherlands)/DFI (Denmark).
A weird summer's day in the life of lift-man Albert.

Lithuanian cinema took great pride when the young director Arunas Matelis received a lot of attention at Cannes in 2003 with his poetic documentary short, *Sunday. The Gospel According to Lift-Man Alberta (Sekmadienis. Evangelija pagal liftininka Alberta).* Matelis combines the documentary artist's eye for unstaged reality with ironic, post-modern touches.

With **Utterly Alone** (*Vienui vieni*), theatre and film director Jonas Vaitkus dramatised the life and adventures of the legendary Lithuanian partisan Juozas Luksa, intertwining his love for a woman and his relationships with his parents and brothers with his heroic exploits against the Soviets. As the country nears integration into the European Union, *Utterly Alone* forcefully reminds audiences of the true human cost of Lithuanian independence.

Two important co-productions are under way. The first is from Lithuanian's best-known director internationally, Sarunas Bartas, who has been at work in Lithuania, Russia, Germany and the Netherlands shooting *Seven Invisible Men* (*Septyni nematomi zmones*). This is a road movie that takes audiences from Lithuania, via Poland, to the southern parts of the former Soviet Union, in the company of characters who are all hostile to society – one is trying to escape the law, another wants to escape his own self. Their desperate journey brings them into inescapable conflict with a world they can neither understand nor reshape according to their own principles.

With financial support from two German companies alongside Lithuania's Sensas, young Audrius Juzenas (previously responsible for the documentary *The Front Line* and the drama *It Also Snows in Paradise*), has taken charge of the most expensive Lithuanian film since independence: *Ghetto* (*Getas*). Adapted by Joshua Sobol from his acclaimed stage play, it tells the story of the Jewish theatre company that operated in the Vilnius ghetto during the war, prolonging for more than a year the lives of its already doomed members, because they entertained not only the inhabitants but also the Nazis. The songs for the film are in Yiddish and the music was created by Anatolijus Senderovas, a famous Lithuanian composer, incorporating some authentic melodies from the Vilnius ghetto.

Sunday. The Gospel According to
Lift-Man Albert

VENECIJAUS GYVENIMAS IR CEZARIO MIRTIS (The Life of Venecijus and Ceasar's Death)

[Documentary, 2002] Script and Dir: Janina Lapinskaite. Phot: Martynas Vidzbelis. Prod: Studio 2000 and National Radio and Television of Lithuania.
Venecijus, in his late forties, is abandoned by his wife and struggles to cope with his newly single existence.

TROLEIBUSU MIESTAS (Trolleybus Town)

[Ironic documentary, 2002] Script and Dir: Giedre Beinoriute. Phot: Vaidotas Digimas. Prod: Studio VG.
A film about human life viewed through the windows of a trolleybus.

PASTABOS GYVENIMO BUDO PARASTESE. V. ZALAKEVICIUS (Remarks Written at the Edge of Life. V. Zalakevicius)

[Documentary, 2002] Script: Almantas Grikevicius, Algimantas Puipa. Dir: Grikevicius. Phot: Algimantas Mikutenas. Prod: Studio 2000/National Radio and Television of Lithuania.
Exploration of the life and work of Lithuania's most celebrated film director, Vytautas Zalakevicius.

SEPTYNI NEMATOMI ZMONES (Seven Invisible Men)

[Drama, forthcoming] Script, Dir, Phot and Prod: Sarunas Bartas. Players: Bartas, Viktorija Kuodyte, Aleksand Esaulov, Aleksandr Bashirov, Axel Neumann, Marina Makshina, Anatolij Gorin.

The doomed performers in **Ghetto**

Audrius Stonys, winner of the Felix for Best European Documentary in 1992, made his fiction debut with the touching short *Last Car* (*Paskutinis vagonas*). Valdas Navasaitis, who won international festival awards for his documentary *The Spring* (*Pavasaris*), completed his trilogy about the seasons with **Summer** (*Vasara*), whose blind 'hero' cannot watch the seasons following each other, but feels and listens to the changes. In Oksana Buraja's intriguing documentary *The Diary* (*Dienorastis*), Larisa, a young girl, finds her late grandmother's old, faded journal, reads it and learns that her grandma knew a lot about her.

In March 2003, the Vilnius Spring festvial screened more than 60 fiction films from various European countries, as well as all of the previous year's Lithuanian productions, allowing audiences and critics to see the complete mosaic of the country's cinema life.

Dr GRAZINA ARLICKAITE is Head of the International Relations Service at Lithuanian Film Studio, Director of the public institution Kino Aljansas and a lecturer in the Film and Theatre Department of the Lithuanian Music Academy.

GETAS (Ghetto)
[Historical drama, forthcoming] Script: Joshua Sobol, based on his play. Dir: Audrius Juzenas. Phot: Andreas Hoefer. Players: Sebastian Hulk, Heino Ferch, Erika Marozsan, Jork Lamprecht, Vytautas Sapranauskas, Andrius Zebrauskas, Margarita Zemelyte, Alvydas Slepikas. Prod: Seansas/Dragon Cene' V.I.E.
(Germany)/New Transit Entertainment (Germany).

VASARA (Summer)
[Documentary, 2003] Script and Dir: Valdas Navasaitis. Phot: Rimvydas Leipus. Prod: Studio VG (Lithuania)/Les Films de l'Observatoire (France)/Danish Film Institute.

Luxembourg Marlene Edmunds

Recent and Forthcoming Films

BYE BYE BLACKBIRD
[Drama, 2004] Script: Arif Alishah, Patrick Faure, Robinson Savary. Dir: Savary. Players: James Thierree, Izabella Miko, Fairuza Balk, Malcolm McDowell, Michael Lonsdale. Producers: Samsa Film/Jani Thiltges (Luxembourg)/Road Movies/Noé Productions/Ipso Facto Films.
Jossef falls in love with a trapeze artist, but complications ensue when her possessive father enters the picture.

THE REVENGE
[Comedy, 2004] Script: Andy Bausch, Jean-Louis Schlesser, Nicolas Steil. Dir: Bausch. Players: Thierry Van Werveke, Myriam Muller, Andre Jung, Marco Lorenzini, Fernand Fox, Luc Feit. Prod: Iris Productions.

I ALWAYS WANTED TO BE A SAINT
[Drama, 2003] Script: Genevieve Mersch, Philippe Blasband. Dir: Mersch. Players: Marie Kremer, Camie Boel, Stasia Kremer, Thierry Lefevre.
Nora, 17, lives alone with her father and, feeling guilty about the world's misfortunes, turns to humanitarian aid work.

DIGGITY: A HOME AT LAST
[Family drama, 2002] Script: Tom Reeve and Michael Burks. Dir: Reeve. Phot: Carlo Thiel. Players: Andrew McCarthy, Louise Lombard, Bill Treacher, Stefan Jurgens. Prod: Carousel Picture Company.
American Raymond Crane inherits an English church. Complications ensue when the

R evenge is likely to taste sweet in Luxembourg in 2004. Filming began in autumn 2003 on *The Revenge*, the sequel to Andy Bausch's *The Unemployment Club*, one of the biggest box-office successes of all time for a local film, bringing in some 8% of the total population of the tiny Grand Duchy. In *The Revenge*, the group of laid-off workers who resisted government efforts to re-train them in the original film are back in business suits, mixing international soccer with fraud, the mob and Eastern European fortune hunters. While *The Unemployment Club* had Luxembourgish dialogue (a local form of German), *The Revenge* will offer a babble of the English, French, German and Luxembourgish spoken locally, as well as a smattering of other tongues commonly used by the many foreign workers in the territory. At press time, the sequel had already secured distribution deals in Austria, Belgium, Germany and France, as well as on home turf.

In a territory whose robust 15-year-old tax incentive scheme has seen its producers rubbing shoulders with some of the world's top lensing and acting talent on visiting productions, local directorial talent and star power have been in short supply. Bausch and Pol Cruchten (*Boys on the run*) are among the few Luxembourgish directors who have brought minor star power to the territory. British-born long-time Luxembourg resident Tom Reeve also directs on a regular basis, although his latest, *George and the Dragon*, which was originally slated to be released in 2002, was only just coming out of post by mid-summer 2003. The delay was caused by the failure of giant German post-production house Das Werk, and the knock-on for other Carousel Picture Company productions also delayed (indefinitely at press time) the release of *Diggity: A Home At Last*.

Delux Productions, at press time, was in development with Pol Cruchten on the comic-strip adaptation *Giacomo*, and respected line producer and associate producer Jean-Claude Schlim has plans to direct *House of Boys*, also for Delux. Both are expected to start shooting in 2004.

Have ambition, must travel

Among the new generation of local directors is Bady Minck, whose debut experimental feature *In the Beginning Was the Eye* was in Directors' Fortnight at Cannes 2003. She was born in Luxembourg

mischievous cherub Diggity tries to help Cane find the church's secret treasure (and his true love) before the conniving Mr Slee gets his hands on it.

GEORGE AND THE DRAGON
[Comedy, 2003] Script: Tom Reeve, Michael Burks. Dir: Reeve. Players: Patrick Swayze, Bill Treacher, James Purefoy, Piper Perabo. Prod: The Carousel Picture Company. George returns from the Crusades and a 1,000-year-old legend begins.

A PIECE OF THE SKY
[Drama, 2002] Script and Dir: Benedicte Lienard. Players: Severinne Caneele, Yolande Moreau, Sofia Leboutte, Andre Wilms, Naima Hireche. Producer: Tarantula Films. Two women, one inside and one outside a prison, correspond.

Quotes of the Year

"Maybe as directors we do end up dispersing across Europe to other territories to find work, but we end up bringing a rucksack full of talent back to Luxembourg."
BADY MINCK, *director of* In the Beginning Was the Eye.

"Just because there are many languages spoken in *The Revenge*, that doesn't make it a Europudding. Luxembourg is a territory where many languages are spoken."
NICOLAS STEIL, *owner of Iris Productions, on the company's comedy sequel.*

but studied in Austria and splits her time between the two territories. Other newcomers include Genevieve Mersch, whose first feature, **I Always Wanted To Be a Saint**, bowed in May 2003, and Laurent Brandenbourger (*Small Miseries*) who both went to Belgium to learn their craft and pick up work. As Luxembourg producer Alexander Dumreicher-Ivanceanu, co-owner with Minck of Minotauraus Film, has noted: "The problem is if you want to be a Luxembourg director, you have to go away from Luxembourg."

Marie Kremer in **I Always Wanted To Be a Saint**

Luxembourg is clearly being affected by the general malaise in the entertainment economy, with tax rebates from the government falling by some distance. "We're feeling the results of some of the funding not coming together internationally," said Heinz Thym, CEO of T-Films, but Luxembourg companies still continue to crank out a steady stream of pics, Delux and Samsa being among the most prolific. Delux was co-producer on Peter Greenaway's *Tulse Luper Suitcases*, and at press time was in co-production with Constantine Films on *Porta Westfalia*.

Samsa, which always has a dizzying schedule of co-productions in the works, is executive producer on *The Immortals* (see Portugal section), and planned to start shooting *Bye Bye Blackbird* in October 2003. Both films rely heavily on local talent for cast and crew, although the directors come from other countries.

MARLENE EDMUNDS is an Amsterdam-based correspondent for *Variety* and other US and European publications.

Malaysia Baharudin A. Latif

Recent Films

EMBUN
*[War melodrama, 2003] Script
and Dir: Erma Fatima. Phot:
Teoh Gay Huan. Players: Umie
Aida, Hani Mohsein, Aqasha.
Prod: Filem Negara
Malaysia/FINAS Film.*

PALOH
*[War melodrama, 2003]
Script: Asman Salleh, based on
Ismail Ahmad's play* Autonomi.
*Dir: Salleh. Phot: Teoh Gay
Huan. Players: Nam Ron, Janet
Khoo. Prod: World Evolution
Brain Film.*

Nasha Aziz as **Laila Isabella**

LAILA ISABELLA
*[Youth comedy-melodrama,
2003] Script and Dir: Rashid
Sibir. Phot: Indra Che Muda.
Players: Rosyam Nor, Hans
Isaac, Saiful. Prod: Tayangan
Unggul Film.*

ISKANDAR
*[Social melodrama, 2003] Script:
Shamsul Cairel. Dir: Nagaraja.
Phot: Muhamma Amal "Aki".
Players: Awie, Jeslina Hashim,
Farouk Hussain. Prod: SV
Production Film.*

GILA-GILA PENGANTIN
(Wedding Blues)
*[Comedy, 2003] Script and Dir:
Aziz M. Osman. Phot: Bada.
Players: Erra Fazira, Juliana
Banos, Norma Hakim. Prod:
Skop and Ace Motion Film.*

With producers duplicating tried – and tired – trends from previous years, local cinemas were deluged with effervescent comedies and teenage romps in 2002-03, and a gullible public lapped them up. Six of the ten titles released in 2002 made more than $500,000 (1.9m Ringgit), apparently a record. The top hit was the sequel **Mame Jarum** (the title translates loosely as *More of the Stupids*). Like the original *Anak Mame*, this was another no-brainer rustic comedy with crude dialogue, slapstick and a sterile plot, all greatly appreciated by easily pleased audiences.

It is shocking to learn that the *Mame* series (the third film was awaiting release at press time) is the brainchild of an associate professor of film at a local university. These films are challenging the box-office supremacy of the *Senario* comedy team, whose first three films all grossed more than $1.5m, with a fourth on the way in a 2003-04 season packed with sequels.

One exhibitor, however, Golden Screen Cinemas, has catered for more discerning viewers by dedicating four screens at its flagship 18-screen multiplex to arthouse fare. It has imported international gems such as *Run Lola Run* (Germany), *Baran* (Iran) and *The Road Back* (China). Encouragingly, a recent World Film Festival, with entries from more than 20 countries, proved enormously popular, demonstrating that some film fans are hungry for variety.

The Information Ministry has implemented an emergency plan to boost local film-making, by investing $3m into production through its agencies, the National Film Development Corporation (FINAS) and Filem Negara Malaysia. The first film shot in this way, **Embun**, was an improbable melodrama about a Japanese lieutenant's love for a resistance leader's wife during the Japanese occupation of Malaysia in 1940. This was old-fashioned hokum that grossed only a third of its budget of $780,000 (about three times the local average for a feature). The battle scenes lacked charge, the histrionic acting was unconvincing and the film was sadly reminiscent of movies of the 1940s. Hopes were high for the second state-backed film, *Paloh* (unreleased at press time), which is also set during the Second World War and is directed by London Film School graduate Adman Salleh.

BAHARUDIN A. LATIF has written on Malaysian cinema for 37 years, contributing to *Variety*, *Asiaweek* and other publications.

Mexico Carlos Bonfil

The Year's Best Films

Carlos Bonfil's selection:
Japón (Dir: Carlos Reygadas)
The Crime of Father Amaro
(Dir: Carlos Carrera)
Un Mundo Raro
(Dir: Armando Casas)
Second Century
(Dir: Jorge Bolado)
A Thousand Clouds
of Peace...
(Dir: Julián Hernández)

Recent and
Forthcoming Films

UN MUNDO RARO
(*literally*, **A Strange World**)
[*Comedy-drama, 2001*] *Script:*
Rafael Tonatiuh, Armando
Casas. Phot:
Alejandro Cantú. Players: Víctor
Hugo Arana, Emilio Guerrero,
Ana Serradilla, Jorge Sepúlveda.
Prod: Cuec/Imcine.

VIVIR MATA
(*literally*, **Living Kills**)
[*Comedy, 2001*] *Script: Juan*
Villoro, Nicolas Echevarría. Dir:
Echevarría. Phot: Pablo Reyes
Monzón. Players: Susana
Zabaleta, Daniel Jiménez Cacho,
Luis Felipe Tovar, Emilio
Echevarría. Prod: Titán
Producciones.
Silvia has a hectic love affair with
a visual artist, until she discovers
that he's an habitual liar.

CORAZONES ROTOS
(**Broken Hearts**)
[*Drama, 2001*] *Script and Dir:*
Rafael Montero. Phot: Rafael
Ortega. Players: Verónica
Merchant, Rafael Sánchez
Navarro, Carmen Montejo,
Odiseo Bichir. Prod:

I n 2002, the dramatic shortcomings for Mexican cinema were again apparent. As the 17 features released during this year attest, box-office success seems to be the driving force for most film-makers, especially those who have had previous hits. Film authorship and the expression of a personal point of view have become synonymous with commercial failure, so few of the leading film-makers want to take chances, go against the grain or experiment, either in their mode of expression or choice of narrative subjects. Many have risked repeating themselves – and tiring their once captivated audiences – by choosing to exploit safe, popular genres, such as light comedy (Nicolas Echevarria's *Vivir mata*, Carlos Sama's *Sin ton ni sonia*) and social melodrama (Fernando Sariñana's *Amar te duele*, Walter Doehner's *La habitación azul*).

In this context, the biggest surprise was the turmoil caused by Carlos Carrera's **The Crime of Father Amaro** (*El crimen de Padre Amaro*), which turns a classic nineteenth-century Portuguese novel into an effective and very acute satire of Catholic corruption in contemporary Mexico and also deals with another difficult subject: abortion. This story of moral decay and hypocrisy in the church and the coming-of-age of a young priest (Gael García Bernal) who falls in love, causes an unwanted pregnancy and gradually becomes as cynical and corrupt as the older priests he once admired, was an explosive combination, which immediately triggered a violent response from the Catholic hierarchy and conservative groups.

Gael García Bernal and Ana Claudia Talancón in **The Crime of Father Amaro**

Their unsuccessful attempt to ban the film only increased public curiosity and the film became an instant hit, placing itself in third in the box-office list, with more admissions than the second *Harry Potter*. Carrera's film is not particularly outstanding in terms of its acting or other artistic achievements, but it is a turning point for the local film industry – challenging taboos concerning religious authority, much as Luis Estrada's *Herod's Law* previously denounced political corruption.

Too much reality?

Armando Casas' **Un mundo raro** (literally, *A Strange World*), takes an ironic look at Mexican showbusiness and its links to political power. When kidnappers discover that the man they've abducted is a famous TV entertainer, the aggression of one naïve young gang member turns to admiration, because he has always wanted to be in showbusiness. As the film implicitly refers to recognisable political and media personalities, and hence may inspire some social debate, it confirms the perception that open political criticism is becoming a reinvigorating feature of a new Mexican cinema.

Alongside Carrera's and Casas' broad canvases, we find more intimate views of local reality, such as Jorge Bolado's **Second Century** (*Secundo siglo*), an intriguing, surrealist and exhilarating road movie in which the half-blind film-maker travels around Scotland, London, New York and Mexico with a small, extravagant crew (including old actor Martin Lasalle and independent cinéaste and photographer Robert Frank). His observations alternate with amusing reflections on Mexican customs, among them chauvinism and the popular mistrust of talent.

Carlos Reygadas' Japón

Carlos Reygadas' **Japón** is yet another introspective experience. A man chooses to end his life in a small town in northern Mexico. An old peasant offers her generous care and her remaining sexual energies to help him out of his existential dilemma. The experience is both disturbing and visually challenging. *Japón* brought Mexican

Imcine/Producciones Volcán.
The daily crises, frustrations and loneliness of several families living in the same big-city housing development.

EL GAVILAN DE LA SIERRA
(The Mountain Hawk)
[Drama, 2001] Script and Dir: Juan Antonio de la Riva. Phot: Ángel Goded. Players: Guillermo Larrea, Juan Ángel Esparza, Claudia Gotilla, Mario Almada. Prod: Imcine/ Conaculta/Videocine.
A road singer from Durango composes a folk song to the memory of his brother, a young rebel shot by bandits, evoking his adventurous life and the violence of northern Mexico.

FRANCISCA (¿DE QUÉ LADO ESTÁS?) (Francisca)
[Drama, 2001] Script: Eva López Sánchez, Jorge Goldenberg. Dir: López Sánchez. Phot: Javier Morón. Players: Ulrich Noethem, Fabiola Campomanes, Arcelia Ramírez, Julio Bracho. Prod: Producciones Odeón/Imcine.
México 1968. A former East German secret agent is hired by the Mexican authorities to infiltrate the student movement and falls in love with Adela, one of the activists.

EL CRIMEN DEL PADRE AMARO (The Crime of Father Amaro)
[Drama, 2002] Script: Vicente Leñero, from a novel by José María Eca de Queiroz. Dir: Carlos Carrera. Phot: Guillermo Granillo. Players: Gael García Bernal, Ana Claudia Talancón, Sancho Gracia, Angélica Aragón. Prod: Alfredo Ripstein/Imcine.

CIUDADES OSCURAS
(*literally*, Dark Cities)
[Drama, 2001] Script: Enrique Rentería, Fernando Sariñana. Dir: Sariñana. Phot: Salvador Cartas. Players: Dolores Heredia, Zaide Silvia Gutiérrez, Jesús Ochoa, Héctor Suárez. Prod: Altavista Films/Veneno Producciones.
Twelve stories about violence

in Mexico City. An acid, albeit melodramatic look at urban decay.

ACOSADA
(*literally,* **Woman Harassed**)
[Thriller, 2001] Script and Dir: Marcela Fernández Violante. Phot: Arturo de la Rosa. Players: Ana Colchero, Esteban Soberanes, María Bernal, Dino García, Beatriz Aguirre. Prod: CNCA/Imcine.
A young woman is terrorised when her apartment is robbed. She is constantly threatened by mysterious criminals and the corrupt police do little to help.

LA HABITACION AZUL
(*literally,* **The Blue Room**)
[Drama, 2002] Script: Vicente Leñero, Walter Doehner. Dir: Doehner. Phot: Serguei Saldivar Tanaka. Players: Patricia Llaca, Juan Manuel Bernal, Elena Anaya, Mario Iván Martínez. Prod: Argos Cine/Televisa Cine/Titán Producciones.
After a long absence, a man returns to his small hometown and falls in love with the wife of his best friend, Nicolas, who is dying. The gossiping townsfolk condemn the adulterous couple.

SEGUNDO SIGLO
(**Second Century**)
[Comedy, 2002] Script and Dir: Jorge Bolado. Phot: Lorenzo Hagerman. Players: Martín Lasalle, Robert Frank, Philippe de Saint Phalle, Eugenia Souza. Prod: La Máquina Gorda/Juan E. García, Jorge Bolado.

BENDITO INFIERNO
(**Don't Tempt Me**)
[Comedy, 2002] Script and Dir: Agustín Díaz Yanes. Phot: Paco Femenia. Players: Victoria Abril, Penélope Cruz, Demián Bichir, Gael García Bernal. Prod: Eduardo Campoy, Thierry Forte, Edmundo Gil.
Social allegory/morality tale with a political subtext. Hell is situated in a big American corporation; heaven is a fancy nightclub in Paris. The characters become the defenceless puppets

cinema further international recognition, particularly in Europe, where it was hailed as a major artistic achievement.

Another independent work, **A Thousand Clouds of Peace Surround the Sky, Love, When Shall You Stop Being Love** (*Mil nubes de paz cercan el cielo, amor, jamas acabaras de ser amor*), deals with unrequited homosexual love. Its depiction of Mexico City suburbs and the sentimental journey of a frustrated male lover is crude and illuminating, a brand of social realism constantly tainted by intimate despair, and inspired by the works of Pasolini and Fassbinder.

Supply vs demand

Although Mexican film production remains very low and, in artistic terms, mostly poor and unimaginative, there is a growing recognition of young independent talent, basically because of its previous acceptance abroad, and the growing demands of local, middle-class audiences for more refined narratives. As commercial fiction films show signs of fatigue, documentaries are becoming an exciting and far more rewarding way of exploring reality.

In Mercedes Moncada's vigorous and uncompromising document on social inequalities in rural Mexico, **The Passion of María Elena** (*La pasión de María Elena*), an indigenous woman from the northern sierra faces local corruption and discrimination when her little son is run over by the car of a white woman. Marcela Arteaga's **Remembrance** (*Recuerdos*) is a sentimental journey through the life and political engagements of Lithuanian emigrant Luis Frank, which interestingly blends Mexican and European twentieth-century history. Juan Carlos Martin's **Gabriel Orozco** is an original portrait of one of Mexico's most outstanding conceptual artists, looking at how he collects industrial waste and ordinary objects and transforms them into instant aesthetic icons.

A number of young film students and dedicated cinéastes have turned to digital technology as an alternative to the high costs of production. Arturo Ripstein has repeatedly gone digital in his recent films, and so has Jaime Humberto Hermosillo for his latest video experience, *Exxxorcismos*. There is a growing challenge from young, independent film-makers to an ageing industry that is still reluctant to embrace artistic innovation and narrative renewal. Fabricating box-office hits has become a reason for survival, but it is not clear how long this surely temporary solution will satisfy the needs of an increasingly demanding audience.

CARLOS BONFIL has since 1989 written a weekly article on film for the leading Mexican national newspaper *La Jornada*, and is the author of *Through the Mirror: Mexican Cinema and its Audience* and a book on Cantinflas.

of angels and devils.

EL TIGRE DE SANTA JULIA
(*literally,* **The Tiger of Santa Julia**)
*[Comedy, 2002] Script: Francisco
Sanchez. Dir: Alejandro Gamboa.
Phot: Alfredo Kassem. Players:
Miguel Rodarte, Irán Castillo,
Isaura Espinoza, Cristina
Michaus. Prod: Videocine.*
The legend of an adventurous
orphan in late nineteenth-century
rural Mexico who robs
highwaymen to help the poor.

PUNTO Y APARTE
(*literally,* **Full Stop**)
*[Drama, 2001] Script: Francisco
del Toro, Monica Maldonado.
Dir: del Toro. Phot: Agustín
Meza. Players: Mauricio Islas,
Evangelina Sosa, Mariagna Prats,
Geraldine Bazan. Prod:
Armaggedón/Francisco del Toro.*
Two couples, from very different
social origins, face the moral and
psychological effects of abortion in
this conservative melodrama
about a crucial public health issue.

AMAR TE DUELE
(**Love Hurts You**)
*[Drama, 2002] Script: Carolina
Rivera. Dir: Fernando Sariñana.
Phot: Salvador Cartas. Players:
Luis Fernando Peña, Martha
Higareda, Ximena Sariñana,
Alfonso Herrera. Prod: Altavista
Films/Videocine.*
A Romeo and Juliet-style
approach to social inequalities.
A young proletarian falls in love
with a rich girl in the suburbs of
Mexico City and they face moral,
racial and class discrimination.

EN LA MENTE DEL ASESINO
(**In the Mind of the Assassin**)
*[Drama, 2002] Script and Dir:
Agustí Villaronga, Lydia
Zimmermann, Isaac Pierre
Racine. Phot: Guillermo
Granillo. Players: Daniel Jiménez
Cacho, Carmen Beato, Zoltán
Jozan, Mariona Castillo. Prod:
Moro Films/Lestes Films/Canal
+/Televisión Española.*
An intriguing false documentary
on the case of Aro Tolbukhin,
a Hungarian accused in 1981 of
having burned alive seven people

in Guatemala. He subsequently
admitted having murdered five
more women.

LA HIJA DEL CANIBAL
(*literally,* **The Cannibal's
Daughter**)
*[Comedy-drama, 2002] Script
and Dir: Antonio Serrano. Phot:
Xavier Pérez Grobet. Players:
Cecilia Roth, Carlos Álvarez-
Novoa, Kuno Becker, Socorrode
la Campa. Prod: Matthias
Ehrenberg, José M. Garacino,
Epigmenio Ibarra.*

LA PASIÓN DE MARÍA ELENA
(**The Passion of María Elena**)
*[Documentary, 2002] Script and
Dir: Mercedes Moncada
Rodríguez. Phot: Javier Morón.
Prod: Moncada Rodríguez, Javier
Morón, Chango Films/Imcine.*

JAPÓN
*[Drama, 2002] Script and Dir:
Carlos Reygadas. Phot: Diego
Martínez Vignatti. Players:
Alejandro Ferretis, Magdalena
Flores, Yolanda Villa, Carlos
Reygadas Barquín. Prod: Carlos
Reygadas, No Dream
Cinema/Mantarraya
Producciones/Imcine.*

SIN TON NI SONIA
*[Comedy, 2002] Script: Luis
Felipe Sabre, Carlos Sama. Dir:
Sama. Phot: Federico Barbabosa.*

*Players: Cecilia Suárez, Juan
Manuel Bernal, Mariana Gajá,
José María Yaspic. Prod: Salvador
de la Fuente, Erwin Neumaier,
Harakiri Producciones.*

EXXXORCISMOS
*[Drama, 2002] Script and Dir:
Jaime Humberto Hermosillo.
Phot: Jorge Z. López. Players:
Alberto Estrella, José Juan
Meraz, Patricia Reyes Spíndola.
Prod: Jaime Humberto
Hermosillo, Fernando Gou,
Resonancia Producciones.*

RECUERDOS (Remembrance)
*[Documentary, 2002] Script and
Dir: Marcela Arteaga. Phot:
Celiana Cárdenas. Prod: Ángeles
Castro, Hugo Rodríguez,
Gustavo Montiel,
CCC/Churubusco/Imcine.*

MIL NUBES DE PAZ CERCAN
EL CIELO, AMOR, JAMAS
ACABARAS DE SER AMOR
(**A Thousand Clouds of Peace
Surround the Sky, Love, When
Shall You Stop Being Love**)
*[Drama, 2002] Script and Dir:
Julián Hernández. Phot: Diego
Arizmendi. Players: Juan Carlos
Ortuño, Juan Carlos Torres,
Perla de la Rosa, Salvador
Álvarez. Prod: Roberto Fiesco,
Cooperativa Cinematográfica
Morelos-Mil nubes.*

The Passion of Maria Elena

Morocco Roy Armes

Recent Films

A LOVE STORY
*[Drama, 2001] Script and Dir:
Hakim Noury. Phot: Kamal
Derkaoui. Players: Younès Megri,
Fatin Layachi, Hamidou, Maria
Sadek, Mohamed Ben Brahim.
Prod: Prod'Action (Morocco).*

A Love Story

**UNE MINUTE DE SOLEIL
EN MOINS**
(One Minute of Sunshine Less)
*[Drama, 2002] Script and Dir:
Nabil Ayouch. Players:
Nouraddin Orahhou, Lubna
Azabal, Hicham Moussoune,
Noor, Majd Mohamed,
Hammadi Tousi. Prod: Arte/BC
Films (France)/Ali N'Productions
(Morocco)/GMT Productions.*

One Minute of Sunshine Less

ET APRÈS... (And Afterwards...)
*[Drama, 2001] Script and Dir:
Mohamed Ismaïl. Phot: Denis*

Morocco's is by far the healthiest of the three North African film industries, even if it has yet to achieve an international reputation to match that acquired by Algeria in the 1970s or Tunisia in the 1990s. The Moroccan government has continued its ambitious funding programme into the early 2000s, backing an average of seven features a year and a similar number of shorts. In 2002 funding reached a record level, with 11 features and six shorts backed to the tune of almost $2.4m (22m dirhams), compared to the previous year's total of about $1.6m. This is a level almost three times greater than in the 1970s and 1980s, and in 2002, for the first time, both the total number of Moroccan directors and the number of feature films they have produced exceeded figures achieved consistently since the 1960s by Algeria.

Newcomers born in the 1960s have again been supported for feature-length work, including, in 2002, Yasmine Kassari and Hassan Legzouli, who have both made excellent short films. The problems in distribution are being resolved. Only one of the 15 films shown at the National Film Festival in Marrakesh in 2001 had failed to secure a commercial release by spring 2003 and every year at least one or two local features draw large audiences. In 2002 the best results were obtained by Hakim Noury's **A Love Story** (original title), one of the contemporary social studies in which the director has specialised. Here, a totally upright and honest bureaucrat falls in love with a beautiful call-girl and tries to help her leave her socially degraded life. With three top-two box-office hits in four years, Noury has confirmed his reputation as Morocco's most commercially successful and prolific director.

Among the established directors working alongside Noury, Souheil Benbarka, head of the Moroccan film institute, the Centre Cinématographique Marocain, showed his new historical drama. Set in 1936, **The Lovers of Mogador** (*Les amants de Mogador*) is a classic tale of star-crossed lovers, separated by class, nationality and religion, and it is animated by Benbarka's customary choice of international actors (Max von Sydow and Marie-Christine Barrault among them). It traces the love of Hélène, a French judge's daughter, for a young Moroccan peasant, Belkacem, at a moment of colonial conflict.

Lahlou's return

The appropriately titled **The Years of Exile** (*Les années de l'exil*) marked the return, after 10 years of silence, of the comic dramatist Nabyl Lahlou, who had made half a dozen features prior to 1992. This film chronicles the misadventures of two policemen sent to a mountain village to arrest a so-called subversive. In addition, Hassan Benjelloun, another prolific director, showed his third film of the new decade, **The Pal** (*Le pote*).

Nabyl Lahlou's **The Years of Exile**

Two of the younger film-makers who achieved their first breakthroughs in the late 1990s also continued their careers. Mohamed Ismaïl followed *Aouchtam* with a new feature, **And Afterwards...** (*Et après...*), yet another study of the lure of Europe for Moroccans living in the north of the country, ending with frustrated hopes and ambitions. Nabil Ayouch, previously responsible for the acclaimed *Ali Zaoua*, mixed thriller and love story elements in his third feature. **One Minute of Sunshine Less** (*Une minute de soleil en moins*) is the story of a policeman investigating the murder of a drug dealer in which the prime suspect is the cop's own mistress. The film encountered problems with the censors and, since Ayouch has refused to make the cuts demanded, had not released by mid-2003.

Two newcomers also made their appearances with first features in 2002: Kamal Kamal with **Taif Nizar**, and Imane Mesbahi with **The Paradise of the Poor** (*Paradis des pauvres*), which she had begun in 1994 and partially reshot in 1999. Mesbahi is a further example of the emergence of a younger generation, as her father, Abdellah Mesbahi, was one of the pioneers of Moroccan cinema in the 1970s. In 1994 he wrote the original script *An Immigrant's Song* which in 1999 became *The Paradise of the Poor*. ∎

Gravoul. *Players: Rachid El Ouali, Mohamed Miftah, Victoria Abril, Fadela Belkebla, Naïma El M'Charqi. Prod: Mia Production (Morocco).*

LES ANNEES DE L'EXIL
(The Years of Exile)
[Drama, 2002] Script and Dir: Nabyl Lahlou. Phot: Mostapha Marjane. Players: Lahlou, Sophia Hadi, Younès Megri, Mohamed Belfkih, Amal Ayouch, Majjoub Raji, Mehdi Piro, Fattouma Belhassan. Prod: Production Loukkos Film (Morocco).

LES AMANTS DE MOGADOR
(The Lovers of Mogador)
[Drama, 2002] Script: Bernard Stora and Souheil Benbarka. Dir: Benbarka. Phot: Vittorio Bagnasco. Players: Mahmoud Mahmoudi, Violante Placido, Max von Sydow, Marie-Christine Barrault, Claude Rich, Bernard Fresson, Boujemâa Oujoud. Prod: Dawliz Rabat/Casablanca (Morocco)/Poetiche Cinematogaphiche Rome (Italy).

Quote of the Year

"There are Moroccan films, but no Moroccan cinema."
MOHAMED ABDERRAHMAN TAZI, *one of Morocco's leading directors.*

Nepal Uzzwal Bhandary

Recent and Forthcoming Films

JE BHO RAMRAI BHO
[literally, **Whatever Happened, It Was a Good Result**]
*[Social comedy-drama, 2003]
Script and Dir: Haribamsa
Aacharya. Players: Aacharya,
Madan K. Shrestha, Rajesh
Hamal, Jal Shah. Pro: Om Sai
Films/Kiran KC.*

Haribamsa Aacharya and Jal Shah in
Je Bho Ramrai Bho

BISWAS (Trust)
*[Social drama, 2003] Script and
Dir: Ujol Ghimire. Players: Dilip
Rayamajhi, Kirti Bhatarai,
Ramesh Adhikari, Sivahari
Mama. Prod: Ayus Films.*

BABUSAHEB (Landlord)
*[Love story, 2003] Dir:
Ramesh. Players: Bhuvan KC,
Karishma Manandhar, Nirshah,
Harihar Sharma. Prod:
Karishma Manandhar.*

BIR GANESHMAN
*[Political biopic, 2003] Script and
Dir: Navindra R. Joshi. Players:
Ram Maharjan, Bharat Adhikari,
Bhairab Bahadur. Prod:
Ganeshman Memorial Trust.*

MUKTIDATA (Liberator)
*[Love story, 2003] Dir: Bijay
Chalise. Players: Rajesh Hamal,
Jal Shah, Jimi Gurung. Prod:
Jimi Gurung.*

Despite the uncomfortable and unstable political situation in Nepal, with violent student protests and Maoist rebel activities continuing to have a direct impact on the movie industry, producers and directors somehow manage to make films. More than 40 new features were completed in 2002, most of them pale imitations of Indian cinema.

Industry estimates put total production investment in Nepalese films at about $2.5m a year, of which only two thirds was recouped at the box-office in 2002, leaving many producers out of pocket. Finance is so scarce that one producer told me: "I have sold my land and home to make this film and if it does not cover my debts I shall be ruined." Typical feature-film budgets are between $35,000 and $70,000, which is a real problem for Nepalese producers who must compete against much more expensive, imported Indian films whose superior production values are inevitably more attractive to Nepalese audiences, whether in the cinemas or at home on VCD or DVD.

However, there was one entertaining local hit in the first half of 2003. **Je bho ramrai bho** (literally, *Whatever Happened, It Was a Good Result*) stayed in Kathmandu theatres for more than seven weeks, a remarkable achievement that more than recouped the film's $80,000 budget. Director, writer and star Haribamsa Aacharya plays a double leading role as two brothers, one clever, the other stupid. The stupid one finds a job in a Gulf state where he becomes involved in crime, is deported back to Nepal and jailed. He and two fellow prisoners (Rajesh Hamal and Madan K. Shrestha) then decide to enter politics and fight government corruption. The plan is so successful that the dumb brother ends up as deputy prime minister.

The director manages to treat the burning issue of corruption with humour and intelligence. The three lead actors give fine performances, but actress Jal Shah is employed simply to entertain the audience with dances and love scenes. This is the second hit production from Om Sai Films, following *Bad Mr Badri* (*Tata sarai bigris Badri*, 2001).

UZZWAL BHANDARY appears as a comedian and satirist on Nepal TV. He has also worked for the past 15 years as a tour guide and tourism executive.

Netherlands Pieter van Lierop

The Year's Best Films

Pieter van Lierop's selection:

Twin Sisters
(Dir: Ben Sombogaart)

Godforsaken
(Dir: Pieter Kuijpers)

Interview
(Dir: Theo van Gogh)

Yes Nurse! No Nurse!
(Dir: Pieter Kramer)

Peter Bell (Dir: Maria Peters)

Recent and Forthcoming Films

ADRENALINE
[Action crime thriller, 2003]
Script, Dir, Phot and Prod: Roel
Reiné. Players: Jason Fijal,
Georgina Verbaan, Daniel Rivas,
Keren Tahor.
A girl is found dead. Her
boyfriend discovers that she was
a member of a gang of thrill-
seekers who go skydiving and
bungee-jumping and perform
other prohibited stunts in Cape
Town. The South African
locations and stunts look great.

GRIMM
[Black comedy, 2003] Script and
Dir: Alex van Warmerdam. Phot:
Tom Erisman. Players: Jacob
Derwig, Halina Reijn, Carmelo
Gomez, Elvira Minguez.
Jacob and his sister are
abandoned by their penniless
Dutch father. They travel to
Spain where the uncle they hoped
might help them appears to be
dead. Modern adaptation of the
Grimms' *Hansel and Gretel.*

INTERVIEW
[Psychodrama, 2003] Script:
Theodor Holman. Dir: Theo van
Gogh. Phot: Thomas Kist.

D utch film-makers are worried. After being tightened up
in 2002, the tax incentive scheme that has made it so
attractive for private investors to support Dutch film
production will expire on December 31, 2003. Fourteen months
of political instability in a period of economic recession have also
created great uncertainty around the government's attitude towards
extending these measures. Furthermore, the Ministry of Finance has
set a maximum of €23m in lost tax revenue from private individuals'
film investments for 2003. This has led to a stampede at the offices
of Senter, the body to which producers must submit their projects
for financial approval (applications are handled strictly in sequence).
Of more than 40 projects submitted, only half have been accepted.

The volume of production is shrinking and is set to shrink even more,
but for the moment Dutch cinema blossoms as never before. And
because both the tax incentives and the current subsidy policies of
the Dutch Film Fund (which has around €12m to hand out each year)
are clearly designed for the benefit of commercially minded film-
makers, there has been a major change in Dutch audiences' attitudes
towards domestic movies. Of the total number of cinema tickets sold
(stable in 2002 at 24 million), the share of Dutch films has increased
from 5.6% in 2000 to 9.3% in 2001 and 10.5% in 2002, this upward
trend continued in the first half of 2003.

The best news is that it is no longer just children's films that attract
larger audiences, although the youth market remains the most
important, and it is becoming normal for a Dutch children's film to sell
a million tickets during the winter months. Following the success of
the delightful feline fairytale *Minoes* late in 2001, the winter 2002 hit
came from Maria Peters, who had earlier filled 1,135,000 seats with
Little Crumb (*Kruimeltje*, 2000). Her new "rascal film", *Peter Bell*, full
of slapstick and adventure, sold 900,000 tickets, and by summer
2003 filming was already complete on *Peter Bell 2*, scheduled for
release in December 2003. Another youth film, *Schippers of The
Chameleon*, became a hit in July 2003.

You don't have to be mad, but...

Suddenly it also seems possible to attract sizeable audiences for
youth films, even outside the winter season, as demonstrated by
two films in the autumn of 2002, both based on television series.

Bobby Eerhart's **Loonies** was something of a *tour de force*, the adventures of psychiatric patients giving rise to good-natured humour, while their particular psychiatric and social situation was also taken seriously.

Pieter Kramer's musical Yes Nurse! No Nurse!

Selected for competition at Berlin, **Yes Nurse! No Nurse!** (*Ja Zuster! Nee Zuster!*), directed by Pieter Kramer, is based on a television series that enjoyed huge popularity 30 years ago. This hilarious musical likewise centres around a home for the mildly deranged. Led by their nurse, the inhabitants are forced to defend themselves against attempts by their underhand neighbour to get his hands on their home. The youngest audience members were delighted, fans of the old series waxed nostalgic and a group somewhere in the middle appreciated the camp qualities of this production from Burny Bos, the brain behind *Minoes*.

Now that children have become accustomed to Dutch films, it is important that teens and twentysomethings overcome their aversion to feature films in their own language. It appears that this is happening, thanks to producers and directors who have previously managed to woo this target group with soaps on television. They are making unpretentious entertainments for the big screen with the same youthful soap actors, among whom Katja Schuurman, Georgina Verbaan, Miryanna van Reeden, Daan Schuurmans and Cas Jansen enjoy star status. Following on from the success of Johan Nijenhuis' Spanish-set *Costa* (675,000 admissions in 2001) have come similarly themed but increasingly well-produced (by Nijenhuis) romantic comedies such as **Full Moon Party** (*Volle maan*) and **I Love To Love** (*Liever verliefd*, directed by Pim van Hoeve). Currently Nijenhuis has *Floris* in the pipeline, a medieval adventure directed by Jean van de Velde.

Players: Katja Schuurman, Pierre Bokma. Prod: Theo van Gogh, Gijs van de Westerlaken. Excellent acting in a clever story about a star reporter from a quality daily paper obliged to interview Holland's most popular soap actress. He hates everything she stands for, but she is not as stupid as he thought and the meeting descends into a kind of guerrilla combat (the collision of high and low culture). Schuurman is indeed Holland's most popular soap star, here stretching her skills.

JA ZUSTER! NEE ZUSTER!
(Yes Nurse! No Nurse!)
[Musical, 2002] Script: Frank Houtappels and Pieter Kramer. Dir: Kramer. Players: Loes Luca, Paul Kooij, Tjiske Reidinga, Paul de Leeuw, Waldemar Torenstra, Beppe Costa. Prod: Burny Bos.

LIEVER VERLIEFD
(I Love To Love)
[Romantic comedy, 2003] Script and Dir: Pim van Hoeve. Phot: Han Wennink. Players: Miryanna van Reeden, Chris Zegers, Romijn Conen. Prod: Nijenhuis/de Levita Films/TV BV. Girl in her early thirties is fed up with boys who go for love without commitment. She wants to reverse the roles and catches two different boys, never guessing they are friends.

Loonies

LOENATIK, DE MOEVIE
(Loonies)
[Children's comedy, 2002] Script: Karen van Holst Pellekaan and Martin van Waardenberg. Dir: Bobby Eerhart. Phot: Jules van

den Steenhoven. Players; Karen van Holst Pellekaan, Martin van Waardenberg, John Buijsman, Dick van der Toorn. Prod: Get Reel Productions.

MOONLIGHT
[Children's drama, 2002] Script: Carel van der Donck. Dir: Paula van der Oest. Phot: Guido van Gennep. Players: Andrew Howard, Laurien van den Broeck, Hunter Bussemaker, Johan Leysen. Prod: Staccato Films.

Quinten Scham as **Peter Bell**

PETER BELL
[Children's adventure, 2002] Script and Dir: Maria Peters. Phot: Hein Groot. Players: Quinten Scham, Felix Strategier, Angela Groothuisen, Katja Hebers, Rick Engelkens. Prod: Shooting Star Filmcompany.
Naughty boy fights criminals with a little help from his friends and becomes a hero.

PHILEINE ZEGT SORRY
(Phileine Says Sorry)
[Romantic comedy, 2003] Script and Dir: Robert Jan Westdijk. Phot: Bert Pot. Players: Kim van Kooten, Michiel Huisman, Liesbeth Kamerling.
Based on a bestseller by Ronald Giphart, the story of a young Dutch couple caught up in the New York theatre scene. Westdijk and leading actress van Kooten earlier had a surprise hit together with *Little Sister (Zusje).*

SWINGERS
[Erotic drama, 2002] Script and Dir: Stephan Brenninkmeijer. Phot: Ron Toekook. Players:

Pim van Hoeve's romantic comedy I Love to Love

Something for the grown-ups

Things also seem to be looking up for features intended predominately for thinking adults who may occasionally also read a book. Paula van der Oest's relationship comedy **Zus & Zo**, released in the spring of 2002, conquered America nine months later, receiving an Oscar nomination. A considerably darker film was van der Oest's English-language **Moonlight**, a kind of allegorical road movie about a 12-year-old girl who finds in her garden a wounded Afghan boy on the run from the gang who forced him to smuggle drugs. *Moonlight* capitalises on the current focus on these drug "swallowers", many of whom are currently incarcerated in Dutch gaols, and more and more film-makers are being attracted to topics of contemporary relevance.

Staccato Films

Paula van der Oest's road movie **Moonlight**

Director Pieter Kuijpers and producer Reinier Selen, for instance, used a notorious real-life case as the inspiration for **Godforsaken** (*Van God los*), in which two boys make a perfectly sober decision to choose a life of crime, and slide from common thuggery to becoming hired assassins. Stylish and psychologically powerful, *Godforsaken* managed to attract a wide audience in spring 2003.

Two young men turn to crime in **Godforsaken**

The same was true of **Twin Sisters** (*De Tweeling*), which drew more than 600,000 spectators. Ben Sombogaart directed this story of two German girls who are separated following the death of their parents in the 1920s. One grows up with a rich family in the Netherlands, while the other ekes out a miserable existence on a farm in Germany. The rise of Nazism and the Second World War create a gaping chasm between the twins and reconciliation is only possible half a century later.

Twin Sisters is a heartbreaking human drama featuring some outstanding acting. Together with *Godforsaken*, the film was a firm favourite to take a Golden Calf this autumn in Utrecht. However, by that time we will also have seen the premiere of *Grimm*, the new film by Alex van Warmerdam, one of the Netherlands' most original directors, who in the past achieved renown at international festivals with *The Dress* (*De Jurk*) and *Little Tony* (*Kleine Teun*).

Dutch films are doing well on the festival circuit, although the fact that no Dutch film has been selected for the competition in Cannes for 27 years is starting to grate. No full-length film, in any event – Esther Rots was selected in 2003 with the mysteriously poetic short *I Sprout* (*Ik Ontspruit*), following her success the previous year with the equally free-floating *Play with Me* (*Speel met me*).

A little pride is being garnered, however, from Dutch participation in

Ellen van der Koogh, Nienke Brinkhuis, Joep Sertons, Danny de Kok. Prod: Roel Reiné and Stephan Brenninkmeijer.
The insecure Diana reluctantly goes along with long-term partner Julian's suggestion that they experiment sexually with another couple.

THE TULSE LUPER SUITCASES, PART I. THE MOAB STORY
[Series of feature films, DVDs and websites] Script and Dir: Peter Greenaway. Phot: Reinier van Brummelen. Players: J. J. Feild, Drew Mulligan, Yorick Van Wageningen, Kevin Tighe, Scot Williams, Tom Bower, Deborah Harry. Prod: Kees Kasander, The Kasander Film Company.
Tulse Luper, a writer and project-maker, is caught up in a life of prisons all over the world, leaving behind 64 suitcases, some filled with fish. The story covers 60 years from the discovery of uranium in 1928 up to the end of the Cold War.

VAN GOD LOS (Godforsaken)
[True-life crime drama, 2002] Script: Paul Jan Nelissen and Pieter Kuijpers. Dir: Kuijpers. Phot: Bert Pot. Players: Egbert-Jan Weeber, Tygo Gernandt, Angela Schijf. Prod: Rinkelfilm.

VOLLE MAAN (Full Moon Party)
[Romantic teen drama, 2002] Script: Johan Nijenhuis and Mischa Alexander. Dir: Nijenhuis. Players: Daan Schuurmans, Georgina Verbaan, Cas Jansen, Ellen ten Damme, Chantal Janzen.
After graduation a group of schoolfriends party hard and fall in love on vacation on a sailing boat on Mallorca.

ZUS & ZO
[Comedy, 2002] Script and Dir: Paula van der Oest. Phot: Bert Pot. Players: Halina Reijn, Jacob Derwig, Monic Hendrickx, Anneke Blok, Sylvia Poorta, Theu Boermans. Prod:

Filmprodukties De Luwte. Very loosely based on *Three Sisters* by Chekhov. Three sisters and their homosexual brother inherit a hotel in Portugal.

Quote of the Year

"I liked the fact that *The Delivery* was in the video rental top three in Moscow for three months and that I saw illegal copies in Bangkok."

ROEL REINÉ, *Dutch director, on his feature debut, which was panned in the Netherlands.*

films by Lars von Trier, Alexander Sokurov and Peter Greenaway. The pride is most justified in the case of Greenaway, as the multimedia trilogy *The Tulse Luper Suitcases* features Dutchman Kees Kasander as principal producer, while Greenaway himself now resides in Amsterdam.

PIETER VAN LIEROP is film editor of the Netherlands Press Association GPD (23 syndicated daily papers). He has been a correspondent for *IFG* since 1981.

Alex van Warmerdam's **Grimm**

KATHARINE HEPBURN with James Stewart in The Philadelphia Story. *She died on June 29, 2003, aged 96.*

New Zealand Peter Calder

The Year's Best Films

Peter Calder's selection:

Whale Rider (Dir: Niki Caro)

The Two Towers
(Dir: Peter Jackson)

Kombi Nation
(Dir: Grant Lahood)

This Is Not a Love Story
(Dir: Keith Hill)

Coffee, Tea or Me
(Docu. Dir: Brita McVeigh)

Recent and Forthcoming Films

WHALE RIDER
[Drama, 2003] Script: Niki Caro, based on the novel by Witi Ihimaera. Dir: Caro. Phot: Leon Narbey. Players: Keisha Castle-Hughes, Rawiri Paratene, Cliff Curtis, Vicki Haughton. Prod: John Barnett, Tim Sanders, Frank Huebner.

PERFECT STRANGERS
[Drama, 2003] Script and Dir: Gaylene Preston. Phot: Alun Bollinger. Players: Sam Neill, Rachael Blake. Prod: Robin Laing.
A chilling romance about a woman (Blake) who finds herself the subject of a man's (Neill) romantic obsession on a deserted island.

Perfect Strangers: *Sam Neill and Rachael Blake*

The New Zealand film biz has always been something of a feast-or-famine affair. And the year 2002 made something of a feast of its famine. For the first year since the 1970s, when *Sleeping Dogs*, Roger Donaldson's first feature, starring the young Sam Neill, kickstarted the modern era of local film-making, not a single Kiwi release lit up a domestic screen. It escaped few people's notice that this occurred in a year bookended by the release of the first two parts of New Line's *Lord of the Rings* trilogy, which showcase this country and its film-making talent better and more widely than ever before.

The problem was largely the result of the collapse of a single production company, Kahukura Productions, which had four films in the works. Kahukura supremo Larry Parr, whose Mirage Entertainment was a 1980s high-flyer which crashed and burned, had, it emerged, diverted funds intended for a television show he was producing, and he also faced tax evasion charges in April 2003. The films included a thriller, *Crime Story*, which had just wrapped, and three micro-budget titles in various stages of post-production.

The New Zealand Film Commission, the state-funded film bank that develops and part-finances most films here, tried to remain aloof from the commercial imbroglio, but came under fire from film-makers who said it should have more closely monitored Kahukura's expenditure. A vicious public spat between the commission and Peter Jackson, who owns the post-production lab that was one of Kahukura's creditors, culminated in the *Rings* meister "disinviting" commission chiefs to the Australasian premiere of *The Two Towers*. By January 2003, the commission had managed to extract at least some of Kahukura's work from the clutches of creditors. But other productions struggled to find local distributors or secure theatrical sales in significant overseas territories.

A *Whale* of a tale

In startling contrast to the general gloom was **Whale Rider**, which was released in late January 2003 and eventually took almost $3.4m (NZ$5.8), a hit performance by local standards, exceeded only by 1994's *Once Were Warriors*. The second film by writer-director Niki Caro, whose ravishing *Memory and Desire* (1998) signalled a real talent, it adapted an early novel by noted Maori writer Witi Ihimaera

TOY LOVE

[Comedy, 2002] Script and Dir: Harry Sinclair. Phot: Grant McKinnon. Players: Dean O'Gorman, Kate Elliott, Marissa Stott. Prod: Juliette Veber.

A young man who routinely cheats on his girlfriend falls head-over-heels with an unpredictable beauty and finds the boot is on the other foot.

THIS IS NOT A LOVE STORY

[Romantic comedy-drama, 2002] Script and Dir: Keith Hill. Phot: Phil Burchell. Players: Sarah Smuts-Kennedy, Stephen Lovatt, Peta Rutter. Prods: Keith Hill, Andrew Calder.

A romantic young woman decides that a troubled neighbouring couple can help her satisfy her need for more life experiences.

TONGAN NINJA

[Martial arts comedy, 2002] Script: Jason Stutter, Jermaine Clement. Dir and Phot: Stutter. Players: Sam Manu, Jermaine Clement, Linda Tseng, Charles Lum. Prods: Jason Stutter, Andrew Calder.

Irreverent comedy involving a comically inept Tongan immigrant martial arts whizz, who defends a Chinese woman against a Mr Big.

THE LOCALS

[Horror, 2003] Script and Dir: Greg Page. Phot: Brett Nichols. Players: John Barker, Dwayne Cameron, Kate Elliott, Aidee Walker. Prod: Steve Sachs.

Two best mates hit the road for a weekend of surfing and boozing, take a short cut and end up in the heartland of evil.

John Barker in **The Locals**

Keisha Castle-Hughes, centre, as Paikea in **Whale Rider**

into a moving film about a young Maori girl who aches to shoulder the mantle of leadership of her tribe against the wishes of her hidebound grandfather, who believes females unfit for chieftainship.

Drenched in a sure sense of place – an isolated seaside Maori community – but rich in universal, mythic associations, it was a revelation for local audiences who customarily ignore domestic productions. The sublime camerawork of Leon Narbey and a guileless performance by child newcomer Keisha Castle-Hughes helped make it an instant local classic, enthusiastically embraced here and in Australia. Notably it was picked up for Australasian distribution by Disney subsidiary Buena Vista, which poured big bucks into the antipodean releases; local movies are usually handled by boutique operators.

Conspicuously less successful was **Toy Love**, the third feature by Harry Sinclair, which dropped off the local Top 20 in its second week of release in May 2003. Sinclair, an anarchic talent whose *Topless Women Talk About their Lives* was not without charm, persists in shooting films without scripts (every evening he writes the following day's pages) and despite the dismal commercial performance of his last film, the beautiful but unfathomable *The Price of Milk*, the commission persists in funding him on the basis of brief treatments, to the puzzlement of all local observers. *Toy Love*, which won an audience award at the Fantasporto Festival in Portugal, was an erratic, episodic comedy about bed-hopping twentysomethings, hampered by hesitant performances and characters who seemed more like collections of personality quirks than real people.

By contrast, **This Is Not a Love Story**, a debut feature from Keith Hill to follow several shorts, was a light look at a love triangle, made without a cent of commission money. A rough cut showed at

Cannes in 2002, where *Variety*'s Robert Koehler welcomed it as "far more adult than most American indie pics treading similar turf" and called Hill a film-maker of "considerable talent". Brandishing the review, Hill went back to the commission to seek completion finance and was turned down. He eventually secured an ex-gratia payment of $20,000, not enough to blow the film up to 35mm, but sufficient to make it ready for a premiere screening in an arts festival in October.

The contrast between the support offered to Sinclair and Hill serves to underline a troubled relationship between the commission – increasingly seen as aloof and arbitrary in its decision-making – and film-makers. The relationship is now at a lower ebb than even seasoned observers can remember, and, coming on the heels of *Whale Rider*'s success, it is doubly puzzling. The government's Screen Production Industry Task Force called in May 2003 for a much stronger and equal partnership between the commission and industry. The task force, which comprised leading figures in film and television, said the commission had a high level of control but was not transparent enough with financing decisions.

Have Kombi, will travel

Of the films caught up in the Kahukura collapse, only **Kombi Nation** had been sighted by press time (in a private screening organised by the director in the hope that critics would put pressure on the commish to free it up). This charming, micro-budget, guerrilla-style road flick set in a VW microbus (known locally as a Kombi) follows a group of Kiwi twentysomethings around Europe on what is known as OE (the "overseas experience"), seen here as a rite of passage. Since so many of its cultural references are specifically Kiwi, its international appeal is probably limited, but it is an enjoyable romp for post-teens and generation X-ers and is due for a winter release here. Of the other freed films, *Crime Story* has been retitled *Fracture* and was scheduled to complete post-production in October 2003, while *All the Way to Her* (formerly *For Good*) and *Aidiko Insane* await local distribution deals.

On a brighter note, the romantic thriller *Perfect Strangers*, the new feature by noted local helmer Gaylene Preston (*Mr Wrong*, *Ruby and Rata*) is in the wings. It stars Sam Neill in his first New Zealand feature since *The Piano* and Australian Rachael Blake (*Lantana*) as a woman who finds herself the object of his obsessive desire. *The Locals*, a traditional horror flick, was in post in mid-2003 and Vincent Ward (*Map of the Human Heart*, *What Dreams May Come*) was at press time looking for the last piece of finance for a period drama called *River Queen*, set in the rugged bush country of central North Island.

NEMESIS GAME
(formerly **Paper, Scissors, Stone***)*
[Psychological thriller, 2003]
Script and Dir: Jesse Warn.
Players: Ian McShane, Adrian Paul, Carly Pope, Rena Owen.
Prod: Matthew Metcalfe.
A woman's fascination with riddles almost costs her her life.

FRACTURE
(formerly **Crime Story***)*
[Psychological thriller, 2003]
Script: Larry Parr, based on the novel by Maurice Gee. Dir: Parr.
Phot: Fred Renata. Players: Kate Elliott, Jared Turner, Cliff Curtis, John Noble. Prod: Charlie McClellan.
A single mother, struggling to cope, is pushed to the brink when her brother bungles a burglary.

ALL THE WAY TO HER
(formerly **For Good***)*
[Psychological drama, 2003]
Script and Dir: Stuart McKenzie.
Phot: Duncan Cole. Players: Michelle Langstone, Adam Gardiner, Tim Gordon, Tim Balme, Miranda Harcourt. Prods: Neil Pardington, Larry Parr.
A young woman, fascinated by the killer of her childhood friend who is being released from prison, impersonates a journalist and enters his world.

COFFEE, TEA OR ME
[Documentary, 2002] Dir: Brita McVeigh Phot: Cameron McLean. Prod: Brita McVeigh, Gaylene Preston.
Entertaining documentary, initially whimsical but ultimately political, about the battles for acceptance endured by air hostesses (known as "trolley dollies") with Air New Zealand.

Quotes of the Year

"In a year when film crews and suppliers of the independent film industry have been abused and vilified by these self-serving bureaucrats, it would be totally inappropriate for the Film Commission to be participating in this event."

PETER JACKSON *explaining why he "disinvited" commission chiefs to the Australasian premiere of* The Two Towers.

"It's a strange experience for a Picton lad. I'm just very, very proud to be here."

MICHAEL HOPKINS, *small town boy and co-winner of a Sound Editing Oscar for* The Two Towers, *adding a Kiwi accent to the Academy acceptance speeches.*

The country continues to enjoy the attention – and empty the wallets – of overseas film-makers who respond to its pitch as the world's most diverse collection of locations. Warner Bros shot large parts of the Tom Cruise actioner *The Last Samurai* here, and a South Korean expedition drama called *Antarctic Journal* was set to shoot mid-year. But there were signs that a strengthening Kiwi dollar and the willingness of other territories – in particular Australia – to offer tax incentives to runaway productions might reduce New Zealand's competitiveness in this area.

PETER CALDER, the New Zealand correspondent for *Variety*, is a journalist and writer who has been a film critic for the *New Zealand Herald* since 1984.

Genevieve McLean and Jason Whyte hit the road in **Kombi Nation.**

KAREL REISZ, a co-founder of Britain's Free Cinema movement in the mid-1950s, and director of the classic Saturday Night and Sunday Morning *(1960), died on November 25, 2002, aged 76.*

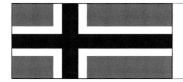

Norway Trond Olav Svendsen

The Year's Best Films

Tron Olav Svendsen's selection:

Kitchen Stories
(Dir: Bent Hamer)

Music for Weddings and Funerals (Dir: Unni Straume)

Falling Sky
(Dir: Gunnar Vikene)

Jonny Vang (Dir: Jens Lien)

My Body
(Docu. Dir: Margreth Olin)

Lena Endré in **Music for Weddings and Funerals**

Recent and Forthcoming Films

MUSIKK FOR BRYLLUP OG BEGRAVELSER (Music for Weddings and Funerals)
[Drama, 2002] Script and Dir: Unni Straume. Phot: Harald Paalgard. Players: Lena Endre, Bjørn Floberg, Goran Bregovic, Wenche Foss, Kristoffer Joner. Prod: Edward A. Dreyer/ Tom Remlov/Unni Straume/ Christiania Film.

VEKTLØS (Weightless)
[Documentary, 2002] Script and Dir: Sigve Endresen. Phot: Torstein Nodland, Kjell Vassdal. Players: Kari Iveland, Else Iveland, Tobias Iveland. Prod: Sigve Endresen/Motlys.

In May 2003, two of the most venerated directors of Norwegian post-war cinema passed away: Edith Carlmar (b. 1911) and Arne Skouen (b. 1913). They made their debuts in 1949 – Carlmar as the first female film director in Norway – with two of the most striking films ever made in this country, the film noir *Death is a Caress* (*Døden er et kjærtegn*) and the neo-realist *Street Urchins* (*Gategutter*) respectively. Carlmar and Skouen were lucky to enter films when cinema attendance in Norway was on the rise (it peaked in the mid-1950s), and they were both able to make half a dozen films or more in their first 10 years as directors.

Even if the overall attendance figures of 50 years ago cannot be matched today, contemporary Norwegian directors can look forward to similarly favourable conditions. In 2003, Norway's small film industry is witnessing a major increase in its production volume, from perhaps 8 to 10 features per year to more than 20, a record. The change is the result of increased government subsidies and a more efficient system of distributing them, most of the funds coming from one central institution, the Norwegian Film Fund. There is a noticeably greater recognition of the achievement of Norwegian film-makers, past and present, and of the art form's role in the cultural life of the nation.

One of the striking things about the 2002-03 season, therefore, was the number and regularity of cinema releases; a new film rolled off the assembly line every month or so. Some feel that this increase alone is cause for celebration, even before the many new projects have been premiered. It is commonly thought that greater opportunities, job security and a strengthened sense of continuity and community for film professionals must yield some results.

It is of course a good omen that attendance figures jumped in the second half of the season. A total of one million admissions a year for domestic films, a figure achieved five times in the last decade, has become something of a magic number, and in 2003 this figure was reached by the end of April, the home product capturing close to 25% of all ticket sales during the winter. And there are many more films in the pipeline. The main reasons for the success were the children's films, but the earnings of a film like Bent Hamer's *Kitchen Stories* also exceeded expectations. "A clear vote of confidence from the public", was what Stein Slyngstad, the first director of the Film Fund, called it.

Margreth Olin in **My Body**

KROPPEN MIN (My Body)
*[Documentary, 2002] Script and
Dir: Margreth Olin. Phot: Kim
Hiorthøy. Player: Olin. Prod:
Thomas Robsahm/Speranza.*

**SMILET I ØYET
(The Smile in the Eye)**
*[Documentary, 2002] Script:
Piotr Kuzinski, Bente Olav
Kuzinski. Dir and Phot: Bente
Olav Kuzinski. Players: Helene,
Carina, Eilén, Gro. Prod: Bente
Olav Kuzinski/Frameline Film.*

**KARLSSON PÅ TAKET
(Karlsson on the Roof)**
*[Children's animation, 2002]
Script: Vibeke Idsøe, based on a
novel by Astrid Lindgren.
Dir: Idsøe. Prod: John M.
Jacobsen/Filmkameratene/
Waldemar Bergendahl/
Svensk Filmindustri.*

**VELKOMMEN HJEM
(Welcome Home)**
*[Documentary, 2002] Script and
Dir: Trond Kvist. Prod: Torstein
Grude/SubFilm.*

Julia Boracco Braaten in **Wolf Summer**

ULVESOMMER (Wolf Summer)
*[Drama, 2003] Script and Dir:
Peder Norlund. Phot: Harald*

Weddings and Funerals (without Hugh Grant)

The season began with Unni Straume's **Music for Weddings and Funerals** (*Musikk for bryllup og begravelser*). Straume, who lives in Italy, has what a Norwegian would call a "continental" approach to film-making, as opposed to the many, somewhat Americanised, youngsters now establishing themselves in Norwegian cinema. There are echoes of Antonioni in this story set in the austere, modernist villa of a divorced writer, Sara (Lena Endré). In the naked interiors, a handful of characters, starting with Sara and her former husband, Peter (Bjørn Floberg), who designed the house, discuss contemporay aesthetics.

Tired of the perfect world Peter has created, Sara has invited Bogdan, a hard-drinking Serb, and his Orchestra for Weddings and Funerals into the house. The band's music, with its vibrant, improvised rhythms from the borderlands between Europe and Asia, becomes an obvious contrast to the self-consciously calculated architecture. The male characters are deliberately one-dimensional, and there is no drama in the conventional sense. The film's energy comes from the contrast between the dialogue's symbolic levels and the actors' natural way with their words, and also from the way cinematographer Harald Paalgard works with Straume to create an interesting, multifaceted surface. An antithesis to the Danish Dogme ethos, the film is lit and shot with careful attention to the unlimited visual possibilities of the film frame.

Also in the autumn season, Gunnar Vikene made his feature debut with **Falling Sky** (*Himmelfall*), the story of two young psychiatric patients, Reidar (Kristoffer Joner) and Juni (Maria Bonnevie). Reidar is afraid that a meteor will destroy the earth; Juni attacks anyone who touches her. Their doctor (Danish actor Kim Bodnia) is a failure, allowing his wife to have an affair with another man. Vikene tempers the gloomy aspects of the film with humour and brings the story, which takes place over the Christmas weekend, slowly forwards. He does well with the actors, getting a goodish performance from Joner and a fine one indeed from Bonnevie. The dramatic climax, however, is a let-down.

Jonny Vang is the story of an ambitious, energetic young man in rural Norway. Jonny has a business idea. He will grow earthworms and sell them to anglers as bait. But his own messy private life and the local community work against him. He is even knocked unconscious by an unknown assailant. The director is Jens Lien, a London International Film School graduate making a very assured feature debut after a decade of advertising work. Lien and his scriptwriter, Ståle Stein Berg, handle a dozen characters and a lot of incident with great ease, the film has great charm and the camerawork is faultless. It is storytelling modelled on the film

Paalgard. *Players: Julia Boracco Braathen, Line Verndal, Jørgen Langhelle, Samuel Fröler, Aksel Hennie. Prod: Ellen Jacobsen/ Kåre Storemyr/Northern Lights.*

PELLE POLITIBIL
(Pelle the Police Car)
[Children's film, 2002] Script: Arthur Johansen. Dir: Thomas Kaiser. Phot: Marius Johansen Hansen. Players: Hege Elise Strømsnes, Gard B. Eidsvold, Bjørn Sundquist, Jørgen Langhelle. Prod: Aage Aaberge/Yellow Cottage.

SALMER FRA KJØKKENET
(Kitchen Stories)
[Comedy, 2003] Script: Jörgen Bergmark, Bent Hamer. Dir: Hamer. Phot: Philip Øgaard. Players: Joachim Calmeyer, Tomas Norström, Bjørn Floberg, Sverre Anker Ousdal, Reine Brynolfsson. Prod: Bent Hamer/BulBul Film/Jörgen Bergmark/Bob Film.

OLSENBANDEN JR. GÅR UNDER VANN (The Junior Olsen Gang Goes under Water)
[Children's adventure, 2003] Dir: Arne Lindtner Næss. Phot: Kjell Vassdal. Players: Aksel Støren Aschjem, Thomas Engeset, Lars Berteig Andersen, Hege Schøyen, Finn Schau, Lasse Kolstad. Prod: Rune Trondsen/Nordisk Film og TV.

HIMMELFALL (Falling Sky)
[Drama, 2002] Script: Gunnar Vikene, Torun Lian. Dir: Vikene. Phot: Sjur Aarthun. Players: Kristoffer Joner, Maria Bonnevie, Kim Bodnia, Hildegun Riise, Endre Hellestveit. Prod: Sigve Endresen/Motlys.

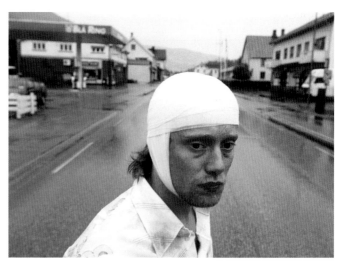

Aksel Hennie in the title role of **Jonny Vang**

classics, old and new, with every scene moving the story forwards and every piece of information paying off. The actors are good. Perhaps the film reveals more about modern cinema trends than about the actual people and environment of rural Norway, yet its qualities are far from negligible.

Good to keep Hamer in the *Kitchen*

One of the season's critical favourites was Bent Hamer's **Kitchen Stories** (Salmer *fra kjøkkenet*). Hamer's subject is, as always, highly original, and makes for rather unlikely film material: a fictional research project in rural Norway in the 1950s, carried out by a Swedish team, on the subject of bachelors' kitchen habits. There are no women in the film, which focuses on the developing friendship between a farmer (veteran Norwegian actor Joachim Calmeyer) and his observer (Tomas Norström), the latter absurdly perched on a specially designed chair in the corner of the kitchen.

Hamer is of course interested in the failure of his characters to live up to the scientists' ideal, however well-intentioned the research is, and finds just the right balance between his realist and absurdist elements. The film becomes a good-natured satire on the post-war era and its profound belief in modern science, while Norwegian audiences certainly appreciated the underplayed humour that permeates the film. Hamer also resists going on too long, even though the dramatic finale is a bit short of breath.

TROND OLAV SVENDSEN earned his BA and MA in history from the University of Oslo. He has worked as a researcher for the Norwegian Film Insitute and as a newspaper film critic. Among his publications is a *Theatre and Film Encyclopaedia*.

Kristoffer Joner in **Falling Sky**

JONNY VANG
*[Drama, 2003] Script: Ståle
Stein Berg. Dir: Jens Lien.
Phot: Philip Øgaard. Players:
Aksel Hennie, Laila Goody,
Fridtjov Såheim, Marit
Andreassen, Bjørn Sundquist,
Nils Vogt. Prod: Dag
Alveberg/Maipo.*

BUDDY
*[Drama, 2003] Script: Lars
Gudmestad. Dir: Morten
Tyldum. Phot: John-Andreas
Andersen. Players: Nicolai Cleve
Broch, Aksel Hennie, Anders
Baasmo Christensen, Pia Tjelta,
Janne Formoe. Prod: Gudny
Hummelvoll/Knut Jensen/
Happy Endings.*

Joachim Calmeyer, left, and Tomas Norström in **Kitchen Stories**

VILLMARK (Dark Woods)
*[Thriller, 2003] Script: Pål Øie,
Christopher Grøndahl. Dir: Øie.
Phot: Sjur Aarthun, Tore Vollan.
Players: Kristoffer Joner, Bjørn
Floberg, Sampda Sharma, Eva
Röse, Marko Kanic. Prod: Jan
Aksel Angeltvedt/Spleis.*

UNITED
*[Comedy, 2003] Script and Dir:
Magnus Martens. Phot: Jakob
Ingimundarson. Players: Håvard
Lilleheie, Berte Rommetveit,
Vegar Hoel, Ole-Jørgen Nilssen,
Gjert Haga. Prod: Håkon
Øveraas/Aagot Skjeldal/4.*

BÁZO
*[Drama, 2003] Script and Dir:
Lars Göran Pettersson. Phot:
Svein Krøvel. Players: Sverre
Porsanger, Issaht Juakim Gaup,
Anitta Suikkari, Göran
Forsmark. Prod: Nils Thomas
Utsi/Filbmagoahti.*

PLAY
*[Drama, 2003] Script and Dir:
John Sullivan. Phot: Knut
Kollandsrud, Martin Otterbeck.
Players: Hege Aga Roastad,
Linda M. Hverven, Nina Ellen
Ødegård, Siren Jørgensen, Jan
Marin Johnsen. Prod: Tom
Remlov/Tomas
Backström/Dinamo Story.*

**LILLE FRØKEN NORGE
(The Beast of Beauty)**
[Children's film, 2003] Script:

*Hilde Heier, Kjetil Indregård.
Dir: Heier. Phot: Philip Øgaard.
Players: Ida Maria Dahr
Nygaard, Amanda Kvakland,
Ingrid Lorentzen, Bård Tufte
Johansen, Marit Åslein. Prod:
Finn Gjerdrum/Paradox.*

**MOT MOSKVA
(Destination Moscow)**
*[Drama, 2003] Script and Dir: Jo
Strømgren, Runar Hodne. Phot:
Patrik Säfström. Players:
Thorbjørn Harr, Espen R.
Bjerke, Kyrre Texnæs, John
Brungot, Jo Strømgren. Prod:
Rune H. Trondsen/Nordisk Film.*

**KVINNEN I MITT LIV
(The Woman in My Life)**
*[Comedy, 2003] Script: Lars
Espen Bakke. Dir: Alexander Eik.
Phot: Jon Gaute Espevold.
Players: Thomas Giertsen, Ane
Dahl Torp, Line Verndal, Gard
Eidsvold, Pia Tjelta, Gjertrud
Jynge, Kjersti Holmen. Prod: John
M. Jacobsen/Filmkameratene.*

FIA OG KLOVNENE (Fia!)
*[Children's film, 2003] Script and
Dir: Elsa Kvamme. Phot: Kjell
Vassdal. Players: Klara Døving,
Sergio Bini, Hanne Lindbekk,
Stig Henrik Hoff, Anne Ryg.
Prod: Petter Borgli/Tomas
Backström/Dinamo Story.*

MORS ELLING (Mother's Elling)
*[Drama, 2003] Script: Axel
Hellstenius, based on a novel by*

*Ingvar Ambjørnsen. Dir: Eva
Isaksen. Phot: Rolv Håan.
Players: Per Christian Ellefsen,
Grete Nordrå. Prod: Dag
Alveberg/Maipo.*

**REVYTRADISJONER PÅ
MAGERØYA (North Cape
Cabaret)**
*[Documentary, 2003] Dir: Knut
Erik Jensen. Phot: Paal Bugge
Haagenrud. Prod: Jan-Erik
Gammleng/Barentsfilm.*

Quotes of the Year

"Norwegian directors
(and critics) rarely refer
to their country's own film
history… They need to
relate to what has been
done before, forget all
dogmas and insist on
recapturing the language
of film."
DAG JOHAN HAUGERUD,
film director, writing in Film &
Kino *magazine.*

"The Norwegian feature
film of today has regrettably
become a film with identifiable
genre elements, and in this
way adapted to the market
place."
KALLE LØCHEN, *editor of*
Film & Kino *magazine.*

Pakistan Aijaz Gul

The Year's Best Films

Aijaz Gul's selection:
This Heart Is Yours
(Dir: Javaid Shaikh)
Dacoit (Dir: Shan)
Beauty Parlour
(Short. Dir: Mehreen Jabbar)
World Center (Short. Dirs:
Faisal Rehman, Bilal Minto)
**Daughters of the Late
Colonial** (Dir: Mehreen Jabbar)

Recent Films

**YEH DIL APP KA HUWA
(This Heart Is Yours)**
*[Urdu. Romantic drama, 2002]
Script: Babar Kashmiri, Javaid
Shaikh. Dir: Shaikh. Players:
Mommar Rana, Saana,
Babar Ali, Javaid Shaikh.
Prod: Akbar Khan.*

DAKU (Dacoit)
*[Urdu. Thriller, 2002] Script:
Shan, Pervaiz Kaleem. Dir: Shan.
Phot: Ali Jan. Players: Shan,
Saima. Prod: Jamshed Zafar.*
The story of a young college
professor (Shan) who is gunned
down saving his kid brother.
The second half brings us
a look-alike, Dacoit
(Shan again), who helps the
kid brother settle scores with
the mafia.

BEAUTY PARLOUR
*[Urdu. Short, 1998]
Script: Azra Babar. Dir and
Prod: Mehreen Jabbar.
Phot: Anu Malik. Players:
Sania Saeed, Nadia Jamal.*
Characters meet in a salon
and their lives are revealed
through trips down memory
lane. The film took five years to
gain exhibition.

All the top actors (Shan, Samima) and directors (Sangeeta, Perviz Rana) worked non-stop in 2002 on Punjabi and Urdu quickies, and a total of 64 features were released (28 in Punjabi, 18 in Pushto and 18 in Urdu). But this was a highly disappointing year on many fronts. The National Film Development Corporation (NAFDEC), set up in 1973, was closed by the government in October 2002. It had imported quality films, held the annual National Film Awards (the big film event of the year in Lahore), set up state-of-the-art cinemas, studios and a film academy, promoted film exports and festival appearances and held film festivals, but lack of funds prevented it from consistently meeting all its goals. Industry figures had expected its closure for years but it was still a big blow – and not the only one of the year.

Lousy film after lousy film bombed at the box-office. The once bankable Syed Noor, having emptied his bag of tricks, completed several flops, including **Oath** (*Khuda qasam*), **Flames** (*Sholey*) and **Dacoit** (*Behram daku*). Actress-director Sangeeta, who's been in the business for 30 years, delivered five blood-soaked actioners. A couple of these orgies did average business, but none of her work addresses the real issues facing women in macho Pakistani society.

Pervaiz Rana made eight disastrous films in 2002 and Shan, the country's highest-paid actor (charging about $15,000 per film, plus plenty of star perks), raised hell in no fewer than 28 films in 2002. The commercial failures of others did nothing to dent his position at number one. Leading actress Saima, now in her early thirties and with her soaring career guided by Syed Noor, was seen in 20 titles, mostly opposite Shan. She now commands about $8,000 per role.

Audiences take *Heart*

The year's only redeeming feature was director-actor Javaid Shaikh's **This Heart Is Yours** (*Yeh dil app ka huwa*), which stayed in cinemas for more than ten months after its release in July 2002. Filmed on picture-postcard locations in Switzerland and Spain (including the obligatory bull-fight), with the most popular music of the year, this drama had relatively weak script about a pair of young lovers (Mommar Rana and Saana) from filthy-rich families whose marriage is opposed by the girl's villainous brother. He eventually bites the dust so that the lovers can walk into the sunset. Impressive wardrobe,

Mommar Rana and Saleem Shaikh in **This Heart Is Yours**

camerawork, locations (posh villas) and enormous TV publicity were part of the film's winning formula.

The dearth of good films owed a great deal to the dearth of professional producers. The experienced ones have either died or retired, to be replaced by milk magnates and other traders in search of a fast buck and keen to enjoy the company of pretty heroines (and heroes). Creative cinema was not their priority.

Hopes that an influx of writers and directors from television might supply fresh blood were dashed by TV director Fahim Burney, whose feature debut **In Love** (*Pyar hi pyar*) was a disaster in 2003. The thin plot involved a hero who heads for Dubai and a heroine who gets married to another man, becomes a mother and then a widow. The hero, Ashal, was average. Two other names from television, Samina Peerzada with **Play** (*Shararat*) and Asif Ali with **Fire**, met the same fate. Both films had unappealing themes and were mis-cast.

The good news was that before NAFDEC was liquidated, it submitted sound recordist Syed Afzal Hussain for the country's highest arts accolade, Pride of Performance, which he received from President Musharraf in March 2003. He began his recording career in Mumbai in the 1940s, and now at 80 is a household name in film circles. The industry lost director Hussnain and composer Nazir Ali, who will be long remembered for many Punjabi hit melodies, sung by the late Noorjehan. Foreign films continued to take a bashing at the box-office. Almost all of them had already been seen uncensored on pirate cable channels or VCD and DVD. *Ocean's Eleven*, *xXx* and *Rush Hour 2* were among the casualties in theatres.

AIJAZ GUL earned his BA and MA from the University of Southern California and has published numerous articles and three books on cinema. He lives in Islamabad.

WORLD KA CENTER
(World Center)
[Urdu. Short drama, 2002]
Script, Dir and Prod: Faisal
Rehman, Bilal Minto. Phot:
Arshad Altaf. Players: Iftikhar
Kasuri, Usman Farooq.
Young boys from Lahore see off their friend, who is heading for the United States on 9/11. Lower middle-class urban life filmed with honesty and simplicity.

MARHOOM COLONIAL KI
BAITYAAN (Daughters of the
Late Colonial)
[Urdu. Drama, 2002] Dir:
Mehreen Jabbar. Phot: Mirza
Mehmood. Players: Samina
Ahmad, Yasmin Ismail. Prod:
Friends Entertainment.
Adaptation of Katherine Mansfield's *Daughters of the Late Colonial*. Two middle-aged spinster sisters try to cope with the world after demise of their strict and disciplined Colonial father. They have a new life and freedom but can they handle it?

Quote of the Year

"I never used glycerine."
MOHAMMAD ALI, *actor, after shedding tears on screen for more than 30 years.*

Peru Isaac Léon Frías

Recent and Forthcoming Films

D'JANGO, LA OTRA CARA
(D'Jango, the Other Face)
[Thriller, 2002] Script: Gastón Vizcarra. Dir: Ricardo Velázquez. Phot: Teo Delgado. Players: Giovanni Ciccia, Melania Urbina, Tatiana Astengo. Prod: Inca Cine.

MUERTO DE AMOR
(Death of Love)
[Romantic drama, 2002] Script and Dir: Edgardo Guerra. Phot: Alberto Arévalo. Players: Diego Bertie, Vanessa Robbiano, Karina Calmet. Prod: Sur Producciones.

OJOS QUE NO VEN (*literally, Eyes That Do Not See*)
[Drama, 2003] Script: Giovanna Pollarolo. Dir: Francisco Lombardi. Phot: Teo Delgado. Players: Paul Vega, Gustavo Bueno, Gianfranco Brero, Patricia Pereyra. Prod: Inca Cine.

BAÑO DE DAMAS
(Ladies' Toilet)
[Drama, 2003] Script and Dir: Michael Katz. Phot: Juan Durán. Players: Andrea Montenegro, Lorena Meritano, Coco Marusix, Sonia Oquendo. Prod: Iguana Films.

POLVO ENAMORADO
(Lovesick Dust)
[Drama, 2003] Script: Giovanna Pollarolo. Dir: Luis Barrios. Phot: Carlos de la Cadena. Players: Paul Vega, Gianella Neyra, Gustavo Bueno. Prod: Inca Cine.

EL DESTINO NO TIENE FAVORITOS (Destiny Has No Favourites)
[Comedy, 2002] Script and Dir: Alvaro Velarde. Phot: Micaela

The local exhibition market has expanded gradually, following the building of many new cinemas, and total admissions in 2002 reached 11 million, the highest for 15 years – though little of the gain was for Peruvian films. Production has increased, too, but several films have stalled in post-production or await local exhibition.

During the second half of 2002, three Peruvian films were released. Ricardo Velázquez's **D'Jango, the Other Face** (*D'jango, la otra cara*) is a crime thriller, inspired by the life of a real bank robber. It is a *Bonnie and Clyde*-type story set in Lima during the 1980s, routinely directed and, unable to conceal its budgetary limitations, no better than an average TV movie. **Death of Love** (*Muerto de amor*), directed by Edgardo Guerra, is a modern romantic comedy about a charming yuppie who falls for a young actress. Its main influences are Howard Hawks' screwball films and it starts promisingly, with a distinctive visual atmosphere, but the rhythm soon flags and the story is unnecessarily stretched.

The Foreigner (*El Forastero*) is a new critical and commercial failure in the long career of Federico García. Made with Spanish co-production investment (the cinematographer and editor were Spaniards), this is a contrived blend of local *costumbrista* comedy and science-fiction, with a "New Age" twist. A blond alien arrives on his spaceship in the small Andean village of Cuzco and helps transform the lives of the villagers, but nothing in this flatly directed film is convincing.

Lombardi *Eyes* his last

In the first half of 2003, three films were released, including the year's best: **Ojos que no ven** (literally, *Eyes That Do Not See*), the last film of the late Francisco Lombardi. It is an ambitious project, inspired by the political corruption under President Alberto Fujimori in the 1990s. The so-called *Vladivideos*, the tapes recorded by intelligence chief Vladimiro Montesinos, showing political bribery, frame a multi layered story that forms a grey and pessimistic mosaic. It reveals the complicity of Peruvian politicians, judges, journalists and military officials. There are uneven moments in this 149-minute picture, which was not quite up to the standard of Lombardi's best works, *Lion's Den* (*La boca del lobo*) and *Fallen from Heaven* (*Caídos del cielo*), but it demonstrated his trademark skills: precise direction of actors and balanced rhythm.

Giancarlo Brero and Patricia Pereyra in political thriller **Ojos que no ven**

Lovesick Dust (*Polvo enamorado*), directed by Peruvian Luis Barrios, charts the passionate relationship between a priest and a young married woman in a small fishing town. The story resembles *The Crime of Father Amaro* (see Mexico section) but lacks the dramatic nerve needed to heighten the conflict inherent in forbidden love. Disappointingly, these two films drew smaller audiences than the worst of the Peruvian features of 2003: **Ladies' Toilet** (*Baño de damas*), directed by Venezuelan Michael Katz. Based on a stage piece, it is a ridiculous flop set in a ladies' restroom where a group of women share different experiences, leading up to a lesbian encounter.

Short film production continues, but despite the surprising and impressive qualities of many of these shorts there are still almost no spaces in which to show them. Many of them are made on analog and digital video outside Lima, in various inland towns. Sadly, this burgeoning audio-visual horizon is virtually unknown in the capital.

The long-awaited new film legislation has remained in a kind of limbo, while Peruvian legislators are preoccupied with more pressing social concerns, strikes and other forms of protest that make the plight of the film industry seem trivial, and make it virtually impossible for CONACINE (Consejo Nacional de Cinematografía) to improve the situation. There were, nonetheless, two films ready for release in summer 2003: Antonio Fortunic's *A Martian Named Desire* (*Un Marciano llamado deseo*) and Alvaro Velarde's *Destiny Has No Favourites* (*El destino no tiene favoritos*), and in all perhaps five or six Peruvian features will open in 2004 – not many compared to the likes of Mexico, Argentina and Brazil, but still an outstanding achievement under the circumstances.

ISAAC LÉON FRÍAS is Professor of Language and Film History at the University of Lima. From 1965 to 1985 he was director of *Hablemos de Cine* magazine and now runs Filmoteca de Lima.

Cajahuaringa. Players: Angie Cepeda, Elena Romero, Bernie Paz, Tatiana Astengo. Prod: Alvaro Velarde Producciones.

UN MARCIANO LLAMADO DESEO
(A Martian Called Desire)
[Comedy, 2003] Script and Dir: Antonio Fortunic. Phot: Micaela Cajahuaringa. Players: Christian Meier, Mónica Sanchez. Prod: Focus Producciones.

IMPOSIBLE AMOR
(Impossible Love)
[Drama, 2002] Script and Dir: Armando Robles Godoy. Phot: Luciano Talledo. Players: Mónica Sanchez, Javier Echevarría, Vanessa Robbiano, Giovanni Ciccia. Prod: Películas del Pacífico.

PALOMA DE PAPEL
(Paper Dove)
[Drama, 2003] Script and Dir: Fabrizio Aguilar. Phot: Micaela Cajahuaringa. Players: Antonio Callirgos, Aristóteles Picho, Sergio Galliani, Melania Urbina. Prod: Luna Llena Films.

MERCURIO NO ES UN PLANETA (Mercury Is Not a Planet) *[working title]*
[Thriller, 2003] Script and Dir: Alberto Durant. Phot: Juan Duran. Players: Fabrizio Aguilar, Mari Pili Barreda, Katia Condos, Gianfranco Brero. Prod: Agua Dulce Films.

EL FORASTERO (The Foreigner)
[Fantasy, 2001] Script and Dir: Federico García. Phot: Fernando Arribas. Players: Carlos Sovera, Nacho Duato, Gabriela Velázquez. Prod: Pilar Roca Producciones/Sociedad Audiovisual Dos Orillas (Spain).

Philippines Tessa Jazmines

The Year's Best Films

Tessa Jazmines' selection:
Kiss the Hand
(Dir: Joel Lamangan)
Small Voices (Dir: Gil Portes)
The 70s Decade
(Dir: Chito Rono)
Spirit Warriors 2: The Short Cut (Dir: Chito Rono)

The 70s Decade

Recent and Forthcoming Films

MANO PO (Kiss the Hand)
[Drama, 2002] Script: Roy Iglesias. Dir: Joel C. Lamangan. Phot: Leslie Garchitorena. Players: Maricel Soriano, Richard Gomez, Eddie Garcia, Gina Alajar, Boots Anson Roa, Amy Austria, Tirso Cruz III, Cogie Domingo, Maxene Magalona, Jay Manalo, Eric Quizon. Prod: Lily Monteverde, Regal Films.
The struggles of Filipino-Chinese families to find their place in Philippine society and retain their Chinese identity. The story starts in 1949 with the marriage of a young Chinese lad and his Filipina wife. Through generations the family proves that blood is always thicker than

The bad news is that the Philippine economy improved only slightly in 2002-03, forcing producers to be more inhibited and preventing them from churning out dozens of films a year, as they did in the 1970s and 1980s. The good news is that, creatively, Filipino film-makers ventured into new genres that redefined their craft. Buoyed by government tax incentives, a new movie bill to support the industry and the dangling of both official honours and monetary rewards in front of anyone who made films that departed from the run-of-the-mill, "kiss-kiss, bang-bang" formula, local producers went for new themes and substance. The result was a richer, more varied tapestry of Filipino films.

The Metro Manila Film Festival, held during the two-week Christmas holidays, reflected this innovative spirit. Previously showcasing crowd pleasing comedies, horror flicks or action movies, with shallow plots and characters, the 2002-03 festival offered original and challenging new subject matter. Adjudged Best Film was Joel C. Lamangan's **Kiss the Hand** (*Mano po;* the title is what you say as you place the back of an older person's hand to your forehead to show respect and humility). It was the first movie ever to explore the islands' Filipino-Chinese community and something of a personal adventure for Regal Films' executive producer, Lily Y. Monteverde, who grew up Chinese in the Philippines. She opened up the padlocked doors of Chinese homes to the public with *Kiss the Hand*, the epic saga of a wealthy

A Filipino-Chinese family dominates **Kiss the Hand**

Chinese family coping with the stress and strains of its divided heritage. The colour and texture of the movie are as rich and opulent as dragon-red Chinese brocade.

The 70s Decade (*Dekada 70*), directed by Chito Rono, was another festival entry that made a valiant attempt to recapture a lost era: martial rule under Ferdinand Marcos. Based on an award-winning novel, the movie stars veteran actress Vilma Santos, who gives a brilliant performance as a mother rising to the many challenges of those trying times. The screenplay was by Lualhati Bautista, winner of the Palanca Award, the country's most prestigious literary gong.

But serious movies were not the only fare on offer at Manila. Fantasy adventures like **Spirit Warriors 2: The Short Cut** also caught public attention. This $1.5m (P80m) production reflected the growing fascination of local film-makers with special effects. Imus Productions' **Grandpa's Legend** (*Ang Alamat ni Lolo*) and high-flying comic-book comedy **Lastikman** were also effects-ridden. *Lastikman* was the surprise hit of the festival, taking $373,000 in just two days. It stars TV comic Vic Sotto as the islands' answer to Spider-Man, a wimpy saviour of the downtrodden whose flexible limbs help him fall in love and save the world. What more could anyone want?

Sex comes back into fashion

In June, the Manila Film Festival showcased another set of films, which some critics judged as mediocre. Here, the *bomba* (sexy) genre, which always makes for good local box-office, made a comeback. Joel Lamangan won nine of the event's 15 awards with **The Last Virgin on Earth** (*Huling birhen sa lupa*) a story of fraudulent miracles by a fake priest and his willing accomplices, the village whore and her retarded sister. The biggest moneymaker, however, was **My Dream Is to Love You** (*Pangarap kong ibigin ka*), an out-and-out love story about an eccentric painter who falls in love at first sight with the hero of the story. Filipinos are pushovers for grand love affairs.

Other entries were **The Power of Mud** (*Bertud ng putik*), the saga of a folk hero studded with amulets; **Balikatan,** an action movie about ongoing joint military training between American and Filipino soldiers (some labelled it propaganda); and **Passion of the Race** (*Alab ng lahi*), which dwells on the plight of Filipino and Japanese soldiers after the Japanese Imperial Army's surrender to American troops in 1945.

Perhaps the most important film of the year was **Small Voices** (*Mga munting tinig*), directed, co-written and co-produced by

water, but identity can be shaped by where you live.

DEKADA 70 (The 70s Decade)
[Drama, 2002] Script: Lualhati Bautista. Dir: Chito Rono. Phot: Neil Daza. Players: Vilma Santos, Christopher de Leon, Marvin Agustin, Danilo Barrios, Carlos Agassi, Dimples Romana, John Wayne Sace, Piolo Pascual. Prod: Star Cinema.
A middle-class couple and their five sons struggle with the realities shaped by the volatile political developments of the early 1970s, when the Philippines was placed under martial law. Family bonds are threatened by changing values and contrasting ideologies, and the mother (Santos) undergoes the most dramatic transformation.

SPIRIT WARRIORS 2: THE SHORT CUT
[Horror fantasy-adventure, 2002] Dir: Chito Rono. Players: The Street Boys (Jhong Hilario, Vhong Navarro, Danilo Barrios, Spencer Reyes, Christopher Cruz). Prod: Lily Monteverde, MaQ Productions.
The Spirit Warriors find an entrance to the underworld as they search for an ancient and powerful amulet. Their problem is how to return a taste of really gruesome underworld hospitality.

LASTIKMAN: ANG BAGONG SUPERHERO NG BAYAN (Lastikman: the Country's New Super Hero)
[Fantasy comedy, 2002] Dir: Toni Y. Reyes. Phot: Ely Cruz. Players: Vic Sotto, Donita Rose, Jeffrey Quizon, Michael V, Oyo Boy Sotto. Prod: Octo Arts.
Noted Filipino comics creator Mars Ravelo's elastic superhero reaches the screen. A meteor strikes a rubber tree, giving the young Hilario special powers of elasticity that render him invincible.

LAPU-LAPU
[Epic drama, 2002] Script: Jerry Tirazona. Dir and Prod: William

Mayo. *Players: Lito Lapid, Joyce Jimenez, Dante Rivero, Roi Vinzon, Ian Veneracion.*
In the sixteenth century, Lapu-Lapu, brave chieftain of Cebu Island and the first Filipino hero, battles and kills Ferdinand Magellan, leader of the Spanish colonisers.

HULING BIRHEN SA LUPA
(**The Last Virgin on Earth**)
[Erotic drama, 2003] Script: Raquel Villavicencio. Dir: Joel C. Lamangan. Players: Jay Manalo, Maui Taylor, Ara Mina. Prod: Neo Films.
Two sisters, one retarded, live with their sickly mother in a remote, small town. To make ends meet, the elder sister is forced to sell her body and engage in other illegal activities. One ruse she pulls is faking a miracle, but their lives really change when the younger sister experiences a genuine miracle: she sees the Blessed Virgin's image tossing among the waves.

MGA MUNTING TINIG
(**Small Voices**)
[Drama, 2002] Script: Gil Portes, Senedy Que, Adolf Alix. Dir: Portes. Phot: Ely Cruz. Players: Alessandra de Rossi, Gina Alajar, Amy Austria, Dexter Doria, Bryan Homecillo, Piero Rodriguez III, Sining Blanco, Keno Agaro, Christian Galindo, Nonie Buencamino, Irina Adlawan, Tony Mabesa.
When Merlinda is sent to Malawig, a remote province, to provide basic education for poor children, she feels compelled to change the outlook of the adults and children there, who think only the rich can afford to dream and achieve. Through the children's singing voices the people find new hope.

TANGING INA
(**Unique Mother**)
[Comedy-drama, 2003] Script : Mel del Rosario. Dir: Wenn Deramas. Players: Ai-Ai de las Alas, Edu Manzano, Tonton Gutierrez, Jestoni Alarcon,

acclaimed Filipino director Gil M. Portes. This heartwarming story of a young teacher who tries to make a difference in a small town by inspiring her young students to join a local singing contest helped to put Filipino cinema on the global stage. It won Best Picture, Director and Screenplay at Palm Springs, played to sold-out festival audiences in Toronto and Los Angeles and has been invited to Cannes, Edinburgh and Karlovy Vary, among other events. Warner Brothers acquired Filipino and international theatrical and home video rights, making *Small Voices* the first Filipino film ever to successfully close a distribution deal with a major Hollywood studio. It was also the Philippines' entry to the Oscars.

A teacher transforms lives in Gil M. Portes' **Small Voices**

Overall, Philippine cinema managed to survive the hostile economic environment in 2002-03, showing patches of brilliance and giving hope for a brighter future when the economy recovers. Video piracy remained a scourge, however, despite the redoubled efforts of the Video Regulatory Board, which made a series of raids on shopping malls and illegal CD factories.

TESSA JAZMINES is *Variety* correspondent for the Philippines and Associate Professor of Journalism, University of the Philippines College of Mass Communication.

Shaina Magdayao, Marvin Agustin, Danilo Barrios, Alwyn Uytingco, Serena Dalrymple. Prod: Star Cinema.
The sad, funny story of an "ideal" mother who marries and is widowed three times and how she copes with the challenges of raising her 12 children through sad and happy (mis)adventures.

CRYING LADIES
[Comedy, forthcoming] Script and Dir: Mark Meily. Phot: Lee Meily. Players: Sharon Cuneta, Hilda Koronel, Angel Aquino. Prod: Tony Gloria/Unitel Pictures.

Comic misadventures of three friends begin when Stella Mate (Cuneta) hires her friends Choleng (Aquino) and Dora (Koronel) and convinces them to act as mourners at a Chinese funeral.

Quote of the Year

"It's time to break the walls in our minds. It's up to us to conquer and make the Filipino film industry fly."
RICHARD GORDON,
Philippines Tourism Secretary.

Poland William Roderick Richardson

Recent and Forthcoming Films

ANIOL W KRAKOWIE
(An Angel in Kracow)
[Comedy, 2002] Script: Witold Beres, Artur Wiecek. Dir: Wiecek. Phot: Piotr Trela. Players: Krzyztof Globisz, Ewa Kaim, Jerzy Trela. Prod: Beres & Baron Media Production/L&L Studio/Kino Swiat International.

KAMELEON (Chameleon)
[Thriller, 2002] Script: Janusz Kijowski, Jacek Janczarski. Dir: Kijowski. Phot: Zdzislaw Najda. Players: Piotr Machalica, Ewa Blaszczyk. Prod: Telewizja Polska SA/Agencja Produkcji Filmowej/ITI Cinema.
A rural policeman under investigation decides to take on the mafia and corrupt officials.

CHOPIN, PRAGNIENIE MILOSCI
(Chopin, Desire for Love)
[Drama, 2002] Script and Dir: Jadwiga Baranska, Jerzy Antczak. Phot: Edward Klosinski. Players: Piotr Adamczyk, Danuta Stenka, Bozena Stachura, Adam Woronowicz. Prod: Antczak Production/PKO Bank Polska SA/TVP SA/Wizja TV/ITI Cinema/Skorpion Art.
Weepy biopic about the Polish composer's tribulations with French author George Sand.

DZIEN SWIRA
(The Day of the Wacko)
[Comedy, 2002] Script and Dir: Marek Koterski. Phot: Jacek Blawut. Players: Marek Kondrat, Janina Traczykowna, Michal Koterski, Joanna Sienkiewicz, Piotr Machalica. Prod: SF Zebra/Vision Film Production/

In 2002 Polish helmers turned generally to satire and cynicism about the ironies of contemporary life in their country. Andrzej Wajda released another popular period piece. Indie prods piqued interest with the provocative *Edi*, winning awards on a shoestring budget. Favourite son Roman Polanski grabbed an Oscar for *The Pianist*, but corruption loomed when *Pianist* producer Lew Rywin became embroiled in a front-page bribery scandal.

In short, Poland is suffering political and cultural chaos as it heads for EU membership. Public trust in Parliament was measured at 12%. Public interest in the film industry is equally low, with locals buying only 4.6 million tickets to Polish films in 2002 (down more than 50% on 2001), and 70% of that market share went to historical pics *Chopin* and *Zemsta*, both made in 2001.

Some might say the best plot occurred off-screen. In December, Mr Rywin was implicated in a scandal, which rocked Polish politics and showbusiness to the core. He was taped during a conversation with Adam Michnik, editor of Poland's leading daily newspaper, *Gazeta Wyborcza*, proposing a $17.5m bribe in order to smooth legislation that would enable the newspaper group to acquire control of one of Poland's major TV stations. The scandal, which has inevitably become known as "Rywingate", had far-reaching consequences, including supposed ties to the Prime Minister and the head of TVP SA, the Polish TV giant.

Against this background, Polish cinema has had an off year. It has always been a micro-business but, following structural changes, a massive reduction in state production financing and a significant drop in vital television funding, the length and number of films have shrunk further. Only 18 films over 90 minutes were produced in 2002 – far below the average of 25 to 30 over the last 15 years.

Indie helmers have picked up some of the slack. Take **Edi**, for example. Made on a shoestring by director Piotr Trzaskalski, without any state support, it is the dire story of a homeless scrap collector struggling to bring up an orphaned baby. It won a number of awards at Poland's feature film festival in Gdynia, including Special Prize of the Jury, Best Cinematography and Best Art Direction. It also took the Grand Prix at the Warsaw International Film Festival and the Best Cinematography award at the

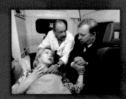

Camerimage Festival of international cinematography. Bleak though the story is, it sheds light on the present situation in which more than one in five Poles is unemployed, showing a society under stress and a protagonist resigned to the will of forces beyond his control. Though not a box-office hit, it struck a cultural chord in troubled times.

Contrast this with Andrzej Wajda's **Zemsta**, starring Roman Polanski and noted actors Janusz Gajos and Andrzej Seweryn. Based on Aleksander Fredro's classic stage comedy, it displays those national characteristics that in time brought on many of Poland's national embarrassments – how fitting in the year that brought Rywingate. Two rival princes, each controlling half of the same castle, seek to usurp the other. Love thickens the plot when a ravishing damsel becomes a further object of their desire. Wajda neatly captures the Polish obsession with self-interest to the point of self-destruction, providing a fitting allegory for current events.

The most inventive recent movie has to be the manic comedy **The Day of the Wacko** (*Dzien Swira*), which was named best Polish film in 2002. This was *Adaptation*, Polish-style, with Marek Kondrat as Adam Miauczynski, 44, a self-obsessed, divorced teacher heading for his 19th nervous breakdown.

Monika Donner-Treliniske and Marek Kondrat in **The Day of the Wacko**

Desperate to make order out of chaos, he resorts to numerology: he exercises until exactly 7am, drinks seven sips of water, washes himself while counting over and over to seven, pours seven handfuls of oatmeal into his bowl, stirs his coffee seven times. Life is boring. Life is necessary. He pops Prozac, takes vitamins, scoffs tonics. Fear and loathing with a pinch of paranoia abound, each minute providing a new form of torture. His solace is the son he loves – a middle-class echo of the theme of *Edi*, which underlines the appropriate Polish propensity, born of calamitous history, to invest hope in new generations.

Non Stop Film Service.

EDEN
[Animation, 2002] Script and Dir: Andrzej Czeczot. Phot: Zbigniew Kotecki, Andrzej Teodorzyk, Jadwiga Zauder-Olesinska, Dorota Bernadowska. Prod: Europe Ltd.
Pleasant fairytale for adults.

EDI
[Drama, 2002] Script and Dir: Piotr Trzaskalski. Phot: Krzystof Ptak. Players: Henryk Golebiewski, Jacek Braciak, Jacek Lenartowicz, Domnik Bak. Prod: Opus Film.

GABI
[Drama, 2002] Script: Roland Rowinski, Malgorzata Sawicka-Owsiany. Dir: Rowinski. Phot: Marian Prokop. Players: Marta Chodorowska, Andrzej Chyra, Jan Frycz, Krzystof Globisz. Prod: Figaro Film Production.
Impossible love between a 16-year-old girl and an older man.

HAKER (Hacker)
[Thriller, 2002] Script: Janusz Zaorski, Marek Nowowieski. Dir: Zaorski. Phot: Lukasz Kosmicki. Players: Bartosz Obuchowicz, Kasia Smutniak, Boguslaw Linda. Prod: Bow & Axe Entertainment/HBO Poland/Monolith Films Ltd.
Adolescent computer freaks strike gold in the virtual world.

JULIA WRACA DO DOMU (Julia Walking Home)
[Drama, 2002] Script: Roman Gren, Arlene Sarner, Agnieszska Holland. Dir: Holland. Phot: Jacek Petrycki. Players: Miranda Otto, William Fichtner, Lothaire Bluteau, Ryan Smith, Bianca Crudo. Prod: SF TOR/TVP SA/Canal + Polska/Art Oko Film (Germany)/Film Works Ltd/IMX Communications Inc. (Canada).
Jilted woman returns to Poland from Canada seeking a faith healer to cure her daughter's cancer.

GOLASY – FILM PSYCHOLOGICZNY
(Naked – A Psychological Film)
[Drama, 2002] Script: Krzysztof Jaworski. Dir: Witold Swietnicki. Phot: Wojciech Rawecki. Players: Anna Pudlowska, Barbara Gasior, Agnieszka Pasko, Waldemar Plotek. Prod: Wytwornia Filmow Amerikanskich.

KARIERA NIKOSIA DZYMY
(Nikos Dyzmy's Career)
[Comedy, 2002] Script: Tomasz Kepski. Dir: Jacek Bromski. Phot: Arkadiusz Torniak. Players: Cezary Pazura, Anna Przybylska, Ewa Kasprzyk, Andrzej Grabowski, Krzysztof Globisz, Lew Rywin. Prod: KASA Balcerak Produkcja Filmowa/Vision Film Production.

ZEMSTA (Revenge)
[Historical comedy, 2002] Script: Andrzej Wajda, from the novel by Aleksander Fredro. Dir: Andrzej Wajda. Phot: Pawel Edelman. Players: Janusz Gajos, Andrzej Seweryn, Roman Polanski, Kasia Figura. Prod: Arka Film/Vision Film Production/TVP SA.

SHOW
[Comedy, 2002] Script and Dir: Maciej Slesicki. Phot: Andrzej Ramiau. Players: Cezary Pazura, Jerzy Stuhr, Dorota Segda. Prod: Studio Filmowe Oko/Syrena Entertainment Group.

THE STAR
[Documentary, 2002] Script and Dir: Sylwester Latkowski. Prod: SPI International Polska/TVP SA/Universal Music Polska. Analyses the success of Poland's most popular singing star, Michal Wisniewski.

SUPERPRODUCKCJA
(Superproduction)
[Comedy, 2002] Script and Dir: Juliusz Machulski. Phot: Edward Klosinski. Players: Rafal Krolikowski, Janusz Rewinski, Anna Przybylska. Prod: SF Zebra, Vision Film Production/Non Stop Film Service.

From an *Angel* to *Eden*

Fantasy featured in three notable indie pics. In **An Angel in Krakow** (*Aniol w Krakowie*) a rock'n'roll-loving angel is sentenced to live on Earth, where he must perform an act of kindness a day. Winding up in Krakow he becomes so entranced with its atmosphere and a particular sausage-selling lady that he begs leave to remain. *Eden* is an enjoyable 80-minute trip through historical and pop culture mythology, with an excellent score by Michal Urbaniak, which alone is worth the ticket price. **Naked – A Psychological Film** (*Golasy – film psychologiczny*) strips office life bare when business proceeds as usual *sans* duds – a kind of *Manager's New Clothes* that proves once and for all that most of us look better with our clothes on.

Three satires reveal anger at the low level of political and cultural elites and their expectations. Juliusz Machulski's **Superproduction** (*Superproduckcja*) satirises Polish film-making, as a critic's killer reviews prompt a local wise-guy to force the know-it-all to write a script that will make his girlfriend a star. Mayhem ensues. Inventive and pointed as usual, Machulski smacks his targets relentlessly.

Rafal Krolikowski, centre, as a critic in **Superproduction**

Maciej Slesicki's **Show** is a different kettle of fish, taking a dark look at the televisual art of audience manipulation and the nihilistic attitudes of TV bosses, as a psychopathic exec tries to kill the stars of the reality show he has created. **Nykos Dyzmy's Career** (*Kariera Nikos Dzymy*) features Poland's most popular actor, Cezary Pazura (who also stars in *Show*), as a bumpkin gravedigger who comes to Warsaw and manipulates the political manipulators, including the Prime Minister (a cameo by Lew Rywin), to triumph and become a bigwig.

WILLIAM RODERICK RICHARDSON is a writer and film-maker, who lives in Poland and the US. He recently completed documentaries about Death Row in Texas and the city of Warsaw. His collection of travel stories, *Wish You Were Here*, will be published in 2004.

Portugal Martin Dale

The Year's Best Films

Martin Dale's selection:
Come and Go
(Dir: João Cesar Monteiro)
The Woman Who Believed
She Was President of
the USA (Dir: João Botelho)
My Voice (Dir: Flora Gomes)
The Jungle (Dir: Leonel Vieira)
Forget Everything I've
Told You
(Dir: António Ferreira)

Recent and Forthcoming Films

A PASSAGEM DA NOITE
(Passing of the Night)
[Drama, 2003] Script and Dir:
Luís Filipe Rocha. Phot: Edgar
Moura. Players: Cristóvão
Campos, João Ricardo, Leonor
Seixas, Maria Rueff. Prod:
Madragoa Filmes.

A MULHER QUE
ACREDITAVA SER
PRESIDENTE DOS EUA
(The Woman Who Believed She
was President of the USA)
[Comedy, 2003] Script and Dir:
João Botelho. Phot: Inês
Carvalho. Players: Alexandra
Lencastre, Rita Blanco, Laura
Soveral. Prod: Madragoa Filmes.

Alexandra Lencastre as
The Woman Who...

Over the 2002-03 season, Portuguese cinema strolled forward in its longstanding tradition of high-brow, niche-audience films, with Paulo Branco's Madragoa Filmes dominating the landscape (it produced around 40% of national films released). The principal themes continue to be isolation, solitude, sadness, pessimism and a poetic longing for the past. These themes also reflect overall concerns in Portuguese society, at a time when the country seems to be going through a profound process of self-analysis and self-criticism.

One of Portugal's most renowned and gifted *auteurs*, João Cesar Monteiro, passed away on February 3, 2003, the day after his 64th birthday and three months before the premiere of his final film **Come and Go** (*Vai e vem*) at Cannes. Cesar Monteiro leaves behind him a unique, idiosyncratic œuvre, including classics such as *Memories of the Yellow House* (*Recordações da casa amarela*) and *God's Comedy* (*A comédia do Deus*). The director appears in his final film as João Vuvu, following in the footsteps of his former incarnation as João de Deus. Monteiro's physical frailty, solitude and bittersweet vision of the world haunt us as he travels every day on the Number 100 bus, from his quaint Lisbon neighbourhood up to his favourite park – seemingly in preparation for his journey to the Other World.

The late João Cesar Monteiro, centre, in Come and Go

VAI E VEM (Come and Go)
[Drama, 2003] Script and Dir:
João Cesar Monteiro. Phot:
Mário Barroso. Players: César
Monteiro, Rita Pereira Marques,
Joaquina Chicau, Miguel Borges.
Prod: Madragoa Filmes.

MULHER POLÍCIA
(Cop Woman)
[Drama, 2003] Script and Dir:
Joaquim Sapinho. Phot: Jacques
Loiseleux. Players: Amélia Corôa,
Ludovic Videira, Maria Silva,
Vitor Norte. Prod: Rosa Filmes.

NHA FALA (My Voice)
[Musical comedy, 2003] Script
and Dir: Flora Gomes. Phot:
Edgar Moura. Players: Fatou
N'Diaye, Jean-Christophe Doll.
Prod: Fado Filmes.

A SELVA (The Jungle)
[Costume drama, 2002] Script:
Izaís Almada, João Nunes. Dir:
Leonel Vieira. Phot: Acácio de
Almeida. Players: Diogo
Morgado, Chico Diaz, Gracindo
Junior, Maitê Proença. Prod:
Costa do Castelo.

A FILHA (The Daughter)
[Drama, 2003] Script and Dir:
Solveig Nordlund. Phot: Acácio
da Almeida. Players: Nuno Melo,
Joana Bárcia, Margarida
Marinho. Prod: Ambar Filmes.

QUARESMA
[Drama, 2003] Script and Dir:
Jose Alvaro Morais. Phot: Acácio
da Almeida. Players: Beatriz
Batarda, Filipe Cary, Rita Durão.
Prod: Madragoa Filmes.

ESQUECE TUDO O QUE TE
DISSE (Forget Everything I've
Told You)
[Drama, 2002] Script: César
Santos, António Ferreira. Dir:
Ferreira. Players: Custódia
Gallego, António Capelo, Amélia
Corôa. Prod: Madragoa Filmes.

A JANGADA DE PEDRA
(The Stone Raft)
[Drama, 2003] Script: Yvette
Biro, George Sluizer, based on
the novel by Jorge Saramago.
Dir: Sluizer. Phot: Goert Giltaij.
Players: Ana Padrão, Diogo

Two other Portuguese films at Cannes in 2003 were João Botelho's **The Woman Who Believed She Was President of the USA** (A mulher que acreditava ser presidente dos EUA) and Jose Alvaro Morais' Quaresma. Botelho's film is a burlesque comedy that revolves around Alexandra Lencastre as a woman who lives under the delusion of the title in Washington Street, Lisbon. The cast is composed exclusively of women and satirises the modern world dominated by male and American values. **Quaresma** is an elliptical road movie. David is about to leave Portugal but on learning of the death of his grandfather returns to his home village where he meets his cousin's wife, Ana, and falls under her mysterious spell.

Friends reunited

Other highly individualistic productions include **The Flaw** (A Falha) by João Mário Grilo, which dramatises a Big Chill-style reunion of former high-school colleagues who find themselves trapped during a visit to a marble quarry and are forced to confront bitter internal tensions that have been buried for 25 years. Solveig Nordlund's **The Daughter** (A Filha) explores an obsessive love between a father (Nuno Melo) and his 18-year-old daughter (Joana Bárcia), in which they progressively reveal their true natures. Despite the fascinating nature of the story, the rather uneven performances by the main actors undermine the film's dramatic force.

Passing of the Night (A Passagem da Noite), by veteran film-maker Luís Filipe Rocha, tells the story of a 17-year-old girl who is raped by a drug addict and falls pregnant. The drug addict is then arrested for murder and realises he will have an alibi only if he confesses to the rape. Dutch director George Sluizer mixes magic realism and biting satire in **The Stone Raft** (A jangada de pedra), based on the novel by Nobel-prize winner Jorge Saramago. The Iberian peninsula floats away from the rest of the European continent and in this strange new world a cast of oddball characters begin to forge new bonds.

Several films were released by Portuguese cinema's younger generation. António Ferreira's debut **Forget Everything I've Told You** (Esquece tudo o que te disse) is a youthful comedy about a dysfunctional family, with a very strong performance by António Capelo as a dentist who dreams of becoming an illusionist. Joaquim Sapinho's **Cop Woman** (Mulher polícia) is the long-awaited but somewhat disappointing follow-up to his 1997 debut feature Haircut (Corte de cabelo). It revolves around the tragic odyssey of a mother and son in the wake of the death of her husband. They are finally rescued by the policewoman of the title. It has haunting cinematography but is dramatically uneven.

Remembering empire

Two films with very different atmospheres explored Portugal's colonial links with Africa and Brazil. Flora Gomes' **My Voice** (*Nha fala*) is a lively musical comedy vibrating with warm melodies and colours. The beautiful Vita has promised never to sing because of a family curse, but is progressively tempted to break her promise. **The Jungle** (*A selva*), by young, mainstream director Leonel Vieira, was heralded as Portugal's most expensive production ($4m). Adapted from the novel by Ferreira de Castro, it tells the story of a young monarchist, Alberto, forced into exile in Brazil in 1812, where he finds work in a rubber plantation and falls in love with the beautiful wife of the estate manager.

Despite its spectacular panoramic images of the Amazon and strong character performances by Brazilian actors Chico Diaz and Gracindo Junior, the central relationship between the hero (Diogo Morgado) and the older woman (Maitê Proença) is unconvincing. It was nonetheless the biggest national hit of the year, with a modest 75,000 admissions (in 2002 Portuguese films claimed 0.5% of the total box-office of $75m; from 20 million admissions at 550 screens).

The most eagerly anticipated forthcoming films include *Talking Film* (*Filme falado*), from Manoel de Oliveira, and *The Immortals* (*Os imortais*), by mainstream director António Pedro Vasconcelos. Oliveira's film stars John Malkovich and Catherine Deneuve, and recounts the tales told by a professor to his daughter on their trip through Europe. *The Immortals* tells the story of an annual get-together for five colonial war veterans that goes haywire when one of the group brings a *femme fatale* (Emmanuelle Seigner) instead of a prostitute to the party.

On the institutional front, the victory of the centre-right government in March 2002 has led to significant restructuring of public institutions, with major downsizing at the public broadcaster, RTP, and a rancorous ousting of the Management Board at the film institute, ICAM, amidst rumours of crippling debts. The main national broadcasters are also suffering losses and cutting back on production, the most notable example being SIC's decision to halt its production of 10 telefilms per year. Overall, Portugal is facing severe economic difficulties and acute problems are likely to be felt in the film and TV industries for some time to come.

MARTIN DALE has lived in Lisbon since 1994 and is currently working as an independent media consultant. He has written several books on the film industry, including *The Movie Game* (Continuum, 1997).

Infante, Federico Luppi. Prod: MGS Film Amsterdam.

Amélia Corôa in **Forget Everything I've Told You**

A FALHA (The Flaw)
[Drama, 2002] Script: Luís Carmelo, João Mário Grilo. Dir: Mário Grilo. Phot: Sabine Lancelin. Players: Rita Blanco, Rogério Samora, João Lagarto, Teresa Roby, Alexandra Lencastre. Prod: Madragoa Filmes.

OS IMORTAIS (The Immortals)
[Drama, 2002] Script and Dir: António Pedro Vasconcelos. Phot: Sabine Lancelin. Players: Nicolau Breyner, Joaquim de Almeida, Emmanuelle Seigner. Prod: Animatografo.

O PRINCÍPIO DA INCERTEZA (The Principle of Uncertainty)
[Drama, 2002] Script and Dir: Manoel de Oliveira. Phot: Renato Berta. Players: Leonor Baldaque, Leonor Silveira, Isabel Ruth. Prod: Madragoa Filmes.

Quote of the Year

"I don't think we can talk about cinema in Portugal. Most of us are not professionals, I'm not a professional. If I lived on cinema alone I would have died of hunger long ago."
ANTÓNIO PEDRO VASCONCELOS, *director of* The Immortals.

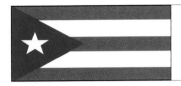

Puerto Rico José Artemio Torres

Recent and Forthcoming Films

DIOS LOS CRIA 2
(literally, **God Raises Them** *2)*
[TV portmanteau drama, 2003]
Script and Dir: Jacobo Morales.
Phot: P. J. López. Players:
Morales, Johanna Rosaly, Teófilo
Torres and Elia Enid Cadilla.
Prod: Cinesí.
Sequel to Morales' first film (*Dios los cría*, 1980), this also features three stories: an aged film director plans a bank robbery to finance a film; a drug addict rehabilitates; a middle-aged woman surprises her husband.

Benicio del Toro in **Julia All in Me**

JULIA, TODA EN MI
(Julia, All in Me)
[Docu-drama, 2003] Script:
Angel Darío Carrero and Ivonne
Belén. Dir: Belén. Phot: Jochi
Melero. Players: Gretchen Colón,
Viriani Rodríguez, Consuelo Sáez
Burgos, Benicio del Toro, Daisy
Granados, Angélica Aragón and
Jorge Perrugoría.
Examination of the life and work of the late Puerto Rican poet Julia de Burgos.

ocal film production continues to be dominated by the burgeoning market for TV movies, with five new titles broadcast in 2002. They included *Bitter Sweat* (*Sudor amargo*), shot on digital video by Sonia Valentín and focusing on the real-life struggles of female workers in the tuna-canning industry. Less impressive was *Fire in the Soul* (*Fuego en el alma*), which told three stories (a jealous baseball player kills his wife; a homosexual pilot comes out of the closet; a female middle-aged painter falls in love with a photographer), and even worse was *The Other Mafia* (*La otra Mafia*), a disappointing political thriller by Vicente Castro, who has a deal to make six TV movies in 2003. While all of these titles were made for commercial channels, state broadcaster Channel 6 made an open call for projects in January 2003, but by mid-June it had yet to announce who would have access to its annual $3m budget for TV movies and mini-series.

The only theatrical feature produced for almost two years is **Julia, All in Me** (*Julia, toda en mi*), a docu-drama about the gifted and tragic Puerto Rican poet Julia de Burgos, who died in 1953. It combines an interview with her nephew with readings of her letters and poems by an international cast including Benicio del Toro and Daisy Granados.

Theatrical feature production is meant to switch into high gear by the end of 2003, sponsored by the new Puerto Rican Film Production Fund, administered by the Puerto Rico Film Commission. The fund will give producers interest-free loans of up to 80% of a film's budget (no loan will exceed $800,000) and made its first call for projects in March 2003, with another scheduled for October. Some 50% of theatrical box-office tax revenue gives the Fund an initial balance of $6m.

Another positive development, in May 2003, saw the signing of a co-production agreement between Puerto Rico and Spain, and Puerto Rico is now also participating in Ibermedia, the co-production fund for Spain and Spanish-speaking Latin America. American companies continue to use Puerto Rico as a location. The *Dirty Dancing* sequel, *Havana Nights*, filmed here, and MTV chose west coast scenery for its modern *Wuthering Heights*. These productions are being attracted by locations, skilled crews and tax breaks.

JOSÉ ARTEMIO TORRES is a film-maker and writer. He heads La Linterna Mágica, a production and distribution company, and is Programming Director of the San Juan Cinemafest.

Romania Cristina Corciovescu

Recent and Forthcoming Films

GARCEA SI OLTENII
(Garcea and the Olt Folk)
[Comedy, 2002] Script: *Mugur Mihaescu.* Dir: *Sam Irvin.* Players: *Mugur Mihaescu, Radu Pietreanu, Mirela Stoian, Florin Petrescu, Alexandra Mutu.* Prod: *MediaPro Pictures.*

FURIA (The Rage)
[Drama, 2002] Script: *Radu Muntean, Ileana Constantin, Mircea Staiculescu.* Dir: *Muntean.* Players: *Dragos Bucur, Andi Vasluianu, Dorina Chiriac, Andrei Tuli.* Prod: *MediaPro Pictures.*

COBAI (*literally,* Guinea Pig)
[Romantic drama, 2003] Script: *Lia Bugnar, Ana-Valentina Florescu.* Dir: *Bogdan Dumitrescu.* Phot: *Silviu Stavila.* Prod: *Titi Popescu (Filmex Romania)/Zutta Production (Germany)/National Centre of Cinematography (Romania).*
Ileana, 27, is the hostess of Candid Camera Live, a new show making its debut on an important TV station. Sebastian, 41, decides to profit from his appearance as one of the show's victims.

FOTOGRAFII DE FAMILIE
(*literally,* Family Pictures)
[Comedy-drama, 2003] Script: *Bogdan Ficeag.* Dir: *Serban Marinescu.* Phot: *Dan Alexandru.* Players: *Dorel Visan, Razvan Vasilescu, Florin Calinescu.* Prod: *MDV Film/National Centre of Cinematography.*
Inspired by a true story about a big media company and its (more or less) clean business practices.

AZUCENA
[Drama, 2003] Script and

The main surprise of 2002 was undoubtedly the fact that two Romanian productions appeared in the local box-office top 10 for the year. The year's biggest hit was the independent production **Garcea and the Olt Folk** (*Garcea si oltenii*), a formulaic comedy of low taste and heavy humour, which was spun off from a highly successful local TV show. In a poor village in Olt (a region in the south-west of Romania), two dumb peasants find an ancient talisman in a lake. They don't realise its great value, but intelligence services from all over the world are alerted to its discovery and despatch agents to the scene, among them a dumb Romanian policeman named Garcea.

At number 10 in the year's chart was the fantastical drama *Filantropica* (see *IFG 2002*) from Nae Caranfil, the only director from the younger generation who has managed to keep working in recent years. His work consistently appeals to the more educated sector of the audience.

No other films pleased the local critics, but several new titles testified that Romanian cinema is still alive – or at least responding to attempts at resuscitation. Three well-regarded directors from the elder generation released new films. Malvina Ursianu's **What a Joyful World!** (*Ce lume minunata!*) was a semi-autobiographical story about the death of a world defined by dignity, aristocracy and intellectual sophistication (all well known to the 76-year-old director) and the birth of the new world of money, sex and 'get rich' preoccupations. Nicolae Margineanu's **Blessed Be the Jail** (*Binecuvintata fie inchisoarea*) was a film about belief and forgiveness, adapted from the memoirs of a woman who had spent years in various communist prisons during the 1950s. It was built around a single character, played by Maria Ploaie, the director's wife.

With **The Tower of Pisa** (*Turnul din Pisa*), Serban Marinescu told the sensational, tragic story of a girl raped on her wedding night who, years later, falls in love with the rapist. He probably hoped to bring in to cinemas the fans of South American telenovelas, but the only thing that his, Ursianu's and Margineanu's films proved was that applying rather old-fashioned styles to realistic stories is not the best route to box-office success.

Dir: Mircea Muresan. Phot: Mihai Sarbusca. Prod: Art Production/National Centre of Cinematography.
At the Romanian-Moldavian border, a young officer falls in love with a beautiful girl. But he discovers she is the daughter of the leader of a gypsy band.

AVENTURILE UNEI ZILE
(*literally,* **One Day Adventures**)
[Supernatural drama, 2003]
Script: Mihai Ispirescu. Dir: Patre Nastase. Phot: Liviu Marghidan. Players: Marcel Iures, Horatiu Malaele, Mircea Diaconu. Prod: Astra Entertainment/National Centre of Cinematography.
An actor returns to his hometown to meet relatives and friends and begin a new life. The people he meets are unchanged, among them his former wife, now married to his best friend. But he finds they are all really dead.

ITALIENCELE
(*literally,* **The Italian Girls**)
[Comedy-drama, 2003] Script and Dir: Napoleon Helmis. Phot: Florin Mihailescu. Players: Mara Nicolescu, Ana Ularu, Vlad Zamfirescu, Emil Hostina. Prod: Ro de Film/National Centre of Cinematography.
Two young girls want to go to Spain to work and become rich. A guy tricks them and sells them into prostitution in Kosovo.

LOTUS
[Drama, 2003] Script and Dir: Ioan Carmazan. Phot: Marian Stanciu. Players: Razvan Vasilescu, Gheorghe Visu. Prod: Filmex/National Centre of Cinematography.

ORIENT EXPRESS
[Drama, 2003] Script: Sergiu Nicoleascu, based on a novel by Eugen Barbu. Dir: Nicoleascu. Phot: Dan Alexandru. Players: Sergiu Nicolaescu, Stefan Iordache, Dan Bitman. Prod: Ro de Film/National Centre of Cinematography.

Rage (on-screen and off)

Much more successful was Radu Muntean's **The Rage** (*Furia*), whose story focuses on the underworld of the local gypsy mafia and its associated networks. Local critics greeted the film as "a punch straight in society's solar plexus", expressing "the most hopeless perspective" on the contemporary state of things in Romania. The general feeling was that a new name had joined the team of younger film-makers following in Caranfil's footprints by depicting post-socialist Romanian society with humorous veracity: after Cristi Puiu and Cristian Mungiu, here comes Radu Muntean.

This quartet joined others in a collective attempt to signal, through an open letter, the deficiencies of the new Law of Cinematography which was put forward in December 2002. The protesters argued that the constraints and ambiguities of the law were meant to conserve the status quo within the local industry and minimise the career prospects of younger film-makers.

Their view was supported by the most recent edition of the contest organised by the National Centre of Cinematography between February and April each year, designed to select the best film projects to be partially supported from public money. Surprisingly, many of the winners in 2003 were themselves members of the Centre of Cinematography, and protests from the non-member film-makers led to the launching of an inquiry into the selection process. Despite these problems, production has remained steady, with six features completed in 2002 and ready for distribution; another 14 secured production finance. However, we will have to wait quite some time until we know whether they will please their public more than this year's films.

CRISTINA CORCIOVESCU is a film critic and the author of several film dictionaries.

Radu Muntean's **Rage**

Russia Kirill Razlogov

The Year's Best Films

Kirill Razlogov's selection:
Be Quiet! (Docu. Dir: Victor
Kosakovsky)
Petersburg
(Dir: Irina Evteeva)
Koktebel (Dirs: Boris
Khlebnikov, Alexei
Popogrebsky)
The Clearings of the Moon
(Dir: Igor Minaev)
The Return (Dir: Andrej
Zvjagintsev)

Recent and Forthcoming Films

BABUSYA (Granny)
[Drama, 2003] Script and Dir:
Lidia Bobrova. Phot: Valery
Revich. Players: Nina Shubina,
Olga Onishchenko, Anna
Ovsyannikova, Sergei Anufriev.
Prod: Lenfilm/3B
Production/CNC (France).
Granny, left alone by her
children, moves to find her
grandchildren.

Oleg Anufriev in **Granny**

BEDNYI, BEDNYI PAVEL
(Poor, Poor Pavel)
[Historical drama, 2003] Script
and Dir: Vitaly Melnikov. Phot:
Sergei Astakhov. Players: Victor
Sukhorukov, Oleg Yankovsky,
Yulia Mavrina, Alexei Barabash,

ast year I suggested hopefully that an emerging young generation of Moscow film-makers (almost all the children of famous parents) might take over film production and aesthetics. Now I must confess that it was a premature hope. Traditional ways of thinking and working are still very much alive, and of the 70 feature films set for release in 2003, 65 have been made with state support. Courting the Ministry of Culture and its resources is still more important than thinking about the public (and box-office potential), but the results were not as disappointing as they might have been.

After the succss of *Antikiller* (the third recent Russian film, after *The Brother* and *The Barber of Siberia,* to gross more than $1m at home), a thriller by debuting director Petr Buslov, **Boomer**, was courting the record at press time, while *Antikiller 2* is in the pipeline. The whole country and especially the film community was shattered by the tragic death, aged 30, of Sergei Bodrov Jr (superstar of *Brother* and director of *Sisters*) and his entire young film crew, swept to their deaths by a landslide while on location in Ossetia in September 2002.

The festival triumphs of *The Cuckoo* in 2002 were followed by its unexpectedly good box-office results at home and healthy international sales. Russian cinema seems (very slowly) to be regaining the interest of local audiences, while its success with TV viewers is beyond question: Russian TV series push virtually all European, Latin American and US programming out of prime time, and Soviet features still generally pull larger viewing figures than Hollywood movies (some local films appear in theatrical versions after success on the small screen).

Nevertheless, there is still a long way to go to counterbalance American dominance in cinemas. As the number of screens and the prevalence of Dolby equipment grows steadily, so does the overall box-office (doubling every year), with new records set by the latest blockbusters (*The Matrix Reloaded* became the first title to gross more than $10m in Russia and CIS). The market share for Russian films officially is 11%, but this actually means 11% of screenings, around 8% of the audience and less than 3% of the total gross.

Svetlana Kryuchkova.
Prod: Lenfilm, with Ministry
of Culture.
The story of the murder of
Russian Emperor Pavel I in 1801.

VTORAYA NEVESTA
IMPERATORA (The Second
Bride of the Emperor)
[Historical drama, 2002] Script:
Svetlana Druzhinina, Pavel Finn-
Khalfin. Dir: Druzhinina. Phot:
Anatoly Mukasei. Players:
Dmitry Verkeenko, Dmitry
Kharatyan, Larisa Luzhina,
Alexei Zharkov, Alexander
Belyavsky, Nina Ruslanova.
Prod: Sagittarius, with Ministry
of Culture.
Eighteenth-century palace
intrigues exile Menshikov to
Siberia. Prince Dolgoruky tries to
marry his daughter Yekaterina to
young Peter II and thus win the
Russian throne.

KAVKAZSKAYA RULETKA
(Caucasian Roulette)
[Psychological drama, 2002]
Script: Viktor Merezhko, Alla
Krinitsyna. Dir: Fyodor Popov.
Phot: Lomer Akhvlediani.
Players: Nina Usatova, Tatyana
Mescherkina, Anatoly
Goryachov, Sergei Garmash.
Prod: Stella, with Ministry of
Culture/Krug.
A young Russian woman who is
a sniper with the Chechens, and
the mother of a Russian soldier
who has been captured by the
Chechens, meet on a train.

Igor Petrenko and Olga Filippova
in **Carmen**

KARMEN (Carmen)
[Love story, 2003] Script: Yuri
Korotkov. Dir: Alexander Khvan.
Phot: Igor Kozhevnikov. Players:

Tolstoy meets Dogme?

The current diversity of film production, as noted by most critics,
is festival-oriented. The winner of the 2003 edition of the national
film festival, Kinotaur, was Gennadiy Sidorov's **Old Women**
(*Starukhi*), an intimate vision of life in a Russian village deserted
by all but its oldest inhabitants. The same type of filmed everyday
routines has made the festival career of Lidia Bobrova, whose
latest, **Granny** (*Babusya*), is a portrait of an old woman. This
type of aesthetics, which might seem over-simplistic, is in reality
a curious symbiosis between classical (Tolstoy, Dostoyevsky,
Chekhov) Russian realism, the remnants of Italian neo-realism
and the Danish Dogme movement (which helps to give these
films their festival appeal).

Young directors, like Larissa Sadilova whose **With Love, Lilya**
(*S lyubovyu, Lilya*) won a Tiger award in Rotterdam, or Boris
Khlebnikov and Alexei Popogrebsky with **Koktebel,** add sincerity
and spontaneity to this tradition (when Agnieszka Holland, gave
Koktebel's first-time directors their Special Jury Prize at Moscow
she offered them a pair of scissors to encourage them to be more
rigorous editors in future). As expected, the officially respected
State Prize went to Nikolai Lebedev's Second World War chronicle
The Star (reviewed in *IFG 2003*).

On the opposite side we find Irina Yvteeva's **St Petersburg**
(*Peterburg*), a post-modern spider's web combining quotes,
real life and fiction, and fragments from classical Soviet films, all
transformed by hand-drawn animation to relate the legends of
the city of Peter the Great. This was one of the best of the (too)
many films marking the tercentenary of the "Northern capital"
of the former Russian Empire. In an academic way its past was
portrayed by the veteran Vitaly Melnikov in **Poor, Poor Pavel**
(*Bednyi, bednyi Pavel*), the final part of his historical trilogy, and
more lightly by Svetlana Druzhinina in **The Second Bride of the**
Emperor (*Vtoraya nevesta Imperatora*), the fifth film in the series
Mysteries of Palace Revolutions. Russia, Eighteenth Century.

Promenade (*Progulka*) was Alexei Uchitel's real-time
reconstruction of a chance meeting between two young boys
and a buxom girl in modern-day St Petersburg. Written by Dunya
Smirnova (daughter of Andrei, the film director and scriptwriter,
and grand-daughter of Sergey, the writer), it reflects the desire
of the new elites to join Europe, their wealth and their lack of
problems, except in love. Igor Minaev, in a Russian-French
co-production, **The Clearings of the Moon** (*Lunnye polyany*),
offered a very "Russian Soul" vision of a creative crisis and incest
that combine to cause a tragedy.

Something for all ages

Meanwhile the old- and middle-generation masters stayed true to their respective traditions. Alexander Sokurov's **Father and Son** (*Otets il syn*) took the FIPRESCI Jury Prize at Cannes. Vadim Abrashitov completed **Magnetic Storms** (*Magnitnye bury*), a dark parable on life in a provincial town, with a brilliant if uncharacteristic performance from Viktoria Tolstoganova, breaking her image as star of the New Russian cinema. Vladimir Khotinenko, with **70 Metres,** presented his own vision of the *Kursk* submarine disaster. Alexander Proshkine's **Trio** is a TV-like road adventure story.

A limited revival of movies for children brought reminders of the glorious Soviet history in this field (with films praised in the almost forgotten past even by the avant-garde New York critics of *Film Culture*). Today's modest achievements include Ivan Popov's **Little Lord Fauntleroy** (*Radosty i pechali malyenkogo Lorda*), Valery Bychenkov's **Chelyabumbia** and many animated films.

The year's big sensation was a documentary masterpiece, **Be Quiet!**, shot by Victor Kosakovsky from the window of his flat in St. Petersburg to record, from this unusual angle, the preparations for the city's anniversary celebrations. Eldar Ryazanov failed to revive the popular success his films enjoyed between the 1950s and 1970s with a traditional vaudeville, **Keys to the Bedroom** (*Klyuch ot spalny*). A CIS/European co-production, **Chic** (*Shik*), by Tadjikistan's Bakhtiyor Khudoynazarov, was, after the acclaimed *Luna Papa,* a disappointment. **Casus Belli,** the debut film of comic star Igor Ugolnikov, was a critical flop and a commercial disappointment.

Director Elgar Ryazanov, second right, on location for **Keys to the Bedroom**

Igor Petrenko, Olga Filippova, Yaroslav Boiko, Ramil Sabitov, Alexander Shein. Prod: Pigmalion, with Ministry of Culture.
A policeman falls for a convict working off her confinement at a tobacco factory.

KLYUCH OT SPALNY
(Keys to the Bedroom)
[Comedy, 2003] Script and Dir: Eldar Ryazanov. Phot: Nikolai Nemolyaev. Players: Nikolai Fomenko, Yevgeniya Kryukova, Sergei Makovetsky, Vladimir Simonov, Sergei Bezrukov. Prod: Gulliver/Luch (Mosfilm), with Ministry of Culture.
Frivolous comedy based on the farce by Georges Feydeau, short stories by Arkady Averchenko and classical French vaudeville.

MAGNITNYE BURY
(Magnetic Storms)
[Melodrama, 2003] Script: Alexander Mindadze. Dir: Vadim Abrashitov. Phot: Yuri Shaigardanov. Players: Maxim Averin, Victoria Tolstoganova, Lyubava Aristarkhova, Boris Shuvalov, Rushana Ziafitdinova. Prod: Ark-Film (Mosfilm), with Ministry of Culture.
In a modern-day provincial town Valery loses his apartment, friends and wife. But he is rescued by Marina.

MARSH SLAVYANKI
(Slav's March)
[Tragic melodrama, 2003] Script and Dir: Natalia Piankova. Phot: Vadim Arapov. Players: Galina Bokashevskaya, Marina Yakovleva, Alexander Bogdanov, Oleg Khusainov, Ilya Narodovoi, Vadim Piankov. Prod: Cinematograph Three Thousand Years.

PRAVDA O SCHELPAKH
(The Truth About Schelps)
[Comedy, 2003] Script: Leonid Porokhnya, Alexei Muradov. Dir: Muradov. Phot: Robert Filatov. Players: Kamil Tukaev, Alexei Shlyamin, Leonid Okunev. Prod: PiE Film (Lenfilm), with Ministry

of Culture.
Three close friends meet in
their home town after many years
apart.

PRITYAZHENIE (Attraction)
[Mystic thriller, 2002] Script:
Alexander Muromtsev. Dir:
Vasily Serikov. Phot: Alexander
Ekimov. Players: Igor Sukachev,
Vladimir Vinogradov, Yelena
Plotnikova, Nikolai Molochkov,
Igor Pismenny. Prod: Illusion.
Provincial Russia in the 1800s.
A series of murders shakes
a small town and Arsenyev,
a detective, arrives to investigate.

RADOSTY I PECHALI
MALYENKOGO LORDA
(Little Lord Fauntleroy)
[Family drama, 2002] Script:
Galina Arbuzova, Vladimir
Zheleznikov, Ivan Popov.
Dir: Popov. Phot: Alexander
Antipenko. Players: Alexei
Veselkin, Stanislav Govorukhin,
Olga Budina, Oleg Shklovsky,
Sergei Gazarov, Nikolai Volkov.
Prod: Angel-Film.
Remake of the classic tale of
the American boy who learns
that he may be related to an
English count.

Valentina Berezutskaya in **Old Women**

STARUKHI (Old Women)
[Tragi-comedy, 2003] Script and
Dir: Gennady Sidorov. Phot:
Anatoly Petriga. Players:
Valentina Berezutskaya, Galina
Smirnova, Zoya Norkina,
Tamara Klimova, Bronislava
Zakharova. Prod: Cinema
Support Foundation (CSF),
with Ministry of Culture.
FOTO (Photo)
[Psychological drama, 2003]
Script and Dir: Alexander Galin.

After *The Kite* (closely modelled on Alexei German's naturalistic
obsessions), Alexei Muradov made **All the Truth About Schelps**
(*Pravda o Schelpakh*), a popular comic parable, based on folklore.
Vasily Serikov, a former student of the late Vladimir Kobrin, who
used the pretext of scientific films to experiment with new
technologies, made a controversial mystic thriller, **Attraction**
(*Prityazhenie*). Alexander Khvan, known for his debut feature *Duba,*
Duba, tried to 'Russify' **Carmen,** proving once again that Russian
paths can intersect with European and universal patterns.

In *Love* and war

We can note also the emergence of a new generation of women
film-makers. Vera Storozheva chose for her debut a modernised
adaptation of a classic, polemical play by Edward Radzinsky,
104 Pages About Love, first filmed more than 30 years ago.
The new film stars cult actress Renata Litvinova, who also wrote
the screenplay. Another actress, Natalia Petrova, directed her
first feature, **The Road,** taking as partner the star of *Antikiller,*
Gosha Kutsenko.

The Chechen war continues to be a touchy subject. The presence
of the Chechen sniper drama **Caucasian Roulette** (*Kavkazskaya*
ruletka) in a Berlin sidebar in 2003 was a shock to most Russian
critics. Andrei Konchalovsky's **House of Fools,** acclaimed in
Venice, also generated controversy at home, especially because
the Chechen terrorist attack on the Nord-Ost Theatre coincided
with the first domestic screening of the film. Most critics preferred
it to the Russian Oscar committee's choice, *The Cuckoo.* Natalia
Pyankova, the former actress and designer who began directing
as part of the recent, short-lived wave of very low-budget films,
tackled the Chechnya situation in **Slav's March** (*Marsh Slavyanki*)
and gave a more humane view of women caught up in the war
than Konchalovsky.

Marina Yakoleva and Alexander Bogdanov in **Slav's March**

The majority of industry discussion is now focused on local distribution issues. Three new projects were launched recently. Initiated by the Ministry of Culture, the Russian Film Distribution plan is mostly concerned with building new theatres, especially multiplexes. The Moscow Cinema project is an attempt by the capital's administration to take charge of the exhibition boom. People's Cinema, the most ambitious idea, proposed by the newly created National Academy of Cinema Arts and Sciences of Russia and supported by the Ministry of Communication, would create a network of budget film theatres all over the country, equipped to receive feature films by satellite. George Lucas' digital exhibition dream might just come true in Russia.

KIRILL RAZLOGOV is Director of the Russian Institute for Cultural Research and Programme Director of the Moscow International Film Festival. On television he hosts *Moviecult* (Kultura Channel) and on radio *Life in the Movies* (Mayak-24).

Phot: Mikhail Agranovich. Players: Alexander Kalyagin, Nikolai Karachentsov, Olga Ostroumova, Valery Khlebnikov, Tamara Kotikova. Prod: Russian Theatre Agency, with Ministry of Culture/ALBUM.
Two old friends meet after many years, one now a successful businessman, the other an ex-con.

SHIK (Chic)
[Tragi-comedy, 2002] Script: Oleg Antonov. Dir: Bakhtiyor Khudoynazarov. Phot: Vladimir Klimov. Players: Artur Smolyaninov, Ivan Kokorin, Alexander Yatsenko, Andrei Panin, Nikolai Fomenko, Rusudan Rukhadze. Prod: Central Partnership/Vvys/Pandora Film Production/Paradise Film/ Poetiche Cinematografiche/ Ministry of Culture.
Three young friends grow up in a small Crimean town.

LUNNYE POLYANY
(The Clearings of the Moon)
[Psychological drama, 2002] Script: Igor Minaev, Olga Mikhailova. Dir: Minaev. Phot: Vladimir Pankov. Players: Alisa Bogart, Andrei Kuzichev, Victoria Tolstoganova, Alexander Berda, Andrei Tolubeev. Prod: NTV-KINO/Artcam International, in association with CNC (France).

A brother and sister meet after 10 years.

S LYUBOVYU, LILYA
(With Love, Lilya)
[Melodrama, 2002] Script: Larisa Sadilova, Gennady Sidorov. Dir: Sadilova. Phot: Anatoly Petriga. Players: Marina Zubanova, Murad Ibragimbekov, Victor Uralsky, Valentina Berezutskaya. Prod: Regional Public Fund for Cinema Support.
Lilya works at a poultry factory in a provincial town. One day at a concert she meets a local pianist who becomes a part of her life.

OTETS I SYN (Father and Son)
[Drama, 2003] Script: Sergei Potepalov. Dir: Alexandr Sokurov. Phot: Alexander Burov. Players: Andrei Schetinin, Alexei Neimyshev, Alexander Razbash, Fyodor Lavrov, Marina Zasukhina. Prod: Zero Film GmbH/Nikola-Film/Lumen Films/Isabella Films/Mikado Films.
Second part of a trilogy about the drama of natural human bonds.

KOKTEBEL
[Psychological drama, 2003] Script and Dir: Boris Khlebnikov, Alexei Popogrebsky. Phot: Shandor Berkeshi R.G.C. Players: Gleb Puskepalis, Igor Chernevich,

Vladimir Kucherenko, Agrippina Steklova. Prod: Roman Borisevich, with Ministry of Culture.
When their life in Moscow hits rock bottom, a father and his 11-year-old son set off on a 1,000-km journey to the sea.

PETERBURG (St Petersburg)
[Fantasy, 2003] Script: Irina Yevteeva, Andrei Chernykh, Yuri Kravtsov. Dir: Yevteeva. Phot: Heinrich Maranjan. Players: Alexander Cherednik, Svetlana Svirko, Smyon Strugachev. Prod: Lenfilm.

CASUS BELLI
[Adventure comedy, 2003] Script: Ivan Kiasashvili. Dir: Igor Ugolnikov. Players: Inna Churikova, Aleksei Petrenko, Vitaly Solomin, Alexander Mikhailov, Barbara Brylska. Prod: 12 A Studio.
Mikhail suspects that his wife is having an affair and hires a private detective, who happens to be an ordinary housewife.

DNEVNIK KAMIKADZE
(Diary of a Kamikaze)
[Drama, 2002] Script: Eduard Volodarsky. Dir: Dmitry Meskhiev. Phot: Sergei Machilsky. Players: Sergei Shakurov, Yuri Kuznetsov, Nikolai Chindyaikin, Victoria Tolstoganova, Yevgenia Dobrovolskaya, Natalia Kolyakanova. Prod: Production Company "Slovo"/Non-Stop Production, with Ministry of Culture.
A 55-year-old dramatist is found dead in Moscow. His old friend, a successful film producer, refuses to believe it was suicide.

ZHIZN ODNA (One Life)
[Melodrama, 2003] Script: Liana Koroleva, with Alexander Borodyansky. Dir: Vitaly Moskalenko. Phot: Yuri Nevsky. Players: Tatyana Yakovenko, Aleksei Nilov, Sergei Bezrukov, Tatyana Lyutaeva, Aleksei Kravchenko. Prod: Narodnoe Kino/Genre (Mosfilm).
Two people meet in a suburban Moscow health resort and their

love creates a miracle.

INTERESNYE MUZHCHINY
(Interesting Men)
[Musical drama, 2002] Script:
Yuri Kara, based on the story by
N. Leskov. Dir: Kara. Phot:
Vadim Semenovykh. Players:
Natalia Fenkina, Nikolai
Kochegarov, Andrei Mezhulis,
Alexei Elistratov, Sergei
Nikonenko. Prod: Master
(Moscow), with Ministry
of Culture.
A young cornet-player is in love
with a girl whose parents have
ordered her to marry his
commanding colonel.

MARSH-BROSOK
(Forward-Rush)
[Action drama, 2003] Script:
Eduard Volodarsky, Sergei
Bratchikov. Dir: Nikolai
Stambula. Phot: Radik Askarov.
Players: Vladimir Volga, Olga
Chursina, Yevgeny Kosyrev,
Alexander Baluev, Fedor Smirnov.
Prod: Artes Production.
Sasha Buida, who grew up in
an orphanage, volunteers to fight
in the Chechen war.

PROGULKA (Promenade)
[Romantic melodrama, 2003]
Script: Dunya Smirnova. Dir:
Alexei Uchitel. Phot: Yuri
Klimenko, Pavel Kostomarov.
Players: Irina Pegova, Pavel
Barshak, Yevgeny Tsyganov.
Prod: ROK.
Escapades of two young
friends and a girl they meet in
St Petersburg.

CHELYABUMBIA
[Melodrama, 2002] Script: Valery
Bychenkov, Andrei Romanov.
Dir: Bychenkov. Phot: Sergei
Lando. Players: Yelena
Korobeinikova, Dmitry Lysenkov,
Mikhail Fedorov, Galina
Bokashevskaya, Alexander
Bashirov. Prod: Barmalei/Lenfilm,
with Ministry of Culture.
Incredibly funny and sad story
about first love, vocation and the
hero's journey from Chelyabinsk
to St Petersburg.

NE DELAITE BISKVITY V
PLOHOM NASTROENII
(Do Not Bake Biscuits
When in a Bad Mood)
[Psychological drama, 2002]
Script: Tatyana Moskvina. Dir:

Grigory Nikulin. Phot: Sergei
Lando, Aleksei Solodov. Players:
Era Ziganshina, Sergei Dontsov,
Semyon Strugachev, Lyudmila
Vagner. Prod: Barmalei/Lenfilm.
One day in the life of a middle-
aged St Petersburg woman.

Quotes of the Year

"It is extremely difficult
for a Russian artist to survive
in Europe or in America...
Many of my Western
colleagues... want to keep
intact the barbed wire
surrounding Russian culture."
ALEXANDER SOKUROV,
director.

"The Cannes Film Festival
is not Formula 1 or the
football World Cup. In film
the final score is known
sometimes many years
after the premiere."
ANDREI PLAKHOV,
critic, reacting to Russian
press attacks on the films at
Cannes 2003.

Kirill Razlogov adds: Russian cinema returned to the limelight in Venice in September 2003, when Andrej Zvjagintsev's **The Return**
(Ozvrasnje), *starring Konstantin Lavronenko (pictured above) as a father who embarks on a mythic journey with his two long-lost sons,
won the Golden Lion for Best Film and the Lion of the Future award. Alexei German Jr.'s* **The Last Train** (Posledniy poezd) *earned a special
mention in the Upstream competition and Murad Ibraguimbekov's* **The Oil** (Neft) *won the Silver Lion for Best Short.*

Serbia & Montenegro Goran Gocic

The Year's Best Films

Goran Gocic's selection:

The Professional
(Dir: Dusan Kovacevic)

Little Night Music
(Dir: Dejan Zecevic)

Bare Ground
(Dir: Ljubisa Samardzic)

Zone (Dir: Zdravko Sotra)

One on One
(Dir: Mladen Maticevic)

Bora Todorovic in **The Professional**

I n many respects, this season was a repeat of the previous one, its 10 films creating a sense of *déjà vu* from 2000-01. Again, the most sought-after cinematic escape route from ever grimmer reality was comedy (half this year's output) and first-time directors again made significant contributions: three out of 10 films, compared to four debuts out of 11 features in 2000-01.

The sole surprise – and one that would have been pleasant in any season during the past decade – was without doubt **Zone** (*Zona zamfirova*), a costume drama based on the classic Serbian novel by Stevan Sremac and set in the southern town of Nis in the early twentieth century. *Zone* is a nicely presented love story in which two pretty people fall in love, but it takes some ingenuity to bind them in marriage, since they are divided by class. By the end, everything falls into place, including the casting and music, and the film won the hearts of the audience, unexpectedly drawing 1.2 million admissions – a triumph for director Zdravko Sotra, who produced his best work at the age of 70. A genuine Serbian blockbuster, *Zone* has been sold to Turkey, Greece, the former Yugoslavia and most of Eastern Europe, including Russia.

The first new release of the 2002-03 season was the comedy **One on One** (*Jedan na jedan*), the feature debut of ethnic Croatian Mladen Maticevic. The hero is a lonesome youth who becomes

A genuine Serbian blockbuster: **Zone**

Recent and Forthcoming Films

SKORO SASVIM OBICNA PRICA (An Almost Totally Ordinary Story)
[Romantic comedy, forthcoming]
Script: Dusan Ristic. Dir: Milos Petricic. Phot: Vladan Pavic. Players: Milica Zaric, Vuk Toskovic. Prod: Premax Group (Belgrade).

LEDINA (Bare Ground)
[Social drama, 2003] Script: Nikola Pejakovic. Dir: Ljubisa Samardzic. Phot: Radoslav Vladic. Players: Dragan Bjelogrlic, Zijah Sokolovic. Prod: Cinema Dizajn (Belgrade).

VOLIM TE NAJVISE NA SVETU (I Love More Than Anything in the World)
[Romantic comedy, 2003]
Script: Radoslav Pavlovic. Dir: Predrag Velinovic. Phot: Radoslav Vladic. Players: Tanja Boskovic, Ana Sofrenovic. Prod: Favi/Zastava Film/Avala Film/RTV Serbia (Belgrade).

KENEDI SE VRACA KUCI (Kennedy Comes Back Home)
[Social drama, forthcoming]
Script and Dir: Zelimir Zilnik. Phot: Miodrag Milosevic. Players: Kenedi Hasani, Denis Ajeti. Prod: Terra Film (Novi Sad).

POLJUPCI (Kisses)
[Drama, forthcoming] Script and Dir: Sasa Radojevic. Phot: Goran Volarevic. Players: Ljuba Tadic, Ljubinka Klaric. Prod: Soul Flower (Belgrade).

SJAJ U OCIMA (Loving Glances)
[Romantic comedy, forthcoming]
Script and Dir: Srdjan Karanovic. Phot: Radan Popovic. Players: Senad Alihodzic, Ivana Bolanca. Prod: Yodi Movie Craftsman/RTV Serbia (Belgrade)/F.A.M.E. (London).

SIROTI MALI HRCKI (Poor Little Hamsters)
[Absurdist comedy, forthcoming]
Script: Gordan Mihic. Dir:

a vigilante and cleans up his neighbourhood, so the plot resembled Srdan Golubovic's *Absolute Hundred* (*Apsolutnih sto*; reviewed in *IFG 2003*) and coincided with a real-life police clean-up of the Serbian mafia in 2003. The screenwriter, Srdjan Andjelic, already had one local blockbuster, *Dudes!*, to his credit.

If the mould ain't broke...

Serbian genre movies have become increasingly common in recent years and **I Love More Than Anything in the World** (*Volim te najvise na svetu*) is a local romantic comedy in which a middle-aged man has no trouble finding a bride, but encounters a lot of static when he meets her mother. Dejan Zecevic swiftly followed up his horror film from last season, *T. T. Syndrome*, with the highly entertaining sexploitation comedy **Little Night Music** (*Mala nocna muzika*), which had a lot in common with **Dead Cool** (*Mrtav ladan*), written and directed by television director Miodrag Milinkovic: both indulge in blackish humour and the central characters in both are corpses. In *Little Night Music* a worker in a morgue decides to trade his identity with a dead mafioso when he finds a mobile phone in the gangster's pocket. In *Dead Cool* two youngsters transport their dead grandpa by train, since they cannot afford any other method.

Close ancestors of most of these films originated in Hollywood, rather than Serbia. *Dead Cool* is a local *The Trouble with Harry* and **Jagoda in a Supermarket** (*Jagoda u supermarketu*), in which a war veteran takes hostages because his grandmother was insulted in a supermarket, takes after *Dog Day Afternoon*, albeit with an unlikely happy ending.

The hostages are tied up in **Jagoda in a Supermarket**

Jagoda is the very first project of Emir Kusturica's newly established production company Rasta International (Kusturica himself has an entertaining cameo as a police chief). However, the most successful Yugoslav film-maker of all time has had a much harder time producing and directing his latest feature, *Life Is a Miracle* (*Zivot je cudo*), which reportedly went a long way beyond its planned budget and schedule. But, unlike Kusturica, few of the film-makers mentioned so far claimed any notable artistic pretensions. They opted instead to please the audience, even if it meant introducing their own idea of entertainment.

From beyond the grave

The best-looking and most costly venture this season was **Labyrinth** (*Lavirint*), a mystery thriller directed and co-scripted by Miroslav Lekic. A middle-aged gambler comes back to Belgrade, haunted by the death of his close friend. There he encounters a mysterious sect of Aryans and a woman seeking revenge for his past deeds. *Labyrinth* also introduced a young and talented actress, Katarina Radivojevic, who later got the lead in *Zone*, becoming a darling of the local tabloids overnight – and a new star to be counted on in future roles.

Dragan Nikolic, left, and Branislav Lecic in **Labyrinth**

After a lot of trouble, both legal and creative, the last work of the late director Zivojin Pavlovic, **Land of the Dead** (*Zemlja mrtvih*), was scraped together and finally released late in 2002, after several years in the can. A harrowing look into the decade of war and crisis, seen through the eyes of a low-ranking Yugoslav officer, it did not live up to expectations and flopped in cinemas. In another overtly political, home-grown social drama, **Bare Ground** (*Ledina*), directed by Ljubisa Samardzic (who habitually completes a new film a year), people from mixed marriages suffer the consequences of Yugoslav partition, like the heroes of *Land of the Dead*.

Slobodan Sijan. Phot: Milorad Glusica. Players: Boro Stjepanovic, Petar Bozovic. Prod: RTV Serbia/Horizont 2000 (Belgrade).

PROFESIONALAC
(The Professional)
[Black comedy, 2003] Script: Dusan Kovacevic, based on his play. Dir: Kovacevic. Phot: Bozidar Nikolic. Players: Bora Todorovic, Branislav Lecic. Prod: VANS (Belgrade).

SIVI KAMION CRVENE BOJE
(Red-Coloured Grey Truck)
[Road movie, forthcoming] Script and Dir: Srdjan Koljevic. Phot: Goran Volarevic. Players: Srdjan Todorovic, Aleksandra Balmazovic. Prod: Komuna (Belgrade).

MALI SVET (Small World)
[Black comedy, forthcoming] Script and Dir: Milos Radovic. Phot: Aleksandar Jovanovic. Players: Miki Manojlovic, Lazar Ristovski. Prod: Cobra Film (Belgrade).

WANDER-FIRE
[Historical drama, forthcoming] Script: Ferenc Deak. Dir: Karolj Vicek. Phot: Gabor Halasz. Players: Attila Magyar, Tibor Szloboda. Prod: Subotica Film.

LAVIRINT (Labyrinth)
[Mystery thriller, 2003] Script: Miroslav Lekic, Igor Bojovic. Dir: Lekic. Phot: Predrag Todorovic. Players: Dragan Nikolic, Branislav Lecic, Katarina Radivojevic. Prod: Vans.

ZONA ZAMFIROVA (Zone)
[Costume drama, 2002] Script: Zdravko Sotra, based on the novel by Stevan Sremac. Dir: Sotra. Phot: Veselko Krcmar. Players: Katarina Radivojevic, Vojin Jetkovic. Prod: Dream Company (Belgrade).

Quotes of the Year

"I always try to combine true drama and true comedy, like a cake with one sweet filling and one sour filling."
DUSAN KOVACEVIC, *writer-director, on* The Professional.

"For me, film directing is a game. I am into film-making because I love to play."
DEJAN ZECEVIC, *director, who has made four features by the age of 30.*

Politics also preoccupy the best contemporary Serbian playwright and prolific screenwriter, Dusan Kovacevic (*Who's Singing Over There, Underground*). He likes to put his own plays on the stage, and occasionally on the screen, with *The Balkan Spy* and now **The Professional** (*Profesionalac*). A comedy of the absurd in which a retired member of the secret service introduces himself to a writer and presents him with a track record of the latter's "works", all acquired by surveillance, this had not been released at press time but, based on Kovacevic's track record, has hit potential.

To sum up, producers' and audiences' preferences for comedy and, increasingly, romantic dramas, continue, as living standards reach their lowest point in years. At the moment, retail prices are sky-high for the average consumer, including cinema tickets, which rose by 75%. As a result, although total admissions for 2002 fell slightly compared to 2001, happy distributors saw their revenue increase by 71%. In spite of poor distribution outside the big cities and the absence of legislation to protect the feeble domestic industry, audiences are still partial towards local films: as in 2001, five of the year's top 10 hits were Serbian.

GORAN GOCIC has written chapters in 11 books on cinema and mass media and is the author of the monographs *Andy Warhol and Strategies of Pop* (1997) and *Notes From the Underground: The Cinema of Emir Kusturica* (2001).

Singapore Yvonne Ng

The Year's Best Films

Yvonne Ng's selection:
I Not Stupid (Dir: Jack Neo)
Talking Cock The Movie
(Dirs: Colin Goh,
Joyceln Woo)
The Eye (Dirs: Danny
and Oxide Pang)
Song of the Stork
(Dirs: Jonathan Foo, Nguyen
Phan Quang Binh)
15 (Dir: Royston Tan)

Royston Tan's **15**

Recent and Forthcoming Films

15
[Drama, 2003] Script and Dir: Royston Tan. Phot: Lim Ching Leong. Players: Melvin Chen, Erick Chun, Melvin Lee, Vynn Soh. Prod: Zhao Wei Films.

THE EYE
[Horror, 2002] Script: Jo Jo Hui Yuet Chun, Danny and Oxide Pang. Dir: Pangs. Phot: Decha Seementa. Players: Angelica Lee, Lawrence Chow, Pierre Png, Edmund Chen. Prod: Applause Pictures/Raintree Pictures.

Angelica Lee in **The Eye**

CITY SHARKS
[Road comedy, 2003] Script and Dir: Esan Sivalingam.

Singapore cinema had a relatively good year in 2002. Theatrical attendance rose by about 3% and box-office increased by 7% to $60m. Encouragingly, the only two non-Hollywood movies on the year's top 10 chart were Singapore productions: Jack Neo's satirical comedy *I Not Stupid* (reviewed in *IFG 2003*), which earned $2.2m, and *The Eye,* with $1.1m. This was a double triumph for Raintree Pictures, the film-making branch of state-owned broadcaster MediaCorp, which produced *I Not Stupid* for $518,000 and co-produced *The Eye* with Hong Kong's Applause Pictures, contributing 30% of the $2.6m budget.

Directed by Thai-based twins Danny and Oxide Pang, **The Eye** tells the story of a blind young woman who receives a corneal transplant that enables her to see the dead. This visually stylish, aurally effective and genuinely creepy horror stars Malaysian-born Taiwanese Angelica Lee as the heroine and Chinese-Canadian singer Lawrence Chow as the psychotherapist who falls for her. It was shot in Hong Kong and Thailand, with dialogue in Cantonese, Mandarin and Thai.

A sequel by the Pangs is in the making, as might be a Hollywood version: Tom Cruise's Cruise-Wagner Productions has acquired remake rights. As part of its attempt to reach new audiences through regional co-production, Raintree teamed up with Hong Kong-based Golden Network Asia on the $690,000 black comedy **Nothing to Lose**, a flashy, style-over-substance crime orgy directed by Danny Pang.

Song of 'Nam

The first Singapore-Vietnam joint effort, **Song of the Stork** (*Vu khuc con co*), was directed by Singaporean Jonathan Foo and Vietnamese Nguyen Phan Quang Binh and produced for under $1m. Based on true accounts, it looks at the Vietnam War from the Vietnamese perspective, following the fates of five young soldiers and concentrating on the human dimension of war, instead of ideology. The first international production allowed into Vietnam to make a film about the war, it blends documentary and fiction narrative styles, and uses documentary footage.

Song won Best Feature at Milan in 2002, has been sold to the US,

Phot: Jamal J. Farley. Players: Nicolas Lee, Sheikh Haikel, Hans Isaac, Lim Kay Tong. Prod: Hoods Inc. Productions. A young man and two pals set out to save their foster parents' debt-ridden orphanage from closure, by collecting debts owed to a dead loan shark.

HOME RUN
[Drama, 2003] Script and Dir: Jack Neo. Phot: Kane Chen Kin Meng. Players: Huang Wen Yong, Xiang Yun, Shawn Lee Chuang Rui, Megan Zheng Zhi Yun. Prod: Raintree Pictures. An adaptation of Majid Majidi's *Children of Heaven*, set in 1965, as Singapore declares independence from Malaysia.

NOTHING TO LOSE
[Action comedy-drama, 2003] Script and Dir: Danny Pang. Players: Arisara Wongchalee, Pierre Png, Yvonne Lim. Prod: Raintree Pictures/Golden Network Asia. Two strangers attempting suicide become partners-in-crime.

PERTH
[Urban social satire, 2003] Script and Dir: Djinn Ong. Prod: Vacant Films/Ground Glass Images. Character study of a wife-beater.

VU KHUC CON CO
(Song of the Stork)
[War drama, 2002] Script: Wayne Karlin, Nguyen Duy Tom, Nguyen Quang Sang, Thu Bon. Dir: Jonathan Foo, Nguyen Phan Quang Binh. Phot: Mohd Jeffri Mohd Yusof. Players: Pham Chi Bao, Ta Ngoc Bao, Quang Hai Prod: Mega Media Pte Ltd/VIVAFILM.

Quote of the Year

"I am a marketer-writer-co-ordinator-manager-accountant-cheerleader most of the time, and a film director every once in a rare while."
KELVIN TONG, *director, on making films in Singapore.*

Europe and Asia and screened at the 2003 Singapore International Film Festival (SIFF), but according to its makers it is not expected to be theatrically released in Singapore (Foo's company would have been obliged to cover most or all of the marketing costs). Foo is also a driving force behind Singapore's new Media Hive academy, a private initiative by experienced television and film professionals to offer practical courses for emerging film-makers.

The Singapore Film Commission (SFC) has launched a Co-Production Investment Fund which matches the funds raised by local producers, up to a maximum $290,000, provided that the foreign investors contribute at least 30% of the budget. The SFC also signed a deal with the Singapore Broadcasting Authority and Raintree Pictures to co-finance four TV movies.

The much anticipated **15**, the feature-length version of director Royston Tan's prize-winning short, premiered at SIFF. As in the original, a cast of non-professionals play themselves in an unflinchingly raw and disturbing depiction of marginalised teenagers. Produced by film-maker Eric Khoo for under $150,000 (with a $30,000 grant from the SFC), the film was shown to much critical acclaim, but at press time its theatrical release was being held up by the censors, concerned by its plentiful Hokkien obscenities and explicit scenes of drug-taking and self-mutilation. Its MTV-inspired style and dream-like still images work better in the short version, but *15* nonetheless confirms Tan as a distinctive voice in Singapore cinema.

The *15* controversy contributed to unusually lively recent censorship debates and developments. In January 2003, the SFC, the Films and Publications Department (Censorship) and the Singapore Broadcasting Authority merged to form the Media Development Authority (MDA). The SFC will continue under the MDA with its own charter, name and logo. It is too early to see the results of this restructuring – especially the impact on the SFC's autonomy, financing and strengthened ties to the censors. In 2002, a Censorship Review Committee was set up to review censorship policies and recommend changes and, with the impact of globalisation and new technologies, the easing of strict censorship laws is inevitable. The question is how far the government will dare to go.

YVONNE NG has written widely on Asian cinema and is on the editorial board of *KINEMA* (published at the University of Waterloo). She is the co-author of *Latent Images: Film in Singapore* (OUP, 2000; CD-ROM version, Singapore, 2003).

Slovakia Hana Cielová

Recent and Forthcoming Films

POKRVNÉ VZT'AHY
(Blood Ties)
[Drama, forthcoming] Script:
Oleg Harencár, Ondrej Sulaj.
Dir: Harencár. Phot: Ján Duris.
Players: Monika Hilmerová,
Roman Luknár, Rudolf Martin,
Sally Kirkland, Max Gail. Prod:
ALEF Film & Media.

ZOSTANE TO MEDZI NAMI
(It Will Stay Between Us)
[Drama, forthcoming] Script:
Slavena Pavlásková, Miro
Sindelka. Dir: Sindelka. Phot:
Ján Duris. Players: Danica
Jurcová, Michal Dlouhy, Tomás
Hanák, Anna Sisková, Bozidara
Turzonovová, Jozef Lenci, Radek
Brzobohaty, Zdena Studénková,
Miro Noga. Prod: Film Factory.

66 Seasons

66 SEZÓN (66 Seasons)
[Documentary, 2003] Script and
Dir: Peter Kerekes. Phot: Martin
Kollár. Prod: Peter Kerekes/Slovak
TV/Czech TV.

NICHOLAS WINTON –
SILA L'UDSKOSTI (Nicholas
Winton – The Power of Good)
[Documentary, 2002] Script and
Prod: Matej Minác, Patrik Pass.
Dir: Minác.

I n January 2003 Slovakia became a member of the EU's Media programme, and Slovak film-makers and distributors should benefit from its initiatives (in April a new Media desk opened in Bratislava). In May, Slovaks voted in a nationwide referendum to enter the EU, but the good news ends there because, disappointingly, no new Slovak feature has been completed since *Cruel Joys* (*Kruté radosti*), Juraj Nvota's early 1900s rural drama (reviewed in *IFG 2003*).

Two new features were in post-production in summer 2003. The ambitious *Blood Ties* (*Pokrvné vzt'ahy*), a Slovak/US co-production that is the first English-language film made in Slovakia, is the fiction direction debut of Oleg Harencár, a Slovak-born independent documentary-maker from San Francisco. An American software specialist finds out that his real mother comes from Slovakia, a country he has never heard of, and travels there to find out more.

Also nearing completion in summer 2003 was *It Will Stay Between Us* (*Zostane to medzi nami*), a second feature from Miro Sindelka. Like his debut, *A Passionate Kiss* (*Vásnivy bozk*), this is another psychological drama about male-female relationships. The main character Danica has a safe, dull life with Michal, a successful businessman whose extremely rational nature virtually eliminates the emotions that Danica craves. So it's not surprising that she falls for the charismatic Tomás, a fascinating, turbulent young man.

There is more activity on the documentary front, most notably with Matej Minác's **Nicholas Winton – The Power of Good** (*Nicholas Winton – Sila l'udskosti*), which won an International Emmy in 2002 and was shown at many festivals. It tells the story of "Britain's Schindler", the man who in 1939 saved the lives of 669 children, most of them Jewish, by bringing them from Nazi-occupied Czechoslovakia across Germany and on to Britain. The children included the late director Karel Reisz, and for nearly 50 years Winton kept his actions secret. Among emerging names, Peter Kerekes made **66 Seasons** (*66 sezón*), an original portrait of a municipal swimming pool and its patrons over the last 66 years, in the multinational town of Kosice in eastern Slovakia.

HANA CIELOVÁ is a freelance writer and works for Czech Television on the monthly film programme *Filmopolis*.

Slovenia Ziva Emersic

The Year's Best Films

Ziva Emersic's selection:

Spare Parts
(Dir: Damjan Kozole)
Rustling Landscapes
(Dir: Janez Lapajne)
Ljubljana (Dir: Igor Sterk)

Recent and Forthcoming Films

REZERVNI DELI (Spare Parts)
*[Drama, 2002] Script and Dir:
Damjan Kozole. Phot: Radoslav
Jovanov Gonzo. Players: Peter
Musevski, Aljosa Kovacic,
Aleksandra Balmazovic, Primoz
Petkovsek. Prod: Emotionfilm.*

**VARUH MEJE (The Guardian
of the Frontier)**
*[Drama, 2002] Script: Brock
Norman Brock, Zoran Hocevar,
Maja Weiss. Dir: Weiss. Phot:
Bojan Kastelic. Players: Iva
Kranjc, Pia Zemljic, Tanja
Potocnik. Prod: Bela Film.*

LJUBLJANA
*[Drama, 2002] Script and Dir:
Igor Sterk. Phot: Ven Jemersic.
Players: Gregor Zorc, Primoz
Pirnat, Manca Dorrer. Prod:
A.A.C. Production.*

SLEPA PEGA (Blind Spot)
*[Drama, 2002] Script and Dir:
Hanna A.W. Slak. Phot: Karina
Maria Kleszcewska. Players:
Manca Dorrer, Kolja Saksida.
Prod: Bindweed Soundvision.*

**SELESTENJE
(Rustling Landscapes)**
*[Drama, 2002] Script: Janez
Lapajne and players. Dir:
Lapajne. Phot: Matej Kriznik.
Players: Barbara Cerar, Rok
Vihar, Gregor Zorc, Masa
Derganc. Prod: Triglav Film.*

As Slovenia prepares to become a full EU member (in May 2004), its film-makers continue to find that artistic passion, talent and effort are not appropriately backed up by production infrastructure and state support. The arrival of democracy and independence in 1991 pushed domestic production to the brink of collapse. Following the immediate dismantling of the state-owned production and distribution company, it took the local industry another five years to re-establish a basis for production – during which time the local media fostered intensively negative opinions about Slovenian and European cinema.

In 1993, sustained lobbying led to the launch of the Film Fund of Slovenia, an independent body responsible for state subsidies, and feature film output rose from one or two films a year to seven in 2002. The public's attitude to local films improved with international successes such as the Lion of the Future awarded in Venice in 2001 to Jan Cvitkovic's *Bread and Milk* and the presence of Damjan Kozole's *Spare Parts* in competition at Berlin in 2003.

However, the recent withdrawal of state-owned TV Slovenija from a co-production agreement with the fund means that it is again the sole source of finance. In cinemas, the American majors consistently claim around 95% of a very small theatrical market. The production cost of an average film is about $750,000 and with average tickets costing $3.5 the handful of independent producers have no chance of making their money back at home. Most domestic titles sell between 2,000 and 25,000 tickets (although *Bread and Milk* and Vojko Anzeljc's black comedy *The Last Supper* both sold more than 50,000 in 2001), so it's easy to understand why producers mostly opt to make small, low-budget, contemporary stories.

Dangerous journies

Kozole's **Spare Parts** (*Rezervni deli*), the fourth feature by this gifted director, is a bleak drama about organ trafficking. It tells the heartbreaking stories of desperate refugees smuggled across Europe as live donors, and also evokes sympathy for two smugglers, themselves lost and desperate souls. It impressed critics at Berlin, but could not pass 27,000 admissions at home. **The Guardian of the Frontier** (*Varuh meje*), directed by Maja Weiss, won the Salzgeber Award at Berlin's Panorama in 2002 for "civil courage". All kinds of real and symbolic frontiers are challenged when three young female students find their 'relaxing' boat trip down the Kolpa River, along the Croatian border, turning into a nightmare which forces them to examine their humanity, courage and sexuality.

Left to right: Pia Zemljic, Tanja Potocnik and Iva Kranjc in **The Guardian of the Frontier**

After his highly accomplished first film, *Express* (a wordless story about lovers on a train), Igor Sterk made the demanding **Ljubljana**, which portrays the "lost generation" of the Slovenian capital: young people wrestling with careers, love, sex and friendships, their lives characterised by emptiness, doubt and alienation. The young and gifted Hanna A. W. Slak made her feature debut with **Blind Spot** (*Slepa pega*), a deep gaze into the lives of a drug addict and the devoted girlfriend who saves him from suicide and insanity. The excellent photography and sound design reveal a director with a special command of cinematic language.

Rustling Landscapes (*Selestenje*), the debut film of Janez Lapajne (b. 1967), was the big winner at the fifth national film festival in Portoroz. The director wrote the screenplay after extensive workshops with his actors, creating an intimate story of two couples on the brink of separation, their strained relationships juxtaposed against the outstanding beauty of Bela Krajina, one of Slovenia's most tranquil resorts.

Andrej Kosak followed his debut, *Outsider* (the biggest domestic hit of the last 20 years), with **Headnoise** (*Zvenenje v glavi*), adapted from the acclaimed novel by Slovenian Drago Jancar. In 1970, the inmates of a Livada state prison revolt when they are stopped from watching a basketball match between Yugoslavia and US. In this tale of yet another revolution condemned to eat its own children, Kosak failed to match the novel's rich, political symbolism but still made a dynamic action drama, with excellent performances.

ZIVA EMERSIC is a film critic, a former director of the National Film Festival at Portoroz and former head of the documentary programme at TV Slovenija.

Jernej Sugman in **Headnoise**

ZVENENJE V GLAVI (Headnoise)

[Drama, 2002] Script: Dejan Dukovski, Andrej Kosak. Dir: Kosak. Phot: Dusan Joksimovic. Players: Jernej Sugman, Ksenija Misic, Radko Polic. Prod: Novi val/Ata Productions.

(A)TORZIJA (A)Torsion)

[Short drama, 2002] Script: Abdulah Sidran. Dir: Stefan Arsenijevic. Phot: Vilko Filac. Players: Davor Janjic, Amir Glamocak, Mirjana Sajinovic, Brane Grubar. Prod: Studio Arkadena. Winner of Golden Bear for Best Short at Berlin, 2003. Stories of great humanity and courage from the tunnel under Sarajevo airport, the only connection to the outside world during the siege.

SLOVENIJA, OBLJUBLJENA DEZELA (Slovenia – The Promised Land)

[Drama, forthcoming] Script: Miha Hocevar, Ozren Kebo. Dir: Hocevar. Phot: Slobodan Trninic. Players: Milena Zupancic, Mustafa Nadarevic, Sasa Tabakovic, Filip Djuric. Prod: Studio Arkadena. Two Bosnian brothers who decide to move to Slovenia after the death of their father.

RUSEVINE (Ruins)

[Drama, forthcoming] Script: Janez Burger, Ana Lasic. Dir: Burger. Phot: Simon Tansek. Players: Darko Rundek, Natasa Matjasec, Matjaz Tribuson. Prod: Vertigo/Emotion Film. Second film by acclaimed Burger (*Idle Running*) explores the charade of theatre and its influence on the cast of a play.

South Africa Martin Botha

The Year's Best Films

Martin Botha's selection:

Judgment Day
(Docu. Dir: Kevin Harris)

Bread and Water
(Docu. Dir: Toni Strasburg)

It's My Life
(Docu. Dir: Brian Tilley)

A Drink in the Passage
(Short. Dir: Zola Maseko)

When the War Is Over
(Docu. Dir: François Verster)

Bread and Water

Recent and Forthcoming Films

'N SPROKIE (A Fairytale)
[Short drama, 2002] Script and Dir: Harold Holscher. Phot: Catherine Hornby, Grant Appleton. Players: Greta Clarence, Bernard Peters. Prod: CityVarsity Film and Television School.

AMANDLA! A REVOLUTION IN FOUR PART HARMONY
[Documentary, 2002] Dir: Lee Hirsch. Prod: Desiree Markgraaf.

A DRINK IN THE PASSAGE
[Short drama, 2002] Dir: Zola Maseko. Prod: M-NET/National Film and Video Foundation.

BREAD AND WATER
[Documentary, 2002] Dir: Toni Strasburg. Prod: Big World Cinema.

The past year was characterised by outstanding documentaries by veteran South African directors. Having already made several acclaimed anti-apartheid documentaries, Kevin Harris made a universal statement about war and the consequences of protracted violent conflict on Israeli and Palestinian society in **Judgment Day,** which, with one eye on the violent anti-apartheid struggle, examines the present cycle of bloodshed in the Middle East and the way in which ordinary people become brutalised by war and sectarian conflict.

Toni Strasburg's **Bread and Water** was filmed over 10 months and gives an intimate and almost poetic insight into the life of a woman and her community as they desperately attempt to get clean water to their village. Brian Tilley's powerful, multi-award-winning **It's My Life** follows internationally famed Aids activist Zackie Achmat, who refuses to take anti-retrovirals until they are available in South African public hospitals and clinics, leads the court battle against the multinational drug companies and takes on the South African government for its confusing policies on HIV/Aids. The film splendidly interweaves personal and public images to provide an intimate look at the complexities of this campaign and its leader.

The American Lee Hirsch won the 2002 Sundance Documentary Audience and Freedom of Expression Awards for **Amandla! A Revolution in Four Part Harmony**, a vivid celebration of music in the struggle against apartheid. It examines how changes in the lyrics, rhythms and melodies of liberation songs reflected the radicalisation of black resistance in response to ever harsher state crackdowns.

Don't blame the iceberg

Veteran film-maker Tim Spring reached a career peak and won numerous local awards with **Why They Sank Titanic**, a documentary that combines documented evidence with speculation to argue that the famous wreck is in fact not the *Titanic*, but her sister ship the *Olympic*. Based on research by Andrew Newton, Spring's film argues that the White Star Line, owners of the luxurious superliners, which cost $10m each, could not afford to write off the *Olympic*, which had been severely damaged in three accidents. Instead they swapped the ships' names, had the crocked ship sunk on April 15, 1912 and collected the $12m insurance payout. Spring constructed a remarkable portrait of the last moments of the famous ship.

Nearly three years in the making, François Verster's **When the War Is Over** deals with the after-effects of the fight against apartheid, as experienced by survivors active in a militant self-defence unit operating in the mid-1980s. One is now an army captain back from exile and still unable to come to terms with life after apartheid, not least the prospect of marriage. Another is trying to abandon a life of violent crime. As in the case of Verster's *Pavement Aristocrats* (reviewed in *IFG 2000*) his latest work is gritty, yet beautiful in its portrayal of human nature and a world seems to have little to offer those who were willing to sacrifice their lives for the struggle against apartheid.

International recognition for South African shorts and features was demonstrated by our award-winning presence at the leading African film festival FESPACO. Director Zola Maseko won Best Short Film for *A Drink in the Passage,* a powerful and touching work in which a celebrated black sculptor recalls the curious events that led him to share a brandy with a white family at the height of apartheid in the 1960s. Jason Xenopoulos' powerful drama about white supremacists, *Promised Land* (reviewed in *IFG 2003*), was awarded a prize in the Best Editing category and also won Best Screenplay at Tokyo.

Short cuts to the future

At home, several award-winning short films by graduates from the CityVarsity Film and Television School in Cape Town left one with much hope for the future. Louis du Toit's sensitive portrayal of racial reconciliation in post-apartheid South Africa, *When Tomorrow Calls,* won two National Television and Video Association Stone Awards. Awards also went to another exploration of racial reconciliation and white angst, *Swing Left Frank,* which was characterised by stunning visuals on 35mm by Grant Appleton and excellent editing by Matthys Pretorius. *'n Sprokie (A Fairytale),* sensitively directed by Harold Holscher and beautifully shot on 16mm by Catherine Hornby and Grant Appleton, is a visual poem about a mother waiting for her son to return from the South African war in Namibia.

Talented film-makers like those mentioned above could blossom if more funding were available to boost local production – and this could happen. The National Film and Video Foundation (NFVF), the primary body for state funding, recently saw a 50% increase in its annual allocation to $2.25m (R18m) and the Arts and Culture Ministry released a further $4.37m for short and feature film production for 2003-05.

GOD IS AFRICAN
[Drama, 2002] Script and Dir: Akin Omotoso. Players: Sami Sabiti, Hakeem Kai-Kazim. Prod: Akin Omotoso, Hakeem Kai-Kazim.

HIJACK STORIES
[Comedy-drama, 2000] Dir: Oliver Schmitz. Players: Tony Kgoroge, Rapulana Seiphemo. Prod: Christoph Meyer-Wiel & Philippe Guez.

HOODLUM & SON
[Gangster drama, 2003] Script and Dir: Ashley Way. Phot: Buster Reynolds. Players: Ron Perlman, Robert Vaughn, Ian Roberts. Prod: Peakviewing Film Productions S.A.

JUDGMENT DAY
[Documentary, 2002] Script, Dir and Prod: Kevin Harris.

THE MAN WHO KNOWS TOO MUCH
[Documentary, 2002] Dir: Liza Key.

PAVEMENT
[Drama, 2003] Dir: Darrell Roodt. Phot: Giulio Biccarri. Players: Robert Patrick, Lauren Holly. Prod: Film Afrika for Apollo Media.

PROMISED LAND
[Drama, 2002] Script and Dir: Jason Xenopoulos. Phot: Giulio Biccarri. Players: Nick Boraine, Ian Roberts, Daniel Brodie. Prod: Moonyeenn Lee, David Wicht.

PROPERTY OF THE STATE: GAY MEN IN THE APARTHEID MILITARY
[Documentary, 2002] Script and Dir: Gerald Kraak. Phot: Pam Laxen. Prod: Jill Kruger, National Film and Video Foundation/Joseph Rowntree Charitable Trust.

PROTEUS
[Drama, 2003] Script and Dir: John Greyson and Jack Lewis. Players: Neil Sandilands, Rouxnet Brown. Prod: Steven Markovitz, Anita Lee, Platon Trakoshis (Big World Cinema

and Pluck Productions).

STANDER
*[Crime drama, 2003] Script:
Bima Staff. Dir: Bronwyn
Hughes. Players: Thomas Jane.
Prod: The Imaginarium
(SA)/Grosvenor Park
(Canada)/Seven Arts (UK).*

Swing Left Frank

SWING LEFT FRANK
*[Short drama, 2002] Script and
Dir: Johan Nel. Phot: Grant
Appleton. Prod: CityVarsity Film
& Television School.*

UBUNTU'S WOUNDS
*[Short drama, 2002] Script and
Dir: Sechaba Morojele. Prod:
American Film Institute/National
Film and Video Foundation.*

WHEN THE WAR IS OVER
*[Documentary, 2002] Script
and Dir: François Verster.*

WHEN TOMORROW CALLS
*[Short drama, 2002] Script and
Dir: Louis du Toit. Phot:
Richard Bellon. Prod: Louis du
Toit, CityVarsity Film and
Television School.*

WHY THEY SANK TITANIC
*[Documentary, 2000] Script
and Dir: Tim Spring.
Prod: Barry Kruger.*

Quote of the Year

"We need to grasp the
fact that we're in the
entertainment business,
not sociology, and that film
is an expensive medium that
cannot serve the whims
of a minority audience."
DAVID WICHT, *producer,
on the challenges facing South
Africa's film industry.*

The NFVF has already backed outstanding films such as *Promised Land*, *A Drink in the Passage* and Akin Omotoso's remarkable and daring **God Is African.** This 90-minute feature, shot for $7,500 over 24 days in 2000, was finally screened in South Africa in 2003. It is a serious, witty drama about xenophobia, and deals with a Nigerian student at a local university drumming up support for writer Ken Saro Wiwa, who was later killed by the Nigerian government. Clearly a labour of love, the film has enjoyed accolades around the world.

The NFVF also invested in **Proteus**, a South Africa/Canada co-production directed by John Greyson and Jack Lewis. Based on a true story, it is a period film that raises issues still of enormous relevance today. Co-director Lewis was fascinated by a court record in the Cape Archives, dated August 18, 1735, giving judgment in the case of two Robben Island prisoners, Dutch sailor Rijkhaart Jacobsz and Khoe convict Class Blank, who received extreme sentences for "the abominable and unnatural crime of Sodomy". This dramatisation of their story features five languages: English, Afrikaans, Dutch, Nama and Latin.

Proteus: *set on Robben Island in 1735*

Finally, in September 2002, one of the pioneers of modern, bold and inventive South African cinema, Jans Rautenbach (*The Candidate*, *Katrina*), was honoured with a retrospective at the up-and-coming domestic showcase, the Apollo Film Festival, held in the small Karoo town of Victoria West.

Dr **MARTIN BOTHA** has written two books and more than 200 articles on South African and African cinema, including an in-depth study of the late director Manie van Rensburg. He is a member of the council of South Africa's National Film and Video Foundation.

South Korea Frank Segers

The Year's Best Films

Frank Segers' selection:
My Teacher, Mr Kim
(Dir: Jang Gyu-sung)
A Good Lawyer's Wife
(Dir: Im Sang-soo)
Conduct Zero
(Dir: Cho Keun-sik)
Tube (Dir: Baek Woon-hak)
*My Virginity Flows through
Her Body* (Short. Dir: Park
Jong Woo)

Recent and Forthcoming Films

**SA-LIN-EUI CHU-EOK
(Memories of Murder)**
*[Drama, 2003] Script: Bong
Joon-ho, Shim Sung-bo. Dir:
Bong. Phot: Kim Hyung-gu.
Players: Song Kang-ho, Kim
Sang-kyung. Prod: Tcha Sung-
jai/Sidus Corp./CJ Entertainment.*
Two detectives track an elusive
serial killer responsible for the
rape and murder of 10 young
women within a 2km radius
in Gyunggi Province in the
mid-1980s.

**JO-POK MA-NU-RA 2
(My Wife Is a Gangster 2)**
*[Comedy-drama, 2003] Script:
Choi Hea-chul, Jung Hung-soon.
Dir: Jung. Phot: Jo Dong-kwan.
Players: Shin Eun-kyung,
Park Jun-kyu. Prod: Park
Mi-jung/Hyunjin Cinema/
CJ Entertainment.*
Sequel to 2002's hit about
a female gangster who marries
a mild-mannered good citizen to
placate her dying sister. This time
a female gangster suffers amnesia
after being conked on the head in
a brawl and falls for a kindly
restaurateur while struggling

Hold the huzzahs about South Korean cinema, please. Although as vital as any film industry outside the US over the last decade (local market share climbed from 15.9% in 1994 to 42.9% in the first quarter of 2003), signs of strain have prompted questions about how much longer such phenomenal growth can be sustained. The industry is said euphemistically to be "in transition" as the boom in overall attendance and box-office revenue, market share and the number of cinemas is mirrored by rising production and marketing costs, and increased competition for the filmgoers' won.

In a nutshell, the extraordinary 1999 success of Kang Je-gyu's *Shiri* led to a flood of production investment, some $181.3m (201.5 billion won) in 2000-01, creating a market bubble. After several big-budget titles bombed with the public – notably Korea's answer to *Heaven's Gate*, Jang Sun-woo's $10m *Resurrection of the Little Match Girl* (2002) – a lot of investment bypassed cinema and went to other, more profitable sectors.

That's hardly surprising when, according to the Korean Film Commission (KOFIC), 2002's films lost an average of nearly $450,000 each. Nonetheless, the legacy of big budgets and big marketing costs continues to dog the market, as does the intensified competition among major distributors. Early in 2003, CJ Entertainment and Cinema Service, accounting for a combined 66% of the market, considered a merger. To sighs of relief from the growing band of smaller distributors (Showbox, Korea Pictures, Aura Entertainment, Big Blue Film, among others), the whole thing was called off in April. The upshot is a renewed emphasis on more "business-minded" commercial films.

Lurking within this commercial calculation is an artistic one. Will further growth come at the price of aesthetic quality? Almost certainly not. South Korean cinema is far too diverse to reduce itself to simple equations of box-office returns versus artistic achievement. If anything, Korean films demonstrate that both can be achieved by the same title. In 2002, for example, among the 11 biggest export earners was Im Kwon-taek's Cannes competition costume drama, *Chihwaseon*. In all, South Korea exported 151 films (including 30 shorts, still an active genre in the market) to 32 countries for total export revenue of $15m.

to remember her past, which resurfaces in odd ways.

AH-KA-SHI-AH (Acacia)
[*Horror, 2003*] *Script: Sung Ki-young, Park Ki-hyeong. Dir: Park. Phot: Oh Hyun-je. Players: Shim Hye-jin. Prod: Yu Young-shik/DaDa Film/Beautiful Film Production/Korea Pictures/Cineclick Asia.*
A childless couple adopt an artistically inclined boy who becomes emotionally attached to an acacia tree in the garden after his adoptive mother finally gives birth. The boy disappears after overhearing talk of being sent back to the orphanage. The tree blossoms, sparking strange phenomena.

TAE GUK GI HUI NAL RI MYEO (Brotherhood)
[*Drama, 2003*] *Script and Dir: Kang Je-gyu. Phot: Hong Kyung-pyo. Players: Jang Dong-gun, Won Bin, Lee Eun-joo. Prod: Choi Jin-wha/Kangjegyu Films.*
The director of Shiri returns with this big-budget action vehicle about two brothers serving in the Korean War. The elder tries to have his academe-bound younger brother released from military service by taking on dangerous missions, but the younger misinterprets his brother's sacrifices. Title refers to South Korea's national flag.

CHOET-SA-RANG SA-SOO GWOL-GI-DAE-HWE (Crazy First Love)
[*Comedy, 2003*] *Script and Dir: Oh Jong-rok. Phot: Jung Gwang-suk. Players: Cha Tae-hyun, Son Ye-jin, Yoo Dong-geun. Prod: Han Sung-goo/Popcorn Film/Cinema Service.*
Father jokingly promises to marry off his daughter to a young boy when latter grows up. The youngster turns out to be the biggest troublemaker at school, but is still determined to marry the daughter, so the dad takes action.

Year of the Moon

The sheer variety of topics covered by some of the most interesting titles this past year is astonishing. There is the sleek sexiness of Im Sang-soo's **A Good Lawyer's Wife**, featuring a stellar, erotically charged turn from the highly supple Moon So-ri as the cheating wife of a cheating barrister husband. In Lee Chang-dong's **Oasis**, Moon portrays the physically handicapped woman who falls for the ex-con responsible for the hit-and-run accident that killed her father. *Oasis* was popular at home, the seventh highest-grossing domestic film of 2002, and played Venice, where Moon was named Best Actress.

Then there is the dazzling visual footwork of Cho Keun-sik's **Conduct Zero**, a madcap examination of a school tough guy whose top-dog status is challenged on a number of interesting fronts. Contrast this crowd-pleaser with Park Jong-woo's riveting 15-minute short, *My Virginity Flows through Her Body* (Sa-yeon), which played the Directors' Fortnight at Cannes, combining unrequited love, sex and a bloody suicide in concise and confounding fashion.

Baek Woon-hak's action thriller **Tube**

In the big-budget action vein is Baek Woon-hak's **Tube**, a lumbering but spiffily made suspenser about an intrepid policeman's effort to foil a terrorist hijacking on the Seoul subway system. The film marks, coincidentally, the comeback of independent producer Tube Entertainment.

Tales out of school

Few will soon forget Cha Seung-won's superlative performance as a dodgy teacher assigned to save a rural school in Jang Gyu-sung's skilfully constructed **My Teacher, Mr Kim**. On the comedy front, Kim Kyung-hyung's **My Tutor Friend** pitted a simple country college girl against a roistering and wealthy high-school senior in a series of revealing private tutorials.

Cha Seung-won, centre, as **My Teacher, Mr Kim**

A major critical and commercial success in 2003 was Bong Joon-ho's **Memories of Murder** (*Sa-lin-eui chu-eok*), a tightly knit, factually based policer about two detectives of different styles tracking down an audacious serial killer. In production at press time were potential blockbusters from Kang Je-gyu, *Brotherhood*, about the intertwining fates of two brothers in the Korean war, and Kang Woo-suk (who founded Cinema Service) with *Silmi Island* (*Tae guk gi hui nal ri myeo*), about an actual 1971 incident in which the South Korean president was nearly assassinated. These are among the varied titles resulting from the more earnest commercial policy of "managing profitability".

Although Korean titles were in relatively short supply at Cannes in 2003, one gem, Shin Sang-okk's *The Evergreen* (1961), was newly printed and revived in the Retrospective section. Shin has achieved great things as a director but is best known for one of the most bizarre events in film history. He and his actress wife were kidnapped and held captive for eight years by the North Koreans, who obliged the director to make propaganda films until the couple's escape in 1986.

KOFIC, which has a $36m budget for 2003, covering investments, loans and other film support, is currently attempting to streamline the market's tallying of national box-office figures. At present, Seoul attendance figures are considered reliable, but those from other major cities and rural areas less so.

Perhaps the year's biggest surprise occurred off-screen, with the appointment of Oasis director Lee Chang-dong to the influential post of Minister of Culture and Tourism. The iconoclastic Lee is likely to shake things up a bit, and industry figures hoped that he would draw the teeth of Korea's censorship apparatus, the Media Ratings Board. One untouchable, Minister Lee quickly declared, was the nation's sacrosanct screen quota system, which ensures that local cinemas must screen South Korean films for at least 126-146 days a year.

OL-DEU BO-I (Old Boy)
[Drama, 2003] Script: Hwang Jo-yoon, Im Joon-hyung. Dir: Park Chan-wook. Phot: Jung Jung-hoon. Players: Choi Min-shik, Kang Hye-jung. Prod: Im Seung-yong/Show East Co./Cineclick Asia.
Man with loving wife and daughter is drugged, kidnapped and incarcerated in a private hospital-prison. During his 15-year confinement his wife is brutally murdered. After a mysterious escape, he seeks vengeance and the reason for his imprisonment. Stars Korea's biggest name actor, Choi Min-shik; director made the hit *JSA: Joint Security Area.*

CHEONG-PUNG-MYEONG-WEOL (Sword in the Moon)
[Historical drama, 2003] Script: Jang Min-suk. Dir: Kim Eui-suk. Phot: Moon Yong-shik. Players: Choi Min-soo, Cho Che-hyun, Kim Bo-kyung. Prod: Lee Chung-soo/White Lee Entertainment/Mirovision Inc.
Seventeenth-century costume drama about assassination of a local government official setting off turmoil throughout a city. An elite military unit is called in to capture the mysterious and elusive assassin.

TONG-GAE (Mutt Boy)
[Drama, 2003] Script and Dir: K. T. Kwak. Phot: Hwang Ki. Players: Jung Woo-sung, Eom Jee-won, Kim Kab-su. Prod: Jung Jong-sub/Zininsa

Cineclick Asia

Jung Woo-sung as **Mutt Boy**

Film/Show East/Cineclick Asia. Disaffected youth beats up 21 members of the local soccer club after they kill and eat his beloved dog. His subsequent notoriety attracts a following of small-time gangsters. Kwak made Korea's box-office champ *Friend*.

MI-SEU-TEO LE-I-DI (Mr Lady)
[Comedy, 2003] Script: Jo Myung-nam. Dir: Jo. Phot: Jang Sang-il. Players: Ahn Sung-gee, So Chan-hwi, Kim Gun-il. Prod: Hwang Yun-kyung/Indecom.
Eldest son of an aristocratic family confounds expectations of marriage and family by singing and dancing at Swan Lake, a club for transsexuals. When misfortune strikes, he and two roommates try to save the club they regard as their true home.

PA-GWE (Ravage)
[Drama, 2003] Script: Jeon Soo-il based on Kim Young-ha's original story. Dir: Jeon. Phot:

Kim Sung-tai. Players: Jung Bo-suk, Kim Young-min. Prod: Hong Seung-hyun/Dongnyuk Film/RGP France.
Modest-budget entry about a taxi driver who picks up a young woman in a nightclub. They begin a relationship, but just as he falls in love she disappears and he desperately searches for her throughout the city.

Quote of the Year

"He is certainly nothing of a bureaucrat. He prefers not to be chauffeured around, drives his own car to work and favours casual dress. This is somewhat disconcerting to some people at the Ministry."

ANONYMOUS *representative of the Korean Film Commission, describing newly appointed*

Minister of Culture and Tourism and film director, Lee Chang-dong.

40th Grand Bell Awards

Best Film:
Memories of Murder.
Best Director: Bong Joon-ho
(Memories of Murder).
Best Screenplay:
Jang Kyu-sung, Lee Won-hyung
(My Teacher, Mr Kim).
Best Actor: Song Kang-ho
(Memories of Murder).
Best Actress:
Lee Mi-yeon *(Addicted).*
Best Supporting Actor:
Baek Yoon-shik
(Save the Green Planet).
Best Supporting Actress:
Song Yoon-ah *(Jail Breakers).*
Best Cinematography:
Jung Kwang-seok *(Jail Breakers).*
Best New Director:
Jang Jun-hwan
(Save the Green Planet).

Cops track a killer in the Grand Bell-winning **Memories of Murder**

Spain Jonathan Holland

The Year's Best Films

Jonathan Holland's selection:

My Life without Me
(Dir: Isabel Coixet)

Where Is Madame Catherine?
(Dir: Marc Recha)

The Hours of the Day
(Dir: Jaime Rosales)

Salamina Soldiers
(Dir: David Trueba)

Life Marks
(Dir: Enrique Urbizu)

Recent and Forthcoming Films

THE MACHINIST
[Thriller, 2003] Script: Scott Alan Kosar. Dir: Brad Anderson. Phot: Xavi Gimenez. Players: Christian Bale, Jennifer Jason Leigh, John Sarian, Aitana Sánchez-Gijón. Prod: Filmax/Castelao Productions.
A hallucinating, insomniac factory worker provokes a nasty accident.

CACHORRO (*literally,* **Puppy**)
[Drama, 2003] Script: Miguel Albadalejo, Salvador García. Dir: Albadalejo. Phot: Alfonso Sanz. Players: José Luis García-Pérez, David Castillo, Diana Cerezo, Mario Arias. Prod: Star Line Productions.
A gay dentist looks after his 11-year-old nephew.

CARMEN
[Drama, 2003] Script: Vicente Aranda, Joaquín Jordá. Dir: Aranda. Phot: Paco Femenía. Players: Paz Vega, Leonardo Sbaraglia, María Botto, Antonio Dechent. Prod: Starline Productions.
Version of the Andalucian

Spanish-language films have enjoyed a mini sales boom in the US and UK of late. *The Son of the Bride, Talk to Her, The Devil's Backbone* and *Y tu mamá también* have all made their mark, and a raft of lesser-known pics have clinched American TV deals. What once seemed a dream has actually happened; so why, then, was the Spanish Film Academy's (SFA) annual report on the state of the industry entitled *The Coming Crisis?*

The answer is the bleak domestic lookout. The SFA's report mixes dark comedy, tragedy and even farce – but the laughs are few and far between. Economic growth is generally down; one estimate says that the major television networks' investment in film in 2002 fell 21%. North American films grabbed 77% of ticket sales. The twin Sogecable-Via Digital digital platform looks set to buy just 60 Spanish films in 2003, and the times when they battled it out to see who could buy the most are now a long-distant memory. Only 2.9% of producers in 2002 made more than four films, while 82.4% made only one.

Market share for Spanish films in 2002 was 13.7%, which is on a par with the last five years – but from double the number of films produced five years ago. In a nutshell, the financing has been available, but the market has not (2002 admissions plummeted from 26.6 million to 15 million). Lots of Spanish films are made – 114 in 2002 – but many wonder whether fewer wouldn't be better, with improved production values and promotion giving projects a better chance of following in the hallowed, giant footsteps of Pedro Almodóvar's *Talk to Her.* And on it goes.

At least 2003 has delivered one major Spanish hit, in the form of Javier Fesser's *Mortadelo and Filemón,* and a survey of the biggest home hits of the last year shows that Spanish audiences have recovered their taste for the off-beat: they've tired, it seems, of standard Civil War romances or low-budget local comedies. On paper, 2002's *The Other Side of the Bed (El otro lado de la cama)* by Emilio Martínez-Lázaro must have looked risky (a teen comedy-musical, anyone?) but its freshness and good humour clicked big-time with the public.

This year's big hit (and the second biggest in Spanish B. O. history) has been the ambitious, technically accomplished take on 1960s passion classic, based not on Bizet but on Mérimée's novel.

ASTRONAUTAS
(*literally,* **Astronauts**)
[*Drama, 2003*] *Script and Dir: Santi Amodeo. Phot: Alex Catalán. Players: Nancho Novo, Teresa Hurtado, Manolo Solo, Julian Villagrán, Alex O'Dogherty. Prod: Tesela PC/La Zanfoña Producciones.*
Off-beat fare from co-director of The Pilgrim Factor.
Artist in rehab finds himself a 15-year-old saviour.

THE BRIDGE OF SAN LUIS REY
[*Historical drama, 2003*]
Script: Mary McGuckian, based on the Thornton Wilder novel. Dir: McGuckian. Phot: Javier Aguirresarobe. Players: Robert de Niro, Harvey Keitel, F. Murray Abraham, Jim Sheridan, Gabriel Byrne, Kathy Bates, Geraldine Chaplin. Prod: Davis/Kanzaman/Pembridge.
A bridge collapses in eighteenth-century Peru, with heavyweight consequences.

DESCONGELATE
(**Chill Out**)
[*Comedy, 2003*] *Script and Dir: Félix Sabroso, Dunia Ayaso. Phot: Kiko de la Rica. Players: Pepón Nieto, Candela Peña, Loles León, Rubén Ochandiano. Prod: El Deseo/MediaPro.*
Almodóvar-produced third feature focuses on a down-at-heel director in multi-ethnic Madrid district.

EL PRINCIPE DE ARQUIMEDES
(*literally,* **The Archimedes Principle**)
[*Drama, 2003*] *Script: Belén Gopegui. Dir: Gerardo Herrero. Phot: Alfredo Mayo. Players: Marta Belaustegui, Roberto Enríquez, Manuel Morón, Alberto Jiménez. Prod: Tornasol Films/Continental Produciones.*
Women in the workplace come under the scrutiny of the director of My Friend's Reasons.

Benito Pocino as Mortadelo in **Mortadelo and Filemón: The Big Adventure**

cartoon secret agents, **Mortadelo and Filemón: The Big Adventure** (*La gran aventura de Mortadelo y Filemón*), which cleverly combined farce, nostalgia and very contemporary special effects, thus keeping three generations (read: more than four million) of Spaniards happy.

The Latin Loach?

It's hard to imagine that Fernando León de Aranoa's **Mondays in the Sun** (*Los lunes al sol*), a gritty, Ken Loach-ish take on the trials and tribulations of a group of unemployed men in the North, would have done quite so well had it not won the Golden Shell at the San Sebastián festival and been Spain's nomination for the Foreign-Language Oscar. Driven by yet another stunning performance from the increasingly chameleon-like Javier Bardem, the film was this year's demonstration that popular and critical success, though increasingly divorced, are not always separate bedfellows.

At the top end of the box-office, it's not all quality and originality, though. Jesus Bonilla's utterly lame local comedy **Moscow Gold** (*El oro de Moscú*), by virtue of a star-studded local cast including Santiago Segura, has generated mucho oro, as has Jaume Balagueró's long-awaited, technically flashy but hollow English-language chiller *Darkness*, which starred Anna Paquin and was quickly snapped up by Dimension.

Thinking equally big but performing below expectations were thesp Jordi Molla's overblown millennial media satire **We Are Nobody** (*No somos nadie*), Alex de la Iglesia's underrated spaghetti Western spoof/homage **800 Bullets** (*800 balas*), which featured one of the performances of the year from veteran Sancho Gracia as an ageing stuntman, and Anton Reixa's debut **The Carpenter's Pencil** (*El lápiz del carpintero*), a lush Civil War romancer which utterly failed to click.

The sincerest form?

Depressingly little work engages with political or social reality. Instead, the last 12 months have seen an avalanche of US-influenced genre work, often by first-time hopefuls working with hopelessly limited budgets (in 2002, only one film in 20 was budgeted at €5m or more, and forthcoming budget levels are splitting between high-end product with large overseas ambitions, and cheapo fare, the mid-range pics looking likely to be consigned to oblivion).

This obsession with imitation gave rise to several movies, which, naming no names, should never have been made. Among genre work that did stand out there were Norberto López Amado's **They're Watching Us** (*Nos miran*), a parallel-worlds psycho-chiller debut starring Carmelo Gómez as a cop breaking down; **Two Tough Guys** (*Dos tipos duros*) by Juan Martínez Moreno, a crowd-pleasing, ketchup-splattered kidnap spoof; Ramón de España's neo-realist black comedy **Kill Me Tender** (*Haz conmigo lo que quieras*), whose appeal is only enhanced by the fact that it features Ingrid Rubio (Saura's *Taxi*) carrying a whip and wearing high heels; and Xavier Villaverde's underrated contempo ghost yarn **Thirteen Bells** (*Trece campanadas*).

Luis Tosar, left, and Javier Bardem in **Mondays in the Sun**

EL SEPTIMO DIA
(*literally,* **The Seventh Day**)
[*Drama, 2003*] Script: Ray Lóriga. Dir: Carlos Saura. Prod: Lola Films.
Controversial recreation of an early 1990s bloody family feud in rural eastern Spain.

HECTOR
[*Drama, 2003*] Script: Gracia Querejeta, David Planell. Dir: Querejeta. Phot: Angel Iguacel. Players: Nilo Mur, Adriana Ozores, Damián Alcázar, Unax Ugalde. Prod: Elías Querejeta PC/DeAPlaneta/Ensueño Films.
Father-son reunion drama from the dependable Querejeta stable.

INCAUTOS
(*literally,* **Incautious**)
[*Thriller, 2003*] Script: Miguel Bardem, Carlos Martin. Dir: Bardem. Phot: Thierry Arbogast. Players: Ernesto Alterio, Victoria Abril, Federico Luppi, Manuel Alexandre. Prod: Alquimia Cinema.
Four grifters face off in Bardem's third solo feature.

LA MALA EDUCACION
(*literally,* **Bad Education**)
[*Thriller, 2003*] Script and Dir: Pedro Almodóvar. Phot: José Luis Alcaine. Players: Gael García Bernal, Fele Martínez, Javier Cámara. Prod: El Deseo.

CRIMEN FERPECTO
(*literally,* **Ferpect Crime**)
[*Comedy, 2003*] Script: Alex de la Iglesia, Jorge Guerricaecheverria. Dir: de la Iglesia. Players: Guillermo Toledo. Prod: Pánico Films.
Hitchcock spoof about a shop assistant who accidentally kills his boss.

LA VIDA QUE TE ESPERA
(*literally,* **The Life Which Awaits You**)
[*Rural drama, 2003*] Script: Manuel Gutiérrez Aragón, Angeles González-Sinde. Dir: Gutiérrez Aragón. Phot: Gonzalo Berridi. Players: Juan Diego, Luis Tosar, Marta Etura. Prod: Continental

Producciones/Tornasol Films.
Neighbours' dispute brings
tragedy to a village in
northern Spain.

*Vincente Romero, left, and Alex
Brendemühl in* **The Hours of the Day**

LAS HORAS DEL DIA
(**The Hours of the Day**)
*[Drama, 2003] Script: Enric
Rufas, Jaime Rosales. Dir:
Rosales. Phot: Oscar Duran.
Players: Alex Brendemühl,
Agata Roca, Maria Antonia
Martinez. Prod: Fresdeval
Films/In Vitro Films.*
Idiosyncratic debut from Jaime
Rosales charts the humdrum life
of a murderer; FIPRESCI prize
winner at Cannes.

TANGER (*literally,* **Tangiers**)
*[Drama, 2003] Script: Juan
Madrid, based on his own novel.
Dir: Madrid. Phot: Federico
Ribes. Players: Jorge Perugorría,
Ana Fernández, José Manuel
Cervino. Prod: World
Entertainment/Abaco Movies.*
Hard-hitting social drama.

TE DOY LOS OJOS (*literally,*
I Give You My Eyes)
*[Drama, 2003] Script: Iciar
Bollain, Alicia Luna. Dir:
Bollain. Phot: Carles Gusi.
Players: Luis Tosar, Laia Marull,
Candela Peña, Rosa María
Sardá. Prod: La Iguana/Alta
Producción.*
Bollain's long-awaited third
feature examines the difficulty of
escaping from domestic violence.

MAR ADENTRO (**Out to Sea**)
*[Drama, 2003] Script: Alejandro
Amenábar, Mateo Gil. Dir:*

Away from genre, we saw Álvaro García-Capelo's *Short Cuts*-
inspired **Dog Days** (*Canícula*), which unfairly sank without trace;
Nobody's Life (*La vida de nadie*) by Eduardo Cortes, an invented-
identity drama starring José Coronado; Jaime Rosales's chilling-
because-unsensational serial killer study, **The Hours of the Day**
(*La horas del día*), which came from left field to win the FIPRESCI
jury's prize at Cannes 2003; and **Silvia's Gift** (*El regalo de Silvia*)
by Dionisio Pérez Galindo, a morbid-sounding but actually strongly
affecting look at the lives of three people who have received organ
transplants from a teenage suicide. Altogether more upbeat was
Pablo Berger's somewhat overrated debut, *Torremolinos 73*,
which looks at a Spanish couple's early 1970s flirtation with the
porn industry.

Other young(-ish) names supplied some superior work. Marc
Recha's French-language **Where Is Madame Catherine?** (*Les
mains buides*) examines the impact of the death of an old woman
on a rural community and was his most accessible effort to date.
Best thriller of the year was Enrique Urbizu's box-office-friendly
Box 507 (*Caja 507*), in which noir meets contemporary Spain.
Urbizu, for too long an undervalued treasure in Spain, was also
responsible for the oblique, off-beat brother buddy piece **Life
Marks** (*La vida mancha*).

Miguel Hermoso, another director who deserves wider exposure,
delivered the elegant **The End of a Mystery** (*La luz prodigiosa*),
which imagines what would have happened had poet Federico
García Lorca not died during the Civil War, and which features
a magnificent performance from vet Alfredo Landa. The relationship
of Spain's past to its present was also dealt with in David Trueba's
third, **Salamina Soldiers** (*Soldados de Salamina*). Based on
a best-selling novel, the film looks at one woman's documentary
approach to the Spanish Civil War, and the result, easily Trueba's
best film to date, is a powerful exploration of memory and desire.

Experience preferred, but not essential

Vet helmers performed with variable success. The comeback of
the year was Basilio Martín Patino, whose **Octavia** (which he says
will be his last) was a throwback to a time when cinema could
be intellectually challenging. Pedro Olea's couples-in-crisis drama
Stormy Weather (*Tiempo de tormenta*) drew a career-best
performance from Jorge Sanz, while Antonio Giménez-Rico's
thriller **Hotel Danubio** lovingly recreated the atmosphere of noir
Hollywood. A more disappointing adaptation was Fernando
Colomo's slight **South from Granada**, an English-language take on
the 1920s experiences of Brit novelist Gerald Brenan in Andalucía.

Some of the year's best works were documentaries, with some, unusually, settling into arthouse theatres for decent runs. One of 2002's few in-cinema glimpses of politics was Pere Joan Ventura's potent **The Iguazú Effect** (*El effecto Iguazú*), shot during the lengthy Madrid protest by a group of former Telefónica employees. Catalan helmer Ventura Pons looked affectionately at the life of legendary Barcelona musician Gato Pérez in **El Gran Gato**, while Ana Diez, in **Galíndez**, took a hard, if one-sided, look at an obscure 1950s political exile in the US. An even more obscure figure – the poet, boxer and Dadaist Arthur Cravan, Oscar Wilde's nephew – was the subject of the year's best Spanish documentary, Isaki Lacuesta's wild and wonderful **Cravan vs Cravan.**

The Spanish industry continues to be testosterone-driven. A brief, unofficial recap reveals that only four features directed by women were released in 2002. Laura Maña's **Killing Words** (*Palabras encadenadas*) had Dario Grandinetti (*Talk to Her*) and Goya Toledo (*Amores perros*) facing off in a Scheherazade-like thriller. María Ripoll's supernatural thriller **Utopia**, starring this year's fastest-rising thesp, Argentina's Leonardo Sbraglia, took a typically male genre and played some interesting games, while Chus Gutierrez's **Poniente** powerfully confronted the problem of immigration and racism in the Spanish south. Female standout of the year, though, is Isabel Coixet's affecting, English-language **My Life without Me**, in which Sara Polley learns she's going to die and makes her plans accordingly. Four hits out of four for Spanish women film-makers in 2002. Industry, please take note.

JONATHAN HOLLAND, a teacher and journalist, is *Variety's* film critic in Spain.

Spain's Goya Awards 2003 are listed on p.306

Alberto Ferreiro, right, in Civil War drama **Salamina Soldiers**

Harvey Keitel in **Galíndez**

Amenábar. Players: Javier Bardem. Prod: Sogecine, Himenóptero.
Real-life story about controversial right-to-die hero Ramón Sampedro marks generic departure for wunderkind Amenábar.

Quotes of the Year

"What is really lacking in Spanish cinema is greater freedom to do what you really want to do, not just what is fashionable."
GONZALO SÚAREZ, *veteran director.*

"In the US, they work with greater resources, but you have to pay a price: you have to sell your soul. But my soul is very cheap, and I'm willing to sell."
ALEX DE LA IGLESIA, *director*

"It's easier to get on television by showing your left testicle than it is by talking about your new film or book."
DAVID TRUEBA, *director of* Salamina Soldiers.

Sri Lanka Amarnath Jayatilaka

The Year's Best Films

Amarnath Jayatilaka's selection:

Little Angel
(Dir: Somaratne Dissanayake)
Thirst of Fire
(Dir: Jayantha Chandrasiri)
Shadows of White
(Dir: Sunil Ariyaratne)
My Left Hand
(Dir: Linton Semage)

Recent and Forthcoming Films

SUDU SEVANALI
(Shadows of White)
[Drama, 2002] Script, Dir and Prod: Sunil Ariyaratne. Players: Irangani Serasinghe, Wasanthi Chathurani, Linton Semage, Roshan Pilapitiya.

PUNCHI SURANGANAVI
(Little Angel)
[Meldodrama, 2002] Script and Dir: Somaratne Dissanayake. Players: Tharaka Hettiarachchi, Nithyavani Kandasamy, Sriyantha Mendis, Dilani Abeywardena. Prod: Renuka Balasooriya.

IRA MEDIYAMA (August Sun)
[Drama, 2003] Script and Dir: Prasanna Vithanage. Phot: M. D. Mahindapala. Players: Peter D'Almeida, Nimmi Harasgama, Namal Jayasinghe, Mohamed Rafiulla. Prod: Soma Edirisinghe for EAP Films & Theatres Ltd. Over two scorching days, three different groups of people face totally different experiences after terrorist attacks.

AGNIDAHAYA (Thirst of Fire)
Script, Dir and Prod: Jayantha Chandrasiri. Players: Jackson

In 2002, which marked the 30th birthday of the National Film Corporation, the film industry experienced significant developments, mostly as a result of the end of the disastrous state monopoly and the privatisation of film distribution in 2000-01. The long overdue modernisation of the nation's cinemas has been spearheaded by EAP Films & Theatres Ltd., which as producer, exhibitor, importer and distributor is now the country's leading film company. It owns 15 theatres, including the spectacularly refurbished Savoy in Colombo, which reopened with *Attack of the Clones.*

EAP also took a giant step forward as a producer. Having hitherto made lowest common denominator movies, it has gone into production on the costliest Sinhala film ever, a drama about terrorism and its victims called *August Sun* (*Ira mediyama*), directed by Prasanna Vithanage, the leading member of the new generation.

In the year under review, 24 Sinhala movies were released, of which six belonged to the *Kama Rella* "sex wave" and flopped badly at the box-office. Part of the current comedy boom, **Parliament Jokes** (the directorial debut of matinee idol Ranjan Ramanayaka) was a record-breaking hit, selling more than 1.4 million tickets in its first 100 days on release. It follows three farmer's sons – clad in spun cloth, lazy and engaged in petty thefts in their village – on a path to becoming MPs, a path laid with corruption, impersonation, intimidation, lies and thuggery.

Written, produced and directed by Sunil Ariyaratne, with a score by the talented Rohana Weerasinghe, **Shadows of White** (*Sudu sevanali*) is woven around a typical Sinhala family in 1848. Sudu Banda, a priest, returns to his home village after fighting the British alongside Weera Puran Appu, and finds that his mother has lost her mind, his elder brother, Heen Banda, is languishing in jail and Heen's wife and two children are destitute. The film follows the families' conflicts, heartaches and despair.

Language barriers

Written and directed by Somaratne Dissanayake, **Little Angel** (*Punchi suranganavi*) is set in 1983, when ethnic tensions between Tamils and Sinhalese were rising. Sampath is a 10-year-old

Sinhalese boy abandoned by his mother and deprived of love by his rich, business-obsessed father, Perera. The family's most devoted servant, Velu, a Tamil who doesn't understand much Sinhalese, worries about Samapath. When he brings his 8-year-old daughter, Sathya, to work alongside him she becomes friendly with Sampath, teaching him Tamil words – to the annoyance of Perera. But doctors advise him that the friendship is good for the boy. This was the first local film to promote national integration and only the second to use both national languages, and it became the second-highest grossing film of 2002.

Linton Semage's **My Left Hand** (*Mage vam atha*) is the story of a Colombo pickpocket, Kamal (Semage), who one day steals a man's wallet and finds that it contains a photo of his wife. Suddenly jealous, he does not tell his wife of his discovery and decides to hunt for the wallet's owner. The search makes him an introverted character, dogged by fear and suspicion, and he ultimately discovers that the photo belonged to his brother-in-law, who kept it as a memento of his sister, whom he'd not seen since her marriage.

Jayantha Chandrasiri followed up several TV dramas with his feature debut, **Thirst of Fire** (*Agnidahaya*). Set 200 years ago, in the Kandyan Kingdom, it is the story of Punchirala (Jackson Anthony), a village leader who holds immense power because of his skills as a shaman and exorcist, and his brutish assistant, Sobana (Kamal Addaraarachchi). Sobana falls in lust with Kirimenike (Yasodha Wimaladhrma), a petite village belle, and murders her husband, Herath, so that he can have her – an act which stokes his dangerous rivalry with Punchirala. The director strikingly portrays the fiery sexual passions raging within these characters without resort to explicit visuals.

AMARNATH JAYATILAKA is a film-maker and one of the leading film personalities in Sri Lanka. His latest film is *A Drop in the Reign of Terror* (2003).

Anthony, Kamal Addaraarachchi, Yasodha Wilmaladharma.

THAHANAM GAHA
(Forbidden Tree)
[Drama, 2002] Script and Dir: Christy Shelton Perera. Phot: Andrew Jayamanna. Players: Anoja Weerasinghe, Sunetra Saratchandra, Asoka Peries and Dilhani Ekanayaka. Prod: Ranjith Perera for Winson Films.
A daughter witnesses her mother having sex with her uncle.

SALELU WARAMA
(Web of Love)
[Drama, 2002] Script and Dir: Vasantha Obesekara. Phot: Jayantha Gunawardhana. Players: Sangeetha Weeraratne, Kamal Addaraarachchi, Pradeep Senanayake. Prod: Soma Edirisinghe for EAP Films & Theatres Ltd.
Tragic tale of star-crossed lovers on a university campus.

MAGE VAM ATHA
(My Left Hand)
Script: Priyankara Ratnayake. Dir and Prod: Linton Semage. Phot: M. D. Mahindapala. Players: Semage, Dilhani Ekanayake, Sarath Kothalawala, Mahendra Perera, Saumya Liyanage.

WEKANDA WALAWWA
(Mansion by the Lake)
[Drama, 2003] Script: Somaweera Senanayake, based on Chekhov's The Cherry Orchard. Dir: Lester James Peries. Phot: K. A. Dharmasena. Players: Malini Fonseka, Vasanthi Chathurani, Ravindra Randeniya, Sanath Gunathilaka. Prod: Chandran Rutnam, Asoka Perrea for Taprobane Pictures.
Selected by the Cannes Film Festival 2003 as a special Tribute to Peries.

Mansion by the Lake: *screened at Cannes as a tribute to Lester James Peries*

Sweden Bengt Forslund

The Year's Best Films

Bengt Forslund's selection:

Lilya 4-ever
(Dir: Lukas Moodysson)
Everyone Loves Alice
(Dir: Richard Hobert)
The Guy in the Grave Next Door (Dir: Kjell Sundvall)
My Name Was Sabina Spielrein
(Docu. Dir: Elisabeth Márton)
The Bricklayer
(Docu. Dir: Stefan Jarl)

Recent and Forthcoming Films

ALLA ÄLSKAR ALICE
(Everyone Loves Alice)
[Drama, 2002] Script and Dir: Richard Hobert. Phot: Lars Crépin. Players: Lena Endre, Marie Richardsson, Mikael Persbrandt. Prod: Sonet Film.

BLODSBRÖDER
(Bloodbrothers)
[Drama, 2003] Script: Grace Maharaj, Liam Norberg, Daniel Fridell. Dir: Fridell. Phot: Johan Bergman. Players: Liam Norberg, Reine Brynolfsson, Marie Richardsson, Thorsten Flinck. Prod: Public Art.

BÄST I SVERIGE
(Marcello & Fatima)
[Drama, 2002] Script: Peter Birro. Dir: Ulf Malmros. Phot: Mats Olofson. Players: Ariel Petsonk, Zamand Hägg, Michael Nyqvist, Anna Pettersson, Ralph Carlsson. Prod: Götafilm.

DETALJER (Details)
[Relationship drama, 2003] Script: Lars Norén, Jonas Frykberg. Dir: Kristian Petri. Phot: Göran Hallberg. Players:

As regards feature films, 2002 was, like the previous year, rather ordinary, so it is not surprising that the market share for Swedish movies has fallen from 25% in 2000 to 17% in 2002 – a sad situation, especially when we compare Sweden to the performance of local films in our neighbour, Denmark.

Artistically, only one film gained international acclaim: **Lilya 4-ever** (*Lilja 4-ever*), by Lukas Moodysson, his third film and his third success. All his films are remarkably different, but still have an *auteur* touch. As he is profiled this year as a Director of the Year, I will here just mention that *Lilja 4-ever* is a black story – based on a real event – about the trafficking of young girls from Eastern Europe, conned into coming to Sweden just to be used as prostitutes. Though it is a tough and pessimistic film it was seen by over 300,000 people in Sweden and was a triumph at the Golden Bug Gala in January 2003, winning five of the main awards.

The public hit of the year was **The Guy in the Grave Next Door** (*Grabben i graven bredvid*), by Kjell Sundvall, always a reliable and professional director. The film is based on a popular novel and is part romantic comedy, part realistic drama. It shows what

Elisabet Carlsson and Michael Nyqvist in **The Guy in the Grave Next Door**

happens when an ordinary farmer and an intellectual librarian fall in love, and is a simple but interesting story, extremely well played by Elisabeth Carlsson and Michael Nyqvist, voted Best Actor at the Golden Bugs.

The third most important movie was Richard Hobert's family drama **Everyone Loves Alice** (*Alla älskar Alice*). In a way it is just another drama about a divorce and 'the other woman', but this time told from the child's perspective, since Alice, the couple's daughter, is the leading character. Lena Endre, the second wife in the film (and, incidentally, of the director) leads a uniformly excellent cast and *Everyone Loves Alice*'s public appeal extended beyond Sweden, winning it the Hollywood European Award at the Hollywood Film Festival, in competition with 20 other titles.

The Reunion (*Klassfesten*), from comedy team Måns Herngren and Hannes Holm, dealt with a high school's 20th anniversary reunion and, though not very original, provided good entertainment while it lasted. More original was Peter Schildt's **Suxxess**, a sharp satire of the hyper-competitive modern business world, set in dot.com company Omniville. It was probably too elaborate and had too many principal characters to grab the public's attention. Meanwhile a new trend has been low-budget films shot on DV by small groups of young people, but the initial results have been woeful and since the trend is likely to continue let us hope it does so with better scripts and more talented directors.

Documentaries as entertainment

The last year was a strong one for a Swedish speciality: long documentaries. The team responsible a few years ago for *Lighthouse* returned with **Tokyo Noise**, described as "a journey into the past, the present and the future of a megacity". The elaborate sound design by Johan Söderberg won a special Golden Bug,

Stefan Jarl, our best-known documentary film-maker, made a portrait of the actor Thommy Berggren, **The Bricklayer** (*Muraren*). Berggren is well known from many Bo Widerberg films, including *Elvira Madigan*, and was for years a leading actor at the Royal Dramatic Theatre. What is less widely known, until this film, is that he is also a magnificent storyteller. I have seldom smiled and laughed at a documentary as I did with this one.

The very best documentary, to my taste, was the docu-drama **My Name Was Sabina Spielrein** (*Mitt namn var Sabina Spielrein*), by Hungarian-born director Elisabet Márton. The psychoanalyst Sabina Spielrein has long been forgotten, though she was close to both Freud and Jung, and an important scientist in her own

Pernilla August, Michael Nyqvist, Jonas Karlsson, Rebecca Hemse. Prod: Göta Film.

ELINA – SOM OM JAG INTE FANNS (Elina)
[Drama, 2003] Script: Kjell Sundstedt. Dir: Klaus Härö. Phot: Jarkko T. Laine. Players: Natalie Minnevik, Maijala Marjaana, Bibi Andersson, Henrik Rafaelsen. Prod: Filmlance International/Kinoproduction Oy (Finland).

GRABBEN I GRAVEN BREDVID (The Guy in the Grave Next Door)
[Drama, 2002] Script: Sara Heldt. Dir: Kjell Sundvall. Phot: Philip Ögaard. Players: Michael Nyqvist, Elisabeth Carlsson. Prod: Filmlance International.

KLASSFESTEN (The Reunion)
[Comedy, 2002] Script and Dir: Måns Herngren, Hannes Holm. Phot: Göran Hallberg. Players: Björn Kjellman, Inday Ba, Cecilia Frode. Prod: S/S Fladen.

Peter Widing

Torkel Petersson in **Kops**

KOPPS (Kops)
[Comedy, 2003] Script: Josef Fares, Mikael Håfström, Vasa. Dir: Fares. Phot: Aril Wretblad. Players: Fares Fares, Torkel Petersson, Sissela Kyle, Göran Ragnerstam, Eva Röse. Prod: Memfis Film.

MIFFO
[Romantic drama, 2003] Script: Malin Lagerlöf. Dir: Daniel Lind Lagerlöf. Phot: Olof Johnson.

Players: Jonas Karlssons, Livia Millhagen, Ingvar Hirdwall. Prod: Hägring AB.

Eva Österberg in **My Name Was Sabina Spielrein**

MITT NAMN VAR SABINA SPIELREIN (My Name Was Sabina Spielrein)
[Drama-documentary, 2002]
Script: Elisabeth Márton, Signe Maehler, Yolande Knobel. Dir: Márton. Phot: Robert Nordström, Gunnar Källberg, Sergej Jurizditskij. Players: Eva Österberg, Lasse Almebäck. Prod: Idé Film.

MURAREN (The Bricklayer)
[Portait documentary, 2002]
Script and Dir: Stefan Jarl. Phot: Halldor Gunnarsson, Joakim Johansson, Per Källberg, Viggo Lundberg. Featuring: Thommy Berggren, actor. Prod: Stefan Jarl AB.

NÄRVARANDE (Presence)
[Portrait documentary, 2003]
Script, Dir and Phot: Jan Troell. Featuring: Georg Oddner, photographer. Prod: Athenafilm.

right. Márton researched this project for years in Russia, Austria and Germany, and the result is stunning from artistic and scientific viewpoints.

Gifts and rifts

The donation of the year was the Bergman Foundation's decision to give all his scripts, letters, diaries and amateur films, from his childhood to the present, to the Swedish Film Institute – material that is sure to be of great use to future film, theatre and television historians. The protest of the year came from the directors Vilgot Sjöman and Claes Eriksson, who were up in arms against the commercial channel TV4 for inserting commercial breaks (ads for jeans, sanitary napkins, etc.) into their feature films. The protest was followed up by other directors, with Bergman to the fore, and at press time TV4 was facing a class action from the film-makers for copyright infringement.

On the industry front, Klas Olofsson, head of Sandrew Metronome, the second biggest film company in Sweden, and former head of the Film Institute, has retired and been succeeded by Morten Kongrød from Shipsted, Norway's leading media group.

In late January 2003, Klaus Härö's excellent children's movie **Elina** (Elina – som om jag inte fanns), about a troubled 9-year-old village girl, became a prize winner in the children's sections of both Berlin and Montreal. The following week, Josef Fares (Jalla! Jalla!) had a new local hit with his humorous **Kops** (Kopps), about the police who fake a crime wave to stave off the imminent closure of their station in a sleepy, crime-free town. It was quickly optioned for a remake by Adam Sandler's Hollywood company. In March 2003 came a beautiful new documentary from Jan Troell, **Presence** (Närvarande), a portrait of legendary Swedish photographer Georg Oddner.

ONDSKAN (Evil)
[Drama, 2003] Script: Hans Gunnarsson, Mikael Håfström. Dir: Håfström. Phot: Peter Mokrosinski. Players: Andreas Wilson, Linda Zilliacus, Henrik Lundström, Gustaf Skarsgård, Kjell Bergqvist. Prod: Moviola Film & Television.

PARADISET (Paradise)
[Thriller, 2003] Script: Colin Nutley, Johanna Hald. Dir: Nutley. Players: Helena Bergström, Suzanna Dilber, Örjan Rahmberg, Reine Brynolfsson. Prod: Sweetwater.

SUXXESS
[Comedy, 2002] Script: Christina Herrström, Peter Schildt. Dir: Schildt. Phot: Jens Fischer. Players: Peter Engman, Göran Ragnerstam, Stina Ekblad, Lennart Jähkel, Sven Wollter. Prod: GF Studios/Trelandsfilm/SVT Fiction.

TILLFÄLLIG FRU SÖKES (Seeking Temporary Wife)
[Romantic comedy, 2003] Script: Lisa Ohlin and Unlimited Stories. Dir: Ohlin. Phot: Marek Wieser. Players: Gustaf Hammarsten, Lotta Östlin Stenshäll, Irina Jonsson, Lars Wäringer. Prod: Illusion Film and Sonet.

TOKYO NOISE
[Documentary, 2002] Script and Dir: Kristian Petri, Jan Röed, Johan Söderberg. Prod: Charon Film/Manden med Cameraet/Chrystal Eye.

Quote of the Year

"If you can get a lorry, just come and pick up the shit."
INGMAR BERGMAN, *calling the head of the Swedish Film Institute, Åse Kleveland, before donating his personal archive.*

Former classmates get together in **The Reunion**

The Golden Bugs 2002

Film: *Lilja 4-ever.*
Direction: Lukas Moodysson *(Lilja 4-ever).*
Script: Lukas Moodysson *(Lilja 4-ever).*
Camera: Ulf Brantås *(Lilja 4-ever).*
Actress: Oksana Akinshina *(Lilja 4-ever).*

Actor: Michael Nyqvist *(The Guy in the Grave Next Door).*
Supporting Acress: Cecilia Frode *(The Reunion).*
Supporting Actor: Göran Ragnerstam *(Suxxess).*
Documentary: Muraren *(The Bricklayer).*
Foreign Film: The Man without a Past *(Finland).*

Tommy Berggren in **The Bricklayer,** *which won Best Documentary at the Golden Bugs 2002*

Switzerland Michael Sennhauser

The Year's Best Films

Michael Sennhauser's
selection:

Burning in the Wind
(Dir: Silvio Soldini)

Love Your Father
(Dir: Jacob Berger)

A Little Colour
(Dir: Patricia Plattner)

Foreign Country
(Dir: Luke Gasser)

On dirait le sud
(Dir: Vincent Pluss)

*Luke Gasser in **Foreign Country***

Recent and Forthcoming Films

A.K.A. Birdseye
*[Satirical drama, 2002] Script
and Dir: Michael Huber, Stephen
Beckner. Phot: Thomas
Wüthrich. Players: Stefan Kurt,
Fred Ward, Amy Hathaway,
Johnny Whitworth, Jaimz
Woolvett, Fred Koehler, Lisa
Blount. Prod: Dschoint Ventschr
Filmproduktion AG/SF
DRS/Teleclub AG.*

The Swiss continue to love films of all kinds, at the cinema and on DVD and video – all kinds but their own, one is tempted to conclude. Films produced in Switzerland took a market share of around 3% in 2002, which was only minimally higher than last year's 2.7%. It was, however, one single comedy, **Crisis in Havana** (*Ernstfall in Havanna*), that, at number 14 in the annual list, gave the Swiss their most successful native production for over a decade and accounted for almost half of all ticket sales for local films.

Directed by expert newcomer Sabine Boss, *Crisis in Havana* tells of the mishaps of Balsinger, a Swiss Embassy clerk in Havana, who, in the absence of his boss, tries to be of service to a visiting US Senator. Swiftly paced and deftly written, the film relies heavily on the popularity of Swiss political satirist and former TV comic Victor Giacobbo as the bungling clerk. Since Giacobbo is popular only in German-speaking Switzerland, the film took the lion's share of its gross there.

Two French-speaking productions from the minority parts of the country were the next most successful at the box-office. Patricia Plattner's **A Little Colour** (*Les petites couleurs*) stars France's Anouk Grinberg as a battered wife and hairdresser who finds refuge and eventually love in a dilapidated motel. Set as a sweetly coloured dramatic comedy and interspersed with glimpses of an overblown American Soap Opera which the heroine and her rescuing boss, the spirited hotel owner Mona, adore, *A Little Colour* aims straight for the heart and does not miss.

*Philippe Bas and Anouk Grinberg in **A Little Colour***

Despite its mainstream appeal, Plattner's film sold fewer than 16,000 tickets, (compared to *Ernstfall*'s 310,000), and fewer than 10,000 turned out for Silvio Soldini's **Burning in the Wind** (*La brûlure du vent*), an adaptation of Agota Kristof's novel *Hier*, which tells of Eastern European refugee Tobias, who falls obsessively in love with a former classmate who works with him in a watch factory and is married to another man. It is at once dark and precise, minutely carving out its characters and their secrets. Christoph Schaub's well-written and well-produced **Quiet Love** (*Stille Liebe*), a tragic love story between a deaf-mute nun and yet another fugitive from an Eastern European country, fared no better with the public.

There is a clear gap between the numbers a film can reach in the larger German-speaking part of Switzerland and the much smaller French-speaking areas. But when a well-made production like Jacob Berger's **Love Your Father** (*Aime ton père*), with father Gérard and son Guillaume Depardieu in the leads (as a successful writer and his frustrated son), fails to attract the public in France and Geneva, distributors understandably tend to reduce their marketing costs for the rest of the country.

Facts and pixels

It is still the documentaries that are the great strength of Swiss *auteurs*-producers, with hits like Friedrich Kappeler's **Mani Matter** (on a beloved Bernese chansonnier who died prematurely) or indefatigable Erich Langjahr's **Shepherd's Journey into the Next Millennium** (*Hirtenreise ins nächste Jahrtausend*), an impressive and meditative documentary on wandering (and of course disappearing) Swiss shepherds and their sheep.

And then, as in most countries, it is the increasingly prevalent guerrilla film-making (mostly, but not exclusively digital) that produces the surprises. One was Vincent Pluss' **On dirait le sud** which won the Swiss feature film prize 2003. Shot over two days on mini-DV, this lively comedy about recently divorced Jean-Louis' increasingly absurd attempts to win back his family had some scripted and some

ACCORDION TRIBE
[*Documentary*, 2003] Script: Stefan Schwietert, Stephan Settele. Dir: Schwietert. Phot: Wolfgang Lehner. Prod: maximage GmbH/FischerFilm.

AU SUD DES NUAGES
(*literally*, **South of the Clouds**) [*Drama*, 2003] Script: Jean-François Amiguet, Anne Gonthier. Dir: Amiguet. Phot: Hugues Ryffel. Players: Bernard Verley, François Morel, Maurice Aufaire. Prod: Bernard Lang AG/Zagora Films SA/King Movies.

Burning in the Wind

LA BRÛLURE DU VENT
(**Burning in the Wind**) [*Drama*, 2002] Script: Doriana Leondeff, Silvio Soldini. Dir: Soldini. Phot: Luca Bigazzi. Players: Ivan Franék, Barbara Lukesová, Ctirad Götz, Caroline Baehr, Cécile Pallas, Petr Forman, Zuzana Mauréry. Prod: Albachiara Spa/Vega Film AG/RAI Cinema/RTSI.

CHAOS AND CADAVERS
[Black comedy, 2003] Script:
Niklaus Hilber, Drew Bird. Dir:
Hilber. Phot: Tony Imi. Players:
Nick Moran, Keeley Hawes,
Steve Huison, Erich Vock.
Prod: Zodiac Pictures
International/Matador Pictures.

**DAS KAMEL, DER MARABUT
UND DAS MÄDCHEN**
(working title)
[Documentary, 2003] Script and
Dir: Ulrike Koch. Phot: Pio
Corradi. Prod: Pegasos Film/
Artcam (Netherlands)/SF DRS.

DES EPAULES SOLIDES
(literally, **Solid Shoulders**)
[Drama, 2002] Script: Ursula
Meier, Frédéric Videau. Dir:
Meier. Phot: Nicolas Guicheteau.
Players: Louise Szpindel, Jean-
François Stévenin, Guillaume
Gouix, Dora Jeema, Nina
Meurisse. Prod: PCT Cinéma
& Télévision SA/TSR/Arte/GMT
Productions/Need Productions.

**ELISABETH KÜBLER-ROSS –
DEM TOD INS GESICHT
SEHEN** (Elisabeth Kübler-Ross –
Facing Death)
[Documentary, 2003] Script and
Dir: Stefan Haupt. Phot: Jann
Erne, Christian Davi, Patrick
Lindenmaier. Prod: Fontana
Film/SF DRS.

**FORGET BAGHDAD – JEWS
AND ARABS – THE IRAQI
CONNECTION**
[Documentary, 2002] Script
and Dir: Samir. Phot: Nurith
Aviv. Prod: Dschoint Ventschr
Filmproduktion
AG/Tag/Traum/SF DRS/
Teleclub AG.

**GLOBI – DER
GESTOHLENE SCHATTEN**
(**Globi and the Stolen Shadows**)
[Animation, 2003] Script: Peter
Lawrence. Dir: Robi Engler.
Prod: Fama Film AG/Motion
Works/Iris Productions
SA/Impuls Home
Entertainment/SF DRS.

Dune Landenberg and Louis Johannides in **On dirait le sud**

improvised dialogue. The other surprise was **Foreign Country**
(*Fremds Land*) by Swiss rock singer-songwriter Luke Gasser. On a
minimal budget (but on film), and with mostly amateur actors, Gasser
shot the story of a Swiss peasant who is first pressed into Napoleon's
Russian army and then emigrates to become a scout and trapper in
the mythical Wild West. It is at once a homecoming story reminiscent
of *The Deer Hunter* and an emigrant tale that reminds us how closely
nineteenth-century Switzerland resembled other poor and over-
populated European countries like Ireland.

Alongside these two fresh and quick efforts were more laborious
and well-meaning productions that deservedly failed to reach
significant audiences, among them Rolando Colla's **Across the
Border** (*Oltre il confine*), a war veteran drama set in contemporary
Italy and starring Anna Galiena, and the ambitious but overblown
media-satire **A.K.A. Birdseye** directed by Stephen Beckner and
Michael Huber and starring reliable US actor Fred Ward.

With total attendance of 18.8 million (up from 17.1 million) and box-
office receipts of $199m (SFr261.9m, up 11.4% on 2001), 2002
was the best year in a long time for commercial distribution. The
four Swiss subsidiaries of the US majors (Warners, Buena Vista, UIP
and Fox) increased their market share by 12.5% to 69.5%, with the
remainder divided among some 25 independents, led by Monopole
Pathé Films (7.59% market share), Elite Film (6.86 %) and Filmcoopi
Zurich (5.78%). The average number of movie tickets sold per capita
reached 2.57 (more than in Germany or Austria) and while American
blockbusters account for two thirds of all tickets sold, there is an
encouragingly wide range of European film-making available in
Swiss cinemas.

MICHAEL SENNHAUSER is Film Editor at Swiss National
Radio SR DRS.

GUERRE SANS IMAGES – ALGERIE, JE SAIS QUE TU SAIS (War without Images – Algeria, I Know that You Know)
[Documentary, 2002] Script: Mohammed Soudani, Michael Von Graffenried. Dir: Soudani. Phot: Paul Nicol, Soudani. Prod: Amka Films/Productions SA/IMTM Film/RTSI.

JE SUIS TON PERE (I Am Your Father)
[Drama, 2003] Script, Dir and Phot: Michel Rodde. Players: Dominique Gubser, Bernard Montini, Attilio Sandro Palese. Prod: Stalker Films/TSR.

LITTLE GIRL BLUE
[Drama, 2003] Script: Anna Luif, Micha Lewinsky. Dir: Luif. Phot: Eeva Fleig. Players: Mark Kuhn, Sabine Berg, Bernarda Reichmuth, Michael Voita. Prod: Dschoint Ventschr Filmproduktion AG/SF DRS/Teleclub AG/SWR.

MANI MATTER – WARUM SYT DIR SO TRUURIG?
[Documentary, 2002] Script and Dir: Friedrich Kappeler. Phot: Pio Corradi. Prod: Catpics Coproductions AG/SF DRS.

MEIN NAME IST BACH, JOHANN SEBASTIAN BACH (working title)
[Historical drama, 2003]. Script: Dominique de Rivaz Knecht, Jean-Luc Bourgeois, Leo Raat. Dir: de Rivaz Knecht. Phot: Ciro Cappellari. Players: Vadim Glowna, Jürgen Vogel, Bernard Liegme, Gilles Tschudi.

Prod: CAB Productions SA/Pandora Filmproduktion GmbH/Twenty Twenty Vision/TSR/WDR – Westdeutscher Rundfunk Köln/Arte.

MISSION EN ENFER (Mission in Hell)
[Documentary, 2003] Script, Dir and Phot: Frédéric Gonseth. Prod: Frédéric Gonseth Productions/TSR/Almaz Film Productions SA.

NAMIBIA CROSSING
[Documentary, 2003] Script and Dir: Peter Liechti. Phot: Peter Guyer, Peter Liechti. Prod: Reck Filmproduktion GmbH/SF DRS.

NI PERDON NI OLVIDO (Neither Forgive nor Forget)
[Documentary, 2003] Script and Dir: Richard Dindo. Phot: Peter Indergand. Prod: Lea Produktion.

ON DIRAIT LE SUD
[Comedy, 2002] Script: Laurent Toplitch, Stéphane Mitchell, Vincent Pluss. Dir: Pluss. Phot: Luc Peter. Players: Jean-Louis Johannides, Céline Bolomey, Frédéric Landenberg, François Nadin, Gabriel Bonnefoy, Dune Landenberg. Prod: Intermezzo Films SA.

SKINHEAD ATTITUDE
[Documentary, 2003] Script and Dir: Daniel Schweizer. Phot: Denis Jutzeler. Prod: Dschoint Ventschr Filmproduktion AG/ADR Productions/Cameo Film/SF DRS/Arte/ZDF.

Quotes of the Year

"Co-production deals keep us alive. But... I have a feeling that we need to reconquer the Swiss market before we can start exporting. Products that hardly sell at home are even harder to sell abroad."
MARC WEHRLIN, *Chief of the Film Section of the Ministry of the Interior.*

"With all my successes, expectations are high and the knives are out."
ARTHUR COHN, *winner of six Oscars as a producer, on his fear with every film he sends into the Academy Awards race.*

Neugasse 6, P.O. Box, 8031 Zürich, Switzerland
Tel. ++41/1/272 53 30 Fax ++41/1/272 53 50
e-mail: info@swissfilms.ch www.swissfilms.ch

. . . swiss films

Syria Mohammed Rouda

Recent Films

SUNDUQ AL-DUNYA
(Sacrifices)
*[Drama, 2002] Script and Dir:
Oussama Mohammad. Phot:
Elso Roque. Players: Rafik Sbeil,
Maha Al Saleh, Ali Mohammad,
Nihal Al Khatib. Prod:
National Film Organisation
(Syria)/AMIP (France).*
The lives of three children born
to a large peasant family in a
remote Syrian village and
brought up according to strict
traditions and loyalties.

Peasant children in **Sacrifices**

QAMARAN WA ZEITOUNA
(Two Moons and an Olive)
*[Drama, 2002] Script and Dir:
Abdulatif Abdulhamid. Phot:
Youcef Bin Youcef. Players:
Asaad Foddah, Norman Asaad,
Hosam Eid. Prod: National Film
Organisation/Al Forsan Films.*
Two little boys and a girl are
severely punished by their
parents when they show
independent tendencies.

**MA YATLOBOHO AL
MOSTAMI'ON**
(Listeners' Requests)
*[Dark comedy, 2003] Script
and Dir: Abdulatif Abdulhamid.
Phot: Youcef Bin Youcef.
Players: Fayez Kuzok, Jamal
Feech, Mohsin Ghazi, Reem Ali,
Ibrahim Isa. Prod: National
Film Organisation.*

RO'AA HALIMA
(A Dreamlike Vision)
[Drama, 2003] Script and

Of the 110 cinemas open in Syria in the 1970s, fewer than 30 are still operating. They are in poor condition and, unable to compete with illegal videos and DVDs, have lost at least 70% of their audience to the pirates. The government issued a decree in 2002 allowing private companies to import foreign films, thereby ending the distribution monopoly of the National Film Organisation (NFO), the state body that has produced almost every Syrian film of the last 25 years. In return, the private sector must refurbish its cinemas and pay a hefty $2,250 tax on each imported title, so the new measure is unlikely to be of significant benefit to distributors and exhibitors.

On the production front, the NFO has been very busy since the appointment in 2001 of its general director, Muhammed Al-Ahmad, a scholar and critic well known in the Arab world. He is very keen to get a stagnant industry moving again, and under his tenure the NFO co-produced the first Syrian film ever to be selected officially at Cannes. **Sacrifices** (*Sunduq al-dunya*), shown in Un Certain Regard in 2002, is by veteran director Oussama Mohammad and demonstrates his personal style: dark in mood and colour. Its message is hard to grasp for international audiences, as the story reveals the impact of previous Arab-Israeli wars on a remote rural community, with a symbol in every name and plot twist.

The NFO also co-produced **Two Moons and an Olive** (*Qamaran wa zeitouna*) by Abdulatif Abdulhamid, the most prolific of today's Syrian directors. This is another look at daily life in a remote village, where ancient methods of teaching leave their scars on two boys and a little girl (whose nicknames give the film its title). There are a number of films in production in 2003-04 and concerted efforts continue to turn the small Damascus Film Festival into a larger, more international event. The sooner the NFO realises the vast opportunities that lie ahead if the industry is freed from some of its excessively strict regulation, the better it will be for all sectors.

*Dir: Waha Al Rahib. Phot:
Mark Colin. Players: Salim Sabri,
Nadin Salama, Reem Ali,
Waha Al Rahib. Prod: National
Film Organisation.*

Quote of the Year

"I love cinema. I don't think I can last a day without it."
MUHAMMED AL-AHMAD,
*director of the National
Film Organisation.*

Taiwan Stephen Cremin

The Year's Best Films

Stephen Cremin's selection:
Blue Gate Crossing
(Dir: Yee Chih-yen)
Better Than Sex (Dir: Su
Chao-pin & Apple Lee)
The Best of Times
(Dir: Chang Tso-chi)
Double Vision
(Dir: Chen Kuo-fu)
A Human Comedy
(Dir: Hung Hung)

Kao Meng-chieh and Wing Fan in
The Best of Times

Recent and
Forthcoming Films

BU SAN (Goodbye, Dragon Inn)
*[Comedy, 2003] Script and Dir:
Tsai Ming-liang. Phot: Liao Pen-
jung. Players: Lee Kang-sheng,
Chen Shiang-chyi, Yang Kuei-
mei, Miao Tien, Shih Jun.
Prod: Liang Hung-
chih/Homegreen Films.*
On closing night at the rundown Fu He cinema, outside
Taipei, a Japanese film-lover
encounters the ghosts of cinema
past when King Hu's titular
movie is projected.

BURNING DREAMS
*[Documentary, 2003] Dir:
Wayne Peng. Phot: He Nanhong.
Featuring: The Dream 52 Dance
School, Liang Yi, Yang Yang.
Prod: Wayne Peng/Pure
Films/Janet Yeo/10AM
Communications.*
Monochrome documentary

There is reason to be cautiously optimistic about the state of Taiwanese cinema in 2003. Audiences returned to local films in 2002, even as box-office figures remain shockingly low, a gross of just $30,000 (NT$1m) in Taipei being considered a success. Six local films reached that psychological milestone – six more than in 2001 – and Taiwanese film claimed 2% of the market, a twentyfold increase, against Hollywood's 95%.

There are other hopes on the horizon. The success of local television dramas has created a talent pool of emerging young stars for cinema, while the collapse of the local music industry has made pop stars more affordable as screen actors. Also, a new generation of directors and producers is entering the industry, with an understanding of international finance, local marketing and the need to tell good stories in an industry where the *auteur* system still dominates.

The first film to break $30,000 in 2002 was Su Chao-pin's directing debut **Better Than Sex** (*Ai qing ling yao*), co-directed by Apple Lee. Su, Taiwan's highest paid and most in-demand scriptwriter, moved behind the camera when he failed to find a director to take on his zany, anti-authoritarian youth comedy. He cast only popular musicians in the leading roles in the story of an over-endowed teenager, Lin (Michael "Quang Liang" Wong), who turns to pornography to come to terms with his body image.

In the tradition of contemporary East Asian melodrama, he uncovers a secret love story in his past that teaches him that love is "better than sex". On the periphery are a biker gang at war with a motorcycle cop, a mystical, 4,000-year-old knife and a Japanese television crew, all filmed in the red, amber and green of Taipei's omnipresent traffic lights. Su tested the limits of local censorship regulations with his low-brow irreverence, while moving his film at a breakneck pace that spoke to the teen generation.

Su also co-wrote the year's biggest domestic hits: Leon Dai's feature debut, *Twentysomething Taipei* (*Taipei wan jiu chao wu*), and Chen Kuo-fu's *Double Vision* (*Shuang tong*). **Twentysomething Taipei** (which took $168,000 locally and three times as much in Hong Kong) was marketed as a movie for "Generation Y", presenting a dynamic vision of life in the capital rarely seen on local

about the students and eccentric founder of a unique Shanghai school that teaches jazz and tap dance.

GONG ZHU CHE YE WEI MIAN (Princess in Wonder)
[Comedy, 2002] Script: Tsai Yi-chun, Ho Ping. Dir: Ho. Phot: Fisher Yu. Players: Ku Jung-kao, Lin Chia-li, Hsia Ching-ting, Tuan Chun-hao, Jerry Huang. Prod: Heat Films.
A woman with amnesia, a fake fortune-teller, a woman in red underwear and an unidentified corpse are caught up in a tale of confused identities and infidelity.

HEI GOU LAI LIAO (Black Dog Go Go!)
[Black comedy, 2003] Script: Christin Huang, Lee Jui-hsun, Hsu Kung-chin. Dir: Yin Chi. Phot: Chang Chan. Players: Tsai Chen-nan, Lee Bing-hui, Tai Bao, Shining 3 Girl. Prod: Chiu Shun-ching/Central Motion Picture Corporation.
A man in heavy debt goes to the local gangster for a quick loan, pretending that his father is dead... and has to stage a fake funeral.

KONG SHOU DAO SHAO NU ZU (Kung Fu Girls)
[Action comedy, 2003] Script and Dir: Alice Wang. Players: Anita Yuen, Lin Yi-chen, Stella Ng, An Yi-shuen, Suen Li-ting. Prod: Alice Wang/Core Image Production.
Four young women are trained in singing, dancing and martial arts to be the next big girl band. But after a disastrous press conference, they return to their normal lives, promising to meet in one year's time.

LIANG ZHU HU DIE MENG (The Dreams of Butterfly)
[Animation, 2003] Script: Tsai Ming-chin, Deng Ya-yan. Dir: Ming-chin. Art: Kao Wen-yu. Voices: Rene Liu, Elva Hsiao. Prod: Chiu Shun-ching/Central Motion Picture Corporation.
A girl born into a wealthy family disguises herself as a man so that

Leon Dai gets to grips with hoodlums in **Better Than Sex**

screens, a world of yuppie twentysomethings whose lives revolve around clubs, sex and drugs.

Supernatural thriller **Double Vision,** launched by Columbia Pictures Film Production Asia with a $500,000 marketing campaign, took local films back to the heady heights of *Crouching Tiger, Hidden Dragon,* with a Taipei gross of more than $1m, greater than all other local releases combined (but still only enough to place it at number 18 on the year's overall chart). At press time Su was preparing to direct teleportation thriller *Tunneling (Chuan sui),* from his own script.

Audiences also responded to teen dramas with attractive casts, notably Chang Tso-chi's **The Best of Times** (*Mei li shi guang*), which helped young Wing Fan cement his reputation as one of the best actors of his generation, and Yee Chih-yen's **Blue Gate Crossing** (*Lan se da men*), whose teenage stars, Chen Bo-lin and Guey Lun-mei, have since become youth icons.

Neo and realism

Despite the upward trend for local features, overall attendance is still in decline and 2003 has been a particularly difficult year, with the SARS crisis decimating box-office in April and May (even *The Matrix Reloaded* could not break $3m in Taipei), and Taiwanese films endured a very lean spell, with none of the seven features released between November 2002 and August 2003 grossing $30,000.

They included Cheng Wen-tang's **Somewhere over the Dreamland** (*Meng huan bu luo*) and Alex Yang's **The Trigger** (*Kou ban ji*). Both directors have a festival following and work primarily within the realist tradition pioneered by Edward Yang and Hou Hsiao-hsien. *Somewhere over the Dreamland* boasts a strong love story, striking cinematography and a haunting score. *The Trigger* employs sharp dialogue to express a multi-layered philosophy that explores violence and redemption.

On the other hand, Wu Mi-sen and Wang Ming-tai favour more visually expressive films. Wang, while employing a traditional narrative, basks **Brave 20 (Xian dou jiang)** in an orange glow to convey nostalgia for the 1980s of his youth. Wu Mi-sen's **Drop Me a Cat (Gei wo yi zhi mao)** creates its own surreal universe, using the camera with poetic freedom. Wu's imagery is among the most exciting to emerge in recent Taiwan film, even if his narrative needs time to mature.

The high concentration of releases in early 2003 does not reflect the plummet in production, as producers waited for delayed government subsidies under a new and confusing points system. Of the six films supported by the production fund, only Sylvia Chang's eagerly anticipated **20:30:40** was due to reach theatres in 2003. An encouraging sign for the future is the increasingly widespread use of digital technologies, supported by various government schemes. Veteran director Chu Yen-ping was the first to embrace this trend with a series of films shot on HD-CAM 24P, including **Kunfu Kid** (*Ye man xiao zi*) and **Let's Go Shaolin** (*Lai qu shaolin*).

Driving the momentum in film production are new companies with an international sensibility, including Flash Forward Entertainment, Good Film Co., Jin Chuan Pictures, Pandasia Entertainment Corporation and Three Dots Entertainment. With stronger producers accessing new sources of funding, directors keen to connect with audiences and advances in film-making technology, 2004 may be the year in which the promises of 2002 finally come to fruition.

STEPHEN CREMIN programmed Udine Far East Film Festival (2002-03), edited the Asian Film Library industry newsletter (2000-01) and directed the London Pan-Asian Film Festival (1998-99).

Taiwan's Golden Horse Awards 2002 are listed on p.306

she can study the classics, only to attract the attentions of a poor young scholar.

SHI QI SUI DE TIAN KONG (Formula 17)
[Comedy, 2003] Script: Rady Fu. Phot: Adili Chen. Dir: D. J. Chen. Players: Tony Yang, Duncan Lai, Jin Chin, Dada Liu, Jason Cheung. Prod: Aileen Li/Michelle Yeh/Three Dots Entertainment.
A pure-hearted teenage boy comes to Taipei from the South and falls in love with the capital's number one playboy. But what he yearns for is true love.

SHA REN JI HUA (My Whispering Plan)
[Suspense, 2002] Script: Lin Chun-hua. Dir: Arthur Chu. Players: Peggy Yang, Sherlly Hsieh, Hsu Shao-yang, Ko I-cheng, Liu Yi-ching. Prod: Arthur Chu/Oxygen Film.
Two schoolgirl friends – one plain, one pretty – drift apart when one befriends a homeless man. Her resentment fuels hateful drawings in a notebook, which mysteriously disappears...

TAIPEI ER YI (Taipei 21)
[Drama, 2003] Script and Dir:
Alex Yang. Phot: Lin Min-kou. Players: Tsai Hsin-hung, Lin Meng-chin. Prod: Mia Chen/Together Production/Chiu Shun-ching/Central Motion Picture Corporation.*
After seven years together, a twentysomething couple are still struggling to make ends meet. With her father in debt and her brother on the run from the police, the girlfriend has to make a difficult decision.

TIAN BIAN YI DUO YUN (Wayward Wind)
[Musical comedy, 2003] Script and Dir: Tsai Ming-liang. Phot: Liao Pen-jung. Players: Lee Kang-sheng, Chen Shiang-chyi, Yang Kuei-mei, Lu Yi-ching. Prod: Arena Films/Homegreen Films.

20:30:40
[Romantic drama, 2003] Script and Dir: Sylvia Chang. Players: Lee Sinje, Rene Liu, Sylvia Chang, Tony Leung, Anthony Wong, Richie Ren. Prod: Hsu Li-Kong/Tang Meng Co. Ltd.
Portrait of three very different women: a twentysomething musician leaving home for the first time, a thirtysomething flight attendant juggling her affairs and a fortysomething divorcee.

XUN ZHAO QIU DAO YU (Sanma)
[Short, 2003] Script and Dir: Chang Tso-chi. Phot: Peng De-cheng. Players: Tseng I-cheh, Chang Shun-wei, Chen Pei-chun, He Pei-chun, Chan Cheng-yun. Prod: Lu Shih-yuan/Chang Tso-Chi Film Studio.
Homage to Ozu, inspired by his final movie, *An Autumn Afternoon*. Teenagers go fishing in an artificial pond.

Quote of the Year

"We have plenty of directors... too many directors. We need more producers."
HOU HSIAO-HSIEN,
director, on the dilemma facing Taiwanese cinema.

Thailand Anchalee Chaiworaporn

The Year's Best Films

Anchalee Chaiworaporn's selection:

One Night Husband
(Dir: Pimpaka Tohveera)
Three (Dirs: Kim Jee-woon, Nonzee Nimibutr, Peter Chan)
February (Dir: Yuthlert Sippapak)

Recent and Forthcoming Films

BEAUTIFUL BOXER
[Drama, 2003] Script: Ekachai Uekrongtham, Desmond Sim. Dir: Uekrongtham. Phot: Choochart Nanti Thanyathada. Players: Asanee Suwan, Soraphong Chatree. Prod: GMM Pictures.

HIAN (The Mother)
[Horror, 2003] Script: Bandit Thongdee and Songsak Mongkolthong. Dir: Thongdee. Phot: Surachet Thongmee. Players: Intira Charoenpura, Aranya Namwong. Prod: Mongkol Cinema.

KUMPHAPHAN (February)
[Drama, 2003] Script and Dir: Yuthlert Sippapak. Phot: Prapope Duangpikool. Players: Sopidnapa Dabbaransi, Chahkrit Yamnam. Prod: GMM Pictures.

KHUEN RAI NGAO (One Night Husband)
[Suspense drama, 2003] Script and Dir: Pimpaka Towira. Phot: Christoph Janetzko. Players: Nicole Tereo, Siriyakorn Pukkawes. Prod: GMM Pictures.

MEKHONG FULL MOON PARTY

Thai cinema is at a crossroads. Statistics seem to indicate a thriving industry, with amazing increases in production (from 16 features in 2001 to 24 in 2002 and up to 50 in 2003) and market share for local films (from 23% in 2002 to 41% in the first quarter of 2003). In response to the boom, RS Films expanded into seven subsidiaries and several investors from other businesses plunged into the film industry hoping for a share of the pie.

But increased quantity does not mean improved quality. Many newcomers were given more opportunities just to make quick, cheap slapstick comedies and horror flicks. The exotic 'period' genre represented by *Suriyothai* has been replaced by the copycatting of recent hits. The local and international success of the transvestite basketball players in **Iron Ladies** was swiftly followed by the military rescue of transvestites in **Saving Private Tootsie**, transvestite cheerleader contests in **Cheerleader Queens,** the life of a transvestite fighter in **Beautiful Boxer** and then a sequel to the original *Iron Ladies,* **Iron Ladies II: The Early Years**. Horror is another popular genre, accounting for about a third of annual domestic releases.

Also, yet again, no Thai films reached Cannes in 2003, and in its centenary year the local industry was very aware that no Thai films had ever been officially selected for competition at Cannes, Berlin or Venice. This ongoing omission is largely attributable to the fact that there are so few Thai directors capable of making films that might tempt the leading festivals. Apart from Nonzee Nimibutr (*Jandara*), Penek Rattanaruang (*Monrak Transistor*), the Pang brothers, Wisit Sassanathieng (*Tears of the Black Tiger*) and Apichatpong Weerasethakul (*Blissfully Yours*), the rest of the directors lag a long way behind festival standards.

At press time, most of the arthouse names were at work on new projects: Nimibutr on *The Truth Untold* (*Buddha Didn't Tell*), Sassanathieng on *Hot Chili Sauce,* about a man whose keen sense of taste brings him a lifetime of love, pain, contentment, depression, jealousy and vengeance, and Weerasethakul on *Tropical Malady,* about a man-man relationship in which one turns into a monster and escapes into the jungle.

Thailand's busiest directors, the Pang brothers, chose commercial horror in **Omen** (*Sanghorn*), the story of three boys caught up in a deadly encounter with three strangers. The older Pang, Oxide, also directed the British-Japanese production of *The Tesseract*, adapted from Alex Garland's crime novel about three people travelling to Thailand and Manila.

Bak to the front

The most talked-about pic in early 2003 was the Thai martial arts vehicle **Ong-Bak**, directed by Pratya Pinklaew. Despite the thin storyline (a rural boy heads for the big city to retrieve the village's stolen Buddha icon), it caught international audiences' attention, thanks to the kick-boxing antics of stuntman-turned-actor Bhanom Jayiram, and became a huge hit at home, taking $2.8m (second only to *The Two Towers*).

Former stuntman Bhanom Jayiram leaps to box-office success in **Ong-Bak**

Penek Ratanaruang's Dutch-French-Japanese-Singapore-Thai co-production **Last Life in the Universe** (*Raknoi noinid mahasan*) had thrilling cinematography by Christopher Doyle and hot Japanese star Asano Tadanobu as the suicide-obsessed Kenji, who runs away to Thailand and spends three days with a Thai girl discovering love and life. It became the first Thai film to compete at Venice.

Thailand's first pair of sister directors, Nida Suthat Na Ayuthaya and Buranee Ratchaiboon, made the thriller **See-ui**, based on the true story of a Chinese serial killer in the early 1960s who ate his child victims' organs. Both sisters have long track records directing TV advertisements and *See-ui* is the first feature from commercials house Matching Motion Pictures, one of the companies taking their first steps into Thai cinema.

ANCHALEE CHAIWORAPORN is a freelance film critic based in Thailand. She has won local awards for Best Film Critic (2000) and Best Feature Writer (2002).

[Drama, 2003] Script and Dir: Jira Malikool. Phot: Somboon Piriyapakdeekul. Players: Anuchid Sapanphong, Tidarat Charoengchaichana. Prod: GMM Pictures.

ONG-BAK
[Martial arts action, 2003] Script and Dir: Pratya Pinklaew. Players: Ja Bhanomyeeram, Mam Jokmok. Prod: Mongkol Cinema.

RAKNOI NOINID MAHASAN (Last Life in the Universe)
[Drama, 2003] Script and Dir: Yuthlert Sippapak. Phot: Prapope Duangpikool. Players: Asano Tadanobu. Prod: Cinemasia.

SANGHORN (Omen)
[Thriller, 2003] Script and Dir: Oxide and Danny Pang. Phot: Decha Srimanta. Players: Kawee Tanjrarak, Apichet Kittikra. Prod: RS Film & Distribution.

SANIMSOI
[Drama, 2003] Script: Khanitha Sangkhathat. Dir: Jaroon Wattanasin. Phot: Suthat Intranupakorn. Prod: Five Star Entertainment.

THAWIPHOB (The Renaissance)
[Epic, 2003] Script and Dir: Surapong Pinijkhar. Player: Wanida Fawer, Rangsiroj Phanpheng. Prod: Film Bangkok.

Quote of the Year

"The new wave is coming, but we are not there yet."
APICHATPONG WEERASETHAKUL, *independent director, on contemporary Thai films.*

Tunisia Roy Armes

Recent Films

LE CHANT DE LA NORIA
(The Noria's Song)
[Drama, 2002] Script: Gérard
Martin and Abdellatif Ben
Ammar. Dir: Ben Ammar. Phot:
Christophe Paturange. Players:
Houyem Rassaa, Hichem
Rostom, Ahmed Hafiène, Ahmed
Snoussi, Jamila Chihi. Prod: Ben
Duran/IMF/ANPA (Tunisia)/Sam
Alta Films/Valentine
(France)/2M-Soread (Morocco).

Ridha Behi's The Magic Box

LA BOITE MAGIQUE
(The Magic Box)
[Drama, 2002] Script and Dir:
Ridha Behi. Phot: Yorgos
Arvanitis. Players: Marianne
Basler, Abdellatif Kechiche,
Hichem Rostom, Lotfi
Bouchnak, Mehdi Rebii. Prod:
Atlas Entertainment.

KHORMA (literally, Stupidity)
[Drama, 2002] Script and Dir:
Jilani Saadi. Phot: Gilles Porte.
Players: Mohamed Graya,
Mohamed Mourali, Ramzi Brari,
Hassen Khalsi, Lazhari Sbaï.
Prod: J S Productions.

EL-KOTBIA (The Bookstore)
[Drama, 2002] Script and Dir:
Nawfel Saheb-Ettaba. Phot:

Despite the frequent brilliance of its best film-makers, the overall situation of Tunisian cinema remains precarious. The distribution system, in particular, is in a parlous state, offering no chance of a profitable return to local producers. Government grants to film-makers are also comparatively low and as a result almost all Tunisian features are co-productions with Europe, made with one eye on French markets.

Nevertheless, there was a burst of releases in 2002, in time for the major North African film festival, the Journées Cinématographiques de Carthage (JCC), held every two years in Tunis, and Neïla Gharbi, editor of *SeptièmArt* magazine, gave an upbeat view of the situation in its 100th issue. The festival included new work by three established directors and debut films from two newcomers (with a third newcomer having her work shown abroad).

Abdellatif Ben Ammar first made a name for himself with a trio of features culminating in the masterly *Aziza* (1980), which looked at urban life through the eyes of a young orphan. Returning to direction after 22 years devoted largely to production activities, Ben Ammar offered **The Noria's Song** (*Le chant de la noria*), which lacks the stylistic originality of his early work and is yet another tale of self-discovery by middle-aged city dwellers, thanks to an exemplary trip to the underdeveloped South (the *noria* of the title is the traditional Arab water pump).

Since his debut in 1977 with his striking indictment of the impact of tourism on North Africa, *Hyena's Sun*, Rida Rehi's work has been aimed largely at an international audience. He used Egyptian melodramatic conventions (and Egyptian dialect) in *The Angels*, and French leading performers in *Bitter Champagne* and *Swallows Don't Die in Jerusalem*. His latest, **The Magic Box** (*La boîte magique*), is in a more personal, even autobiographical vein and tells of Raouf, a disillusioned film-maker in his forties. As he fulfils a commission from a European television channel, Raouf looks back at his own relationship with the cinema as a child.

Exploitation films

Nouri Bouzid has established himself as the leading creative figure in Tunisian cinema through his own features and the scripts he has written for others, including Ferid Boughedir and Moufida Tlatli. For his fifth feature, **Clay Dolls** (*Poupées d'argile*), Bouzid has chosen a subject familiar from the work of his Moroccan contemporaries Hakim Noury (*Stolen Childhood*) and Jillali Ferhati (*Reed Dolls*): the exploitation of young village children who are hired as maids by middle-class families living in the capital. The plot traces the attempts by the middle-man Omrane, accompanied by a new 9-year-old recruit, Fedhah (who makes the clay dolls of the title), to fulfil his obligations to the parents when one of his young charges absconds.

Three new film-makers, all born in the 1960s, also made their appearance in 2002, two of them at the JCC. **Khorma** (literally, *Stupidity*), directed by Jilani Saadi (b. 1962), tells the story of a young man, nicknamed Khorma, who takes over from his aged benefactor the role of dealing with the dead in their small town, with unexpected results. Nawfel Saheb-Ettala (b. 1959), who had studied film and media in Canada, made **The Bookstore** (*El-Kotbia*), another study of a return from abroad, this time by a young man broken by his overseas experiences. He finds comfort in the bookstore where he works and where he becomes emotionally involved with an older woman, the mother of the shop's owner.

A young man finds comfort in Nawfel Saheb-Ettala's **The Bookstore**

Nadia El Fani (b. 1960), who has worked extensively in production activities and is well-known for her short films, made her first feature, **Bedwin Hacker**. This is the somewhat confused tale of a young Tunisian woman who, from a base in the south Tunisian desert, begins to hack into European satellite broadcasts, inserting Arab slogans into sports programmes and other transmissions. ∎

Gilles Porte. Players: Hend Sabri, Ahmed El Hafienne, Martine Gafsi, Yadh Beji, Raouf Ben Amor, Mustapha El Adouani. Prod: Stratus Films/ANPA (Tunisia)/YMC Productions (France)/2M (Morocco).

BEDWIN HACKER
[Drama, 2002] Script and Dir: Nadia El Fani. Phot: Tarak Ben Abdallah. Players: Sonia Hamza, Tomer Sisley, Muriel Solvay, Xavier Desplas. Prod: Z'Yeux Noirs Movies/ERTT (Tunisia)/ 2M/Soread (Morocco)/Canal+ Horizons (France).

Clay Dolls

POUPEES D'ARGILE
(Clay Dolls)
[Drama, 2002] Script and Dir: Nouri Bouzid. Phot: Tarek Ben Abdallah and Gilberto Azevedo. Players: Hend Sabri, Ahmed Hafiane, Oumeyma Ben Hafsia, Lotfi Abdelli. Prod: Nouveau Regard Production (Tunisia)/Les Films de l'Observatoire (France)/Lamy Films (Belgium).

Quote of the Year

"I don't believe that the film-maker is bound to deal with so-called priority problems, though that may have been the case in the 1960s and 1970s."
ABDELLATIF BEN AMMAR, *veteran Tunisian director.*

Turkey Atilla Dorsay

The Year's Best Films

Atilla Dorsay's selection:
Distant
(Dir: Nuri Bilge Ceylan)
Innowhereland
(Dir: Tayfun Pirselimoglu)
The Fall of the Red Sultan
(Dir: Ziya Öztan)
Nine (Dir: Ümit Ünal)
He's in the Army Now
(Dir: Mustafa Altioklar)

Recent and Forthcoming Films

O SIMDI ASKER
(**He's in the Army Now**)
[Comedy, 2002] Script: Levent Kazak, Mustafa Altioklar. Dir: Altioklar. Phot: Soykut Turan. Players: Ozcan Deniz, Ali Poyrazoglu, Yavuz Bingöl, Mehmet Günsur, Pelin Batu. Prod: ANS Yapim Yayin A.S.

UZAK (Distant)
[Drama, 2002] Script, Dir, Phot and Prod: Nuri Bilge Ceylan. Players: Muzaffer Özdemir, Mehmet Emin Toprak, Zuhal Gencer Erkaya, Ebru Ceylan.

SIR COCUKLARI
(**Children of Secret**)
[Drama, 2002] Script and Dir: Aydin Sayman and Ümit Cin Güven. Phot: Eyüp Boz. Players: Firat Tanis, Özgü Namal, Mehmet Ali Alabora. Prod: Atadeniz Film/Tivoli Film.

GÖNLÜMDEKI KÖSK
OLMASA (House of Hearts)
[Drama, 2002] Script: Elizabeth Rygard, Yüksel Isik. Dir: Rygard. Phot: Hans Welin. Players: Mazlum Cimen, Sebnem Köstem, Menderes Samancilar, Serra

I n 2002, 17 Turkish films were commercially released, a 50% increase on 2001. There were some astonishing artistic and commercial successes and a significant number of debuts. The new government has shown serious interest in solving the problems of cinema, promising to stimulate production with greater state subsidy and tax breaks for investors.

In the popular comedy genre (films of little artistic value, but respectable on their own terms), first-timer Erdal Murat Aktas had a moderate hit with the first Egyptian-Turkish co-production for years, **Mummy on the Run** (*Mumya firarda*), a bizarre film about a mummy kidnapped in Egypt and brought to Turkey. Debutants Ercan Durmus and Hakan Haksun also did well with **Easy Money** (*Kolay para*), about a trio of charming bums in pursuit of fast cash.

Other newcomers chose more serious stories. Bülent Pelit's **When the Seagulls are Hungry** (*Martilar acken*) was an awful melodrama about a bunch of big-city outcasts. Aydin Sayman and Ümit Cin Güven co-directed **Children of Secret** (*Sir cocuklari*), about the lost children on the streets of Istanbul. It had a certain sincerity and warmth, but was too closely modelled on Italian neo-realism.

Painter and writer Tayfun Pirselimoglu's first feature, *Innowhereland* (*Hicbiryerde*, see *IFG 2003*), about a woman whose son suddenly disappears, successfully toured the festival circuit (Jury Grand Prix, Montreal 2002). Shot on digital, Ümit Ünal's debut, **Nine** (*Dokuz*), followed an investigation into the murder of a street girl. A formalist essay, it relied on breathtaking ensemble acting.

The popular comedy writer-actor Zeki Alasya had a busy year, completing both **The Russian Bride** (*Rus gelin*), about a gorgeous Russian athlete's forced marriage to a retired wrestler with a young heart, and **Ömerçip**, an effective parody exploiting the clichés of old Turkish melodramas. Already famous as a TV comic, Levent Kirca followed *The End* (*Son*) with **Where Is the Devil to It?** (*Seytan bunun neresinde?*), a rather obvious comedy about a TV personality lost in remote Anatolia. In **He's in the Army Now** (*O simdi asker*), Mustafa Altioklar (already responsible for huge hits such as *Istanbul under My Wings* and *Cholera Street*) tackled a sacred period of every Turkish man's life: military service. Sacred, but also apparently untouchable, because nobody had previously

Military service is mocked in **He's in the Army Now**

dared analyse it on film, let alone ridicule it. Altioklar's reward for doing so was the year's biggest box-office success.

Inquisitive visitors

Foreign directors have recently explored Turkish life. The Italian Alberto Rondelli shot **The Dervish** (*Dervis*), with mostly Turkish actors in a story about an adept of the great mystic, Mevlana. Denmark's Elisabeth Rygaard, also thrilled by Sufi music and philosophy, shot **House of Hearts** (*Gönlümdeki kösk olmasa*), which focuses on the problems of a small rural community coping with emigration in the 1970s. The Iraqi-Kurd Ravin Asfa shot **Yellow Days** (*Sari günler*), a burning story about ethnic conflict, seen through the eyes of a 12-year-old boy. All three films were interesting, but not entirely persuasive.

Two veterans returned after lengthy absences. Zeki Ökten, prestigious director of Yilmaz Güney scripts (*The Heard*, *The Enemy*), gave us a very old-fashioned, sentimental story about the disintegration and subsequent reunion of a big family in **My Rose** (*Gülüm*). Yusuf Kurcenli, once responsible for radical, socially conscious films, presented a love story about two elderly people trying to revive their affair 25 years on, *Unsent Letters* (*Gönderilmemis Mektuplar*). Both films had some commercial success but added nothing to the glory of their creators. Ziya Öztan, known for his successful TV serials, made an impressive historical epic, **The Fall of the Red Sultan** (*Abdulhamid düserken*), about the last days of Abdulhamid, one of the last chiefs of the Ottoman Empire.

Far away, so close

The year's greatest surprise came from Nuri Bilge Ceylan. He is one of the few directors who insist on working on a very small scale, with non-professional actors and practically no music, and is a genuine *auteur*, taking care of writing, directing, shooting and editing. His third feature, **Distant** (*Uzak*), is even more mature and

Yilmaz. Prod: Alfa Film/Zentropa Productions.
GÖNDERILMEMIS MEKTUPLAR (Unsent Letters)
[Drama, 2003] Script and Dir: Yusuf Kurcenli. Phot: Mehmet Aksin. Players: Türkan Soray, Kadir Ananir, Suna Selen, Melike Demirag, Aytac Arman. Prod: Film F Filmcilik/Tivoli Film.

GÜLÜM (My Rose)
[Drama, 2002] Script: Fatih Altinöz. Dir: Zeki Ökten. Phot: Ertunc Senkay. Players: Tarik Akan, Okan Bayülgen, Rutkay Aziz, Idil Firat, Güler Ökten. Prod: FilmPop.

RUS GELIN (The Russian Bride)
[Comedy, 2003] Script: Umur Bugay. Dir: Zeki Alasya. Phot: Eyüp Boz. Players: Alasya, Metin Akpinar, Tatsyana Tsvikevich, Murat Akkoyunlu. Prod: Bugay Film/Türk Film.

KARSILASMA (Encounter)
[Drama, 2003] Script: Ömer Kavur and Macit Koper. Dir: Kavur. Phot: Ali Utku. Players: Ugur Polat, Lale Mansur, Cetin Tekindor, Aytac Arman. Prod: Alfa Film/Objective Film Studio. A man comes to believe that he has been given a chance for a new life and that he can achieve all he ever dreamed of.

SARI GÜNLER (Yellow Days)
[Drama, 2002] Script and Dir: Ravin Asaf. Phot: Erdal Kahraman. Players: Sandra Steffl, Nur Sürer, Hama A. Chan, Hogar Tanya. Prod: Film Fabrik/Sözen Film.

MARTILAR ACKEN (When the Seagulls Are Hungry)
[Drama, 2002] Script and Dir: Bülent Pelit. Phot: Levent Pelit. Players: Meral Oguz, Umut Ulas, Ümit Belen, Murat Sen. Prod: Galata Film Ltd/Sirketi.

ICERDEKI (Inside)
[Drama, 2002] Script: Ahmet Kücükkayali, Aytekin Cakmakci. Dir: Kücükkayali. Phot: Ulas Zeybek. Players: Pelin Batu, Tan Sagtürk, Semsi Inkaya, Toprak Sergen, Melisa Sözen. Prod: New

Films International.
A French painter comes to
Turkey on holidays and finds
love in an unexpected way.

ABDÜLHAMIT DÜSERKEN
(The Fall of the Red Sultan)
*[Historical drama, 2003] Script
and Dir: Ziya Öztan. Phot:
Colin Mounier. Players: Meltem
Cumbul, Mehmet Kurtulus, Halil
Ergün, Nur Sürer. Prod: TRT.*

HITITLER (The Hittites)
*[Docu-drama, 2003] Script and
Dir: Tolga Örnek. Phot: Ferhan
Akgün. Players: Haluk Bilginer,
Sanem Celik, Cüneyt Türel,
Burak Sergen. Prod: Ekip Film.*

MUMYA FIRARDA
(Mummy on the Run)
*[Comedy, 2002] Script: Haluk
Özenc. Dir: Erdal Murat Aktas.
Phot: Haik Kirakosian. Players:
Teoman, Nurgül Yesilcay,
Selami Sahin, Dilek Türker.*

SEYTAN BUNUN
NERESINDE?
(Where Is the Devil to It?)
*[Comedy, 2002] Script: Yasar
Arak, Müfit Can Sacinti. Dir:
Levent Kirca. Phot: Cengiz Tacer.
Players: Kirca, Sezai Alptekin,
Fatma Murat, Ali Demirel.
Prod: Hodri Meydan.*

ÖMERÇIP
*[Comedy, 2003] Script: Kemal
Kenan Ergen. Dir: Zeki Alasya.
Phot: Kamil Cetin. Players:
Mehmet Ali Erbil, Askin Nur
Yengi, Onur Selimbeyoglu,
Zeki Alasya. Prod: Erler Film.*

DOKUZ (Nine)
*[Thriller, 2002] Script and Dir:
Ümit Ünal. Phot: Aydin
Sarioglu. Players: Ali Poyrazoglu,
Cezmi Baskin, Serra Yilmaz.
Prod: PTT Film.*

HICBIRYERDE (Innowhereland)
*[Political drama, 2002]
Script and Dir: Tayfun
Pirselimoglu. Phot: Colin
Mounier. Players: Zuhal Olcay,
Parkan Özturan. Prod:
Mine Film.*

accomplished than *The Town* (*Kasaba*) and *Clouds in May* (*Mayis sikintisi*).

Distant follows the heroes of his previous films, who have settled in Istanbul. The elder (Muzaffer Özdemir) finds an almost-successful niche as a photographer in a petit-bourgeois circle. His young cousin (Mehmet Emin Toprak) is still searching for meaning in his life, and dreams of going far away by boat. While living in the photographer's apartment he discovers the hidden charms of Istanbul, which is blanketed by the absolute white of heavy snow. In this dream-like city, Ceylan makes us share the deepest feelings of his two unforgettable protagonists, and feel the passing of time.

Snow-covered Istanbul is the setting for Nuri Bilge Ceylan's **Distant**

Distant won the Jury Grand Prix at Cannes and an unexpected Best Actor prize for Özdemir and Toprak. Tragically, the latter had been killed in a traffic accident a few months earlier. *Distant* also claimed the three major national awards at the Istanbul festival in April 2003 (a successful event, despite having the fewest international visitors in its history, because of the Iraq war).

Finally, a real rarity: a documentary made by a young director and commercially released in Turkey. Tolga Örnek's **The Hittites** (*Hititler*) is a docu-drama about one of the most important but lesser-known ancient civilisations of the Anatolian land.

ATILLA DORSAY, founder and president of SIYAD (Association of Turkish Critics), has written about film since 1966 and is the author of 30 books, including biographies of Yilmaz Güney and Türkan Soray.

Quote of the Year

"I know a lot of film-makers who, after a few prizes, tried their hands at big-budget films and therefore lost their creativity and personality. I will try not to fall into this trap."

NURI BILGE CEYLAN, *director,
after his double triumph in Cannes.*

Ukraine Goga Lomdize

Recent and Forthcoming Films

SHUM VETRA (Sound of Wind)
*[Drama, 2002] Script and Dir:
Sergei Masloboishikov. Phot:
Bogdan Verzhbitski. Players:
Nikon Romanchenko, Alla
Sergiiko, Dmitri Lalenkov, Denis
Karasev, Vadim Skuratovski,
Natalia Dolia, Andrei Dimentiev,
Viktor Andrienko.*

**MALENKOE PUTISHESTVIE
(Short Journey)**
*[Short, 2002] Script and Dir:
Mikhail Ilienko. Players: Ilienko,
Anatoli Diachenko, Dmitri
Linartovich, Kostia Marinochkin.*

TELEGA (Cart)
*[Short, 2001] Script and Dir:
Sergei Shakhvorostov. Players:
Vladimir Pavelko, Pavel
Makarchenko, Olga Oleksi.*

Les Sanin's **Mamay**

MAMAY
*[Historical drama, 2002] Script
and Dir: Oles Sanin. Players:
Victoria Spesivceva, Nazl
Seitablaev, Sergei Romaniuk,
Andrei Belous, Akhtem
Seitablaev, Eldar Akimov,
Emil Rafilov.*

On Christmas Day 2002 a new law supporting the state-funded development of the Ukrainian film industry came into effect – a vital piece of legislation for a country in which feature production has plummeted from 40 films in 1991 to fewer than 10 in 2002. The great production hubs of the Soviet period, Dovzhenko National Film Studio, Odessa Film Studio and Yalta Film Studio (privatised in 2002), lie virtually abandoned at a time when Ukraine is blessed with many gifted actors and film-makers whose work gains international recognition.

The exhibition network has also collapsed. In 1957 there were 10,210 screens in Ukraine, today only 509 (70 with Dolby) serving a population of 51 million. The 220 films released sold six million tickets in 2002, grossing $7.2m, mostly for Hollywood films (about 15 blockbusters are imported each year, mainly by Ukrainian-Russian joint ventures or local agents for the American majors). Domestic productions (six features, two TV dramas and more than 20 shorts and documentaries) claimed about 5% of the market. The state promised production funding of $4m (22.5m Grivna), but only about a third of that was used during the year. Support now goes directly to independent producers; not, as in former days, to the studios.

The local festival scene is quite healthy. In June 2002, the fifth International Film Festival Brigantina had competition entries from Ukraine, Russia and Belarus, and non-competing films from Georgia, Greece, Israel and Turkmenistan. In July, the second Russian-Ukrainian film festival took place in Yalta, and in October the thirty-second International Film Festival Molodist, Kiev, was again a great opportunity for Ukrainian film-makers, especially the younger ones, to meet foreign colleagues.

The intimate and the epic

The memorable films of 2002 explored traditional Ukrainian leitmotivs: historical, poetic and social. Poetic drama **Sound of Wind** (*Shum vetra*) by Sergei Masloboishikov, famous as a stage production designer, is based on Goethe's *Elfkönig*. It is an irrational parable, full of visual metaphors and flashbacks, following the lives of a husband, a wife and their son, all caught up in their dreams and seeking an ideal world. The son, Aliosha, is fascinated by

CHIORNAYA RADA
(Black Rada)
*[Historical drama, 2002] Script
and Dir: Nikolai Zaseev-
Rudenko. Players: Aleksei
Petrenko, Bogdan Stupka,
Aleksandr Bondarenko, Sergei
Romaniuk. Prod: National Film
Studio Dovzhenko.*

TAYNA CHINGIZKHANA
(Mystery of Genghis Khan)
*[Historical drama, 2002] Script:
Ivan Drach. Dir: Vladimir
Saveliev. Players: Bogdan Stupka,
Polina Lazova, Sergei Romaniuk,
Raisa Nedashkivska. Prod:
National Film Studio
Dovzhenko.*

Quotes of the Year

"I want my films and plays to
be interesting to the public.
But if we do not share the
same values, it is quite
another matter."
SERGEI MASLOBOISHIKOV,
director.

"I can't even find out to
whom and for how much
my films have been sold. Is
this a commercial secret? I
am an author of these films!"
VLADIMIR SAVELIEV, *director,
on copyright problems in the
former USSR.*

nature and harmony. The parents are searching for a soul-mate. The film's introspective approach prompted Russian critics (who admired the film more than local reviewers) to compare it to Tarkovsky's *The Mirror*. For his magnificent camerawork, Bogdan Verzhbitski won Best Cinematographer at Kinoshok 2002.

A married couple confront their dreams in **Sound of Wind**

After Yuri Ilienko's grandiose historical epic *Hetman Mazepa* (see *IFG 2003*), the Ukrainian fondness for this type of film continued early in 2003 with debutant Oles Sanin's triptych **Mamay**, based on Ukrainian and Tartar medieval legends. In the first part, three Ukrainian brothers escape from Tartar captivity on horses which turn out to be important totems for their captors. In the next story, three Tartar brothers go to Ukraine to recover the horses. These two tales are connected by an original story written by Sanin, about the tragic love of a Tartar woman for a Ukrainian cossack.

Nikolai Zaseev-Rudenko's **Black Rada** (*Chornaya rada*) is a costume drama filled with action, romance and intrigue, based on a nine-part TV series about the crisis that hit Ukraine in 1663, after the death of headman Bogdan Khmelnitski, when rival factions devastated the country in their fight for supremacy. The founder of the Mongolian empire in the thirteenth century is the hero of Vladimir Saveliev's biopic **The Mystery of Genghis Khan** (*Tayna Chingizkhana*), which traces his journey across Europe from southern Siberia. Finally, Ukraine has a fine record in short film-making, and at Berlin in 2002 Stepan Koval's animated *The Tram N°9 Goes*, filled with simple conversations between streetcar passengers, won awards.

United Kingdom Philip Kemp

The Year's Best Films

Philip Kemp's selection:

The Magdalene Sisters
(Dir: Peter Mullan)

Young Adam
(Dir: David Mackenzie)

Dirty Pretty Things
(Dir: Stephen Frears)

The Emperor's New Clothes (Dir: Alan Taylor)

28 Days Later
(Dir: Danny Boyle)

Recent and Forthcoming Films

ALL OR NOTHING
[Drama, 2002] Script and Dir: Mike Leigh. Phot: Dick Pope. Players: Timothy Spall, Lesley Manville, James Corden, Alison Garland. Prod: Thin Man/Alain Sarde.

ANITA & ME
[Social comedy, 2002] Script: Meera Syal. Dir: Metin Hüseyin. Phot: Cinders Forshaw. Players: Chandeep Uppal, Anna Brewster, Lynn Redgrave, Meera Syal. Prod: Portman Film/Film Council/BBC Films.

Chandeep Uppal and Anna Brewster in **Anita & Me**

BLACKBALL
[Comedy, 2003] Script: Tim Firth. Dir: Mel Smith. Phot: Vernon Layton. Players: Paul

Judged purely on the BOS factor (Bums on Seats), cinema in Britain is alive and exceedingly well. Annual admissions in 2002 continued the seemingly inexorable rise that began in the mid-1980s, increasing by 13% to 170 million, the highest figure since 1972. Also for the first time since the 1970s, the UK overtook Germany to become the second biggest market in Europe in terms of admissions – only just behind France's 183 million. With seat prices well above the European average – many would say British tickets are too expensive – the UK already generates Europe's largest box-office gross by some distance.

Can the boom continue indefinitely? Exhibitors may think not; it's been widely mooted that the UK market may be approaching saturation point. The headlong expansion, which saw 730 new screens added between 1996 and 2000, has slowed virtually to a standstill. Few new builds are in the pipeline; instead exhibitors are looking to maximise revenue from existing sites through refitting and reprogramming. And some people are prudently getting out altogether. In March 2003, Venture capital company Cinven, which bought the Odeon circuit from Rank in 2000 and merged it with the former ABC chain to form the UK's largest circuit (99 sites with 614 screens), sold it on for $688m to a consortium that includes the fast-growing British independent Entertainment Film Distributors. Only weeks later, the second biggest circuit, Warner Village Cinemas (42 sites, 405 screens), was sold to SBC International, which plans to rebrand its new acquisitions as Vue.

Whoever owns them, the vast bulk of these screens will as usual be showing heavily marketed Hollywood studio product. The arthouse sector continues to suffer from a dwindling number of potential outlets and the prohibitive cost of prints. This may change, though, if a scheme proposed by the overall government support body, the UK Film Council (FC), comes to fruition. The Council plans to invest $22m in setting up a nationwide circuit of digital screens, hired from mainstream outlets and dedicated to specialist films. Films will be distributed on HDD5 tape, at a fraction of the cost of conventional prints. Initial industry response has been cautiously supportive, though doubts have been raised whether audiences will come to see arthouse movies at multiplexes and whether exhibitors will be prepared to meet the cost of installing the digital equipment – especially given the rapid obsolescence factor

BBC/Film Council

Paul Kaye in **Blackball**

Kaye, Imelda Staunton, Alice
Evans, Johnny Vegas. Prod:
Midfield.

BRIGHT YOUNG THINGS
*[Comedy, 2003] Script: Stephen
Fry, based on Vile Bodies by
Evelyn Waugh. Dir: Fry. Phot:
Henry Braham. Players: Stephen
Campbell Moore, Emily
Mortimer, Michael Sheen, Peter
O'Toole, Jim Broadbent. Prod:
Doubting Hall/Revolution.*

*Stephen Campbell Moore and Emily
Mortimer in* **Bright Young Things**

THE BUM'S RUSH
*[Comedy-drama, 2003] Script:
Stewart Svaasand, Gill
Humpherston. Dir: Svaasand.
Phot: Svein Krovel. Players:
Jamie Sives, Kevin McKidd, Iain
Robertson, Neve McIntosh.
Prod: Scott Three/Hero/Motlys.*

CALENDAR GIRLS
*[Comedy, 2003] Script: Tim
Firth, Julette Towhidi. Dir: Nigel
Cole. Phot: Ashley Rowe.
Players: Helen Mirren, Julie
Walters, Penelope Wilton, Celia
Imrie. Prod: Buena Vista.*

Helen Mirren and Julie Walters in
Calendar Girls

in digital technology. HDD5, according to some exhibitors, is
already old hat.

At the same time, in a classic case of giving with one hand to take
away with the other, the British Film Institute (which falls under the
FC umbrella) cut the annual support it gives to small independent
cinemas by $263,000. Both these sums, in any case, are dwarfed
by the much-criticised cost of running the FC itself, currently some
$116m per annum, representing 20% of its turnover. A lot of
money for fairly unimpressive results, some would argue. "After
three years, precious little strategy is actually in place [at the FC],"
noted the trade journal *Screen International* in April 2003. Not
surprisingly, a Council-commissioned report, written by veteran
producer Simon Relph, that recommended UK production
companies should cut their costs prompted widespread muttering
about pots and kettles.

Still, if the FC's digital scheme is intelligently executed it could
help the provision for foreign-language cinema to recover from the
additional blow it received in May 2003, when FilmFour (taken over,
according to Roger Clarke in *The Independent on Sunday,* by
"a cabal of marketing men and former bankers with little or no
knowledge of film") closed down its Film Four World and Film Four
Extreme subscription TV channels and replaced them with one
showing wall-to-wall *Four Weddings and a Funeral* and similar
bland, mainstream fare. Since BBC2 and (to a lesser extent)
Channel Four have virtually abdicated any commitment to showing
foreign-language movies, the FC scheme could offer a much-
needed replacement.

From boom to slump

In the beleaguered UK production sector, things look a lot less
healthy than on the exhibition side. Production in 2002 slumped by
some 40%, most of the fall being accounted for by indigenous films
– unlike the previous year, when the slump mainly affected visiting
productions. Some of the decline in UK investment can be put
down to uncertainty over the government's plans for tax breaks.
Over-ingenious bending of the rules, allowing foreign productions
with only the most marginal UK connections (such as Roberto
Benigni's *Pinocchio*) to benefit from substantial tax write-offs, are
souring relations between the industry and the Treasury. Already the
government has shown its teeth, excluding TV production and the
use of deferrals from tax breaks; yet more stringent measures, it's
feared, are in the pipeline. And one or two high-profile cases of
abuse, with the Treasury exacting stringent penalties, could scare
away a lot of potential investors.

Still, it could be argued that in terms of overall quality a drop in UK production might not be a bad thing. The embarrassment of two years ago, when a production boom failed to deliver a single British film considered worthy of inclusion at Cannes, underlined the fact that at least half of recently completed British films were not only unlikely ever to get a theatrical release, but scarcely deserved one in the first place. The UK redeemed itself at Cannes in 2002, with both Ken Loach (*Sweet Sixteen*) and Mike Leigh (*All or Nothing*) operating at only slightly below top form, and Lynne Ramsay following her acclaimed debut *Ratcatcher* with the intriguingly enigmatic *Morvern Callar*. But striking new British voices were absent.

Adam's a long way from Eden

Cannes 2003, however, featured at least one impressive British newcomer: David Mackenzie, writer-director of *Young Adam*. Mackenzie wasn't a complete novice, since his debut feature, **The Last Great Wilderness**, was released in the UK a week before *Young Adam* premiered at Cannes, and taken together the two films gave evidence of a highly individual talent. *The Last Great Wilderness* had atmosphere and inventiveness to spare but lacked focus, its plot and mood veering wildly – if often divertingly – from road movie to black comedy to Polanskian *grand guignol,* all leavened with a hint of *The Wicker Man*.

Young Adam, adapted from Alexander Trocchi's 1954 cult novel, establishes its tone from the outset with far more assurance, and sticks to it. Set on and around the grim industrial canals where coal barges ply between Glasgow and Edinburgh, it starts with a young woman's body being retrieved from the water and ends with its anti-hero, Joe Taylor (Ewan McGregor), drifting no less aimlessly, and emotionally no less dead than the corpse.

Recorded Pictures Company

Ewan McGregor, left, and Peter Mullan in **Young Adam**

Trocchi's novel is written in the first person, but Mackenzie rejects the obvious solution of giving his hero a doomy, noirish voice-over. Instead we get Joe's affectless state of mind from the film's gritty

CHEEKY
[Drama, 2003] Script and Dir: David Thewlis. Phot: Oliver Stapleton. Players: Thewlis, Trudie Styler, Johnny Vegas, Ian Hart. Prod: Europa/Xingu.

DIRTY PRETTY THINGS
[Urban thriller, 2002] Script: Steven Knight. Dir: Stephen Frears. Phot: Chris Menges. Players: Audrey Tatou, Chiwetel Ejiofor, Sergi Lopez, Sophie Okonedo. Prod: Miramax/ BBC/Celador.

THE EMPEROR'S NEW CLOTHES
[Historical drama, 2001] Script: Kevin Molony. Dir: Alan Taylor. Phot: Alessio Gelsini Torresi. Players: Ian Holm, Iben Hjelje, Tim McInnerny, Nigel Terry. Prod: Film Four/Mikado/ Rai/Redwave.

THE GOOD THIEF
[Crime caper, 2002] Script and Dir: Neil Jordan. Phot: Chris Menges. Players: Nick Nolte, Tcheky Karyo, Saïd Taghmaoui, Gérard Darmon. Prod: Alliance Atlantis.

IN THIS WORLD
[Docu-drama, 2002] Script: Tony Grisoni. Dir: Michael Winterbottom. Phot: Marcel Zyskind. Players: Jamal Udin Torabi, Enyatullah, Wakeel Khan. Prod: Revolution/Film Consortium/BBC.

KISS OF LIFE
[Drama, 2003] Script and Dir: Emily Young. Phot: Wojciech Szepel. Players: Ingeborga Dapkunaite, Peter Mullan, David Warner, Millie Findlay. Prod: Wild Horses/BBC/France3.

THE LAST GREAT WILDERNESS
[Thriller, 2002] Script: Michael Tait, Alastair Mackenzie, Gillian Berrie, David Mackenzie. Dir: David Mackenzie. Phot: Simon Dennis. Players: Alastair Mackenzie, Johnny Phillips, Ewan Stewart, Victoria Smurfit. Prod: Sigma.

LOST IN LA MANCHA
[Documentary, 2002] Script and Dir: Keith Fulton, Louis Pepe. Phot: Louis Pepe. Featuring: Terry Gilliam, Jean Rochefort, Johnny Depp. Prod: Quixote Films/Low Key Pictures/Eastcroft Productions.

Johnny Depp and Terry Gilliam in
Lost in La Mancha

LOVE ACTUALLY
[Romantic comedy, 2003] Script and Dir: Richard Curtis. Phot: Michael Coulter. Players: Laura Linney, Liam Neeson, Martine McCutcheon, Keira Knightley, Hugh Grant. Prod: Universal/DNA.

Nora-Jane Noone in
The Magdalene Sisters

THE MAGDALENE SISTERS
[Period drama, 2002] Script and Dir: Peter Mullan. Phot: Nigel Willoughby. Players: Geraldine McEwan, Nora-Jane Noone, Anne-Marie Duff, Dorothy Duffy, Eileen Walsh. Prod: PFP.

MORVERN CALLAR
[Drama, 2002] Script: Liana Dognini, Lynne Ramsay, based on the novel by Alan Warner. Dir: Ramsay. Phot: Alwin Kuchler. Players: Samantha Morton, Kathleen McDermott,

visual texture and cold, grey-blue palette, from the flat, detached dialogue and, above all, from McGregor's performance. Paring away the streetwise perkiness of his earlier roles, the star brings a hungry, raw dissatisfaction to the part, his mouth skewed in a grimace of anticipated distaste. This is a man who seeks sexual encounters with restless, grim compulsion, as if to confirm what he already knows – that they bring him no closer to anyone.

For all the film's sense of existential futility, Mackenzie handles his material with a light touch and an intimate attention to physical detail. The sense of grimy, sweaty flesh – especially in the sex scenes between Joe and the married Ella (Tilda Swinton) on the barge – is startlingly vivid. In a moment of supreme post-coital disaffection, Joe watches expressionless as a fat black fly takes a leisurely stroll around Ella's nipple. Mackenzie resists the temptation to jazz up his story with any spurious sense of urgency or passion. Barring one brief bizarre scene of erotic violence – involving custard and spanking with a wooden slat – *Young Adam* moves with the torpid, inexorable pace of the coal-barge, abetted by David Byrne's moody score.

Ella's cuckolded husband is played, with saturnine resignation, by the Scots actor Peter Mullan, whose second feature as director, **The Magdalene Sisters**, was awarded the Golden Lion at Venice. Based closely on real-life cases, it is a harrowing study in how the individual can not only be ruthlessly crushed by overweening social pressure, but can be brainwashed into acquiescing in the process. The Magdalene Laundries, run by the Irish Catholic Sisters of Mercy, held an estimated 30,000 women, convicted of no crime, denied all contact with the outside world, subjected to harsh discipline and forced labour for years, often for the rest of their lives. The last laundry closed only in 1996.

As Sister Bridget, chief jailor, Geraldine McEwan gives a chilling display of genteel sadism, her tight little smile and well-bred tones becoming increasingly sinister. The power of Mullan's film, amply confirming the promise of his first feature, *Orphans*, lies in the way he relates his story to the wider picture of a cramped, repressed society in which sexual impulses are twisted by shame and ignorance, and a conspiracy of state, church and family could be sustained against women deemed "morally irresponsible" without a voice being raised in protest. The film's success at Venice aroused screams of protest from the Vatican, suggesting that Mullan was pretty much on target.

28 Days of the undead

As was to be expected, *The Magdalene Sisters* also hit trouble from Catholic pressure groups in the US, but other British films had

Optimum/Kobal

Film Council/Momentum/Kobal

an easier run Stateside. Following the utterly unlooked-for transatlantic success of the anodyne girls-football comedy *Bend It Like Beckham,* Danny Boyle and his regular producer Andrew Macdonald scored an even more substantial American hit with **28 Days Later,** an apocalyptic thriller set in a plague- and zombie-ridden Britain. Pacy and energetic, the film marks a return to *Trainspotting* form for the Boyle-Macdonald team after the glossy misfires of *A Life Less Ordinary* and *The Beach.*

DNA/Figment/Fox

Cillian Murphy in Danny Boyle's **28 Days Later**

Sharing *28 Days*' post-apocalyptic setting and scabrous energy – though on a far smaller budget – as well as Christopher Eccleston in a lead role, Alex Cox's lively punk reworking of a Jacobean gore-fest in **Revengers Tragedy** takes a blithely irreverent attitude to its source. The original play (traditionally ascribed to Cyril Tourneur, but more likely by Thomas Middleton) is a studiedly artificial concoction, giving few handholds to naturalism, and Cox gleefully seizes the opportunity to go all out for ultra-stylised black comedy. His chosen setting, Liverpool a decade hence, seemingly after some unspecified national disaster, is a city of wrecked cars and burnt-out buildings, ruled by Mafiosi and populated by roaming gangs of street thugs. The costumes, especially the baddies', are heightened into rampant hyperbole. Playing almost every scene close to parody, Cox tosses in sly visual references to other dystopian movie fantasies – a hint of Cocteau's *Orphée* (1949) in the black-leather outriders of the ruling Duke (Derek Jacobi), more than a touch of Kubrick's *A Clockwork Orange* (1971) in the rococo treatment of urban squalor.

From an *Emperor* to a *King*

The reckless trashing of FilmFour, Channel 4's semi-autonomous film production arm, in 2002 left several films undeservedly stranded. Among them was Alan Taylor's **The Emperor's New**

Raife Patrick Burchell, Dan Cadan. Prod: Company/BBC.

THE MOTHER
[Comedy-drama, 2003] Script: Hanif Kureishi. Dir: Roger Michell. Phot: Alwin Kuchler. Players: Anne Reid, Peter Vaughan, Anna Wilson-Jones, Daniel Craig. Prod: Renaissance/BBC.

MY LITTLE EYE
[Horror, 2002] Script: David Hilton, James Watkins. Dir: Marc Evans. Phot: Hubert Taczanowski. Players: Sean CW Johnson, Kris Lemche, Laura Regan, Jennifer Sky. Prod: Momentum/Universal/Studio Canal/Working Title.

THE PRINCIPLES OF LUST
[Drama, 2003] Script and Dir: Penny Woolcock. Phot: Graham Smith. Players: Alec Newman, Marc Warren, Sienna Guillory, Lara Clifton. Prod: Blast/Film Four Lab/Yorkshire Media.

PURE
[Drama, 2002] Script: Alison Hume. Dir: Gillies MacKinnon. Phot: John de Borman. Players: Molly Parker, David Wenham, Geraldine McEwan, Keira Knightley, Harry Eden. Prod: Little Wing/Kudos.

REVENGERS TRAGEDY
[Melodrama, 2002] Script: Frank Cottrell Boyce, based on the play by Cyril Tourneur. Dir: Alex Cox. Phot: Andy Collins. Players: Christopher Eccleston, Eddie Izzard, Derek Jacobi, Diana Quick. Prod: Exterminating Angel.

SWEET SIXTEEN
[Drama, 2002] Script: Paul Laverty. Dir: Ken Loach. Phot: Barry Ackroyd. Players: Martin Compston, William Ruane, Annmarie Fulton, Michelle Abercromby. Prod: Alta/BBC/Road Movies.

TO KILL A KING
[Historical drama, 2002] Script: Jenny Mayhew. Dir: Mike Barker. Phot: Eigil Bryld.

Players: Tim Roth, Dougray Scott, Rupert Everett, Olivia Williams. Prod: Hanway/Future Film Group.

28 DAYS LATER
[Sci-fi horror, 2002] Script: Alex Garland. Dir: Danny Boyle. Phot: Anthony Dod Mantle. Players: Cillian Murphy, Naomie Harris, Megan Burns, Brendan Gleeson, Christopher Eccleston. Prod: Fox Searchlight/DNA Films.

WONDROUS OBLIVION
[Comedy-drama, 2003] Script and Dir: Paul Morrison. Phot: Nina Kellgren. Players: Sam Smith, Delroy Lindo, Emily Woof, Stanley Townsend. Prod: APT.

YOUNG ADAM
[Period drama, 2003] Script and Dir: David Mackenzie. Phot: Giles Nuttgens. Players: Ewan McGregor, Tilda Swinton, Peter Mullan, Emily Mortimer. Prod: HanWay/Recorded Picture Co.

Clothes, a "What if...?" historical fantasy in which Napoleon (Ian Holm), having left a lookalike in his place, escapes from Saint Helena in a bid to regain his throne. At the time of writing, this warmly likeable if slightly old-fashioned movie had been on the shelf for two years.

Tim Roth as Cromwell and Dougray Scott as Fairfax in **To Kill a King**

Still more unlucky was Mike Barker's **To Kill a King** (previously known as *Cromwell and Fairfax*), which contrived to go bankrupt twice during the course of production when backers pulled out. What finally emerged was a rare attempt at an intelligent historical epic, with the passion invested in fervent political debate rather than in spectacle and swordplay. It was let down, though, by an increasingly tendentious script, which settled for demonising Cromwell to the point of Pythonesque parody.

With UK cinemas swamped by a tsunami of megabudget, CGI-packed fantasies in 2002-03 – *Spider-Man, The Hulk,* the latest in the *Harry Potter, Lord of the Rings, Matrix* and *X-Men* franchises – small, intelligent movies tackling contemporary problems tended to have a poor time of it. Stephen Frears' **Dirty Pretty Things** enjoyed widespread critical acclaim but performed disappointingly at the box-office. A sympathetic, at times angry portrayal of London's illegal immigrant community, Frears' film offers an intriguing glimpse into a parallel world of desperate, demeaning survival tactics that few tourists – and not many Londoners – ever realise exists. To sugar the dirty-realist pill, Frears and screenwriter Stephen Knight mix in thriller elements involving the trade in human organs, but the two strands never quite mesh. The film boasts an eloquent, stoic performance from Chiwetel Ejiofor as a Nigerian doctor, although Audrey Tautou (*Amélie*) never quite convinces as a Turkish asylum seeker.

Refugees, currently much in the news thanks to British tabloids' attempts to whip up synthetic panics, also featured in **In This**

BBC/Celador Productions/Kobal

Audrey Tautou as an illegal immigrant in **Dirty Pretty Things**

World, the latest feature from the prolific and bewilderingly versatile Michael Winterbottom. A raw, chilling docu-drama tracing the perils and discomforts of the overland journey from Peshawar to London of two young Afghan refugees, it stars two non-professionals, genuine Afghan refugees, in effect playing themselves and recreating their own experiences.

Again, warm critical reception failed to translate into box-office success, although Winterbottom had better luck than Gillies MacKinnon with **Pure**, a vivid study of drug addiction in the mean streets of east London, seen through the eyes of the 10-year-old son of a junkie single mother. This was thrown away on a half-hearted release and vanished almost without notice, despite a prodigious performance from newcomer Harry Eden as the resilient boy.

Optimists spring eternal

To end on a more upbeat note, two instances of unquenchable optimism – one from a complete newcomer, the other from one of the industry's most respected veterans. Stelios Haji-Joannou, maverick Anglo-Greek founder of the cut-price EasyJet airline and several other Easy-branded ventures, has been trying to extend his no-frills tactics into exhibition.

Having rented a 10-screen multiplex in Milton Keynes (one of the first to be built in the UK, now looking more than a little tatty), Haji-Joannou is offering tickets over the internet which, if booked far enough in advance, will cost only 20p ($0.30). No foyer service, no popcorn, no box-office – just the movies. That is, if he can get them, since at press time distributors were still proving reluctant to make first-run product available on EasyCinema's bargain-basement terms. Still, Haji-Joannou has overcome cries of "It'll never work!" several times; he may yet shake up the sector.

British Academy of Film and Television Awards 2002

Film: *The Pianist* (Roman Polanski, Robert Benmussa, Alain Sarde).
British Film: *The Warrior* (Bertrand Faivre, Asif Kapadia).
Direction: Roman Polanski (*The Pianist*).
Actor: Daniel Day-Lewis (*Gangs of New York*).
Actress: Nicole Kidman (*The Hours*).
Supporting Actor: Christopher Walken (*Catch Me If You Can*).
Supporting Actress: Catherine Zeta-Jones (*Chicago*).
Original Screenplay: Pedro Almodóvar (*Talk to Her*).
Adapted Screenplay: Charlie Kaufman (*Adaptation*).
Film Music: Philip Glass (*The Hours*).
Cinematography: Conrad L. Hall (*Road to Perdition*).
Production Design: Dennis Gassner (*Road to Perdition*).
Costume Design: Ngila Dickson, Richard Taylor (*The Lord of the Rings: The Two Towers*).
Editing: Daniel Rezende (*City of God*).
Sound: Michael Minkler, Dominick Tavella, David Lee, Maurice Schell (*Chicago*).
Visual Effects: Jim Rygiel, Joe Letteri, Randall William Cook, Alex Funke (*The Two Towers*).
Make-Up & Hair: Judy Chin, Beatrice De Alba, John Jackson, Regina Reyes (*Frida*).
Best Foreign-Language Film: *Talk to Her.*
Carl Foreman Award: Asif Kapadia (*The Warrior*).
Audience Award: *The Two Towers.*
Fellowship: Saul Zaentz.
Michael Balcon Award: Michael Stevenson (2nd Assistant Director), David Tomblin (1st Assistant Director).

Quotes of the Year

"You'd be saying extraordinary things like 'Deep down in the lake there is slime and lichen – that is how you are, Mary!' Things that made literally no sense." **HUGH GRANT** *recalls his glory years as king of the Europuddings.*

"No more boring British films. That is my slogan." **STEPHEN FREARS,** *director, giving hostages to fortune.*

"A movie is like the Alien in Ridley Scott's movie: it lives inside you and then one day it bursts out of your stomach and you're left lying in a bloody pool on the floor." **SAM MENDES,** *director.*

Meanwhile, the venerable Lord Attenborough – "Dickie" to one and all – turned 80 in August 2003, showing not the least signs of slowing down. Not content with having more directorial projects in the pipeline, he is overseeing the construction of huge, state-of-the-art film studios in Wales. Long-mooted plans for the first-ever Scottish studio may have run aground, but Dragon Studios, near Cardiff, are currently being built at a projected cost of $500m and are scheduled to be ready in 2005, with Attenborough as company chairman. It will be, says Dickie with boundless enthusiasm, "the greatest studio in the world".

Molly Parker, centre, in Gillies MacKinnon's **Pure**

Spain – Goya Awards 2003

Film: *Mondays in the Sun* (Los lunes al sol).
Director: Fernando Leon (*Mondays in the Sun*).
New Directors: Julio Wallovits and Roger Gual (*Smoking Room*).
Original Screenplay: Antonio Hernandez and Enrique Braso (*The City without Limits*).
Adapted Screenplay: Adolfo Aristarain and Kathy Saavedra (*Common Places/Lugares Comunes*).
Actor: Javier Bardem (*Mondays in the Sun*).
Actress: Mercedes Sampietro (*Common Places*).
Supporting Actor: Luis Tosar (*Mondays in the Sun*).
Supporting Actress: Geraldine Chaplin (*The City without Limits*).
New Actor: Jose Angel Egido (*Mondays in the Sun*).
New Actress: Lolita Flores (*Rencor*).
European Film: *The Pianist* (Roman Polanski).
Foreign Spanish-Language Film: *The Last Train* (Diego Arsuaga).

Taiwan – 39th Golden Horse Awards

Presented in Kaohsiung on November 16, 2002.

Picture: *The Best of Times*.
Director: Fruit Chan (*Hollywood Hong Kong*).
Actor: Leon Lai (*Three: Going Home*).
Actress: Angelica Lee Sinje (*The Eye*).
Supporting Actor: Anthony Wong (*Princess D*).
Supporting Actress: Karena Lam (*July Rhapsody*).
New Actor: Karena Lam (*July Rhapsody*).
Screenplay: Ivy Ho (*July Rhapsody*).
Cinematography: Christopher Doyle (*Three: Going Home*).
Special Effects: Centro Digital Pictures Limited (*The Eye*).
Art Direction: Huang Mao-sen (*Drop Me a Cat*).
Costuming: Jessie Dai Mei-ling (*Hollywood Hong Kong*).
Action Choreography: Bruce Mang (*Running Out of Time 2*).

United States Eddie Cockrell

Recent and Forthcoming Films

21 GRAMS
[Drama, 2003] Script: Guillermo Arriaga. Dir: Alejandro González Iñárritu. Phot: Rodrigo Prieto. Players: Sean Penn, Naomi Watts, Benicio Del Toro, Charlotte Gainsbourg, Danny Huston. Prod: This is That Productions.
The lives of a former drug addict (Watts), a terminally ill maths teacher (Penn) and a spiritual ex-convict (Del Toro) intersect in unexpected ways.

ALEXANDER
[Historical epic, 2004] Script and Dir: Oliver Stone. Players: Colin Farrell, Anthony Hopkins. Prod: Pacifica/Intermedia Films/Pathe.
Farrell plays the Macedonian conqueror.

BIRTH (aka BEFORE BIRTH)
[Supernatural romantic drama, 2004] Script: Jean-Claude Carrière, Jonathan Glazer, Milo Addica. Dir: Glazer. Phot: Harris Savides. Players: Nicole Kidman, Cameron Bright, Danny Huston, Lauren Bacall. Prod: Academy Prods/Lou-Yi Prods.
In modern-day New York, a thirtysomething woman (Kidman) is surprised to meet a 10-year-old boy who seems to have a crush on her and claims to be the reincarnation of her dead husband.

BROTHERS GRIMM
[Fantasy adventure, 2004] Script: Ehren Kruger. Dir: Terry Gilliam. Phot: Nicola Pecorini. Players: Matt Damon, Heath Ledger, Robin Williams, Jonathan Pryce. Prod: Summit Entertainment.

At press time, the quirkiest industry-related story, as reported by Lew Irwin's invaluable Studio Briefing service, concerned one Michael Kinney, a reporter for the *Sedalia Democrat,* Missouri. Seems that Kinney had been taking entire paragraphs of *Chicago Sun-Times* critic Roger Ebert's reviews and passing them off as his own, in a heartland spin on the work of discredited *New York Times* reporter Jayson Blair (shades, too, of Sony Pictures, who two years ago admitted to cooking up a fake critic to deliver bogus quotes hyping its new releases).

Ebert, the dean of mainstream American movie critics, was in the news as well, trading *bons mots* with actor-director Vincent Gallo during and after Cannes 2003 over the former's fiercely eccentric one-man road-trip **The Brown Bunny**. Explaining a very strange insult, Gallo conceded, "The only thing I am sorry about is putting a curse on Roger Ebert's colon... If a fat pig like Roger Ebert doesn't like my movie then I'm sorry for him." Ebert shot back with, "I had a colonoscopy once, and they let me watch it on TV. It was more entertaining than *The Brown Bunny...*" And so on, and so forth. Memo to one and all: doesn't Hollywood's current feast-or-famine strategy, in which autumn and spring line-ups are punctuated by year-end logjams of prestige titles and summers of mindless eye candy, provide enough grist for the mill without film-makers and critics pouncing on one another?

Now to business. In early summer 2003, Hollywood's fortunes looked rosy indeed (on paper, anyway). Propelled during 2002 by the requisite action spectacles (goosed along with the $250m taken by sleeper smash *My Big Fat Greek Wedding*), the industry basked in the glow of a boffo holiday season, weathered a dismal first quarter 2003 prompted in part by a general nervousness over the second Gulf War (not to mention tepid pictures), and saw *X2: X-Men United, The Matrix Reloaded, Bruce Almighty, Finding Nemo* and *2 Fast 2 Furious* kick off a fine summer of mindless moviegoing. More on these developments later.

For the record, box-office revenue for 2002 swelled to $9.5 billion, up 13.2% over 2001 – the greatest annual jump in two decades. The charge was led by seven films that broke the $200m mark (five in 2001). Total admissions were up from 1.49 billion to 1.639 billion, despite the average increase in ticket price from $5.66 to $5.81.

THE BROWN BUNNY

[Drama, 2004] Script, Dir, Phot, Prod: Vincent Gallo. Players: Gallo, Chloe Sevigny. Morose motorcyclist Bud Clay (Gallo) commandeers a black van for an introspective drive through the American Midwest.

CASA DE LOS BABYS

[Drama, 2003] Script and Dir: John Sayles. Phot: Maurizio Rubinstein. Players: Maggie Gyllenhaal, Marcia Gay Harden, Daryl Hannah, Mary Steenburgen, Lili Taylor. Prod: Blue Magis Pictures/Springall Pictures/IFC Productions. Six American women from very different backgrounds travel to a Latin American country to take custody of adopted infants, only to find they're now required by law to live there.

THE CLEARING

[Thriller, 2004] Script: Justin Haythe. Dir: Pieter Jan Brugge. Phot: Denis Lenoir. Players: Robert Redford, Helen Mirren, Willem Dafoe, Alessandro Nivola. Prod: Thousand Words/The Clearing. Following the kidnapping of a wealthy executive (Redford) by a disgruntled employee (Dafoe) who hides him in the North Carolina woods, the exec's wife (Mirren) must pay the ransom or rescue her husband.

COLD MOUNTAIN

[Historical drama, 2003] Script: Anthony Minghella, from the novel by Charles Frazier. Dir: Minghella. Phot: John Seale. Players: Jude Law, Nicole Kidman, Renée Zellweger, Eileen Atkins, Brendan Gleeson, Philip Seymour Hoffman, Natalie Portman, Giovanni Ribisi, Donald Sutherland. Prod: Mirage Enterprises. In the final days of the Civil War, wounded soldier Inman (Law) rises from his deathbed and begins the long trek back to his North Carolina home and girlfriend (Kidman).

The jump occurred despite a 4% drop in screens (from 36,764 to 35,280) and theatres (down 14.4% to 6,020, from 7,070). Exhibition's dodo bird, the drive-in, lost four more ozoners, sinking to 650. The number of released films also dropped, from 482 in 2001 (the most since 1998, when there were 509) to 467. They seem to be shorter, too, which comes as a relief to just about everyone. Call it the year of big, fat deceptive numbers.

One man's remake...

Any discussion of 2002 in American films should begin at the end – specifically, the spectacular fourth quarter, which ended up accounting for some $2.7 billion in revenue (28% of the year's gross). It was also among the most consistently rich, diverse and rewarding slate of holiday releases in memory, including the second instalments in the *Harry Potter* and *Lord of the Rings* franchises and virtually all of the high-profile Oscar contenders.

Even the rare misfires were dazzling: Steven Soderbergh's glossy, stripped-down, defiantly moody remake of Andrei Tarkovsky's **Solaris** drew the attentive viewer in as surely as the planet that reads the minds of those who pass too close. Few passed near cinemas playing the film (an odd choice indeed for a major studio's Thanksgiving release slate).

Julianne Moore and Dennis Quaid in **Far from Heaven**

At around the same time *Solaris* was polarising audiences, Todd Haynes' sublimely crafted **Far from Heaven** proved that remakes (well, in this case more of a homage) can be thoughtful and respectful advances on original works. Haynes' film shows a tender, even reverent attitude towards the Douglas Sirk movies on which it is based (chiefly *All That Heaven Allows*). Here, perfect 1950s suburban housewife Cathy Whitaker (Julianne Moore) watches her marriage crumble around her, even as she finds herself drawn to her handsome, decent black gardener (Dennis Haysbert). A superb period piece (both physically and emotionally), the film's often jarring sequences involving the emerging homosexuality of Cathy's seemingly straight-arrow husband, Frank (Dennis Quaid), are handled without condescension or sensationalism.

Another film that used its time period to shrewd effect was **Auto Focus**, the most prominent work by writer-director Paul Schrader since 1997's *Affliction*. The story of 1960s TV star and closet sex addict Bob Crane (Greg Kinnear), it manages to be both mischievous and sorrowful, following Crane from the soundstages of the truly weird network hit *Hogan's Heroes* (love and laughter in a Nazi prison camp) to the parties with a seemingly endless stream of admiring women organised by reptilian enabler John Carpenter (Willem Dafoe). Kind of a cross between Schrader's *Hardcore* and *American Gigolo*, *Auto Focus* saw him back on familiar ground.

Like Schrader, Brian De Palma proved himself an old master on top of his game. His latest work, **Femme Fatale**, is vintage De Palma, a dazzling display of technical prowess married to a story so rich and complicated that all hope of figuring it out is quickly dashed, leaving the grateful moviegoer time to appreciate the boldness of it all. Rebecca Romijn-Stamos seems born to play a brassy De Palma heroine, here a master thief who returns to the scene of her Paris crimes after seven years, now married to the American ambassador (Peter Coyote) but still linked to a celebrity photographer (Antonio Banderas) hot on the trail of her secrets. Few films in 2002 felt as swaggeringly confident – an appealing trait in these formulaic times.

In praise of Denzel, George and Jack

Two films either unjustly ignored or physically swept aside by this tsunami of quality were *Antwone Fisher* and *Confessions of a Dangerous Mind,* a pair of directorial debuts by high-profile actors that synthesise their makers' public personas in the telling of true-life biographical stories. As an actor, Denzel Washington is admired for his measured intensity and quiet authority and he brings that even-keeled clarity to every frame of **Antwone Fisher**, imbuing the troubled navy recruit's rocky maturation with a dignity that is at once sobering and exhilarating. Mysteriously, this directorial debut

Drew Barrymore and Sam Rockwell in **Confessions of a Dangerous Mind**

Miramax/Takashi Seida/Kobal

CRIMINAL
[Comedy-thriller, 2004] Script: Gregory Jacobs, Steven Soderbergh. Dir: Jacobs. Phot: Chris Menges. Players: John C. Reilly, Diego Luna, Maggie Gyllenhaal. Prod: Warner Bros./Section Eight.
Remake of Argentine hit *Nine Queens.*

THE DAY AFTER TOMORROW
(aka **TOMORROW**)
[Sci-fi action-thriller, 2004] Script: Roland Emmerich, Jeffrey Nachmanoff. Dir: Emmerich. Phot: Ueli Steiger. Players: Dennis Quaid, Jake Gyllenhaal, Ian Holm, Arjay Smith, Tamlyn Tomita. Prod: Tomorrow Films.
The greenhouse effect and global warming trigger worldwide catastrophes. Paleoclimatologist Adrian Hall (Quaid) must rescue his son (Gyllenhaal) from a new Ice Age in New York City.

ELEPHANT
[Drama, 2003] Script and Dir: Gus Van Sant. Phot: Harris Savides. Players: Alex Frost, Eric Deulen, John Robinson, Elias McConnell, Jordan Taylor, Carrie Finklea, Timothy Bottoms. Prod: Metro Films/Blue Relief.
Multi-award winner at Cannes dramatises the Columbine massacre, reimagined in an Oregon high school.

ETERNAL SUNSHINE OF THE SPOTLESS MIND
[Romantic comedy, 2003] Script: Charlie Kaufman. Dir: Michel Gondry. Phot: Ellen Kuras. Players: Jim Carrey, Kate Winslet, Kirsten Dunst, Mark Ruffalo, Tom Wilkinson, Elijah Wood. Prod: Blue Ruin/This is That Productions/Anonymous Content.
When the girlfriend (Winslet) of Joel (Carrey) undergoes an experimental memory erasure procedure under the care of a psychiatrist (Wilkinson), the young man decides to have the same treatment – then changes his mind.

EXORCIST: THE BEGINNING
[Horror thriller, 2004] Script: William Wisher. Dir: Paul Schrader. Phot: Vittorio Storaro. Players: Stellan Skarsgård, Billy Joe Crawford, Gabriel Mann, Clara Bellar, Julian Wadham. Prod: Dominion Productions.
Prequel to the groundbreaking horror film follows the formative years of Father Merrin (Skarsgård), the priest originally played by Max von Sydow.

GOTHIKA
[Horror, 2004] Script: Sebastian Gutierrez. Dir: Mathieu Kassovitz. Phot: Matthew Libatique. Players: Halle Berry, Penélope Cruz, Robert Downey Jr, Charles S. Dutton. Prod: Dark Castle Entertainment.
After awakening as an inmate in the asylum where she works as a criminal psychologist, Dr Miranda Grey stands accused of a murder she can't remember committing and must fight a malevolent spirit.

HELLBOY
[Action-adventure, 2004] Script and Dir: Guillermo del Toro. Phot: Guillermo Navarro. Players: Ron Perlman, Selma Blair, Doug Jones, John Hurt, Jeffrey Tambor. Prod: Revolution Studios/Dark Horse Entertainment.

A HOME AT THE END OF THE WORLD
[Drama, 2004] Script: Michael Cunningham, Keith Bunin. Dir: Michael Mayer. Phot: Enrique Chediak. Players: Colin Farrell, Robin Wright Penn, Dallas Roberts, Sissy Spacek. Prod: Killer Films/Hart Sharp.
Two gay men (Farrell, Roberts), childhood friends, move from Cleveland to New York. When one of them impregnates Clarie (Wright Penn), the trio decide to raise the child.

I LOVE HUCKABEE'S
[Romantic comedy, 2004] Script: David O. Russell, Jeff Baena. Dir: Russell. Players: Mark Wahlberg, Naomi Watts, Jude

(every bit as satisfying as Robert Redford's Oscar-winning *Ordinary People*) didn't garner the Academy nominations it so richly deserved.

For his part, George Clooney cultivates a public image as a strong-willed yet happy-go-lucky actor who sticks by his friends and plays practical jokes on his sets. **Confessions of a Dangerous Mind** plays just that way: a visually busy and tongue-in-cheek adaptation (by *Being John Malkovich*'s Charlie Kaufman) of the hard-to-believe saga of Chuck Barris. While making a very public fortune as the host of TV variety hit *The Gong Show*, he was also, he would have us believe, a contract killer for the American government. Clooney is clearly influenced by the mischievous irony of the Coen Brothers (for whom he starred in *O Brother, Where Art Thou?*), but proves himself a capable storyteller in his own right. *Confessions* was a casualty of the crowded holiday season.

Also playing against type, to sublime effect, was Jack Nicholson, whose canny performance as a retired Midwestern insurance wonk in Alexander Payne's **About Schmidt** neatly submerged all his trademark, exaggerated tics beneath a befuddled sincerity that signalled new depths in an actor all Americans thought they had pegged. In much the same way that Jack Torrance was a turning point for Nicholson in *The Shining,* Warren Schmidt suggests that the Hollywood veteran's sunset years might find him exploring the ageing process onscreen. He promptly followed *About Schmidt* by playing opposite Adam Sandler in the over-the-top 2003 comedy **Anger Management**.

As these "little" movies were attracting critical attention, such high-profile films as *The Hours, The Pianist, Gangs of New York* and *Catch Me If You Can* were doing good business at the multiplexes. Fittingly, the subsequent Oscar race was suspenseful, with awards evenly spread among a clutch of films. Sadly, *Far from Heaven* walked away empty-handed, as did Scorsese's **Gangs of New York**, the former perhaps a victim of its own sophistication and

Daniel Day-Lewis and Leonardo DiCaprio in **Gangs of New York**

the latter of overkill. Scorsese seems to have travelled far from the nervous urgency of his best work; there's nothing particularly propulsive about *Gangs,* a rather ploddingly paced work with jagged flashes of what its maker does best and puzzlingly flabby stretches that look as if they could have been shot by any of a dozen competent technicians.

From curvy *Women* to *Spellbound* kids

The most distinctive American independent films of the period followed no set thematic pattern, but offered distinctive voices, solid storytelling and breakout acting. A sunny teenager named America Ferrera sparked director Patricia Cardozo's **Real Women Have Curves**, the inspirational story of a young Mexican American who learns to be happy with who she is. Film-maker Miguel Arteta and writer Mike White followed their noteworthy 2000 collaboration *Chuck and Buck* with the equally satirical and confident **The Good Girl**. American television star Jennifer Aniston comes into her own on the big screen as Justine, a bored, married store clerk who becomes involved with college drop-out Tom (Jake Gyllenhaal, star of *Donnie Darko*). Gyllenhaal's sister Maggie provoked early Oscar talk for her fearless performance as sado-masochistic office worker Lee Holloway in director Steven Shainberg's **Secretary**, who enters into a most odd – and rewarding – relationship with her remote boss Mr Grey (James Spader).

The period was similarly fertile for stimulating documentary fare. The year's most infuriating movie was Michael Moore's Cannes- and Oscar-winning **Bowling for Columbine**, in which the shambling showman pondered the genuinely provocative issue of guns in America. Unfortunately, his stridently subjective methodology undercut the importance of his message, and his grating Oscar acceptance speech constituted grandstanding of the most distasteful sort.

Similarly manipulative but not as controversial, **The Kid Stays in the Picture** employs its subject, flamboyant producer Robert Evans, to narrate the picaresque story of his rise from child actor to studio honcho, and his string of hits at Paramount in the late 1960s and early 1970s (*The Odd Couple, Rosemary's Baby, Love Story, The Godfather, Urban Cowboy*). It's a remarkable life, for sure, but the way in which directors Brett Morgen and Nanette Burstein manipulate their source material – basically, still photos that move – seems somehow dubious, as if they don't trust this wealth of information to impress on its own.

Far more satisfying as classically constructed documentaries were Jeffrey Blitz's Oscar-nominated **Spellbound**, about the teenage finalists in a national spelling competition, and Christian Charles'

Law, Jason Schwartzman, Dustin Hoffman, Lily Tomlin, Catherine Deneuve. Prod: Scott Rudin Productions/Qwerty Films.
A pair of married detectives help people through their existential crises.

I, ROBOT
[Sci-fi thriller, 2004] Script: Jeff Vintar, Hillary Seitz, Akiva Goldsman, from the short stories by Isaac Asimov. Dir: Alex Proyas. Phot: Simon Duggan. Players: Will Smith, Bridget Moynahan, Alan Tudyk, Chi McBride. Prod: Davis Entertainment/Mystery Clock Cinema/Laurence Mark Productions.
Cop Del Spooner (Smith) leads a murder investigation which reveals that domesticated servant robots may be plotting to gain control of the human world.

JERSEY GIRL
[Dramatic comedy, 2003] Script and Dir: Kevin Smith. Phot: Vilmos Zsigmond. Players: Ben Affleck, Jennifer Lopez, Casey Affleck, Jason Biggs, George Carlin, Jason Lee, Jason Mewes, Liv Tyler, Matt Damon, Will Smith. Prod: Miramax Films/View Askew Productions.
A comedy about fatherhood, inspired by Smith's recent marriage and domesticity.

KING ARTHUR
[Historical action-adventure, 2004] Script: John Lee Hancock, David Franzoni. Dir: Antoine Fuqua. Players: Clive Owen, Stephen Dillane, Keira Knightley, Ioan Gruffudd, Stellan Skarsgård, Ray Winstone. Prod: Jerry Bruckheimer Films/Touchstone Pictures.

LADDER 49
[Action, 2004] Script: Lewis Colick. Dir: Jay Russell. Phot: James Carter. Players: Joaquin Phoenix, John Travolta, Robert Patrick, Balthazar Getty, Jay Hernandez, Bille Burke, Tim Guinee. Prod: Touchstone Pictures/Beacon Pictures/Casey

Silver Productions.
While trapped in a burning building, a Baltimore firefighter (Phoenix) reflects on his life.

THE LADYKILLERS
[Caper comedy, 2004] Script: Ethan Coen, Joel Coen, from the 1955 film written by William Rose. Dir: Coens. Players: Tom Hanks, Marlon Wayans. Prod: The Jacobson Company, Sonnenfeld/Josephson Productions.
In contemporary New Orleans, an eccentric professor (Hanks) plots to rob a massive riverboat casino, but is thwarted by his landlady.

MAN ON FIRE
[Action thriller, 2004] Script: Brian Helgeland, from the novel by A. J. Quinnell. Dir: Tony Scott. Phot: Paul Cameron. Players: Denzel Washington, Dakota Fanning, Christopher Walken, Giancarlo Giannini, Marc Anthony, Radha Mitchell. Prod: Regency Enterprises/ Scott Free.
An ex-Marine bodyguard (Washington) hunts down the killer of the young girl he'd been hired to protect.

MISSION: IMPOSSIBLE 3
[Action adventure, 2004] Script: Robert Towne, Dean Georgaris. Dir: Joe Carnahan. Players: Tom Cruise, Ving Rhames. Prod: Cruise/Wagner Productions.

THE NOTEBOOK
[Romantic drama, 2004] Script: Jeremy Leven, Nick Cassavetes, from the novel by Nicholas Sparks. Dir: Cassavetes. Phot: Robert Fraisse. Players: Ryan Gosling, Gena Rowlands, James Garner, Joan Allen, Sam Shepard. Prod: Avery Pix.
As a retired salesman (Garner) reads to an elderly Alzheimer's patient (Rowlands), the story emerges of their adventures in 1946 South Carolina.

THE PASSION
[Religious drama, 2004] Script: Ben Fitzgerald, Mel Gibson,

unexpectedly sincere **Comedian**, in which Jerry Seinfeld, having made untold millions from his eponymous TV show, reveals his continuing apprehension at telling jokes in front of a live audience. These were complex stories, straightforwardly told – the hallmarks of good documentary movie-making.

New year, same old problems

As has become a dismaying American tradition, the period from January to April 2003 represented the march of the mediocre. Weekend after weekend, the top-grossing films failed to quicken either bloodstream or revenue stream. By May, box-office lagged almost 25% behind the previous year. *Kangaroo Jack, Darkness Falls, The Recruit, How to Lose a Guy in 10 Days, Daredevil, Cradle 2 the Grave, Bringing Down the House, Head of State, Phone Booth, Anger Management, Holes, Identity*: who will remember these competent programmers?

Tellingly, most of them were comedies (or aspired to be, anyway), suggesting that during times of war and economic uncertainty, Americans acted much as they did during the Great Depression, by soothing themselves with laughter (or music: it's hardly a coincidence that **Chicago** was the first tuner in a generation to win the Best Picture Oscar). By mid-year, four comedies (*Bringing Down the House, How to... , Anger Management* and *Bruce Almighty*) had already passed the $100m mark.

It wasn't until **X2: X-Men United** jumpstarted the summer season in early May that revenues began to come in line with the previous year. **The Matrix Reloaded** set a record for an R-rated opening two weeks later with $91.7m. The Disney/Pixar release **Finding Nemo** set a record for an animated opening, hauling in $70.6m ("wholly mackerel", opined *Variety*). Clearly, summer had returned to America.

Move from the figures to the front lines of the American googolplex, and these results take on a decidedly sinister air. More people are piling in to fewer theatres in a shorter period of time, running from one event movie to the next. As Exhibitor Relations chief Paul Dergarabedian pointed out, only a decade ago the summer's top 10 films earned half their total revenue in a span of three weeks, while the top 10 performers of summer 2002 opened on nearly twice as many screens and earned three quarters of their total revenue in the same timespan.

X2 dropped 53% its second weekend; *The Matrix Reloaded* by 60%. This is a risky business indeed: if Hollywood forces the already distracted consumer to develop an even shorter attention span, pictures that could use the time to overcome tepid reviews and build word of mouth (*Solaris, Confessions...*) will sink without a trace.

Mainstream thunder aside, two of the best films released in the first half of 2003 grappled with the documentary form in very different ways. Christopher Guest's charming mockumentary **A Mighty Wind** is covered in the profile of Guest at the front of this book, and proved a sincere and almost heartwarming antidote to the pandering mindset of the more popular movies.

Far more sinister – terrifying, in fact – is Andrew Jarecki's **Capturing the Friedmans**, which won the documentary prize at the 2003 Sundance festival. When the creator of the popular Moviefone cinema ticketing service set out to document the antics of popular New York City childrens' party clown David Friedman, little did he know the dark story that would emerge. David's father, Arnold, and his youngest brother, Jesse, were arrested in late 1987 and charged with child molestation. But evidence of their guilt proves maddeningly elusive. What elevates the film to an altogether different level is the existence of hours and hours of videotape (Friedman was a camera buff) showing the family debating the case each step of the way. "We wanted the audience to be like the jury," editor Richard Hankin told audiences at special screenings surrounding the film's June 2003 theatrical release, and at that *Capturing the Friedmans* is frighteningly effective

George Argerolos/Magnolia Pictures

Arnold and Jesse Friedman, centre and right, in **Capturing the Friedmans**

For now, *The Matrix*'s Neo, Harry Potter, Frodo Baggins and various comic book-derived superheroes may be the engines pulling the train, but it's the characters back in steerage, the Antwone Fishers, Cathy Whitakers, Warren Schmidts and Arnold Friedmans (as well as those who create and/or document them), who quicken the pulse and provide the emotional and intellectual sustenance to the serious cineaste. Hollywood may be fat now, but if it continues systematically to leach the originality and spontaneity from its high-season product, it could become very thin very fast. Yet knowing Americans and their love of presold social phenomena, they'll probably still go to the movies. ∎

translated into Latin and Aramaic by Prof Bill Fulco. Dir: Gibson. Phot: Caleb Deschanel. Players: James Caviezel, Monica Bellucci, Rosalinda Celentano, Sergio Rubini. Prod: Marquis Films/Icon Productions.
The last 12 hours in the life of Jesus Christ.

THE PERFECT SCORE
[Teen caper comedy, 2004]
Script: Jon Zack. Dir: Brian Robbins. Phot: J. Clark Mathis. Players: Erika Christensen, Scarlett Johansson. Prod: Roger Birnbaum Productions/Tollin-Robbins/Spyglass Entertainment.
Five high-school seniors try to ensure perfect scores on their SATs by breaking into the Princeton Testing Centre.

ROSE AND THE SNAKE
[Drama, 2004] Script and Dir: Rebecca Miller. Phot: Ellen Kuras. Players: Daniel Day-Lewis, Catherine Keener, Camilla Belle, Paul Dano, Beau Bridges. Prod: IFC Films.
A widower (Day-Lewis) learns that he's terminally ill and helps introduce his 16-year-old daughter (Belle) to the world from which he's sheltered her on an abandoned commune off the Canadian coast.

SHALL WE DANCE?
[Romantic comedy-musical, 2004] Script: Audrey Wells, based on the 1996 Japanese film written by Masayuki Suo. Dir: Peter Chelsom. Players: Jennifer Lopez, Richard Gere. Prod: Miramax Films.
An overworked accountant (Gere) glimpses a beautiful dance teacher (Lopez) and the subsequent lessons transform his outlook on life.

A SOUND OF THUNDER
[Sci-fi action-thriller, 2004] Script: Thomas Dean Donnelly, Joshua Oppenheimer, from the short story by Ray Bradbury. Dir: Peter Hyams. Players: Ben Kingsley, Catherine McCormack, Edward Burns. Prod: Crusader Entertainment/Franchise Pictures.

In the near future, a packaged big-game hunting trip back to the days of dinosaurs goes awry when one of the hunters accidentally alters the future.

SPARTAN
[Thriller, 2004] Script and Dir: David Mamet. Phot: Juan Ruiz Anchia. Players: Val Kilmer, Derek Luke, William H. Macy, Clark Gregg. Prod: Spartan Productions.
While investigating the kidnapping of the president's daughter, maverick federal agent Scott (Kilmer) discovers a major White House conspiracy.

THE STEPFORD WIVES
[Sci-fi, 2004] Script: Paul Rudnick, from the novel by Ira Levin. Dir: Frank Oz. Phot: Rob Hahn. Players: Nicole Kidman, Matthew Broderick, Bette Midler, Glenn Close, Christopher Walken. Prod: Scott Rudin Productions.

SUSPECT ZERO
[Crime thriller, 2004] Script: Zak Penn, Billy Ray. Dir: Elias Merhige. Phot: Michael Chapman. Players: Aaron Eckhart, Ben Kingsley, Carrie-Ann Moss, Harry J. Lennix. Prod: Intermedia Film Equities/Cruise-Wagner Productions.

TAKING LIVES
[Crime thriller, 2004] Script: Jon Bokenkamp, Hillary Seitz, from the novel by Michael Pye. Dir: D. J. Caruso. Phot: Amir Mokri. Players: Angelina Jolie, Ethan Hawke, Kiefer Sutherland, Gena Rowlands, Olivier Martinez. Prod: Taking Lives Films.

TROY
[Historical action epic, 2004] Script: David Benioff, from Homer's The Iliad. Dir: Wolfgang Petersen. Phot: Roger Pratt. Players: Brad Pitt, Eric Bana, Orlando Bloom, Diane Kruger, Peter O'Toole, Julie Christie, Brian Cox, Sean Bean, Brendan Gleeson. Prod: Warner

Bros/Village Roadshow Pictures Entertainment/ Radiant Productions.

UNCHAIN MY HEART
[Musical biography, 2004] Script: James L. White. Dir: Taylor Hackford. Phot: Pawel Edelman. Players: Jamie Foxx, Kerry Washington, Regina King, Clifton Powell, Harry Lennix, Richard Schiff. Prod: Crusader Entertainment.
The life of Ray Charles.

VAN HELSING
[Action-horror, 2004] Script and Dir: Stephen Sommers. Phot: Allen Daviau. Players: Hugh Jackman, Kate Beckinsale, Richard Roxburgh. Prod: Carpathian Pictures.

Quotes of the Year

"You can get many kinds of balance toward any seemingly grinding postulate of life."
JACK NICHOLSON, in coversation with Newsweek's Jeff Giles.

"It's a bloodbath out there."
JAMES SCHAMUS, writer-producer, on pre-Oscar frenzy, December 2002.

"Saddam Hussein, George Bush – no one will stop me from getting my gift bag."
JOHN WATERS, director, getting his priorities straight at the Independent Spirit Awards, March 2003.

"My research was to go see the [stage] show, and each time I saw the show, I thought, 'Well, how are they going to do this [as a movie]?'"
JOHN TRAVOLTA explaining why he turned down Richard Gere's role in Chicago.

The 75th Academy Awards (2002)

Film: Chicago.
Animated Feature Film: Spirited Away.
Direction: Roman Polanski (The Pianist).
Actor: Adrien Brody (The Pianist).
Actress: Nicole Kidman (The Hours).
Supporting Actor: Chris Cooper (Adaptation).
Supporting Actress: Catherine Zeta-Jones (Chicago).
Original Screenplay: Pedro Almodóvar (Talk to Her).
Adapted Screenplay: Ronald Harwood (The Pianist).
Cinematography: Conrad L. Hall (Road to Perdition).
Film Editing: Martin Walsh (Chicago).
Sound: Michael Minkler, Dominick Tavella, David Lee (Chicago).
Sound Editing: Ethan Van der Ryn, Michael Hopkins (The Lord of the Rings: The Two Towers).
Visual Effects: Jim Rygiel, Joe Letteri, Randall William Cook and Alex Funke (The Two Towers).
Costume Design: Colleen Atwood (Chicago).
Art Direction: John Myhre, Gordon Sim (Chicago).
Make-Up: John Jackson and Beatrice De Alba (Frida).
Original Score: Elliot Goldenthal (Frida).
Original Song: "Lose Yourself", Music by Eminem, Jeff Bass and Luis Resto, Lyrics by Eminem (8 Mile).
Foreign-Language Film: Nowhere in Africa (Germany).
Documentary Feature: Bowling for Columbine.

Uruguay Jorge Jellinek

The Year's Best Films

Jorge Jellinek's selection:

Aside (Dir: Mario Handler)

25 Watts (Dirs: Juan Pablo Rebella, Pablo Stoll)

The Last Train
(Dir: Diego Arsuaga)

Waiting (Dir: Aldo Garay)

El Viaje Hacia el Mar
(Dir: Guillermo Casanova)

Recent and Forthcoming Films

EL ULTIMO TREN
(**The Last Train**)
[Drama, 2002] Script: Diego Arsuaga, Beda Docampo Feijóo, Fernando León de Aranoa. Dir: Arsuaga. Phot: Hans Burman. Players: Federico Luppi, Héctor Alterio, Osvaldo Soriano, Gastón Pauls, Eduardo Migliónico. Prod: Taxi Films, Uruguay.

LA ESPERA (**Waiting**)
[Drama, 2002] Script: Sebastián Bednarik and Coral Godoy, based on the novel Torquator *by Henry Trujillo. Dir: Aldo Garay. Phot: Diego Varela. Players: Verónica Perrota, Elena Zuasti, Walter Reyno, Roberto Suárez. Prod: Austero Producciones.*

EL VIAJE HACIA EL MAR
(*literally,* **The Trip to the Sea**)
[Comedy, 2003] Script: Guillermo Casanova and Julio César Castro, based on the short story by Juan José Morosoli. Dir: Casanova. Phot: Bárbara Alvarez, Daniel Rodríguez. Players: Hugo Arana, Diego Delgrossi, Julio Calcagno, Héctor Guido, Walter Reyno, Julio César Castro. Prod: Natacha López, Jorge Rocca,

Something really surprising has been going on in Uruguayan cinema in recent years. Somehow, with almost no state support and very limited independent finance, around five local feature films are released each year (some of them shot on video), creating a new impulse in national production. This increasing output has gone hand in hand with improving artistic quality, with films such as *In This Tricky Life, The Last Train, 25 Watts* and *Waiting* winning important prizes at festivals such as Huelva, Rotterdam, Buenos Aires, Montreal and Miami.

This achievement is the result of intense work by a new generation of determined film-makers. With a population of around three million (half in the capital, Montevideo), the local theatrical market is too small to support feature budgets of around $100,000 to $1m, so films are feasible only through co-production (mainly with Argentina and Spain) and contributions from international organisations like the Hubert Bals Fund or Ibermedia.

Two film-making trends predominate: the industrial and the independent. The former involves films that shoot in 35mm and use respected foreign actors and technicians. Examples include Esteban Schroder's police story *The Vineyard* (*El viñedo*, 2000) and Beatriz Flores Silva's comedy-drama *In This Tricky Life* (*En la puta vida*, 2001), which recreated the true story of a young woman who escaped from a European prostituion ring. It set an all-time record

Old-timers hijack a locomotive in **The Last Train**

*Yvonne Roucco/
Lavorágine Films.*
In the 1950s, a group of typical inhabitants of a little hillside town have a very eventful trip to the seaside in an old red truck.

Mario Handler's **Aside**

APARTE (Aside)
[Docu-drama, 2002] Dir, Phot and Prod: Mario Handler.

WHISKY
[Comedy-drama, 2003] Script: Juan Pablo Rebella, Pablo Stoll, Gonzalo Delgado. Dir: Stoll and Rebella. Players: Jorge Bolani, Mirela Pascual. Prod: CTRL/Z Films.
When his successful brother returns from abroad, a frustrated middle-aged man's decision to pretend that he is married to a woman who works for him sparks a series of deceptions in a triangle of passion and jealousy.

LA PERRERA (Dog Pound)
[Comedy-drama, forthcoming] Script and Dir: Manuel Nieto. Prod: CTRL/Z Films.
A failed student loses his scholarship and must return to a house in a small, isolated beach town, where his authoritarian father spends the weekends. Dogs become an important part of the young man's life as he starts building his own home on an abandoned lot.

TOKYO BOOGIE
[Comedy, 2003] Script: Pablo Casacuberta, Yukihiko Goto, Viki Anderson, Inés Bortagaray.

for a Uruguayan film (more than 140,000 admissions).

Other 'industrial' films are Luis Nieto's **Southern Star** (*Estrella del sur*, 2002), which explored, with mixed results, the violent past of a former leftist militant. The main character returns to present-day Uruguay with his family after many years in exile in Spain and must confront his involvement with the violent *Tupamaros* guerrilla movement in the late 1960s and early 1970s, after his teenage son discovers old guns buried in the backyard of the family's seaside house.

Firmly directed by Diego Arsuaga and sold for a possible Hollywood remake, the pleasant but superficial **The Last Train** (*El último tren*) is a dramatic adventure about three retired train workers (splendidly played by Argentine actors Federico Luppi, Héctor Alterio and Osvaldo Soriano) who decide to run away with an old locomotive. The picture drew more than 50,000 admissions and also did quite well in Spain, where it received the Goya Prize for Best Latin American Film.

Surprising power from *25 Watts*

The more independent, lower-budget style was inaugurated by **25 Watts** (2001), made for less than $50,000 in 16mm black-and-white by Juan Pablo Rebella and Pablo Stoll as they were finishing off at film school. With its off-beat humour and refined visuals, this ironic, dark portrait of a group of juvenile middle-class friends spending a very boring Sunday together was a fresh breeze that helped to reinvigorate Uruguayan cinema. It received several prizes, including the Tiger Award in Rotterdam and the FIPRESCI Award in Buenos Aires, and the same team's new project, **Whisky**, has already won the Sundance NHK International Film-makers Award.

Another low-budget production is Aldo Garay's **Waiting** (*La espera*), a minimalistic story of frustrated passions and deception in the relationship between a young woman, her bedridden, dying mother and a mature neighbour who harbours a secret attraction. Based on Henry Trujillo's novella *Torquator,* it resembles the pessimistic universe of Juan Carlos Onetti's writings. With its dense, oppressive atmosphere, it marks an interesting fiction debut from Garay, already known for his documentaries.

Documentary production has also developed. Virginia Martínez's **Acratas** (2000) is the richly documented and tightly edited story of a group of anarchists who travelled from Spain to Argentina and Uruguay in the 1920s and 1930s. Their audacious actions, including a massive underground jailbreak, made quite an impact in the press at the time, and they are presented as the forefathers of the political activists of the 1960s and 1970s.

A daughter looks after her dying mother in Aldo Garay's **Waiting**

Also successfully exhibited in local cinemas was Gerard Stawsky's **Despite Treblinka** (*A pesar de Treblinka*, 2002), a deeply emotional and sometimes hilarious story about endurance in the face of horror. With music by acclaimed composer John Zorn, it combines achival footage and interviews with three of the last 10 survivors of the Nazi extermination camp in Poland, one of whom lives in Uruguay.

Of special interest is **Aside** (*Aparte*), released in spring 2003, because it marks the comeback of Mario Handler, acclaimed internationally in the 1960s for his political films. Produced, shot (on digital video) and edited by Handler, this extreme and personal exploration of the margins of Uruguayan society follows for more than a year the fight for survival of young people living in extreme poverty in the Montevideo suburbs. They are invisible to the rest of society, caught in a vicious circle of drugs, violence and jail. *Aside* has been acclaimed as one of Handler's most important works.

It is also important that Uruguayan cinema has room for animation, especially the work of internationally acclaimed Walter Tournier, whose last short, *In Spite of Everything* (*A pesar de todo*), is an eloquent anti-war tale demonstrating excellent use of stop-motion.

Recession and devaluation, which have severely restricted the grants passed on to film-makers by FONA (the fund created by the government in 1996, in collaboration with Uruguay's commercial TV channels), could still jeopardise the future of the fragile Uruguayan industry. But it surely won't stop the new generation of writers and directors from pursuing their dreams.

JORGE JELLINEK has been a film critic and journalist for 20 years, contributing to radio, newspapers and magazines, including pan-American weekly *Tiempos del Mundo*. He is vice-president of the Uruguayan Critics Association.

Dir: Casacuberta, Goto. Prod: Casacuberta.
In the 1950s, a Japanese film crew arrives by mistake in a small town in Uruguay, looking for locations to make a Western. The film shoot stalls as confusion grows.

Quote of the Year

"One character in the film says, 'What you see is what you get' and that sums up my intention of showing real people living their lives – the opposite of what you see in 'reality' TV shows."
MARIO HANDLER, *director of* Aside.

Uzbekistan Eugene Zykov

Recent and Forthcoming Films

MALCHIKI V NEBE
(Boys in the Sky)
[Comedy, 2003] Script and Dir: Zulfikar Musakov. Phot: Abdurakhim Ismailov. Players: Murad Abdulaev, Timur Musakov, David Gulyamov, Artyom Sultanov. Prod: Uzbek Film Studios.

Comrade Boikendjaev

TOVARISCH BOIKENDJAEV
(Comrade Boikendjaev)
[Satirical drama, 2002] Script and Dir: Yusuf Razykov. Phot: Khafis Faiziev. Players: Farkhad Abdullaev, Miryam Alimova, Umar Alikhodjaev. Prod: Uzbek Film Studios.

TANK
[Comedy, 2003] Script and Dir: Tureniyas Kalimbetov. Phot: Abdurakhim Ismailov. Players: Amir Sultanov. Prod: Karakalpak Film Studios/Uzbek Film Studios.

VLYUBLENNYE 2
(Tenderness 2)
[Romantic drama, 2003] Script and Dir: Ilyer Ishmukhamedov. Players: Rodion Nakhapetor, Martiana Verinskaya, Rustam Sagdullaev, Olgha Kabo, Tabara Akulova. Prod: Ishmukhamedov, Studio Vatan, with Russia's Ministry of Culture.

n 2003, two Uzbek films broke into the local box-office top 10 alongside the Hollywood imports. The first, **Boys in the Sky** (*Malchiki v nebe*), from award-winning director Zulfikar Musakov (b.1958), followed the bittersweet adolescence (school friendship and first loves) of four boys in Tashkent and stayed in cinemas for five months. The second, **The Scorpio Flower**, is an eternal triangle drama about an unhappily married woman who takes a lover. Such success is still a far cry from the 1970s, when the Tashkent Film Festival was the entertainment Mecca of central Asia. Now Uzbek Film Studios, the principal state-run producer, releases perhaps four or five features annually, with an average budget of $200,000. The state provided about $1m (one billion Sum) for 2003, enough to support three features and some documentary and animation work.

Traditionally, Uzbekistan offers great opportunities to its seasoned film veterans, led by Yusuf Razykov, director general of Uzbek Film Studios, whose *Orator,* a political satire about Soviet times, won numerous festival awards. Those young film-makers who do get a chance to work have the guts to show Uzbeks the grim state of their nation. Furkatbet Yakvalkhodzhaev's shocking docu-drama short *Podyenschitsy* (literally, *Day Labourers*) focuses on Uzbek cleaning women who work as speechless, underpaid slaves.

Uzbek comedies are a combination of Russian and Indian styles (both film cultures influenced Uzbekistan for decades). Their charismatic heroes often make extravagant, romantic gestures to please beautiful women or even bureaucrats. In **Tank**, an old man uses all his personal charm and new friends to avoid giving a bribe to a ruthless official, and in Zulfikar Musakov's short, *Old Good Boots* (*Kaloshi*), an ageing tinker sneaks away from his house to visit his lover just before Christmas.

Some major Uzbek directors work in Moscow, among them Ali Khamraev, who is following the award-winning *Ba Bo Bu* with plans for an epic drama, *Tamer an*. After a smashing success 30 years ago with *Tenderness* (*Vlyublennye*), a heart-warming musical about male friendships and teenagers' first loves, director Ilyer Ishmukhamedov has been shooting *Tenderness 2* at Mosfilm. "I find it quite exciting to bring my heroes [from *Tenderness*] into the present," he said. "It's like the three musketeers showing up today and encountering skinheads or racketeers."

Venezuela Andréina Lairet and Suzanne García

Recent and Forthcoming Films

LA PLUMA DEL ARCÁNGEL
(The Archangel's Feather)
[Drama, 2001] Script: Juan Carlos Gené, César Sierra, based on a novel by Arturo Uslar Pietri. Dir: Luis Manzo. Phot: Cezary Jaworski. Players: Iván Tamayo, Roque Valero, Elba Escobar, Alejo Felipe, Julio Mota, Armando Gota. Prod: Luis Pinto G, Martha Pabón.

YOTAMA SE VA VOLANDO
(*literally,* Yotama Flies Away)
[Drama, 2001] Script: Carlos Brito, Jacques Espagne. Dir: Luis Armando Roche. Phot: Vitelbo Vásquez. Players: Beatriz Vázquez, Edgar Ramírez, Martha Tarazona, Asdrúbal Meléndez. Prod: Marie Françoise Roche.
A musician, Emilio, 60, returns to Venezuela for Christmas to meet his grandson, Manuel. Yotama, a young female criminal, takes them hostage.

EL NUDO (The Knot)
[Thriller, 2002] Script, Dir and Prod: Alejandro Wiedemann. Players: Fabiola Colmenares, Rafael Romero, Edgar Ramírez.
A tropical film noir. Two middle-class men want to get out of Venezuela to start a prosperous new life. So they plan a robbery.

PASO AL FRENTE (*literally,* One Step Forward)
[Drama, 2002] Dir: Elia Schneider. Players: Ramiro Meneses, Edgar Ramírez, Juan David Restrepo.
Two soldiers become best friends on the Venezuela/Colombia border. Through war and confusion their relationship endures.

Although Venezuelan directors and writers have been criticised for addressing political issues in their films, national politics and film-making continue to walk hand in hand. In 2002, the local audience welcomed several pictures that, although set in different periods, mirrored the nation's ongoing crisis. Enrique Lazo's *Starting from Scratch (Borrón y cuenta nueva)*, which took $250,000 to be the year's most successful Venezuelan film, and Malena Roncayolo's *Acosada en Lunes de Carnival* (a $28,000 gross) all deal with the hardships of living in an unstable country. Lazo's box-office tally was impressive, even though the average budget for a local feature is more than $500,000.

Venezuela's nominee for the Foreign-Language Oscar, Luis Manzo's **The Archangel's Feather** (*La pluma del arcángel*) is also overtly political. In a small town in the 1930s, a telegraphist starts an undercover information revolution that blatantly defies the local authorities and their abuse of power. Despite its good reviews, the film took less than $12,000. With such high inflation in 2002, ticket prices went up by 18%, but total box-office fell by 12.5%, because many people could no longer afford a night at the movies, and in December all cinemas were closed by the general strike.

Four films completed in 2002 awaited release at press time, three of them debuts. Alejandro Wiedemann, writer-director of *The Knot* (*El nudo),* spent $375,000 on his film, and said: "I made it with the intention of people liking the film. If things turn out well, I will be able to do a second movie. If not, I'll contemplate suicide."

The local industry remained almost paralysed in 2003 because of the chronic shortage of private and government funding. Venezuelan film-makers have been more successful overseas, with local films gaining distribution in seven countries, participating in 100 festivals and winning 27 awards in 2002. Finally, the Venezuelan Film Commission's efforts to attract visiting productions are predicted to attract inward investment of more than $500,000 for 2003, but it remains to be seen whether this revenue will breathe life back into the local industry.

ANDRÉINA LAIRET has directed one short film and worked on several others. **SUZANNE GARCÍA** directs TV reports and advertisements for Nochinoma Productions and Cinesa, Caracas.

JOHN SCHLESINGER *shooting* An Eye for an Eye *(1995).*
The Oscar-winning director of Midnight Cowboy *(1969) died on July 25, 2003, aged 77.*

ELIA KAZAN, right, with Marlon Brando on the set of A Streetcar Named Desire *(1951).*
Kazan died on September 28, 2003, aged 94.

World Box-Office Survey 2002

ARGENTINA

		Admissions
1.	Spider-Man	1,718,000
2.	Ice Age	1,407,000
3.	The Two Towers	1,391,000
4.	The Chamber of Secrets	1,130,000
5.	Passionate (Argentina)	1,123,000
6.	Ocean's Eleven	1,010,000
7.	Signs	998,000
8.	Lilo & Stitch	901,000
9.	A Beautiful Mind	803,000
10.	Men in Black II	778,000

Population:	37 million
Admissions:	32.3 million
Total box-office:	$50m
Local films' market share:	9.5%
Screens:	782
Avge. ticket price:	$1.50

Source: INCAA.

AUSTRALIA

		$m
1.	Attack of the Clones	18.39
2.	The Fellowship of the Ring	17.35
3.	Spider-Man	16.86
4.	The Chamber of Secrets	16.48
5.	My Big Fat Greek Wedding	13.00
6.	Ocean's Eleven	12.08
7.	Ice Age	11.10
8.	A Beautiful Mind	10.72
9.	Austin Powers in Goldmember	10.50
10.	Scooby-Doo	9.90

Population:	19.8 million
Admissions:	92.5m
Total box-office:	$459.57m
Local films' market share:	5%
Screens:	1,872
Avge ticket price:	$4.97

$1 = A$0.544
Sources: Aust. Bureau of Statistics/MPDAA.

AUSTRIA

		Admissions
1.	The Fellowship of the Ring	1,019,500
2.	The Two Towers	839,762
3.	The Chamber of Secrets	757,379
4.	Ice Age	722,774
5.	Spider-Man	589,903
6.	Men in Black II	535,136
7.	Attack of the Clones	503,314
8.	Ocean's Eleven	490,711
9.	Monsters, Inc.	489,659
10.	Die Another Day	483,436

Population:	8 million
Admissions:	19,316,023
Total box-office:	$12.91m
Sites/screens:	198/562

Source: Wirtschaftskammer Österreich.

BELARUS

1.	The Two Towers
2.	Men in Black II
3.	Attack of the Clones
4.	Femme Fatale
5.	xXx
6.	Vanilla Sky
7.	Minority Report
8.	The Chamber of Secrets
9.	A Beautiful Mind
10.	Spider-Man

Films' admissions totals not available.

Population:	10.5 million
Admissions:	10.5 million
Total box-office:	$22 m
Screens:	152
Avge. ticket price:	$2

1$ = 2.0 Roubles
Source: Department Filmvideoart Belarus.

BELGIUM

	Admissions
1. The Chamber of Secrets	1,085,971
2. Asterix & Obelix... (Fr/Ger)	782,107
3. Ocean's Eleven	679,164
4. Spider-Man	654,709
5. Die Another Day	565,114
6. The Two Towers	527,994
7. Attack of the Clones	512,613
8. Ice Age	453,714
9. Minority Report	446,630
10. Signs	422,880

Population:	10.31 million
Admissions:	24.5 million
Sites/screens:	127/514
Avge. ticket price:	€5.67

Source: Federation of Belgian Cinemas.

BOSNIA AND HERZEGOVINA

	Admissions
1. Remake (Bosnia)	63,156
2. My Big Fat Greek Wedding	15,349
3. The Chamber of Secrets	11,018
4. Signs	9,017
5. The Princess Diaries	8,344
6. Sweet Home Alabama	5,631
7. Attack of the Clones	5,521
8. The Count of Monte Cristo	4,256
9. Bad Company	4,238
10. The Hot Chick	3,156

Population:	3 million
Screens:	25
Avg. ticket price:	$1-$2

$1 = 2 marks.
Source: Kino Meeting Point, Sarajevo.

BRAZIL

	Admissions
1. Spider-Man	8,488,182
2. The Fellowship of the Ring	4,286,797
3. The Chamber of Secrets	3,933,328
4. Men in Black II	3,445,424
5. Scooby-Doo	3,186,201
6. City of God (Brazil)	3,117,220
7. Signs	2,710,249
8. Xuxa and the Gnomes (Brazil)	2,657,091
9. Ice Age	2,495,665
10. Ocean's Eleven	2,438,408

Population:	170 million
Admissions:	90.87 million
Total box office:	$150.44m
Local films' market share:	8%
Screens:	1,635
Avge. ticket price:	$2.18

Source: Filme B.

BULGARIA

	Admissions
1. The Fellowship of the Ring	117,539
2. The Philosopher's Stone	140,431
3. Attack of the Clones	91,576
4. xXx	86,318
5. Ocean's Eleven	58,417
6. Men in Black II	54,056
7. The Chamber of Secrets	65,417
8. Rush Hour 2	55,996
9. Spider-Man	54,509
10. A Beautiful Mind	43,171

Population:	7.85 million
Admissions:	2.02 million
Total box-office:	$4.19m
Local films' market share:	Less than 1%
Sites/screens:	179/202
Avge. ticket price:	$2.08

Sources: National Statistical Institute/Geopoly Ltd.

CANADA

	$m
1. Spider-Man	34
2. The Fellowship of the Ring	26
3. Attack of the Clones	24
4. The Chamber of Secrets	21
5. My Big Fat Greek Wedding	20
6. Austin Powers in Goldmember	18
7. Signs	16
8. A Beautiful Mind	14
9. The Two Towers	14
10. Ice Age	14

Population:	31.4 million
Admissions:	154 million
Total box office:	$690m
Local films' market share:	3%
Sites/screens:	714/2,953
Avge. ticket price:	$4.47

Source: Motion Picture Theatre Associations of Canada.

CHILE

	Admissions
1. The Fellowship of The Ring	890,258
2. Spider-Man	776,123
3. Attack of The Clones	599,418
4. Ice Age	579,342
5. Lilo & Stitch	471,816
6. The Chamber of Secrets	383,929
7. Ocean's Eleven	343,609
8. Signs	341,486
9. Men in Black II	339,359
10. A Beautiful Mind	283,363

Population:	15.12 million
Admissions:	11.45 million
Total box-office:	$33.34 million
Local films' market share:	3.4%
Screens:	216
Avge. ticket price:	$2.9

Sources: Instituto Nacional de Estadística/Cámara Chilena de Comercio Cinematográfico.

CHINA

	$m
1. Big Shot's Funeral (China/US)	4.84*
2. The Touch (HK/Taiwan/China)	3.39
3. Together (China/S.Korea)	1.69
4. Ghosts (China)	1.33
5. The Lion Roars (Hong Kong)	1.21
6. I Love You (China)	1.09
7. The Missing Gun (China)	1.08
8. Charging Out Amazon (China/US)	0.85
9. The Faded Beauty (China)	0.72
10. Red Snow (China)	0.60*

Estimate. $1 = 8.25 RMB.
Sources: Chinese Film Market/Asian Film Connections.

Admissions:	200 million (Est.)
Local films' market share:	55% (Est.)
Screens:	10,000-plus.

COLOMBIA

1. Spider-Man
2. The Fellowship of the Ring
3. Ice Age
4. The Philosopher's Stone
5. Monsters, Inc.
6. Men in Black II
7. Signs
8. A Beautiful Mind
9. The Two Towers
10. Ocean's Eleven

Films' admissions totals not available.

Population:	42 million (est.)
Admissions:	16.8 million
Total box-office:	$42m (est.)
Avge. ticket price:	$2.30

Sources: Acocine/Cine Colombia.

CROATIA

	Admissions
1. The Fellowship of the Ring	289,666
2. The Chamber of Secrets	174,984
3. The Philosopher's Stone	129,008
4. Attack of the Clones	122,411
5. Spider–Man	110,561
6. Die Another Day	98,722
7. Men in Black II	83,448
8. Ocean's Eleven	81,532
9. Minority Report	59,136
10. Amélie (France)	53,994

Population:	4,381,352
Admissions:	2,656,543
Local films' market share:	Less than 2%
Screens:	55
Avge. ticket price:	$3

Sources: Central Bureau of Statistics/Hollywood magazine.

CZECH REPUBLIC

	Admissions
1. The Fellowship of the Ring	957,223
2. The Philosopher's Stone	766,359
3. Men in Black II	315,391
4. Ice Age	315,359
5. Attack of the Clones	277,637
6. The Chamber of Secrets	261,885
7. Spider-Man	233,065
8. Max, Sally & the Magic Phone (Cz)	207,751
9. Year of the Devil (Czech)	204,617
10. Minority Report	198,082

Population:	10.27 million
Admissions:	10.92 million
Total box-office:	$32.5m
Local films' market share:	9.5%
Screens:	754
Avge. ticket price:	$3 (approx.)

Source: Czech Film Centre.

DENMARK

	Admissions
1. The Fellowship of the Ring	1,021,252
2. The Chamber of Secrets	602,849
3. The Two Towers	515,062
4. My Sister's Kids 2 (Denmark)	506,312
5. Open Hearts (Denmark)	502,236
6. Attack of the Clones	458,169
7. Spider-Man	423,543
8. Monsters, Inc.	384,484
9. Old Men in New Cars (Denmark)	337,098
10. Ice Age	272,557

Population:	5.4 million
Admissions:	12.9 million
Total box-office:	$99.5m
Local films' market share:	19.8%
Sites/screens:	162/358
Avge. ticket price:	$8.7

Source: Danmarks Statistik.

EGYPT

	$
1. El Limby	3,760,350
2. Mafia	2,252,835
3. Thieves in Kindergarten II	1,811,728
4. Prince of Darkness	1,718,967
5. His Friend's Friend	1,202,114
6. Khul Lawyer	1,061,269
7. What's On?	506,597
8. The Magician	482,701
9. The Mediterranean	480,920
10. Sehr El Eyoun	410,239

All titles are Egyptian.

Population:	68 million
Admissions:	16 million (approx.)
Total box-office:	$22.06m
Local films' market share:	74%
Sites/screens:	160/202
Avge. Ticket price:	$2:50

$1 = 6.5 Pounds. Source: United Motion Picture (Cairo).

ESTONIA

		Admissions
1.	Names in Marble (Estonia)	136,171
2.	The Fellowship of the Ring	91,222
3.	Ice Age	89,109
4.	Ocean's Eleven	45,138
5.	Men in Black II	43,586
6.	Spider-Man	39,635
7.	xXx	39,095
8.	Die Another Day	38,663
9.	The Chamber of Secrets	35,460
10.	Attack of the Clones	33,031

Population:	1.36 million
Admissions:	1.56 million
Total box-office:	$5.49m
Local films' market share:	9.5%
Screens:	81
Avge. ticket price:	$3.53

$1 = 16.606 EEK
Source: Estonian Film Foundation.

FINLAND

		Admissions
1.	The Fellowship of the Ring	548,384
2.	The Chamber of Secrets	340,390
3.	Attack of the Clones	320,268
4.	Spider-Man	267,443
5.	Rollo & The Spirit... (Finland)	259,524
6.	Me and Morrison ((Finland)	245,647
7.	Die Another Day	223,202
8.	Lovers and Leavers (Finland)	215,417
9.	Ocean's Eleven	213,275
10.	Hayflower and Quiltshoe (Finland)	204,630

Population:	5.2 million
Admissions:	7.7 million
Total box-office:	€55m
Local films' market share:	17.7%
Screens:	345
Avge. cinema ticket price:	€7.14

Source: Finnish Film Foundation.

FRANCE

		Admissions (millions)
1.	Asterix & Obelix... (Fr/Ger)	14.22
2.	The Chamber of Secrets	6.94
3.	Spider-Man	6.32
4.	Attack of the Clones	5.58
5.	Men in Black II	4.52
6.	Ocean's Eleven	4.45
7.	The Two Towers	4.25
8.	Die Another Day	3.57
9.	8 Women (France)	3.54
10.	Minority Report	3.46

Population:	58.52 million
Admissions:	184.5 million
Total box-office:	€1.027 billion
Local films' market share:	35%
Sites/screens:	2,167/5,280
Avge. ticket price:	€5.57

Source: Centre National du Cinéma.

GERMANY

		$m
1.	The Chamber of Secrets	51.31
2.	The Two Towers	38.57
3.	Ice Age	36.38
4.	Attack of the Clones	35.65
5.	Spider-Man	28.70
6.	Men in Black	27.08
7.	Die Another Day	26.73
8.	Ocean's Eleven	25.22
9.	Minority Report	16.40
10.	Monsters, Inc.	16.28

Population:	82,474,729
Admissions:	163.9 million
Total box-office:	$905.7m
Local films' market share:	11.9%
Sites/screens:	1,049/4,868
Avge. ticket price:	$5.53

$1 = €1.06
Source: Federal Film Board.

GREECE

		Admissions
1.	The Two Towers	910,000
2.	My Big Fat Greek Wedding	800,000
3.	The Chamber of Secrets	600,000
4.	Die Another Day	430,000
5.	The Matrix Reloaded	425,000
6.	Signs	325,000
7.	Catch Me If You Can	290,000
8.	Chicago	280,000
9.	Gangs of New York	270,000
10.	Minority Report	260,000

July 2002 to June 2003. Figures unconfirmed officially.

Population:	10.9 million
Admissions:	14.8 million
Screens:	440
Avge. ticket price:	$5.50

Source: Cinema Department, Ministry of Culture.

HONG KONG

		$m
1.	Infernal Affairs (Hong Kong)	7.06
2.	The Chamber of Secrets	4.90
3.	Spider-Man	3.66
4.	Hero (China/Hong Kong)	3.42
5.	Monsters, Inc.	3.31
6.	Minority Report	2.92
7.	Marry A Rich Man (Hong Kong)	2.78
8.	Men in Black II	2.67
9.	My Left Eye Sees Ghosts (HK)	2.66
10.	Fat Choi Spirit (Hong Kong)	2.46

Source: City Entertainment/Industry data.

Population:	6,815,800
Admissions:	20.1 million
Total box-office:	$110.6m
Local films' market share:	40.2%
Sites/screens:	58/184
Avge. ticket price:	$5.40

$1 = HK$7.8. Sources: HK Theatres Association/City Entertainment/South China Morning Post/Far East Film.

HUNGARY

	Admissions
1. Attack of the Clones	811,603
2. The Two Towers	691,645
3. The Chamber of Secrets	668,388
4. Ice Age	574,329
5. A Kind of America (Hungary)	531,474
6. Men in Black II	469,050
7. My Big Fat Greek Wedding	353,000
8. Taxi 3 (France)	341,211
9. Asterix & Obelix... (Fr/Ger)	309,044
10. Spider-Man	295,372

April 2002 to May 2003.

Population:	10.5 million
Admissions:	15,228,000
Total Box-Office:	$39m
Local films' market share:	7.5 %
Screens:	585
Avge. ticket price:	$2.58

$1 = 250 forints. Sources: UIP Dunafilm Budapest/Skyfilm Studio/Assoc. of Film Distributors.

IRELAND

	$m
1. The Fellowship of the Ring	5.12
2. The Chamber of Secrets	4.63
3. Spider-Man	4.28
4. Monsters, Inc.	4.27
5. Ocean's Eleven	3.79
6. The Two Towers	3.34
7. Die Another Day	3.19
8. Attack of the Clones	3.18
9. Austin Powers in Goldmember	3.1
10. Scooby-Doo	2.89

Population:	3.91 million
Admissions:	17.3 million
Total box-office:	$88.21m
Local films' market share:	2%
Screens:	326
Avge. ticket price:	$5.40

Source: AC Nielsen EDI/Carlton Screen Advertising.

ITALY

	$m
1. Christmas on the Nile (Italy/Spain)	26.6
2. Pinocchio (Italy)	24.62
3. Legend of Al, John & Jack (Italy)	20.94
4. The Chamber of Secrets	19.62
5. The Two Towers	19.34
6. My Big Fat Greek Wedding	13.02
7. Signs	10.47
8. Facing Window (Italy/UK/Turkey/Port.)	9.72
9. Minority Report	9.62
10. Remember Me (Italy/UK)	9.53

August 2002 to June 2003 (approx. 65% of annual gross).

Population:	57.8 million
Admissions:	49.7 million
Total box-office:	$284.72m
Local films' market share:	30.1%
Screens:	3,700
Avge. ticket price:	$6

Sources: Cinetel/Agis.

JAPAN

	$m
1. The Philosopher's Stone	172
2. The Chamber of Secrets	152.5
3. Monsters, Inc.	79.4
4. Attack of the Clones	79.2
5. The Fellowship of the Ring	76.9
6. Spider-Man	63.6
7. Ocean's Eleven	59.3
8. The Cat Returns (Japan)	54.7
9. Men in Black II	33.9
10. I Am Sam	29.3

Population:	126.9 million
Admissions:	160.8 million
Total box-office:	$1.67 billion
Local films' market share:	27.1%
Screens:	2,635
Avge. ticket price:	$10.37

$1 = 118 Yen.
Source: Japan Motion Picture Producers Association.

KAZAKHSTAN

	Admissions
1. The Fellowship of the Ring	69,920
2. Men in Black II	63,283
3. The Mummy Returns	59,538
4. Attack of the Clones	56,238
5. Spider-Man	56,063
6. X-Men	49,573
7. The Philosopher's Stone	48,944
8. The Scorpion King	47,524
9. Planet of the Apes	46,415
10. Jurassic Park III	38,100

Figures are for Almaty only. Source: Ottau Cinema.

LATVIA

	Admissions
1. The Fellowship of the Ring	47,912
2. The Philosopher's Stone	40,415
3. Men in Black II	34,117
4. Die Another Day	30,393
5. Spider-Man	30,269
6. Stuart Little 2	30,042
7. Ocean's Eleven	29,519
8. Attack of the Clones	29,517
9. xXx	28,150
10. Ice Age	24,115

Population:	2.4 million
Admissions:	1,908,380
Total box-office:	$3.33m
Local films' market share:	1.2%
Sites/screens:	32/35
Avge. ticket price:	$3.14

$1 = 0.566 Lats
Sources: UN Human Development Report/ National Film Centre.

LEBANON

	Admissions
1. Die Another Day	129,194
2. Spider-Man	85,036
3. A Trip (Lebanon)	74,357
4. Ocean's Eleven	69,072
5. A Beautiful Mind	60,591
6. My Big Fat Greek Wedding	50,203
7. Behind Enemy Lines	47,899
8. The Fellowship of the Ring	47,628
9. Unfaithful	46,259
10. Men in Black II	43,762

LITHUANIA

	Admissions
1. The Fellowship of the Ring	50,679
2. The Chamber of Secrets	38,790
3. A Beautiful Mind	38,024
4. Spirit: Stallion of the Cimarron	36,443
5. Vanilla Sky	29,874
6. xXx	32,002
7. Ocean's Eleven	31,290
8. Die Another Day	28,268
9. Ice Age	32,495
10. The Scorpion King	30,504

Population:	3,698,500
Sites/screens:	67/83
Avge. ticket price:	$2.78

LUXEMBOURG

	Admissions
1. The Chamber of Secrets	63,000*
2. Spider-Man	49,800
3. The Fellowship of the Ring	48,800
4. Die Another Day	43,500*
5. Ocean's Eleven	41,700
6. Asterix & Obelix ...(Fr/Ger)	39,000
7. Ice Age	40,000
8. Monsters, Inc.	36,500
9. Men in Black II	36,300
10. The Unemployment Club (L'bourg)	33,800

*includes 2001 figures.

Population:	441,300
Admissions:	1.4 million
Local films' market share:	0.3%
Screens:	25
Avge. ticket price:	$7

MALAYSIA

	$m
1. Spider-Man	1,700,000
2. The Two Towers	1,200,000
3. The Chamber of Secrets	1,050,000
4. Attack of the Clones	870,000
5. The Scorpion King	850,000
6. Die Another Day	850,000
7. The Tuxedo	750,000
8. Mami Jarum (Malaysia)	750,000
9. Baba (Malaysia)	660,000
10. Men in Black II	550,000

$1= 3.80 Ringit. Figures net of entertainment tax.

Population:	24 million
Admissions:	10.235 million
Total box-office:	$19.7m
Sites:	195
Avge. Ticket price:	$1.85

Sources: National Film Development Corp./Golden Screen Cinemas.

MEXICO

	$m
1. Spider-Man	29.4
2. Ice Age	18.6
3. The Crime of Father Amaro (Mexico)	16.1
4. The Chamber of Secrets	15.8
5. Signs	11.6
6. Lilo & Stitch	11.3
7. Men in Black II	10.6
8. Scooby-Doo	10.6
9. The Two Towers	10.4
10. Shallow Hal	9.8

Population:	99.7 million
Admissions:	152 million
Total box-office:	$445m
Local films' market share:	9.8%
Sites/screens:	498/2,823
Avge. ticket price:	$3.25

$1US = M$9.90. Sources: Instituto Mexicano de Cinematografía/Cineteca Nacional.

THE NETHERLANDS

	Admissions
1. The Chamber of Secrets	1,478,000
2. The Fellowship of the Ring	1,348,000
3. Ocean's Eleven	807,00
4. The Two Towers	725,000
5. Attack of the Clones	649,000
6. Spider-Man	624,000
7. The Philosopher's Stone	559,000
8. Signs	510,000
9. Full Moon (Netherlands)	455,000
10. A Beautiful Mind	440,000

Population:	16.1 million
Admissions:	24.1 million
Total box-office:	$180m
Local films' market share:	10.5%
Screens:	596
Avge. ticket price:	$7.46

Source: Netherlands Cinematographic Federation.

NEW ZEALAND

		$m
1.	The Fellowship of the Ring	14.6
2.	The Philosopher's Stone	4.51
3.	Attack of the Clones	3.21
4.	Spider-Man	3.06
5.	Scooby-Doo	2.12
6.	Men in Black II	2.05
7.	Ocean's Eleven	2.03
8.	A Beautiful Mind	1.82
9.	Monsters, Inc.	1.80
10.	Ice Age	1.80

Population:	4 million
Admissions:	17,837,000
Total box-office:	$82.77m
Local films' market share:	1%
Screens:	323
Avge. ticket price:	$4.65

$NZ1 = $0.58
Source: Motion Picture Distributors' Association.

NORWAY

		Admissions
1.	The Fellowship of the Ring	667,920
2.	The Chamber of Secrets	610,703
3.	Ice Age	575,318
4.	Spider-Man	498,329
5.	The Two Towers	466,684
6.	Attack of the Clones	396,471
7.	Monsters, Inc.	395,409
8.	I Am Dina (Norway)	310,905
9.	About a Boy (US/UK)	296,375
10.	Lilo & Stitch	293,971

Population:	4.5 million
Admissions:	12 million
Total box office:	$100.5m
Local films' market share:	7.5%
Screens:	401
Avge. ticket price:	$8.38

Source: National Association of Municipal Cinemas.

PERU

		$
1.	Spider-Man	1,950,000
2.	The Fellowship of the Ring	1,470,000
3.	Attack of the Clones	1,160,000
4.	The Chamber of Secrets	1,060,000
5.	Ice Age	1,000,000
6.	Stuart Little 2	950,000*
7.	Signs	730,000*
8.	A Beautiful Mind	600,000*
9.	Ocean's Eleven	500,000*
10.	Shallow Hal	450,000*

*Estimate

Population:	82 million
Admissions:	18.37 million

PHILIPPINES

1. Spider-Man
2. The Chamber of Secrets
3. Attack of the Clones
4. The Two Towers
5. Die Another Day
6. Minority Report
7. The Tuxedo
8. Men in Black II
9. A Walk to Remember
10. The Scorpion King

Films' admissions totals not available.
Sources: Ayala Cinemas/SM Cinemas.

Population:	27.14 million
Admissions:	11,804,545
Total box-office:	$20.81m
Avge. ticket price:	$2.75

POLAND

		Admissions
1.	The Fellowship of the Ring	2,520,000
2.	The Philosopher's Stone	2,507,000
3.	Revenge (Poland)	1,958,000
4.	The Pianist (UK/Ger/Fr/Poland)	1,154,000
5.	Attack of the Clones	868,000
6.	A Beautiful Mind	749,000
7.	Ice Age	709,000
8.	Asterix & Obelix... (Fr/Ger)	665,000
9.	Minority Report	496,000
10.	Chopin: Desire for Love (Poland)	446,000

Population:	40 million
Admissions:	25.9 million
Total box-office:	$85.76m
Local films' market share:	16.6%
Avge. ticket price:	$3.31

Sources: Film Polski/Agropos Info.

PUERTO RICO

		$m
1.	Spider-Man	4.15
2.	xXx	2.44
3.	Attack of the Clones	1.88
4.	Men in Black II	1.75
5.	Scooby-Doo	1.64
6.	Ice Age	1.57
7.	Stuart Little 2	1.44
8.	The Ring	1.35
9.	Die Another Day	1.34
10.	The Chamber of Secrets	1.33

Source: 20th Century Fox Puerto Rico.

Population:	3.9 million
Total box-office:	$40m
Screens:	253
Avge. ticket price:	$5

ROMANIA

	Admissions
1. Garcea & the Olt Folk (Romania)	232,050
2. Attack of the Clones	172,859
3. Spider-Man	152,659
4. The Fellowship of the Ring	130,478
5. Men in Black II	116,674
6. Ocean's Eleven	113,681
7. A Beautiful Mind	110,588
8. The Scorpion King	107,361
9. xXx	95,635
10. Filantropica (Romania)	91,958

Population:	21.68 million
Admissions:	5.32 million
Local films' market share:	25%
Screens:	247
Avge. ticket price:	$1.5

Source: Statistical Report of Romanian Cinematography.

RUSSIA

	Admissions
1. The Fellowship of the Ring	2,697,161
2. Men in Black II	2,282,712
3. The Philosopher's Stone	2,120,431
4. Attack of the Clones	1,935,484
5. Die Another Day	1,235,275
6. Spider-Man	1,237,659
7. Ocean's Eleven	1,090,129
8. Minority Report	1,009,318
9. xXx	1,014,115
10. Signs	1,009,983

Population:	150 million
Admissions:	45 million
Total box-office:	$118m
Local films' market share:	8%
Sites/screens: 1,200 urban sites/17,000 provincial screens	

Avge. ticket price: $4 (in modernised cinemas)
Sources: Rossiiskaya Kinematografia/Kinoprocess.

SERBIA AND MONTENEGRO

	Admissions
1. Zone (Serbia)	962,871
2. The Philosopher's Stone	371,069
3. The Fellowship of the Ring	339,061
4. Dead Cool (Serbia)	175,590
5. Little Night Music (Serbia)	152,625
6. Spider-Man	150,787
7. Asterix & Obelix... (Fr/Ger)	145,115
8. Labyrinth (Serbian)	120,291
9. One on One (Serbia)	102,486
10. Ocean's Eleven	101,671

Population:	8.5 million
Admissions:	4.68 million
Total box-office:	$8.95m (est.)
Local films' market share:	34%
Sites/screens:	180/195 (est.)
Avge. ticket price:	$1.91

Source: Film Distributors' Association of Yugoslavia.

SINGAPORE

	$m
1. Spider-Man	3.07
2. The Chamber of Secrets	2.95
3. The Two Towers	2.32
4. I Not Stupid (Singapore)	2.20
5. Attack of the Clones	2.13
6. Die Another Day	1.56
7. The Tuxedo	1.37
8. Minority Report	1.35
9. Men in Black II	1.33
10. The Eye (S'pore/Hong Kong)	1.15

Population:	4.16 million
Admissions:	14 million
Total box-office:	$58m
Local films' market share:	5%
Screens:	154
Avge. ticket price:	$4.35

SG$1 = $0.58
Sources: S'pore Film Commission/Straits Times/
S'pore Film Society.

SLOVAKIA

	Admissions
1. The Philosopher's Stone	253,294
2. The Fellowship of the Ring	220,104
3. The Chamber of Secrets	98,123
4. Spider-Man	90,068
5. Men in Black II	73,114
6. Monsters, Inc.	71,893
7. Ice Age	71,180
8. Signs	70,404
9. Attack of the Clones	62,629
10. Ocean's Eleven	61,427

Population:	5.4 million
Admissions:	3.01 million
Total box-office:	$6.6m
Local films' market share:	1.18%
Sites/screens:	294/312
Avge. ticket price:	$2.20

$1 = 37 crowns
Source: Slovakian Distributors' Association.

SLOVENIA

	Admissions
1. The Fellowship of the Ring	81,515
2. A Beautiful Mind	42,171
3. Men in Black II	41,446
4. Asterix & Obelix... (Fr/Ger)	33,905
5. Amélie (France)	33,121
6. Attack of the Clones	31,763
7. About a Boy (US/UK)	30,970
8. Stuart Little 2	30,049
9. The Chamber of Secrets	29,672
10. Vanilla Sky	27,698

Population:	1.98 million
Admissions:	3 million
Total box-office:	$11.32m
Screens:	100
Average ticket price:	$3.3

Source: Slovenian Film Fund.

SOUTH AFRICA

		$m
1.	Spider-Man	2.78
2.	Die Another Day	2.61
3.	The Two Towers	2.41
4.	Ocean's Eleven	2.10
5.	The Chamber of Secrets	2.08
6	My Big Fat Greek Wedding	1.89
7.	Ice Age	1.77
8.	xXx	1.71
9.	A Beautiful Mind	1.50
10.	The Bourne Identity	1.31

Population:	45 million
Admissions:	25 million (Est.)
Total box-office:	$40m (Est.)
Screens:	530
Average ticket price:	$3

$1 = 8 rand
Sources: Ster-Kinekor/National Film & Video Foundation.

SOUTH KOREA

		Admissions
1.	Marrying the Mafia (South Korea)	1,604,219
2.	The Way Home (South Korea)	1,596,521
3.	Minority Report	1,400,757
4.	The Fellowship of the Ring	1,375,101
5.	The Chamber of Secrets	1,199,616
6.	Public Enemy (South Korea)	1,161,500
7.	Spider-Man	1,107,600
8.	The Two Towers	951,952
9.	Spirited Away (Japan)	936,250
10.	Jail Breakers (South Korea)	911,315

Figures are for Seoul only (approx. 40% of national totals).

Population:	48 million
Admissions:	107 million
Total box-office:	$506m
Local films' market share:	48.3%
Screens:	850
Avge. ticket price:	$5.45

Sources: Korean Film Commission/Federation of Theatre Owners.

SPAIN

		$m
1.	Spider-Man	21.32
2.	The Chamber of Secrets	18.39
3.	The Fellowship of the Ring	16.14
4.	Attack of the Clones	15.84
5.	The Two Towers	15.29
6.	Monsters, Inc.	15.04
7.	Ocean's Eleven	13.23
8.	Ice Age	11.66
9.	The Other Side of the Bed (Spain)	11.48
10.	A Beautiful Mind	11.32

$1 = €1.06

Population:	40.08 million
Admissions	19.02 million
Total box-office:	$719.48m
Local films' market share:	13.66%
Sites/screens:	1,223/4,039

Source: Instituto de la Cinematografía y de las Artes Audiovisuales.

SWEDEN

		Admissions
1.	The Fellowship of the Ring	1,795,000
2.	The Guy in the Grave... (Sweden)	970,300
3.	The Chamber of Secrets	900,100
4.	Die Another Day	770,000
5.	Attack of the Clones	727,000
6.	Spider-Man	620,000
7.	Monsters, Inc	605,000
8.	Ocean's Eleven	540,000
9.	Lilo & Stitch	420,000
10.	The Reunion (Sweden)	402,000

Population:	8.9 million
Admissions:	18.3 million
Total box-office:	$157m
Local films' market share:	17%
Screens:	1,176
Avge. ticket price:	$8.5

Source: Swedish Film Institute.

SWITZERLAND

		Admissions
1.	The Chamber of Secrets	754,200
2.	Die Another Day	693,684
3.	The Fellowship of the Ring	688,473
4.	Ocean's Eleven	535,424
5.	Ice Age	513,349
6.	Spider-Man	508,690
7.	Asterix & Obelix... (Fr/Ger)	494,719
8.	The Two Towers	468,686
9.	A Beautiful Mind	414,746
10.	Attack of the Clones	378,660

Population:	7.26 million
Total box-office:	$198.97m
Admissions:	18.81 million
Sites/screens:	337/511
Avge. ticket price:	$10.58

Sources: Pro Cinema/State Statistics Office/Swiss Film Centre.

TAIWAN

		$m
1.	The Two Towers	4.722
2.	The Chamber of Secrets	4.694
3.	The Fellowship of the Ring	3.758
4.	Spider-Man	3.331
5.	Minority Report	2.857
6.	Men in Black II	2.472
7.	Ocean's Eleven	2.066
8.	Ice Age	1.652
9.	Attack of the Clones	1.440
10.	Monsters, Inc.	1.433

Population:	2,646,474
Admissions:	10,006,614
Total box-office:	$67.37m
Local films' market share:	2%
Sites/screens:	186/668
Avge. ticket price:	US$6.73

$1 = NT$0.028. All figures for Taipei only.

TURKEY

	Admissions
1. He's in the Army Now (Turkey)	1,630,000
2. The Two Towers	1,452,000
3. The Matrix Reloaded	1,195,000
4. The Chamber of Secrets	1,110,000
5. The Russian Bride (Turkey)	655,000
6. Signs	650,000
7. Ghost Ship	605,000
8. Catch Me If You Can	602,000
9. The Ring	547,000
10. Minority Report	532,000

May 2002 to May 2003.

Population:	65 million
Admissions:	23 million
Total box-office:	$70m
Sites/screens:	438/980
Avge. ticket price:	$4

Source: Antrakt-Sinema magazine.

UNITED KINGDOM

	$m
1. The Chamber of Secrets	78.74
2. The Two Towers	59.52
3. Monsters, Inc.	58.41
4. Attack of the Clones	58.01
5. Die Another Day	52.37
6. Spider-Man	44.53
7. Ocean's Eleven	40.86
8. Austin Powers in Goldmember	36.31
9. Men in Black II	34.35
10. Scooby-Doo	33.41

£1 = $1.55

Population:	58.7 million
Admissions:	175.9 million
Total box-office:	$1.2 billion
Local films' market share:	6.2%*
Sites/screens:	668/3,258
Avg. Ticket Price:	$7.20

Sources: Film Distributors' Association
* Incl. non-US co-prods; incl. US co-prods, share is 18.2%.

UNITED STATES

	$m
1. Spider-Man	403.7
2. Attack of the Clones	310.1
3. The Chamber of Secrets	245.9
4. The Two Towers	230.9
5. Signs	227.6
6. My Big Fat Greek Wedding	224.9
7. Austin Powers in Goldmember	213.1
8. Men in Black II	190.4
9. Ice Age	176.3
10. Scooby-Doo	153.2

Population:	288.37 million
Admissions:	1.639 billion
Total box-office:	$9.5 billion
Sites/screens:	6,050/35,280
Avge. ticket price:	$5.81

Sources: MPAA/Variety.

URUGUAY

	Admissions
1. Ice Age	168,585
2. Spider-Man	135,390
3. The Fellowship of the Ring	116,363
4. A Beautiful Mind	98,708
5. Ocean's Eleven	84,707
6. Lilo & Stitch	82,574
7. The Chamber of Secrets	82,400
8. Men in Black II	68,053
9. Signs	62,493
10. Passionate (Argentina)	55,727

Population:	3.24 million
Total box-office:	$5.29m
Local films' market share:	2.5%
Admissions:	2.03 million
Screens:	52
Avge. ticket price:	$3

Source: RBS Distribution Company.

VENEZUELA

	$
1. Spider-Man	1,620,000
2. Ice Age	1,430,000
3. Ocean's Eleven	870,000
4. Lilo & Stitch	720,000
5. A Beautiful Mind	700,000
6. Signs	650,000
7. Stuart Little 2	620,000
8. Scooby-Doo	600,000
9. Attack of the Clones	580,000
10. Shallow Hal	560,000

Population:	24.2 million
Admissions:	17 million (est.)
Total box-office:	$31.28m
Local films' market share:	1.1%
Sites/screens:	213/330
Avge. ticket price:	$1.88

$1 = 1,600 Bolivares. Source: ASOINCI (film industry association).

WORLD-WIDE

	$m
1. Spider-Man	821.6
2. The Chamber of Secrets	728.2
3. Attack of the Clones	647.7
4. The Fellowship of the Ring	525.0
5. The Two Towers	487.4
6. Men in Black II	441.8
7. Signs	401.3
8. Ice Age	378.4
9. Minority Report	335.8
10. Die Another Day	322.3

Source: Variety.

[Unless otherwise indicated, all titles are US productions and all figures are for January to December 2002. The Lord of the Rings: The Two Towers (US/New Zealand), Harry Potter and the Chamber of Secrets (US/UK) and Die Another Day (UK/US) were all still in world-wide release in 2003. Iran chart appears on p.53. Asterix & Obelix... (Fr/Ger) denotes Asterix & Obelix: Mission Cleopatra.

FESTIVAL DES 3 CONTIN

The Festival of Three Continents' First 25 years

by Charles Tesson

An event as essential as the Festival of Three Continents (Le festival des trois continents; F3C for short), which has broadened our cinematic horizons in a salutory and definitive manner, credits its undeniable success to the encounter of films and a city, orchestrated by the bubbling and stimulating personalities of the Jalladeau brothers, Alain and Philippe.

Nantes is an introverted harbour city, positioned between the promise of an ocean and a river, the Loire, eager to free itself. Like Bordeaux, its twin sister on the Atlantic coast, by the estuary of the Gironde, Nantes the bourgeois made the best of its fortune by trafficking slaves. To atone, in part, for this burdensome history and the wealth of its colonial harbour, Nantes developed two institutions which have become the pride of the city: its football club, known as the Canaries, and its film festival, known as F3C, both of which established model practices that have been much imitated.

The Canaries tapped the reservoir of black African players and today every French football club does the same. F3C has demonstrated, from 1979 to 2003, that cinema from beyond Europe's borders is great and beautiful, and the new cinematic horizons it opened up have been explored by famous festivals like Cannes. Satyajit Ray was the guest of honour at Nantes in 1980, before *La Maison et le Monde* (1984) had officially entered the competition at Cannes in 1985. Im Kwon-taek initially stopped over at Nantes with his films before Cannes gave him the honour he deserved (*Chunhyang, Chihwaseon*).

Likewise, it was in Nantes that we in France discovered the films of Hou Hsiao-hsien: *Boys from Fengkwei*, *Dust in the Wind*. Afterwards,

Venice and Cannes took over. Nantes received Wong Kar-wai and Edward Yang long before Cannes opened up to their work. Jia Zhangke is the latest to date to benefit from Nantes' sixth sense, which has made F3C the centre of cinema's authors of tomorrow. He came in person to present *Xiao Wu*; then *Platform* was in official competition at Venice and *Unknown Pleasures* at Cannes in 2002.

Wong Kar-wai's **Days of Being Wild**: *F3C was one of Wong's earliest champions*

In the beginning...

The festival's origins lie in the autumn of 1972, when Henri Langlois came to Nantes to reopen a local branch of the French Cinémathèque, that had been closed since the mid-1960s. In his suitcases were some rare films, among them an Oshima (*Pleasures of the Flesh*) and Sternberg's last film, *The Saga of Anatahan*, shot in Japan (already the seeds of an Asian focus were being sown).

Subsequently, the different events organised by the Jalladeau brothers between 1972 and 1979 (Italian cinema, the unforgettable visit of Jean-Luc Godard and Jean-Pierre Gorin for the Dziga

Helène Cayeux

Left to right: actress Carmi Martin, Philippe Jalladeau, director Lino Brocka and Alain Jalladeau at F3C in 1984

Vertov group's films, numerous debates with writers from *Cahiers du cinéma*) all helped to cement the spirit of the future festival, which owes a lot to the personality of Serge Daney (occult traveller-scout-adviser of the festival in its earliest days) and to the presence of numerous indestructible travel companions, among them Pierre Rissient.

Today, there is a genuine (and wholly justified) pride in Nantes. If a football team can possess a core play (for the Canaries, a game based on short, one-touch passes), we can add that there exists a core spirit for Nantes' cinema enthusiasts, unique in France, for whom F3C is a most fortunate event. It's often said that the Canaries' playing style is close to Brazil's and, as if by chance, the cinema event organised in 1978 by the Jalladeau brothers, which would give birth the following year to F3C, was devoted to Brazilian cinema and the unknown marvels of *Cinema Novo* (Joaquim Pedro de Andrade, Leon Hirszman et al).

Fraternal passions

In Nantes, there are three continents and two brothers. One favours Latin America and the Arab world (Philippe), the other (Alain) is more attracted by Asia (from India to Japan, stopping off in China and Korea). That leaves Africa,

which continues its love affair with the city (and the rest of France). In addition, the festival made its debut in 1979 with an important retrospective on black American film-makers, up to and including Melvin van Peebles, who brought his most recent films.

In France as elsewhere, May 1968 changed the face of cinema. We developed an interest in cinema said to be Third World, militant, committed, anti-Hollywood. The festival always refused, with much courage and reason in the face of widespread criticism, to be exclusively associated with this socio-militant cinema. By stepping back from this movement and being born on the threshold of a new decade (the 1980s, which was carried by and towards Asia), the festival was able to find a good balance between healthy political awareness and sheer love of cinema. It was a gamble, but cinema itself has proved it to have been a winning one.

This exceptional annual meeting of film enthusiasts, on the brink of winter, in beautiful Nantes, around the Place Graslin and the Cigale restaurant (immortalised by Jacques Demy's *Lola* and a Mecca of festival conviviality over river fish-sauce 'beurre blanc', Muscadet or Gros Plant), is held together by the Jalladeau brothers' acute intuition. Experienced travellers, as soon as they detect in a country the first signs of cinematic stirring, its films find their way into the programme. If Argentine cinema has become a recent topic of conversation, and rightly so, we note that two Argentine films competed at the festival as long ago as 1997.

It is one of the festival's great strenghts that it doesn't aim for an exhaustive ecumenical panorama, in which all films have an equal position. A great detector of new talents, F3C knows how to be selective, while other festivals discredit themselves with quantitative choices, flashily tasteless. When the Jalladeau brothers say there is something happening in a country, and then construct their programme around it (most recently with Kazakh cinema), we are rarely disappointed by the journey.

When Lino Brocka visited Nantes in 1981,

Manila, *directed by Lino Brocka*

accompanied by his friend, the critic and *IFG* contributor Agustin Sotto, they brought in their luggage some vintage films, among them the superb works of Geraldo de Leon. In Nantes we also discovered the work of Guru Dutt and, especially, the great Ritwik Ghatak. Retrospectives have been the festival's strong

point because they have always been reclaimed with an interest anchored in the present.

Young generations are discovering Bollywood through the recent *Devdas*. What better reason to remind us of what came before and what we have a tendency to forget? Thus Bollywood will be the guest of honour at the festival's 25th edition, in particular the films of Raj Kapoor. But let's not forget that the festival's regulars remember meeting Kapoor in person in 1984, at a time when commercial Hindi cinema was not yet in fashion - yet another example to illustrate how F3C and the Jalladeau brothers stay ahead of cinema's future. Did anyone mention Nantes pride?

CHARLES TESSON began writing for *Cahiers du cinéma* in 1979, was on its editorial staff from 1981-91, then chief editor (1998-2003). He teaches history and aesthetics of cinema at Sorbonne Nouvelle University, Paris, and is the author of several books, including *Satyajit Ray* (l'Etoile, 1992) and *Luis Bunuel* (l'Etoile, 1995). Article translated by Enid Pifeteau.

Phil Journé

Philippe and Alain Jalladeau celebrate the festival's 20th anniversary in 1999 with actress Anna Karina and director Melvin van Peebles, who'd both also attended the inaugural F3C

The Jalladeau Brothers' Favourite F3C Films

The festival's founders were each asked by *IFG* to choose ten of their favourites from the 1,500 titles screened at F3C in the last 25 years. Their selections are listed in alphabetical order by country of origin.

Philippe Jalladeau's Selection

La Cienaga (*The Swamp*, Lucrecia Martel, Argentina, 2001)
"Like Godard's *Breathless* in its own time, Martel's innovative film is symbolic of a movement which broke new ground in Latin American cinema."

Deus e o diablo na terra do sol (*Black God, White Devil*, Glauber Rocha, Brazil, 1964)
"Rocha's most accomplished and iconic film."

Meghe dhaka tara (*Hidden Star*, Ritwik Gathak, India, 1960)
"In 1980, the festival made this astounding discovery of a then unknown genius."

Aryaner din ratri (*Days and Nights in the Forest*, Satyajit Ray, India, 1969)
"One of Ray's major works, casual and unusual, containing one of the most erotic scenes in film history."

Kamigami no fukaki (*Deep Desire of Gods*, Shohei Imamura, Japan, 1968)
"Imamura's maddest film."

Kayrat (Darezhan Omirbayev, Kazakhstan, 1991)
"A restrained, moving film from an expert in the unspoken and the suggestive."

Bakai pasture (*The Sky of Our Childhood*, Tolomush Okeyev, Kirgystan, 1967)
"Delicate, moving and extremely modern – one of the most beautiful films on childhood."

El Rey del Barrio (*The King of the Neighbourhood*, Gilberto Martinez Solares, Mexico, 1949)
"One of the greatest and funniest (a rarity!) films of the festival, featuring the tremendously funny Tin Tan."

Segell Ikhtifa (*Chronicle of a Disappearance*, Elia Suleiman, Palestine, 1996)
"Suleiman's first film is a fully accomplished work in which politics serves art, not, as in most films, the other way around."

Les baliseurs du désert (*The Wanderers*, Nacer Khemir, Tunisia, 1984)
"One of the rare films able to convey Arab culture through time and space.

Gilberto Martinez Solares' **The King of the Neighbourhood**, *one of Philippe Jalladeau's F3C favourites*

Alain Jalladeau's Selection

Da yue bing (*The Big Parade*, Chen Kaige, China, 1985)
"After *Yellow Earth*, Chen brilliantly dealt with the relationships between the individual and society in contemporary China, confirming his talent as one of the major representatives of the Fifth Generation."

Xiao Wu (Jia Zhang-ke, China, 1997)
"With his first film, Jia established himself as one of tomorrow's major film-makers, through a formally accomplished evocation of today's China."

Bab el-hadid (*Cairo Station*, Youssef Chahine, Egypt, 1958)
"One of his major films, as director and actor. Chahine invented a free, rebellious way of making films."

Ah fei zheng zhuan (*Days of Being Wild*, Wong Kar-wai, Hong Kong, 1990)
"A major first film by a director who was to become one of the best in the world."

Mother India (Mehboob Khan, India, 1957)
"One of the best examples of the golden age of popular Hindi cinema. An ultimate masterpiece."

Kaagaz ke phool (*Paper Flowers*, Guru Dutt, India, 1959)
"A flamboyant melodrama and a very personal film, which made Dutt a unique figure within Indian cinema."

Kaneh, ye doust kojast (*Where's the Friend's House?*, Abbas Kiarostami, Iran 1987)
"A new way to think in terms of film by a very unusual film-maker."

Sibaji (*Surrogate Mother*, Im Kwon-taek, South Korea, 1986)
"One of Korean cinema's most accomplished films, a masterpiece of direction."

Touki Bouki (Djibril Diop Mambety, Senegal, 1973)
"Unique, inimitable, like nothing else we know in cinema."

Fen-Kuei-lai-te jen (*The Boys from Feng-kuei*, Hou-Hsia-hsien, Taiwan, 1984)
"A joyful marvel of a film in which Hou Hsiao-hsien already displayed his talent. He is the film-maker of modernity.

"Such a limited choice obliged me to leave out dozens of great film-makers, including Leonardo Favio (Argentina), Nelson Pereira dos Santos (Brazil), Ning Ying, Sun Yu, Xie Jin (China), Hong Sang-soo, Sin Sang-ok (Korea), King Hu, Stanley Kwan, Tsui Hark (Hong Kong), Ritwik Ghatak, Adoor Gopalakrishnan, Raj Kapoor, Satyajit Ray (India), Abolfazl Jalili, Moshen Makhmalbaf, Amir Naderi (Iran), Shoei Imamura, Yasuzo Masumara, Nagisa Oshima (Japan), Souleymane Cisse (Mali), Arturo Ripstein (Mexico), Lino Brocka, Gerardo de Leon (Philippines), Ousmane Sembene (Senegal), Lester James Peries (Sri Lanka), Tsai Ming-liang, Edward Yang (Taiwan), Metin Erksan (Turkey)."

Chen Kaige's **The Big Parade**

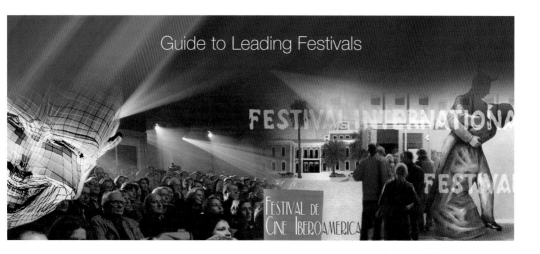

Guide to Leading Festivals

American Film Market,
February 25 – March 3, 2004

Founded in 1981, AFM has become the world's largest movie industry event. For eight days, the Loews Santa Monica Beach Hotel becomes an international market and all 23 screens on the Promenade are used to present more than 400 feature films for more than 7,000 delegates (producers, distributors, agents, attorneys, acquisition and development executives), representing hundreds of companies. Hundreds of films are financed, packaged and licensed, sealing more than $500m of business. *Inquiries to*: 10850 Wilshire Blvd, 9th Floor, Los Angeles, CA 90024-4311, USA. Tel: (1 310) 446 1000. Fax: 446 1600. e: afm@afma.com. Web: www.americanfilmmarket.com.

Amiens
November 5-14, 2004

Discovery of new talents, new cinematography and reassessment of film masters. A competitive festival in northern France for shorts, features, animation and documentaries. Also retrospectives, tributes and the "Le monde comme il va" series, which includes works from Africa, Latin America and Asia. A growing section for more than 10 years, "Europe, Europes", presents new works from Young European Talents (Shorts, Documentaries and Animation). *Inquiries to:* Amiens International Film Festival, MCA, Place Léon

Gontier, 80000 Amiens, France. Tel: (33 3) 2271 3570. Fax: 2292 5304. e: contact@filmfestamiens.org. Web: www.filmfestamiens.org.

AWARDS 2002
Golden Unicorn (Feature): **Rachida** (Algeria), Yamina Bachir-Chouikh.
Special Prize: **Meisje** (Belgium), Dorothée van den Berghe.
Golden Unicorn (Short): **Journey Man** (UK), Dictynna Hood.
Special Prize: **Mboutoukou** (Cameroon), Victor K Viyuoh; **Matadero** (Spain), Xuan Acosta and Manuel F. Torres.
Best Actor: Luis Sziembrowski aka El Pampa, **Sudeste** (Argentina), Sergio Bellotti.
Best Actress: Charlotte Vanden Eynde, **Meisje.**
Audience Prize: **Rachida** (Algeria).

Report 2002
At the 22nd festival, more than 63,000 spectators enjoyed 400 new and classic films at 22 venues. Highlights included tributes to Gaston Kabore (Burkina Faso), one of the key figures in African cinema, along with Ousmane Sembene and Souleymane Cisse. The festival also paid tribute to the American "Prince of the B Movie", Edgar G. Ulmer, and several authors contributed to *Edgar G. Ulmer: The Unmasked Bandit* (published by the festival and Yellow Now). In the Great World's Studios series, more than 30 films shot at Churubusco (Mexico) were screened, including David Lynch's *Dune*.

Austin Film Festival
October 2004

Celebrating its 10th anniversary, the Screenwriter's Conference is a celebration of screenwriting and narrative film. For four days, industry professionals reveal secrets of the trade to aspiring screenwriters and film-makers. The Bronze Typewriter Award is given to Featured Screenwriters and Film-makers and to Screenplay and Film Competition Winners. The Austin Film Festival starts on the same day as the Conference and runs for four days afterwards, screening more than 80 movies, including competition films. *Inquiries to:* Austin Film Festival, 1604 Nueces, TX 78701, USA. Tel: (1 512) 478 4795. Fax: 478 6205. e: austinfilm@aol.com. Web: www.austinfilmfestival.com.

Report 2002
This year's Conference panelists included David Benioff (*Troy, 25th Hour*), Linwood Boomer (creator of *Malcolm in the Middle*), Bill Broyles (*Unfaithful, Cast Away*), Ted Elliott (*Shrek, Aladdin*), Anne Rapp (*Dr T and the Women*), Mike Rich (*The Rookie*), Terry Rossio (*Shrek, Aladdin*), Chris and Paul Weitz (*About a Boy*).

BERGEN INTERNATIONAL FILM FESTIVAL, BERGEN – NORWAY

BIFF

MID OCTOBER 2004

BERGEN INTERNATIONAL FILM FESTIVAL Georgernes verft 12 N-5011 Bergen, Norway
biff@biff.no • www.filmweb.no/biff • tel: + 47 55 32 25 90 fax: + 47 55 32 37 40

Bergen
October 2004

Norway's beautiful capital of the fjords launches the fifth BIFF. The festival's Competition Programme consists of arthouse films. There are sidebars on documentary and digital productions, as well as premieres of the upcoming theatrical Christmas releases, through extensive collaboration with Norway's theatrical distributors. Bergen has a special focus on new British films, in co-operation with The British Council. *Inquiries to:* Bergen International Film Festival, Georgernes verft 12, NO-5011 Bergen, Norway. Tel: (47) 5532 2590. Fax: 5532 3740. e: biff@biff.no. Web: www.biff.no.

Report 2002
The Opening Film Gala was the world premiere of the Bergen production *Falling Sky* by Gunnar Vikene. The International competition programme consisted of 16 films and the Austrian film *Hundstage* (*Dog Days*) by Ulrich Seidl won the Jury Award. Michael Moore's *Bowling for Columbine* won the Audience Award. The Jury gave special mention to *Oasis* by Lee Chang-dong (South Korea) and *House of Fools* by Andrei Konchalovsky (Russia).
– **Tor Fosse**, Festival Director.

Berlin, Internationale Filmfestspiele
February 5-15, 2004

Situated at the Potsdamer Platz, the Berlinale has increased its popularity with the public and film professionals. In 2003, it had 15,545 accredited guests and a remarkable 368,400 tickets were sold for 1,384 screenings in 10 cinemas. The website registered 6.3 million hits. Some 3,675 journalists from about 80 countries reported on the programme and visits by the likes of Nicole Kidman, Catherine Zeta-Jones, Richard Gere, Dustin Hoffmann and Claude Chabrol. The European Film Market recorded another increase in participants, screenings and turnover. The inaugural Berlinale Talent Campus, consisting of panels and workshops on film-making, theory and marketing, involved 476 young film-makers from 61 countries (see www.berlinale-talentcampus.de). *Inquiries to:* Internationale Filmfestspiele Berlin, Potsdamer Str 5, D-10785 Berlin, Germany. Tel: (49 30) 259 200. Fax: 2592 0299. e: info@berlinale.de. Web: www.berlinale.de.

AWARDS 2003
Golden Bear: **In This World** (Great Britain), Michael Winterbottom.
Jury Grand Prix: **Adaptation** (US), Spike Jonze.
Best Director: Patrice Chéreau, **Son Frère** (France).

Best Actor: Sam Rockwell, **Confesions of a Dangerous Mind** (US).
Best Actress: Julianne Moore, Nicole Kidman and Meryl Streep, **The Hours** (UK).
Best Short: **(A)Torzija** (Slovenia), Stefan Arsenijevic.

Bermuda International Film Festival
March 19-25, 2004

Features the best of international independent film in three competition categories (features, documentaries and shorts). Q&A sessions with directors, and the popular lunchtime "Chats with..." sessions give filmgoers and film-makers a chance to mix. A win in any of the three competition categories earns the director an invitation to sit on the festival jury the following year. Submission deadline: November 1.
Inquiries to: Bermuda International Film Festival, PO Box 2963, Hamilton HM MX, Bermuda. Tel: (441) 293 3456. Fax: 293 7769. e: bdafilm@ibl.bm. Web: www.bermudafilmfest.com.

AWARDS 2003
Feature: **Kops** (Sweden), Josef Fares.
Documentary: **Discovering Dominga** (US), Patricia Flynn.
Short: **Sophie** (US), Helen Lee.
Audience Choice: **The Pianist** (UK/Poland/Italy/France), Roman Polanski.
Special Jury Mention: **1/2 The Rent** (Germany), Marc Ottiker; **The Other Final** (Netherlands), Johan Kramer; **10 Again** (UK), Simon Ellis; **Katherine** (US), Mary Louise Stoughton.

Brisbane International Film Festival
Late July – early August 2004

There was something for everyone at the 12th BIFF. The 2003 programme featured a diverse range of internationally acclaimed titles, with many films having won awards at Hong Kong, Venice, New York, Cannes, Rotterdam and Sydney. The opening night film was *Gettin' Square* and the Showcase screenings included Ben Lee in *The Rage in Placid Lake* (Australia), and *Laurel Canyon*, starring Frances McDormand and Kate Beckinsale.

Retrospectives showcased Yasujiro Ozu and Abel Ferrara. *Inquiries to:* Helen Kaye, Brisbane International Film Festival, GPO Box 909, Brisbane, QLD, 4001, Australia. Tel: (61 7) 3007 3020. Fax: 3220 0400. e: publicist@biff.com.au. Web: www.biff.com.au.

Cannes
May 12-23, 2004

Cannes remains the world's top festival, attracting key films, personalities and industry personnel. The official selection includes the Competition, "Un Certain Regard", the Short Film Competition and the Cinéfondation. The much-improved market (Marché du Film), whose facilities were extended and improved in 2000, is part of the official organisation. There are also the Directors' Fortnight, the Critics' Week and other useful screenings (e.g. Australian, New Zealand and Scandinavian films). The 2003 festival jury, presided over by Patrice Chéreau, included Aishwarya Rai, Meg Ryan, Karin Viard, Erri de Luca, Jean Rochefort, Steven Soderbergh, Danis Tanovic and Jiang Wen.
Inquiries to: Festival de Cannes, 3, rue Amélie 75007 Paris, France. Tel: (33 1) 5359 6100. Fax: 5359 6110. e: festival@festival-cannes.fr. Web: www.festival-cannes.org.

AWARDS 2003
Palme d'Or: **Elephant** (US), Gus Van Sant.
Grand Prix: **Uzak** (Turkey), Nuri Bilge Ceylan.
Best Actor: Muzaffer Ozdemir and Mehmet Emin Toprak, **Uzak**.
Best Actress: Marie-Josée Croze, **Les Invasions Barbares** (Canada).
Best Director: Gus Van Sant, **Elephant**.
Best Screenplay: Denys Arcand, **Les Invasions Barbares**.
Jury Prize: **Panje Asr** (Iran), Samira Makhmalbaf.
Caméra d'Or: **Reconstruction** (Denmark), Christoffer Boe.

Cartagena
Feb/March 2004

Ibero-Latin American films, including features, shorts, documentaries, tributes to Latin American directors and a film and TV market.

A competitive section for Colombian films was added in 2000. *Inquiries to:* Victor Nieto Nuñez, Director, Cartagena International Film Festival, Centro, Calle San Juan de Dios, Baluarte San Francisco Javier, Cartagena, Colombia. Tel: (57 5) 660 1702. e: info@festicinecartagena.com. Web: www.festicinecartagena.com.

Chicago
October 7-21, 2004

Now in its fourth decade, the Chicago International Film Festival is the oldest competitive event in North America. It spotlights the latest work by established international directors and newcomers. It bestows its highest honour, the Gold Hugo, on the best feature in the International Competition, with separate prizes for documentaries, student films and shorts. Chicago is one of two US sites to award the FIPRESCI prize for first- and second-time directors, judged by a jury of top international critics. *Inquiries to:* Philip Bajorat (Entries and Awards Co-ordinator), Chicago International Film Festival, 32 W Randolph St, Suite 600, Chicago, IL 60601, USA. Tel: (1 312) 425 9400. Fax: 425 0944. e: info@chicagofilmfestival.com. Web: www.chicagofilmfestival.com.

AWARDS 2002
Gold Hugo: **Madame Satã** (Brazil/France), Karim Ainouz.
Best Director: Andreas Dresen, **Grill Point** (Germany).
FIPRESCI Prize: **El Bonaerense** (Argentina), Pablo Trapero.
Special Jury Prize: **Divine Intervention** (Palestine/France/Morocco), Elia Suleiman.
Best Ensemble Acting: **Grill Point.**
Gold Plaque: **Marooned in Iraq** (Iran), Bahman Ghobadi.
Gold Plaque (Acting): Vincent Rottiers, **The Devils** (France/Spain).
Best Documentary (Gold Hugo): **Sister Helen** (USA), Rob Fruchtman and Rebecca Cammisa.
Best Documentary (Silver Hugo): **Daughter from Yan'an** (Japan), Kaoru Ikeya.
Best Documentary (Gold Plaque): **Blind Spot: Hitler's Secretary** (Austria), Andre Heller and Othmar Schmiderer.

Best Documentary (Silver Plaque): **Bellaria As Long As We Live!** (Germany/Austria), Douglas Wolfsperger.
1st Place Audience Choice Award: **Bowling for Columbine** (US), Michael Moore.
2nd Place Audience Choice Award: **Real Women Have Curves** (US), Patricia Cardoso.
Lifetime Achievement Award: Clint Eastwood.
Career Achievement Award: Pierce Brosnan.
Black Perspectives Career Achievement Award: Charles S. Dutton.

Report 2002
Our 38th festival presented more than 100 features and 40 shorts making their regional, national or world premieres. Film-makers in town to present their films included Julie Taymor, Lynne Ramsay, Paul Greengrass, Maximillian Schell, D.A. Pennebaker and Phillip Noyce. The competition jury was headed by John Russell Taylor.
– **Joanna Slotkin**, (Film Programming Intern) and **Philip Bajorat** (Entries and Awards Co-ordinator).

Cinéma Tout Ecran
November 2004

The first and, until recently, only festival devoted to films of artistic quality produced by television. The main criteria for selection are the film-maker's distinctive view of the world and storytelling style. Highlights include the International Competition (three major prizes), New TV Series, Retrospective, Thematic Night and professional seminars. *Inquiries to:* Cinéma Tout Ecran, International Cinema & Television Festival, Maison des Arts du Grutli, 16 rue Génèral Dufour, CP 5305 CH-1211 Geneva 11, Switzerland. Tel: (41 22) 809 6908. Fax: 329 3747. e: info@cinema-tout-ecran.ch. Web: www.cinema-tout-ecran.ch.

Report 2002
The festival's 8th edition attracted more than 25,000 spectators. Highlights included the Atom Egoyan retrospective, attended by the director, and the screening of *Kedma* with director Amos Gitai. Other guests included Edouard Baer, Bruno Nuytten, Rashid Mashrawi (Palestine), Marco Raat (Estonia) and Henner Winckler

(Germany). The Jury awarded the Grand Prix to *The High School Girl's Friend* (*Jogakusei no tomo*; Japan) by Tetsuo Shinohara and three prizes went to *Des épaules solides* (Switzerland/France/Belgium) by Ursula Meier.
– **Léo Kaneman**, Festival Director.

Clermont-Ferrand
January 30 – February 7, 2004

International and National competitions for 16mm, 35mm films and digital works on DigiBeta, all completed after January 1, 2003 and shorter than 40 minutes. All the entries will be listed in the Market catalogue. Many other side programmes (retrospectives and panoramas). *Inquiries to:* Clermont-Ferrand Short Film Festival, La Jete, 6 place Michel-de L'Hospital 63058 Clermont-Ferrand Cedex 1, France. Tel: (33 473) 916 573. Fax: 921 193. e: info@clermont-filmfest.com.
Web: www.clermont-filmfest.com.

AWARDS 2003
Grand Prix: **De Beste Gr Frst** (Norway), Hans Petter Moland; **N[eon]** (UK), Dave McKean; **La Patience d'une Mère** (France), Dodine Herry-Grimaldi.
Audience Prizes: **Der Er En Yndig Mand** (Denmark), Martin Strage-Hansen; **Pigly** (Belgium/France), Philippe Tailliez; **La Chatte Andalouse** (France), Gérald Hustache-Mathieu.

Report 2003
Our 25th festival attracted some 133,000 spectators and welcomed 2,600 industry delegates. Festival and market confirmed their position as the world's top short films event. Some 189 films representing 48 countries were shown in three juried competitions: national (65 films), international (81) and digital (43). The non-competitive programmes showcased Algeria and Germany. Other programmes focused on Aboriginal cinema, Venice and the Cinémathèque Québécoise, as well as the usual African perspectives, American universities, Children's and Pupil's programmes. A tribute was paid to animator Borislav Sajtinac.
– **Christian Guinot**, Festival Delegate.

Denver
October 2004

The Starz Denver International Film Festival, an invitation event, presents approximately 150 films and welcomes more than 80 film artists. Includes new international features, cutting-edge independent fiction films and documentaries, animation, experimental works, children's programmes and shorts. Festival awards include the Mayor's Lifetime Achievement Award, the Krzysztof Kieslowski Award for Best European Film (juried), the Stan Brakhage Award for Poetic Film and the Starz People's Choice Awards.

Chen Kaige at Denver in 2002

Entry fee: $35 ($20 for students). The Denver Film Society also produces the Denver Jewish Film Festival in March, the Denver Pan-African Film Festival in April, the Aurora Asian Film Festival in June and programmes the new Starz FilmCenter, Denver's only cinémathèque, daily throughout the year. *Inquiries to:* Denver Film Society, 1725 Blake St, Denver, Colorado 80202, USA. Tel: (1 303) 595 3456. Fax: 595 0956. e: dfs@denverfilm.org. Web: www.denverfilm.org.

AWARDS 2002

John Cassavetes Award: Nick Nolte
Mayor's Award: John Wells, producer.
Krzysztof Kieslowski Award: **Sweet Sixteen** (UK), Ken Loach
Starz People's Choice Award: (Fiction)
Rabbit-Proof Fence (Australia), Phillip Noyce; (Documentary) **Standing in the Shadows of Motown** (US), Paul Justman.

Report 2002

Our Silver Anniversary festival saw more than 30,000 people sample 175 films and interact with more than 100 film artists. Highlights included tributes to Phillip Noyce and Chen Kaige, a Salute to Chinese Cinema (with 11 new films from China), a 20-minute work-in-progress sneak peek at Zhang Yimou's *Hero*, An Evening with Cheng Pei-pei and a closing night screening of *Bowling for Columbine*, with Michael Moore and several survivors of the Columbine tragedy taking part in a lively Q&A session.
– **Britta Erickson**, Director of Media and Industry Relations.

Edinburgh International Film Festival
August 11-22, 2004

The world's longest continually running film festival, Edinburgh is also one of the most accessible. The emphasis is on new films, innovation and excellence worldwide, UK films and young directors, retrospectives and seminars. There's an off-beat sparkle to the mix of local audiences and visitors. Edinburgh also encapsulates Film UK, a focus for all matters concerning UK Film. FilmFour is the principal sponsor. *Inquiries to:* Edinburgh International Film Festival, 88 Lothian Rd, Edinburgh EH3 9BZ, Scotland. Tel: (44 131) 228 4051. Fax: 229 5501. e: info@edfilmfest.org.uk. Web: www.edfilmfest.org.uk.

AWARDS 2002

Saltire Society Grierson Award for Short Documentary: **Sky High** (UK), Anna Jones.
Michael Powell Award for Best New British Feature: **Out of Control**, Dominic Savage.
Guardian New Director's Award: **Japón**, (Mexico/Spain), Carlos Reygadas.
Standard Life Audience Award: **Rabbit-Proof Fence** (Australia), Phillip Noyce.

Report 2002

More than 400 film-makers came to the 2002 event, contributing to the unique sense of congregation generated by an international film festival. Highlights included the masterclass with Oscar-winning editor Anne Coates (*Lawrence of Arabia, Erin Brockovich*) and the visit of Bollywood superstar Shah Rukh Khan, whose arrival literally stopped the Edinburgh traffic.
– **Shane Danielsen**, Artistic Director.

Espoo Ciné International Film Festival
August 24-29, 2004

Espoo Ciné has established itself as the annual showcase of contemporary European, primarily long feature, cinema in Finland. The traditional section should appeal to every movie buff in Finland, and the growing fantasy selection should attract those hungry for stimulation of the imagination. It is a member of the European Fantastic Film Festivals Federation and organises every year a Méliès d'Argent fantastic

film competition. Also US indies, new films from other continents, the best of contemporary Finnish cinema, outdoor screenings, retrospectives, sneak previews, seminars and distinguished guests. *Inquiries to:* Espoo Ciné, PO Box 95, FIN-02101 Espoo, Finland. Tel: (358 9) 466 599. Fax: 466 458. e: office@espoocine.org. Web: www.espoocine.org.

Report 2002

At our 13th festival, more than 20,000 spectators enjoyed more than 80 films at three venues. Highlights included the Finnish premieres of François Ozon's *8 Femmes* and Tom Tykwer's *Heaven*. At a special gala, Eisenstein's *Strike* was screened with live music from popular St. Petersburg band Tequilajazzz. Other events included the interactive cinema showcase, orchestrated by Chris Hales and Teijo Pellinen, and an audience seminar about film music. The Méliès d'Argent went to *Fausto 5.0* (Spain, Isidro Ortiz, Álex Ollé and Carlos Padrissa) and the Audience Award to *Son de Mar* (Spain, Bigas Luna.
– **Satu Elo**, Co-ordinator.

Fajr International Film Festival
February 1-11, 2004

The Fajr Festival has flourished as a competitive event and aims to provide a bridge between eastern and western cinemas. Caters mainly for Iranian films, but since 1999 has incorporated an international competition. For the past seven years it has included a film market for domestic production, but for 2004 this will be expanded to an international scale. *Inquiries to:* Farhang Cinema, Dr Shariati Ave, Gholhak, Tehran 19139, Iran. Tel: (98 21) 200 2088-90. Fax: 267 082. e: fcf2@dpi.net.ir.

AWARDS 2003
Best Film: **The Son** (Belgium), Jean-Pierre and Luc Dardenne.
Best Director: Alexi Muradov, **The Kite** (Russia).
Best Performance: Olivier Gourmet,
The Son (Belgium).
Best Screenplay: Aki Kourismäki,
The Man Without a Past (Finland).

Best Technical and Artistic Achievement:
Laissez-Passer (France), Bertrand Tavernier.
Best Narrative Short Film: **Hidden** (Sweden), Hanna Hellborn, David Aronowiteh and Mats Johansson.
Special Jury Prize: **Dance in the Mist** (Iran), Asghar Farhadi.

Report 2003
At our 21st festival, some 240 new and classic films were viewed by more than 350,000 spectators at a dozen venues across Tehran. Highlights included tributes to Charlie Chaplin, Yasujiro Ozu and Swiss documentary film-maker Richard Dindo, as well as seminars on Experiments in Documentary Narrative Cinema and Sound in Contemporary Cinema. For the first time, the competition included shorts. The festival jury was Krzysztof Zanussi (Poland; president), Cedomir Kolar (Croatia), Todd Solondz (USA) and Dariush Mehrjuie (Iran).

Fantasporto
February 20-28, 2004

The Oporto International Film Festival, now going into its 24th edition, specialises in fantasy and science-fiction films in its Official Competitive section. Also includes the 14th New Directors' Week (official competition and retrospective section). Festival director Mário Dorminsky is preparing, with the help of the Portuguese Film Institute, a programme of Portuguese Films for foreign guests. The festival uses five theatres and screens nearly 200 features. All major Portuguese print and

Danny Boyle, left, at Fantasporto 2003

broadcast media cover the festival (yielding some 4,000 cuttings) and average public attendance is around 115,000 (112,000 in 2003). *Inquiries to:* Fantasporto, Rua Anibal Cunha 84, Sala 1.6, 4050-048 Porto, Portugal. Tel: (35 1) 222 076 050 Fax: 222 076 059. e: info@fantasporto.online.pt. Web: www.fantasporto.com.

AWARDS 2003
Fantasy Section
Best Film: **Intacto** (Spain), Juan Carlos Fresnadillo.
Special Jury Award: [Ex-aequo] **Cypher** (Canada), Vincenzo Natali; **A Snake of June** (Japan), Shynia Tsukamoto.
Best Director: Danny Boyle, **28 Days Later** (UK).
Best Actor: Jeremy Northam, **Cypher**.
Best Actress: Asuka Kurosawa, **A Snake of June**.
Best Screenplay: Juan Carlos Fresnadillo and Andrés Koppel, **Intacto**.
Best Visual Effects: Bret Culp and Bob Monroe, **Cypher**.
Best Short Film: **Atraksion** (Belgium), Raoul Servais.
Directors' Week
Best Film: **L.I.E.** (US), Michael Cuesta.

Best Director: Michael Cuesta, **L.I.E.** (US).
Special Jury Award: **The Last Minute** (UK), Stephen Norrington.
Best Actor: Paul Franklin Dano, **L.I.E.** (US).
Best Actress: Maggie Gyllenhaal, **Secretary** (US).
Best Screenplay: Phil Hay, **Bug** (US).
Critics Jury: [Ex-aequo] **Cube 2: Hypercube** (Canada), Andrzej Sekula; **Nos Miran** (Spain), Norberto Lopez.
Audience Award: **Toy Love** (New Zealand), Harry Sinclair.

Report 2003
At our 23rd edition, highlights included an Austrian Film retrospective, a New Zealand Focus and Stephen King Homage. Directors and producers like Danny Boyle, Jaume Balagueró and Paco Plaza were among the 100 personalities who presented their films. Other events included round-table discussions about Fantasy Spanish cinema, Austrian cinema and the presentation of several books.
– **Mário Dorminsky**, Director.

Far East Film Festival
April 23-30, 2004

Annual themed event which, since 1998, has focused on Eastern Asian cinema. *Inquiries to:* Centro Espressioni Cinematografiche, Via Villalta 24, 33100 Udine, Italy. Tel: (39 04) 3229 9545. Fax: 3222 9815. e: fareastfilm@cecudine.org, Web: www.fareastfilm.com/.

Report 2003
Attendance at Teatro Nuovo reached 35,000 and we had more accredited guests (600-plus) than ever (even though many visitors from areas

affected by SARS were unable to attend). The Audience Awards crowned the excellent *Infernal Affairs* (Hong Kong), Miike Takashi's intense *Shangri-la* (Japan) and *The Way Home* by Lee Jeong-hyang (South Korea). The most favourable critical receptions were reserved for Johnnie To's *PTU* (Hong Kong) and the irresistible black comedy *Out* by Japanese director Hirayama Hideyuki. The King of Cult, director Ishii Teruo, was the subject of a career tribute.
– **Sabrina Baracetti & Max Mestroni**.

Festival Des 3 Continents
November 25 – December 2, 2003

The only annual competitive festival in the world for films originating solely from Africa, Asia and Latin and Black America. It's one of the few festivals where genuine discoveries may still be made. From Hou Hsiao-hsien or Abbas Kiarostami in the 1980s to Darejan Omirbaev or Jia Zang Ke in recent years, unknown names have been discovered in Nantes. F3C has also charted the film history of the southern countries through retrospectives (genres, countries, actors and actresses), showing more than 1,000 films and bringing to light large pieces of the world's cinematographic heritage. *Inquiries to:* Alain and Philippe Jalladeau, Directors, Festival des 3 Continents, BP 43302, 44033 Nantes Cedex 1, France. Tel: (33 2) 4069 7414. Fax: 4073 5522. e: festival@3continents.com.

AWARDS 2002
Golden Montgolfier: **Altyn Kyrgho/My Brother Silk Road** (Kirghizstan), Marat Sarulu.
Silver Montgolfier: **Emtehan/Exam** (Iran), Nasser Refaie.
Special Jury Award: **Historias Mínimas/Minimal Stories** (Argentina), Carlos Sorín.
Best Director: Jacques Demy, **La Espera/The Wait** (Uruguay).
Best Actress: Zhou Wenkian, **Jia Zhuang Mei Gan Jué/Shanghai Women** (China).
Best Actor: Fang Chih-wei, **Chang Duo Chiang/Brave 20** (Taiwan).
ARTE Award: **Tan De Repente/Suddenly** (Argentina), Diego Lerman.

Young Audience Award: **Historias Mínimas.**
Audience Award: **Araïs Al Teïn/Clay Dolls** (Tunisia), Nouri Bouzid.

Report 2002
During the 24th festival, more than 35,000 spectators enjoyed 80 films, including 12 in the Official Competition. Special sections included "Maggie Cheung: from Hong Kong to Paris" and "About the Rio de la Plata". There was a retrospective on the great Kirghize director Tolomouch Okeev, a short history of Moroccan cinema from S. Ben Barka to Aoulad Syad and a focus on Portuguese African cinema. The International Jury comprised president Christine Laurent, scriptwriter (France), Léonor Baldaque, actress (Portugal), Michel Braudeau, writer (France), Mario Dondero, photographer (Italy), Gerard Huisman, distributor (Netherlands) and Thaddeus O'Sullivan, director (Ireland).
– **Marie-Annick Ranger**, Festival Co-Ordinator.

Filmfest Hamburg
September 24 – October 1, 2004

Filmfest Hamburg is Germany's premiere springboard for independent productions. It focuses on young cinema from around the world, screening 80-100 features and up to 40 shorts. It previews some Hollywood productions and shows homegrown TV movies. The Douglas Sirk Prize honours outstanding contributions to film culture and business. This year the third annual digi@ward will be given to two productions using new digital technologies. There are more than 30,000 admissions and about 1,000 industry professionals attend. *Inquiries to:* Steintorweg 4, D-20099 Hamburg, Germany. Tel: (49 40) 3991 9000. Fax: 3991 90010. e: info@filmfesthamburg.de. Web: www.filmfesthamburg.de.

Report 2002
Highlights included the German premieres of *The Magdalene Sisters*, presented by the three lead actresses, *All Or Nothing*, with a lively discussion with Mike Leigh, and *The Man Without a Past*, which earned Aki Kaurismäki the Douglas Sirk Award. The audience vote gave the Tesafilm Award for Best First Feature to Joel

€81,000*

*From this year onwards the Flanders International Film Festival-Ghent will present prizes for a total value of €81,000 to local distributors who release the winning films.

5-16 OCTOBER, 2004
www.filmfestival.be

For more facts and figures: **www.filmfestival.be** / info@filmfestival.be

Bergvall and Simon Sandquist for *The Invisible* (Sweden). The jury gave the digi@ward to Michel Schonnemann, producer of *Old Men in New Cars* (Denmark), and Joakim Hansson, producer of *The Invisible*.
– **Kathrin Kohlstedde**, Programme Co-Ordinator.

Flanders International Film Festival (Ghent)

October 5-16, 2004

Belgium's most prominent annual film event attracts attendance of 90,000-plus. Principally focused on "The Impact of Music on Film", this competitive festival awards grants worth up to $75,000 and screens around 150 features and 80 shorts, most without a Benelux distributor. Other sections include the World Cinema spectrum (world, European or Benelux premieres), film music concerts, retrospectives, seminars and workshops, and a tribute to an important film-maker. The festival's Joseph Plateau Awards are the highest film honours in Benelux. Presented for the first time in 2001, the World Soundtrack Awards, judged by 180 internatonal composers, celebrate excellence in film scoring. *Inquiries to:* Flanders International Film Festival-Ghent, 40B Leeuwstraat, B-9000 Ghent, Belgium. Tel: (32 9) 242 8060. Fax: 221 9074. e: info@filmfestival.be. Web: www.filmfestival.be.

AWARDS 2002
Best Film: **The Man Without a Past** (Finland), Aki Kaurismäki.
Best Music: Howard Shore, **Spider** (Canada)
Best Screenplay: Rolf de Heer, **The Tracker** (Australia).
Best Director: Andreas Dresen, **Halbe Treppe**

(Germany).
Special Jury Prize: David Cronenberg.
FNAC Audience Award: **Piedras** (Spain), Ramón Salazar.
Young Jury Award: **Mein Bruder der Vampir** (Germany), Sven Taddicken.
Special Mention: **Snapshot** (Belgium), Jakob Verbruggen.
Prix UIP/Ghent 2002: **La Chanson-Chanson** (Belgium), Xavier Diskeuve.

Fort Lauderdale

October 22 – November 16, 2004

Screens more than 100 international films, including features, documentaries, shorts and student works. The festival presents Lifetime Achievement Awards to outstanding actors, directors, producers, writers and composers. It also offers film competition and a host of gala events on the beaches and waterways of South Florida. *Inquiries to:* The Fort Lauderdale International Film Festival, 1314 East Las Olas Blvd. Suite 007, Fort Lauderdale, FL 33301, USA. Tel: (1 954) 760 9898. Fax: 760 9099. e: brofilm@aol.com. Web: www.fliff.com.

AWARDS 2002
Best Film: **Laissez-Passer** (France), Bertrand Tavernier.
People's Choice: **Chaos** (France).
Best Director: Bertrand Tavernier.
Best Actor: Alexander Senderovich, **Trumpet in the Wadi** (Israel).
Best Actress: Khawleh Hag-Debsy, **Trumpet in the Wadi**.

Report 2002
Our 17th festival drew 68,500 admissions and

design by tangledspider.com

The Fort Lauderdale International Film Festival 2004

OCTOBER 20th to NOVEMBER 14th

Over 150 films, nightly parties, blacktie opening gala

FLIFF2004

The Fort Lauderdale International Film Festival
October 20th - November 14th 2004 • www.fliff.com • 954-525-FILM

featured 100 films. The 2002 Star on the Horizon honoree was Maria Bello (*Auto Focus, Coyote Ugly*) and the Robert Wise Director of Distinction Award went to Irvin Kershner (*Robocop 2, The Empire Strikes Back*). Matt Damon received the Renaissance Award for writing, producing and acting, conducted a sold-out Q&A and hosted an evening fundraiser to help a friend with leukaemia.
– **Lily Pardo**, PR Director.

Freedom Film Festival
February 21-25, 2004

Founded in 1997 by the American Cinema Foundation, this showcase of films from Eastern and Central Europe is dedicated to illuminating Europe's recent history and creating opportunities for its film-makers. The films relate to the struggle for personal, political, economic and artistic freedom during Stalin's times and in the wake of the Cold War. Coincides with the Berlin International Film Festival and the American Film Market in Los Angeles, and has

activities at Karlovy Vary and Moscow. *Inquiries to:* American Cinema Foundation, 9911 W Pico Blvd, Suite 1060, Los Angeles, CA 90035, USA. Tel: (1 310) 286 9420. Fax: 286 7914. e: acinema@cinemafoundation.com. Web: www.cinemafoundation.com.

Fribourg
March 21-28, 2004

Features, shorts and documentaries from Asia, Africa and Latin America unspool at this Swiss event with a competitive section. *Inquiries to:* Fribourg Film Festival, Rue Nicolas-de-Praroman 2, Case Postale 550, 1701 Fribourg, Switzerland. Tel: (41 26) 347 4200. Fax: 347 4201. e: info@fiff.ch. Web: www.fiff.ch.

AWARDS 2003
Le Regard d'Or: **Historias Mínimas** (Argentina), Carols Sorin.
Special Mention: **Caja Negra** (Argentina), Luis Ortega.
Political Press Award: **Kaddim Wind, Morrocan**

Chronicles (Israel), David Benchetrit.
Ecumenical Award: **Araïs al-Teïn** (Tunisia),
Nouri Bouzid.
E-changer Award: **Caja Negra** (Argentina),
Luis Ortega.
Special Mention: **Zendan-e Zanan** (Iran),
Manijeh Hekmat.
FICC Award: **Caja Negra**.
Special Mention: **Gei Wo Zhi Mao** (Taiwan),
Wu Mi-sen.
FIPRESCI Award: **Narradores de Javé** (Brazil),
Eliane Caffé
Public Award: **Lugares Comunes** (Argentina),
Adolfo Aristarain.

Giffoni
July 17-24, 2004

Located in Giffoni Valle Piana, a small town
about 40 minutes from Naples, the Giffoni
International Film Festival for Children and Young
People was founded in 1971 by Claudio
Gubitosi to promote films for youthful audiences
and families. Now includes four competitive
sections: Kidz (animated and fiction shorts that
tell fantastic stories, juried by 70 children aged
six to nine); First Screens (fiction features and
animated shorts, mainly fantasy and adventure,
juried by 400 children aged nine to 11); Free 2
Fly sees 350 teenagers (aged 12 to 14)
assessing features and shorts about the pre-
adolescent world; Y GEN has 250 jurors (aged
15 to 19) and takes a curious look at cinema for
young people. *Inquiries to:* Giffoni Film Festival,
Cittadella del Cinema, Via Aldo Moro 4, 84095
Giffoni Valle Piana, Salerno, Italy. Tel: (39 089)
802 3001. Fax: 802 3210. e: info@giffoniff.it.
Web: www.giffoniff.it.

Gijón International Film Festival
November 20-28, 2003

One of Spain's oldest festivals (41st edition in
2003), Gijón is now at the peak of its popularity.
Having firmly established itself as a barometer of
new film trends worldwide, it draws a large and
enthusiastic public. Gijón has built on its niche
as a festival for young people, programming
innovative and independent films made by and
for the young, including retrospectives,

panoramas, exhibitions and concerts. Alongside
the lively Official Section, sidebars celebrate
directors who forged new paths in film-making.
Inquiries to: Gijón International Film Festival,
Paseo de Begona, 24-Ent, 33201 Gijon, Spain.
Tel: (34 98) 518 2940. Fax: 518 2944.
e: festivalgijon@telecable.es.
Web: www.gijonfilmfestival.com.

AWARDS 2002
International Jury
Best Feature: **Lilya 4-Ever** (Sweden),
Lukas Moodysson.
Best Short: **Am See** (Germany),
Ulrike Von Ribbeck.
Young Jury
Best Feature: **Lilya 4-Ever**.
Best Short: **Rosso Fango** (Italy), Paolo Ameli.

Göteborg
January 23 – February 2, 2004

Now in its 27th year, Göteborg Film Festival is
the major international film festival in Scandinavia
and one of Europe's key events. Large
international programme and a special focus on
Nordic films, including the Nordic Competition.
In 2003, more than 400 films were screened.
International seminars and the market place
Nordic Event attract buyers and festival
programmers to the newest Scandinavian films.
Some 2,000 professionals attend and more than
110,000 tickets are sold. *Inquiries to:* Göteborg
Film Festival, Olof Palmes Plats, S- 413 04
Göteborg, Sweden. Tel: (46 31) 339 3000. Fax:
(46 31) 410 063. e: goteborg@filmfestival.org.
Web: www.filmfestival.org.

Haugesund – Norwegian International Film Festival
August 2004

Held in Haugesund, on the West coast of
Norway, the festival has become the country's
major film event, attended by many international
visitors and more than 1,000 representatives
from the Norwegian and Scandinavian film
industries. Award-winning films receive Amanda
Statuettes, and the New Nordic Film market
runs for three days at the beginning of the

festival. Festival Director: Gunnar Johan Løvvik. Programme Director: Håkon Skogrand. Inquiries to: PO Box 145, N-5501 Haugesund, Norway. Tel: (47 52) 743 370. Fax: 743 371. e: info@filmfestivalen.no. Web: www.filmfestivalen.no.

Helsinki Film Festival – Love & Anarchy
September 16-26, 2004

An important festival for current cinema in Finland, now in its 16th year, Helsinki promotes high-quality international film-making to Finnish audiences and distributors. True to its subtitle, "Love and Anarchy", the event challenges limits of cinematic expression and experience. Non-competitive. Submission deadline: June 30. *Inquiries to:* Helsinki Film Festival, PO Box 889, FIN-00101 Helsinki, Finland. Tel: (358 9) 6843 5230. Fax: 6843 5232. e: office@hiff.fi. Web: www.hiff.fi.

Report 2002
Attendance hit a record-breaking 40,000 and many intriguing film-makers visited, including cinematographer Robby Müller, who opened the festival with Michael Winterbottom's *24 Hour Party People*, Lukas Moodysson, actress Anne Parillaud, Hector Herrera, Brian Hill and Roger Michell. Bollywood film was introduced to Finland, with producer Yash Johar bringing *K3G* – an instant festival hit.

Hong Kong
April 6-21, 2004

A leading showcase for Asian cinema since 1977, Hong Kong is also recognised as an efficient, friendly event with a high-quality global

programme. It introduced an International Competition for young cinema in 2003, with cash prizes up to $20,000. The Hong Kong – Asia Film Financing Forum (HAF) will most probably be held again during the festival. *Inquiries to:* Hong Kong International Film Festival, 22/F, 181 Queens Rd Central, Hong Kong. Tel: (852) 2970 3300. Fax: 2970 3011. e: hkiff@hkadc.org.hk. Web: www.hkiff.org.hk.

AWARDS 2003
Golden Firebird Award: **Hukkle** (Hungary), György Pálfi.
Silver Firebird Award: **Blind Shaft** (China), Li Yang.
Golden DV Award: **Love Is Not a Sin** (Macau), Doug Chan.
Silver DV Award: **Welcome to Destination Shanghai** (China), Andrew Cheng.
Best Documentary: **Clown in Kabul** (Italy), Enzo Balestrieri and Stefano Moser.
Outstanding Documentary: **The Day I Will Never Forget** (UK), Kim Longinotto.
FIPRESCI Award: **Chicken Poets** (China), Meng Jinghui.

Johnny To, far right, director of PTU, with its stars, Ruby Wong, Simon Yam and Maggie Shiu, at Hong Kong 2003

People's Choice: **War Photographer** (Switzerland), Christian Frei.

Report 2003

At our 27th festival, more than 90,000 spectators enjoyed 330 new and classic films. In spite of the SARS outbreak, which prevented 80% of foreign guests from attending, the local audience was very supportive (attendance was about 60% of normal). Highlights included the Yasujiro Ozu Centenary Retrospective, which featured all 36 of his existing films.
– **Peter Tsi**, Festival Director.

Huelva
November 2004

The main aim of Huelva Latin American Film Festival is to show and promote films of artistic quality which contribute to a better knowledge of Latin American production, including works from the Hispanic US. Huelva has become a key rendezvous, enabling European buyers and film buffs to catch up with the latest developments. It includes a competition for films from Latin America and the Hispanic US, tributes and round-table discussions. *Inquiries to:* Casa Coln,

Plaza del Punto s/n, 21003 Huelva, Spain. Tel: (34 95) 921 0170/0171/0299. Fax: 921 0173. e: festival@festicinehuelva.com. Web: www.festicinehuelva.com.

AWARDS 2002

Best Film: **Madame Satã** (Brazil/France), Karim Aïnouz.
Best Director: Suzana Amaral, **Uma Vida Em Segredo** (Brazil).
Best Actor: Lázaro Ramos, **Madame Satã**.
Best Actress: Sabina Greve, **Uma Vida Em Segredo**.
Best Script: Diego Lerman and Maria Meira, **Tan De Repente** (Argentina).
Best Photography: Walter Carvalho, **Madame Satã**.
Best First Film: **Tan De Repente**.
Special Jury Prize: **Uma Vida Em Segredo**.

IFP Market
September 19-24, 2004

The only selective film market in the US focused on presenting film and TV works in development exclusively to industry professionals. More than 2,000 buyers, distributors, agents, producers, programmers and others gather to discover works by the best emerging film-makers. It accepts approximately 200 projects across three sections: Emerging Narrative, Spotlight on Documentaries and the No Borders International Co-Production Market. Projects include works-in-progress, feature-length screenplays and completed documentary features. *Inquiries to:* Michelle Byrd, Executive Director, IFP/New York, 104 West 29th St, 12th Floor, New York, NY, 10001, USA. Tel: (1 212) 465 8200. Fax: 465 8525. e: ifpny@ifp.org. Web: www.ifp.org.

India
October 2004

Annual, government-funded event recognised by FIAPF and held under the aegis of India's Ministry of Information and Broadcasting. Comprehensive "Cinema of the World" section, foreign and Indian retrospectives and a film market, plus a valuable panorama of the year's best Indian films, subtitled in English. Every even year the festival is held in Delhi (which hosts a competitive section of New Asian Cinema) and every odd year the festival is non-competitive and held in another city. *Inquiries to:*

The Director, Directorate of Film Festival, Siri Fort Auditorium 1, August Kranti Marg, Khel Gaon, New Delhi 110049, India. Tel: (91 11) 649 9371/9357. Fax: 649 7214/0457). e: dffiffi@bol.net.in. Web: www.mib.nic/dff.

Internationale Hofer Filmtage/Hof International Film Festival
October 26-31, 2004

Dubbed "Home of Film" (HOF) by Wim Wenders, Hof is famous for its thoughtful selection of some 50 features. Founded by the directors of the New German Cinema, Hof enjoys a high reputation among German film-makers and American cult figures such as Roger Corman and Monte Hellman. Directed by one of the most respected German film enthusiasts, Heinz Badewitz, Hof has enjoyed a rising reputation these past 37 years. A screening here often results in a distribution deal. Inquiries to: Postfach 1146, D-95010 Hof, Germany or Heinz Badewitz, Lothstr 28, D-80335 Munich, Germany. Tel: (49 89) 129 7422. Fax: 123 6868. e: info@hofer-filmtage.de. Web: www.hofer-filmtage.de.

Report 2002

Some 58 features and documentaries and 27 shorts celebrated their German premiere at our 36th festival. In five days, 27,000 people visited 150 screenings showing films from Australia, Austria, Canada, Denmark, France, Greece, Hungary, Italy, Japan, New Zealand, Norway, Switzerland, Turkey, UK, US and Germany. The retrospective was dedicated to Paul Morrissey, who presented his own choice of films. As in the last 36 years, the directors' soccer team, 1 FC Hofer Filmtage, played a select Hof Team. The thrilling match ended 4-4.
– **Heinz Badewitz**, Festival Director.

Istanbul

April 10-25, 2004

The only film festival which takes place in a city where two continents meet, the Istanbul International Film Festival, recognised as a specialised competitive event by FIAPF, acts as a valuable showcase for distributors internationally. Attendance exceeds 100,000. Now in its 23rd edition, this dynamic event focuses on features dealing with the arts, with other thematic sections such as tributes, selections from World Festivals, "A Country – A Cinema", and a panorama of Turkish cinema. *Inquiries to:* Mrs Hulya Ucansu, Istanbul Kultur ve Sanat Vakfi, Istiklal Caddesi Luvr Apt 146, Beyoglu 34435, Istanbul, Turkey. Tel: (90 212) 334 0721. Fax: (90 212) 334 0702. e: film.fest@istfest-tr.org. Web: www.istfest.org.

AWARDS 2003

Golden Tulip: **Tan De Repente/Suddenly** (Argentina), Diego Lerman.
Special Prize of the Jury: **Personal Velocity**

(US), Rebecca Miller.
FIPRESCI Awards: **Hafid/The Sea** (Iceland), Balthasar Kormakur (International Competition); **Uzak/Distant** (Turkey), Nuri Bilge Ceylan National Competition.
Best Turkish Film of the Year: **Uzak**.
Best Turkish Director of the Year: Nuri Bilge Ceylan, **Uzak**.
Honorary Award: Estela Bravo.

Jerusalem International Film Festival

July 2004

Israel's most prestigious cinematic event showcases more than 180 films: Best of International Cinema, Documentaries, Israeli Cinema, Animation, Short Films, American Independents, Avant Garde, New Directors, Jewish Themes, Classics, Restorations and Special Tributes. Prize categories include the Wolgin Awards for Israeli Cinema, Lipper Award for Best Israeli Screenplay, international awards like the Wim van Leer "In the Spirit of Freedom" for films focusing on human rights, and the Films on Jewish Themes Award. *Inquiries to:* Jerusalem Film Festival, PO Box 8561, Jerusalem 91083, Israel. Tel: (972 2) 565 4333. Fax: 565 4334. e: festival@jer-cin.org.il. Web: www.jff.org.il.

Report 2002

More than 7,500 people (a record), attended the 19th festival's Opening Gala below the ancient walls of the Old City to watch Almodóvar's *Talk to Her*. The "In The Spirit of Freedom Award" was given to Paul Greengrass' *Bloody Sunday* and the Mayor's "Jewish Experience" Award to Caroline Link's *Nowhere in Africa*. Guest of Honour was David Mamet. Special Events included Moonlight Cinema in the Park (three nights of free screenings with music and dance).

JERUSALEM FILM FESTIVAL

Director: Lia van Leer

July 8 - 17 2004

Karlovy Vary International Film Festival
July 2-10, 2004

Founded in 1946, Karlovy Vary is one of the most important film events in Central and Eastern Europe. It includes international competitions for features and documentaries and every year foreign visitors welcome the chance to see new productions from former Eastern Bloc countries. *Inquiries to:* Film Servis Festival Karlovy Vary, Panská 1, CZ 110 00 Prague 1, Czech Republic. Tel: (420 2) 2141 1044. Fax: 2141 1033. e: festival@kviff.com. Web: www.kviff.com.

Report 2003
At the 38th festival, 122,000 spectators enjoyed around 250 new and classic films. The Jury, presided over by Canadian producer Rock Demers, awarded the Grand Prix, the Crystal Globe, to *Facing Window* (Italy, Ferzan Ozpetek), which also won Best Director and Best Actress. Further awards were given to *Babusya* (Russia, Lidia Bobrova), *Fear and Trembling* (France, Alain Corneau) and Old, *New, Borrowed and Blue* (Denmark, Natasha Arthy). The Audience Prize went to *Buddy* (Norway, Morten Tyldum). Highlights included tributes to Joseph Strick and Amos Gitai, and Focus on Baltic Films. Special Crystal Globes were awarded to Stephen Frears, Jiří Menzel and Morgan Freeman.

La Rochelle
Late June – early July 2004

In a friendly atmosphere, this non-competitive festival showed 120 films to audiences of 78,000 in 2003. Five films are screened a day in each of the six theatres situated around the old port. There is a daily 4pm meeting for public and press with a film-maker. The festival includes Retrospective celebrations of the work of six or seven film-makers or actors; tributes to important but unjustly neglected directors or actors; The World As It Is: a selection of new international films receiving their French premiere. Films for children are shown every morning and the festival ends with an all-night programme of five films, followed by breakfast in cafés overlooking the old port. *Inquiries to:* La Rochelle International Film Festival, 16 rue Saint Sabin, 75011 Paris, France. Tel: (33 1) 4806 1666. Fax: 4806 1540. e: info@festival-larochelle.org. Web: www.festival-larochelle.org.

Le Giornate del Cinema Muto
October 9-16, 2004

The world's first festival dedicated to silent cinema, in the historic town of Sacile, close to the festival's original home of Pordenone. It is invaded by international archivists, historians, scholars, collectors and enthusiasts, along with cinema students chosen to attend the internationally recognised "Collegium". The Film Fair, which features books, CD-ROMs and DVDs, continues to provide a valued meeting place for authors and publishers. Festival director: David Robinson. *Inquiries to:* Le Giornate del Cinema Muto, c/o La Cineteca del Friuli, Palazzo Gurisatti, Via Bini 50, 33013 Gemona (UD), Italy. Tel: (39 04) 3298 0458. Fax: 3297 0542. e: info.gcm@cinetecadelfriuli.org. Web: www.cinetecadelfriuli.org/gcm/.

Report 2002
A wealth of rediscovered and restored works was shown with live musical accompaniment. The inaugural masterclass series enabled the festival's outstanding resident musicians to pass on their experience to a new generation of artists. "Cooper, Schoedsack & Friends" showcased the American film-makers who exploited exotic locations as settings for fictional stories. "Ivan Mozhukhin – Paths of Exile" was a tribute to a legendary figure, a mesmeric actor who was a superstar in Tsarist Russia and

1920s France. Other presentations featured Thai silents and the seventh instalment of the Griffith Project, which covered 1913.

Leeds
October 2004

The UK's largest regional film festival, based in the country's fastest-growing city. Competitive for debut/sophomore features, short films and animation. Leeds is buzzing with more than a dozen strands, including Fanomenon, the 'cultural' heart of the festival (a feast of fantasy film); 'evolution', a focus on new ways of seeing film; Eureka, a major spotlight on new and archive European cinema. *Inquiries to:* Leeds International Film Festival, The Town Hall, The Headrow, Leeds, LS1 3AD, UK. Tel: (44 113) 247 8398. Fax: 247 8494. e: filmfestival@leeds.gov.uk. Web: www.leedsfilm.com.

Report 2002
The 16th festival saw record attendance (16,000 spectators enjoyed 300 screenings and events). Opening night guests included Ken Loach, who introduced *Sweet Sixteen*, and Marc Evans opened Fanomenon with *My Little Eye*. A rare retrospective of the work of Peter Watkins and a three-day seminar exploring digital and time-based arts practice took place alongside the previews and premieres. After a very close contest, *Rabbit-Proof Fence* won the Audience award, with Peter Næss' *Elling* in second place.

Locarno
August 4-14, 2004

Locarno, the world's second oldest festival, has become a place where world and European premieres are regular occasions and serious buyers come to discover creative filmmakers. More than 1,000 accredited journalists from 30-plus countries are surrounded by an international attendance of 187,000. Every night more than 7,000 people sit in front of the giant screen in Piazza Grande.
Inquiries to: Festival Internazionale del Film Locarno, Via Luini 3A, CH-6601 Locarno, Switzerland. Tel: (41 91) 756 2121. Fax: 756 2149. e: info@pardo.ch. Web: www.pardo.ch.

London

Late October – early November 2004

The UK's largest and most prestigious festival, presented at the National Film Theatre and in the West End, and at cinemas throughout the capital, the programme comprises around 200 features and documentaries, as well as a showcase for shorts. There is a British section and a very strong international selection from Asia, Africa, Europe, Latin America, US independents and experimental and avant-garde work. More than 1,200 UK and international press and industry representatives attend and there is a buyers/sellers liaison office. *Inquiries to:* Sarah Lutton, London Film Festival, National Film Theatre, South Bank, London SE1 8XT, UK. Tel: (44 20) 7815 1322. Fax: 7633 0786. e: sarah.lutton@bfi.org.uk. Web: www.lff.com.

Report 2002

The festival screened 180 features, including 22 documentaries, and 122 shorts; 118 of the screenings were sold out, as were many of the public and educational events. The festival welcomed 424 film-makers and the exceptionally strong and eclectic selection included *Russian Ark, City of God, Lola Montes* and *Dracula: Pages from a Virgin's Diary*.

Málaga

April 23 – May 1, 2004

After six editions, the Festival of Málaga is firmly established as the key national showcase for Spanish cinema. Used as a launch pad for spring releases in Spain, Málaga enjoys large turnouts from local audiences and Spanish actors, producers and directors. Besides a competition for features and shorts, tributes and retrospectives, the festival has a documentary section, exhibits, round-tables and the Market of European and Latin American Documentaries, MERCADOC, and Market Screenings for Spanish films. The cash prizes, in the form of distribution aid, are worth $170,000. *Inquiries to:* Salomón Castiel, Director, Málaga Spanish Film Film Festival, Ramos Marín 2, 1-C, 29012, Málaga, Spain. Tel: (34 95) 222 8242. Fax: 222 7760. e: info@festivaldemalaga.com. Web:
www.festivaldemalaga.com.

AWARDS 2003

Best Film: **Torremolinos 73** (Spain), Pablo Berger.
Special Jury Prize: **Tiempo de Tormenta/Stormy Weather** (Spain), Pedro Olea.
Best Director: Pablo Berger, **Torremolinos 73**.
Best Actress: Javier Cámara, **Torremolinos 73**.
Audience Prize: **Dos Tipos Duros** (Spain), Juan Martínez Moreno.

Mannheim-Heidelberg

November 20-29, 2003

The Newcomers' Festival: for young independent film-makers. Presents around 35 new features and around 10 shorts in two main sections, International Competition and International Discoveries (entry deadline: August 9). The Newcomers' Market & Industry Screenings: reserved for international buyers and distributors. The Mannheim Meetings: Part 1 is one of only four worldwide co-production meetings for producers (alongside Rotterdam, New York and Pusan) and runs in parallel to the main event (entry deadline: July 31). Part 2 is the unique European Sales & Distribution Meetings for theatrical distributors and sales agents. The Distribution Market will take place during the festival. *Inquiries to:* Dr Michael Koetz, International Filmfestival Mannheim-Heidelberg, Collini-Center, Galerie, D-68161 Mannheim, Germany. Tel: (49 621) 102 943. Fax: 291 564. e: ifmh@mannheim-filmfestival.com. Web: www.mannheim-filmfestival.com.

Zhang Yimou, left, with festival director Michael Koetz at Mannheim-Heidelberg in 2002

AWARDS 2002

Best Fiction Film: **The Devils** (France),
Christophe Ruggia.
Best Short Film: **Tomorrow** (Netherlands),
Jacqueline van Vugt.
Rainer Werner Fassbinder Prize: **Utopia –
Nobody Is Perfect in the Perfect Country**
(Norway), Morten Tyldum, Arild Frølich, Sara
Johnson, Ingeborg Torgersen, Terje Ragnes,
Magnus Martens, Martin Asphaug, Hans Petter
Moland and Thomas Robsahm.
Special Award of the Jury: **The Exam** (Iran),
Nasser Refaie.
Audience Award: **Charlie Butterfly** (Denmark),
Dariusz Steiness; **La Spagnola** (Australia),
Steve Jacobs.

Report 2002

At our 51st festival, more than 60,000
spectators enjoyed 40 films from 30 countries.
Highlights included the tribute to guest of
honour Zhang Yimou, and 170 professionals
met in more than 750 one-on-one meetings at
the Co-production and Sales & Distribution
Meetings. The jury comprised Thomas Mai
(Denmark), Trine Dyrholm (Denmark), Karen
Moon (Korea), Margarita Segui (France) and
Jaana Puskala (Finland).
– **Sigrid Scherer**, Public Relations.

Melbourne International Film Festival

July 21 – August 8, 2004

The longest-running festival in the Southern
hemisphere will present its 53rd edition in 2004,
with 400-plus features, shorts, documentaries
and new media works, presented in five venues.
Inquiries to: PO Box 2206, Fitzroy Mail Centre
3065, Melbourne, Victoria, Australia.

Tel: (61 3) 9417 2011. Fax: 9417 3804.
e: miff@melbournefilmfestival.com.au.
Web: www.melbournefilmfestival.com.au.

Report 2003

The 52nd festival drew to a close with a gala
screening of Australian director Gregor Jordan's
long-delayed *Buffalo Soldiers*, at the end of 19
days which saw record attendances and almost
double the number of sold-out sessions
compared to 2002 (year-on-year box-office rose
by 17%). Among the sold-out screenings were
Distant (Turkey), The Best Shorts of the
Festival/FIPRESCI Awards, *Ten* (Iran),
Spellbound (US) and *Infernal Affairs* (Hong
Kong). World premieres included the Australian
features *The Rage in Placid Lake* (winner of the
Audience Award) and *Travelling Light*.

MIFED (Milan)

November 2004

Long-established market held in the
expansive Milan Fair, particularly well-attended
by international buyers and sellers. Third on
the annual calendar after the American Film
Market and Cannes, MIFED's atmosphere is
considered by many to be more sober and
business-like. MIFED is unique because its
exhibition and screening facilities are all under
one roof. Its 28 screening rooms have Dolby
stereo, and it continues to invest substantially
in technological and logistical improvements.
Inquiries to: Fiera Milano International, Largo
Domodossola 1, Palazzina FMI, 20145 Milan,
Italy. Tel: (39 02) 485 501. e: mifed@fmi.it.
Web: www.mifed.com.

Mill Valley
October 7-17, 2004

The Mill Valley Film Festival presents a wide variety of international programming, shaped by a commitment to cultural and artistic excellence. This intimate, welcoming event of unusually high calibre and dedication is set in a beautiful small town just north of San Francisco. The non-competitive festival includes the innovative VFest, as well as the Children's Film Fest, tributes, seminars and special events. *Inquiries to:* Mill Valley Film Festival, 38 Miller Ave, Suite 6, Mill Valley, CA 94941, USA. Tel: (1 415) 383 5256. Fax: 383 8606. e: info@cafilm.org. Web: www.mvff.com.

Report 2002
Our 25th festival saw 44,000 tickets sold for almost 200 films (including four world and 14 US premieres) at venues including the California Film Institute's state-of-the-art Christopher B. Smith Rafael Film Center. At a screening of *Bowling for Columbine*, Michael Moore publicly thanked 2002 Tribute recipient Ed Asner, who was the only person in Hollywood to send Moore money for his first film, *Roger and Me*. Other highlights: a fascinating Tribute to Milos Forman and a lively actors' panel with Asner, Diane Wiest, Tony Shalhoub and Brooke Adams. The anniversary party had George Lucas and Saul Zaentz as honorary co-hosts.
– **Rama Dunayevich**, Associate Director, Public Relations

Montreal World Film Festival
August 26 – September 6, 2004

Every year, films from more than 70 countries are selected and more and more cinemagoers attend. The different sections have been reorganised to reflect more fully Montreal's vocation as "World Film Festival". It will present the "World Competition" and the following sections: Cinema of Europe, Cinema of the Americas (Panorama Canada, Cinema of the USA, Latin American Cinema), Cinema of Asia, Cinema of Africa, Cinema of Oceania and Documentaries of the World. All the theatres are within walking distance and this contributes to the relaxed atmosphere. Festival guests have included: Jane Fonda, Clint Eastwood, Gérard Depardieu, Jackie Chan, Gong Li, Jeanne Moreau and Liv Ullmann. *Inquiries to:* Montreal World Film Festival 1432 de Bleury St, Montreal, Quebec, Canada H3A 2J1. Tel: (1 514) 848 3883 Fax: 848 3886. e: info@ffm-montreal.org. Web: www.ffm-montreal.org.

AWARDS 2002
Grand Prix of the Americas (Best Film): **Il Piu Bel Giorno Della Mia Vita/The Best Day of My Life** (Italy), Cristina Comencini.
Special Grand Prix of the Jury: **Hiçbiryerde/In Nowhereland** (Turkey), Tayfun Pirselimoglu.
Best Director: Sophie Marceau, **Parlez-Moi D'Amour** (France).
Best Artistic Contribution: Carlos Saura, **Salomé** (Spain).
Best Actress: Maria Bonnevie, **I Am Dina** (Norway/Denmark/Sweden/Germany/France), Ole Bornedal; Leila Hatami for **Aandoned Station** (Iran), Alireza Raisian.
Best Actor: Alexei Chadov for **The War** (Russia), Alexei Balabanov.
Best Screenplay: Diego Arsuaga, **El Ultimo Tren** (Uruguay/Spain/Argentina).
Lifetime Achievement: Kon Ichikawa.

Netherlands Film Festival, Utrecht
September 22 – October 1, 2004

Since 1981, Holland's only event presenting an overview of the year's entire output of Dutch film-making. The festival opens the new cultural season with Dutch retrospectives, seminars, talk shows and premieres of many new Dutch films. In the competition, Dutch features, shorts, documentaries and TV dramas compete for local cinema's grands prix, the Golden Calf, in 18 categories. The Holland Film Meeting, the sidebar for international and national film professionals, includes a Market Programme and the Netherlands Production Platform for Dutch and European producers. *Inquiries to:* Nederlands Film Festival, PO Box 1581, 3500 BN Utrecht, Netherlands. Tel: (31 30) 230 3800 Fax: 230 3801. e: info@filmfestival.nl. Web: www.filmfestival.nl.

AWARDS 2002

Best Feature Film: **Minoes**, Burny Bos.
Best Director: Alejandro Agresti, **Valentin**.
Best Actor: Jacob Derwig, **Zus & Zo**.
Best Actress: Carice van Houten, **Minoes**.
Best Feature Documentary: **Ramse**,
Pieter Fleury.

New York

October 2004

The festival highlights the best of American and international cinema. Deadline will be around July. Application forms and details available from May. No entry fee. Non-competitive. All categories and lengths accepted. Formats accepted: VHS (NTSC or PAL), u-matic, 16mm, 35mm. For acceptance, you must have a 16mm or 35mm print available. Works must be New York City premieres. *Inquiries to:* Sara Bensman, Film Society of Lincoln Center, 70 Lincoln Center Plaza, New York, NY 10023-6595, USA. Tel: (1 212) 875 5638. Fax: 875 5636. e: sbensman@filmlinc.com. Web: www.filmlinc.com.

Nordische Filmtage Lubeck

Late October – early November 2004

Annual event held in the charming medieval town of Lubeck, north of Hamburg. Spotlights Scandinavian and Baltic cinema, enabling members of the trade, critics and other filmgoers to see the best new productions. Also features a large documentary section. Artistic director Linde Fröhlich reports that the 44th event in 2002 was a huge success, with more than 18,000 people attending 131 screenings. *Inquiries to:* Janina Prossek, Nordische Filmtage Lubeck, Schildstrasse 12, D-23539 Lubeck, Germany. Tel: (49 451) 122 1742. Fax: 122 1799. e: info@filmtage.luebeck.de. Web: http://filmtage.luebeck.de.

AWARDS 2002

NDR Promotion Prize: **Dragonflies** (Norway), Marius Holst.
Baltic Film: **Open Hearts** (Denmark), Susanne Bier.
Audience Prize: **The Man Without a Past** (Finland), Aki Kaurismäki.
Children's Film: **Marcello & Fatima** (Sweden),

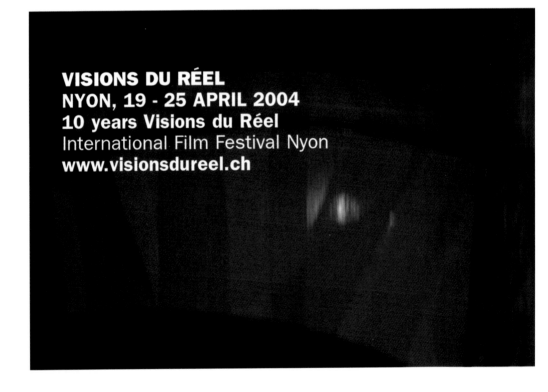

Ulf Malmros.
Documentary Film: **Now You're Hamlet**
(Finland), Ulrika Bengts.
Video Prize: **Marcello & Fatima**.
Children's Jury: **My Sister's Kids 2** (Denmark),
Tomas Villum Jensen.

Nyon
April 19-25, 2004

Visions du Réel, the International Film Festival of
Nyon, aims to promote independent films and
audiovisual productions classified as creative
documentaries. Documentary is treated as a
specific and committed form of cinema. The
works (irrespective of length or format) are
divided into six sections: International
Competition; Regards Neufs (international
competition for first films); Traverses; Etat des
lieux and its Ateliers; Séances spéciales;
Grandes Enquêtes. Deadline: January 15
(regulations and entry form available each
autumn on festival website). *Inquiries to:* Visions
du Réel, 18, rue Juste Olivier, PO Box 593, CH-
1260 Nyon 1, Switzerland. Tel: (41 22) 365
4455. Fax: 365 4450. e:
docnyon@visionsdureel.ch. Web:
www.visionsdureel.ch.

Oberhausen
April 29 – May 4, 2004

In 2004, the International Short Film Festival
Oberhausen will celebrate its 50th anniversary.
The likes of Martin Scorsese, George Lucas,
David Lynch and Werner Herzog, and more
recently Jean-Pierre Jeunet and François Ozon,
have presented their first films here. It has
competitions for international, national, children's
and youth shorts and a German music video
competition, short film market and numerous
non-competitive special programmes. Closing
date for entries: January 15. Festival director:
Dr Lars Henrik Gass. *Inquiries to:* Oberhausen
International Short Film Festival, Grillostrasse 34,
D-46045 Oberhausen, Germany.
Tel: (49 208) 825 2652. Fax: 825 5413.
 e: info@kurzfilmtage.de.
Web: www.kurzfilmtage.de.

AWARDS 2003
International Competition
Grand Prize: **Portret** (Russia), Sergej Loznitsa.
Two Principal Prizes: **No Me Importa Que Se
Mueran Las Jirafas** (Argentina), Gustavo Sidlin;
Dansa Med Dvärgar (Sweden), Emelie Carlsson
Gras,
German Competition
Best Contribution: **Manual** (Germany/UK),
Christoph Girardet, Matthias Müller; **Auto
Center Drive** (Germany), Bjørn Melhus.

Odense
August 2004

Denmark's only international short film festival
invites unusual films with original, surprising and
imaginative content. All 16mm, 35mm and Beta
SP can participate. Maximum length: 45 mins.
At the 18th festival, more than 100 short films
were screened and there were numerous 'Meet
the Audience' sessions, three seminars, several
film professional get-togethers, one exhibition
and four open-air screenings. *Inquiries to:*
Odense Film Festival, Vindegade 18, DK-5000
Odense C, Denmark. Tel: (45) 6613 1372, ext
4044. Fax: 6591 4318. e: off.ksf@odense.dk.
Web: www.filmfestival.dk.

AWARDS 2002
International Grand Prix: **Aria** (Norway),
Pjort Sapegin.
Most Surprising: **Square Couine/Squealing
Square** (France), Fabrice Luang-Vija.
Most Imaginative: **Cherchez la femme**
(Germany), Daniel Höpfner.
Personal Jury Prizes: **Bamboleho** (Spain), Luis
Prieto; **Wahlverwandtschaften** (Germany), Nils
Loof; **Copy Shop** (Austria), Virgil Widrich.
Press Jury Prize: **In Search of Mike** (Australia),
Andrew Lancaster.

Oulu International Children's
Film Festival
November 15-21, 2004

Annual festival with competition for full-length
feature films for children, it screens recent titles
and retrospectives. Oulu is set in northern
Finland on the coast of the Gulf of Bothnia.

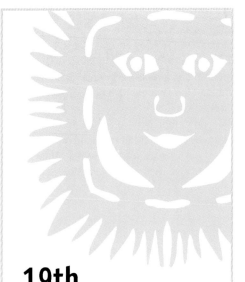

Inquiries to: Oulu International Children's Film Festival, Torikatu 8, 90100 Oulu, Finland.
Tel: (358 8) 881 1293, 881 1294. Fax: 881 1290.
e: oek@oufilmcenter.inet.fi. Web: www.ouka.fi/lef.

Report 2002

The 21st festival attracted 10,000 spectators to 100 screenings in three cinemas. Fourteen films competed for the children's jury Star Boy Award. The adult jury comprised director John Hay, festival director Kathleen Aubry and theatre and circus director Anna-Kaisa Järvi. The retrospective of famous puppet animators Finnish Katariina Lillqvist and Czech Jan Balej was complemented with a successful puppet exhibition. Latvian animators were showcased in a comprehensive programme. Best Film (Children's Jury) was *Catch That Girl* (Denmark, Hans Fabian Wullenweber) and Best Film (CIFEJ Jury) was *Scars* (Norway, Lars Berg).

Palm Springs

January 8-19, 2004

Each year Palm Springs honours individuals with awards, including the Charles A. Crain Desert Palm Achievement, International Film-maker,

27th Portland International Film Festival
February 13-28, 2004

nwFilmCenter

Entry Deadline: October 31

www.nwfilm.org 503.221.1156

Director's Lifetime Achievement, Frederick Loewe Achievement and the Outstanding Achievement in Craft. The festival has more than 600 entries and 65,000 attendees. *Inquiries to:* Rhea Lewis-Woodson, 1700 E. Tahquitz Canyon Way, Suite 3, Palm Springs, CA 92262, USA. Tel: (1 760) 322 2930. Fax: 322 4087. e: info@psfilmfest.org. Web: www.psfilmfest.org.

Pesaro, Italy
June 2004

Focuses on new directors and emerging, innovative cinemas, including non-fiction, animation, shorts and videos. For the past 38 years, this Mediterranean resort has hosted lively screenings and debates. In recent seasons, the programme has been devoted in part to a specific country or culture. The main festival is coupled each October with a five-day themed retrospective of Italian cinema. *Inquiries to:* Mostra Internazionale del Nuovo Cinema (Pesaro Film Festival), Via Villafranca 20, 00185 Rome, Italy. Tel: (39 06) 445 6643/491 156. Fax: 491 163. e:pesarofilmfest@mclink.it. Web: www.pesarofilmfest.it.

Portland
February 13-28, 2004

The 27th Portland International Film Festival will be an invitational event presenting more than 100 films from 30-plus countries. New international features, documentaries and shorts are seen by 35,000 people from throughout the Northwest. The 2003 audience award winners were *Spellbound* (US), *To Be and To Have* (France) and *Kamchatka* (Argentina). Guest directors included Peter Sollett (*Raising Victor Vargas*) and Eliseo Subiela (*Dark Side of the*

Heart 2). *Inquiries to:* Portland International Film Festival, Northwest Film Center, 1219 SW Park Ave, Portland, OR 97205, USA. Tel: (1 503) 221 1156. Fax: 294 0874. e: info@nwfilm.org. Web: www.nwfilm.org.

Raindance
Late October – early November 2004

Raindance aims to reflect the cultural, visual and narrative diversity of international independent film-making by screening features and shorts. It also accepts children's films for Raindance Kids. Held during the Pre-MIFED London Screenings, Raindance targets international film acquisition executives in London prior to the Milan market, and attracts leading industry professionals and film fans. It has premiered and showcased films as diverse as *Pulp Fiction, The Blair Witch Project, Chuck and Buck, Audition, 101 Reykjavik* and *Memento. Inquiries to:* Oli Harbottle, Festival Producer, Raindance Film Festival, 81 Berwick St, London, W1F 8TW, UK. Tel: (44 20) 7287 3833. Fax: 7439 2243. e: festival@raindance.co.uk. Web: www.raindance.co.uk/festival.

AWARDS 2002
Official Selection Feature: **Getting My Brother Laid** (Germany), Sven Taddicken.
Official Selection Short: **Home Road Movies** (UK), Robert Bradbrook.
UK Feature: **Mr In-Between**, Paul Sarossy.
UK Short: **Shadow Man**, Amanda Rudman.
Digital Cinema: **Strass** (Belgium), Vincent Lannoo.

Report 2002
At our 11th festival, 21,000 spectators enjoyed more than 70 features and 200 shorts.

Highlights included the opening night screening of *Tadpole*, the huge success of *Showboy* and the festival's 'Underground' strand, which included *The Bikini Bandits Experience* and *Hey Is Dee Dee Home*. Maverick director Tony Kaye gave an illuminating discussion on his work as film-maker in residence. The Official Selection jury included actor Nick Moran.
– **Oli Harbottle**, Festival Producer.

Rio de Janeiro International Film Festival
Late September – early October 2004

The Rio de Janeiro International Film Festival was created in 1999 by the merger of Mostra Rio and Rio Cine and boasts a spectacular backdrop (screenings on Copacabana Beach), an eclectic programme and the ambition to become a key springboard for film sales to, from and in Latin America. Admissions: 130,000-plus. Key sections include Premiere Brazil, World Panorama and a national film industry tribute. *Inquiries to:* Ilda Santiago, Rua Voluntários da Pátria, 53, 4th Floor, Botafogo – 22270-000, Rio de Janeiro, Brazil. Tel: (55 21) 2579 0352. Fax: 2539 3580. e: films@festivaldorio.com.br. Web: www.festivaldorio.com.br.

International Film Festival Rotterdam
January 21 – February 1, 2004

For 32 years, Rotterdam has showcased the best of contemporary independent and experimental film. With more than 200 features, including 60 world, international or European premieres, it supports diversity and discoveries. It also hosts the leading co-production market, the CineMart. Rotterdam's Hubert Bals Fund (HBF) supports film-makers from non-Western countries. Recently acclaimed HBF-backed films include Carlos Reygadas' *Japón* (Mexico) and Nuri Bilge Ceylan's *Distant* (Turkey). In 2004, returning sidebars like the VPRO Tiger Awards Competition for first and second features, Film-makers in Focus and Exploding Cinema will be complemented by themed programmes, exhibitions and public debates. The festival draws 350,000 spectators and 2,500 professionals. *Inquiries to:* International Film

Festival Rotterdam, PO Box 21696, 3001 AR Rotterdam, Netherlands. Tel: (31 10) 890 9090. Fax: 890 9091.
e: tiger@filmfestivalrotterdam.com.
Web: www.filmfestivalrotterdam.com.

San Francisco International Film Festival
April 2004

The oldest film festival in the Americas, in its 47th year, San Francisco continues to grow in importance and popularity. It presents more than 200 international features and shorts. Special awards include the Skyy Prize ($10,000 cash for an emerging director). *Inquiries to:* San Francisco International Film Festival, San Francisco Film Society, 39 Mesa St, Suite 110, The Presidio, San Francisco, CA 94129, USA. Tel: (1 415) 561 5000. Fax: 561 5099.
e: sffs@sffs.org. Web: www.sffs.org.

AWARDS 2003
Skyy Prize: **The Man of the Year** (Brazil), José Henrique Fonseca.
Golden Gate Award Grand Prizes
Best Short: **Painting with Light in a Dark World** (Australia), Sascha Ettinger-Epstein.
Best Documentary: **The Weather Underground** (US), Sam Green and Bill Siegel.
Best Bay Area Short: **The Children of Ibdaa: To Create Something Out of Nothing** (US/Palestine), S. Smith Patrick.
Best Bay Area Documentary: **Lost Boys of the Sudan** (US), Jon Shenk and Megan Mylan.
New Visions: **Fall (3 Parts)** (US/France), Leighton Pierce.
Best Narrative Short: **The Way Back** (Australia), Samuel MacGeorge.
Best Bay Area Narrative Short: **Frequency Response-Observations** (US), Christopher Arcella.
Best Animated Short: **Pan With Us** (US), David Russo.

Report 2003
Attendance topped 94,500 (a 5% increase over 2002 and a third consecutive record) for 250 screenings of 202 films in San Francisco, Berkeley and Palo Alto. The annual gala raised

$230,000 to support the San Francisco Film Society. Robert Altman received the Award for Lifetime Achievement in Directing from Lily Tomlin, who performed her classic character, Ernestine. Dustin Hoffman received the Peter J. Owens Award. Also in attendance for Awards Night were Robin Williams, Delroy Lindo, Peter Coyote and Daniel Benzali.

San Sebastian
September 16-25, 2004

Held in an elegant Basque seaside city known for its superb gastronomy and beautiful beaches, the Donostia-San Sebastian Festival remains Spain's most important event in terms of glamour, competition, attendance (200,000 spectators, 1,300 reporters and 1,490 professionals in 2002), facilities, partying and number of films. Events include the Official Competitive section, Zabaltegi, Horizontes Latinos (with an €18,000 Horizontes Award) and meticulous retrospectives. The juried New Director's Prize gives €120,000 to a first or second film. In partnership with the Rencontres Cinémas Amérique Latine in Toulouse, the Films in Progress industry platform aims to aid the completion of six Latin American and two Spanish projects. Director: Mikel Olaciregui.
Inquiries to: San Sebastian International Film Festival, Apartado de Correos 397, 20080 Donostia, San Sebastian 20080, Spain. Tel: (34 943) 481 212. Fax: 481 218. e: ssiff@sansebastianfestival.com. Web: www.sansebastianfestival.ya.com.

AWARDS 2002
Golden Shell for Best Film: **Los Lunes al Sol/Mondays in the Sun** (Spain/France/Italy),
Fernando León de Aranoa.
Special Jury Award: **Historias Mínimas/Minimal Stories** (Argentina/Spain), Carlos Sorín.
Best Director: Chen Kaige, **Han Ni Zai Yiki/Together** (China).
Best Actress: Mercedes Sampietro, **Lugares Comunes/Common Places** (Argentina/Spain).
Silver Shell for Best Actor: Liu Peiqi, **Together** (China).
Jury Award for Best Photography: Sergey Mikhalchuk, **Lubovnik/The Lover** (Russia).
Jury Award for Best Screenplay: Adolfo Aristaráin, Katy Saavedra, **Lugares Comunes**; Gennadiy Ostrovsky, **Lubovnik** (Russia).
New Director's Award: Alice Nellis, **Vylet/Some Secrets** (Czech Republic).
Pearl of the Audience Award: **Bowling for Columbine** (Canada/US), Michael Moore.
Made in Spanish Award: **Raising Victor Vargas** (US), Peter Sollett.
Youth Award: **Real Women Have Curves** (US), Patricia Cardoso.
Donostia Award: Dennis Hopper, Jessica Lange, Bob Hoskins.
50th Anniversary Special Award: Francis Ford Coppola.

Santa Barbara
January 30 – February 8, 2004

Established in 1986 in the glamorous seaside resort 90 minutes north of LA, Santa Barbara International Film Festival has received worldwide recognition for its diverse programming. A jury of industry professionals selects winners in several categories, including Best US Feature, Best Foreign Feature, Best Director, Best Documentary Feature and Best

Short. *Inquiries to:* SBIFF, 2064 Alameda Padre Serra, Suite 120 Santa Barbara, CA 93103, USA. Tel: (1 805) 963 0023. Fax: 962 2524. e: info@sbfilmfestival.org. Web: www.sbfilmfestival.org.

Sarasota
January 23 – February 1, 2004

Dedicated to presenting the best new stars over 10 days of independent film, symposiums and events. Hospitable, inquisitive audiences plus a well-organised and publicised programme. Past guests include Todd Haynes, Sydney Pollack, Gena Rowlands, Ismail Merchant and William H. Macy. *Inquiries to:* Cemantha Crain, Marketing Director, Sarasota Film Festival, 635 S Orange Ave, Suite 10B, Sarasota, Florida 34236, USA. Tel: (1 941) 364 9514. Fax: 364 8411. e: info@sarasotafilmfestival.com. Web: www.sarasotafilmfestival.com.

AWARDS 2003
Critics' Award Best Feature: **Saint Monica** (Canada), Terrance Odette.
Critics' Award Best Documentary: **Deconstructing the Myth of Aids** (US), Gary Null.
Audience Award Best Comedy: **Bollywood/Hollywood** (Canada), Deepa Mehta.
Audience Award Best Drama: **A Beautiful Secret** (Mexico), Leopoldo Laborde.
Festival Programmer's Choice: **Last Dance** (US), Mirra Bank.

Report 2003
The 5th festival opened with indie hit *Kiss the Bride* and "CineSymphony: A Musical Tribute to Elmer Bernstein", hosted by Todd Haynes. Nearly 30,000 patrons took in the 65-plus features, breakfast round-tables with film-makers, InFocus Discussions and other sessions with the likes of Haynes, Rita Moreno and

Olympia Dukakis. Richard Dreyfuss received Regal Entertainment's Career Achievement Award, and Aerosmith brought the festival to a close at the Late Night Wrap Party in a tribute to veteran producer Jack Douglas.
– **Cemantha Crain**, Marketing Co-Ordinator.

Seattle International Film Festival
May 20 – June 13, 2004

Largest festival in the US, presenting 215 features, 100 shorts; New Directors Competition, American Indie Competition, Emerging Masters section, Contemporary World Cinema, Tributes, Archival section. *Inquiries to:* 911 Pine St, 6th Floor, Seattle, WA 98101, USA. Tel: (1 206) 464 5830. Fax: 264 7919. e: mail@seattlefilm.com. Web: www.seattlefilm.com.

Sitges International Film Festival of Catalonia
November 27 – December 7, 2003

Now preparing for its 37th edition in a pleasant town on the Catalan coast, 30 km from Barcelona, Sitges focuses on fantasy films and is considered one of Europe's leading specialised festivals, but is also open to new trends. The one official category, "Fantàstic", brings together the year's best genre productions. Other wide-reaching categories include Gran Angular (contemporary cinema with a language of its own), Orient Express (Asian genre films), Anima't (animation), Seven Chances (seven discoveries made by film critics), Audiovisual Català (Catalan productions) and Retrospectives. *Inquiries to:* Sitges Festival Internacional de Cinema de Catalunya, Avenida Josep Tarradellas, 135 Esc A 3r 2a, 08029 Barcelona, Spain. Tel: (34 93) 419 3635. Fax: 439 7380. e: info@cinema.sitges.com. Web: www.sitges.com/cinema.

Sithengi, The Southern African International Film & TV Market
November 2004

Sithengi marked its eighth year in 2003 and has become Africa's leading media event, attended by many international broadcasters, directors and producers. It features a Film & TV Market and trade expo, a Pitching Forum, Conferences and Training Workshops and the Sithengi Film Festival. Business conducted at Sithengi exceeds $75m. *Inquiries to:* Sithengi, PO Box 52120, Waterfront 8002, Cape Town, South Africa. Tel: (27 21) 430 8160. Fax: 430 8186. e: info@sithengi.co.za. Web: www.sithengi.co.za.

Slamdunk
January 17-22, 2004

Founded in Park City, Utah, alongside the 1998 Sundance Film Festival, Slamdunk began as an alternative showcase to Robert Redford's renowned event. It has established itself as a genuinely alternative festival for the indie film community, and hosts screenings at three of the world's most prestigious gatherings: Sundance, Cannes and Toronto. *Inquiries to:* Slamdunk Events, 202 Main St, Suite 14, Venice, California 90291, USA. Tel: (1 310) 399 3358. Fax: 399 8909. e: festival@slamdunk.cc. Web: www.slamdunk.cc.

Report 2003
Our sixth festival saw more than 5,000 people view 12 features and 25 shorts. The Audience Award winner *You'll Never Wieze in this Town Again*, written and directed by Pauly Shore, was given a $1m P&A commitment by Palisades Entertainment Group. Ben Coccio's *Zero Day* was named Best of the Festival. Slamdunk continues to help independent film-makers find their way in to the larger markets; 2003 included Slamdunk's fourth annual screening series at Cannes.
– **Justin W. Henry**, President.

Solothurn Film Festival
January 19-25, 2004

The most important forum for Swiss film-making, Solothurn is popular with media and public. For 38 years it has been the place to see new Swiss films, make discoveries and form opinions. There are Swiss retrospectives, a film school section, an annual focus on a guest country, international shorts and discussions and seminars. The annual Swiss Film Prizes (for feature, documentary, short film, actor and actress) guarantee suspense and the appearance of well-known faces. *Inquiries to:* Solothurn Film Festival, Postfach 1564, CH-4502 Solothurn, Switzerland. Tel: (41 32) 625 8080. Fax: 623 6410. e: info@solothurnerfilmtage.ch. Web: www.solothurnerfilmtage.ch.

39th Solothurn Film Festival
www.solothurnerfilmtage.ch

Stockholm
November 11-21, 2004

The Stockholm International Film Festival is in its 15th year as one of Europe's leading festivals. Recognised by FIAPF, it hosts a FIPRESCI jury and is a member of European Co-ordination of Film Festivals. Quentin Tarantino, Joel and Ethan Coen, Lars von Trier, Lauren Bacall and Dennis Hopper have all enjoyed the festival. It heads the regional film fund, Film Stockholm, which has produced Swedish shorts and documentaries since 2001. Some 150 films have gained distribution in connection with the festival, which launched distribution company Edge Entertainment in 2000. *Inquiries to:* The Stockholm International Film Festival, PO Box 3136, S-103 62 Stockholm, Sweden. Tel: (46 8) 677 5000. Fax: (46 8) 200 590. e: program@filmfestivalen.se. Web: www.filmfestivalen.se.

AWARDS 2002
Best Film: **Irréversible** (France), Gaspar Noé.
Best First Feature Film: **Piedras** (Spain), Ramon Salazar.
Best Actress: Victora Peña, **Piedras**.
Best Actor: James Nesbitt, **Bloody Sunday** (UK/Ireland).
Best Screenplay: Delphine Gleizer, **Carnages** (France).
Lifetime Achievement: Erland Josephson.
Audience Award: **Japón** (Spain/Mexico), Carlos Reygadas.

Report 2002

The 13th festival screened 164 films by emerging and established names for 60,000 spectators. The launch of the Stockholm Sales Office further strengthened the festival as the main platform for creative minds and film industry professionals in Scandinavia, in tandem with the initiatives of Film Stockholm.

15TH
STOCKHOLM
INTERNATIONAL
FILM FESTIVAL
NOVEMBER 11-21, 2004
PHONE: +46 8 677 50 00
E-MAIL: PROGRAM@FILMFESTIVALEN.SE
WWW.FILMFESTIVALEN.SE
www.filmfestivalen.se

Sundance Film Festival

January 15-24, 2004

Sundance is the premiere showcase for American and international independent films. The Dramatic and Documentary Feature Film Competitions are the highlights, open to independently produced features (dramatic features must be 70 minutes-plus; documentary features 50 minutes-plus), which must be US premieres, have at least 50% US financing and have been completed after October 2002. All films submitted for the Competition are also considered for American Spectrum, Showcase, Frontier, Native Forum and Park City at Midnight programmes. International films are considered for World Cinema, World Documentary, World

Shorts, Frontier, Native Forum and Park City at Midnight. *Inquiries to:* Geoffrey Gilmore, Director, Festival Programming Department, Sundance Institute, 8857 West Olympic Blvd, Beverly Hills, CA 90211, USA. Tel: (1 310) 360 1981. Fax: 360 1969. e: institute@sundance.org. Web: www.sundance.org.

AWARDS 2003

Grand Jury Prize (Documentary): **Capturing the Friedmans** (US), Andrew Jarecki.
Grand Jury Prize (Dramatic): **American Splendor** (US), Shari Springer Berman and Robert Pulcini.
Audience Award (Documentary): **My Flesh and Blood** (US), Jonathan Karsh.
Audience Award (Dramatic): **The Station Agent** (US), Tom McCarthy.
Audience Award (World Cinema): **Whale Rider** (New Zealand), Niki Caro.
Directing Award (Documentary): Jonathan Karsh, **My Flesh and Blood** (US).
Directing Award (Dramatic): Catherine Hardwick, **Thirteen** (US).
Freedom of Expression Award: **What I Want My Words to Do to You** (US), Judith Katz, Madeleine Gavin and Gary Sunshine.
Waldo Salt Screenwriting Award: Tom McCarthy, **The Station Agent** (US).

Tampere

March 3-7, 2004

The 34th year of one of the world's leading short film festivals. Famous for its international sauna party, it attracts entries from more than 60 countries. The 700 professionals and nearly 30,000 spectators can see 400-plus shorts in some 100 screenings: international competition (with a Grand Prix and other awards); international retrospectives and tributes; training seminars for professionals. The market includes shorts and documentaries from northern and eastern Europe. *Inquiries to:* Tampere Film Festival, PO Box 305, 33101 Tampere, Finland. Tel: (358 3) 213 0034. Fax: 223 0121. e: office@tamperefilmfestival.fi. Web: www.tamperefilmfestival.fi.

AWARDS 2003

Grand Prix International: **The Projectionist**

(Australia), Michael Bates.
Special Prize of the Jury: **Kazan-Moscow-Kazan** (Russia), Alexei Shipulin.
Best Animation: **Dog** (UK), Suzie Templeton.
Best Documentary: **Dokhtaran-E-Aftab** (Iran), Mehdi Naderi.
Best Fiction: **15** (Singapore), Royston Tan.
Prix UIP Tampere: **Redd Barna** (Norway), Terje Ragnes.
Best Finnish Short: **My Little Elephants** (Finland), Selma Vilhunen.
Jameson Short Film Award: **Treevil** (Finland), Aiju Salminen, Aino Ovaskainen, Christer Lindströ.

Telluride
September 3-6, 2004

A unique, friendly gathering in the historic mining town of Telluride – a spectacular location in the mountains of Colorado. The festival continues to be one of the world's most influential, as famous directors, players and critics descend on the Sheridan Opera House and other theatres. The dedication of organisers and participants to cinema gives Telluride a sincere, authentic feel – not forgetting the "surprise" element, with the programme only announced on the first day.
Inquiries to: The Telluride Film Festival, 379 State St, Portsmouth, NH 03801, USA. Tel: (1 603) 433 9202. Fax: 433 9206. e: mail@ telluridefilmfestival.org. Web: www.telluridefilmfestival.org.

Thessaloniki International Film Festival
November 21-30, 2003 / **Thessaloniki Documentary Festival** March 1-7, 2004

In its 44th year, the oldest and one of the most important film events in Southeastern Europe targets a new generation of film-makers as well as independent films by established directors. The International Competition (for first or second features) awards the Golden Alexander (€37,000) – shared in 2002 by Hodenori Sugimori's *Woman of Water* (Japan) and Apichatpong Weerasethakul's *Blissfully Yours* (Thailand) – and the Silver Alexander (€22,000). Other sections include Greek Film Panorama, retrospectives, Balkan Survey, New Horizons

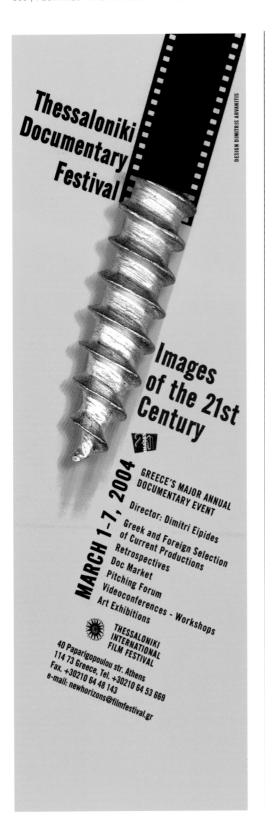

information section, plus galas and exhibitions. Also organises the Thessaloniki Documentary Festival each March, with Greek and international productions, retrospectives and a Pitching Forum. *Inquiries to:* International Thessaloniki Film Festival, 40 Paparigopoulou St, 114 73 Athens, Greece. Tel: (30 210) 645 3669. Fax: 644 8143. e: info@filmfestival.gr. (International Festival); newhorizons@filmfestival.gr (Documentary Festival). Web: www.filmfestival.gr.

Torino Film Festival
November 2004

Well-organised annual event (formerly known as the Festival Internazionale Cinema Giovani), with competitive sections for international films (Best Feature in 2002 was Raja Amari's *Satin Rouge* and Best Short was Jean-Louis Gonnet's *Comme un seul homme*), Italian documentaries and Italian shorts, as well as retrospectives, spotlights and premieres. The festival celebrated its 20th anniversary in 2002, moving from the three screens of the Massimo cinema to the 11-screen Pathé. Many discoveries have been made here, including Chinese and Portuguese films, that were later picked up by other festivals. Dubbed second only to Venice on the crowded Italian festival circuit. *Inquiries to:* Torino Film Festival, Via Monte di Pietà 1, 10121 Torino, Italy. Tel: (39 011) 562 3309 Fax: 562 9796. e: info@torinofilmfest.org. Web: www.torinofilmfest.org.

Toronto International Film Festival
September 2004

A rich diversity of world cinema is featured, offering more than 300 films in 10 days in several programmes: Galas, Special Presentations, Contemporary World Cinema, Planet Africa, Dialogues, Talking with Pictures, Reel to Reel, Directors Spotlight, Midnight Madness, Perspective Canada Discovery and Masters. The Rogers Industry Centre includes a Sales Office and industry programming. *Inquiries to:* Toronto International Film Festival, 2 Carlton St, 16th Floor, Toronto, Ontario, M5B 1J3, Canada. Tel: (1 416) 967 7371. Fax: 967 9477. e: tiffg@torfilmfest.ca. Web: www.bell.ca/filmfest.

Tromsø International Film Festival
January 13-18, 2004

Possibly the world's northernmost film event, far beyond the Arctic Circle, this "Winter Wonderland" focuses on contemporary art films and documentaries, 35mm feature films from all continents. *Inquiries to:* Tromsø International Film Festival, PO Box 285, N-9253 Tromsø, Norway. Tel: (47) 7775 3090. Fax: 7775 3099. e: filmfestival@tiff.no. Web: www.tiff.no.

Umeå
September 2004

Umeå International Film Festival, now in its 18th year, is an annual, competitive event screening around 100 features and 100 shorts. It has considerable standing as a gateway for distribution in Sweden and the Nordic countries and is the largest film festival in Northern Scandinavia. The lively programme includes an international panorama, innovative shorts, Swedish and Nordic documentaries, seminars, workshops and special guests. The popular "Camera Obscura" section includes obscure films and restored or neglected classics. Artistic Director: Thom Palmen. *Inquiries to:* Umeå International Film Festival, Box 43, S-901 02 Umeå, Sweden. Tel: (46 90) 133 388. Fax: 777 961. e: info@ff.umea.com. Web: www.ff.umea.com.

Valencia International Film Festival – Mediterranean Cinema
October 2004

Launched in 1980 and organised by the Valencia Municipal Film Foundation, the Valencia Mostra/Cinema del Mediterrani entered a new era in 2003, introducing well known film-makers José Antonio Escrivá as director and Juan Piquer as deputy director. They will retain a competitive section focusing on Mediterranean-rim countries, but strengthen a parallel section dedicated mostly to European films. Sidebars will draw on Escrivá and Piquer's extensive contacts in Spain. *Inquiries to:* José Antonio Escrivá, Director, Valencia Mostra/Cinema del Mediterrani, Plaza de Arzobispo 2, acc B, 46003 Valencia, Spain. Tel: (34 96) 392 1506. Fax: 391 5156. e: festival@mostravalencia.com. Web: www.mostravalencia.org.

OFFICIAL SECTION (Feature lengths and shorts)
«MEETING POINT» (Parallel showcase)
«TIME OF HISTORY» (Documentaries)
SPANISH CINEMA 2003-2004
TRIBUTES

22nd-30th OCTOBER

VALLADOLID INTERNATIONAL FILM FESTIVAL

Teatro Calderón, Calle Leopoldo Cano, s/n-4°
47003 VALLADOLID (SPAIN) • Tel.: +34-983-426 460 • Fax: +34-983-426 461 • festvalladolid@seminci.com • www.seminci.com

Valladolid
October 22-30, 2004

Now in its 48th edition, this is one of Europe's oldest and most prestigious festivals, with an excellent reputation for professionalism and hospitality. Features, shorts and documentaries are screened in competition and a non-competitive section offers films worthy of special consideration. Sidebars in 2003 were dedicated to Costa Gavras, José Luis Ozores, Focus on Belgium, Tehran: Portrait of a City, ECAM School of Cinema (Madrid) and Spanish Cinema 2002-03. The annual exhibition displayed photographs by Magritte and his contemporaries. *Inquiries to:* Fernando Lara, Director, Teatro Calderón, Calle Leopoldo Cano, s/n 4th floor, 47003 Valladolid, Spain. Tel: (34 983) 426 460. Fax: 426 461. e: festvalladolid@seminci.com. Web: www.seminci.com.

Vancouver
Late September – early October 2004

Now in its 22nd year, this festival has grown into an event of considerable stature. Approximately 150,000 people attend more than 300 international films. Festival also hosts an Annual Film & Television Trade Forum. *Inquiries to:* Alan Franey, 410-1008 Homer St, Vancouver, British Columbia, Canada V6B 2X1. Tel: (1 604) 685 0260. Fax: 688 8221. e: viff@viff.org. Web: www.viff.org.

Venice
Late August – early September 2004

The Venice Biennale is still going through a dark period because of the Berlusconi government's heavy cuts. In Moritz de Hadeln's expert hands the Mostra has been streamlined but it still badly needs updated theatres and modern facilities along old-fashioned Lido beach. The 2003 edition, its 60th, celebrated great Italian tycoons of the past and present, including Carlo Ponti, Dino De Laurentiis and Franco Cristaldi. *Inquiries to:* La Biennale di Venezia, San Marco, 1364/A, Cà Giustinian, 30124 Venezia, Italy. Tel (39 041) 521 8711. Fax 523 6374. e: cinema@labiennale.org. Web: www.labiennale.org.

MAIN AWARDS 2002
Golden Lion for Best Film: **The Magdalene Sisters** (UK/Ireland), Peter Mullan.
Grand Jury Prize: **Dom Durakov/House of Fools** (Russia/France), Andrei Konchalovsky.
Best Direction: Lee Chang-dong, **Oasis** (South Korea).
Coppa Volpi for Best Actor: Stefano Accorsi, **Un Viaggio Chiamato Amore/A Journey Called Love** (Italy).
Coppa Volpi for Best Actress: Julianne Moore, **Far From Heaven** (US).
Controcorrente Section/Prix San Marco: **Xiao Cheng Zhi Chun/Springtime in a Small Town** (China), Tian Zhuangzhuang.

MAIN AWARDS 2003
Golden Lion for Best Film: **Ozvrasnje/The Return** (Russia), Andrej Zvjagintsev.
Grand Jury Prize: **Le Cerf-Volant/The Kite** (Lebanon), Randa Chahal Sabbag.
Best Direction: Takeshi Kitano, **Zatoichi** (Japan).
Coppa Volpi for Best Actor: Sean Penn, **21 Grams** (US).
Coppa Volpi for Best Actress: Katja Riemann,

Rosenstrasse (Germany).
Controcorrente Section/Prix San Marco: **Vodka Lemon** (Fr/Switz/Armenia/It), Hiiner Saleem.

Victoria Independent Film & Video Festival
January 30 – February 8, 2004

From the mainstream to the original, the Victoria Festival offers up the finest contemporary international independent cinema. It has a strong interest in putting programmers, media and industry professionals together with emerging film-makers, and is dedicated to raising awareness of film and its artistic insights. Set in beautiful Victoria, the 10th festival will include a film forum, new media event, lectures and a film-related art exhibition. *Inquiries to:* Victoria Independent Film & Video Festival, 808 View St, Victoria, British Columbia, V8W 1K2, Canada. Tel: (1 250) 389 0444. Fax: 389 0406. e: festival@vifvf.com. Web: www.vifvf.com.

AWARDS 2003
Best Feature: **Roger Dodger** (US), Dylan Kidd.
Famous Players Award for Best Canadian Feature: **Flower & Garnet**, Keith Behrman.
Chum Television Award for Best Canadian First Feature: **Expecting**, Deborah Day.
Best Documentary: **Criminal Acts** (Canada), Tony Snowsill.
Best Short: **The Provider** (US), Matt Smith.
Audience Favourite: **Standard Time** (US), Robert Carey.

Report 2003
More than 12,000 spectators enjoyed 160 contemporary features and shorts, unique events, distinguished visitors and Victoria's natural beauty. Highlights included the opening gala screening of Alan Rudolph's only available print of *Investigating Sex*. Rudolph later hosted a masterclass. Fabulous finds included the world premieres of

Final Draft, Want and *Stormy Weather*, along with popular entries *Bug* and *Open Hearts*.
– **Kathy Kay**, Festival Director.

Wellington International Film Festival
July 2004

The 32nd Wellington International Film Festival launched its 2003 programme of 125 features from 38 countries with the hilarious *A Mighty Wind* (US). The festival provides a non-competitive New Zealand premiere showcase and weclomes many international film-makers, restorers and musicians. Brimming with animation, arthouse, documentaries and silent films enriched by live orchestral music, the festival and its 35 year-old Auckland sibling – under the direction of Bill Gosden – always set out to set new records for attendance. *Inquiries to:* Wellington Film Festival, Box 9544, Marion Square, Wellington, New Zealand. Tel: (64 4) 385 0162. Fax: 801 7304. e: festival@enzedff.co.nz. Web: www.nzff.co.nz.

Wine Country Film Festival
July 22 – August 8, 2004

Set in the heart of Northern California's premium wine region, this gently-paced, mainly non-competitive event accepts features, shorts, documentaries, animation and music videos. All genres are considered for five categories: independent features, international films, films making social comment, films about the arts and films about the culinary arts. Many of the films are shown outdoors in spectacular wine country settings. *Inquiries to:* PO Box 303, Glen Ellen, CA 95442, USA. Tel: (1 707) 996 2536. Fax: 996 6964. e: wcfilmfest@aol.com. Web: www.winecountryfilmfest.com.

Report 2002
The 16th edition screened 101 films from 31 countries, with scores of film-makers on hand. Tributes celebrated the works of master film-maker Eliseo Subiela (Argentina) and actor Richard Dreyfuss. Best Documentary Grand Prix went to Mika Kaurismäki's *Sounds of Brazil*, Best Documentary (International) was Inara Kolmane's *Poco a Poco* (Latvia), Best

Documentary (Domestic) was Maryanne Galvin's *Amuse Bouche* and Best of the Fest was Thomas Robsahm's *The Greatest Thing* (Norway).

WorldFest – Houston
April 6-15, 2004

Celebrating its 37th year, the festival offers competition for independent features, shorts, documentaries, student films, TV productions, commercials and screenplays. WorldFest is the largest competition in the world in terms of number of entries received. It is the only truly independent festival in North America, as it does not accept major studio films. Founding Director J. Hunter Todd automatically notifies the leading 200 international film festivals of the WorldFest winners. Co-ordinators also submit all student, short and screenplay winners to the top US talent agencies. Deadlines: early/discount: Nov 15, 2003; regular: Dec 15, 2003; final/late fee: Jan 15, 2004. *Inquiries to:* WorldFest – Houston, PO Box 56566, Houston, TX 77256, USA. Tel: (1 713) 965 9955.
Fax: 965 9960. e: mail@worldfest.org.
Web: www.worldfest.org.

Report 2003
The 36th WorldFest enjoyed a remarkable increase in attendance from public (25,000-plus) and film-makers (450-plus, representing 37 nations), despite the international situation. It premiered 55 new indie features and 104 shorts. Nine professional production seminars covered topics such as Special Effects by Steve Wolf (*The Firm, Cast Away*) and Writing & Selling Screenplays by John Truby. The major winners were both from Holland: Pieter Verhoeff's *Nynke* won Best Feature and Michael Dudok de Wit's *Father and Daughter* won Best Short.

Other Festivals and Markets of Note

AFI FEST, 2021 N Western Ave, Los Angeles, CA 90027-1657, USA. Tel: (1 323) 856 7896. Fax: 462 4049. e: afifest@afi.com. Web: www.afifest.com. (*One of North America's fastest growing film events, and the premier international festival in LA – Nov.*)

Alcalá de Henares/Comunidad de Madrid Film Festival, Plaza del Empecinado 1, 28801 Alcalá de Henares, Madrid, Spain. Tel: (34 91) 881 3934. Fax: 881 3906. e: festival@festivalcinealcala.com. Web: www.festivalcinealcala.com. (*Competition for Spanish shorts, new directors and Madrid-made videos, plus international shorts and Spanish director sidebars – Nov.*)

Alexandria International Film Festival, 9 Orabi St, Cairo 1111, Egypt. Tel: (202) 574 1112. Fax: (202) 576 8727. e: info@alexandriafilmfestival.com. Web: www.alexandriafilmfestival.com. (*Competitive for Mediterranean countries and internationally for first films – Sept.*)

Almería International Short Film Festival, Diputación de Almería, Departamento de Cultura y Juventud, Calle Navarro Rodrigo 17, 04071 Almería, Spain. Tel: (34 950) 211 100 Fax: 269 785. e: coordinator@almeriaencorto.net. Web: www.almeriaencorto.net. (*Competition for international shorts – May/June.*)

Ann Arbor Film Festival, PO Box 8232, Ann Arbor, MI 48107, USA. Tel: (1 734) 995 5356. Fax: 995 5396. e: aafilmfest@aol.com. Web: www.aafilmfest.org. (*Experimental films from all over the world – March 16-21, 2004.*)

Angelus Awards Student Film Festival, 7201 Sunset Blvd., Hollywood, CA 90046, USA. Tel: (800) 874 0999. Fax: 874 1168. e: info@angelus.org. Web: www.angelusawards.org. (*International competition honouring college-level student films of uncommon artistic calibre that reflect compassion and respect for the human condition. All genres: drama, comedy, animation, documentary and narrative. $23,000-plus in cash prizes, including the $10,000 Patrick Peyton Excellence in Film-making Award and the $5,000 Triumph of the Human Spirit Award. Past winners include Patricia Cardoso (Real*

Women Have Curves). *Call for entries is July Entry forms available online. Screening and awards ceremony held at the Directors' Guild of America, Hollywood – late Oct or early Nov.*)

Annecy/International Animated Film Festival and International Animated Film Market (MIFA), Centre International du Cinéma d'Animation, 18 Avenue du Trésum, BP 399, 74013 Annecy Cedex, France. Tel: (33 4) 5010 0900. Fax: 5010 0970. e: info@annecy.org. Web: www.annecy.org. (*Long established international and competitive festival with a useful sales/distribution market (MIFA) – Festival: June 7-12; MIFA: June 7-10, 2004.*)

Animerte Dager, The Nordic and Baltic Animation Festival, Kasernen Gamlebyen, Box 1405, N-1602 Fredrikstad, Norway. Tel: (47) 6932 0075. Fax: 6932 0077. e: ad@animertedager.no. Web: www.animertedager.no. (*Nordic, Baltic and international animation, with retrospectives and student films. Competitive – May.*)

Aspen Shortsfest & Filmfest, 110 E Hallam, Ste 102, Aspen, CO 81611, USA. Tel: (1 970) 925 6882. Fax: 925 1967. e: filmfest@aspenfilm.org. Web: www.aspenfilm.org. (*Shortsfest: Short subject competition – March 30-April 5, 2004; Filmsfest: Feature-length invitational – Sept/Oct 3.*)

Atlantic Film Festival, PO Box 36139, 220-5600 Sackville St, Halifax, NS, B3J 3S9, Canada. Tel: (1 902) 422 3456. Fax: 422 4006. e: festival@atlanticfilm.com. Web: www.atlanticfilm.com. (*Film and video features, shorts, documentaries and animation; also includes industry workshops and panels – Sept 17-25, 2004.*)

Auckland International Film Festival, PO Box 9544, Marion Sq, Wellington 6001, New Zealand. Tel: (64 4) 385 0162. Fax: 801 7304. e: festival@nzff.co.nz. Web: www.nzff.co.nz. (*Leading showcase for more than 110 features and 50 shorts. Twinned with the Wellington Film Festival – July.*)

Augsburg Children's Film Festival, Filmbüro Augsburg, Schroeckstrasse 8, 86152 Augsburg, Germany. Tel: (49 821) 349 1060. Fax: 155 518. e: filmbuero@t-online.de. Web: www.lechfremmem.de. (*International features for children – Nov.*)

BAF, National Museum of Photography, Film & Television, Bradford, BD1 1NQ, UK. Tel: (44 1274) 203 308. Fax: 394 540. e: a.pugh@nmsi.ac.uk. Web: www.baf.org.uk. (*Industry-based animation festival; masterclasses, seminars, workshops and screenings with some of animation's top names. Home to the BAF Awards, which open for entries in April – Nov.*)

Banff Mountain Film Festival, Mountain Culture, The Banff Centre, Box 1020, Banff, AB, T1L 1H5, Canada. Tel: (1 403) 762 6675. e: mountainculture@banffcentre.ca. Web: www.banffmountainfestivals.ca. (*International competition for films and videos related to mountains and the spirit of adventure – Nov.*)

Bilbao International Documentary and Short Film Festival, Calle Colón de Laurreategui, 37-4 Derecha, 48009 Bilbao, Spain. Tel: (34 94) 424 8698/5507. Fax: 424 5624. e: info@zinebi.com. Web: www.zinebi.com. (*Long-running competitive festival for shorts and documentaries – Nov; Deadline: mid-Sept.*)

Birmingham Film & TV Festival, 9 Margaret St, Birmingham B3 3BS, UK. Tel: (44 121) 212 0777. Fax: 212 0666. e: info@film-tv-

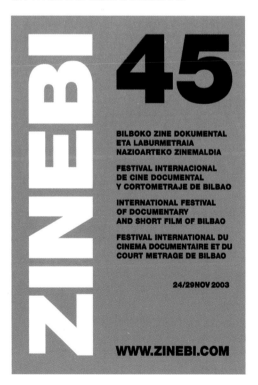

ZINEBI 45

BILBOKO ZINE DOKUMENTAL ETA LABURMETRAIA NAZIOARTEKO ZINEMALDIA

FESTIVAL INTERNACIONAL DE CINE DOCUMENTAL Y CORTOMETRAJE DE BILBAO

INTERNATIONAL FESTIVAL OF DOCUMENTARY AND SHORT FILM OF BILBAO

FESTIVAL INTERNATIONAL DU CINEMA DOCUMENTAIRE ET DU COURT METRAGE DE BILBAO

24/29NOV 2003

WWW.ZINEBI.COM

festival.org.uk. Web: www.film-tv-festival.org.uk. (*International event. Includes local showcase and respected South Asian film focus – March 5-11, 2004.*)

Bite the Mango Film Festival, National Museum of Photography, Film & TV, Bradford, BD1 1NQ, UK. Tel: (44 1274) 203 311. Fax: 394 540. e: i.ajeeb@nmsi.ac.uk. Web: www.bitethemango.org.uk. (*A celebration of cultural cinema from China and Japan, to Malaysia and Pakistan – June tbc.*)

Bogotá Film Festival, Residencias Tequendama, Centro Internacional Tequendama, Bogotá, Colombia. Tel: (57 1) 341 7562 e: direccion@bogocine.com. Web: www.bogocine.com. (*Competitions for Colombian films and new directors – Oct.*)

Boston Film Festival, PO Box 516, Hull, MA 02045, USA. Tel: (1 617) 331 9460. e: gemsad@aol.com. Web: www.bostonfilmfestival.org. (*Approximately 50 films, including studio releases, American independents, documentaries and shorts – Sept.*)

Bradford Film Festival, National Museum of Photography, Film & TV, Bradford, BD1 1NQ, UK. Tel: (44 1274) 203 320. Fax: 394 540. e: a.earnshaw@nmsi.ac.uk. Web: www.bradfordfilmfestival.org.uk. (*Includes the Lumière Lecture, retrospectives, the Shine Awards for the best new European film-makers and the Widescreen Weekend – March 12-27, 2004.*)

British Silent Cinema, Broadway, 14-18 Broad St, Nottingham, NG1 3 AL, UK. Tel: (44 115) 952 6600. Fax: 952 6622. e: laraine@broadway.org.uk. Web: www.broadway.org.uk. (*Screenings and presentations, with the 2004 focus on the Great War – April 8-11, 2004.*)

Brussels Animation Film Festival, Folioscope, Avenue de Stalingrad 52, B-1000 Brussels, Belgium. Tel: (32 2) 534 4125. Fax: 534 2279. e: info@folioscope.be. Web: www.awn.com/folioscope. (*Showcase for the newest, most interesting animation – Feb 19-29, 2004.*)

Brussels International Festival of Fantastic Film, 8 Rue de la Comtesse de Flandre 1020 Brussels, Belgium. Tel: (32 2) 201 1713. Fax: 201 1469. e: peymey@bifff.org. Web:

www.bifff.org. (*Competitive international and European selection. Special side events include the Unusual Fashion Show – March 12-27, 2004.*)

Buenos Aires Independent Film Festival, Avenida Corrientes 1530, Piso 8, Oficina 7, Capital Federal C1042AAO, Argentina. Tel: (54 11) 4373 8930. Fax: 4374 0320. e: produccion@bafilmfest.com. Web: www.bafilmfest.com. (*Four year-old event with a strong independent, international flavour – April.*)

Cph:Dox – Copenhagen International Documentary Festival, Store Kannikestraede 6, 1169 Copenhagen K, Denmark. Tel: (45) 3312 0005. Fax: 3312 7505. e: info@cphdox.dk. Web: www.cphdox.dk. Producer: Niels Lind Larsen. Programmer: Tine Fischer. (*Nov.*)

Cairo International Film Festival, 17 Kasr el Nil St, Cairo, Egypt. Tel: (20 2) 392 3562. Fax: 393 8979. e: info@cairofilmfest.com. Web: www.cairofilmfest.com. (*Competitive, aims to show major international films that would usually not be available – Oct.*)

Cairo International Children's Film Festival, 17 Kasr El Nil St, Cairo, Egypt. Tel: (20 2) 392 3562. Fax: 393 8979. e: info@cairofilmfest.com. Web: www.cairofilmfest.com. (*Organised by the General Union of Arab Artists. Competitive – March.*)

Camerimage, Rynek Nowomiejski 28, 87-100 Torun, Poland. Tel/Fax: (48 56) 621 0019. e: office@camerimage.pl. Web: www.camerimage.pl. (*Competition, Special Screenings, William Fraker's Retrospective, Student Festival, World Panorama Retrospective, seminars, workshops, press conferences, exhibitions – Nov 29-Dec 6, 2003.*)

Cape Town International Film Festival, Institute for Film & New Media, University of Cape Town, Private Bag, Rondebosch 7700, Cape Town, South Africa. Tel/Fax: (27 21) 423 8257. e: ctfilmfest@ananzi.co.za. (*Oldest film festival in South Africa. Non-competitive, transgressive in tone, emphasis on new technologies and digital productions – April/May 2004.*)

Cartoons on the Bay, Rai Trade, Via Umberto Novaro 18, 00195 Rome, Italy. Tel: (39 06) 3749 8315. Fax: 3751 5631. e: cartoonsbay@raitrade.it. Web:

www.cartoonsbay.com. (*International Festival and Conference on television animation, organised by RAI Trade – April 21-25, 2004; Deadline: Jan 20.*)

Chicago International Children's Film Festival, Facets Mulimedia, 1517 W Fullerton, Chicago, IL 60614, USA. Tel: (1 773) 281 9075. Fax: 929 0266. e: kidsfest@facets.org. (*Largest and oldest festival of children's films in US – late Oct-early Nov.*)

Chicago Latino Film Festival, International Latino Cultural Center of Chicago, c/o Columbia College Chicago, 600 S Michigan Ave, Chicago, IL 60605-1996, USA. Tel: (1 312) 431 1330. Fax: 344 8030. e: info@latinoculturalcenter.org. Web: www.latinoculturalcenter.org. (*ILCC promotes awareness of Latino culture through the arts, including this festival – April.*)

Cinekid, Korte Leidsedwarstraat 12, 1017 RC Amsterdam, Netherlands. Tel: (31 20) 531 7890. Fax: 531 7899. e: info@cinekid.nl. Web: www.cinekid.nl. (*International film, TV and new media festival for children and young people – Oct 16-24, 2004.*)

Cinema Jove International Film Festival, Calle Jerónimo de Monsoriu 19, 46022 Valencia, Spain. Tel: (34 96) 331 1047. Fax: 331 0805. e: cinemajove@ivaj.gva.es Web: www.gva.es/cinemajove. (*Low-glam, high-fun foray into state-of-the-art youth cinema – June.*)

Cinéma Mediterranéen Montpellier, 78 Avenue du Pirée, 34000 Montpellier, France. Tel: (33 4) 9913 7373. Fax: 9913 7374. e:info@cinemed.tm.fr. Web: www.cinemed.tm.fr. (*Competitive festival for fiction works by directors from the Mediterranean Basin, the Black Sea states, Portugal or Armenia. Categories: Feature, Short, Documentary. Formats: 16mm, 35mm. Preview on VHS – late Oct-early Nov.*)

Cinéma Italien Rencontres D'Annecy, Bonlieu Scène Nationale, 1 rue Jean Jaures, BP 294, 74007 Annecy Cedex, France. Tel: (33 450) 334 400. Fax: 518 209. e: com@annecycinemaitalien.com. Web: www.annecycinemaitalien.com. (*Feature films from Italy, with tributes and retrospectives. Competitive – early Oct.*)

Cinemagic World Screen Festival for Young People, 3rd Floor, Fountain House, 17-21 Donegall Place, Belfast, BT1 5AB, Northern Ireland. Tel: (44 28) 9031 1900. Fax: 9031 9709. e: info@cinemagic.org.uk. Web: www.cinemagic.org.uk. (*Children's films in competition – Dec 4-14, 2003.*)

Cinemayaat (Arab Film Festival), 2 Plaza Ave, San Francisco, CA 94116, USA. Tel (1 415) 564 1100. Fax: 564 2203. e: info_aff@yahoo.com. Web: www.aff.org. (*Arab films – Sept/Oct.*)

Cinequest, PO Box 720040, San Jose, CA 95172-0040, USA. Tel: (1 408) 995 5033. Fax: 995 5713. e: info@cinequest.org. Web: www.cinequest.org. (*Maverick films, film-makers and technologies. Competition for features, documentaries and shorts, plus tributes, seminars, entertainment – March 3-14, 2004.*)

Cleveland International Film Festival, 2510 Market Ave, Cleveland, OH 44113-3434, USA. Tel: (1 216) 623 3456. Fax: 623 0103. e: cfs@clevelandfilm.org. Web: www.clevelandfilm.org. (*International "World Tour" progamme with specials such as family films, American independents and lesbian and gay films – March.*)

Cognac International Thriller Film Festival, Le Public Système Cinéma, 40, rue Anatole France, 92594 Levallois-Perret Cedex, France. Tel: (33 1) 4134 2033. Fax: 4134 2077. e-mail : fbataille@le-public-systeme.fr. Web: www.festival.cognac.fr. (*International thrillers and "films noir"; competitive for features and French-speaking shorts – April 2004.*)

Cork Film Festival, 10 Washington St, Cork, Republic of Ireland. Tel: (353 21) 427 1711 Fax: 427 5945. e: info@corkfilmfest.org. Web: www.corkfilmfest.org. (*Features, documentaries, competitive shorts, animation – Oct 10-17, 2004; Deadline: July.*)

Cottbus Film Festival – Festival of East European Cinema, Werner-Seelenbinder-Ring 44/45, D-03048 Cottbus, Germany. Tel: (49 355) 431 070. Fax: 4310 720. e: info@filmfestivalcottbus.de. Web: www.filmfestivalcottbus. (*International festival for East European films: features and shorts (competitive), children's film focus, spectrum, national hits – late Oct to early Nov.*)

Deauville Festival of American Film, Le Public Système Cinéma, 40, rue Anatole France, 92594 Levallois-Perret Cedex, France. Tel: (33 1)

4134 2033. Fax: 4134 2077. e: fbataille@le-public-systeme.fr. Web: www.festival-deauville.com. (*Showcase for US features and independent films – Sept 5-14, 2004.*)

Divercine International Film Festival for Children and Youth, Lorenzo Carnelli 1311, PO Box 1170, 11200 Montevideo, Uruguay. Tel: (59 82) 418 2460/5795. Fax: 419 4572. e: cinemuy@chasque.apc.org. Web: www.cinemateca.org.uy. Contact: Ricardo Casas (Director). (*July 5-16, 2004; Deadline: May 2.*)

Duisburg Film Week, Am König Heinrich Platz, D-47049 Duisburg, Germany. Tel: (49 203) 283 4187. Fax: 283 4130. e: filmwoche.vhs@duisburg.de. Web: www.duisburg.de/filmwoche. (*German-language documentaries from Germany, Switzerland and Austria – Nov 4-10, 2004; Deadline: Aug 23.*)

25th Durban International Film Festival, 14-27 June 2004,Centre for Creative Arts,University of Natal ,Durban 4041 South Africa Tel: +27 (0) 31 260 2506. Fax: +27 (0) 31 260 3074. e: diff@nu.ac.za Web: http://www.und.ac.za/und/carts/

Edmonton International Film Festival, Edmonton International Film Society, 006-11523 100 Avenue NW, Edmonton, Alberta, T5K 0J8, Canada. Tel: (1 780) 423 0844. Fax: 447 5242. e: mailbox@edmontonfilm.com. Web: www.edmontonfilm.com. (*March.*)

Emden International Film Festival, An der Berufschule 3, 26721 Emden, Germany. Tel: (49 21) 915 531. Fax: 915 599. e: filmfest@vhs-emden.de. Web: www.filmfest-emden.de. (*Focus on North Western European films, particularly Germany and UK – June 2-9, 2004.*)

L'Etrange Festival, Le Forum Des Images, Les Halles, Paris, France. Tel (33 1) 5320 4860. e: gilles@etrangefestival.com. (*Created in 1993 and dedicated to international features, documentaries and shorts by maverick directors – Aug/Sept.*)

European First Film Festival (Premiers Plans), Festival d'Angers, 54 rue Beaubourg, 75003 Paris, France. Tel: (33 1) 4271 5370. Fax: 4271 0111. e: paris@premiersplans.org. Web: www.premiersplans.org. (*Competitive festival for European debut features, shorts and student works – Jan 15-26, 2004.*)

Femme Totale International Women's Film Festival, Dortmund, c/o Kulturbüro Stadt Dortmund, Küpferstrasse 3, D-44122 Dortmund, Germany. Tel: (49 231) 502 5162. Fax: 502 5734. e: info@femmetotale.de. Web: www.femmetotale.de. (*Biennial festival with changing themes, highlighting films made by women. Non-competitive – Spring 2005.*)

Festival International du Film Francophone de Namur, 175, Rue des Brasseurs, 5000 Namur, Belgium Tel: (32 81) 241 236. Fax: 234 091. e: presse@fiff.be. Web: www.fiff.namur.be. (*Sept/Oct.*)

Festival Dei Popoli, Borgo Pinti 82 Rosso, 50121 Firenze, Italy. Tel: (39 055) 244 778. Fax: 241 364. e: fespopol@dada.it. Web: www.festivaldeipopoli.org. (*Partly competitive and open to documentaries on social, anthropological, historical and political issues – Nov 28-Dec 4, 2003.*)

Festival du Cinema International en Abitibi-Temscamingue, 215 Mercier Avenue, Rouyn-Noranda, Quebec J9X 5WB, Canada. Tel: (1 819) 762 6212. Fax: 762 6762. e: festivalcinema@lino.com. Web: www.lino.com/festivalcinema. (*International shorts, medium- and full-length features; animation, documentary and fiction – Oct.*)

Festroia, Forum Luisa Dodi, 2900-461 Setúbal Codex, Portugal. Tel: (351 265) 525 908. Fax: 525 681. e: geral@festroia.pt. Web: www.festroia.pt. (*Held in Setúbal, near Lisbon. Official section for countries producing fewer than 25 features per year – June.*)

Figueira da Foz International Film Festival, Apartado de Correios 5407, 1709-001 Lisbon, Portugal. Tel: (351 11) 346 9556. (*One of Portugal's leading film events – Sept.*)

Filmfest München, Sonnenstr 21, D-80331, Munich, Germany. Tel: (49 89) 381 9040. Fax: 381 90426. e: festivalleitung@filmfest-muenchen.de. Web: www.filmfest-muenchen.de. (*International screenings, TV movies and retrospectives – June/July.*)

Filmfestival Max Ophüls Prize, Mainzerstrasse 8, 66111 Saarbruecken, Germany. Tel: (49 681) 906 8910. e: cruth@max-ophuels-preis.de. Web: www.filmfestival-max-ophüls.de. (*Competitive event for young directors from German-speaking countries – Jan.*)

Florida Film Festival, Enzian Theatre, 1300 South Orlando Ave, Maitland, Florida 32751, USA. Tel: (1 407) 629 8587. Fax: 629 6870. e: filmfest@gate.net. Web: www.enzian.org. (*Specialises in independent American films: features, shorts, documentaries and non-competitive spotlight films – March.*)

Focus on Asia Fukuoka International Film Festival, c/o Fukuoka City Hall, 1-8-1, Tenjin, Chuo-ku, Fukuoka 810 8620, Japan. Tel: (81 92) 733 5170. Fax: 733 5595. e: info@focus-on-asia.com. Web: www.focus-on-asia.com. (*Dedicated to promoting Asian film. Non-competitive – Sept.*)

Future Film Festival – New Technologies in Animation Cinema, Via del Pratello 21/2 Bologna, Italy. Tel: (39 051) 296 0664. Fax: 656 7133. e: future@futurefilmfestival.org. Web: www.futurefilmfestival.org. (*Jan 14-18, 2004.*)

Galway Film Fleadh, Cluain Mhuire, Monivea Road, Galway, Ireland. Tel: (353 91) 751 655. Fax: 735 831. e: gafleadh@iol.ie. Web: www.galwayfilmfleadh.com. (*Irish and international features. Accompanied by the Galway Film Fair, Ireland's only film market – July 6-11, 2004.*)

Gerardmer International Fantasy Film Festival, Le Public Système Cinéma, 40, rue Anatole France, 92594 Levallois-Perret Cedex, France. Tel: (33 1) 4134 2033. Fax: 4134 2077. e-mail : fbataille@le-public-systeme.fr. Web: www.gerardmer-fantasticart.com. (*International fantasy, sci-fi, psychological thriller and horror films, with competition for features and French-speaking shorts – Jan 28-Feb 1, 2004.*)

Go East Festival of Central and Eastern European Film in Wiesbaden, [organiser] Deutsches Filminstitut, Schaumainkai 4, 60596 Frankfurt. Tel: (49 69) 9612 2027/6637 2946. Fax: 6637 2947. e: info@filmfestival-goeast.de. Web: www.filmfestival-goeast.de. (*Established in 2001 for audiences interested in Eastern European film, with mix of current productions and historical series, an academic symposium and related events. Member of FIAPF and hosts FIPRESCI jury. Deadline: January 31. Films from the newest EU member countries will be the main focus in 2004 – April 21-27, 2004.*)

Guadalajara Mexican Film Showcase, Avenida Alamenaia 1367, Planta Alta, Colonia Moderna, 44190 Guadalajara, Mexico. Tel: (52) 3810 1148/1151. Fax: 3810 1146. e: muestra@cencar.udg.mx. Web: www guadalajaracinemafest.com. (*Competition for unreleased Mexican features. Latin American films also invited out of competition – March 19-25, 2004.*)

Haifa International Film Festival, 142 Hanassi Ave, Haifa 34 633, Israel. Tel: (972 4) 8353 521/4. Fax: 8384 327. e: film@haifaff.co.il. Web: www.haifaff.co.il. (*Broad spectrum of new international films, special tributes, retrospectives – Oct.*)

Hawaii International Film Festival, 1001 Bishop St, Honolulu, Hawaii 96813, USA. Tel: (1 808) 528 3456. Fax: 528 1410. e: info@hiff.org. Web: www.hiff.org. (*Seeks to promote cultural understanding between East and West through film – late Oct-early Nov.*)

Heartland Film Festival, 200 S Meridian, Suite 220, Indianapolis, Indiana 46225-0176, USA. Tel: (1 317) 464 9405. Fax: 464 9409. e: info@heartlandfilmfestival.org. Web: www.heartlandfilmfestival.org. (*Established in 1991 to honour film-makers whose work expresses hope and respect for positive values – Oct.*)

Hébraïca Montpellier, 500 Boulevard d'Antigone, 34000 Montpellier, France. Tel: (33 4) 6715 0876. Fax: 6715 0872. (*Theatre Festival, conferences; showcases Jewish and Israeli films. Competitive – March.*)

Holland Animation Film Festival, Hoogt 4, 3512 GW Utrecht, Netherlands. Tel: (31 30) 233 1733. Fax: 233 1079. e: info@haff.nl. Web: www.awn.com/haff. (*International competitions for independent and applied animation; special programmes, retrospectives, student films, exhibitions – Nov.*)

Hometown Video Festival, Alliance for Community Media, 666 11th Street NW, Suite 740, Washington, DC 20001, USA. Tel: (1 202) 393 2650. Fax: 393 2653. e:

acm@alliancecm.org. Web: www.alliancecm.org. (*US and international community productions – July.*)

Huesca Film Festival, Avenida del Parque 1,2, 22002 Huesca, Spain. Tel: (34 974) 212 582. Fax: 210 065. e: huescafest@tsai.es. Web: www.huesca-filmfestival.com. (*Well-established competitive shorts festival in country town, with features sidebars – June 4-13, 2004.*)

Hungarian Film Week, Magyar Filmunió, Városligeti, Fasor 38, 1068 Budapest, Hungary. Tel: (36 1) 351 7760. Fax: 352 6734. e: filmunio@filmunnio.hu. Web: filmunio.hu. (*Competitive national festival showcasing Hungarian production from the previous year – Feb.*)

Il Cinema Ritrovato, Mostra Internazionale del Cinema Libero, Cineteca del Comune di Bologna, Via Riva di Reno 72, 40122 Bologna, Italy. Tel: (39 051) 204 820. Fax: 204 821. e: cinetecamanifestazioni1@comune.bologna.it. Web: www.cinetecadibologna.it. (*A selection of the best film restorations from all over the world; 30,000 spectators, 400 films and 500 guests. Four theatres and open-air screenings – June/July.*)

Independent Film Days, Filmbüro Augsburg, Schroeckstrasse 8, 86152 Augsburg, Germany. Tel: (49 821) 153 078. Fax: 155 518. e: filmbuero@t-online.de. Web: www.filmfest-augsberg.de. (*International event for documentary and independent features, with retrospectives, national focus and student symposium – Nov.*)

International Animated Film Festival – Cinanima, Apartado 743, 4500-901 Espinho, Portugal. Tel: (351) 227 331 350/51. Fax: 227 331 358. e: cinanima@mail.telepac.pt. Web: www.cinanima.pt. (*Competition and retrospectives; seminars and exhibitions – Nov.*)

International Documentary Film Festival - Amsterdam (IDFA), Kleine-Gartmanplantsoen 10, 1017 RR Amsterdam, Netherlands. Tel: (31 20) 627 3329. Fax: 638 5388. e: info@idfa.nl. Web: www.idfa.nl. (*Creative documentaries, including numerous awards and a special "Kids & Docs" section. Includes the Forum, a market for international co-financing – Nov 18-28, 2004.*)

International Film Camera Festival "Manaki

Brothers", UI 8 Mart #4, 1000 Skopje, Republic of Macedonia. Tel/Fax: (389 2) 211 811. e: ffmanaki@mt.net.mk. Web: www.manaki.com.mk (*Held in remembrance of Yanaki and Milton Manaki, the first cameramen of the Balkans – Sept.*)

International Festival of New Latin American Cinema, Calle 2 No 411, Entre 17/19, Vedado, Havana, Cuba. Tel: (53 7) 552 841. Fax: 334 273. e: festival@icaic.inf.cu. Web: www.havanafilmfestival.com. (*Competitive event and market – Dec.*)

International Film Festival Innsbruck, Museumstrasse 31, A-6020 Innsbruck, Austria. Tel: (43 512) 5785 0014. Fax: 5785 0013. e: info@iffi.at. Web: www.iffi.at. (*Films about Africa, Latin America and Asia, Austrian premieres – June 9-13, 2004.*)

International Film Festival of Uruguay, Lorenzo Carnelli 1311, 11200 Montevideo, Uruguay. Tel: (59 82) 418 2460/5795. Fax: 419 4572. e: cinemuy@chasque.net. Web: www.cinemateca.org.uy. (*Organised by the highly respected Uruguayan Cinematheque director Manuel Martínez Carril. Presents independent and documentary films – April 3-18, 2004. Deadline: Feb 5.*)

International Film Forum "Arsenals", Marstalu 14, Riga, LV-1050, Latvia Tel: (371) 7221 620. Fax: 7820 445. e:programm@arsenals.lv. Web: www.arsenals.lv. (*Biannual competitive festival with $10,000 international competition and latest releases from Latvia, Lithuania and Estonia in features, documentary, shorts and animation – Sept 18-26, 2004.*)

International Student Film Festival, Dept of Film & Television, Tel Aviv University, Ramat Aviv 69978, Israel. Tel: (972 3) 640 9936. Fax: 640 9935. e: filmfest@post.tau.ac.il. Web: www.taufilmfest.com. (*Workshops, retrospectives, tributes, premieres – June.*)

International Women's Film Festival, Maison des Arts, Palace Salvador Allende, 94000 Créteil, France. Tel: (33 1) 4980 3898. Fax: 4399 0410. e: filmsfemmes@wanadoo.fr. Web: www.filmdefemmes.com. (*Features, shorts and animation made by women – March 12-21, 2004.*)

Israel Film Festival, Israfest Foundation, 6404 Wilshire Blvd, Suite 1240, Los Angeles, CA

90048, USA. Tel: (1 323) 966 4166. Fax: 658 6346. e: israfest@earthlink.net. Web: www.israelfilmfestival.com. (*US showcase for Israeli features, shorts, documentaries and TV dramas – late May/early June in LA; May in Chicago; June/July in NY; Nov in Miami.*)

Kidfilm/USA Film Festival, 6116 N Central Expressway, Suite 105, Dallas, Texas 75206, USA. Tel: (1 214) 821 6300. Fax: 821 6364. e: usafilmfestival@aol.com. (*Non-competitive; accepts US and international shorts and features – Jan 17-18, 2004.*)

Kiev International Film Festival "Molodist", 6 Saksagansky St, Suite 115, 01033 Kiev, Ukraine. Tel: (380 44) 461 9803. Fax: 227 4557. e: novikova@molodist.com. Web: www.molodist.com. (*Ukraine's largest international film event and annual competition, dedicated to first professional and student films – late Oct-early Nov.*)

Kracow Film Festival, Ul Pychowicka 7, 30-364 Krakow, Poland. Tel: (48 12) 427 1355. Fax: 267 2340/1060. e: festiwal@apollofilm.pl. Web: www.cracowfilmfestival.pl. (*Poland's oldest international film festival and respected short film showcase – May 28-June 1, 2004.*)

London Lesbian & Gay Film Festival, National Film Theatre, South Bank, London SE1 8XT, UK. Tel: (44 20) 7815 1323. Fax: 7633 0786. e: anna.dunwoodie@bfi.org.uk. Web: www.llgff.org.uk. (*Films of special interest to lesbian and gay audiences. Selected highlights tour regional film theatres April to September – March/April, 2004 tbc.*)

Lucas International Children's Film Festival, Schaumainkai 41, 60596 Frankfurt/Main, Germany. Tel: (49 69) 9637 6380. Fax: 9637 6382. e: lucas@deutsches-filmmuseum.de. Web: www.lucasfilmfestival.de. (*New international productions for children – Sept 19-26, 2004.*)

Mar de Plata International Film Festival, Lima 319, Piso 9°, C1073AAG, Buenos Aires, Argentina. Tel: (54 11) 6779 0900 ext 190. Fax: 6779 0985. e: marplafest.director@incaa.gov.ar. (*The only A-grade festival in Latin America – March, 2004.*)

Margaret Mead Film & Video Festival, American Museum of Natural History, 79th St at Central Park W, New York, NY 10024, USA. Tel: (1 212) 769 5305. Fax: 769 5329. e: meadfest@amnh.org. Web: www.amnh.org/mead. (*International documentaries: shorts, animation and features – Nov.*)

Marseilles Documentary Film Festival, 14, Allée Léon Gambetta, 13001 Marseilles, France. Tel: (33 4) 9504 4490. Fax: 9504 4491. e: welcome@fidmarseille.org. Web: www.fidmarseille.org. (*The best international documentaries – June/July.*)

"Message to Man" International Documentary, Short and Animated Film Festival, Karavannaya 12, 191011, St Petersburg, Russia. Tel: (7 812) 235 2660/230 2200. Fax: 235 3995. e: info@message-to-man.spb.ru. Web: www.message-to-man.spb.ru. (*International competition, international debut competition, national documentary competition and special programmes – June 15-22, 2004.*)

Miami International Film Festival, Florida International University, University Park PC 230, Miami, Florida 33199, USA. Tel: (1 305) 348 4722. (1 305) 348 7055. e: info@miamifilmfestival.com. Web: www.miamifilmfestival.com. Director - Nicole Guillemet. (*The best of world cinema; special focus on Ibero-American films – Jan 30-Feb 8, 2004.*)

Midnight Sun Film Festival, Lapintie 16 As 2, 99600 Sodankylä, Finland. Tel: (358 16) 614 524. Fax: 618 646. e: office@msfilmfestival.fi. Web: www.msfilmfestival.fi. (*International and silent films, plus award-winners from Cannes, Berlin, Locarno and Stockholm – June, 2004.*)

Minneapolis/St Paul International Film Festival, University Film Society, Minnesota Film Arts, 309 Oak St Ave SE, Minneapolis, MN 55414, USA. Tel: (1 612) 331 7563. Fax: 627 4111. e: filmsoc@tc.umn.edu. Web: www.ufilm.org. (*Built up over 20 years by the reliable Al Milgrom. Screens scores of foreign films, especially Scandinavian – April 2004.*)

Montreal International Festival of New Cinema and New Media, 3530 Boulevard St-Laurent, Bureau 304 Montreal, Quebec, Canada H2X 2V1. Tel: (1 514) 847 9272. Fax: 847 0732. e: info@fcmm.com. Web: www.fcmm.com. (*Seeks to explore quality experimental films as* *an alternative to conventional commercial cinema – Oct.)*

Moscow International Film Festival, 10/1 Khokhlovsky per., Moscow, 109028, Russia. Tel: (7 095) 917 2486. Fax: 916 0107. e: info@miff.ru. Web: www.miff.ru. (*Competitive only for full-length features – June.*)

Mumbai International Film Festival, Rajkamal Studio, S. S. Rao Road, Parel, Mumbai 400 012, India. Tel: (91 22) 2413 6571/6572. Fax: 2412 5268. e-mail: iffmumbai@yahoo.com. Web: www.iffmumbai.com. (*Established in 1997, the only independent film festival in India, organised by Mumbai Academy of the Moving Image, whose chairman is renowned film-maker Shyam Benegal. Full-length feature films only. Sections: World Cinema, with a FIPRESCI award, Retro, Tribute, Focus on Film-maker, Focus on One Country, Film India Worldwide & Competition for Indian Films, judged by an international jury. Entry form and other information available online – Nov 20-27, 2003.*)

Munich International Festival of Film Schools, Sonnenstrasse 21, D-80331 Munich, Germany. Tel: (49 89) 3819 040. Fax: 3819 0426. e: festivalleitung@filmfest-muenchen.de. Web: filmfest-muenchen.de. (*Competition for student productions from about 30 film schools – late Nov.*)

NatFilm Festival, Store Kannikestraede 6, 1169 Copenhagen, Denmark. Tel: (45) 3312 0005. Fax: 3312 7505. e: info@natfilm.dk. Web: www.natfilm.dk. Producer: Andreas Steinmann. Programmer: Kim Foss. (*Off-beat international retrospectives and tributes – Mar 26-April 11, 2004.*)

New Directors/New Films, Film Society of Lincoln Center, 70 Lincoln Center Plaza, New York, NY 10023, USA. Tel: (1 212) 875 5638. Fax: 875 5636. e: sbensman@filmlinc.com. Web: www.filmlinc.com. (*Works by new directors; co-sponsored by the Film Society and MOMA – March/April, 2004.*)

New England Film and Video Festival, Boston Film & Video Foundation, 119 Braintree St, Box 159, Suite 104, Boston, MA 02134, USA. Tel: (1 617) 783 9241. Fax: 783 4368. e: festival@bfvf.org. Web: www.bfvf.org. (*Since 1976, competitive festival for new works by professionals and students resident in New England – March.*)

New Orleans Film Festival, 843 Carondelet St, New Orleans, LA 70130, USA. Tel: (1 504) 523 3818. Fax: 975 3478. e: incompetition@neworleansfilmfest.com. Web: www.neworleansfilmfest.com. (*Competition for all lengths, genres and formats and non-competitive programme that includes re-mastered classics and cutting-edge new releases – Oct 7-24, 2004.*)

New York EXPO of Short Film and Video, 224 Centre St, New York, NY 10013, USA. Tel: (1 212) 505 7742. e: nyexpo@aol.com. Web: www.nyexpo.org. (*America's longest-running shorts festival seeks fiction, animation, documentary and experimental works under 60 minutes and completed in the previous two years. Student and international entries welcome – Dec 12-14, 2003.*)

Nordic Film Festival, 75 rue General le Clerc, 76000 Rouen, France. Tel: (33 232) 767 322. Fax: 767 323. e: festival-cinema-nordique@festival-cinema-nordique.asso.fr. Web: www.festival-cinema-nordique.asso.fr. (*Competitive festival of Nordic cinema, including retrospectives – March 17-28, 2004.*)

Northwest Film and Video Festival, Northwest Film Center, 1219 SW Park Ave, Portland, Oregon 97205, USA. Tel: (1 503) 221 1156. Fax: 294 0874. e: info@nwfilm.org. Web: www.nwfilm.org. (*Annual survey of new moving-image art produced in the Northwest US and British Columbia; features, shorts and documentaries – Nov; Deadline: Aug 1.*)

OFFICINEMA, Cineteca del Comune di Bologna, Via Riva di Reno 72, 40122 Bologna, Italy. Tel/Fax: (39) 051 204 820. e: cinetecamanifestazioni1@comune.bologna.it. Web: www.cinetecadibologna.it. (*Competition for final projects from European schools; deadline: July. Visioni Italiane competition for Italian shorts and first features: deadline: Sept. 8,000 spectators, 200 films, 150 guests, 10 awards – Nov.*)

OKOMEDIA – International Environmental Film Festival, Oekomedia Institute Nussmannstr 14, D-79098 Freiburg, Germany. Tel: (49 761) 52 024. Fax: 555 724. e: oekomedia@t-online.de. Web: www.oekomedia-institute.de. (*International* film and TV productions about contemporary ecological/environmental issues – late Oct-early Nov.)

Open Air Filmfest Weiterstadt, Film Fest Weiterstadt, Kommunales Kino Im Buergerzentrum, Carl-Ulrich-Strasse 9-11, D-64331 Weiterstadt, Germany. Tel: (49 61) 501 2185. Fax: 501 4073. e: filmfest@weiterstadt.de. Web: www.filmfest-weiterstadt.de. (Aug 12-16, 2004; Deadline: May 15.)

Palm Beach International Film Festival, PO Box 880419, Boca Raton, Florida 33071, USA. Tel: (1 561) 218 1370. Fax: 345 0004. e: randiem@aol.com. Web: www.pbifilmfest.org. (More than 80 films: American and international features, shorts, documentaries and large format. Competitive – April 15-22, 2004.)

Palm Springs International Festival of Short Films, 1700 E Tahquitz Canyon Way, Suite 3, Palm Springs, CA 92262, USA. Tel: (1 760) 322 2930. Fax: 322 4087. e: info@psfilmfest.org. Web: www.psfilmfest.org. Contact: Rhea Lewis-Woodson. (Largest competitive shorts festival in US. Student, animation, documentary and international competition with Audience and Juried Awards. Attracts 1,200 entries and 7,500 spectators. Seminars and workshops – Sept.)

Panorama of European Cinema, c/o Eleftherotypia, 10-16 Minoos St, 11 743 Athens, Greece. Tel: (30 21) 0929 96001. Fax: 0864 7730. e: ninos@enet.gr. Contact: Ninos Feneck Mikelides. (Includes European Competition – Oct.)

Peñíscola International Comedy Film Festival, Patronato Municipal de Turismo, Festival de Cine, Plaza Constitución, s/n, 12598 Peñíscola, Castellón, Spain. Tel: (34 964) 480 483. Fax: 481 079. e: info@festivalpeniscola.com. Web: www.festivalpeniscola.com. (Hugely enjoyable festival in spectacular Mediterranean resort – May/June.)

Philadelphia International Film Festival, Philadelphia Film Society, 4th Floor, 234 Market St, Philadelphia, PA 19106, USA. Tel: (1 215) 733 0608. Fax: 733 0668. e: festival@phillyfests.com. Web: www.phillyfests.com. (International features, documentaries and shorts – April.)

Portland International Film Festival,

Northwest Film Center, 1219 SW Park Ave, Portland, Oregon 97205, USA. Tel: (1 503) 221 1156. Fax: 294 0874. e: info@nwfilm.org. Web: www.nwfilm.org. (Non-competitive; focuses primarily on international work but includes American features, documentaries and shorts. Deadline for unsolicited preview tapes: Oct 30 – Feb 13-28, 2004.)

Prix Italia, Via Monte Santo 52, 00195 Rome, Italy. Tel: (39 06) 372 8708. Fax: (39 06) 372 3966. e: l.pinelli@rai.it. Web: www.prixitalia.rai.it. (International competition for radio, TV programmes and multi-media; open only to 75 member organisations – Sept.)

Punta del Este International Film Festival, Sala Cantegril, Maldonado, Uruguay. Tel/Fax: (598 42) 241266. e: cultmal@adinet.com.uy. (European and Latin American films meet at splendid international sea resort; non competitive – Jan.)

Pusan International Film Festival, Yachting Center, Annex 2-1, #1393 Woo 1 Dong, Haeundae-Gu, Pusan, Korea. Tel: (82 51) 747 3010. Fax: 747 3012. e: program@piff.org. Web: www.piff.org. (Launched in 1996; celebrates the best in world cinema, with emphasis on Asian films – Oct.)

RAI Trade Screenings, Rai Trade, Via Umberto Novaro 18, 00195 Rome, Italy. Tel: (39 06) 3749 8257. Fax: 3701 343. e: giandrea@raitrade.it. Web: www.raitrade.rai.it. (International programming buyers view RAI productions for broadcast, video and other rights – March, 2004.)

Saint Louis International Film Festival, 394 AN Euclid Ave, St Louis, MO 63108, USA. Tel: (1 314) 454 0042. Fax: 454 0540. e: chris@sliff.org. Web: www.sliff.org. (Showcases approximately 180 US and international independent films, documentaries and shorts. Competitive, with awards in 15 categories – Nov.)

St Petersburg Festival of Festivals, 190 Kamennostrovsky Ave, St Petersburg 197101, Russia. Tel: (7 812) 237 0072. Fax: 237 0304. e: info@filmfest.ru. Web: www.filmfest.ru. (International and local productions – June 23-29, 2004; Deadline: April 15.)

San Francisco International Asian American Film Festival, c/o NAATA, 145 9th Street, Suite

350, San Francisco, CA 94103, USA. Tel: (1 415) 863 0814. Fax: (1 415) 863 7428. e: festival@naatanet. Web: www.naatanet.org. (*Film and video works by Asian-American and Asian artists – March 4-14, 2004.*)

San Francisco International Lesbian and Gay Film Festival, Frameline, 145 9th St, Suite 300, San Francisco, CA 94103, USA. Tel: (1 415) 703 8650. Fax: (1 415) 861 1404. e: info@frameline.org. Web: www.frameline.org. (*Focus on gay, lesbian, bisexual and transgender themes – June.*)

San Sebastian Horror and Fantasy Film Festival, Donostia Kultura, Plaza de la Constitucion 1, 20003 Donostia-San Sebastian, Spain. Tel: (34 943) 481 197/53/57. Fax: (34 943) 430 621. e: cinema_cinema@donostia.org. Web: www.donostiakultura.com/terror. (*Cult, cutting-edge horror fantasy festival; short film and feature competition – Oct 29-Nov 6, 2004.*)

San Sebastian Human Rights Film Festival, Donostia Kultura, Plaza de la Constitucion 1, 20003 Donostia-San Sebastian, Spain. Tel: (34 943) 481 197/53/57. Fax: 430 621. e: cinema_cinema@donostia.org. Web: www.donostiakultura.com. (*Short films and features about human rights – March 2004.*)

Sao Paulo International Film Festival, Rua Antonio Carlos, 288 2° andar, 01309-010 Sao Paulo, Brazil. Tel: (55 11) 3141 1068/2548. Fax: 3266 7066. e: info@mostra.org. Web: www.mostra.org. (*Competitive event for new film-makers and international panorama – Oct 15-28, 2004.*)

Seville Film and Sport Film Festival, Estadio Olímpico de Sevilla Puerta J, local A, 41092 Seville, Spain. Tel: (34 954) 460 786. Fax: 460 356. e: festival@festivaldesevilla.com. Web: www.festivaldesevilla.com (*Competition for sport-themed films, tributes and general panorama, run by festival veteran Jose Luis Ruiz – Nov.*)

Siberian International Festival – Spirit of Fire, Festival Committee, 1 Mosfilmovskaya St, Moscow, 119992 Russia. Tel: (7 095) 143 9484. Fax: 938 2312. e: festival@spiritoffire.ru. Web: www.spiritoffire.ru. (*Showcases 15 films directed by young talents; all formats eligible. The Grand Prix is worth $150,000 and three runners-up share a similar prize fund. Numerous debates –*

Jan/Feb).

Singapore International Film Festival, 45A Keong Saik Road, Singapore 089149. Tel: (65) 6738 7567. Fax: 6738 7578. e: filmfest@pacific.net.sg. Web: www.filmfest.org.sg. (*Showcases the best of Asian and world cinema. Competitive Asian section – April.*)

Sydney Film Festival, PO Box 96, Strawberry Hills, NSW 2012, Australia. Tel: (61 2) 9280 0511. Fax: 9280 1520. e: info@sydneyfilmfestival.org. (*Broad-based, non-competitive event screening new Australian and international features and shorts – June.*)

Taormina International Film Festival, Corso Umberto 19, 98039 Taormina Messina, Italy. Tel: (39 094) 221 142. Fax: 223 348. e: info@taormina-arte.com. Web: www. taormina-arte.com. (*Films by English-language directors. Restorations. Silver Ribbons awarded by Italian film critics – June.*)

Tel Aviv-Yafo International Film Festival, 68 Ibn Gvirol St, Tel Aviv 64162, Israel. Tel. (972 3) 521 7868. Fax: 521 7869. e: info@tafilmfest.co.il. Artistic Director: Edna Fainaru. (*Dedicated to actors; competition for young actors in their first significant roles. Films directed by actors, or films about acting; plus tributes and masterclasses – March.*)

Tokyo International Film Festival, 5F Ginza 8 Building, 4-14-6 Ginza, Chuo-ku, Tokyo 104-0061, Japan. Tel: (81 3) 3524 1081. Fax: 3524 1087. e: info@tiff-jp.net. Web: www.tiff-jp.net. Director: Tsuguhiko Kadokawa. (*Major competitive international event; cash prize of $80,000; sidebars – Nov.*)

Tribeca Film Festival, 375 Greenwich St, New York, NY 10013, USA. Tel: (1 212) 941 2400. Fax: 941 3939. e: festival@tribecafilmfestival.org. Web: www.tribecafilmfestival.org. Contact: Peter Scarlet. (*Established in 2002; features and shorts – May 4-9, 2004; Deadline: January.*)

Tudela First Film Festival, Centro Cultural Castel Ruiz, Plaza Mercadal, 7, 31500, Tudela, Navarra, Spain. Tel: (34 948) 825 868. Fax: 412 003. e: jasone.cr@tudela.com. Web: www.geocities.com/operaprimafestival. (*Late Oct-early Nov.*)

Uppsala International Short Film Festival, PO Box 1746, S-751 47 Uppsala, Sweden. Tel: (46

18) 120 025. Fax: 121 350.
e: info@shortfilmfestival.com. Web:
www.shortfilmfestival.com. (*Sweden's only
international shorts festival. Competitive.
Deadline: June – Oct 2004.*)
USA Film Festival, 6116 N Central Expressway,
Suite 105, Dallas, Texas 75206, USA. Tel: (1
214) 821 6300. Fax: 821 6364.
e: usafilmfestival@aol.com. Web:
www.usafilmfestival.com. (*Non-competitive for
US and international features. Academy-
qualifying National Short Film/Video competition
with cash awards – April 2004.*)
Valdivia International Film Festival, Cine Club,
Universidad Austral de Chile, Campus Isla Teja
s/n, Valdivia, Chile. Tel: (56 63) 215 622.
Fax: 221 209. e: cineclub@uach.cl. Web:
www.festivalcinevaldivia.com. (*International
feature contest for young directors and/or
maiden works; Chilean cinema contest; plus
Chilean and international shorts, documentaries
and animation – Oct.*)
Valley International Film Festival, PO Box
3609, Chatsworth, CA 91313, USA. Tel: (1 818)
968 0052. Fax: 709 8597. e: info@viffi.org. Web:
www.viffi.org. Executive Director/Programmer:
Patte Dee. President: Clancy Grass.
(*Competition for films and screenplays;
showcase for film-makers and writers who
believe in entertainment that should not contain
gratuitous violence or profanity – Nov; Deadline:
mid-Sept.*)
VIENNALE Vienna International Film Festival,
Siebensterngasse 2, 1070 Vienna, Austria.
Tel: (43 1) 526 5947. Fax: 523 4172.
e: office@viennale.at. Web: www.viennale.at.
(*New international films, creative documentaries,
shorts and tributes – Oct 15-27, 2004.*)

**Viewfinders International Film Festival for
Youth**, PO Box 36139, 220-5600 Sackville St,
Halifax, NS, B3J 3S9, Canada. Tel: (1 902) 422
3456. Fax: 422 4006.
e: festival@atlanticfilm.com.
Web: www.atlanticfilm.com. (*April 20-24, 2004.*)
Vila do Conde, Festival Internacional de Curtas
Metragens Auditório Municipal, Praa da
República, 4480-715 Vila do Conde, Portugal.
Tel: (351 252) 248 469/646 516. Fax: 248 416.
e: festival@curtasmetragens.pt Web:
www.curtasmetragens.pt. (*National and
International shorts competitions. Special
programme and retrospectives – July.*)
Warsaw International Film Festival, PO Box
816, 00-950 Warsaw 1, Poland. Tel: (48 22) 621
4647. Fax: 621 6268. e: festiv@wff.org.pl. Web:
www.wff.org.pl. (*Key event in Poland. Fiction
and documentary features. New Films' and New
Directors' competition – Oct 7-18, 2004.*)
**Washington, DC International Film Festival
(Filmfest DC)**, PO Box 21396, Washington, DC
20009, USA. Tel: (1 202) 724 3456. Fax: 724
6578. e: filmfestdc@filmfestdc.org. Web:
www.filmfestdc.org. (*Celebrates the best in
world cinema – April 21-May 2, 2004.*)
World Animation Celebration, 30941 West
Agoura Road, Suite 102, Westlake Village, CA
91361, USA. Tel: (1 818) 991 2884. Fax: 991
3773. e: info@animationmagazine.net.
Web: www.animationmagazine.net. (*Aug.*)

ALGERIA
Cinémathèque Algérienne, 49 rue Larbi Ben M'Hidi, Algiers. Tel: (213 2) 737 548/50. Fax: 738 246. www.cinematheque.art.dz/.

ARGENTINA
All Tel/Fax numbers begin (54 11)

Useful Addresses
Cinemateca Argentina, [Archive], Salta 1915, CP 1137 Buenos Aires. Tel: 4306 0562. Fax: 4306 0592. www.cinemateca.org.ar.
Critics Association of Argentina, Maipu 621 Planta Baja, 1006 Buenos Aires. Tel/Fax: 4322 6625. cinecronistas@yahoo.com.
Directors Association of Argentina (DAC), Río Bamba 67, 2°, 1025 Buenos Aires. Tel/Fax: 4954 0080. dac1@infovia.com.ar.
Directors of Photography Association, San Lorenzo 3845, Olivos, 1636 Buenos Aires. Tel/Fax: 4790 2633. www.adfcine.com.ar.
Exhibitors Federation of Argentina, Ayacucho 457, 1° 13, Buenos Aires. Tel/Fax: 4953 1234. empcinemato@infovia.com.ar.
Film University, Pasaje Giufra 330, 1064 Buenos Aires. Fax: 4300 1413. www.ucine.edu.ar.
General Producers Association, Lavalle 1860, 1051 Buenos Aires. Tel/Fax: 4371 3430. argentinasonofilm@ impsat1.com.ar.
National Cinema Organisation (INCAA), Lima 319, 1073 Buenos Aires. Tel: 6779 0900. Fax: 4383 0029. info@incaa.gov.ar.
Producers Guild of Argentina (FAPCA), Godoy Cruz 1540, 1414 Buenos Aires. Tel: 4777 7200. Fax: 4778 0046. recepcion@patagonik.com.ar.
Sindicato de la Industria Cinematográfia de Argentina (SICA), Juncal 2029, 1116 Buenos Aires. Tel: 4806 0208. Fax: 4806 7544. www.sicacine.com.ar.

ARMENIA
All Tel/Fax numbers begin (374 1)

Useful Addresses
Armenian National Cinematheque, 25A Tbilisyan Highway, 375052 Yerevan. Tel: 285 406. filmadaran@yahoo.com.
Armenian Union of Film-makers, 318 Vardanants, Yerevan. Tel: 540 528. Fax: 540 136.
Association of Film Critics & Cinema Journalists, 26 Amiryan Str, 2nd Bldg, 2nd Floor, Yerevan. Tel: 535 889. Fax: 583 287. www.arm-cinema.am.
Hayfilm Studio, 50 Gevork Chaush, 375088 Yerevan. Tel: 343 000. Fax: 393 538. hayfilm@arminco.com.
Hayk Documentary Studio, 50 Gevork Chaush, 375088 Yerevan. Tel: 357 032.
Yerevan Studio, 47 Nork, 375047 Yerevan. Tel: 558 022. tx-yes@media.am.

AUSTRALIA

Archives
Archives Office of Tasmania, 77 Murray St, Hobart, Tasmania 7000. Tel: (61 3) 6233 7488. Fax: 6233 7490. www.archives.tas.gov.au.
Screensound Australia, The National Screen and Sound

Archive, GPO Box 2002, Caberra ACT 2601. Tel: (61 2) 6248 2000. Fax: 6248 2222. enquiries@screensound.gov.au.

Useful Addresses
AFC News, [Magazine], GPO Box 3984, Sydney NSW 2001. Tel: (61 2) 9321 6444. Fax: 9357 3737. www.afc.gov.au/newsandevents. Monthly.
Australian Entertainment Industry Association (AEIA), 8th Floor, West Tower, 608 St Kilda Rd, Melbourne VIC 3004. Tel: (61 3) 9521 1900. Fax: 9521 2285. aeia@aeia.org.au.
Australian Film Commission (AFC), 150 William St, Woolloomooloo NSW 2011. Postal address: GPO Box 3984, Sydney NSW 2001. Tel: (61 2) 9321 6444. Fax: 9357 3737. www.afc.gov.au.
Australian Film Finance Corporation (AFFC), 130 Elizabeth St, Sydney NSW 2000. Postal address: GPO Box 3886, Sydney NSW 2001. Tel: (61 2) 9268 2555. Fax: 9264 8551. www.ffc.gov.au.
Australian Film Television & Radio School (AFTRS), Postal address: PO Box 126, North Ryde NSW 2113. Tel: (61 2) 9805 6611. Fax: 9887 1030. direct.sales@syd.aftrs.edu.au.
Australian Screen Directors Association (ASDA), Postal address: PO Box 211, Rozelle NSW 2039. Tel: (61 2) 9555 7045. Fax: 9555 7086. www.asdafilm.org.au.
Electric Shadows Bookshop, City Walk, Akuna St, Canberra ACT 2601. Tel: (61 2) 6248 8352. Fax: 6247 1230. www.electricshadowsbook shop.com.au.
Film Australia, 101 Eton Rd, Lindfield NSW 2070. Tel: (61 2) 9413 8777. Fax: 9416 9401.

www.filmaust.com.au.
Film Victoria, Level 7, 189 Flinders Lane, Melbourne VIC 3000. Tel: (61 3) 9660 3200. Fax: 9660 3201. www.film.vic.gov.au.
Office of Film & Literature Classification (OFLC), 23 Mary St, Surry Hills NSW 2010. Tel: (61 2) 9289 7100. Fax: 9289 7101. oflcswitch@oflc.gov.au.
Screen Producers Association of Australia (SPAA), Level 7, 235 Pyrmont St, Pyrmont NSW 2009. Tel: (61 2) 9518 6366. Fax: 9518 6311. www.spaa.org.au.

More information can be found at www.nla.gov.au/oz/gov/. Also www.sna.net.au for Screen Network Australia, a gateway to 250 film/TV sites.

AUSTRIA

Archives
Austrian Film Museum, Augustinerstr 1, A-1010 Vienna, Tel: (43 1) 5337 0540. Fax: 5337 0562. www.filmmuseum.at.
Filmarchiv Austria, Obere Augartenstr 1, A-1020 Vienna. Tel: (43 1) 216 1300. Fax: 216 1300-100. www.filmarchiv.at.

Useful Addresses
Association of Austrian Film Directors, Burggasse 51, A-1070 Vienna. Tel/Fax: (43 1) 524 5429. www.austrian-directors.com.
Association of Austrian Film Producers, Speisingerstrasse 121, A-1230 Vienna. Tel/Fax: (43 1) 888 9622. www.austrian-film.com.
Association of the Audiovisual & Film Industry, Wiedner Hauptstrasse 53, PO Box 327, A-1045 Vienna. Tel:

(43 1) 5010 53010. Fax: 5010 5276. www.fafo.at.
Austrian Film Commission, Stiftgasse 6, A-1070 Vienna. Tel: (43 1) 526 3332-200. Fax: 526 6801. www.afc.at.
Austrian Film Institute (OFI), Spittelberggasse 3, A-1070 Vienna. Tel: (43 1) 526 9730-400. Fax: 526 9730-440. www.filminstitut.at.
Celluloid, [Magazine], Carl Zwillinggasse 32/19, A-2340 Mödling. Tel: (43 664) 462 5444. Fax: 23240. www.celluloid.at. Austria's leading international cinema magazine.
Location Austria, Opernring 3, A-1010 Vienna. Tel: (43 1) 588 5836. Fax: 586 8659. www.location-austria.at.
ORF, Austrian Broadcasting Corporation, Würzburggasse 30, A-1136 Vienna. Tel: (43 1) 878 780. www.orf.at.
University of Music & Performing Arts, Dept of Film & TV, Metternichgasse 12, A-1030 Vienna. Tel (43 1) 7115 5290. Fax: 7115 5299. www.mdw.ac.at.

AZERBAIJAN
Azerbaijan Film Fond, 69 Zardabi Ave, 370122 Baku. Tel: (994 12) 933 164.

BELARUS

Useful Addresses
All Tel/Fax numbers begin (375 17)

Belarusfilm, Scaryna Prospect 98, 220023 Minsk. Tel: 264 1002. Fax: 264 3132.
Ministry of Culture Department of Filmvideoart, Masherov Street 11, 220004 Minsk. Tel: 223 7114. Fax: 223 5030.

BELGIUM

Magazines
FilmMagie VZW,
Cellebroerstraat 16 Bus 2,
B-1000 Brussels. Tel: (32 2)
546 0811. Fax: 546 0819.
www.filmmagie.be. Extensive
coverage of films.
Signis Media, Rue du Saphir
15, B-1030 Brussels. Tel (32 2)
734 9708. Fax: 734 7018.
sg@signis.org. www.signis.net.
Trilingual bi-monthly.

Useful Addresses
Artémis Productions,
[Producer], 50 Ave Dailly, B-
1030 Brussels. Tel: (32 2) 216
2324. Fax: 216 2013. www.
artemisproductions.com.
**Communauté Française de
Belgique,** Centre du Cinéma et
de l'Audiovisuel, Bld Léopold II,
44, B-1080 Brussels. Tel: (32
2) 413 2519. Fax: 413 2415.
Flanders Image, Handelskaai
18/3, B-1000 Brussels. Tel: (32
2) 226 0630. Fax: 219 1936.
flandersimage@vaf.be.
**Flemish Audiovisual Fund
(VAF),** Handelskaai 18/3, B-
1000 Brussels. Tel: (32 2) 226
0630. Fax: 219 1936.
info@vaf.be. www.vaf.be.
**Help Desk for the Audiovisual
Arts in Flanders (IAK),**
Bijlokekaai 7E, 9000 Ghent.
Tel: (32 9) 235 2260.
Fax: 233 0709. info@iak.be.
**Institut National des Arts du
Spectacle et Techniques de
Diffusion (INSAS),** [Film
school], 8 Rue Thérésienne,
B-1000 Brussels. Tel (32 2)
511 9286. Fax: 511 0279.
www.insas.be
**Ministry of the Flemish
Community,** Dept of Media &
Film, North Plaza B, 3rd Floor,
Koning Albert II-Laan 7, B-
1210 Brussels. Tel: (32 2) 553
4650. Fax: 553 4672.

media@vlaanderen.be or
film@vlaanderen.be.
Royal Film Archive, Palais des
Beaux-Artes, 2nd Floor, 23 Rue
Ravenstein, B-1000 Brussels.
Tel: (32 2) 507 8370.
www.ledoux.be.
**Wallonie Bruxelles Image
(WBI),** Place Flagey 18,
B-1050 Brussels. Tel: (32 2)
223 2304. Fax: 218 3424.
www.cfwb.be.

BOSNIA & HERZEGOVINA
All Tel/Fax numbers begin (387 33)

Useful Addresses
**Academy for Performing
Arts,** Obala, Sarajevo.
Tel/Fax: 665 304.
Association of Film-makers,
Strosmajerova 1, Sarajevo. Tel:
667 452.
**Cinemateque of Bosnia &
Herzegovina,** Alipasina 19,
Sarajevo. Tel/Fax: 668 678.
kinoteka@bih.net.ba.
Sarajevo Film Festival,
Sarajevo. Tel: 209 411.
www.sff.ba.

BRAZIL

Archives
Cinemateca Brasileira, Largo
Senador Raul Cardoso, Vila
Clementino 207, 04021-070
São Paulo. Tel: (55 11) 5084
2318 Fax: 5575 9264.
www.cinemateca.com.br.
**Cinemateca do Museu de
Arte Moderna,** Ave Infante
Dom Henrique 85, Parque do
Flengo, 20021-140 Rio de
Janeiro. Tel: (55 21) 2240
4913. cinemateca
@mamrio.com.br.

Useful Addresses
**ANCINE (National Agency for
Cinema),** Praça Pio X, 54, 10th
Floor, 22091-040 Rio de
Janeiro. Tel: (55 21) 3849

1339. www.ancine.gov.br.
**Brazilian Cinema Congress
(CBC),** (Federation of Cinema
Unions/Associations), Rua
Cerro Cora 550, Sala 19,
05061-100 São Paulo.
Tel/Fax: (55 11) 3021 8505.
www.congressocinema.com.br.
Grupo Novo de Cinema,
(Distributor), Rua Capitao
Salomao 42, 22271-040 Rio
de Janeiro.
Tel: (55 21) 2539 1538.
www.gnctv.com.br.
Ministry of Culture, Films &
Festivals Dept, Esplanada dos
Ministerios, Bloco B, 3rd Floor,
70068-900 Brasilia.
www.cultura.gov.br.

BULGARIA
All Tel/Fax numbers begin (359 2)

Useful Addresses
**Bulgarian Film Producers
Association,** 19 Skobelev
Blvd, 1000 Sofia. Tel: 8860
5350. Fax: 963 0661.
geopoly@mail.techno-link.com.
**Bulgarian National Film
Library,** 36 Gurko St, 1000
Sofia. Tel: 987 0296. Fax: 987
6004. bmateeva@bnf.bg.
Geopoly Ltd, [Producer], 16
Kapitan Andreev St, 1421
Sofia. Tel/Fax: 963 0661.
geopoly@mail.techno-link.com.
Ministry of Culture, 17
Stamboliiski St, 1000 Sofia. Tel:
980 6191. Fax: 981 8559.
www.culture.government.bg/.
National Film Centre, 2A
Dondukov Blvd, 1000 Sofia.
Tel.: 987 4096. Fax: 987 3626.
nfc@mail.bol.bg.
**Union of Bulgarian Film
Makers,** 67 Dondukov Blvd,
1504 Sofia. Tel: 946 1068. Fax:
946 1069. sbfd@bitex.com.

CANADA

Archives

La Cinémathèque Québécoise, 335 Blvd de Maisonneuve E, Montréal, Quebec, H2X 1K1.Tel: (1 514) 842 9763. Fax: 842 1816. www.cinematheque.qc.ca.

National Archives of Canada, Visual & Sound Archives, 344 Wellington St, Ottawa, Ontario, K1A 0N3. Tel: (1 613) 995 5138. Fax: 995 6274. www.archive.ca.

Film Schools

Queen's University, 160 Stuart St, Kingston, Ontario, K7L 3N6. Tel: (1 613) 533 2178. Fax: 533 2063. www.film.queensu.ca.

Sheridan College, School of Animation, Arts & Design, 1430 Trafalgar Rd, Oakville, Ontario, L6H 2L1.
Tel: (1 905) 845 9430. www.sheridanc.on.ca.

Simon Fraser University, School for the Contemporary Arts, 8888 Univeristy Drive, Burnaby, British Columbia, V5A 1S6. Tel: (1 604) 291 3363. Fax: 291 5907. www.sfu.ca/sca.

University of Manitoba, Film Studies Program, 367 University College, Winnipeg, Manitoba, R3T 2N2. Tel: (1 204) 474 9581. Fax: 474 7684. www.umanitoba.ca.

University of Windsor, 401 sunset Ave, Windsor, Ontario, N9B 3P4. Tel: (1 519) 253 3000. Fax: 973 7050. www.uwindsor.ca.

Vancouver Film School, 198 West Hastings St, Suite 200, Vancouver, British Columbia, V6B 1H2. Tel: (1 604) 685 5808. Fax: 685 5830. www.vfs.com.

York University, Film & Video Dept, 4700 Keele St, Toronto, Ontario, M3J 1P3. Tel: (1 416) 736 5149. Fax: 736 5710.

www.yorku.ca.

Magazines

Ciné-Bulles, 4545 Ave Pierre-de-Coubertin, CP 1000, Succursale M, Montréal, Quebec, H1V 3R2. www.cinemasparalleles.qc.ca. Informative Québécois quarterly.

Film Canada Yearbook, Moving Pictures Media, Box 720, Port Perry, Ontario, L9L 1A6. Tel (1 905) 986 0050. Fax: 986 1113. www.filmcanadayearbook.com.

Kinema, Fine Arts & Film Studies, University of Waterloo, 200 University Ave, Waterloo, Ontario, N2L 3G1. Tel: (1 519) 888 4567 ext. 3709. Fax: 746 4982. www.kinema.uwaterloo.ca. A journal of history, aesthetics of world film.Twice yearly.

Sequences, 1850 rue Joliette, Montréal, Quebec, H1W 3G3. Tel: (1 514) 598 9573. Fax: 598 1789. cast49@hotmail.ca.

Useful Addresses

Academy of Canadian Cinema & Television, 172 King St E, Toronto, Ontario, M5A 1J3. Tel: (1 416) 366 2227. Fax: 366 8454. www.academy.ca.

Canadian Association of Film Distributors & Exporters, 30 Chemin des Trilles, Laval, Quebec, H7Y 1K2. Tel: (1 450) 689 9950. Fax: 689 9822. cic@total.net.

Canadian Film & Television Production Association, 151 Slater St, Suite 605, Ottawa, Ontario, K1P 5H3. Tel: (1 613) 233 1444. Fax: 233 0073. ottawa@cftpa.ca.

Canadian Motion Picture Distributors Association (CMPDA), 22 St Clair Ave E, Suite 1603, Toronto, Ontario,

M4T 2S4. Tel: (1 416) 961 1888. Fax: 968 1016.

Directors Guild of Canada, 1 Eglinton Ave E, Suite 604, Toronto, Ontario, M4P 3A1. Tel: (1 416) 482 6640. Fax: 486 6639. www.dgc.ca.

Motion Picture Theatre Associations of Canada, (Exhibitors), 146 Bloor St W, 2nd Floor, Toronto, Ontario, M5S 1P3. Tel: (1 416) 969 7057. Fax: 969 9852. www.mptac.ca.

National Film Board of Canada, PO Box 6100, Station Centre-Ville, Montréal, Quebec, H3C 3H5. Tel: (1 514) 283 9246. Fax: 283 8971. www.nfb.ca.

Telefilm Canada, 360 St Jacques St W, Suite 700, Montréal, Quebec, H2Y 4A9. Tel: (1 514) 283 6363. Fax: 283 8212. www.telefilm.gc.ca.

Theatrebooks, [Bookshop], 11 St Thomas St, Toronto, Ontario, M5S 2B7. Tel: (1 416) 922 7175. Fax: 922 0739. www.theatrebooks.com.

CHILE
All Tel/Fax numbers begin (56 2)

Área de Cine y Artes Audiovisuales de la División de Cultura del Ministerio de Educación, Fray Camilo Henríquez 262, 4° Piso, Santiago. Tel: 731 9880. Fax: 665 0797. www.mineduc.cl/cultura.

Chile Chitá, Gerona 3450, Ñuñoa, Santiago. Tel: 326 3521. Fax: 326 3520. www.ladoizquierdo.com.

Chilefilms, La Capitanía 1200, Las Condes, Santiago. Tel: 220 30 86. Fax: 229 6406/212 9053. www.chilefilms.cl.

Corporación de Fomento de la Producción (CORFO), Moneda 921, Santiago. Tel:

631 8597. Fax: 671 7735.
www.corfo.cl.
Filmocentro Sonido, Rodolfo
Lenz 3399, Ñuñoa, Santiago.
Tel: 341 2110. Fax: 204 2054.
www.filmosonido.cl.
Transeuropa Chile Limitada,
Seminario 152, Providencia,
Santiago. Tel/Fax: 634 6077.
seminario@adsl.tie.cl.

CHINA

Magazines
Film Art, (Dianying yishu), 77
Beisanhuan Zhonglu, Beijing
100088. Quarterly, leading
mainland academic film journal.
Popular Cinema, (Dazhong
dianying), 22 Beisanhuan
Donglu 22, Beijing. Leading
mainland Chinese magazine,
published fortnightly.
World Screen, China Film
Press, 22 Beisanhuandonglu,
Beijing 100013. Monthly.
Useful Addresses
August First Film Studio, A1,
Beili, Liuliqiao,
Guanganmenwai, Beijing
100073. Tel: (86 10) 6681
2329. Fax: 6326 7324.
**Asian Union Film &
Entertainment**, 5/F, Nanyin
Mansion 2, Dongsanhuan,
North Rd, Chaoyang District,
Beijing 100027. Tel: (86 10)
6410 8181. Fax: 6410 0089.
Beijing Film Institute, 4
Xitucheng Rd, Haidian District,
Beijing 100088. Tel: (86 10)
6201 8899. Fax: 6201 3895.
Beijing Film Studio, 77
Beisanhuan Central Rd, Haidan
District, Beijing 100088.
Tel: (86 10) 6201 2067.
Fax: 6201 2312.
China Film Archive, 3 Wen Hui
Yuan Rd, Xiao Xi Tian, Haidian
District, Beijing 100088. Tel: (86
10) 6225 0916. Fax: 225 9315.
cfafad@263.net.
China Film Co-Production

Corp, 5 Xinyuan South Rd,
Chaoyang District, Beijing
100027. Tel: (86 10) 6466
3330. Fax: 6466 3983.
Guangxi Film Studio, 26
Youai North Rd, Nanning
530001. Tel: (86 771) 313
4261. Fax: 313 3739.

COLOMBIA

Useful Addresses
**Association of Film & Video
Producers & Directors**, Calle
97, No 10-28, Bogotá. Tel: (57
1) 218 2455. Fax: 610 8524.
gustavo@centauro.com.
**Colombian Association of
Cinemas**, Calle 23, No 5-85,
Int 202, Bogotá. Tel: (57 1) 284
5752. Fax: 334 0809. e-mail :
acocine@hotmail.com.
**Colombian Association of
Documentary Film Directors**,
Calle 35, No 4-89, Bogotá.
Tel: (57 1) 245 9961.
aladoscolombia@netscape.net.
www.enmente.com/alados.
**Colombian Association of
Film Directors**, Carrera 6, No
55-10, Apartado 202, Bogotá.
Tel: (57 1) 235 9798. Fax: 212
2586. lisandro@inter.net.co.
**Colombian Association of
Film Distributors**, Carrera 11,
No 93A-22, Bogotá. Tel: (57 1)
610 6695. Fax: 618 5417.
fabogado@impsat.net.co.
Colombian Film Archives,
Carrera 13, No 13-24, Piso 9,
Bogotá. Tel: (57 1) 281 5241.
Fax: 342 1485.
www.patrimoniofilmico.org.co.
Film Promotion Fund, Calle
35, No 4-89, Bogotá. Tel: (57
1) 287 0103. Fax: 288 4828.
www.proimagenescolombia.com.
Kinetoscopio, [Magazine],
Carrera 45, No 53-24,
Apartado 8734, Medellin. Tel:
(57 4) 513 4444, ext 178.
Fax: 513 2666.
www.colomboworld.com/kinet

oscopio. Quarterly covering
international and Latin
American cinema, Colombian
directors and festival news.
Ministry of Culture, Film
Division, Calle 35, No 4-89,
Bogotá. Tel: (57 1) 288 2995.
Fax: 285 5690.
www.mincultura.gov.co.
National Film Council, Calle
35, No 4-89, Bogotá. Tel: (57
1) 288 4712. Fax: 285 5690.
www.mincultura.gov.co.

CROATIA
All Tel/Fax numbers begin (385 1)

Useful Addresses
Croatia Film d.o.o,
Katanciceva 3, 10000 Zagreb.
Tel: 481 3711. Fax: 492 2568.
Croatian Film Directors Guild,
Britanski Trg 12, 10000
Zagreb. Tel: 484 7026.
info@dhfr.hr. www.dhfr.hr.
**Croatian Film Clubs
Association**, Dalmatinska 12,
10000 Zagreb. Tel: 484 8764.
vera@hfs.hr. www.hfs.hr.
HRT (Croatian Television),
Prisavlje 3, 10000 Zagreb.
Tel: 634 3683. Fax: 634 3692.
Interfilm Produkcija, Nova Ves
45, 10000 Zagreb. Tel: 466
7296. Fax: 466 7291.
Jadran Film, Oporovecka l2,
Dugi dol 13, 10000 Zagreb.
Tel: 298 7222. Fax: 285 1394.
Maxima Film d.o.o,
Belostenceva 6, 10000 Zagreb.
Tel: 618 4731.
M.B.M. d.o.o, 10000 Zagreb.
Tel: 487 3292.
Zagreb Film, Vlaska 72,
10000 Zagreb. Tel: 455 0489.

CUBA

Film Schools
**Escuela Internacional de Cine
y TV**, Finca San Tranquilino,
Carretera Vereda Nueva, KM 4,
San Antonio de Los Baños,

Havana. Tel: (53 650) 383 152.
Fax: 382 366.
eictv@eictv.org.cu.
Instituto Superior de Arte,
Facultad de Comunicación
Audiovisual, 5ta, Avenida Esq
A20, Miramar, Playa, Havana.
Tel: (53 7) 209 1302.
isafaud@cubarte.cult.cu.

Useful Addresses
Cine Cubano, [Magazine],
Calle 23 No 1115, El Vedado,
Havana.
Cinematografía Educativa,
[Producer of Government
Educational Films], Calle 7MA
2802, Entre 28 y 30, Miramar,
Playa, Havana. Tel: (53 7) 202
6971. cined@ceniai.inf.cu.
**National Film Institute
(ICAIC),** Calle 23, No 1155,
Entre 8 y 10, Vedado, Havana.
Tel: (53 7) 833 4826. Fax: 333
281. cinemateca@icaic.inf.cu.
www.cubacine.cu.

CZECH REPUBLIC
All Tel/Fax numbers begin (420 2)

Useful Addresses
**Association of Czech
Filmmakers (FITES),** Pod
Nuselskymi Schody 3, 120 00
Prague 2. Tel: 691 0310. Fax:
691 1375.
Association of Producers,
Národní 28, 110 00 Prague 1.
Tel: 2110 5321. Fax: 2110
5303. www.apa.iol.cz.
**Czech Film & Television
Academy,** Na Îertvách 40, 180
00 Prague 8. Tel: 8482 1356.
Fax: 8482 1341.
Czech Film Centre, Národní
28, 110 00 Prague 1. Tel: 2110
5302. Fax: 2110 5303.
www.filmcenter.cz.
FAMU, Film & Television
Faculty, Academy of
Performing Arts, Smetanovo 2,
116 65 Prague 1. Tel: 2422
9176. Fax: 2423 0285.

kamera@f.amu.cz.
Ministry of Culture, Audiovisual
Dept, Milady Horákové 139,
160 00 Prague 6. Tel: 5708
5310. Fax: 2431 8155.
National Film Archive,
Malesická 12, 130 00 Prague
3. Tel: 7177 0509. Fax: 7177
0501. nfa@nfa.cz. www.nfa.cz.
**Union of Czech Film
Distributors,** Národní 28, 110
00 Prague 1. Tel: 2494 5220.
Fax: 2110 5220.

DENMARK
All Tel/Fax numbers begin (45)

Film Schools
European Film College, DK-
8400 Ebeltoft. Tel: 8634 0055.
Fax: 8634 0535.
**National Film School of
Denmark,** Theodor
Christensen's Plads 1, DK-
1437 Copenhagen K. Tel: 3268
6400. Fax: 3268 6410.
info@filmskolen.dk.

Useful Addresses
Danish Film & TV Producers,
Allégade 24A, DK-2000
Frederiksberg. Tel: 3386 2880.
Fax: 3386 2888.
www.producentforeningen.dk.
Danish Film Directors,
Vermundsgade 19, DK-2100
Copenhagen Ø. Tel: 3583
8005. Fax: 3583 8006.
mail@filmdir.dk.
**Danish Film Institute/Archive
& Cinemateque** Gothersgade
55, DK-1123 Copenhagen K.
Tel: 3374 3400. Fax: 3374
3401. dfi@dfi.dk. Publishes the
film magazine Kosmorama.
Danish Film Studio,
Blomstervaenget 52, DK-2800
Lyngby. Tel: 4587 2700.
Fax: 4587 2705.
FILM, [Magazine],
Gothersgade 55, DK-1123
Copenhagen K. Tel: 3374
3400. susannan@dfi.dk and

agnetes@dfi.dk. Published by
the Danish Film Institute. Eight
issues per year (two to three in
English).
Film Distributors in Denmark,
Langelinie Allé 35, DK-2100
Copenhagen Ø. Tel: 3391
9199. Fax: 3391 9973.

EGYPT
All Tel/Fax numbers begin (20 2)

Useful Addresses
**Central Audio-Visual
Censorship Authority,** Opera
Ground, Gezira, Cairo.
Tel: 738 1674. Fax: 736 9479.
Chamber of Film Industry,
1195 Kornish El Nil, Industries
Union Bldg, Cairo. Tel: 578
5111. Fax: 575 1583.
Egyptian Radio & TV Union,
Kornish El Nil, Maspero St,
Cairo. Tel: 576 0014.
Fax: 579 9316.
Higher Film Institute,
Pyramids Rd, Gamal El-Din El-
Afaghani St, Guiza. Tel: 537
703. Fax: 561 1034.
aoarts@idsc.gov.eg.
**National Egyptian Film
Archive,** c/o Egyptian Film
Centre, City of Arts, Al Ahram
Rd, Guiza. Tel: 585 4801. Fax:
585 4701.
National Film Center, Al-
Ahram Ave, Giza. Tel: 585
4801. Fax: 585 4701.

ESTONIA

Useful Addresses
**Association of Professional
Actors of Estonia,** Uus 5,
10111 Tallinn. Tel: (372 6) 464
512. Fax: 464 516.
www.hot.ee/enliit.
Black Nights Film Festival,
Gonsiori 27, 10147 Tallinn. Tel:
(372 6) 284 510. Fax: 284 542.
poff@poff.ee. www.poff.ee.
**Estonian Association of Film
Journalists,** Narva Mnt 11E,

10151 Tallinn. Tel: (372 5) 533
894. Fax: 698 154.
jaan@ekspress.ee.
**Estonian Film & Video
Studios Association**, Kaare
15, 11618 Tallinn. Tel: (372 6)
706 485. afilm@online.ee or
efvsl@solo.ee.
Estonian Film Foundation,
Vana-Viru 3, 10111 Tallinn. Tel:
(372 6) 276 060. Fax: 276 061.
film@ efsa.ee. www.efsa.ee.
Estonian Film-makers Union,
Uus 3, 10111 Tallinn. Tel/Fax:
(372 6) 464 068.
kinoliit@online.ee.
Estonian National Archive,
Ristiku 84, 10318 Tallinn.
Tel: (372 6) 938 613.
www.filmi.arhiiv.ee.
**Pärnu International
Documentary & Anthropology
Film Festival**, Esplanaadi 10,
80010 Pärnu. Tel: (372 4) 430
772. Fax: 430 774.
www.chaplin.ee
Union of Estonian Cameramen,
Faehlmanni 12, 15029 Tallinn.
Tel: (372 6) 568 401. Fax: 568
401. bogavideo@infonet.ee.

FINLAND

Magazines
Filmihullu, Malminkatu 36,
FIN-00100, Helsinki.
Tel: (358 9) 685 2242.
Filmjournalen, Finlandssvenskt
Filmcentrum, Nylandsgatan 1,
FIN-20500, Åbo. Tel: (358 2)
250 0431.
www.fsfilmcentrum.fi/fj/.

Useful Addresses
Artista Filmi Oy, [Producer],
Post Box 69, FIN-28401, Ulvila.
Tel: (338 2) 647 7441.
timo.koivusalo@
artistafilmi.com.
Blind Spot Pictures Oy,
[Producer], Kalliolanrinne 4,
FIN-00510, Helsinki.
Tel: (358 9) 7742 8360.

Dada Filmi Oy, 3 Linja 5, FIN-
00530 Helsinki.
Tel: (358 9) 774 4780.
fennada@dada.pp.fi.
Finnish Film Archive,
Pursimiehenkatu 29-31A, PO
Box 177, FIN-00151, Helsinki.
Tel: (358 9) 615 400.
Kinotar Oy, [Producer],
Meritullinkatu 33E, FIN-00170,
Helsinki. Tel: (358 9) 135 1864.
kinotar@kinotar.com.
**MRP Matila & Röhr
Productions**, [Producer],
Tallbrginkatu 1A 141, FIN-
00180, Helsinki. Tel: (358 9)
540 7820. Fax: 685 2229.
mrp@matilarohr.com.
**University of Art & Design
Helsinki (UIAH)**, Dept of Film,
Hämeentie 135 C, FIN-00560,
Helsinki. Tel: (358 9) 756 31.

FRANCE

Archives
Archives du Film, 7 bis rue
Alexandre Turpault, 78395 Bois
d'Arcy. Tel: (33 1) 3014 8000.
Fax: 3460 5225.
Cinémathèque de Toulouse,
BP 824, 31080 Toulouse
Cedex 6. Tel: (33 5) 6230
3010. Fax: 6230 3012.
www.lacinemathequedet
oulouse.com.
Cinémathèque Française,
4 rue de Longchamp, 75116
Paris. Tel: (33 1) 5365 7474.
Fax: 5365 7465.
www.cinemathequefrancaise.
com.
Cinémathèque Universitaire,
3 rue Michelet, 75006 Paris.
Tel: (33 1) 4325 5099.
cinematheque-
universitaire@univ-paris3.fr.
Institut Lumière, 25 rue du
Premier-Film, BP 8051, 69352
Lyon Cedex 8. Tel: (33 4) 7878
1895. Fax: 7878 3656.
www.institut-lumiere.org.

Bookshops
Atmosphère, Librairie du
Cinema, 10 rue Broca, 75005
Paris. Tel: (33 1) 4331 0271.
Fax: 4331 0369.
librairie.atmosphere@frisbee.fr.
Wide range of publications,
stills, postcards, posters.
Cine-Folie, La Boutique du
Cinéma, 14 rue des Frères
Pradignac, 06250 Cannes.
Tel/Fax: (33 4) 9339 2299.
Gilda, 36 rue de Boudonnais,
75001 Paris.
Tel: (33 1) 4233 6000.
Librairie Contacts, 24 rue du
Colisée, 75008 Paris. Tel: (33
1) 4359 1771. Fax: 4289 2765.
www.medialibrarie.com. Amply
stocked with French and
foreign-language books.
Reliable mail order service.

Film Schools
**Conservatoire Libre du
Cinéma Français**, 9 quai de
l'Oise, 75019 Paris. Tel: (33 1)
4036 1919. Fax: 4036 0102.
www.clcf.com.
**ESEC (Ecole Superieure
d'Etudes Libres
Cinematographique)**, 21 rue
de Citeaux, 75012 Paris. Tel:
(33 1) 4342 4322. Fax: 4341
9521. www.esec.edu.
**Femis (École Nationale
Supérieure des Métiers de
L'Image et du Son)**, 6 rue
Francoeur, 75018 Paris. Tel:
(33 1) 5341 2100. Fax: 5341
0280. www.femis.fr.

Magazines
Cahiers du Cinema,
9 passage de la Boule
Blanche, 75012 Paris. Tel: (33
1) 5344 7575. Fax: 4343 9504.
cducinema@lemonde.fr.
Celebrated monthly journal.
Le Film Français, 150 rue
Gallieni, 92514 Boulogne
Cedex. Tel: (33 1) 4186 1600.

Fax: 4186 1691.
www.lefilmfrancais.com.
Lightweight weekly.
Positif, 3 rue Lhomond, 75005
Paris. Tel: (33 1) 4432 0590.
Fax: 4432 0591.
www.jmplace.com. Europe's
best film magazine.
Premiere, 151 rue Anatole
France, 92534 Levallois-Perret.
Tel: (33 1) 4134 9111. Fax:
4134 9119. eduperray@hfp.fr.
www.premiere.fr. Monthly.
Studio Magazine, 4 rue de
Berri, 75008 Paris. Tel: (33 1)
5688 8888. Fax: 5688 8899.
studiomag@emapfrance.com.
Glossy.

Useful Addresses
**Centre National de la
Cinématographie**, 12 rue de
Lubeck, Paris 75016. Tel: (33
1) 4434 3440. Fax: 4755 0491.
webmaster@cnc.fr. www.cnc.fr.
Unifrance, 4 Villa Bosquet,
Paris 75007. Tel: (33 1) 4753
9580. Fax: 4705 9655.
www.unifrance.org.

GEORGIA
All Tel/Fax numbers begin (995 32)

Useful Addresses
**Georgian Cinematographic
Union**, Dzmebi Kakabadzeebi
Qucha 2, 380008 Tbilisi. Tel:
999 460. Fax: 935 097.
**Georgian Society of Audiovisual
Authors & Producers**, Dzmebi
Kakabadzeebis Qucha 2,
380008 Tbilisi. Tel: 999 324.
Fax: 988 325. www.gsaap.ge.
**Georgian State Institute of
Theatre & Film**, Rustavelis
Gamziri 37, 380008 Tbilisi.
Tel: 983 074. Fax: 991 153.
eliso@geo.net.ge.
**National Centre of
Cinematography**, Rustavelis
Gamziri 37, 380008 Tbilisi.
Tel: 984 201. Fax: 999 037.
www.kinocentre.myweb.ge.

GERMANY

Archives
Deutsches Filminstitut-DIF,
Schaumainkai 41, 60596
Frankfurt am Main. Tel: (49 69)
961 2200. Fax: 620 060. www.
deutsches-filminstitut.de.
**Deutsches Filmmuseum
Frankfurt am Main**,
Schaumainkai 41, 60596
Frankfurt am Main. Tel: (49 69)
2123 8830. Fax: 2123 7881.
www.deutsches-
filmmuseum.de.
**Filmmuseum Berlin-Deutsche
Kinemathek**, Potsdamer Str 2,
10785 Berlin. Tel: (49 30) 300
9030. Fax: 3009 0313.
www.filmmuseum-berlin.de.
**Kino Arsenal/Home of
Independent Cinema**,
Potsdamer Str 2, 10785 Berlin.
Tel: (49 30) 2695 5100. Fax:
2695 5111. www.fdk-berlin.de.
Münchner Filmmuseum, St
Jakobsplatz 1, 80331 Munich.
Tel: (49 89) 2332 2348. Fax:
2332 3931.
www.stadtmuseum-
online.de/filmmu.htm.

Bookshops
Buchhandlung Langenkamp,
Beckergrube 19, 23552
Lübeck. Tel: (49 451) 76479.
Fax: 72645.
Buchhandlung Walther König,
Ehrenstr 4, 50672, Cologne.
Tel: (49 221) 205 9625.
Fax: 205 9625.
www.buchhandlung-walther-
koenig.de.
H Lindemann's Bookshop,
Nadlerstr 4 & 10, 70173
Stuttgart 1. Tel: (49 711) 2489
9977. Fax: 236 9672.
fotobuecher@lindemanns.de.
www.lindemanns.de.
Photography and film literature.
Sautter & Lackmann,
Filmbuchhandlung,
Admiralitädstr 71/72, 20459

Hamburg. Tel: (49 40) 373 196.
Fax: 365 479. info@
sautter-lackmann.de.
**Marga Schoeller
Buecherstube**, Knesebeckstr
33, 10623 Berlin. Tel: (49 30)
881 1122. Fax: 881 8479.
schoeller.buecher@gmx.net.
**Verlag fur Filmschriften
Christian Unucka**, Postfach
63, 85239 Hebertshausen.
Tel: (49 8131) 13922. Fax:
10075. www.unucka.de.

Film Schools
**Deutsche Film und
Fernsehakademie Berlin**,
Potsdamer Str 2, 10785
Berlin.Tel: (49 30) 257 590.
Fax: 257 59161. info@dffb.de.
www.dffb.de. Four-year course.
**Filmakademie Baden-
Würtenberg**, Mathildenstr 20,
71638 Ludwigsburg. Tel: (49
7141) 969 108. Fax: 969 292.
www.filmakademie.de.
**Hochschule für Fernsehen
und Film**, Frankenthaler Str 23,
81539 Munich. Tel: (49 89) 689
570. Fax: 689 57189. www.hff-
muc.de. Four-year course.

Magazines
Blickpunkt Film, Einsteinring
24, 85609 Dornach. Tel: (49
89) 4511 4124. Fax: 4511
4451. www.blickpunktfilm.de.
Strong on box-office and
marketing; weekly.
EPD Medien, Postfach 50 05
50, 60439 Frankfurt am Main.
Tel: (49 69) 5809 8141. Fax:
5809 8261. medien@epd.de.
www.epd.de/medien.
Highbrow publication.
Twice weekly.
Film-Echo/Filmwoche,
Marktplatz 13, 65183
Wiesbaden. Tel: (49 611) 360
980. Fax: 372 878.
www.filmecho.de. Doyen of
the German trade; weekly.
Kino, Export-Union des

Deutschen Films GmbH, Sonnenstr 21, 80331 Munich. Tel: (49 89) 599 7870. Fax: 5997 8730. www.german-cinema.de. Published quarterly in English; yearbook also available.

Kino German Film & Intl Reports, Helgoländer Ufer 6, 10557 Berlin. Tel: (49 30) 391 6167. Fax: 391 2424. ronaldholloway@aol.com. Excellent twice-yearly.

Useful Addresses
Association of Distributors, Kreuzberger Ring 56, 65205 Wiesbaden. Tel: (49 611) 778 920. Fax: 778 9212. vdfkino@aol.com.
Association of Exhibitors, Grosse Praesidentenstr 9, 10178 Berlin. Tel: (49 30) 2300 4041. Fax: 2300 4026. info@kino-hdf.de.
Association of German Film Exporters, Tegernseer Landstr 75, 81539 Munich. Tel: (49 89) 692 0660. Fax: 692 0910. vdfe@kanziel-wedel.de.
Export Union, Sonnenstr 21, 80331 Munich. Tel: (49 89) 599 7870. Fax: 5997 8730. export-union@german-cinema.de. www.german-cinema.de.
Federal Film Board (FFA), Grosse Praesidentenstr 9, 10178 Berlin. Tel: (49 30) 275 770. Fax: 2757 7111. www.ffa.de.
New German Film Producers Association, Agnesstr 14, 80798 Munich. Tel: (49 89) 271 7430. Fax: 271 9728. ag-spielfilm@t-online.de.
Umbrella Organisation of the Film Industry, Kreuzberger Ring 56, 65205 Wiesbaden. Tel: (49 611) 778 9114. Fax: 778 9169. statistik@spio-fsk.de.

HONG KONG
All Tel/Fax numbers begin (852)

Useful Addresses
City Entertainment, [Magazine], Flat B2, 17/F, Fortune Factory Bldg, 40 Lee Chung Rd, Chai Wan. Tel: 2892 0155. Fax: 2838 4930. www.cityentertainment.com.hk. Indispensible bi-weekly. In Chinese.
Film Services Office, 40/F, Revenue Tower, 5 Gloucester Rd, Wan Chai. Tel: 2594 5745. Fax: 2824 0595. www.fso-tela.gov.hk.
Hong Kong Academy for Performing Arts, School of Film & Television, 1 Gloucester Rd, Wan Chai. Tel: 2584 8500. Fax: 2802 4372. www.hkapa.edu.
Hong Kong Film Academy, Room 908, 1066 Tung Chau West St, Lai Chi Kok, Kowloon. Tel: 2786 9349. Fax: 2742 7017. www.filmacademy.com.hk.
Hong Kong Film Archive, 50 Lei King Rd, Sai Wan Ho. Tel: 2739 2139. Fax: 2311 5229. www.filmarchive.gov.hk.
Hong Kong Film Awards Association, 8/F, Lokville Commercial Bldg, 25-27 Lock Rd, Tsim Sha Tsui, Kowloon. Tel: 2367 7892. Fax: 2723 9597. www.hkfaa.com.
Hong Kong Film Critics Society, Unit 104, 1/F, Corn Yan Centre, 1-5 Jupiter St, Tin Hau. Tel: 2575 5149. Fax: 2891 2048. www.filmcritics.org.hk.
Hong Kong Film Directors Guild, 2/F, 35 Ho Man Tin St, Kowloon. Tel: 2760 0331. Fax: 2713 2373.
Hong Kong Film Institute, 6/F, 295 Lai Chi Kok Rd, Kowloon. Tel: 2728 2690. Fax: 2728 5743. www.hkfilm.com.
Hong Kong, Kowloon and New Territories Motion Picture Industry Association, 13/F, Tung Wui Commercial Bldg, 27

Prat Ave, Tsim Sha Tsui, Kowloon. Tel: 2311 2692. Fax: 2311 1178. www.mpia.org.hk.
Hong Kong Theatres Association, 21/F, Hong Kong-Chinese Bank, 42 Yee Woo St, Causeway Bay. Tel: 2576 3833. Fax: 2576 1833.

HUNGARY
All Tel/Fax numbers begin (36 1)

Useful Addresses
Academy of Drama & Film, Szentkiralyi Utca 32A, H-1088, Budapest. Tel: 338 4855.
Association of Hungarian Film Artists, Városligeti Fasor 38, H-1068 Budapest. Tel/Fax: 342 4760. filmszovetseg@axelero.hu.
Filmvilag, [Magazine], Hollan Ernö Utca 38A, H-1137 Budapest. filmvilag@c3.hu. www.filmvilag.hu. Monthly.
Hungarian Film Union, Városligeti Fasor 38, H-1068 Budapest. Tel: 351 7760/1. Fax: 352 6734. filmunio@filmunio.hu.
Hungarian Motion Picture Foundation, Városligeti Fasor 38, H-1068 Budapest. Tel: 351 7696. Fax: 352 8789. www.mma.hu.
Hungarian National Film Archive, Budakeszi Ut 51B, H-1021 Budapest. Tel: 200 8739. Fax: 398 0781. filmintezet@ella.hu.

ICELAND
All Tel/Fax numbers begin (354)

Film Schools
Icelandic Film & Television Academy, Brautarholti 8, 105 Reykjavík. Tel: 562 6660. Fax: 562 6665. bjorn@hugsjon.is. www.spark.is.
Icelandic Film School, Laugarvegur 176, 105 Reykjavík.

kvikmyndaskoli@kvikmyndaskol
i.is. www.kvikmyndaskoli.is.

Useful Addresses
**Association of Icelandic Film
Directors**, Hverfisgata 46, 101
Reykjavík. Tel: 551 2260. Fax:
552 5154. icecorp@icecorp.is.
**Association of Icelandic Film
Distributors**, SAM-Bíóin,
Álfabakka 8, 109 Reykjavík.
Tel: 575 8900. Fax: 587 8910.
thorvaldur@sambio.is.
**Association of Icelandic Film
Producers**, Túngötu 14, PO
Box 5367, 125 Reykjavík. Tel:
863 3057. Fax: 555 3065.
www.producers.is.
Film Censor, Túngötu 14, 101
Reykjavík. Tel: 562 8020.
www.mmedia.is/~kvikmynd/.
Icelandic Film Centre,
Túngötu 14, 101 Reykjavík.
Tel: 562 3580. Fax: 562 7171.
www.icelandicfilmcentre.is.
**Icelandic Film Makers
Association**, PO Box 5162,
125 Reykjavík. Tel: 562 6660.
Fax: 562 6665.
bjorn@hugsjon.is.
**Icelandic Film & Television
Academy/EDDA Awards**,
Túngötu 14, 101 Reykjavík.
Tel: 562 3580. Fax: 562 7171.
bjorn@hugsjon.is.
National Film Archive,
Vesturgötu 11-13, 220
Hafnarfjordur. Tel: 565 5993.
Fax: 565 5994.
www.kvikmyndasafn.is.

INDIA

Magazines
Cinemaya, B 90 Defence
Colony, New Delhi 110 024.
Tel: (91 11) 461 7127.
Fax: 462 7211.
cinemaya@mantraonline.com.
Quarterly in English. The official
journal of NETPAC (Network for
Promotion of Asian Cinema).
Film India Worldwide, Uma

da Cunha, PO Box 11158,
Bombay 400020.
Fax: 2287 3513.
ugmedius@hathway.com.
News, views, reviews, interactive
databank. Published quarterly;
$5/issue + $5 annual postage.

Useful Addresses
Calcutta Film Festival,
Nandan Festival Complex, 1/1
AGC Bose Rd, Calcutta 700
020. www.calfilmfestival.org.
**Confederation of Indian
Industry**, 105 Kakad
Chambers, 132 Dr Annie
Besant Rd, Worli, Mumbai 400
018. Tel: (91 22) 24931790.
Fax: 2493 9463.
www.ciionline.org
Film Federation of India, B/3
Everest Bldg, Tardeo, Bombay
400 034. Tel/Fax: (91 22) 2351
5531. Fax: 2352 2062.
supransen22@hotmail.com.
**Film & Television Institute of
India**, [School], Law College
Rd, Pune 411 004. Tel: (91
020) 543 1817. Fax: 543 0416.
www.ftiindia.com.
**International Film Festival of
Kerala**, Kerala State
Chalachitra Academy, Elankom
Gardens, Trivandrum 695 010,
Kerala. Tel: (91 471) 310 323.
Fax: 310 322.
www.keralafilm.com.
**Mumbai International Film
Festival for Documentary,
Short & Animation Films**,
Films Division, 24 Dr G
Deshmukh Rd, Bombay 400
026. filmsd@bom4.vsnl.net.in.
www.filmsdivision.org.
National Film Archive, Law
College Rd, Pune 411 004.
Tel: (91 020) 565 8049.
Fax: 567 0027.
www.filmindia.com
/orgs/nfai/nfai.html.
**National Film Development
Corporation Ltd**, Discovery of
India Bldg, Nehru Centre, Dr

Annie Besant Rd, Worli,
Bombay 400 018. Tel: (91 22)
2492 6410.
www.nfdcindia.com.

IRAN
Listings appear on p.54.

IRELAND

Film Schools
**Ballyfermot College of Further
Education**, Ballyfermot Rd,
Dublin 10. Tel: (353 1) 626
9421. Fax: 626 6754.
www.bcfe.ie.
**Institute of Art, Design &
Technology**, Kill Ave, Dun
Laoghaire, Co Dublin. Tel: (353
1) 214 4600. Fax: 214 4700.
www.iadt.ie.

Useful Addresses
Ardmore Studios, Herbert Rd,
Bray, Co Wicklow. Tel: (353
404) 286 2971. Fax: 286 1894.
www.ardmore.ie.
Arts Council, 70 Merrion Sq,
Dublin 2. Tel: (353 1) 661 1840.
Fax: 676 0436.
www.artscouncil.ie.
Film Censor's Office, 16
Harcourt Terrace, Dublin 2. Tel:
(353 1) 676 1985. Fax: 676
1898.
Film Institute of Ireland, 6
Eustace St, Dublin 2. Tel: (353
1) 679 5744. Fax: 679 9657.
www.fii.ie.
Film Makers Ireland, The
Studio Bldg, Meeting House
Sq, Temple Bar, Dublin 2.
Tel: (353 1) 671 3525.
Fax: 671 4292. www.fmi.ie.
Irish Film Board, Rockfort
House, St Augustine St,
Galway, Co Galway. Tel: (353
91) 561 398. Fax: 561 405.
www.filmboard.ie.
Irish Film Centre, 6 Eustace
St, Dublin 2. Tel: (353 1) 679
5744. Fax: 679 9657.
www.cinemas@ifc.ie.

ISRAEL

Useful Addresses
Department of Cinema & Television, [Film school], David & Yoland Katz Faculty of the Arts, Tel Aviv University, Mexico Bldg, Tel Aviv. Tel: (972 3) 640 9483. Fax: 640 9935. www.tau.ac.il/arts.
Israel Film Archive, Jerusalem Film Centre, Derech Hebron, PO Box 8561, Jerusalem 91083. Tel: (972 2) 565 4333. Fax: 565 4335. www.jercin.org.il. Organisers of the Jerusalem Film Festival.
Israel Film Centre, Ministry of Industry & Trade, PO Box 299, Jerusalem. Tel: (972 2) 622 0608. Fax: 623 6303. www.moit.gov.il.
Israel Film Fund, 12 Yehudith Blvd, Tel Aviv 67016. Tel: (972 2) 562 8180. Fax: 562 5992. www.filmfund.org.il.

ITALY

Archives
Cineteca del Comune, Via Riva di Reno, 40122 Bologna. Tel: (39 051) 204 820. www.cinetecadibologna.it.
Cineteca del Friuli, Via Bini 50, Palazzo Gurisatti, 33013 Gemona del Friuli, Udine. Tel: (39 04) 3298 0458. Fax: 3297 0542. cdf@cinetecadelfriuli.org. http://cinetecadelfriuli.org. This excellent Italian archive conceived the idea for the Pordenone Silent Film Festival.
Cineteca Nazionale, Via Tuscolana 1524, 00173 Rome. Tel: (39 06) 722 941. Fax: 721 1619.
Fondazione Cineteca Italiana, Villa Reale, Via Palestro 16, 20121 Milan. Tel: (39 02) 799 224. Fax: 798 289. www.cinetecamilano.it/.
Fondazione Federico Fellini, Via

Oberdan 1, 47900 Rimini. Tel (39 0541) 50085. Fax: 57378. www.federicofellini.it/.
Museo Nazionale del Cinema, Via Montebello 15, 10124 Turin. Tel: (39 011) 812 2814. www.museonazionaledel cinema.org.

Film Schools
Magica (Master Europeo in Gestione di Impresa Cinematografica e Audiovisiva), Via Lucullo 7 Int 8, 00187 Rome. Tel: (39 06) 420 0651. Fax: 4201 0898. www.mediamaster.org.
Scuola Nazionale di Cinema, Via Tuscolana 1524, 00173 Rome. Tel: (39 06) 722 941. Fax: 721 1619. www.snc.it.

Magazines
Griffithiana, Cineteca del Friuli, Via Bini 50, Palazzo Gurisatti, 33013 Gemona, Udine. Tel: (39 04) 3298 0458. Fax: 3297 0542.www.cinetecadelfriuli.org. Silent cinema and animation, in English and Italian; quarterly.
Nocturno, Via Trieste 42, 20064 Gorgonzola, Milan. Tel: (39 02) 9534 0057. www.nocturno.it.
Rivista del Cinematografo, Via Giuseppe Palombini 6, 00165 Rome. Tel: (39 06) 663 7514. Fax: 663 7321. www.cinematografo.it. Important Italian monthly.

Useful Addresses
Anica, Viale Regina Margherita 286, 00198 Rome. Tel: (39 06) 442 5961. Fax: 440 4128. anica@anica.it. www.anica.it.
Associazione Generale Italiana Dello Spettacollo (AGIS), Via di Villa Patrizi 10, 00161 Rome. Tel: (39 06) 884 731. Fax: 4423 1838. www.agisweb.it.
Cinecittà Holding Spa, Via Tuscolana 1055, 00173 Rome.

Tel: (39 06) 722 861. Fax: 722 1883. www.cinecitta.com.
Istituto Luce, Via Tuscolana 1055, 00173 Rome. Tel: (39 06) 729 921. Fax: 722 1127. luce@luce.it. www.luce.it.
Italia Cinema, Via Aureliana 63, 00187 Rome. Tel: (39 06) 4201 2539. Fax: 4200 3530. www.italiacinema.net.
Libreria Il Leuto, [Bookshop], Via Di Monte Brianzo 86, 00186 Rome. Tel: (39 06) 686 9269.
Rai Cinema, Piazza Adriana 12, 00193 Rome. Tel: (39 06) 684 701. Fax: 687 2141. www.raicinema.it.

JAPAN
All Tel/Fax numbers begin (81 3)

Archives
Kawakita Memorial Film Institute, Kawakita Memorial Bldg, 18 Ichiban-cho, Chiyoda-ku, Tokyo 102-0082. Tel: 3265 3281. Fax: 3265 3276. info@kawakita-film.or.jp. www.kawakita-film.or.jp.
National Film Center, 3-7-6 Kyobashi, Chuo-ku, Tokyo 104-0031. Tel: 5777 8600.

Useful Addresses
Motion Picture Producers Association of Japan, Tokyu Ginza Bldg 3F, 2-15-2 Ginza, Chuo-ku, Tokyo 104-0061. Tel: 3547 1800. Fax: 3547 0909. eiren@mc.neweb.ne.jp.
Nihon University College of Art, [Film schoo], 4-8-24 Kudanminami, Chiyoda-ku, Tokyo 102. Tel: 5275 8110. Fax: 5275 8310. www.nihon-u.ac.jp.
Shochiku Co Ltd, Intl Business Division, Togeki Bldg, 1-1 Tsukiji, 4-Chome, Chuo-ku, Tokyo 104-8422. Tel: 5550 1623. Fax: 5550 1654. ibd@shochiku.co.jp.

Toei Co Ltd, Intl Dept, 2-17 Ginza, 3 Chome, Chuo-ku, Tokyo 104-8108. Tel: 3535 7621. Fax: 3535 7622. www.international@toei.co.jp.
Toho International Co Ltd, 15th Floor, Yurakucho Denki Bldg, 1-7-1 Yurakucho, Chiyoda-ku, Tokyo 100-0006. Tel: 3213 6821. Fax: 3213 6825. www.toho.co.jp.
Tokyo International Anime Fair, 29F No 1 Bldg, 2-8-1 Nishi-Shinjuku, Shinjuku-ku, Tokyo 163-8001. Tel: 5320 4786. Fax: 5388 1463. tokyo-anime-fair@nifty.com.
UniJapan Film, 6-5 Ginza, 1-Chome, Chuo-ku, Tokyo 104-0061. Tel: 3538 0621. Fax: 3538 0622. t-nishimura@unijapan.org.

KAZAKHSTAN
All Tel/Fax numbers begin (7 3262)

Useful Addresses
Film ASU Anima, 29 Kurmangazy, Suite 319, 480067 Almaty. Tel: 796 768. Fax: 930 113. aksai.ltd@nursat.kz.
Firm-Kino, [Producer], 16 Al-Farabi Ave, 480067 Almaty. Tel: 482 606. Fax: 932 978. aksai.ltd@nursat.kz.
Kazakh Film Studios, 16 Al-Farabi Ave, 480067 Almaty. Tel: 482 211. Fax: 480 909. filmcompany@nursat.kz.
Otau Cinema, 62 Aiteke Bi, 480067 Almaty. Tel/Fax: 507 250. saltanat@oc.kz.

LATVIA
All Tel/Fax numbers begin (371 7)

Archives
Arsenals, Marstalu 14, Riga, LV-1050. Tel: 210 114. Fax: 782 0445. arsenals@latnet.lv. www.arsenals.lv.
Riga Film Museum, 3 Smerla

St, Riga LV-1006. Tel/Fax: 754 5099. kinomuz @com.latnet.lv.

Useful Addresses
EHO Filma, Bruninieku 18 K/3, Riga LV-1001. Tel/Fax: 845 309. eho@eho.lv. www.eho.lv.
Kaupo Filma, Lacplesa 27, Riga, LV-1011. Tel: 281 720. Fax: 240 542. kaupo@latnet.lv.
National Film Centre, Elizabetes 49, Riga, LV-1010. Tel: 505 074. Fax: 505 077. nfc@nfc.gov.lv. www.nfc.lv.
Platforma Filma, Dzintaru Prospekts 19, Jurmala LV-2015. Tel: 754 647. Fax: 811 308.
Rija Films, Meness 4, Riga LV-1013. Tel: 362 656. Fax: 339 198. rijafilms@rijafilms.lv.

LEBANON
All Tel/Fax numbers begin (961 1)

Mideast Film Foundation, PO Box 175088, Beirut. Tel: 202 411. Fax: 585 693. info@mefilmfestival.org.
National Film Centre, Ministry of Culture, Unisco Palace, Beirut. Tel: 807 181. Fax: 807 206.

LITHUANIA

Film Schools
Educational Film & TV Studio of Lithuanian Music Academy, Kosciuskos 12, 2001 Vilnius. Tel/Fax: (370 5) 212 4560. tvac2@takas.lt.
Vilnius Academy of Art, Laboratory of Art of Photography & Media, Maironio 6, 2600 Vilnius. Tel: (370 5) 261 0539. Fax: 261 9962. www.media.vda.lt.

Useful Addresses
Association of Independent Producers, Sevcenkos 16A, 2009 Vilnius. Tel: (370 5) 233

2379. Fax: 233 2374. juzenas@takas.lt.
International Film Festival-Film Spring, Nemencines 4, 2016 Vilnius. Tel: (370 5) 276 4218. Fax: 276 3463. info@kino.lt. www.kino.lt.
Lithuanian Association of Cinema Distributors, Savanoriu 192, 3000 Kaunas. Tel: (370 7) 333 433. Fax: 333 833. film@acme.lt.
Lithuanian State Archive of Vision & Sound, O Milasiaus 19, 2016 Vilnius. Tel: (370 5) 276 8209. Fax: 276 4489. lvga@takas.lt.
Lithuanian Union of Cinematographers, Birutes 18, 2004 Vilnius. Tel/Fax: (370 5) 212 0759. lks1@auste.elnet.lt.
Ministry of Culture, Basanaviciaus 5, 2600 Vilnius. Tel: (370 5) 261 9486. Fax: 262 0768. culture@muza.lt. www.muza.lt.
Museum of Theatre, Music & Cinema, Vilniaus 41, 2001 Vilnius. Tel: (370 5) 279 1051. Fax: 262 2406. www.teatras.mch.mii.lt.
Public Institution-Kino Aljansas, Ozo G 4, 2600 Vilnius. Tel: (370 6) 164 5643. info@kino.lt.

LUXEMBOURG
All Tel/Fax numbers begin (352)

Useful Addresses
Association des Techniciens et des Acteurs du Cinema (ATAC), 57 Rue de l'Hippodrome, L-1730 Luxembourg. Tel: 483 823. Fax: 490 605.
Association Luxemboureoise des Realisateurs et Scenaristes, 102 Rue Ermesinde, L-1469 Luxembourg. Tel/Fax: 227 681. pkmw@pt.lu
Cinémathèque Municipale de la Ville de Luxembourg,

[Archive], 10 Rue Eugene Ruppert, L-2453 Luxembourg. Tel: 4796 2644. Fax: 407 519. cinematheque@vdl.lu.

Film Fund Luxembourg, 5 Rue Large, L-1917 Luxembourg. Tel: 478 2165. Fax: 220 963. www.filmfund.lu.

Media Desk Luxembourg, 5 Rue Large, L-1917 Luxembourg. www.mediadesk.lu.

MALAYSIA

National Film Development Corporation (FINAS), Merdeka Studio Complex, Jalan Hulu Kelang, 68000 Ampang, Selangor DE. Tel: (603) 4108 5722. Fax: 4107 5216.

MEXICO

All Tel/Fax numbers begin (52 5)

Useful Addresses
Association of Mexican Film Producers & Distributors, Avenida División del Norte 2462, Piso 8, Colonia Portales, México DF. Tel: 688 0705. Fax: 688 7251.

Cineteca Nacional, [Archive], Avenida México-Coyoacán 389, Col Xoco, México DF. Tel: 5422 1110. www.cinetecanacional.net.

Dirección General de Radio, Televisión y Cinematografía (RTC), Roma 41, Col Juárez, México DF. Tel: 140 8010. ecardenas@segob.gob.mx.

Instituto Mexicano de Cinematografía (IMCINE), Insurgentes Sur 674 Col del Valle, CP 03100, México DF. Contact: Miguel Ángel Ortega: mercaint@institutomexicanodec inematografía.gob.mx.

MOROCCO
Moroccan Cinematographic Centre, Quartier Industriel, Ave

Al Majd, BP 421, Rabat. Tel: (212 7) 798 110. Fax: 798 105. www.mincom.gov.ma/ cinemaroc/ccm.

NETHERLANDS

Archives
Filmmuseum, Rien Hagen, Vondelpark 3, PO Box 74782, 1070 BT Amsterdam. Tel: (31 20) 589 1400. Fax: 683 3401. www.filmmuseum.nl.

Netherlands Institut voor Beeld en Geluid, PO Box 1060, 1200 BB Hilversum. Tel: (31 35) 677 2672/7. Fax: 677 2835. www.naa.nl.

Film Schools
Maurits Binger Film Institute, Nieuwezijds Voorburgwal 4-10, 1012 RZ Amsterdam. Tel: (31 20) 530 9630. Fax: 530 9631. www.binger.ahk.nl.

Netherlands Film & Television Academy (NFTA), Markenplein 1, 1011 MV Amsterdam. Tel: (31 20) 527 7333. Fax: 527 7344. www.nfta.ahk.nl.

Magazines
Holland Animation Newsbrief, Hoogt 4, 3512 GW Utrecht. Tel/Fax: (31 30) 240 0768. info@holland-animation.nl. www.holland-animation.nl. Twice yearly.

Skrien, Vondelpark 3, 1071 AA Amsterdam. Tel: (31 20) 689 3831. skrien@xs4all.nl. Excellent, enthusiastic monthly.

Useful Addresses
Ciné-Qua-Non, [Bookshop], Staalstraat 14, 1011 JL Amsterdam. Tel: (31 20) 625 5588.

Circle of Dutch Film Critics (KNF), PO Box 10650, 1011 ER Amsterdam. Tel: (31 6) 2550 0668. Fax: 627 5923. knfilm@xs4all.nl.

Dutch Film Fund, Jan Luykenstraat 2, 1071 CM Amsterdam. Tel: (31 20) 570 7676. Fax: 570 7689. info@filmfund.nl.

Ministry of Education, Culture & Science, Arts Dept, Sector Film, Europaweg 4, PO Box 25000, 2700 LZ Zoetermeer. Tel: (31 79) 323 4321. Fax: 323 4959. j.j.cassidy@minocw.nl.

Netherlands Cinematographic Federation (NFC), Jan Luykenstraat 2, PO Box 75048, 1070 AA Amsterdam. Tel: (31 20) 679 9261. Fax: 675 0398. info@nfc.org.

Netherlands Institute For Animation Film, PO Box 9358, 5000 HJ Tilburg. Tel: (31 13) 535 4555. Fax: 580 0057. niaf@niaf.nl.

More information can be found on www.hollandfilm.nl (click on Who's Where).

NEW ZEALAND

Useful Addresses
Film New Zealand, PO Box 24142, Wellington. Tel: (64 4) 385 0766. Fax: 385 8755. info@filmnz.org.nz.

New Zealand Film Archive, PO Box 11449, Wellington. Tel: (64 4) 384 7647. Fax: 382 9595. nzfa@actrix.gen.nz.

New Zealand Film Commission, PO Box 11546, Wellington. Tel: (64 4) 382 7680. Fax: 384 9719. marketing@nzfilm.co.nz.

Office of Film & Literature Classification, PO Box 1999, Wellington. Tel: (64 4) 471 6770. Fax: 471 6781. information@ censorship.govt.nz.

Onfilm, [Magazine], PO Box 5544, Wellesley St, Auckland. Tel: (64 9) 630 8940. Fax: 630 1046. www.profile.co.nz. Film,

TV and video for New Zealand.
Screen Producers &
Directors Association, PO
Box 9567, Wellington. Tel: (64
4) 802 4931. Fax: 385 8755.
info@spada.co.nz.

NORWAY
All Tel/Fax numbers begin (47)

Useful Addresses
Film & Kino, [Magazine],
National Association of
Municipal Cinemas, PO Box
446 Sentrum, 0104 Oslo. Tel:
2247 4610. Fax: 2247 4699.
www.filmweb.no/filmogkino/tids
skriftet. The best film magazine
in Scandinavia.
Henie-Onstad Art Centre,
[Archive], 1311 Hovikodden.
Director: Gavin Jantjens. Tel:
6780 4880. Fax: 6754 3270.
www.hok.no.
Norwegian Film & TV
Producers Association,
Dronningens Gt 16, 0152 Oslo.
Tel: 2311 9313.
Fax: 2311 9316.
produsentforeningen@produse
ntforeningen.no.
Norwegian Film Censorship
Board, PO Box 371 Sentrum,
0102 Oslo. Tel: 2247 4660.
Fax: 2247 4694.
post@filmtilsynet.no.
Norwegian Film Development,
PO Box 904 Sentrum, 0104
Oslo. Tel: 2282 2400. Fax:
2282 2422.
mail@norskfilmutvikling.no.
Norwegian Film Fund, PO
Box 752 Sentrum, 0106 Oslo.
Tel: 2247 8040. Fax: 2247
8041. post@filmfondet.no.
Norwegian Film Institute, Dept
of International Relations, PO
Box 482 Sentrum, 0105 Oslo.
Tel: 2247 4759. Fax: 2247
4597. int@nfi.no. [Also archive].
Norwegian Film Workers
Association, Dronningens Gt
16, 0152 Oslo. Tel: 2247 4640.

Fax: 2247 4689.

PAKISTAN

Useful Addresses
Ministry of Culture, Block D,
Pak Secretariat, Islamabad.
Tel: (92 51) 920 1970.
Pakistan Film Producers
Association, Regal Cinema
Bldg, Sharah-e-Quaid-e-Azam,
Lahore. Tel: (92 42) 732 2904.
Fax: 724 1264.

PERU
All Tel/Fax numbers begin (51 1)

Useful Addresses
Asociación de Cineastas del
Peru, Calle Manco Capac 236,
Lima-18. Tel: 446 1829.
cineperu@chavin.rcp.net.pe.
Consejo Nacional de
Cinematografía (Conacine),
Museo de la Nación, Avenida
Javier Prado 2465, Lima.
Tel/Fax: 225 6479.
Encuentro Latinoamericano
de Cine, Centro Cultural de la
Universidad Católica, Avenida
Camino Real 1075, Lima-27.
Tel/Fax: 616 1616.
elcine@pucp.edu.pe.
Filmoteca de Lima, Museo de
Arte, Paseo Colón 125, Lima-
1. Fax: 331 0126.
filmolima@terra.com.pe.
Sociedad Peruana de
Productores y Realizadores
Cinematográficos (SOCINE),
Calle Manuel A Fuentes 671,
Lima-27. Tel/Fax: 221 3746.

POLAND

Archives
Muzeum Kinematografi, Pl
Zwyciestwa 1, 90 312 Lódz.
Tel: (48 42) 674 0957.
Fax: 674 9006.
National Film Library, Ul
Pulawska 61, 00 975 Warsaw.
Tel: (48 22) 845 5074.

www.fn.org.pl.

Magazines
Film, Ul Pulawska 61, 02 595
Warsaw. Tel: (48 22) 455 235.
Fax: 453 908. Popular monthly
with international slant.
Kino, Ul Chelmska 21, 00 724
Warsaw. Tel: (48 22) 841 1211.
Fax: 841 9057.
www.kino.onet.pl. Monthly.

Useful Addresses
Film Polski, Ul Mazowiecki
6/8, 00 048 Warsaw.
www.filmpolski.com.pl.
National Film, Television &
Theatre School, 63 Targowa
Str, 90 323 Lódz.
Tel: (48 42) 634 5820.
www.filmschool.lodz.pl.
Polish TV (TVP), Ul JP
Woronicza 17, 00-999 Warsaw.
Tel: (48 22) 547 6139. Fax: 547
7583. tvp@tvp.pl. www.tvp.pl.

PORTUGAL

Useful Addresses
Cinemateca Portuguesa,
[Archive], Rua Barata Salgueiro
63, 1269-059 Lisbon. Tel: (351
21) 359 6200. Fax: 352 3180.
www.cinemateca.pt.
Estreia, [Magazine], Rua de
Anibal Cunha 84, Sala 1.6,
4050-846 Porto Tel: (351 22)
207 6050. Fax: 207 6059.
www.estreia.online.pt. Bi-
monthly; international and
Portuguese topics.
Institute of Cinema,
Audiovisual & Multimedia
(ICAM), Rua de S Pedro de
Alcântara 45, 1°, 1250 Lisbon.
Tel: (351 21) 323 0800. Fax:
343 1952. mail@icam.pt.
www.icam.pt.
Short Film Agency, Apartado
214, 4481-911 Vila do Conde.
Tel: (351 25) 264 6683.
Fax: 263 8027.
www.curtasmetragens.pt.

PUERTO RICO

All Tel/Fax numbers begin (1 787)

Useful Addresses
Film & Audiovisual Producers Association, PO Box 190399, San Juan 00919-0399. Tel: 725 3565. Fax: 724 4333. tvegsjpr@prtc.net.
Puerto Rico Film Commission, PO Box 2350, San Juan 00936-2360. Tel: 754 7110. Fax: 756 5706. lavelez@pridco.com. Contact: Laura A Vélez.

ROMANIA

All Tel/Fax numbers begin (40 1)

Useful Addresses
Arhiva Nationala de Filma, [Archive], 4-6 Dem I Dobrescu Str, Sector 1, Bucharest. Tel: 313 4904. Fax: 313 4904. anf@xnet.ro.
National Film Council, Str Dem I Dobrescu 4-6, Bucharest. Tel: 310 4301. Fax: 310 4300. cncin@pcnet.ro.
Romania Film, Bd Aviatorilor 106, Bucharest . Tel: 230 5063. Fax: 230 7372.
Universitatea de Arta Teatrala si Cinematografica, [Film school], Str Matei Voievod 75-77, Bucharest. Tel: 252 8001. www.edu.ro/uatcb.htm.

RUSSIA

All Tel/Fax numbers begin (7 095)

Useful Addresses
Alliance of Independent Distribution Companies. Tel: 243 4741. Fax: 243 5582. felix_rosental@yahoo.com.
Double D Research & Information Group, 13 Vassilyevskaya St, Moscow 123825/Postal address: 28-2-16 Bol Polyanka St, Moscow 119180. Tel/Fax: 238 2984. vengern@df.ru.

Gosfilmofond of Russia, [Archive], Belye Stolby, Moscow 142050. Tel: 546 0520. Fax: 548 0512. www.gosfilmofond.ru.
Iskusstvokino, [Magazine], 9 Ul Usievich, Moscow 125319. Tel: 151 5651. Fax: 151 0272. www.kinoart.ru. The most authoritative Russian monthly.
Ministry of Culture of the Russian Federation, Film Service, 7 Maly Gnezdnikovsky Lane, Moscow 103877. Tel: 923 8677/229 7055. Fax: 299 9666.
National Academy of Cinema Arts & Sciences, 13 Vassilyevskaya St, Moscow 123825. Tel: 200 4284. Fax: 251 5370. unikino@aha.ru.
Russian Guild of Film Directors, 13 Vassilyevskaya St, Moscow 123825. Tel: 251 5889. Fax: 254 2100.
Russian Guild of Producers, 1 Mosfilmovskaya St, Moscow 119858. Tel: 745 5635/ 143 9028. plechev@mtu-net/ru.
Union of Film makers of Russia13 Vassilyevskaya St, Moscow 123825. Tel: 250 4114. Fax: 250 5370. unikino@aha.ru.

SERBIA & MONTENEGRO

All Tel/Fax numbers begin (381 11)

Useful Addresses
Association of Film Producers, Kneza Viselava 88, 11000 Belgrade. Tel: 323 1943. Fax: 324 3482. info@afp.yu. www.afp.co.yu.
Beograd Film, (Chain of Theatres), Terazije 40, 11040 Belgrade. Tel: 688 940. Fax: 687 952. www.beogradfilm.com.
FEST Belgrade International Film Festival, Majke Jevrosime 20, 11000 Belgrade. Tel: 334

6837. Fax: 334 6946. info@fest.org.yu. www.fest.org.yu.
Film Distributors' Association of Yugoslavia (Tuck Film), Velikomoravska 11-15, 11000 Belgrade. Tel: 262 2555. Fax: 413 177. www.tuck.co.yu.
International Festival of Auteur Films, Makedonska 22/VII, 11000 Belgrade. Tel: 324 8554. Fax: 324 8659. yugofilm@yufilm.org.
Yugoslav Film Archive, Knez Mihailova 19, 11000 Belgrade. Tel: 622 555. Fax: 622 587. www.kinoteka.org.yu.
Yugoslav Film Institute, Cika Ljubina 15/II, 11000 Belgrade. Tel: 625 131. Fax: 634 253. ifulm@eunet.yu.

SINGAPORE

All Tel/Fax numbers begin (65)

Useful Addresses
Cinematograph Film Exhibitors Association, 13th & 14th Storey, Shaw Centre, 1 Scotts Rd, Singapore 228208. Tel: 6235 2077. Fax: 6235 2860.
School for Film & Media Studies, Ngee Ann Polytechnic, Block 52, 535 Clementi Rd, Singapore 599489. Tel: 6460 6992. Fax: 6462 5617. www.np.edu.sg.
Singapore Film Commission, 140 Hill St, Mita Bldg #04-01, Singapore 179369. Tel: 6837 9943. Fax: 6336 1170. www.sfc.org.sg.
Singapore Film Society, Golden Village Marina, 5A Raffles Ave, #03-01 Marina Leisureplex, Singapore 039801. Fax: 6250 6167. www.sfs.org.sg.

SLOVAKIA

All Tel/Fax numbers begin (421 2)

Useful Addresses
Academy of Music & Dramatic Art (VSMU), Film & Television Faculty, Ventúrska 3, 813 01 Bratislava. Tel: 5930 1461/5443 2306. www.vsmu.sk.
Association of Slovak Film & TV Directors, Konventná 8, 800 00 Bratislava. hledik@artfilm.sk.
Association of Slovak Film Producers, Tekovská 7, 821 09 Bratislava. Tel: 4445 8511/5556 1045. Fax: 4445 8510. unfilm@webdesign.sk.
Slovak Film Institute, Grösslingova 38, 811 09 Bratislava. Tel: 5710 1501/27. sfu@sfu.sk. www.sfu.sk.
Union of Slovak Film Distributors, Priemyselná 1, 821 09 Bratislava. Tel: 5557 3311. Fax: 5556 1051.

SLOVENIA
All Tel/Fax numbers begin (386 1)

Useful Addresses
Association of Slovenian Film Makers, Miklosiceva 26, Ljubljana. e-mail. dsfu@guest.arnes.si.
Association of Slovenian Film Producers, Brodisce 23, Trzin, 1234 Menges. dunja.klemenc@guest.arnes.si
Slovenian Cinematheque, Miklosiceva 38, Ljubljana. Tel: 434 2520. silvan.furlan@kinoteka.si.
Slovenian Film Fund, Miklosiceva 38, 1000 Ljubljana. Tel: 431 3175. info@film-sklad.si.

SOUTH AFRICA

Useful Addresses
Apollo Film Festival, Victoria West. Mobile: (27) 08257 21682. www.apollotheatre.co.za.

Cape Film Commission, 9th Floor, Tarquin House, Corner Loop & Shortmarket St, Cape Town 8001. Tel: (27 21) 487 2795. Fax: 487 2977. www.capefilmcommission. co.za.
CityVarsity Film, Television & Multimedia School, 32 Kloof St, Cape Town 8000. Tel: (27 21) 423 3366. Fax: 423 6300. www.cityvarsity.co.za.
Durban International Film Festival, Centre for Creative Arts, Durban 4001. Tel: (27 31) 260 2949. Fax: 260 3074. rorvikp@nu.ac.za.
Film Afrika, PO Box 53357, Kenilworth, Cape Town 7745. Tel: (27 21) 461 7950. Fax: 461 7951. www.film-afrika.com.
Gauteng Film Office, 88 Fox St, Johannesburg/PO Box 61840, Marshalltown 2107. Tel: (27 11) 833 8750. Fax: 833 8930. andy@gfo.co.za. Contact: Andy Stead.
Independent Producers Organisation, PO Box 2631, Saxonwold 2132. Tel: (27 11) 726 1189. Fax: 482 4621. www.ipo.org.za.
M-Net Local Productions, PO Box 2963, Randburyg 2123. Tel: (27 11) 686 6123. Fax: 686 6643. www.mnet.co.za..
National Film & Video Foundation, Aida House, 40 Central Ave, Illovo, Johannesburg 2196. Tel: (27 11) 268 2900. Fax: 268 2909. www.nvfv.co.za.

SOUTH KOREA
All Tel/Fax numbers begin (82 2)

Useful Addresses
CJ Entertainment, [Producer/Distributor], 11th Floor, Cheiljedang Bldg, 500 5 Ga, Namdaemoon-No, Chung-ku, Seoul 100-802. Tel: 726 8565. Fax: 726 8291.

Cineclick Asia, [Producer/Distributor], Incline Bldg, 3rd Floor, 891-37 Daechi-Dong, Kangnam-gu, Seoul 135-280. Tel: 538 0211 ext 212. Fax: 538 0479.
Cinema Service, [Producer/Distributor], 5th Floor, Yeoksam Bldg, 824 Yeoksam-dong, Kangnam-gu, Seoul 135-080. Tel: 2192 8730. Fax: 2192 8791.
Kangjegyu Films, [Producer/Distributor], 2F, Olympia Center B/D 828-10, Yoksam-dong, Kangnam-ku, Seoul 135-080. Tel: 2193 2001. Fax: 2193 2199. paragon@kjgfilm.com.
Korean Film Archive, 700 Seocho-dong, Seocho-gu, Seoul 137-718. Tel: 521 3147/9. Fax: 582 6213. www.koreafilm.or.kr.
Korean Film Commission (KOFIC), 206-46, Cheongnyangni-dong, Dongdaemun-gu, Seoul 130-010. Tel: 958 7581. Fax: 958 7592. www.kofic.or.kr.
Mirovision, [Producer/Distributor], 1-151 Shinmunro, 2 Ga, Chongro-gu, Seoul 110-062. Tel: 737 1185. Fax: 737 1184. cassie@mirovision.com.
Tube Entertainment, [Producer/Distributor], 664-21 Shinsa-dong, Kangnam-ku, Seoul 135-120. Tel: 547 6026. Fax: 547 8691. cat@tube-entertainment.co.kr.

SPAIN

Archives
Filmoteca de la Generalitat de Catalunya, Carrer del Portal de Santa Madrona 6-8, Barcelona 08001. Tel: (34 93) 316 2780. Fax: 316 2783. www.cultura.gencat.net.
Filmoteca Espanola, Calle Magdalena 10, 28012 Madrid.

Tel: (34 91) 467 2600.
Fax: 467 2611.
www.cultura.mecd.es/cine/film/
filmoteca.isp.
Filmoteca Vasca, Avenida
Sancho el Sabio, 17 Trasera,
Donostia, 20010 San
Sebastian. Tel: (34 943) 468
484. Fax: 469 998.
www.filmotecavasca.com.

Film Schools
**Academia de las Artes y las
Ciencias Cinematograficas
de Espana**, Sagasta 20, 3°
Derecha., 28004 Madrid.
Tel: (34 91) 593 4648.
Fax: 593 1492.
inforaca@infonegocio.com.
**Centre d'Estudis
Cinematogràfics de Catalunya**,
Calle Torre Velez 33, 08041
Barcelona. Tel: (34 93) 433
5501. Fax: 450 4283.
www.cecc.es.
**Escola Superior de Cinema
Audiovisuals de Catalunya
(ESCAC)**, Carrer Colom 84-90,
08222 Terrassa. Tel: (34 93)
736 1555. www.escac.es.
**Escuela de Cinematografía y
de la Audiovisual de la
Comunidad de Madrid (ECAM)**,
Juan de Orduna 3, Ciudad de
la Imagen, 28223 Pozuelo de
Alarcón, Madrid. Tel: (34 91)
512 1060. Fax: 512 1070.
www.ecam.es.
**Instituto de la Cinematografía
y de las Artes Audiovisuales
(ICAA)**, Plaza del Rey 1, 28004
Madrid. Tel: (34 91) 701 7000.
www.cultura.mecd.es/cine.
Media Business School,
Velazquez 14, 28001 Madrid,
Spain. Tel: (34 91) 575 9583.
Fax: 431 3303.
www.mediaschool.org.

Magazines
Academia & Boletín, Sagasta
20, 3° Derecha, 28004 Madrid.
Tel: (34 91) 593 4648/448

2321. Fax: 593 1492.
www.sie.es/acacine/boletin.
Excellent twice yearly.
Cine & TV Informe, Gran Via
64, 4° Derecha, 28013 Madrid.
Tel: (34 91) 541 5402.
Fax: 559 8110.
www.cineytele.com. Monthly.
Cinevideo 20, Clara del Rey
71, Bajo B, 28002 Madrid.
Tel: (34 91) 519 6586.
Fax: 519 5119.
www.cinevideo20.es.
Fotogramas, Gran Via de les
Corts Catalanes 133, 08014
Barcelona. Tel: (34 93) 223
2790. Fax: 432 2907.
www.fotogramas.es. Monthly.

Useful Addresses
Andalucia Film Commission,
Avenida Matemáticos Rey
Pastor y Castro s/n, 41092
Seville. Tel: (34 95) 446 7310/3.
Fax: 446 1516.
www.andaluciafc.org/afc.
Catalan Films & TV, Portal
Santa Madrona 6-8, 08001
Barcelona. Tel: (34 93) 316
2780. Fax: 316 2781.
**Federación de Entidades de
Empresarios de Cine de
España**, Gran Vía 66, 2°
Izquierda, 28013 Madrid. Tel:
(34 91) 542 0996. Fax: 548
2780. www.feece.com.
**Federation of Associations of
Spanish Audiovisual Producers
(FAPAE)**, Calle Luis Bunuel 2-2°
Izquierda, Ciudad de la
Imagen, Pozuelo de Alarcón,
28223 Madrid. Tel: (34 91) 512
1660. Fax: 512 0148.
web@fapae.es. www.fapae.es.
**Federation of Cinema
Distributors (FEDICINE)**,
Orense 33, 3°B, 28020 Madrid.
Tel: (34 91) 556 9755. Fax: 555
6697. www.fedicine.com.
Ocho y Medio, [Bookshop],
Martin de los Heros 23, 28008
Madrid. Tel: (34 91) 559 0628.
Fax: 540 0672.

www.ochoymedio.com.

SRI LANKA
All Tel/Fax numbers begin (94 1)

Useful Addresses
Ceylon Theatres Ltd,
[Producer, Exhibitor &
Importer], 8 Sir C Gardiner
Mawatha, Colombo 02.
Tel: 431 242/109.
Cinesith, [Magazine], Asian
Film Centre, 118 Dehiwala Rd,
Boralesgamuwa. Fax: 509 553.
afc@sri.lanka.net.
www.lanka.net/asianfilm/.
Sri Lanka's only serious film
magazine; quarterly.
Eap Film & Theaters (PVT) Ltd,
[Producer, Distributor, Exhibitor
& Importer], Savoy Bldg, 12
Galle Rd, Wellawatta, Colombo
06. Tel: 552 877. Fax: 552
878. eapfilms@sltnet.lk.
National Film Corporation,
[Distributor & Importer], 303
Bauddhaloka Mawatha,
Colombo 07. Tel: 580 247.
Fax: 585 526.
filmcorp@sltnet.lk.

SWEDEN

Archives
Cinemateket, Swedish Film
Institute, Box 27126, SE-102
52 Stockholm. Tel: (46 8) 665
1100. Fax: 666 3698.
info@sfi.se. www.sfi.se.
**Swedish National Archive for
Recorded Sound & Moving
Images**, Box 24124, SE-
10451 Stockholm. Tel: (46 8)
783 3700. Fax: 663 1811.
info@ljudochbildarkivet.se.

Film Schools
**University College of Film,
Radio, Television & Theatre**,
Box 27090, SE-102 51
Stockholm. Tel: (46 8) 665
1300. Fax: 662 1484.
www.draminst.se.

University of Stockholm,
Department of Cinema Studies,
Borgvägen 1-5, Box 27062,
SE-102 51 Stockholm. Tel: (46
8) 674 7000.

Magazines
Film International, Lilla
Fiskaregatan 10, SE-222 22
Lund. Tel/Fax: (46 46) 137 914.
www.filmint.nu.
Teknik& Mnniska (TM),
Borgvgen 1-5, PO Box 27126,
SE-102 52 Stockholm. Tel: (46
8) 665 1100. Fax: 662 2684.
tm@sfi.se. www.sfi.se/tm. Bi-
monthly; Swedish production.

Useful Addresses
Movie Art Gallery,
[Bookshop], Sodra Hamngatan
2, SE-411 06 Goteborg.
Tel/Fax: (46 31) 151 412.
www.movieartofsweden.com.
Swedish Film Distributors
Association, Box 23021, SE-
10435 Stockholm. Tel: (46 8)
441 5570. Fax: 343 810.
Swedish Film Institute, Box
27126, SE-10252 Stockholm.
Tel: (46 8) 665 1100. Fax: 666
3698. info@sfi.se.
Swedish Film Producers
Association, Box 27298, SE-
102 53 Stockholm. Tel: (46 8)
665 1255. Fax: 666 3748.
info@frf.net.
Swedish Institute, Cultural Film
Events, Box 7434, SE-10391
Stockholm. Tel: (46 8) 453
7800. Fax: 207 248. si@si.se.

SWITZERLAND

Bookshops
Hans Rohr, Rathausgasse 30,
CH-3011, Bern. Tel: (41 31)
311 4480. Fax: 311 4470.
Librairie du Cinema, 9 rue de
la Terrassiere, CH-1207,
Geneva. Tel: (41 22) 736 8888.
Fax: 736 6616.
www.librairieducinema.ch.

Magazines
Avant Premiere, CP 5615,
1211 Geneva. Tel: (41 22) 809
9455. Fax: 809 9499.
promoedition@quorum-
com.ch. Colourful monthly.
Cine-Bulletin, Swiss Film
Centre, PO Box, Neugasse 6,
CH-8031 Zürich. Tel: (41 1)
272 5330. Fax: 272 5350.
www.swissfilms.ch. Serious
monthly in French and German.
Film Bulletin, Hard 4, Postfach
68, CH-8408 Winterthur.
Tel: (41 52) 226 0555. Fax: 226
0556. info@filmbulletin.ch.
www.filmbulletin.ch. Bi-monthly.

Useful Addresses
Cinémathèque Suisse,
[Archive], Casino de
Montbenon, 3 Allée Ernest
Ansermet, CP 2512, 1002
Lausanne. Tel: (41 21) 331
0101. Fax: 320 4888.
www.cinematheque.ch.
Federal Office of Culture, Film
Dept, Hallwylstrasse 15, PO
Box, CH-3003 Bern. Tel: (41
31) 322 9271. Fax: 322 5771.
www.kultur-schweiz.admin.ch.
Film Location Switzerland,
Avenue Du Grey 123, CH-1000
Lausanne. Tel: (41 21) 648
0380. Fax: 648 0381.
www.filmlocation.ch.
Gruppe Autoren, Regisseure,
Produzenten (GARP),
Dienerstrasse 7, 8004 Zürich.
Tel: (41 1) 241 1656.
www.garp-cinema.ch.
Pro Helvetia, Arts Council of
Switzerland, Film Dept,
Hirschengraben 22, PO Box,
CH-8024 Zürich. Tel: (41 1)
267 7171. Fax: 267 7106.
www.pro-helvetia.ch.
Swiss Film & Video Producers
(SFA), Theaterstrasse 4, CH-
8001 Zürich. Tel: (41 1) 258
4110. Fax: 262 4111.
www.swissfilm.org.
Swiss Film Center, Neugasse

6, PO Box, CH-8031 Zürich.
Tel: (41 1) 272 5330. Fax: 272
5350. www.swissfilms.ch.
Swiss Film Producers
Association (SFP), Zinggstrasse
16, CH-3007 Bern. Tel: (41 31)
372 4001. Fax: 372 4053.
www.swissfilmproducers.ch.
Swiss Short Film Agency,
Maupas 2, CH-1004 Lausanne.
Tel: (41 21) 311 0906. Fax: 311
0325. www.shortfilm.ch.

SYRIA
National Film Organisation,
Rawda 26 Takritt, Damascus.
Tel: (963 11) 333 1884. Fax:
332 3556. cinema@mail.sy.
Publishes quarterly *Al Haya Al
Cinemaia* magazine.

TAIWAN
All Tel/Fax numbers begin (886 2)

Useful Addresses
Central Motion Picture Corp,
6/F, 116 Han Chung St, Taipei
108. Tel: 2371 5191.
Fax: 2331 9241.
Chinese Taipei Film Archive,
4F, 7 Ching-Tao East Rd,
Taipei. Tel: 392 4243. Fax:
2392 6359. www.ctfa.org.
**Digital Content Industry
Promotion Office**, Suite 1105,
18 Chang-An E Rd, Sec 1,
Taipei 104. Tel: 2536 1226.
Fax: 2536 2100.
Film Appreciation, 4F, 7
Ching-Tao East Rd, Taipei. Tel:
392 4243. Fax: 2392 6359.
www.ctfa.org. Taiwan's leading
serious film journal; quarterly.
**Government Information
Office**, Department of Motion
Picture Affairs, 2 Tien-Tsin St
Taipei 100. Tel: 3356 7870.
Fax: 2341 0360.
**Motion Picture Association
of Taipei**, 5F, 196 Chung Hwa
Rd, Sec 1, Taipei. Tel: 2331
4672. Fax: 2381 4341.
Taipei Golden Horse Film

Festival, 3F, 37 Kaifeng St, Sec 1, Taipei 100. Tel: 2388 3880. Fax: 2388 3874.

THAILAND
All Tel/Fax numbers begin (66 2)

Useful Addresses
Film Bangkok, [Producer/Distributor], 622 Emporium Bldg, Sukhumvit, Bangkok 10110. www.filmbangkok.com.
Film Board Secretariat, 7th Floor, Public Relations Dept, Soi Aree Samphan, Rama VI Rd, Bangkok 10400. Fax: 618 2364/72. thaifilmboard@hotmail.com.
GMM Pictures, [Producer/Distributor], 50 GMM Grammy Place, Sukhumvit 21, Bangkok 10110. Fax: 665 8147. jate@gmmgrammy.com.
Kick the Machine, [Producer/Distributor], 44/17 Lad Prao 15, Jatujak , Bangkok 10900. www.kickthemachine.com.
National Film Archive, 93 Moo 3, Phutthamonton 5 Rd, Salaya, Nakorn Prathom 73170. Tel: 441 0263/4.

TURKEY
All Tel/Fax numbers begin (90 212)

Useful Addresses
Association of Directors (FILM-YON), Ayhan Isik Sokak 28/1, Beyoglu, Istanbul. Tel: 293 9001.
Association of Film Critics (SIYAD), Hakki Sehithan Sokak-Barlas Apt 33/13, Ulus, Istanbul. Tel: 279 5998. Fax: 269 8284. al.dorsay@superonline.com. Contact: Atilla Dorsay.
Istanbul Culture & Arts Foundation (IKSV), Istiklal Caddesi, Louvre Apt 146, 800070 Beyoglu, Istanbul.

Tel: 334 0700. Fax: 334 0702. film.fest@istfest-tr.org.
Turkish Cinema & Audiovisual Culture Foundation (TÜRSAK), Gazeteci Erol Dernek Sokak, 11/ 2 Hanif Han, Beyoglu, Istanbul. Tel: 244 5251. Fax: 251 6770. tursak@superonline.com.
Turkish Film & Television Institute, [Archive], 80700 Kislaönü-Besiktas, Istanbul. Tel: 266 1096. Fax: 211 6599. sinematv@msu.edu.tr.

UKRAINE
All Tel/Fax numbers begin (380 44)

Useful Addresses
Central State Archives of Film, Photo & Sound Documents, 24 Solomyanska St, Kiev 252601. Tel: 277 3777. Fax: 277 3655.
Karpenko-Kary Theatre Arts Institute, 40 Yaroslaviv St, Kiev 252034. Tel: 212 1142/0200. Fax: 212 1003.
Ministry of Culture & Art, 19 Franka St, Kiev 252030. Tel: 226 2645. Fax: 225 3257.
Ukrainian Film-makers Union, 6 Saksaganskogo St, Kiev 252033. Tel: 227 7557. Fax: 227 3130.

UNITED KINGDOM
Unless otherwise indicated, all Tel/Fax numbers begin (44 20)

Archives
Imperial War Museum, Lambeth Rd, London SE1 6HZ. Tel: 7416 5291/2. Fax: 7416 5299. www.iwmcollections.org.uk.
National Film & Television Archive, British Film Institute, 21 Stephen St, London W1P 1LN. Tel: 7255 1444. Fax: 7436 0439. www.bfi.org.uk.
Scottish Screen Archive, 1 Bowmont Gardens, Glasgow

G12 9LR. Tel: (44 141) 337 7400. Fax: 337 7413. www.scottishscreen.com.

Bookshops
Cinema Bookshop, 13-14 Great Russell St, London WC1B 3NH. Tel: 7637 0206. Fax: 7436 9979. Prompt, friendly service; rare items.
Cinema Store, Unit 4B/C, Orion House, Upper Saint Martin's Lane, London WC2H 9NY. Tel: 7379 7838. Fax: 7240 7689. . www.thecinemastore.com.
Flashbacks, 6 Silver Place, Beak St, London, W1F 0JS. Tel/Fax: 7437 8562. www.dacre.org/.
Greenroom Books, 9 St James Rd, Ilkley, West Yorkshire LS29 9PY. Tel: (44 1943) 607662. greenroombooks@blueyonder.c o.uk. Mail order for second-hand books on the arts.
Ed Mason, Room 301, Riverbank House, 1 Putney Bridge Approach, London, SW6 3JD. Tel: 7736 8511.
Movie Boulevard, 3 Cherry Tree Walk, Leeds LS2 7EB. Tel: (44 113) 242 2888. Fax: 243 8840. www.movieboulevard.co.uk.
Offstage Film & Theatre Bookshop, 37 Chalk Farm Rd, London, NW1 8AJ. Tel: 7485 4996. Fax: 7916 8046. offstagebookshop@aol.com.
Rare Discs, 18 Bloomsbury St, London WC1B 3QA. Tel: (44 20) 7580 3516. masheter@softhome.net.
Reel Poster Gallery, 72 Westbourne Grove, London W2 5SH. Tel: 7727 4488. Fax: 7727 4499. www.reelposter.com.

Film Schools
London International Film School, 24 Shelton St, London WC2H 9UB. Tel: 7836 9642. Fax: 7497 3718.

info@lfs.org.uk. www.lfs.org.uk. Principal: Ben Gibson. Offers a practical, two-year MA course to professional levels. Facilities include two cinemas, shooting stages, rehearsal stages, and 15 cutting rooms. Faculty made up of permanent and visiting professionals.

Middlesex University, School of Arts, Cat Hill, Barnet, Herts EN4 8HT. Tel: 8411 5066. Fax: 8411 5013. www.mdx.ac.uk.

National Film & Television School, Station Rd, Beaconsfield, Bucks, HP9 1LG. Tel: (44 1494) 731 425/413 Fax: 674042. admin@nftsfilm-tv.ac.uk. www.nftsfilm-tv.ac.uk. MA Courses in: Directing (Animation, Documentary or Fiction); Cinematography; Editing; Post-production Sound; Producing; Production Design; Composing for Film & TV; Screenwriting. Diploma in Sound Recording. Project Development Labs for experienced professionals. Short courses for freelancers. Short courses in digital post-production.

School of Art, Media & Design, University of Wales College, Newport, Caerleon Campus, PO Box 179, NP18 3YG. Tel: (44 1633) 432643. Fax: 432610. www.newport.ac.uk. BA (Hons) Film and Video, Animation, and Media and Visual Culture. MA Film.

Surry Institute of Art & Design, Farnham Campus, Falkner Rd, Farnham, Surrey GU9 7DS. Tel: (44 1252) 722441. Fax: 892616. www.surrart.ac.uk

University of Bristol, Dept of Drama, Film & Television Studies, Cantocks Close, Woodland Rd, Bristol BS8 1UP. Tel: (44 117) 928 7838. Fax:

928 7832. www.bris.ac.uk.

University of Derby, School of Arts, Design & Technology, Kedleston Rdk Derby DE22 1GB. Tel: (44 1332) 591736. Fax: 597739.www.derby.ac.uk.

University of Stirling, Dept of Film & Media Studies, Stirling FK9 4LA. Tel: (44 1786) 467520. Fax: 466855. www.fms.stir.ac.uk.

University of Westminster, Media Art & Design, Watford Rd, Northwick Park, Harrow, HA1 3TP. Tel: 7911 5903. Fax: 7911 5955. www.wmin.ac.uk.

Magazines

Empire, 4th Floor, Mappin House, 4 Winsley St, London W1W 8HF. Tel: 7436 1515. Fax: 7343 8703. empire@emap.com. www.empireonline.co.uk. Supercharged monthly.

Image Technology – Journal of the BKSTS, Pinewood Studios, Iver Heath, Buckinghamshire, SL0 0NH. Tel: (44 1753) 656656. Fax: 657016. info@bksts.com. www.bksts.com. Technology coverage. Ten times yearly.

Screen International, 33-39 Bowling Green Lane, London, EC1R 0DA. Tel: 7505 8080. Fax: 7505 8116. www.screendaily.com. International trade magazine.

Sight & Sound, British Film Institute, 21 Stephen St, London W1T 1LN. Tel: 7255 1444. Fax: 7436 2327. www.bfi.org.uk/sightandsound. The UK's leading film journal.

Total Film, Future Publishing, 99 Baker St, London W1U 6FP. Tel: 7317 2455. Fax: 7317 2642. totalfilm@futurenet.co.uk. Mainstream magazine, monthly.

Useful Addresses

British Academy of Film &

Television Arts (BAFTA), 195 Piccadilly, London, W1J 9LN. Tel: 7734 0022. Fax: 7734 1792. www.bafta.org.

British Board of Film Classification (BBFC), 3 Soho Sq, London, W1D 3HD. Tel: 7440 1570. Fax: 7287 0141. www.bbfc.co.uk.

British Council, Films & Literature Dept, 10 Spring Gardens, London, SW1A 2BN. Tel: 7389 3051. Fax: 7389 3175. www.britishcouncil.org.

British Film Institute, 21 Stephen St, London, W1T 1LN. Tel: 7255 1444. Fax: 7436 7950. www.bfi.org.uk.

Cinema Exhibitors Association, 22 Golden Sq, London, W1F 9JW. Tel: 7734 9551. Fax: 7734 6147. cea@cinemauk.ftech.co.uk.

Directors Guild of Great Britain (DGGB), Acorn House, 314-320 Grays Inn Rd, London, WC1X 8DP. Tel: 7278 4343. Fax: 7278 4742. www.dggb.org.

Film Distributors Association, 22 Golden Square, London W1F 9JW. Tel: 7437 4383. Fax: 7734 0912. www.launchingfilms.com.

Film London, 20 Euston Centre, Regent's Place, London, NW1 3JH. Tel: 7387 8787. Fax: 7387 8788. www.filmlondon.org.uk.

PACT, 45 Mortimer St, London, W1W 8HJ. Tel: 7331 6000. Fax: 7331 6700. www.pact.co.uk.

Scottish Screen, 249 West George St, 2nd Floor, Glasgow, G2 4QE. Tel: (44 141) 302 1700. Fax: 302 1711. www.scottishscreen.com.

UK Film Council, 10 Little Portland St, London, W1W 7JG. Tel: 7861 7861. Fax: 7861 7862.

www.ukfilmcouncil.org.uk.

UNITED STATES

Archives

Academy of Motion Picture Arts & Sciences, Academy Film Archive, Pickford Center, 1313 North Vine St, Los Angeles, CA 90028. Tel: (1 310) 247 3000. Fax: 657 5431. www.oscars.org.

American Film Institute/National Center for Film & Video Preservation, 2021 North Western Ave, Los Angeles, CA 90027. Tel: (1 323) 856 7600. Fax: 467 4578. info@afi.com. www.afi.com.

Getty Images Motion Collections, 75 Varick St, 5th Floor, New York, NY 10013. Tel: (1 646) 613 4100. Fax: 613 3601. www.gettyimages.com.

Library of Congress, Motion Picture, Broadcasting and Recorded Sound Division, Washington, DC 20540-4690. Tel: (1 202) 707 8572. Fax: 707 2371. www.loc.gov/rr/mopic.

Museum of Modern Art, Dept of Film and Video, 11 West 53rd St, New York, NY 10019. Tel: (1 212) 708 9400. Fax: 333 1145. iwww.moma.org.

Bookshops

Applause, 211 West 71st St, New York, NY 10023. Tel: (1 212) 496 7511. Fax: 721 2856. www.applausebooks.com.

Cinema Books, 4753 Roosevelt Way NE, Seattle, WA 98105. Tel: (1 206) 547 7667. www.cinemabooks.net.

Cinemonde, 478 Allied Drive, Suite 105, Nashville, TN 37211. Tel: (1 615) 832 1997. Fax: 832 2082. www.cinemonde.com. Posters.

Déja Vu Enterprises Inc, 2934 Beverly Glen Circle, Suite 309, Los Angeles, CA 90077. Tel: (1 818) 996 6137. Fax: 996 6147. dejavugallery@socal.rr.com. .

Dwight Cleveland, PO Box 10922, Chicago, IL 60610-0922. Tel: (1 773) 525 9152. Fax: 525 2969. www.movieposterbiz.com.

Larry Edmund's Bookshop, 6644 Hollywood Blvd, Hollywood, CA 90028. Tel: (1 323) 463 3273. Fax: 463 4245. www.larryedmunds.com. Huge collection.

Samuel French's Theatre & Film Bookshop, (2 Locations) 7623 Sunset Blvd, Hollywood, CA 90046. Tel: (1 323) 876 0570. Fax: 876 6822. Extended evening hours at 11963 Ventura Blvd, Studio City, CA 91604. Tel: (1 818) 762 0535. www.samuelfrench.com. Worldwide mail-order. Meticulous catalogues.

Gotham Book Mart, 41 W 47th St, New York, NY 10036. Tel: (1 212) 719 4448. Fax: 719 3481.

Limelight Film & Theatre Bookstore, 1803 Market St, San Francisco, CA 94103. Tel: (1 415) 864 2265. www.limelightbooks.com.

Movie Madness, 1083 Thomas Jefferson St, Washington, DC 20007. Tel: (1 202) 337 7064. Current, classic posters.

Movie Star News, 134 West 18th St, New York, NY 10011. Tel: (1 212) 620 8160. Fax: 727 0634. www.moviestarnews.com.

Jerry Ohlinger's Movie Material Store Inc, 242 West 14th St, New York, NY 10011. Tel: (1 212) 989 0869. Fax: 989 1660. www.moviematerials.com.

Film Schools
Information on thousands of US film courses is available in the *American Film Institute's Guide to College Courses in Film and Television*, available from Publications, The American Film Institute, 2021 North Western Ave, Los Angeles, CA 90027. Tel: (1 323) 856 7600.

Magazines

American Cinematographer, ASC Holding Corp, 1782 North Orange Drive, Hollywood, CA 90028. Tel: (1 323) 969 4333. Fax: 876 4973. www.theasc.com. Monthly.

Animation Journal, 108 Hedge Nettle, Crossing, Savannah, GA 31406. www.animationjournal.com. Quarterly.

Audience, PO Box 215, Simi Valley, CA 93062. Tel: (1 805) 584 6651. editoraud@aol.com. www.audiencemag.com.

Box Office, 155 South El Molino Ave, Suite 100, Pasadena, California, 91101. Tel: (1 626) 396 0250. Fax: 396 0248. www.boxoffice.com. Business monthly.

Film Comment, Film Society of Lincoln Center, 70 Lincoln Center Plaza, New York, NY 10023. Tel: (1 212) 875 5614. Fax: 875 5636. rtvfc@aol.com. Still the best US cinema bi-monthly.

Film Criticism, Allegheny College, Box D, Meadville, PA 16335. Tel: (1 814) 332 4333/4343. Fax: 332 2981. lmichael@alleg.edu. Scholarly essays. Tri-quarterly.

Film Literature Index, Film & Television Documentation Centre, State University of New York, 1400 Washington Ave, Albany, NY 12222. Tel: (1 518) 442 5745. Fax: 442 5367. www.albany.edu/sisp/fatdoc/index.html.

Film Quarterly, University of California Press, 2000 Center

St, Suite 303, Berkeley, CA 94704-1223. Tel: (1 510) 642 9740. Fax: 642 9917. www.ucpress.edu/journals/fq.

Filmmaker Magazine, 501 5th Ave, New York, NY 10017. Tel: (1 212) 983 3150. Fax: 973 0318. www.filmmakermagazine.com. Quarterly.

Hollywood Reporter, 5055 Wilshire Blvd, Los Angeles, CA 90036-4396. Tel: (1 323) 525 2000. Fax: 525 2377. www.hollywoodreporter.com.

Movieline's Hollywood Life, 10537 Santa Monica Blvd, Suite 250, Los Angeles, CA 90025. Tel (1 310) 234 9501. Fax: 234 0332. www.movieline.com.

Moviemaker, 349 Broadway, 3rd Floor, Suite 9, New York, NY 10013. Tel 212 625 3377 (1 212) 625 3377. www.moviemaker.com. Quarterly.

Variety, 5700 Wilshire Blvd, Suite 120, Los Angeles, CA 90036. www.variety.com. World's foremost entertainment industry newspaper.

Useful Addresses
American Film Institute, John F Kennedy Center for the Performing Arts, Washington, DC 20566. Tel: (1 202) 833 2348. Fax: 659 1970. www.afi.com.

Directors Guild of America, 7920 Sunset Blvd, Los Angeles, CA 90046. Tel: (1 310) 289 2000. Fax: 289 2029. www.dga.org.

Independent Feature Project, 104 W 29th St, 12th Floor, New York, NY 10001. Tel: (1 212) 465 8200. Fax: 465 8525. ifpny@ifp.org. www.ifp.org.

International Documentary Association, 1201 W 5th St, Suite M320, Los Angeles, CA 90017-1461. Tel: (1 213) 534 3600. Fax: 534 3610. www.documentary.org. Publishes magazine ten times a year.

Motion Picture Association of America, 15503 Ventura Blvd, Encino, CA 91436. Tel: (1 818) 995 6600. Fax: 382 1784. www.mpaa.org.

URUGUAY
All Tel/Fax numbers begin (598 2)

Useful Addresses
Asociación de Críticos de Cine del Uruguay (ACCU), Canelones 1280, Montevideo. Tel: 622 0085. Fax: 908 2685. gusiribarne@yahoo.com.

Asociación de Productores y Realizadores de Cine y Video del Uruguay (ASOPROD), Maldonado 1792, Montevideo. Tel: 418 7998. www.asoprod.org.uy.

Cinemateca Uruguaya, [Archive], Lorenzo Carnelli 1311, 11200 Montevideo. Tel: 418 2460. Fax: 419 4572. www.cinemateca.org.uy. Fondo Para el Fomento y **Desarrollo de la Producción Audiovisual Nacional (FONA)**, Palacio Municipal, Piso 1º, Montevideo. Tel: 902 3775. www.montevideo.gub.uy/cultur

a/c_fona.htm.
Instituto Nacional del Audiovisual (INA), Reconquista 535, 8º Piso, 11100 Montevideo. Tel/Fax: 915 7489/916 2632. www.mec.gub.uy/ina. **Tournier Animación**, Anzani 2015, Montevideo. Tel/Fax: 486 1779. tournier@adinet.com.uy.

UZBEKISTAN
Uzbek Film Studios, 1 Chilanzarskaya St, Tashkent 700065. Tel: (9987 12) 452 963. Fax: 206 972. www.uzbekfilm.com.

VENEZUELA
All Tel/Fax numbers begin (58 212)

Useful Addresses
Chamber For The Film & Video Industry. Tel: 283 4829/7156. Fax: 285 9237. **National Association of Film Authors (ANAC)**, Urbanización Avila, Avenida San Gabriel, Quinta Primavera, Municipal Libertador, Caracas. Tel: 578 3628. anac@cantv.net. **National Film Centre (CNAC)**, Avenida Principal de los Ruices, Edificio Centro Monaca Ala Sur, Piso 2, Los Ruices, Municipal Sucre, Caracas. Tel: 238 1870/1564. presidencnac@true.net. **Venezuelan Chamber of Feature Film Producers (CAVEPROL)**, 4ª, Avenida Entre 9 y 10, Transversal, Quinta Turandot, Los Palos Grandes, Municipal Chacao, Caracas. Tel: 283 4829/7156. Fax: 285 9237. **Venezuela Film Commission**, Avenida Principal de Los Ruices, Edificio Centro Monaca Ala Sur, Piso 2, Los Ruices, Municipal Sucre, Caracas. Tel: 238 1870/1564.

Index to Advertisers